Gravel Edition / Pentagon Papers / Volume I

The Senator Gravel Edition

The Pentagon Papers

*The Defense Department
History of United States
Decisionmaking on Vietnam*

Volume I

Beacon Press   *Boston*

90934

Introduction copyright © 1971 by Mike Gravel

The contents of this volume are drawn from the
official record of the U.S. Senate Subcommittee
on Public Buildings and Grounds. No copyright is claimed
in the text of this official Government document.

Library of Congress catalog card number: 75–178049

International Standard Book Number: 0–8070–0526–6 (hardcover)
0–8070–0527–4 (paperback)

Beacon Press books are published under the
auspices of the Unitarian Universalist Association

Printed in the United States of America

Contents

[*At the end of each volume is a collection of documents, a section entitled
"Justification of the War—Public Statements," and a Glossary*]

Contents of Volume I

Introduction

These are agonizing times for America. This nation has been torn apart by a war that has seared its conscience. We have spent lives and wealth without limit in pursuit of an unworthy goal, preserving our own power and prestige while laying waste the unfortunate lands of Southeast Asia.

For twenty years this nation has been at war in Indochina. Tens of thousands of Americans have been killed, half a million have been wounded, a million Asians have died, and millions more have been maimed or have become refugees in their own land. Meanwhile, the greatest representative democracy the world has even seen, the nation of Washington, Jefferson, and Lincoln, has had its nose rubbed in the swamp by petty war lords, jealous generals, black marketeers, and grand-scale dope pushers.

And the war still goes on. People are still dying, arms and legs are being severed, metal is crashing through human bodies, as a direct result of policy decisions conceived in secret and still kept from the American people.

H. G. Wells, the English novelist and historian, once wrote:

> The true strength of rulers and empires lies not in armies or emotions, but in the belief of men that they are inflexibly open and truthful and legal. As soon as a government departs from that standard, it ceases to be anything more than "the gang in possession," and its days are numbered.

This is nowhere more true than in the conduct of a representative democracy.

Free and informed public debate is the source of our strength. Remove it and our democratic institutions become a sham. Perceiving this, our forefathers included with our Constitution a Bill of Rights guaranteeing the maximum competition in the marketplace of ideas, and insuring the widest opportunity for the active and full participation of an enlightened electorate.

The American people have never agreed that the performance of their elected officials should be immune from public discussion and review. They have never failed to support their government and its policies, once they were convinced of the rightness of those policies. But they should not be expected to offer their support merely on the word of a President and his close advisors. To adopt that position, as many do today, is to demonstrate a basic mistrust in the collective wisdom of the people and a frightening lack of confidence in our form of government.

Our nation was founded at the town meeting, where all citizens had a voice in the decisions of government. Support for policies was insured, for they were made by the people affected. But, with the passage of time, the center of decision-making has escaped the people, and has even moved beyond their representatives in the Congress. With its array of specialists, its technology, and its ability to define state secrets, the Executive has assumed unprecedented power of national decision. The widespread and uncontrolled abuse of secrecy has especially fostered distrust and created division between the government and its people.

We now find policies on the most fundamental of issues, war and peace, adopted without the support or understanding of the people affected by them. As a result of these practices, especially with respect to our involvement in Southeast

Asia, our youth has virtually abandoned hope in the ability of their government to represent them, much less to stand for the ideals for which the Republic once stood. The trust between leaders and their people, without which a democracy cannot function, has been dangerously eroded, and we all fear the result.

For it is the leaders who have been found lacking, not the people. It is the leaders who have systematically misled, misunderstood, and, most of all, ignored the people in pursuit of a reckless foreign policy which the people never sanctioned. Separated from the public by a wall of secrecy and by their own desires for power, they failed to heed the voice of the people, who saw instinctively that America's vital interests were not involved in Southeast Asia. Nor could they bring themselves to recognize the knowledge and insight of that large number of private citizens who foresaw the eventual failure of their plans. As we now know, they were able even to ignore the frequently accurate forecasts of the government's own intelligence analysts.

The barriers of secrecy have allowed the national security apparatus to evolve a rigid orthodoxy which excludes those who question the accepted dogma. The result has been a failure to reexamine the postulates underlying our policy, or to give serious attention to alternatives which might avoid the kinds of disastrous choices that have been made in the past decade.

Nothing in recent history has so served to illuminate the damaging effects of secrecy as has the release of the Pentagon Papers, the Defense Department's history of American decisionmaking on Vietnam. This study is a remarkable work, commissioned by the men who were responsible for our Vietnam planning but who, by 1967, had come to see that our policy was bankrupt. The study was thus a unique attempt, by the Administration that had developed the policy, to look at its foundations and to see what had gone wrong.

A special task force was assembled, composed of outside experts and civilian and military analysts from within the Defense Department. They were given access to all the documentary evidence available to the Pentagon. The result was the most complete study yet performed of the policymaking process that led to our deepening involvement in Vietnam, and the most revealing insight we have had into the functioning of our government's national security apparatus.

We were told that we had to make sacrifices to preserve freedom and liberty in Southeast Asia. We were told that South Vietnam was the victim of aggression, and it was our duty to punish aggression at its source. We were told that we had to fight on the continent of Asia so that we would not have to battle on the shores of America. One can accept these arguments only if he has failed to read the Pentagon Papers.

However, the publc has not had access to this study. Newspapers in possession of the documents have published excerpts from them and have prepared their own summary of the study's findings. In doing this, they have performed a valuable public service. But every American is entitled to examine the study in full and to digest for himself the lessons it contains. The people must know the full story of their government's actions over the past twenty years, to ensure that never again will this great nation be led into waging a war through ignorance and deception.

It is for this reason that I determined, when I came into possession of this material, that it must be made available to the American public. For the tragic history it reveals must now be known. The terrible truth is that the Papers do not support our public statements. The Papers do not support our good intentions. The Papers prove that, from the beginning, the war has been an American war, serving only to perpetuate American military power in Asia. Peace has never been on the American agenda for Southeast Asia. Neither we nor the South Vietnamese have been masters of our Southeast Asian policy; we have been its victims, as the leaders of America sought to preserve their reputation for toughness and determination.

No one who reads this study can fail to conclude that, had the true facts been made known earlier, the war would long ago have ended, and the needless deaths of hundreds of thousands of Americans and Vietnamese would have been averted. This is the great lesson of the Pentagon Papers. No greater argument against unchecked secrecy in government can be found in the annals of American history.

The Pentagon Papers tell of the purposeful withholding and distortion of facts. There are no military secrets to be found here, only an appalling litany of faulty premises and questionable objectives, built one upon the other over the course of four administrations, and perpetuated today by a fifth administration.

The Pentagon Papers show that we have created, in the last quarter century, a new culture, a national security culture, protected from the influences of American life by the shield of secrecy. As *New York Times* reporter Neil Sheehan has written, "To read the Pentagon Papers in their vast detail is to step through the looking glass into a new and different world. This world has a set of values, a dynamic, a language, and a perspective quite distinct from the public world of the ordinary citizen and of the other two branches of the republic— Congress and the judiciary."

The Pentagon Papers reveal the inner workings of a government bureaucracy set up to defend this country, but now out of control, managing an international empire by garrisoning American troops around the world. It created an artificial client state in South Vietnam, lamented its unpopularity among its own people, eventually encouraged the overthrow of that government, and then supported a series of military dictators who served their own ends, and at times our government's ends, but never the cause of their own people.

The Pentagon Papers show that our leaders never understood the human commitments which underlay the nationalist movement in Vietnam, or the degree to which the Vietnamese were willing to sacrifice in what they considered to be a century-long struggle to eliminate colonialism from their land. Like the empires that have gone before us, our government has viewed as legitimate only those regimes which it had established, regardless of the views of those governed. It has viewed the Viet Minh and their successors, the Viet Cong, as insurgents rebelling against a legitimate government, failing to see that their success demonstrated the people's disaffection from the regime we supported. Our leaders lived in an isolated, dehumanized world of "surgical air strikes" and "Viet Cong infrastructure," when the reality was the maiming of women and children and the rise of a popular movement.

The Papers show that there was no concern in the decisionmaking process for the impact of our actions upon the Vietnamese people. American objectives were always to preserve the power and prestige of this country. In the light of the devastation we have brought to that unhappy land, it is hard to believe that any consideration was given to the costs of our policies that would be borne by the very people we claimed to be helping.

But the American people too were treated with contempt. The Pentagon Papers show that the public statements of optimism, used to sustain public support for an increasingly unpopular policy, were contrary to the intelligence estimates being given our leaders at the time. While we were led to believe that just a few more soldiers or a few more bombing runs would turn the tide, the estimates were quite clear in warning that escalation would bring no significant change in the war.

The Pentagon Papers show that the enemy knew what we were not permitted to know. Our leaders sought to keep their plans from the American people, even as they telegraphed their intentions to the enemy, as part of a deliberate strategy to cause him to back down. The elaborate secrecy precautions, the carefully contrived subterfuges, the precisely orchestrated press leaks, were intended not to deceive "the other side," but to keep the American public in the dark. Both we and the enemy were viewed as "audiences" before whom various postures of determination, conciliation, inflexibility, and strength were portrayed. The American public, which once thought of itself as a central participant in the democratic process, found itself reduced to the status of an interested, but passive, observer.

The people do not want, nor should they any longer be subjected to, the paternalistic protection of an Executive which believes that it alone has the right answers. For too long both the people and Congress have been denied access to the needed data with which they can judge national policy. For too long they have been spoon-fed information designed to sustain predetermined decisions and denied information which questioned those decisions. For too long they have been forced to subsist on a diet of half-truths or deliberate deceit, by executives who consider the people and the Congress as adversaries.

But now there is a great awakening in our land. There is a yearning for peace, and a realization that we need never have gone to war. There is a yearning for a more free and open society, and the emerging recognition of repression of people's lives, of their right to know, and of their right to determine their nation's future. And there is a yearning for the kind of mutual trust between those who govern and those who are governed that has been so lacking in the past.

If ever there was a time for change, it is now. It is in this spirit that I hope the past, as revealed in the Pentagon Papers, will help us make a new beginning, toward that better America which we all seek.

Mike Gravel
U.S. Senator

Washington, D.C.
August 1971

Preface

The text of this book consists of public documents drawn from the official record of the Senate Subcommittee on Public Buildings and Grounds.

Early in June 1971, the *New York Times,* and then other newspapers, began printing reports on, and excerpts from, a lengthy Defense Department study of American decisionmaking on Vietnam. Shortly thereafter, the Justice Department succeeded in obtaining injunctions halting further publication of these stories. On the evening of June 29, 1971, while there was still doubt as to whether the newspapers would be permitted to continue publishing their stories, United States Senator Mike Gravel of Alaska attempted to read a collection of the Pentagon Papers in his possession on the floor of the Senate. However, his effort was frustrated by a parliamentary maneuver which prevented him from gaining access to the Senate floor.

As Chairman of the Senate Subcommittee on Public Buildings and Grounds, Senator Gravel immediately convened a hearing, to receive testimony from Congressman John Dow of New York on the war-related lack of funds to meet our nation's needs for public buildings. As his opening remarks, and during the course of the evening, Senator Gravel read part of the Pentagon Papers into the record. The remaining portions of the Papers were incorporated into the record of the subcommittee and then were released to the press.

The material from the Pentagon Papers that was entered into the record, and is reprinted here, consisted of about 2900 pages of narrative, 1000 pages of appended documents, and a 200-page collection of public statements by government officials justifying U.S. involvement in Vietnam. According to information reported in the press, the Defense Department study included in total a narrative of about 3000 pages and documents amounting to about 4000 pages.

The material presented here includes a full history of U.S. decisionmaking on Vietnam from the early 1940s through March of 1968. Even though the documents included with the narrative were only a portion of those appended to the original study, they were of sufficient interest and importance to warrant inclusion in these volumes. (There are extensive quotations within the narrative from many of the other documents included with the original study.) In its published account of the study, the *New York Times* included a number of documents which did not appear in the subcommittee record. These have been reprinted here also, in proper chronological sequence, and their source is indicated. The collection of public statements was drawn from the U.S. Department of State Bulletins and the Public Papers of the Presidents, and was prepared in the form shown here by the Defense Department task force which performed the study.

The preparation of the subcommittee record was performed under the direction of Senator Gravel. The chapter sequence was arranged to provide a convenient, nearly chronological four-volume format. The documents and public statements pertaining to each period are appended to the material in each volume.

No material was added to or changed in the study or appended documents and statements. In some cases, material was illegible or missing. If this occurred within a direct quotation, the omission was indicated with a bracketed statement. If it occurred in narrative text, it was bridged by removing the entire sentence in which it appeared, when it was evident that no substantive material would be lost by this procedure; otherwise, the omission was indicated by a bracketed statement. All other bracketed insertions appear in the original study. Some maps were removed when they were not of sufficient quality to be adequately reproduced as unretouched facsimiles; these omissions have been indicated in the text. Footnotes in the original study, referring primarily to internal government reports, have been removed. A glossary of specialized terms and acronyms was added.

These volumes provide the most complete text of this history of American involvement in Vietnam yet made available, in a form which should make it fully accessible to the American people.

Letter of Transmittal of the Study

January 15, 1969

TO: Clark M. Clifford
       Secretary of Defense

On June 17, 1967, Secretary Robert S. McNamara directed that a task force be formed to study the history of United States involvement in Vietnam from World War II to the present. Mr. McNamara's guidance was simply to do studies that were "encyclopedic and objective." With six full-time professionals assigned to the task force, we were to complete our work in three months. A year and a half later, and with the involvement of six times six professionals, we are finally done to the tune of 37 studies and 15 collections of documents in 43 volumes.

In the beginning, Mr. McNamara gave the task force full access to OSD [Office of the Secretary of Defense] files, and the task force received access to CIA materials, and some use of State Department cables and memoranda. We had no access to White House files. Our guidance prohibited personal interviews with any of the principal participants.

The result was not so much a documentary history, as a history based solely on documents—checked and rechecked with ant-like diligence. Pieces of paper, formidable and suggestive by themselves, could have meant much or nothing. Perhaps this document was never sent anywhere, and perhaps that one, though commented upon, was irrelevant. Without the memories of people to tell us, we were certain to make mistakes. Yet, using those memories might have been misleading as well. This approach to research was bound to lead to distortions, and distortions we are sure abound in these studies.

To bring the documents to life, to fill in gaps, and just to see what the "outside world" was thinking, we turned to newspapers, periodicals, and books. We never used these sources to supplant the classified documents, but only to supplement them. And because these documents, sometimes written by very clever men who knew so much and desired to say only a part, and sometimes written very openly but also contradictorily, are not immediately self-revealing or self-explanatory, we tried both to have a number of researchers look at them and to quote passages liberally. Moreover, when we felt we could be challenged with taking something out of context, we included the whole paper in the documentary record section of the task force studies [Documentary Appendix]. Again seeking to fend off inevitable mistakes in interpretation and context, what seemed to us key documents were reviewed and included in several overlapping in substance, but separate, studies.

The people who worked on the task force were superb—uniformly bright and interested, although not always versed in the art of research. We had a sense of doing something important and of the need to do it right. Of course, we all had our prejudices and axes to grind, and these shine through clearly at times, but we tried, we think, to suppress or compensate for them.

These outstanding people came from everywhere—the military services, State,

O.S.D., and the "think tanks." Some came for a month, for three months, for six months, and most were unable, given the unhappiness of their superiors, to finish the studies they began. Almost all the studies had several authors, each heir dutifully trying to pick up the threads of his predecessor. In all, we had 36 professionals working on these studies, with an average of four months per man.

The quality, style, and interest of the studies varies considerably. The papers in Chapters [1–5], concerning the years 1945 to 1961, tend to be generally nonstartling—although there are many interesting tidbits. Because many of the documents in this period were lost or not kept (except for the Geneva conference era) we had to rely more on outside resources. From 1961 onwards, the records were bountiful, especially on the first Kennedy year in office, the Diem coup, and on the subjects of the deployment of ground forces, the decisions surrounding the bombing campaign against North Vietnam, US–GVN relations, and attempts at negotiating a settlement of the conflict.

Almost all the studies contain both a summary and analysis and a chronology. The chronologies highlight each important event or action in the monograph by means of date, description, and documentary source. The summary and analysis sections, which I wrote, attempt to capture the main themes and facts of the monographs—and to make some judgments and speculations which may or may not appear in the text itself. The monographs themselves stick, by and large, to the documents and do not tend to be analytical.

Writing history, especially where it blends into current events, especially where that current event is Vietnam, is a treacherous exercise. We often could not tell whether something happened because someone decided it, decided against it, or, most likely, because it unfolded from the situation. History, to me, has been expressed by a passage from Herman Melville's *Moby Dick* where he writes: "This is a world of chance, free will, and necessity—all interweavingly working together as one; chance by turn rules either and has the last featuring blow at events." Our studies have tried to reflect this thought; inevitably in the organizing and writing process, they appear to assign more and less to men and free will than was the case.

Leslie H. Gelb
Director
Study Task Force

1. Background to the Conflict, 1940–1950

Summary

INDOCHINA IN U.S. WARTIME POLICY, 1941–1945

Significant misunderstanding has developed concerning U.S. policy towards Indochina in the decade of World War II and its aftermath. A number of historians have held that anti-colonialism governed U.S. policy and actions up until 1950, when containment of communism supervened. For example, Bernard Fall (e.g. In his 1967 post-mortem book, *Last Reflections on a War*) categorized American policy toward Indochina in six periods: "(1) Anti-Vichy, 1940–1945; (2) Pro-Viet Minh, 1945–1946; (3) Non-involvement, 1946–June 1950; (4) Pro-French, 1950–July 1954; (5) Non-military involvement, 1954–November 1961; (6) Direct and full involvement, 1961– ." Commenting that the first four periods are those "least known even to the specialist," Fall developed the thesis that President Roosevelt was determined "to eliminate the French from Indochina at all costs," and had pressured the Allies to establish an international trusteeship to administer Indochina until the nations there were ready to assume full independence. This obdurate anti-colonialism, in Fall's view, led to cold refusal of American aid for French resistance fighters, and to a policy of promoting Ho Chi Minh and the Viet Minh as the alternative to restoring the French bonds. But, the argument goes, Roosevelt died, and principle faded; by late 1946, anti-colonialism mutated into neutrality. According to Fall: "Whether this was due to a deliberate policy in Washington or, conversely, to an absence of policy, is not quite clear. . . . The United States, preoccupied in Europe, ceased to be a diplomatic factor in Indochina until the outbreak of the Korean War." In 1950, anti-communism asserted itself, and in a remarkable volte-face, the United States threw its economic and military resources behind France in its war against the Viet Minh. Other commentators, conversely—prominent among them, the historians of the Viet Minh—have described U.S. policy as consistently condoning and assisting the reimposition of French colonial power in Indochina, with a concomitant disregard for the nationalist aspirations of the Vietnamese.

Neither interpretation squares with the record; the United States was less concerned over Indochina, and less purposeful than either assumes. Ambivalence characterized U.S. policy during World War II, and was the root of much subsequent misunderstanding. On the one hand, the U.S. repeatedly reassured the French that its colonial possessions would be returned to it after the war. On the other hand, the U.S. broadly committed itself in the Atlantic Charter to support national self-determination, and President Roosevelt personally and vehemently advocated independence for Indochina. F.D.R. regarded Indochina as a flagrant example of onerous colonialism which should be turned over to a trusteeship rather than returned to France. The President discussed this proposal with the Allies at the Cairo, Teheran, and Yalta Conferences and received the endorsement of Chiang Kai-shek and Stalin; Prime Minister Churchill demurred. At one point, Fall reports, the President offered General de Gaulle Filipino advisers to help France establish a "more progressive policy in Indochina"—which offer the General received in "pensive silence."

Ultimately, U.S. policy was governed neither by the principles of the Atlantic Charter, nor by the President's anti-colonialism, but by the dictates of military strategy, and by British intransigence on the colonial issue. The United States, concentrating its forces against Japan, accepted British military primacy in Southeast Asia, and divided Indochina at 16th parallel between the British and the Chinese for the purposes of occupation. U.S. commanders serving with the British and Chinese, while instructed to avoid ostensible alignment with the French, were permitted to conduct operations in Indochina which did not detract from the campaign against Japan. Consistent with F.D.R.'s guidance, the U.S. did provide modest aid to French—and Viet Minh—resistance forces in Vietnam after March, 1945, but refused to provide shipping to move Free French troops there. Pressed by both the British and the French for clarification of U.S. intentions regarding the political status of Indochina, F.D.R. maintained that "it is a matter for postwar."

The President's trusteeship concept foundered as early as March 1943, when the U.S. discovered that the British, concerned over possible prejudice to Commonwealth policy, proved to be unwilling to join in any declaration on trusteeships, and indeed any statement endorsing national independence which went beyond the Atlantic Charter's vague "respect the right of all peoples to choose the form of government under which they will live." So sensitive were the British on this point that the Dumbarton Oaks Conference of 1944, at which the blueprint for the postwar international system was negotiated, skirted the colonial issue, and avoided trusteeships altogether. At each key decisional point at which the President could have influenced the course of events toward trusteeship—in relations with the U.K., in casting the United Nations Charter, in instructions to allied commanders—he declined to do so; hence, despite his lip service to trusteeship and anti-colonialism, F.D.R. in fact assigned to Indochina a status correlative to Burma, Malaya, Singapore and Indonesia: free territory to be reconquered and returned to its former owners. Non-intervention by the U.S. on behalf of the Vietnamese was tantamount to acceptance of the French return. On April 3, 1945, with President Roosevelt's approval, Secretary of State Stettinius issued a statement that, as a result of the Yalta talks, the U.S. would look to trusteeship as a postwar arrangement only for "territories taken from the enemy," and for "territories as might voluntarily be placed under trusteeship." By context, and by the Secretary of State's subsequent interpretation, Indochina fell into the latter category. Trusteeship status for Indochina became, then, a matter for French determination.

Shortly following President Truman's entry into office, the U.S. assured France that it had never questioned, "even by implication, French sovereignty over Indo-China." The U.S. policy was to press France for progressive measures in Indochina, but to expect France to decide when its peoples would be ready for independence; "such decisions would preclude the establishment of a trusteeship in Indochina except with the consent of the French Government." These guidelines, established by June, 1945—before the end of the war—remained fundamental to U.S. policy.

With British cooperation, French military forces were reestablished in South Vietnam in September, 1945. The U.S. expressed dismay at the outbreak of guerrilla warfare which followed, and pointed out that while it had no intention of opposing the reestablishment of French control, "it is not the policy of this government to assist the French to reestablish their control over Indochina by force, and the willingness of the U.S. to see French control reestablished assumes that [the] French claim to have the support of the population in Indochina is borne out by future events." Through the fall and winter of 1945–1946, the U.S. received a series of requests from Ho Chi Minh for intervention in Vietnam; these were, on the record, unanswered. However, the U.S. steadfastly refused to assist the French military effort, e.g., forbidding American flag vessels to carry troops or war materiel to Vietnam. On March 6, 1946, the French and Ho signed an Accord in which Ho acceded to French reentry into North Vietnam in return for recognition of the DRV as a "Free State," part of the French Union. As of April 1946, allied occupation of Indochina was officially terminated, and the U.S. acknowledged to France that all of Indochina had reverted to French control. Thereafter, the problems of U.S. policy toward Vietnam were dealt with in the context of the U.S. relationship with France.

U.S. NEUTRALITY IN THE FRANCO–VIET MINH WAR, 1946–1949

In late 1946, the Franco–Viet Minh War began in earnest. A chart (pp. A37 ff) summarizes the principal events in the relations between France and Vietnam, 1946–1949, describing the milestones along the route by which France, on the one hand, failed to reach any lasting accommodation with Ho Chi Minh, and, on the other hand, erected the "Bao Dai solution" in its stead. The U.S. during these years continued to regard the conflict as fundamentally a matter for French resolution. The U.S. in its representations to France deplored the prospect of protracted war, and urged meaningful concessions to Vietnamese nationalism. However, the U.S., deterred by the history of Ho's communist affiliation, always stopped short of endorsing Ho Chi Minh or the Viet Minh. Accordingly, U.S. policy gravitated with that of France toward the Bao Dai solution. At no point was the U.S. prepared to adopt an openly interventionist course. To have done so would have clashed with the expressed British view that Indochina was an exclusively French concern, and played into the hands of France's extremist political parties of both the Right and the Left. The U.S. was particularly apprehensive lest by intervening it strengthen the political position of French Communists. Beginning in 1946 and 1947, France and Britain were moving toward an anti-Soviet alliance in Europe and the U.S. was reluctant to press a potentially divisive policy. The U.S. [words illegible] Vietnamese nationalism relatively insignificant compared with European economic recovery and collective security from communist domination.

It is not as though the U.S. was not prepared to act in circumstances such as these. For example, in the 1945–1946 dispute over Dutch possessions in Indonesia, the U.S. actively intervened against its Dutch ally. In this case, however, the intervention was in concert with the U.K. (which steadfastly refused similar action in Indochina) and against the Netherlands, a much less significant ally in Europe than France. In wider company and at projected lower cost, the U.S. could and did show a determination to act against colonialism.

The resultant U.S. policy has most often been termed "neutrality." It was, however, also consistent with the policy of deferring to French volition announced by President Roosevelt's Secretary of State on 3 April 1945. It was a policy characterized by the same indecision that had marked U.S. wartime policy. Moreover, at the time, Indochina appeared to many to be one region in the troubled postwar world in which the U.S. might enjoy the luxury of abstention.

In February, 1947, early in the war, the U.S. Ambassador in Paris was instructed to reassure Premier Ramadier of the "very friendliest feelings" of the U.S. toward France and its interest in supporting France in recovering its economic, political and military strength:

> In spite any misunderstanding which might have arisen in minds French in regard to our position concerning Indochina they must appreciate that we have fully recognized France's sovereign position in that area and we do not wish to have it appear that we are in any way endeavoring undermine that position, and French should know it is our desire to be helpful and we stand ready assist any appropriate way we can to find solution for Indochinese problem. At same time we cannot shut our eyes to fact that there are two sides this problem and that our reports indicate both a lack French understanding of other side (more in Saigon than in Paris) and continued existence dangerously outmoded colonial outlook and methods in area. Furthermore, there is no escape from fact that trend of times is to effect that colonial empires in XIX Century sense are rapidly becoming thing of past. Action Brit in India and Burma and Dutch in Indonesia are outstanding examples this trend, and French themselves took cognizance of it both in new Constitution and in their agreements with Vietnam. On other hand we do not lose sight fact that Ho Chi Minh has direct Communist connections and it should be obvious that we are not interested in seeing colonial empire administrations supplanted by philosophy and political organizations emanating from and controlled by Kremlin. . . .
>
> Frankly we have no solution of problem to suggest. It is basically matter for two parties to work out themselves and from your reports and those from Indochina we are led to feel that both parties have endeavored to keep door open to some sort of settlement. We appreciate fact that Vietnam started present fighting in Indochina on December 19 and that this action has made it more difficult for French to adopt a position of generosity and conciliation. Nevertheless we hope that French will find it possible to be more than generous in trying to find a solution.

The U.S. anxiously followed the vacillations of France's policy toward Bao Dai, exhorting the French to translate the successive "agreements" they contracted with him into an effective nationalist alternative to Ho Chi Minh and the Viet Minh. Increasingly, the U.S. sensed that French unwillingness to concede political power to Vietnamese heightened the possibility of the Franco-Viet Minh conflict being transformed into a struggle with Soviet imperialism. U.S. diplomats were instructed to "apply such persuasion and/or pressure as is best calculated [to] produce desired result [of France's] unequivocally and promptly approving the principle of Viet independence." France was notified that the U.S. was willing to extend financial aid to a Vietnamese government not a French puppet, "but could not give consideration of altering its present policy in this regard unless real progress [is] made in reaching non-Communist solution in Indochina based on cooperation of true nationalists of that country."

As of 1948, however, the U.S. remained uncertain that Ho and the Viet Minh were in league with the Kremlin. A State Department appraisal of Ho Chi Minh in July 1948, indicated that:

> 1. Depts info indicates that Ho Chi Minh is Communist. His long and well-known record in Comintern during twenties and thirties, continuous support by French Communist newspaper *Humanite* since 1945, praise given

him by Radio Moscow (which for past six months has been devoting increasing attention to Indochina) and fact he has been called "leading communist" by recent Russian publications as well as *Daily Worker* makes any other conclusion appear to be wishful thinking.

2. Dept has no evidence of direct link between Ho and Moscow but assumes it exists, nor is it able evaluate amount pressure or guidance Moscow exerting. We have impression Ho must be given or is retaining large degree latitude. Dept considers that USSR accomplishing its immediate aims in Indochina by (a) pinning down large numbers of French troops, (b) causing steady drain upon French economy thereby tending retard recovery and dissipate ECA assistance to France, and (c) denying to world generally surpluses which Indochina normally has available thus perpetuating conditions of disorder and shortages which favorable to growth communism. Furthermore, Ho seems quite capable of retaining and even strengthening his grip on Indochina with no outside assistance other than continuing procession of French puppet govts.

In the fall of 1948, the Office of Intelligence Research in the Department of State conducted a survey of communist influence in Southeast Asia. Evidence of Kremlin-directed conspiracy was found in virtually all countries except Vietnam:

> Since December 19, 1946, there have been continuous conflicts between French forces and the nationalist government of Vietnam. This government is a coalition in which avowed communists hold influential positions. Although the French admit the influence of this government, they have consistently refused to deal with its leader, Ho Chi Minh, on the grounds that he is a communist.
>
> To date the Vietnam press and radio have not adopted an anti-American position. It is rather the French colonial press that has been strongly anti-American and has freely accused the U.S. of imperialism in Indochina to the point of approximating the official Moscow position. Although the Vietnam radio has been closely watched for a new position toward the U.S., no change has appeared so far. Nor does there seem to have been any split within the coalition government of Vietnam. . . .
>
> *Evaluation.* If there is a Moscow-directed conspiracy in Southeast Asia, Indochina is an anomaly so far. Possible explanations are:
>
> 1. No rigid directives have been issued by Moscow.
> 2. The Vietnam government considers that it has no rightest elements that must be purged.
> 3. The Vietnam Communists are not subservient to the foreign policies pursued by Moscow.
> 4. A special dispensation for the Vietnam government has been arranged in Moscow.
>
> Of these possibilities, the first and fourth seem most likely.

ORIGINS OF U.S. INVOLVEMENT IN VIETNAM

The collapse of the Chinese Nationalist government in 1949 sharpened American apprehensions over communist expansion in the Far East, and hastened U.S. measures to counter the threat posed by Mao's China. The U.S. sought to create and employ policy instruments similar to those it was bringing into play against the Soviets in Europe: collective security organizations, economic aid, and military assistance. For example, Congress, in the opening paragraphs of the law it passed in 1949 to establish the first comprehensive military assistance program, expressed itself "as favoring the creation by the free countries and the free peoples of the Far East of a joint organization, consistent with the Charter of the United Nations, to establish a program of self-help and mutual cooperation designed to develop their economic and social well-being, to safeguard basic rights and liberties, and to protect their security and independence. . . ." But, the negotiating of such an organization among the disparate powers and political entities of the Far East was inherently more complex a matter than the North Atlantic Treaty nations had successfully faced. The U.S. decided that the impetus for collective security in Asia should come from the Asians, but by late 1949, it also recognized that action was necessary in Indochina. Thus, in the closing months of 1949, the course of U.S. policy was set to block further communist expansion in Asia: by collective security if the Asians were forthcoming; by collaboration with major European allies and commonwealth nations, if possible; but bilaterally if necessary. On that policy course lay the Korean War of 1950–1953, the forming of the Southeast Asia Treaty Organization of 1954, and the progressively deepening U.S. involvement in Vietnam.

January and February, 1950, were pivotal months. The French took the first concrete steps toward transferring public administration to Bao Dai's State of Vietnam. Ho Chi Minh denied the legitimacy of the latter, proclaiming the DRV as the "only legal government of the Vietnam people," and was formally recognized by Peking and Moscow. On 29 January 1950, the French National Assembly approved legislation granting autonomy to the State of Vietnam. On February 1, 1950, Secretary of State Acheson made the following public statement:

> The recognition by the Kremlin of Ho Chi Minh's communist movement in Indochina comes as a surprise. The Soviet acknowledgment of this movement should remove any illusions as to the "nationalist" nature of Ho Chi Minh's aims and reveals Ho in his true colors as the mortal enemy of native indepedence in Indochina.
>
> Although timed in an effort to cloud the transfer of sovereignty by France to the legal Governments of Laos, Cambodia and Vietnam, we have every reason to believe that those legal governments will proceed in their development toward stable governments representing the true nationalist sentiments of more than 20 million peoples of Indiochina.
>
> French action in transfering sovereignty to Vietnam, Laos and Cambodia has been in process for some time. Following French ratification, which is expected within a few days, the way will be open for recognition of these local governments by the countries of the world whose policies support the development of genuine national independence in former colonial areas. . . .

Formal French ratification of Vietnamese independence was announced on 2 February 1950; on the same date, President Truman approved U.S. recognition for Bao Dai. French requests for aid in Indochina followed within a few weeks. On May 8, 1950, the Secretary of State announced that:

> The United States Government convinced that neither national independence nor democratic evolution exist in any area dominated by Soviet im-

perialism, considers the situation to be such as to warrant its according economic aid and military equipment to the Associated State of Indochina and to France in order to assist them in restoring stability and permitting these states to pursue their peaceful and democratic development.

The U.S. thereafter was deeply involved in the developing war. But it cannot be said that the extension of aid was a volte-face of U.S. policy precipitated solely by the events of 1950. It appears rather as the denouement of a cohesive progression of U.S. policy decisions stemming from the 1945 determination that France should decide the political future of Vietnamese nationalism. Neither the modest O.S.S. aid to the Viet Minh in 1945, nor the U.S. refusal to abet French recourse to arms the same year, signaled U.S. backing of Ho Chi Minh. To the contrary, the U.S. was very wary of Ho, apprehensive lest Paris' imperialism be succeeded by control from Moscow. Uncertainty characterized the U.S. attitude toward Ho through 1948, but the U.S. incessantly pressured France to accommodate "genuine" Vietnamese nationalism and independence. In early 1950, both the apparent fruition of the Bao Dai solution, and the patent alignment of the DRV with the USSR and Communist China, impelled the U.S. to more direct intervention in Vietnam.

(End of Summary)

I.   INDOCHINA IN U.S. WARTIME POLICY, 1941–1945

In the interval between the fall of France in 1940, and the Pearl Harbor attack in December, 1941, the United States watched with increasing apprehension the flux of Japanese military power into Indochina. At first the United States urged Vichy to refuse Japanese requests for authorization to use bases there, but was unable to offer more than vague assurances of assistance, such as a State Department statement to the French Ambassador on 6 August 1940 that:

> We have been doing and are doing everything possible within the framework of our established policies to keep the situation in the Far East stabilized; that we have been progressively taking various steps, the effect of which has been to exert economic pressure on Japan; that our Fleet is now based on Hawaii, and that the course which we have been following, as indicated above, gives a clear indication of our intentions and activities for the future.

The French Ambassador replied that:

> In his opinion the phrase "within the framework of our established policies," when associated with the apparent reluctance of the American Government to consider the use of military force in the Far East at this particular time, to mean that the United States would not use military or naval force in support of any position which might be taken to resist the Japanese attempted aggression on Indochina. The Ambassador [feared] that the French Government would, under the indicated pressure of the Japanese Government, be forced to accede . . .

The fears of the French Ambassador were realized. In 1941, however, Japan went beyond the use of bases to demands for a presence in Indochina tantamount to occupation. President Roosevelt himself expressed the heightening U.S. alarm to the Japanese Ambassador, in a conversation recorded by Acting Secretary of State Welles as follows:

> The President then went on to say that this new move by Japan in Indochina created an exceedingly serious problem for the United States . . . the cost of any military occupation is tremendous and the occupation itself is not conducive to the production by civilians in occupied countries of food supplies and new materials of the character required by Japan. Had Japan undertaken to obtain the supplies she required from Indochina in a peaceful way, she not only would have obtained larger quantities of such supplies, but would have obtained them with complete security and without the draining expense of a military occupation. Furthermore, from the military standpoint, the President said, surely the Japanese Government could not have in reality the slightest belief that China, Great Britain, the Netherlands or the United States had any territorial designs on Indochina nor were in the slightest degree providing any real threats of aggression against Japan. This Government, consequently, could only assume that the occupation of Indochina was being undertaken by Japan for the purpose of further offense and this created a situation which necessarily must give the United States the most serious disquiet . . .
>   . . . The President stated that if the Japanese Government would refrain from occupying Indochina with its military and naval forces, or, had such steps actually been commenced, if the Japanese Government would withdraw such forces, the President could assure the Japanese Government that he would do everything within his power to obtain from the Governments of China, Great Britain, the Netherlands, and of course the United States itself a binding and solemn declaration, provided Japan would undertake the same commitment, to regard Indochina as a neutralized country in the same way in which Switzerland had up to now been regarded by the powers as a neutralized country. He stated that this would imply that none of the powers concerned would undertake any military act of aggression against Indochina and would remain in control of the territory and would not be confronted with attempts to dislodge them on the part of de Gaullist or Free French agents or forces.

The same date, Secretary of State Cordell Hull instructed Sumner Welles to see the Japanese Ambassador, and

> Make clear the fact that the occupation of Indochina by Japan possibly means one further important step to seizing control of the South Sea area, including trade routes of supreme importance to the United States controlling such products as rubber, tin and other commodities. This was of vital concern to the United States. The Secretary said that if we did not bring out this point our people will not understand the significance of this movement into Indochina. The Secretary mentioned another point to be stressed: there is no theory on which Indochina could be flooded with armed forces, aircraft, et cetera, for the defense of Japan. The only alternative is that this venture into Indochina has a close relation to the South Sea area and its value for offense against that area.

In a press statement of 2 August 1941, Acting Secretary of State Welles deplored Japan's "expansionist aims" and impugned Vichy:

Under these circumstances, this Government is impelled to question whether the French Government at Vichy in fact proposes to maintain its declared policy to preserve for the French people the territories both at home and abroad which have long been under French sovereignty.

This Government, mindful of its traditional friendship for France, has deeply sympathized with the desire of the French people to maintain their territories and to preserve them intact. In its relations with the French Government at Vichy and with the local French authorities in French territories, the United States will be governed by the manifest effectiveness with which those authorities endeavor to protect these territories from domination and control by those powers which are seeking to extend their rule by force and conquest, or by the threat thereof.

On the eve of Pearl Harbor, as part of the U.S. attempt to obtain Japanese consent to a non-aggression pact, the U.S. again proposed neutralization of Indochina in return for Japanese withdrawal. The events of 7 December 1941 put the question of the future of Indochina in the wholly different context of U.S. strategy for fighting World War II.

A. ROOSEVELT'S TRUSTEESHIP CONCEPT

U.S. policy toward Indochina during World War II was ambivalent. On the one hand, the U.S. appeared to support Free French claims to all of France's overseas dominions. The U.S. early in the war repeatedly expressed or implied to the French an intention to restore to France its overseas empire after the war. These U.S. commitments included the August 2, 1941, official statement on the Franco–Japanese agreement; a December, 1941, Presidential letter to Pétain; a March 2, 1942, statement on New Caledonia; a note to the French Ambassador of April 13, 1942; Presidential statements and messages at the time of the North Africa invasion; the Clark–Darlan Agreement of November 22, 1942; and a letter of the same month from the President's Personal Representative to General Henri Giraud, which included the following reassurance:

> . . . The restoration of France to full independence, in all the greatness and vastness which it possessed before the war in Europe as well as overseas, is one of the war aims of the United Nations. It is thoroughly understood that French sovereignty will be re-established as soon as possible throughout all the territory, metropolitan or colonial, over which flew the French flag in 1939.

On the other hand, in the Atlantic Charter and other pronouncements the U.S. proclaimed support for national self-determination and independence. Moreover, the President of the United States, especially distressed at the Vichy "sell-out" to Japan in Indochina, often cited French rule there as a flagrant example of onerous and exploitative colonialism, and talked of his determination to turn Indochina over to an international trusteeship after the war. In early 1944, Lord Halifax, the British Ambassador in Washington, called on Secretary of State Hull to inquire whether the President's "rather definite" statements "that Indochina should be taken away from the French and put under an international trusteeship"—made to "Turks, Egyptians and perhaps others" during his trip to Cairo and Teheran—represented "final conclusions in view of the fact that they would soon get back to the French . . ." (The French marked well the

President's views—in fact as France withdrew from Vietnam in 1956, its Foreign Minister recalled Roosevelt's assuring the Sultan of Morocco that his sympathies lay with colonial peoples struggling for independence. Lord Halifax later recorded that:

> The President was one of the people who used conversation as others of us use a first draft on paper . . . a method of trying out an idea. If it does not go well, you can modify it or drop it as you will. Nobody thinks anything of it if you do this with a paper draft; but if you do it with conversation, people say that you have changed your mind, that "you never knew where you have him," and so on.

But in response to a memorandum from Secretary of State Hull putting the question of Indochina to F.D.R., and reminding the President of the numerous U.S. commitments to restoration of the French empire, Roosevelt replied (on January 24, 1944), that:

> I saw Halifax last week and told him quite frankly that it was perfectly true that I had, for over a year, expressed the opinion that Indo-China should not go back to France but that it should be administered by an international trusteeship. France has had the country—thirty million inhabitants for nearly one hundred years, and the people are worse off than they were at the beginning.
>
> As a matter of interest, I am wholeheartedly supported in this view by Generalissimo Chiang Kai-shek and by Marshal Stalin. I see no reason to play in with the British Foreign Office in this matter. The only reason they seem to oppose it is that they fear the effect it would have on their own possessions and those of the Dutch. They have never liked the idea of trusteeship because it is, in some instances, aimed at future independence. This is true in the case of Indo-China.
>
> Each case must, of course, stand on its own feet, but the case of Indo-China is perfectly clear. France has milked it for one hundred years. The people of Indo-China are entitled to something better than that.

1. *Military Strategy Pre-eminent*

Throughout the year 1944, the President held to his views, and consistent with them, proscribed U.S. aid to resistance groups—including French groups—in Indochina. But the war in the Asian theaters moved rapidly, and the center of gravity of the American effort began to shift northward toward Japan. The question of U.S. strategy in Southeast Asia then came to the fore. At the Second Quebec Conference (September, 1944), the U.S. refused British offers of naval assistance against Japan because Admiral King believed "the best occupation for any available British forces would be to re-take Singapore, and to assist the Dutch in recovering the East Indies," and because he suspected that the offer "was perhaps not unconnected with a desire for United States help in clearing the Japanese out of the Malay States and Netherlands East Indies." Admiral King's suspicions were not well-founded, at least insofar as Churchill's strategic thought was concerned. The Prime Minister was evidently as unwilling to invite an active American role in the liberation of Southeast Asia as the U.S. was to undertake same; as early as February, 1944, Churchill wrote that:

A decision to act as a subsidiary force under the Americans in the Pacific raises difficult political questions about the future of our Malayan possessions. If the Japanese should withdraw from them or make peace as the result of the main American thrust, the United States Government would after the victory feel greatly strengthened in its view that all possessions in the East Indian Archipelago should be placed under some international body upon which the United States would exercise a decisive concern.

The future of Commonwealth territories in Southeast Asia stimulated intense British interest in American intentions for French colonies there. In November and December of 1944, the British expressed to the United States, both in London and in Washington, their concern "that the United States apparently has not yet determined upon its policy toward Indochina." The head of the Far Eastern Department in the British Foreign Office told the U.S. Ambassador that:

> It would be difficult to deny French participation in the liberation of Indochina in light of the increasing strength of the French Government in world affairs, and that, unless a policy to be followed toward Indochina is mutually agreed between our two governments, circumstances may arise at any moment which will place our two governments in a very awkward situation.

President Roosevelt, however, refused to define his position further, notifying Secretary of State Stettinius on January 1, 1945:

> I still do not want to get mixed up in any Indo-China decision. It is a matter for postwar.— . . . I do not want to get mixed up in any military effort toward the liberation of Indo-China from the Japanese.—You can tell Halifax that I made this very clear to Mr. Churchill. From both the military and civil point of view, action at this time is premature.

However, the U.S. Joint Chiefs of Staff were concurrently planning the removal of American armed forces from Southeast Asia. In response to approaches from French and Dutch officials requesting aid in expelling Japan from their former colonial territories, the U.S. informed them that:

> All our available forces were committed to fighting the Japanese elsewhere in the Pacific, and Indochina and the East Indies were therefore not included within the sphere of interest of the American Chiefs of Staff.

American willingness to forego further operations in Southeast Asia led to a directive to Admiral Lord Mountbatten, Supreme Commander in that theater, to liberate Malaya without U.S. assistance. After the Yalta Conference (February, 1945), U.S. commanders in the Pacific were informed that the U.S. planned to turn over to the British responsibility for operations in the Netherlands East Indies and New Guinea. The President, however, agreed to permit such U.S. military operations in Indochina as avoided "alignments with the French," and detraction from the U.S. military campaign against Japan. The latter stricture precluded, in the U.S. view, the U.S. cooperation with the French at Mountbatten's headquarters, or the furnishing of ships to carry Free French forces to Indochina to undertake its liberation. This U.S. position came under particularly severe French criticism after 11 March 1945, when the Japanese overturned the Vichy regime in Vietnam, and prompted the Emperor Bao Dai to declare Vietnam unified and independent of France under Japanese protection. On 16 March 1945, a protest from General de Gaulle led to the following exchange between the Secretary of State and the President:

DEPARTMENT OF STATE
Washington
March 16, 1945

MEMORANDUM FOR THE PRESIDENT

Subject: *Indo-China.*

Communications have been received from the Provisional Government of the French Republic asking for:

(1) Assistance for the resistance groups now fighting the Japanese in Indo-China.

(2) Conclusion of a civil affairs agreement covering possible future operations in Indo-China.

These memoranda have been referred to the Joint Chiefs of Staff in order to obtain their views concerning the military aspects of the problems, and I shall communicate with you further on the subject upon receipt of the Joint Chiefs' reply.

Attached herewith is the text of a recent telegram from Ambassador Caffery describing his conversation with General de Gaulle on the subject of Indo-China. From this telegram and de Gaulle's speech of March 14, it appears that this Government may be made to appear responsible for the weakness of the resistance to Japan in Indo-China. The British may likewise be expected to encourage this view. It seems to me that without prejudicing in any way our position regarding the future of Indo-China we can combat this trend by making public [material illegible] a suggested statement, subject to your approval, by the State Department.

/s/ E. R. Stettinius, Jr.

Enclosures:
1. Proposed Statement.
2. Copy of telegram
   from Ambassador Caffery
   [not included here]

[Enclosure 1]

PROPOSED STATEMENT

The action of the Japanese Government in tearing away the veil with which it for so long attempted to cloak its domination of Indo-China is a direct consequence of the ever-mounting pressure which our arms are applying to the Japanese Empire. It is a link in the chain of events which began so disastrously in the summer of 1941 with the Franco–Japanese agreement for the "common defense" of Indo-China. It is clear that this latest step in the Japanese program will in the long run prove to be of no avail.

The Provisional Government of the French Republic has requested armed assistance for those who are resisting the Japanese forces in Indo-China. In accordance with its constant desire to aid all those who are willing to take up arms against our common enemies, this Government will do all it can to be of assistance in the present situation, consistent with plans to which it is already committed and with the operations now taking place in the Pacific. It goes without saying that all this country's available resources are being devoted to the defeat of our enemies and they will continue to be employed in the manner best calculated to hasten their downfall.

[Response]

THE WHITE HOUSE
Washington
March 17, 1945

MEMORANDUM FOR

The Secretary of State

By direction of the President, there is returned herewith Secretary of State Memorandum of 16 March, subject Indo-China, which includes a proposed statement on the Japanese action in Indo-China.

The President is of the opinion that it is inadvisable at the present time to issue the proposed statement.

/s/ William D. Leahy

The French were also actively pressuring the President and his key advisors through military channels. Admiral Leahy reported that, following Yalta:

The French representatives in Washington resumed their frequent calls to my office after our return from the Crimea. They labeled most of their requests "urgent." They wanted to participate in the combined intelligence group then studying German industrial and scientific secrets; to exchange information between the American command in China and the French forces in Indo-China; and to get agreement in principle to utilizing the French naval and military forces in the war against Japan (the latter would assist in returning Indo-China to French control and give France a right to participate in lend-lease assistance after the defeat of Germany.)

Most of the time I could only tell them that I had no useful information as to when and where we might make use of French assistance in the Pacific.

However, we did attempt to give a helping hand to the French resistance groups in Indo-China. Vice Admiral Fenard called me on March 18 to say that planes from our 14th Air Force in China were loaded with relief supplies for the undergrounders but could not start without authority from Washington. I immediately contacted General Handy and told him of the President's agreement that American aid to the Indo-China resistance groups might be given provided it involved no interference with our operations against Japan.

2. *Failure of the Trusteeship Proposal*

In the meantime, the President's concept of postwar trusteeship status for dependent territories as an intermediate step toward autonomy had undergone study by several interdepartmental and international groups, but had fared poorly. In deference to British sensibilities, the United States had originally sought only a declaration from the colonial powers setting forth their intention to liberate their dependencies and to provide tutelage in self-government for subject peoples. Such a declaration would have been consistent with the Atlantic Charter of 1941 in which the U.S. and the U.K. jointly agreed that, among the "common principles . . . on which they base their hopes for a better future for the world," it was their policy that:

> . . . they respect the right of all peoples to choose the form of government under which they will live; and they wish to see sovereign rights and self-government restored to those who have been forcibly deprived of them. . . .

In November, 1942, Secretary Hull submitted to the President a proposed draft US–UK declaration entitled "The Atlantic Charter and National Independence," which the President approved. Before this draft could be broached to the British, however, they submitted a counter-proposal, a statement emphasizing the responsibility of "parent" powers for developing native self-government, and avoiding endorsement of trusteeships. Subsequent Anglo-American discussions in March 1943 addressed both drafts, but foundered on Foreign Secretary Eden's opposition. Secretary Hull reported in his memoirs that Eden could not believe that the word "independence" would be interpreted to the satisfaction of all governments:

> . . . the Foreign Secretary said that, to be perfectly frank, he had to say that he did not like our draft very much. He said it was the word "independence" that troubled him, he had to think of the British Empire system, which was built on the basis of Dominion and colonial status.
>
> He pointed out that under the British Empire system there were varying degrees of self-government, running from the Dominions through the colonial establishments which had in some cases, like Malta, completely self-government, to backward areas that were never likely to have their own government. He added that Australia and New Zealand also had colonial possessions that they would be unwilling to remove from their supervisory jurisdiction.

U.S. inability to work out a common policy with the U.K. also precluded meaningful discussion, let alone agreement, on the colonial issue at the Dumbarton Oaks Conversations in 1944. Through March, 1945, the issue was further occluded by debates within the U.S. Government over the postwar status of Pacific islands captured from the Japanese: in general, the War and Navy Departments advocated their retention under U.S. control as military bases, while State and other departments advocated an international trusteeship.

3.　*Decision on Indochina Left to France*

Secretary of State Stettinius, with the approval of President Roosevelt, issued a statement on April 3, 1945, declaring that, as a result of international discussions at Yalta on the concept of trusteeship, the United States felt that the postwar trusteeship structure:

. . . should be designed to permit the placing under it of the territories mandated after the last war, and such territories taken from the enemy in this war as might be agreed upon at a later date, and also such other territories as might be voluntarily placed under trusteeship.

Indochina thus seemed relegated to French volition.

Nonetheless, as of President Roosevelt's death on April 12, 1945, U.S. policy toward the colonial possessions of its allies, and toward Indochina in particular, was in disarray:

—The British remained apprehensive that there might be a continued U.S. search for a trusteeship formula which might impinge on the Commonwealth.

The French were restive over continued U.S. refusal to provide strategic transport for their forces, resentful over the paucity of U.S. support for French forces in Indochina, and deeply suspicious that the United States—possibly in concert with the Chinese—intended to block their regaining control of Vietnam, Laos and Cambodia.

B. TRUMAN AND THE OCCUPATION OF INDOCHINA, 1945

Within a month of President Truman's entry into office, the French raised the subject of Indochina at the United Nations Conference at San Francisco. Secretary of State Stettinius reported the following conversation to Washington:

. . . Indo-China came up in a recent conversation I had with Bidault and Bonnet. The latter remarked that the French Government interprets [Under Secretary of State] Welles' statement of 1942 concerning the restoration of French sovereignty over the French Empire as including Indo-China, the press continues to imply that a special status will be reserved for this colonial area. It was made quite clear to Bidault that the record is entirely innocent of any official statement of this government questioning, even by implication, French sovereignty over Indo-China. Certain elements of American public opinion, however, condemned French governmental policies and practices in Indo-China. Bidault seemed relieved and has no doubt cabled Paris that he received renewed assurances of our recognition of French sovereignty over that area.

In early June 1945, the Department of State instructed the United States Ambassador to China on the deliberations in progress within the U.S. Government and its discussions with allies on U.S. policy toward Indochina. He was informed that at San Francisco:

. . . the American delegation has insisted upon the necessity of providing for a progressive measure of self-government for all dependent peoples looking toward their eventual independence or incorporation in some form of federation according to circumstances and the ability of the peoples to assume these responsibilities. Such decisions would preclude the establishment of a trusteeship in Indochina except with the consent of the French Government. The latter seems unlikely. Nevertheless it is the President's intention at some appropriate time to ask that the French Government give some positive indication of its intentions in regard to the establishment of civil liberties and increasing measures of self-government in Indochina before formulating further declarations of policy in this respect.

The United Nations Charter (June 26, 1945) contained a "Declaration Regarding Non-Self-Governing Territories":

Article 73

Members of the United Nations which have or assume responsibilities for the administration of territories whose peoples have not yet attained a full measure of self-government recognize the principle that the interests of the inhabitants of these territories are paramount, and accept as a sacred trust the obligation to promote to the utmost, within the system of international peace and security established by the present Charter, the well-being of the inhabitants of these territories, and, to this end:
    a. to ensure, with due respect for the culture of the peoples concerned, their political, economic, social, and educational advancement, their just treatment, and their protection against abuses;
    b. to develop self-government, to take due account of the political aspirations of the peoples, and to assist them in the progressive development of their free political institutions, according to the particular circumstances of each territory and its peoples and their varying stages of advancement; . . .

Again, however, military considerations governed U.S. policy in Indochina. President Truman replied to General de Gaulle's repeated offers for aid in Indochina with statements to the effect that it was his policy to leave such matters to his military commanders. At the Potsdam Conference (July, 1945), the Combined Chiefs of Staff decided that Indochina south of latitude 16° North was to be included in the Southeast Asia Command under Admiral Mountbatten. Based on this decision, instructions were issued that Japanese forces located north of that line would surrender to Generalissimo Chiang Kai-shek, and those to the south to Admiral Lord Mountbatten; pursuant to these instructions, Chinese forces entered Tonkin in September, 1945, while a small British task force landed at Saigon. Political difficulties materialized almost immediately, for while the Chinese were prepared to accept the Vietnamese government they found in power in Hanoi, the British refused to do likewise in Saigon, and deferred to the French there from the outset.

There is no evidence that serious concern developed in Washington at the swiftly unfolding events in Indochina. In mid-August, Vietnamese resistance forces of the Viet Minh, under Ho Chi Minh, had seized power in Hanoi and shortly thereafter demanded and received the abdication of the Japanese puppet, Emperor Bao Dai. On V-J Day, September 2nd, Ho Chi Minh had proclaimed in Hanoi the establishment of the Democratic Republic of Vietnam (DRV). The DRV ruled as the only civil government in all of Vietnam for a period of about 20 days. On 23 September 1945, with the knowledge of the British Commander in Saigon, French forces overthrew the local DRV government, and declared French authority restored in Cochinchina. Guerrilla war began around Saigon. Although American OSS representatives were present in both Hanoi and Saigon and ostensibly supported the Viet Minh, the United States took no official position regarding either the DRV, or the French and British actions in South Vietnam. In October, 1945, the United States stated its policy in the following terms:

US has no thought of opposing the reestablishment of French control in Indochina and no official statement by US GOVT has questioned even by implication French sovereignty over Indochina. However, it is not the policy of this GOVT to assist the French to reestablish their control over Indochina by force and the willingness of the US to see French control reestablished assumes that French claim to have the support of the population of Indochina is borne out by future events.

French statements to the U.S. looked for an early end to the hostilities, and spoke reassuringly of reforms and liberality. In November, Jean Chauvel, Secretary-General to the French Minister for Foreign Affairs, told the U.S. Ambassador that:

> When the trouble with the Annamites broke out de Gaulle had been urged by the French Mission in India to make some sort of policy statement announcing France's intention to adopt a far-reaching progressive policy designed to give the native population much greater authority, responsibility and representation in govt. De Gaulle considered the idea but rejected it because in the state of disorder prevailing in Indochina he believed that no such policy could be implemented pending restoration of French authority and would therefore just be considered by everyone as "merely more fine words." Furthermore de Gaulle and the Foreign Minister believe that the present situation is still so confused and they have so little information really reliable on the overall Indochina picture that such plans and thoughts as they held heretofore may have to be very thoroughly revised in the light of recent developments.
>
> Despite the fact that the French do not feel that they can as yet make any general statements outlining specific future plans for Indochina, Chauvel says that they hope "very soon" to put into operation in certain areas programs including local elections which will be designed to grant much greater authority and greater voice in affairs to the natives. This he said would be a much better indication of the sincerity of French intentions than any policy statement. . . . The French hope soon to negotiate an agreement with [the King of Cambodia] which will result in the granting of much greater responsibility and authority to the Cambodians. He mentioned specifically that there would be many more natives integrated into the local administrative services and it was also hoped that local elections could soon be held. The French he said intend to follow the same procedure in Laos when the situation permits and eventually also in Annam and Tonkin. When order is restored throughout Indochina and agreements have been reached with the individual states Chauvel said the French intend to embody the results of these separate agreements into a general program for all of Indochina.

From the autumn of 1945 through the autumn of 1946, the United States received a series of communications from Ho Chi Minh depicting calamitous conditions in Vietnam, invoking the principles proclaimed in the Atlantic Charter and in the Charter of the United Nations, and pleading for U.S. recognition of the independence of the DRV, or—as a last resort—trusteeship for Vietnam under the United Nations. But while the U.S. took no action on Ho's requests, it was also unwilling to aid the French. On January 15, 1946, the Secretary of War was advised by the Department of State that it was contrary to U.S. policy to "employ American flag vessels or aircraft to transport troops of any nationality to or from the Netherlands East Indies or French Indochina, nor to permit use of such craft to carry arms, ammunition or military equipment to these areas." However, the British arranged for the transport of additional French troops to Indochina, bilaterally agreed with the French for the latter to assume British occupation responsibilities, and signed a pact on 9 October, 1945, giving "full recognition to French rights" in Indochina. French troops began arriving in Saigon that month, and subsequently the British turned over to them some 800 U.S. Lend-Lease jeeps and trucks. President Truman approved the latter transaction on the grounds that removing the equipment would be impracticable.

The fighting between the French and the Vietnamese which began in South Vietnam with the 23 September, 1945, French *coup d'etat,* spread from Saigon throughout Cochinchina, and to southern Annam. By the end of January, 1946, it was wholly a French affair, for by that time the British withdrawal was complete; on 4 March, 1946, Admiral Lord Mountbatten deactivated Indochina as territory under the Allied Southeast Asia Command, thereby transferring all control to French authorities. From French headquarters, via Radio Saigon, came announcements that a military "mopping-up" campaign was in progress, but pacification was virtually complete; but these reports of success were typically interspersed with such items as the following:

> 20 March 1946:
> Rebel bands are still (wreaking destruction) in the areas south of Saigon. These bands are quite large, some numbering as many as 1,000 men. Concentrations of these bands are to be found . . . in the villages. Some have turned north in an attempt to disrupt (communications) in the Camau Peninsula, northeast of Batri and in the general area south of (Nha Trang). In the area south of Cholon and in the north of the Plaine des Jenes region, several bands have taken refuge. . . .
> 21 March 1946:
> The following communique was issued by the High Commissioner for Indochina this morning: "Rebel activities have increased in the Bien Hoa area, on both banks of the river Dong Nai. A French convoy has been attacked on the road between Bien Hoa and Tan Uyen where a land mine had been laid by the rebels.
> "In the (Baclo) area, northwest of Saigon, a number of pirates have been captured in the course of a clean-up raid. Among the captured men are five Japanese deserters. The dead bodies of three Japanese, including an officer, have been found at the point where the operation was carried out.
> "A French detachment was ambushed at (San Jay), south Annam. The detachment, nevertheless, succeeded in carrying out its mission. Several aggressions by rebel parties are reported along the coastal road."

Violence abated in South Vietnam somewhat as Franco–DRV negotiations proceeded in spring, 1946, but in the meantime, French forces moved into further confrontation with Vietnamese "rebels" in Tonkin. In February, 1946, a French task force prepared to force landings at Haiphong, but was forestalled by diplomatic maneuver. A Franco–Chinese agreement of 28 February 1946 provided that the Chinese would turn over their responsibilities in northern Indochina to the French on 31 March 1946.

On March 6, 1946, a French–DRV accord was reached in the following terms:

> 1. The French Government recognizes the Vietnamese Republic as a Free State having its own Government, its own Parliament, its own Army

and its own Finances, forming part of the Indochinese Federation and of the French Union. In that which concerns the reuniting of the three "Annamite Regions" [Cochinchina, Annam, Tonkin] the French Government pledges itself to ratify the decisions taken by the populations consulted by referendum.

2. The Vietnamese Government declares itself ready to welcome amicably the French Army when, conforming to international agreements, it relieves the Chinese Troops. A Supplementary Accord, attached to the present Preliminary Agreement, will establish the means by which the relief operations will be carried out.

3. The stipulations formulated above will immediately enter into force. Immediately after the exchange of signatures, each of the High Contracting Parties will take all measures necessary to stop hostilities in the field, to maintain the troops in their respective positions, and to create the favorable atmosphere necessary to the immediate opening of friendly and sincere negotiations. These negotiations will deal particularly with:

a. diplomatic relations of Viet-nam with Foreign States
b. the future law of Indochina
c. French Interests, economic and cultural, in Viet-nam.

Hanoi, Saigon or Paris may be chosen as the seat of the conference.

> DONE AT HANOI, the 6th of March 1946
> Signed: Sainteny

Signed: Ho-chi Minh
and Vu Hong Khanh

French forces quickly exercise their prerogative, occupying Hanoi on 18 March 1946, and negotiations opened in Dalat in April.

Hence, as of April 10, 1946, allied occupation in Indochina was officially over, and French forces were positioned in all of Vietnam's major cities; the problems of U.S. policy toward Vietnam then shifted from the context of wartime strategy to the arena of the U.S. relationship with France.

II. U.S. NEUTRALITY IN THE FRANCO–VIET MINH WAR, 1946–1949

A. FAILURES OF NEGOTIATED SETTLEMENT

The return of the French to Tonkin in March, 1946, created an explosive situation. North Vietnam, a traditionally rice-deficit area, had experienced an extraordinarily bad harvest in 1945. Severe famine was scarcely helped by the concentration of armies in the Red River Delta—Vietnamese irregular forces, the most numerous belonging to the Viet Minh; some 150,000 Chinese; and then the French Expeditionary Corps. The people were not only hungry, but politically restive; the popular appetite for national independence had been thoroughly whetted by the Viet Minh and the formation of the DRV. While feeling against all foreign occupiers ran high, the French remained the primary target of enmity. But the March 6 Accord deferred a reckoning, serving to mollify extremists in Tonkin, and to dampen guerrilla operations in South Vietnam. The accord in any event underwrote peaceful cooperation between France and the DRV in North Vietnam for eight months.

Yet the March 6 Accord constituted an admission of defeat for Ho Chi Minh, because his policy had been directed toward internationalizing the Indochina problem. Ho made repeated overtures to the United States, to the United Nations, and to China, the USSR, and the U.K. His letters presented eloquent appeals for U.S. or U.N. intervention in Vietnam on the grounds of the principles embodied in the Atlantic Charter, the U.N. Charter, and on humanitarian grounds. The last such to be forwarded to the U.S. prior to the Accord of 6 March 1946, is summarized in the following telegram from an American diplomat in Hanoi, received in Washington 27 February 1946:

> Ho Chi Minh handed me 2 letters addressed to President of USA, China, Russia, and Britain identical copies of which were stated to have been forwarded to other governments named. In 2 letters to Ho Chi Minh request [sic] USA as one of United Nations to support idea of Annamese independence according to Philippines [sic] example, to examine the case of the Annamese, and to take steps necessary to maintenance of world peace which is being endangered by French efforts to reconquer Indochina. He asserts that Annamese will fight until United Nations interfere in support of Annamese independence. The petition addressed to major United Nations contains:
>
> A. Review of French relations with Japanese where French Indochina allegedly aided Japs:
>
> B. Statement of establishment on 2 September 1945 of PENW [sic] Democratic Republic of Viet Minh:
>
> C. Summary of French conquest of Cochin China begun 23 Sept 1945 and still incomplete:
>
> D. Outline of accomplishments of Annamese Government in Tonkin including popular elections, abolition of undesirable taxes, expansion of education and resumption as far as possible of normal economic activities:
>
> E. Request to 4 powers: (1) To intervene and stop the war in Indochina in order to mediate fair settlement and (2) to bring the Indochinese issue before the United Nations organization. The petition ends with statement that Annamese ask for full independence in fact and that in interim while awaiting UNO decision the Annamese will continue to fight the reestablishment of French imperialism. Letters and petition will be transmitted to Department soonest.

There is no record that the U.S. encouraged Ho Chi Minh thus to submit his cause to the U.S., beyond the O.S.S. support he received during and immediately after World War II; nor does the record reflect that the U.S. responded affirmatively to Ho's petitions. Rather, the U.S. Government appears to have adhered uniformly to a policy of looking to the French rather than to Vietnamese Nationalists for constructive steps toward Vietnamese independence. On 5 December, 1946, after the November incidents, but before the fighting broke out in earnest, State instructed the U.S. diplomatic representative in Hanoi as follows:

> Assume you will see Ho in Hanoi and offer following summary our present thinking as guide.
>
> Keep in mind Ho's clear record as agent international communism, absence evidence recantation Moscow affiliations, confused political situation France and support Ho receiving French Communist Party. Least desirable eventuality would be establishment Communist-dominated Moscow-oriented state Indochina in view DEPT, which most interested INFO

strength non-communist elements Vietnam. Report fully, repeating or requesting DEPT repeat Paris.

Recent occurrences Tonkin cause deep concern. Consider March 6 accord and modus vivendi as result peaceful negotiation provide basis settlement outstanding questions between France and Vietnam and impose responsibility both sides not prejudice future, particularly forthcoming Fontainebleau Conference, by resort force. Unsettled situation such as pertains certain to offer provocations both sides, but for this reason conciliatory patient attitude especially necessary. Intransigence either side and disposition exploit incidents can only retard economic rehabilitation Indochina and cause indefinite postponement conditions cooperation France and Vietnam which both agree essential.

If Ho takes stand non-implementation promise by French of Cochinchina referendum relieves Vietnam responsibility compliance with agreements, you might if you consider advisable raise question whether he believes referendum after such long disorder could produce worthwhile result and whether he considers compromise on status Cochinchina could possibly be reached through negotiation.

May say American people have welcomed attainments Indochinese in efforts realize praiseworthy aspirations greater autonomy in framework democratic institutions and it would be regrettable should this interest and sympathy be imperilled by any tendency Vietnam administration force issues by intransigence and violence.

May inform Ho [U.S. Ambassador Paris] discussing situation French similar frankness. For your INFO, [Foreign Office] in DEC 3 conversation stated (1) no question reconquest Indochina as such would be counter French public opinion and probably beyond French military resources, (2) French will continue base policy March 6 accord and modus vivendi and make every effort apply them through negotiation Vietnam, (3) French would resort forceful measures only on restricted scale in case flagrant violation agreements Vietnam, (4) d'Argenlieu's usefulness impaired by outspoken dislike Vietnam officials and replacement perhaps desirable, (5) French Communists embarrassed in pose as guardian French international interests by barrage telegraphic appeals from Vietnam. [Ambassador] will express gratification this statement French policy with observation implementation such policy should go far obviate any danger that (1) Vietnamese irreconcilables and extremists might be in position make capital of situation (2) Vietnamese might be turned irrevocably against West and toward ideologies and affiliations hostile democracies which could result perpetual foment Indochina with consequences all Southeast Asia.

Avoid impression US Govt making formal intervention this juncture. Publicity any kind would be unfortunate.

Paris be guided foregoing.

Acheson, Acting.

For a while, the French seemed genuinely interested in pursuing a policy based on the March 6 Accord and the *modus vivendi,* and in avoiding a test of arms with the DRV. If there were contrary utterances from some, such as Admiral d'Argenlieu, the High Commissioner of Indo-China,—who recorded his "amazement that France has such a fine expeditionary corps in Indochina and yet its leaders prefer to negotiate rather than to fight. . . ."—there were many such as General Leclerc, who had led French forces into Hanoi on 18 March 1946, and promptly called on Ho Chi Minh, announcing every intention of honoring the March 6 Accord. "At the present time," he said, "there is no question of imposing ourselves by force on masses who desire evolution and innovation." The French Socialist Party—the dominant political party in France—consistently advocated conciliation during 1946. In December, 1946, even after the armed incidents in November between French and DRV armed forces in North Vietnam, Leon Blum—who had become Premier of France, at the head of an all-Socialist Cabinet—wrote that France had no alternative save to grant the Vietnamese independence:

> There is one way and only one of preserving in Indochina the prestige of our civilization, our political and spiritual influence, and also those of our material interests which are legitimate: it is sincere agreement [with Viet Nam] on the basis of independence. . . .

The Communists, the other major Leftist party in France, were also vocally conciliatory; but, expectant of controlling the government, if not alone at least as part of a coalition, they tended to be more careful than the Socialists of their ability to sway nationalist sentiment. In July of 1946, *L'Humanité,* the Communist newspaper, had emphasized that the Party did not wish France to be reduced to "its own small metropolitan territory," but warned that such would be the consequence if the colonial peoples turned against France:

> Are we, after having lost Syria and Lebanon yesterday, to lose Indochina tomorrow, North Africa the day after?

In the National Assembly in September, 1946, a Communist deputy had declared that:

> The Communists are as much as the next person for the greatness of the country. But . . . they have never ceased to affirm that the French Union . . . can only be founded on the confident, fraternal, and above all, democratic collaboration of all the peoples and races who compose it. . . .

However, Ho Chi Minh was unable to capitalize upon this connection with the French Left (Ho had been one of the founding members of the French Communist Party in the early 1920's) to turn the expressed convictions of either the Socialists or the Communists to the advantage of the DRV. The Communists were not prepared to press the case for the Vietnamese at the cost of votes in France. The Socialists in power paid only lip service to conciliation, and allowed the more militant colonialists, especially those in Vietnam, to set France's policy in Indochina; thus, Admiral d'Argenlieu, not General Leclerc, spoke for the French Government.

In mid-December, 1946, as soon as Blum took office, Ho sent him a telegram with proposals for easing tension in Vietnam, but the message did not reach Paris until December 26. By that time the flashpoint had been passed. In Hanoi, on 19 December 1946, Vietnamese troops, after several days of mounting animosity punctuated with violence, cut off the city's water and electricity, and attacked French posts using small arms, mortar and artillery. The issue of who was the aggressor has never been resolved. The fighting flared across North Vietnam, and two days later, the guerrilla war in South Vietnam quickened pace.

The French responded to the initial attacks with an occasional savagery which rendered increasingly remote restoration of *status quo ante.*

On 23 December 1946, Premier Leon Blum addressed the National Assembly on the Indochina crisis. His speech was characteristically principled, and characteristically ambiguous: he talked peace, but endorsed militant French officials in Vietnam. Although he declared that "the old colonial system founded on conquest and maintained by constraint, which tended toward exploitation of conquered lands and peoples is finished today," he also stated that:

> We have been obliged to deal with violence. The men who are fighting out there, the French soldiers and the friendly populations, may count unreservedly on the vigilance and resolution of the government.
> It was our common task to try everything to spare the blood of our children—and also the blood that is not ours, but which is blood all the same, that of a people whose right to political liberty we recognized ten months ago, and who should keep their place in the union of peoples federated around France. . . ,
> Before all, order must be reestablished, peaceful order which is necessarily the basis for the execution of contracts.

Premier Blum was succeeded within a week of his speech by the first government of the Fourth Republic under Paul Ramadier. France sent three emissaries to Vietnam at this juncture: Admiral d'Argenlieu, General Leclerc, and the Socialist Minister of Overseas France, Marius Moutet. Admiral d'Argenlieu became the High Commissioner of Indochina, and accused the Vietnamese of breaking faith with France. He stated emphatically that France intended to preserve in Indochina:

> . . . the maintenance and development of its present influence and of its economic interests, the protection of ethnic minorities with which it is entrusted, the care of assuring the security of strategic bases within the framework of defense of the Federation and the French Union. . . .
> France does not intend in the present state of evolution of the Indochinese people to give them unconditional and total independence, which would only be a fiction gravely prejudicial to the interests of the two parties.

The other two representatives of France were dispatched on fact-finding missions. Their reports contained diametrically opposing policy recommendations. General Leclerc wrote:

> In 1947 France will no longer put down by force a grouping of 24,000,000 inhabitants which is assuming unity and in which there exists a xenophobic and perhaps a national ideal. . . .
> The capital problem from now on is political. It is a question of coming to terms with an awakening xenophobic nationalism, channeling it in order to safeguard, at least in part, the rights of France.

The General had been sent to examine the military situation, and returned recommending a political solution. The Socialist Marius Moutet had been sent to inquire into the political prospects, and returned with the conclusion that only a military solution was promising. Like Admiral d'Argenlieu, Moutet believed that there could be no negotiations with Ho Chi Minh. He wrote of the "cruel disillusionment of agreements that could not be put into effect . . . ," and he declared that:

> We can no longer speak of a free agreement between France and Vietnam. . . .
> Before any negotiations today, it is necessary to have a military decision. I am sorry, but one cannot commit such madness as the Vietnamese have done with impunity.

It was the politician's ideas, rather than the general's, which prevailed in Paris. Premier Ramadier—himself a Socialist—spoke of peace in Vietnam, and announced that his government favored independence and unity for Vietnam:

> Independence within the French Union [and] union of the three Annamese countries, if the Annamese people desire it.

At the same time, however, his government permitted Admiral d'Argenlieu to launch a military campaign of major proportions and punitive intent.

Very early in the war, the French raised the spectre of Communist conspiracy in Vietnam. Admiral d'Argenlieu in Saigon called for an internationally concerted policy to array the Western powers against the expansion of communism in Asia, beginning with Vietnam. In the National Assembly debated in March, 1947, a Rightist deputy introduced the charge that the violence in Vietnam had been directed from Moscow:

> Nationalism in Indochina is a means, the end is Soviet imperialism.

Neither the government nor the people of France heeded General Leclerc's statement of January, 1947:

> Anti-communism will be a useless tool as long as the problem of nationalism remains unsolved.

Ho Chi Minh, for his part, issued repeated appeals to France for peace, even offering to withdraw personally:

> When France recognizes the independence and unity of Vietnam, we will retire to our village, for we are not ambitious for power or honor.

In February, 1947, the French offered terms to Ho tantamount to unconditional surrender. Ho flatly rejected these, asking the French representative, "If you were in my place, would you accept them? . . . In the French Union there is no place for cowards. If I accepted their conditions I should be one." On 1 March 1947, Ho appealed again to the French government and the French people:

> Once again, we declare solemnly that the Vietnamese people desire only unity and independence in the French Union, and we pledge ourselves to respect French economic and cultural interests. . . . If France would but say the word to cease hostility immediately, so many lives and so much property would be saved and friendship and confidence would be regained.

But the French displayed little interest in negotiations. Premier Ramadier stated in March, 1947, that:

We must protect the life and possessions of Frenchmen, of foreigners, of our Indochinese friends who have confidence in French liberty. It is necessary that we disengage our garrisons, re-establish essential communications, assure the safety of populations which have taken refuge with us. That we have done.

Ramadier and his ministers spoke repeatedly in the spring of 1947 of an imminent end to the "military phase" of the crisis, and of the beginning of a "constructive phase," in which presumably economic and political assistance would supplant the military instrument; but in what was to become a pattern of expectation and frustration, the Fourth Republic discovered that its military forces were incapable of controlling even the principal lines of communication in Vietnam, and that the military solution severely taxed the full resources of the French Union. In March, 1947 an additional division of troops for the French Expeditionary Corps, dispatched to Vietnam per General Leclerc's recommendation, had to be diverted en route to quell an insurgency in Madagascar.

By the summer of 1947, the French Government was aware that the situation in Indochina was at an impasse. Having failed in its attempt to force a military decision, it turned to a political solution, as suggested by General Leclerc. But again the ideas of Admiral d'Argenlieu weighed heavily. In January, 1947, d'Argenlieu wrote that:

> If we examine the problem basically, we are led to inquire whether the political form unquestionably capable of benefiting from the political prestige of legitimacy is not the traditional monarchic institution, the very one that existed before the Japanese surrender. . . . The return of the Emperor [Bao Dai] would probably reassure all those who, having opposed the Viet Minh, fear they will be accused of treason.

It was with Bao Dai, not Ho Chi Minh, that the French elected to negotiate for a political settlement with Vietnamese Nationalists.

French emissaries approached Bao Dai with terms not unlike those Ho Chi Minh had negotiated on 6 March 1946: unity and independence within the French Union, provided Bao Dai formed a government which would furnish a clear alternative to Ho Chi Minh's DRV. With French encouragement, a group of Vietnamese Nationalists formed a political party advocating the installation of Bao Dai at the head of a non-Viet Minh Vietnamese regime. Bao Dai was at first evasive and skeptical, but was eventually convinced that the French situation in Indochina was sufficiently desperate that they would have to honor commitments they made to him. Bao Dai also seems to have believed that he could attract American support and material aid—a view which may have stemmed in part from a 1947 *Life* magazine article by William C. Bullitt, the influential former U.S. Ambassador to France, endorsing Bao Dai as a solution to France's dilemma.

France then proceeded to contract with Bao Dai a series of agreements, each of which ostensibly brought Bao Dai closer to genuine autonomy for Vietnam. It was not, however, until February, 1950, that the French National Assembly acceded to political independence and unification for Vietnam. Chronicled below are the principal steps by which France failed on the one hand to reach an accommodation with Ho Chi Minh, and on the other hand erected the "Bao Dai solution" in its stead.

PRINCIPAL EVENTS
FRANCE–VIETNAM RELATIONS, 1946–1950

Description	*Outcome*
Accord of 6 March 1946	
Agreement signed by Ho Chi Minh with French provides that: 1. France recognizes DRV as: "Free State . . . forming part of the Indochina Federation and the French Union." 2. DRV welcomes French Army into Tonkin for 5 years. 3. Further negotiations to spell out details for DRV independence.	1. Led to French occupation of Tonkin Delta. 2. No significant step taken by France toward DRV autonomy.
First Dalat Conference, 19 April–11 May 1946	
French and DRV delegates attempt to negotiate differences, but are able to enact only minor agreements on cultural and educational matters.	1. Overshadowed by continuing guerrilla war in Cochinchina. 2. A commission was set up to arrange an armistice; futile.
Establishment of Provisional Government of Cochinchina, 1 June 1946	
French announce formation of an independent Cochinchina within the Indochina Federation and the French Union. [Material missing] 6. Referendum to decide Cochinchina's relationship to DRV. 7. France–DRV talks to resume in January, 1947.	1. Touched off new wave of guerrilla war in South Vietnam. 2. Possibility of divided Vietnam pressured DRV in negotiations with France; stiffened DRV attitudes.
"Incidents" at Haiphong, Langson, and Tourane, November, 1946	
Local disputes lead to clashes between French and DRV troops.	1. French seized unilateral control over Haiphong and Langson. 2. French reinforcements landed at Tourane in violation of March 6 Accord.

(Continued on next page)

Hanoi Incident, 19 December 1946

Large-scale conflict begins, spreads throughout Vietnam.

Complete breakdown of relations between France and DRV

Declaration of the Freedom of Cochinchina, 4 February 1947

French High Commissioner extends powers of the Saigon Government to include:

1. Legislative and executive action on all internal affairs.
2. Universal suffrage for election of legislature.

1. President Le Van Hoach of Cochinchina admitted Viet Minh controlled greater part of Cochinchina.
2. Elections repeatedly postponed because of civil disorder.

First Ha Long Bay Agreement, 7 December 1947

1. Bao Dai associates himself with French-sponsored nationalist movement.
2. French promise in vague terms national independence for Vietnam.

1. French took no action toward releasing their control in Vietnam.
2. Bao Dai withdrew to Europe.
3. Agreement condemned by non-Viet Minh [words missing]

Second Ha Long Bay Agreement, 5 June 1948

1. France solemnly recognizes the independence of Vietnam within the French Union.
2. Bao Dai reassociates himself with the attempt to form a nationalist government.

1. France transferred no significant political power to Vietnamese.
2. Led only to further negotiations between Bao Dai and France.

Elysee Agreement, 8 March 1949

In an exchange of letters between Bao Dai and President Auriol, France:
1. Reconfirms Vietnam's status as an independent Associated State within the French Union.
2. Agrees to unifying Vietnam, and placing it under Vietnamese administration, under terms to be negotiated subsequently.

1. French economic and political primacy remained unchanged, even in principle.
2. Cochinchina formally merged with Annam and Tonkin in State of

(Continued on next page)

Elysee Agreement, 8 March 1949 (continued)

3. Retains control of Vietnamese armed forces and foreign relations.	Vietnam in June, 1949.
	3. Plans for internal administrative transfer announced 30 December 1949.
	4. Practical matters of transfer of administrative functions in principal external affairs were deferred to Pau Negotiations of 1950.

Recognition of the Independence of the State of Vietnam, 14 June 1949

French High Commissioner for Indochina and Emperor Bao Dai exchange letters in Saigon formalizing Elysee Agreement.	1. Cochinchina government tendered resignation to Bao Dai, merging in principle with new State of Vietnam.

French Ratification of the Independence of Vietnam 2 February 1950

Following National Assembly approval (29 January 1950), France announces ratification of the status for Vietnam. [words missing]	1. U.S. recognized State of Vietnam (3 February 1950).
	2. Details of transfer of powers strained Pau Negotiations (March–November, 1950).

B.   U.S. POLICY TOWARD THE CONFLICT, 1947–1949

The U.S. manifested increasing concern over the conflict in Indochina, but through 1949 American policy continued to regard the war as fundamentally a matter for French resolution. It is clear on the record that American policy-makers of the day perceived the vacuity of French policies in 1946 and 1947. The U.S., in its representations to France, consistently deplored the prospect of protracted war in Vietnam, and urged meaningful concessions to Vietnamese nationalism. However, the U.S. always stopped short of endorsing Ho Chi Minh, deterred by Ho's history of communist affiliation. Accordingly, U.S. policy gravitated with that of France toward the Bao Dai solution. At no point was the U.S. prepared to adopt an openly interventionist course. To have done so would have clashed with the expressed British view that Indochina was an exclusively French concern, and played into the hands of France's extremist political parties of both the Right and the Left. The U.S. was particularly apprehensive lest by intervening it strengthen the political position of French Communists. Moreover, in 1946 and 1947, France and Britain were moving toward an anti-Soviet alliance in Europe, and the U.S. was reluctant to press a potentially divisive policy. Compared with European recovery, and escape from communist domination, the U.S. considered the fate of Vietnamese nationalism relatively insignificant. Further, the dispute in 1946 and 1945 over the Dutch possession in Indonesia had furnished a precedent: there the U.S. had moved cautiously, and only after long delays, to internationalize the conflict. Extensive American and British investments in Indonesia, moreover, afforded common ground for intervention. No similar rationale or commonality existed for intervention in Indochina, since Indochina was almost exclusively a French economic preserve, and a political morass which the U.K. was manifestly interested in avoiding.

The resultant U.S. policy has most often been termed "neutrality." It was, however, also consistent with the policy of deferring to French volition announced by President Roosevelt's Secretary of State on 3 April 1945. It was a policy characterized by the same indecision that had marked U.S. wartime policy. It was, moreover, a policy formulated with an undertone of indifference: at the time, Indochina appeared to be one region in which the U.S. might enjoy the luxury of abstention.

When open warfare broke out between the DRV and France in December, 1946, John Carter Vincent, Director of the Office of Far Eastern Affairs, in a memorandum to Under Secretary Acheson of 23 December 1946, recommended that the latter call in the French Ambassador to highlight inherent dangers. The memorandum included this acute analysis:

> Although the French in Indochina have made far-reaching paper-concessions to the Vietnamese desire for autonomy, French actions on the scene have been directed toward whittling down the powers and the territorial extent of the Vietnam "free state." This process the Vietnamese have continued to resist. At the same time, the French themselves admit that they lack the military strength to reconquer the country. In brief, with inadequate forces, with public opinion sharply at odds, with a government rendered largely ineffective through internal division, the French have tried to accomplish in Indochina what a strong and united Britain has found it unwise to attempt in Burma. Given the present elements in the situation, guerrilla warfare may continue indefinitely.

Secretary Acheson acted on Mr. Vincent's suggestion, and expressed to the Ambassador views summarized as follows:

> We had anticipated such a situation developing in November and events have confirmed our fears. While we have no wish to offer to mediate under present conditions we do want the French GOVT to know that we are ready and willing to do anything which it might consider helpful in the circumstances. We have been gratified to learn of Moutet's mission and have confidence in his moderation and broad viewpoint. We believe however that the situation is highly inflammatory and if present unsettled conditions continue, there is a possibility that other powers might attempt to bring the matter up before the Security Council. If this happens, as in the case of Indonesia, the question will arise whether the matter is one of purely French internal concern or a situation likely to disturb the peace. Other powers

might likewise attempt some form of intervention as has been suggested in the Chinese press. We would be opposed to such steps, but from every point of view it seems important that the question be settled as soon as possible. Mr. Acheson added that he wondered whether the French would attempt to reconquer the country through military force which was a step that the British had found unwise to attempt in Burma.

On 8 January, 1947, the Department of State instructed the American Ambassador in Paris that the U.S. would approve sale of arms and armaments to France "except in cases which appear to relate to Indochina." On the same date, 8 January 1947, the French conveyed to the Department of State a message that:

> . . . the French Government appreciated the understanding attitude that Mr. Acheson had shown in discussing the problem of Indochina; that it had taken note of Mr. Acheson's offer of "good offices" and appreciated the spirit in which the offer was made; and that the French Government did not feel that it could avail itself of our offer but must continue to handle the situation single-handedly along the lines stated by Moutet. [The emissary] went on to say that the principal objective of the French military was to restore order and reopen communications. He said that after this was done the French Government would be prepared to discuss matters with the Vietnamese. He said that the French Government had every intention of living up to the agreement of last March 6 and the *modus vivendi* of September 15, once order was restored. [He was] asked . . . whether he thought the French military could restore order within any foreseeable future time. He seemed to think, without much evidence of conviction, that they could.

There then ensued an interesting exchange between the U.S. official and the French representative in which the Frenchman sketched a claim of American culpability for the war:

> Speaking personally, I told him that I thought there was one flaw in the French approach to the problem worth mentioning. I had in mind an apparent assumption by the French that there was an equality of responsibility as between the French and the Vietnamese. I said that this did not seem to me to be the case; that the responsibility of France as a world power to achieve a solution of the problem was far greater than that of the Vietnamese; and that the situation was not one which could be localized as a purely French-Vietnamese one but might affect adversely conditions throughout Southeast Asia.
>
> [The emissary] quickly substituted the word "authority" for "responsibility" and said that the French were now faced with the problem of reasserting their authority and that we must share the responsibility for their delay in doing so because we had not acceded to French requests in the autumn of 1945 for material assistance.

Early in February, the U.S. Ambassador in Paris was instructed to reassure Premier Ramadier of the "very friendliest feelings" of the U.S. toward France and its interest in supporting France's recovering economic, political and military strength:

> In spite any misunderstanding which might have arisen in minds French in regard to our position concerning Indochina they must appreciate that we

have fully recognized France's sovereign position in that area and we do not wish to have it appear that we are in any way endeavoring undermine that position, and French should know it is our desire to be helpful and we stand ready assist any appropriate way we can to find solution for Indochinese problem. At same time we cannot shut our eyes to fact that there are two sides this problem and that our reports indicate both a lack French understanding of other side (more in Saigon than in Paris) and continued existence dangerously outmoded colonial outlook and methods in area. Furthermore, there is no escape from fact that trend of times is to effect that colonial empires in XIX Century sense are rapidly becoming thing of past. Action Brit in India and Burma and Dutch in Indonesia are outstanding examples this trend, and French themselves took cognizance of it both in new Constitution and in their agreements with Vietnam. On other hand we do not lose sight fact that Ho Chi Minh has direct Communist connections and it should be obvious that we are not interested in seeing colonial empire administrations supplanted by philosophy and political organizations emanating from and controlled by Kremlin, .

Frankly we have no solution of problem to suggest. It is basically matter for two parties to work out themselves and from your reports and those from Indochina we are led to feel that both parties have endeavored to keep door open to a settlement. We appreciate fact that Vietnam started present fighting in Indochina on December 19 and that this action has made it more difficult for French to adopt a position of generosity and conciliation. Nevertheless we hope that French will find it possible to be more than generous in trying to find a solution.

Thus, the U.S. chose to remain outside the conflict; the announced U.S. position was, in the words of Secretary of State George C. Marshall, to hope that "a pacific basis of adjustment of the difficulties could be found." Events conspired against this hope, however, and as the fighting continued, the prospect of a Moscow-controlled state in Vietnam continued to draw the U.S. nearer to involvement. On 13 May 1947, the Department of State furnished the following guidance to U.S. diplomats in Paris, Saigon, and Hanoi:

Key our position is our awareness that in respect developments affecting position Western democratic powers in southern Asia, we essentially in same boat as French, also as British and Dutch. We cannot conceive setbacks to long-range interests France which would not also be setbacks our own. Conversely we should regard close association France and members French Union as not only to advantage peoples concerned, but indirectly our own.

In our view, southern Asia in critical phase its history with seven new nations in process achieving or struggling independence or autonomy. These nations include quarter inhabitants world and their future course, owing sheer weight populations, resources they command, and strategic location, will be momentous factor world stability. Following relaxation European controls, internal racial, religious, and national differences could plunge new nations into violent discord, or already apparent anti-Western Pan-Asiatic tendencies could become dominant political force, or Communists could capture control. We consider as best safeguard against these eventualities a continued close association between newly-autonomous peoples and powers which have long been responsible their welfare. In particular we recognize Vietnamese will for indefinite period require French material and technical assistance and enlightened political guidance which can be provided only by nation steeped like France in democratic tradition and confirmed in respect human liberties and worth individual.

We equally convinced, however, such association must be voluntary to be lasting and achieve results, and that protraction present situation Indochina can only destroy basic voluntary cooperation, leave legacy permanent bitterness, and irrevocably alienate Vietnamese from France and those values represented by France and other Western democracies.

While fully appreciating difficulties French position this conflict, we feel there is danger in any arrangement which might provide Vietnamese opportunity compare unfavorably their own position and that of other peoples southern Asia who have made tremendous strides toward autonomy since war.

While we are still ready and willing do anything we can which might be considered helpful, French will understand we not attempting come forward with any solution our own or intervene in situation. However, they will also understand we inescapably concerned with situation Far East generally, upon which developments Indochina likely have profound effect. . . .

For your INFO, evidence that French Communists are being directed accelerate their agitation French colonies even extent lose much popular support France (URTEL 1719 Apr 25) may be indication Kremlin prepared sacrifice temporary gains with 40 million French to long range colonial strategy with 600 million dependent people, which lends great urgency foregoing views. . . . DEPT much concerned lest French efforts find QUOTE true representatives Vietnam UNQUOTE with whom negotiate result creation impotent puppet GOVT along lines Cochinchina regime, or that restoration Baodai [sic] may be attempted, implying democracies reduced resort monarchy as weapon against Communism. You may refer these further views if nature your conversations French appears warrant.

The U.S. position may have influenced the French to revise the first Ha Long Bay Agreement (December, 1947) and when the second agreement was signed in June, 1948, the U.S. promptly instructed the U.S. Ambassador to "apply such persuasion and/or pressure as is best calculated [to] produce desired result" of France's "unequivocally and promptly approving the principle of Viet independence." Again, however, the Ambassador was instructed to avoid ostensible intervention while making it clear that the U.S. foresaw France's losing Indochina if it persisted to ignore American advice. These instructions were repeated at the end of August, 1948, with the assertion that the Department of State "believes nothing should be left undone which will strengthen truly nationalist groups in Indochina and induce present supporters of the Viet Minh to come to the side of that group."

The first suggestions that the U.S. became tangibly involved in Vietnam appear in a reported conversation of the U.S. Ambassador with the French Foreign Office in September, 1948. The U.S. Ambassador again urged on France legislation or other definite action to move toward the unification of Vietnam, and the immediate negotiation of concrete steps toward autonomy as envisaged by the Ha Long Bay Agreement. He then told the French representative that:

. . . US is fully appreciative difficulties which face French Government in Indochina at this time and reminds him that US had already indicated its willingness, if French Government so desired, to give public indication its approval of concrete steps by French Government to come to grips with basic political problem of Indochina. I informed him that US also willing under similar circumstances to consider assisting French Government with respect to matter of financial aid for Indochina through ECA but could not give consideration to altering its present policy in this regard unless real progress made in reaching non-Communist solution in Indochina based on cooperation of true nationalists of that country.

As negotiations proceeded with Bao Dai preliminary to the Elysee Agreement, the Department of State instructed the American Ambassador in Paris, on 17 January 1949, that:

> While the Department is desirous of the French coming to terms with Bao Dai or any truly nationalist group which has a reasonable chance of winning over the preponderance of Vietnamese, we cannot at this time irretrievably commit the U.S. to support of a native government which by failing to develop appeal among Vietnamese might become virtually a puppet government separated from the people and existing only by the presence of French military forces.

Following the Elysee Agreement, the U.S. was better disposed toward providing aid in Indochina. On 10 May 1949, the American Consul in Saigon was informed that the U.S. desired the "Bao Dai experiment" to succeed, since there appeared to be no other alternative:

> At the proper time and under the proper circumstances, the Department will be prepared to do its part by extending recognition to the Bao Dai government and by expressing the possibility of complying with any request by such a government for U.S. arms and economic assistance. It must be understood, however, that an aid program of this nature would require Congressional approval. Since the U.S. could, however, scarcely afford backing a government which would have the color and be likely to suffer the fate of a puppet regime, it must be clear that France will offer all necessary concessions to make the Bao Dai solution attractive to the nationalists. This is a step of which the French themselves must see the urgency and necessity in view of the possibly short time remaining before Communist successes in China are felt in Indochina. Moreover, the Bao Dai government must through its own efforts demonstrate the capacity to organize and conduct affairs wisely so as to insure the maximum opportunity for obtaining requisite popular support.

But "anti-communism" initially proved to be no better guideline for the formulation of American policy in Indochina than it had been for the French. Indeed, early U.S. attempts to discern the nature and extent of communist influence in Vietnam devolved to the seeming paradox that if Ho Chi Minh were communist, he seemed to have no visible ties with Moscow. For example, a State Department appraisal of Ho Chi Minh provided to the U.S. Ambassador in China in July, 1948, was admittedly speculative:

> 1. Depts info indicates that Ho Chi Minh is Communist. His long and well-known record in Comintern during twenties and thirties, continuous support by French Communist newspaper *Humanite* since 1945, praise given

him by Radio Moscow (which for past six months has been devoting increasing attention to Indochina) and fact he has been called "leading communist" by recent Russian publications as well as *Daily Worker* makes any other conclusion appear to be wishful thinking.

2. Dept has no evidence of direct link between Ho and Moscow but assumes it exists, nor is it able evaluate amount pressure or guidance Moscow exerting. We have impression Ho must be given or is retaining large degree latitude. Dept considers that USSR accomplishing its immediate aims in Indochina by (a) pinning down large numbers of French troops, (b) causing steady drain upon French economy thereby tending retard recovery and dissipate ECA assistance to France, and (c) denying to world generally surpluses which Indochina normally has available thus perpetuating conditions of disorder and shortages which favorable to growth communism. Furthermore, Ho seems quite capable of retaining and even strengthening his grip on Indochina with no outside assistance other than continuing procession of French puppet govts.

In the fall of 1948, the Office of Intelligence Research in the Department of State conducted a survey of communist influence in Southeast Asia. Evidence of Kremlin-directed conspiracy was found in virtually all countries except Vietnam:

Since December 19, 1946, there have been continuous conflicts between French forces and the nationalist government of Vietnam. This government is a coalition in which avowed communists hold influential positions. Although the French admit the influence of this government, they have consistently refused to deal with its leader, Ho Chi Minh, on the grounds that he is a communist.

To date the Vietnam press and radio have not adopted an anti-American position. It is rather the French colonial press that has been strongly anti-American and has freely accused the U.S. of imperialism in Indochina to the point of approximating the official Moscow position. Although the Vietnam radio has been closely watched for a new position toward the U.S., no change has appeared so far. Nor does there seem to have been any split within the coalition government of Vietnam. . . .

Evaluation. If there is a Moscow-directed conspiracy in Southeast Asia, Indochina is an anomoly so far. Possible explanations are:

1. No rigid directives have been issued by Moscow.
2. The Vietnam government considers that it has no rightest elements that must be purged.
3. The Vietnam Communists are not subservient to the foreign policies pursued by Moscow.
4. A special dispensation for the Vietnam government has been arranged in Moscow.
Of these possibilities, the first and fourth seem most likely.

III.   ORIGINS OF THE U.S. INVOLVEMENT IN VIETNAM

A.   THE POLICY CONTEXT

Events in China of 1948 and 1949 brought the United States to a new awareness of the vigor of communism in Asia, and to a sense of urgency over its containment. U.S. policy instruments developed to meet unequivocal communist challenges in Europe were applied to the problem of the Far East. Concurrent with the development of NATO, a U.S. search began for collective security in Asia; economic and military assistance programs were inaugurated; and the Truman Doctrine acquired wholly new dimensions by extension into regions where the European empires were being dismantled. In March, 1947, President Truman had set forth the following policy guidelines:

> I believe that it must be the policy of the United States to support free peoples who are resisting attempted subjugation by armed minorities or by outside pressures. I believe we must assist free peoples to work out their own destinies in their own way. . . .

The President went on to underscore the U.S. determination to commit its resources to contain communism. While he clearly subordinated military aid to economic and political means, he did assert the U.S. intent to assist in maintaining security:

> To insure the peaceful development of nations, free from coercion, the United States has taken a leading part in establishing the United Nations. The United Nations is designed to make possible freedom and independence for all its members. We shall not realize our objectives, however, unless we are willing to help free peoples to maintain their free institutions and their national integrity against aggressive movements that seek to impose upon them totalitarian regimes.

In the year 1947, while U.S. military assistance began to flow into Greece to ward off subversive aggression, the U.S. inaugurated the European Recovery Plan (ERP). ERP was aimed at economic recovery in Western Europe, especially in countries such as France and Italy where post-war depression was fostering marked leftward political trends. In one of the high level appraisals of the situation that the U.S. had to counter in 1947, the Harriman Committee on Foreign Aid has concluded that:

> The interest of the United States in Europe . . . cannot be measured simply in economic terms. It is also strategic and political. We all know that we are faced in the world today with two conflicting ideologies. . . . Our position in the world has been based for at least a century on the existence in Europe of a number of strong states committed by tradition and inclination to the democratic concept. . . .

The fall of the Czechoslovakian Government in February 1948 brought about the Brussels Pact, a Western European collective defense and economic collaboration arrangement. The blockade of Berlin, which began on 1 April 1948, accelerated U.S. movement toward membership in the alliance. On June 11, 1948 the U.S. Senate adopted a resolution advising the Executive to undertake the:

> . . . Progressive development of regional and other collective arrangements for individual and collective self-defense in accordance with the purposes, principles, and provisions of the Charter [of the UN], association of the United States, by constitutional process, with such regional and other

collective arrangements as are based on continuous and effective self-help and mutual aid, and as affect its national security.

That same month, Congress passed the Economic Cooperation Act, and in July, 1948, opened negotiations for a North Atlantic Alliance. The North Atlantic Treaty was signed in April, 1949, and entered into force in August of that year.

In the same omnibus foreign assistance legislation which had authorized ECA in June, 1948, Congress had provided for a China Aid Program. This measure met almost immediate failure, for Mao's armies spread unchecked over the China mainland, and by mid-1949 the position of the nationalists there was untenable. The "failure" of U.S. aid—which was termed such by Congressional critics—no less than the urgent situation in Europe and the exploding of the first Soviet nuclear device in September, 1949, figured in Congressional action on military assistance legislation.

On October 6, 1949, Congress passed the Mutual Defense Assistance Program (MDAP) through which U.S. arms, military equipment and training assistance might be provided world-wide for collective defense. In the first appropriations under MDAP, NATO countries received 76% of the total, and Greece and Turkey (not yet NATO members), 16%. But Korea and the Philippines received modest aid, and the legislators clearly intended the law to underwrite subsequent appropriations for collective security in Asia. The opening paragraph of the law not only supported NATO, but foreshadowed the Southeast Asia Collective Defense Treaty:

> An Act to Promote the Foreign Policy and Provide for the Defense and General Welfare of the United States by Furnishing Military Assistance to Foreign Nations, Approved October 6, 1949.
>
> Be it enacted by the Senate and House of Representatives of the United States of America in Congress assembled, That this Act may be cited as the "Mutual Defense Assistance Act of 1949."

FINDINGS AND DECLARATION OF POLICY

The Congress of the United States reaffirms the policy of the United States to achieve international peace and security through the United Nations so that armed force shall not be used except in the common interest. The Congress hereby finds that the efforts of the United States and other countries to promote peace and security in furtherance of the purposes of the Charter of the United Nations require additional measures of support based upon the principle of continuous and effective self-help and mutual aid. These measures include the furnishing of military assistance essential to enable the United States and other nations dedicated to the purposes and principles of the United Nations Charter to participate effectively in arrangements for individual and collective self-defense in support of those purposes and principles. In furnishing such military assistance, it remains the policy of the United States to continue to exert maximum efforts to obtain agreements to provide the United Nations with armed forces as contemplated in the Charter and agreements to achieve universal control of weapons of mass destruction and universal regulation and reduction of armaments, including armed forces, under adequate safeguards to protect complying nations against violation and evasion.

The Congress hereby expresses itself as favoring the creation by the free countries and the free peoples of the Far East of a joint organization, consistent with the Charter of the United Nations, to establish a program of self-help and mutual cooperation designed to develop their economic and social well-being, to safeguard basic rights and liberties and to protect their security and independence.

The Congress recognizes that economic recovery is essential to international peace and security and must be given clear priority. The Congress also recognizes that the increased confidence of free peoples in their ability to resist direct or indirect aggression and to maintain internal security will advance such recovery and support political stability.

While Congress was deliberating on MDAP, the staff of the National Security Council, at the request of the Secretary of Defense, had been reexamining U.S. policy toward Asia. In June, 1949, the Secretary had noted that he was:

> . . . increasingly concerned at the . . . advance of communism in large areas of the world and particularly the successes of communism in China. . . .
> A major objective of United States policy, as I understand it, is to contain communism in order to reduce its threat to our security. Our actions in Asia should be part of a carefully considered and comprehensive plan to further that objective.

The NSC study responding to the Secretary's request is remarkable for the rarity of its specific references to Indochina. The staff study focused, rather, on generalities concerning the conflict between the interests of European metropoles and the aspirations of subject Asian peoples for independence. The following extract is from the section of the study dealing with Southeast Asia:

> The current conflict between colonialism and native independence is the most important political factor in southeast Asia. This conflict results not only from the decay of European imperial power in the area but also from a widening political consciousness and the rise of militant nationalism among the subject peoples. With the exception of Thailand and the Philippines, the southeast Asia countries do not possess leaders practiced in the exercise of responsible power. The question of whether a colonial country is fit to govern itself, however, is not always relevant in practical politics. The real issue would seem to be whether the colonial country is able and determined to make continued foreign rule an overall losing proposition for the metropolitan power. If it is, independence for the colonial country is the only practical solution, even though misgovernment eventuates. A solution of the consequent problem of instability, if it arises, must be sought on a non-imperialist plane. In any event, colonial-nationalist conflict provides a fertile field for subversive communist activities, and it is now clear that southeast Asia is the target of a coordinated offensive directed by the Kremlin. In seeking to gain control of southeast Asia, the Kremlin is motivated in part by a desire to acquire southeast Asia's resources and communication lines, and to deny them to us. But the political gains which would accrue to the USSR from communist capture of southeast Asia are equally significant. The extension of communist authority in China represents a grievous political defeat for us; if southeast Asia also is swept by communism we shall have suffered a major political rout the repercussions of which will be felt through-

out the rest of the world, especially in the Middle East and in a then critically exposed Australia. The United States should continue to use its influence looking toward resolving the colonial nationalist conflict in such a way as to satisfy the fundamental demands of the nationalist-colonial conflict, lay the basis for political stability and resistance to communism, and avoid weakening the colonial powers who are our western allies. However, it must be remembered that the long colonial tradition in Asia has left the peoples of that area suspicious of Western influence. We must approach the problem from the Asiatic point of view in so far as possible and should refrain from taking the lead in movements which must of necessity be of Asian origin. It will therefore be to our interest wherever possible to encourage the peoples of India, Pakistan, the Philippines and other Asian states to take the leadership in meeting the common problems of the area. . . .

It would be to the interest of the United States to make use of the skills, knowledge and long experience of our European friends and, to whatever extent may be possible, enlist their cooperation in measures designed to check the spread of USSR influence in Asia. If members of the British Commonwealth, particularly India, Pakistan, Australia and New Zealand, can be persuaded to join with the United Kingdom and the United States in carrying out constructive measures of economic, political and cultural cooperation, the results will certainly be in our interest. Not only will the United States be able thus to relieve itself of part of the burden, but the cooperation of the white nations of the Commonwealth will arrest any potential dangers of the growth of a white-colored polarization.

On December 30, 1949, the National Security Council met with President Truman presiding, discussed the NSC staff study, and approved the following conclusions:

As the basis for realization of its objectives, the United States should pursue a policy toward Asia containing the following components:

a. The United States should make known its sympathy with the efforts of Asian leaders to form regional associations of non-Communist states of the various Asian areas, and if in due course associations eventuate, the United States should be prepared, if invited, to assist such associations to fulfill their purposes under conditions which would be to our interest. The following principles should guide our actions in this respect:

1) Any association formed must be the result of a genuine desire on the part of the participating nations to cooperate for mutual benefit in solving the political, economic, social and cultural problems of the area.

2) The United States must not take such an active part in the early stages of the formation of such an association that it will be subject to the charge of using the Asiatic nations to further United States ambitions.

3) The association, if it is to be a constructive force, must operate on the basis of mutual aid and self-help in all fields so that a true partnership may exist based on equal rights and equal obligations.

4) United States participation [words illegible] association formed will be in accord with Chapter VIII of the Charter of the United Nations dealing with regional arrangements.

b. The United States should act to develop and strengthen the security of the area from Communist external aggression or internal subversion. These steps should take into account any benefits to the security of Asia which may flow from the development of one or more regional groupings. The United States on its own initiative should now:

　　1) Improve the United States position with respect to Japan, the Ryukyus and the Philippines.

　　2) Scrutinize closely the development of threats from Communist aggression, direct or indirect, and be prepared to help within our means to meet such threats by providing political, economic, and military assistance and advice where clearly needed to supplement the resistance of the other governments in and out of the area which are more directly concerned.

　　3) Develop cooperative measures through multilateral or bilateral arrangements to combat Communist internal subversion.

　　4) Appraise the desirability and the means of developing in Asia some form of collective security arrangements, bearing in mind the following considerations:

　　　　a) The reluctance of India at this time to join in any anti-Communist security pact and the influence this will have among the other nations of Asia.

　　　　b) The necessity of assuming that any collective security arrangements which might be developed be based on the principle of mutual aid and on a demonstrated desire and ability to share in the burden by all the participating states.

　　　　c) The necessity of assuring that any such security arrangements would be consonant with the purposes of any regional association which may be formed in accordance with paragraph 3-a above.

　　　　d) The necessity of assuring that any such security arrangement would be in conformity with the provisions of Article 51 of the Charter relating to individual and collective self-defense.

　　c. The United States should encourage the creation of an atmosphere favorable to economic recovery and development in non-Communist Asia, and to the revival of [words illegible] non-discriminatory lines. The policy of the United States should be adapted to promote, where possible, economic conditions that will contribute to political stability in friendly countries of Asia, but the United States should carefully avoid assuming responsibility for the economic welfare and development of that continent. . . .

　　h. The United States should continue to use its influence in Asia toward resolving the colonial-nationalist conflict in such a way as to satisfy the fundamental demands of the nationalist movement while at the same time minimizing the strain on the colonial powers who are our Western allies. Particular attention should be given to the problem of French Indo-China and action should be taken to bring home to the French the urgency of removing the barriers to the obtaining by Bao Dai or other non-Communist nationalist leaders of the support of a substantial proportion of the Vietnamese. . . .

　　i. Active consideration should be given to means by which all members of the British Commonwealth may be induced to play a more active role in collaboration with the United States in Asia. Similar collaboration should be obtained to the extent possible from other non-Communist nations having interests in Asia.

j. Recognizing that the non-Communist governments of South Asia already constitute a bulwark against Communist expansion in Asia, the United States should exploit every opportunity to increase the present Western orientation of the area and to assist, within our capabilities, its governments in their efforts to meet the minimum aspirations of their people and to maintain internal security.

Thus, in the closing months of 1949, the course of U.S. policy was set to block further communist expansion in Asia: by collective security if the Asians were forthcoming, by collaboration with major European allies and commonwealth nations, if possible, but bilaterally if necessary. On that policy course lay the Korean War of 1950–1953, the forming of the Southeast Asia Treaty Organization of 1954, and the progressively deepening U.S. involvement in Vietnam.

B. THE U.S. ENTERS THE WAR

On December 30, 1949, the French signed over ten separate implementing agreements relating to the transfer of internal administration in Vietnam to Bao Dai's State of Vietnam, in accordance with the Elysee Agreement of March 8, 1949. By January, 1950, Mao's legions had reached Vietnam's northern frontier, and North Vietnam was moving into the Sino–Soviet orbit. A Department of State statement enunciated U.S. policy as of 20 January 1950:

DEPT still hopeful Bao Dai will succeed in gaining increasing popular support at Ho's expense and our policy remains essentially the same; to encourage him and to urge FR toward further concessions.

The start made by Bao Dai, the qualities exhibited by him, and his initial reception seem to have been better than we might have anticipated, even discounting optimism of FR sources. Transfer of power apparently well received. FR success in disarming and interning fleeing CHI Nationalists without serious intervention to the present by CHI COMMIES also encouraging.

However, more recently, marked opposition has been encountered which demonstrates at least that Bao Dai's popular support has not yet widened. Increased Viet Minh MIL activity is disquieting. This CLD be special effort by Ho, timed to coincide with transfer of power and the arrival of CHI COMMIES armies on frontier, and to precede Bangkok Conference, or CLD be evidence of increasing strength reinforced by hopes of CHI COMMIE support, direct or indirect.

DEPT has as yet no knowledge of negotiations between Ho and Mao groups although radio intercept of New China News Agency release of JAN 17 indicates that Ho has messaged the "GOVTS of the world" that "the GOVT of the Democratic Republic of Vietnam is the only legal GOVT of the Vietnam people" and is "ready to establish DIPL relations with any GOVT which WLD be willing to cooperate with her on the basis of equality and mutual respect of national sovereignty and territory so as to defend world peace and democracy." Ho's radio making similar professions. . . .

Nature and timing of recognition of Bao Dai now under consideration here and with other GOVTS. . . .

First the Chinese Communists, and then the Soviets recognized the DRV. On 29 January 1950, the French National Assembly approved legislation granting autonomy to the State of Vietnam. On February 1, 1950, Secretary of State Acheson made the following public statement:

> The recognition by the Kremlin of Ho Chi Minh's communist movement in Indochina comes as a surprise. The Soviet acknowledgment of this movement should remove any illusions as to the "nationalist" nature of Ho Chi Minh's aims and reveals Ho in his true colors as the mortal enemy of native independence in Indochina.
>
> Although timed in an effort to cloud the transfer of sovereignty by France to the legal Governments of Laos, Cambodia, and Vietnam, we have every reasonable [words illegible] governments will proceed in their development toward stable governments representing the true nationalist sentiments of more than 20 million peoples of Indochina.
>
> French action in transferring sovereignty to Vietnam, Laos and Cambodia has been in process for some time. Following French ratification, which is expected within a few days, the way will be open for recognition of these legal governments by the countries of the world whose policies support the development of genuine national independence in former colonial areas. Ambassador Jessup has already expressed to Emperor Bao Dai our best wishes for prosperity and stability in Vietnam, and the hope that closer relationship will be established between Vietnam and the United States.

Formal French ratification of Vietnamese independence was announced on 2 Febuary 1950. President Truman approved U.S. recognition for Bao Dai the same date, and on 4 February, the American Consul General in Saigon was instructed to deliver the following message to Bao Dai:

> Your Imperial Majesty:
>
> I have Your Majesty's letter in which I am informed of the signing of the agreements of March 8, 1949 between Your Majesty, on behalf of Vietnam, and the President of the French Republic, on behalf of France. My Government has also been informed of the ratification on February 2, 1950 by the French Government of the agreements of March 8, 1949.
>
> Since these acts establish the Republic of Vietnam as an independent State within the French Union, I take this opportunity to congratulate Your Majesty and the people of Vietnam on this happy occasion.
>
> The Government of the United States of America is pleased to welcome the Republic of Vietnam into the community of peace-loving nations of the world and to extend diplomatic recognition to the Government of the Republic of Vietnam. I look forward to an early exchange of diplomatic representatives between our two countries. . . .

Recognition of Bao Dai was followed swiftly by French requests for U.S. aid. On May 8, 1950, Secretary of State Acheson released the following statement in Paris:

> The [French] Foreign Minister and I have just had an exchange of views on the situation in Indochina and are in general agreement both as to the urgency of the situation in that area and as to the necessity for remedial action. We have noted the fact that the problem of meeting the threat to the security of Viet Nam, Cambodia, and Laos which now enjoy independence within the French Union is primarily the responsibility of France

and the Governments and peoples of Indochina. The United States recognizes that the solution of the Indochina problem depends both upon the restoration of security and upon the development of genuine nationalism and that United States assistance can and should contribute to these major objectives.

The United States Government, convinced that neither national independence nor democratic evolution exist in any area dominated by Soviet imperialism, considers the situation to be such as to warrant its according economic aid and military equipment to the Associated States of Indochina and to France in order to assist them in restoring stability and permitting these states to pursue their peaceful and democratic development.

On May 11, 1950, the Acting Secretary of State made the following statement:

A special survey mission, headed by R. Allen Griffin, has just returned from Southeast Asia and reported on economic and technical assistance needed in that area. Its over-all recommendations for the area are modest and total in the neighborhood of $60 million. The Department is working on plans to implement that program at once.

Secretary Acheson on Monday in Paris cited the urgency of the situation applying in the associated states of Viet-Nam, Laos and Cambodia. The Department is working jointly with ECA to implement the economic and technical assistance recommendations for Indochina as well as the other states of Southeast Asia and anticipates that this program will get underway in the immediate future.

Military assistance for Southeast Asia is being worked out by the Department of Defense in cooperation with the Department of State, and the details will not be made public for security reasons.

Military assistance needs will be met from the President's emergency fund of $75 million provided under MDAP for the general area of China.

Economic assistance needs will be met from the ECA China Aid funds, part of which both Houses of Congress have indicated will be made available for the general area of China. Final legislative action is still pending on this authorization but is expected to be completed within the next week.

The United States thereafter was directly involved in the developing tragedy in Vietnam.

IV. THE CHARACTER AND POWER OF THE VIET MINH— A SUMMARY

One of the recurrent themes of criticism of U.S. policy in Vietnam has been that from the end of World War II on, there was a failure to recognize that the Viet Minh was the principal vehicle for Vietnamese nationalism and that it, in fact, was in control of and effectively governing all of Vietnam. Evidence on issues like popularity and control is always somewhat suspect—especially when dealing with an exotic country like Vietnam at a time when what Americans knew about it was largely dependent on French sources. Nonetheless, some generalizations can be made and supported.

First, the Viet Minh was the main repository of Vietnamese nationalism and anti-French colonialism. There were other such groups promoting Viet independence but none were competitive on a country-wide scale. It is also true that the disciplined, well-organized, and well-led Indochinese Communist Party was the controlling element in the Viet Minh. The ICP was not, however, in the numerical majority either in total membership or in leadership posts held. This gap between control and numbers can be explained by two factors: (a) ICP strategy was to unify nationalist elements to achieve the immediate objective of independence; and (b) the other components of the Viet Minh were sizable enough to fractionalize the whole movement. In other words, from World War II on, the ICP was strong enough to lead, but not to dominate Vietnamese nationalism.

Second, the Viet Minh was sufficiently popular and effective to turn itself into a Vietnam-wide government that could have extended its authority throughout the country after World War II—except for the obstacle of reasserted French power, and, to a lesser degree, of indigenous political opposition in Cochinchina. The Viet Minh was always more powerful in Tonkin and Annam than in South Vietnam. However, it seems likely that in the absence of the French, the Viet Minh through its governmental creation, the DRV, would have overridden indigenous tribal, religious, and other opposition in short order.

Vietnamese nationalism developed three types of political parties or movements:

Reform parties. Narrowly based among the small educated Vietnamese elite, these parties made little pretense at representing the masses of the peasantry— except in the ancient mandarinal sense of paternal leadership. In general, they advocated reform of the relationship between France and Vietnam to establish an independent and united nation, but would neither sever beneficial bonds with the metropole, nor alter drastically the Vietnamese social structure. Members included many men of impeccable repute and undoubted nationalist convictions —among them Ngo Dinh Diem—but also a number of known opportunist and corrupt Vietnamese. The reformist parties were further discredited by collaboration with the Japanese during World War II. These parties formed the basis for the "Bao Dai solution" to which France and the U.S. gravitated in the late 1940's.

Theocratic parties. In Cochinchina—and almost exclusively there—during the 1930's there emerged religious sects commanding firm loyalties of hundreds of thousands of peasants. Two of these—the Cao Dai and the Hoa Hao—aspired to temporal as well as spiritual power, fielded armed forces, and formed local governments. They opposed both French political and cultural hegemony, and domination by other Vietnamese parties. Some elements collaborated openly with the Japanese during 1940–1945. Because these parties were of local and religious character, any parallel with other Viet political organizations would be inexact. These movements account in large measure for the distinctive character of South Vietnamese nationalism as compared with that of Annam or Tonkin.

Revolutionary parties. The numerous remaining Vietnamese political parties fall into the revolutionary category: they advocated Vietnam's independence from France and some degree of radical reorganization of the Viet polity. Their political coloration ranged from the deep red of the Saigon-centered Trotskyites (who advocated anti-imperialist revolution throughout the world, and within Vietnam, expropriation for the workers and peasants) through the less violent hues of communism and Kuomintang-styled nationalism, to the indistinct, eclectic nationalism of the Binh Xuyen criminal fraternity (another Saigon phenomenon).

Only two of these movements developed a Vietnam-wide influence: the Indo-chinese Communist Party (ICP), and the Vietnam Nationalist Party (VNQDD). Both these parties were troubled throughout their history by factionalism, and by repeated (French police) purges. Both aspired to politicizing the peasants; neither wholly succeeded. Of the two, the ICP consistently demonstrated the greater resiliency and popularity, attributable to superior conspiratorial doctrine and technique, and to more coherent and astute leadership. Both the ICP and the VNQDD figured in peasant uprisings in 1930–1931, and 1940–1941. Each played a role in the Vietnamese resistance against the Vichy French and the Japanese during World War II: the ICP as the nucleus of the Viet Minh, and the VNQDD as the principal component of the Chinese Nationalist-sponsored Dong Minh Hoi.

The Viet Minh—*Viet Nam Doc Lap Dong Minh Hoi,* League for the Inde-pendence of Vietnam—came into being in May, 1941, at the 8th Plenum of the Indochinese Communist Party, held in South China. It was formed as a "united front" organization initially composed of the ICP, Revolutionary Youth League, the New Vietnam Party, and factions of the Vietnam Nationalist Party (VNQDD). Membership was held open to any other individuals or groups willing to join in struggling for "national liberation." The announced program of the Viet Minh called for a wide range of social and political reforms designed mainly to appeal to Viet patriotism. Emphasis was placed on an anti-Japanese crusade and preparation for "an insurrection by the organization of the people into self-defense corps," not on communist cant.

Though a Kuomintang general originally sponsored the Viet Minh, Ho soon became suspect, and in 1942 was jailed by the Chinese. While he was in prison, probably to offset the Viet Minh's growing appeal, and to assure tighter Chinese control of the Vietnamese, the KMT fostered a rival Viet "popular front," the Vietnam Revolutionary League (Dong Minh Hoi), which was based on the VNQDD, the Great Vietnam Nationalist Party (Dai Viet), and a number of smaller groups, but was supposed to include the Viet Minh. In fact, however, the Dong Minh Hoi never acquired more than a nominal control over the Viet Minh. In 1943, Ho was released from prison and put in charge of the Dong Minh Hoi—a status apparently conditioned on his accepting overall Chinese guidance and providing the allies with intelligence. But as the war progressed, Ho and the Viet Minh drew apart from the Dong Minh Hoi, and the latter never succeeded in acquiring apparatus within Vietnam comparable to the Viet Minh's.

During the war, some Vietnamese political parties collaborated with the Japanese or the Vichy French. These were put at a disadvantage during and after the war in competition with the ICP, the Viet Minh, or the Dong Minh Hoi—all of which developed an aura of unwavering faith to resistance against all foreign domination. But only the ICP and the Viet Minh established their reputations by extensive wartime operations among the people of Vietnam. In Cochinchina, up until surfacing in April 1945, the ICP continued to operate largely under-ground and without much regard for the Viet Minh mantle; in Annam and Tonkin, however, all ICP undertakings were given Viet Minh identity. Through-out Vietnam, the ICP initiated patient political action: the dissemination of propaganda, the training of cadres, the establishment of a network of cells down to hamlet level. The ICP was during the war the hard core of the Viet Minh, but the bulk of the Viet Minh membership were no doubt quite unaware of that fact: they served the Viet Minh out of a patriotic fervor.

The American O.S.S. during World War II dealt with the Viet Minh as the sole efficient resistance apparatus within Vietnam, depending upon it for reliable intelligence, and for aid in assisting downed allied pilots. However, the Viet Minh itself assigned priority to political tasks ahead of these military missions. The first permanent Viet Minh bases were established in 1942–43 in the mountains north of Hanoi. Only after its political network was well established did it field its first guerrilla forces, in September 1943. The first units of the Viet Minh Liberation Army came into being on December 24 of that year, but there is no evidence of large scale, concerted guerrilla operations until after March 1945.

At the end of 1944, the Viet Minh claimed a total membership of 500,000, of which 200,000 were in Tonkin, 150,000 in Annam, and 150,000 in Cochinchina. The Viet Minh political and military structure was significantly further developed in North Vietnam. In May 1945, a Viet Minh "liberated zone" was established near the Chinese border. As the war drew to a close the Viet Minh determined to preempt allied occupation, and to form a government prior to their arrival. The Viet Minh ability to do so proved better in the north than in the south. In August 1945, Ho Chi Minh's forces seized power from the Japanese and Bao Dai in North Vietnam, forced the emperor to abdicate, and to cede his powers to Ho's Democratic Republic of Vietnam (DRV). In Cochinchina, however, the Viet Minh were able to gain only tenuous control of Saigon and its environs. Nonetheless, when the allies arrived, the Viet Minh were the *de facto* government in both North and South Vietnam: Ho Chi Minh and his DRV in Hanoi, and an ICP-dominated "Committee of the South" in Saigon.

On 12 September 1945, the British landed a Gurkha battalion and a company of Free French soldiers in Saigon. The British commander regarded the Vietnamese government with disdain because of its lack of authority from the French and because of its inability to quell civil disorder in South Vietnam. Saigon police clashed with Trotskyites, and in the rural areas, fighting broke out between Viet Minh troops and those of Cao Dai and Hoa Hoa. Spreading violence rendered futile further attempts to draw together the Vietnamese factions, and prompted the French to importune the British commander to permit them to step in to restore order. On the morning of 23 September, French troops overthrew the Vietnamese government after a tenure of only three weeks. The official British account termed the French method of executing the coup d'etat "unfortunate" in that they "absolutely ensured that countermeasures would be taken by the [Vietnamese]. . . ." Vietnamese retaliation was quick and violent: over one hundred Westerners were slain in the first few days, and others kidnapped; on 26 September, the U.S. commander of the O.S.S. in Saigon was killed. Thus, the first Indochina War began in Cochinchina in late September, 1945, and American blood was shed in its opening hours.

At that juncture, the ICP in Cochinchina was in a particularly vulnerable position. The ICP had permitted the Viet Minh to pose as an arm of the Allies, and had supported cooperation with the British and amnesty for the French. The Party had even undertaken, through the Committee of the South, to repress the Trotskyites. But violence undermined its advocacy of political moderation, of maintaining public order, and of negotiations with the French. Further, the ICP in Saigon was assured by French communists that they would receive no assistance from Party brethren abroad. The French coup d'etat thrust conflict upon the Vietnamese of Cochinchina. The question before the communists was how to respond; the ICP leadership determined [words illegible] and that to maintain leadership of the nationalist movement in South Vietnam they had to make the Viet Minh the most unbending foe of compromise with the French.

The situation in all of Vietnam at the end of the war was confused—neither the French, nor the Viet Minh, nor any other group exercised clear authority. While the Viet Minh was far and away the single most powerful Vietnamese organization, and while it claimed dominion over all Vietnam, its authority was challenged in the North by the Chinese and in the South by the British. The French position was patently more tenuous than that of the Viet Minh until 9 October 1945. On that date, France and the UK concluded an agreement whereby the British formally recognized French civil administration in Indochina and ceded its occupation rights to France south of the 16th parallel. This ceding of authority in the South did not, as a practical matter, ensure French rule. With only 35,000 French soldiers in South Vietnam, the Viet Minh and other parties were well able to contest the French.

Viet Minh authority in Annam and Tonkin was less ambiguous, but by no means unchallenged. In the North, the salient political fact of life for the Viet Minh was the presence of the Chinese Nationalist Army of Occupation numbering 50,000 men. Through this presence, the Chinese were able to force the Viet Minh to accommodate Chinese–Viet Nationalists within the DRV and to defer to Chinese policy in other respects.

The Viet Minh had to go further still in accommodating the wishes of the Chinese. In setting up the DRV government of 2 September 1945, pro-Chinese, non-Viet Minh politicians were included, and the ICP took only 6 of 16 cabinet posts. On 11 November 1945, the Viet Minh leadership went even further, and formally dissolved the ICP in the interest of avoiding "misunderstandings." Even this, however, was not sufficient. Compelled by opposition demands, Ho agreed to schedule national elections for January of 1946. The results of these elections were arranged beforehand with the major opposition parties, and the Assembly thus "elected" met on 2 March 1946. This Assembly approved a new DRV government, with the ICP holding only 2 of 12 cabinet posts.

By then, France was ready to pose a stronger challenge. French reinforcements had arrived in Indochina, so that Paris could contemplate operations in North Vietnam as well as in Cochinchina. In early 1946, the Chinese turned over their occupation rights in the North to France. Faced with increased French military power and Chinese withdrawal, and denied succor from abroad, Ho decided that he had no recourse save to negotiate with the French. On 6 March 1946, Ho signed an Accord with the French providing for French re-entry into Vietnam for five years in return for recognizing the DRV as a free state within the French union.

This Accord taxed Ho's popularity to the utmost, and it took all Ho's prestige to prevent open rebellion. On 27 May 1946, Ho countered these attacks by merging the Viet Minh into the Lien Viet, a larger, more embracing "national front." Amity within the Lien Viet, however, lasted only as long as the Chinese remained in North Vietnam. When they withdrew a few weeks later, in mid-June, the Viet Minh, supported by French troops, attacked the Dong Minh Hoi and the VNQDD, as "enemies of the peace," effectively suppressed organized opposition, and asserted Viet Minh control throughout North Vietnam.

But even this ascendancy proved transitory. Ho Chi Minh, though he tried hard, was unable to negotiate any durable *modus vivendi* with the French in the summer and fall of 1946. In the meantime, the DRV and the Viet Minh were drawn more and more under the control of the "Marxists" of the former ICP. For example, during the session of the DRV National Assembly in November, nominal opposition members were whittled down to 20 out of more than 300 seats, and a few "Marxists" dominated the proceedings. Nonetheless, the DRV government maintained at least a facade of coalition. Through 1949, ICP members remained in the minority, and nominally oppositionist VNQDD and Dong Minh Hoi politicians were consistently included.

Although the Cochinchina war continued throughout 1946, with the Viet Minh assuming a leading role in resistance, war in North Vietnam did not break out until December, 1946. A series of armed clashes in November were followed by a large scale fighting in Hanoi in late December. The DRV government took to the hills to assume the status of shadow state. The Viet Minh transformed itself back into a semi-covert resistance organization and committed itself throughout the nation to the military defeat of the French. During the opening year of the war, 1947, the Viet Minh took steps to restore its image as a popular, patriotic, anti-foreign movement, and again to play down the ICP role in its leadership. The DRV government was reorganized and prominent communists excluded. As the Viet Minh gathered strength over the years, however, these same leaders reentered the DRV government.

In February 1951, addressing the Congress of the Vietnamese Communist Party (Lao Dong), Ho Chi Minh stated that the Communist Party had formed and led the Viet Minh, and founded and ruled the DRV. When the French colonialists reappeared in South Vietnam and a Nationalist Chinese-sponsored government seemed in prospect in North Vietnam, Ho averred, the Party went underground, and entered into agreements with the French:

> Lenin said that even if a compromise with bandits was advantageous to the revolution, he would do it. . . .

But Ho's explanation notwithstanding, the Viet Minh was irrefutably nationalist, popular, and patriotic. It was also the most prominent and successful vehicle of Viet nationalism in the 1940's. To a degree it was always non-communist. Available evidence indicates, however, that from its inception, Ho Chi Minh and his lieutenants of the Indochinese Communist Party conceived its strategy, directed its operations, and channeled its energies consistent with their own goals —as they subsequently claimed. Whether the non-communist elements of the Viet Minh might have become dominant in different circumstances must be relegated to speculation. It seems clear that, as matters developed, all of the non-communist nationalist movements—reformist, theocratic, or revolutionary— were too localized, too disunited, or too tainted with Japanese or Nationalist Chinese associations to have competed successfully with the ICP for control of the Viet Minh. And none could compete effectively with the Viet Minh in gaining a following among Vietnam's peasants.

[Supporting text not available]

V.   HO CHI MINH: ASIAN TITO?—A SUMMARY

Among the more cogent critiques of U.S. policy toward Vietnam is the contention that the U.S. failed to recognize in Ho Chi Minh a potential Asian "Tito." This view holds that Ho has always been more concerned with Vietnam's independence and sovereign viability than with following the interests and dictates of Moscow and Peking. With U.S. support, the argument runs, Ho would have adopted some form of neutrality in the East–West conflict and maintained the DRV as a natural and durable bulwark against Chinese expansion southward. Thus, were it not for "U.S. communist blinders," Ho would have served the larger purposes of American policy in Asia. Though the focus of inquiry in this study is the period immediately following World War II, when it would have been relatively easy to support an anti-Japanese, anti-colonial Ho, it is often argued that the U.S. neglected another opportunity after the Geneva Conference of 1954—and indeed, that U.S. acceptance of Ho, and a communist dominated Vietnam, may be the only path to peace in Southeast Asia today. The historical (1945–1954) argument has a persuasive ring. In the light of the present costs and repercussions of U.S. involvement in Vietnam, any prior way out can seem attractive. It is possible, however, that a dynamic and unified communist Vietnam under Ho Chi Minh could have been vigorously expansionist, thus causing unanticipated difficult problems in some ways comparable to current ones.

Many authors have advanced one version or another of the "Tito" hypothesis. Some develop the principal thesis that a different U.S. policy could have moved Ho to non-alignment and opposition to Peking; others stress the corollary that Ho was forced into dependence upon Peking and Moscow by American opposition or indifference. Whether Ho was a nationalist or a communist is not at issue; all of the authors quoted seem to accept that Ho was a communist, and that a communist Vietnam would probably have eventuated under his leadership. Rather, their arguments center on what they perceive to be Ho's willingness to subordinate communist goals, forms, and international discipline to attaining Vietnam's independence and unity. A few openly favor a communist Vietnam on the grounds that only a national communism led by Ho would be sufficiently strong to survive adjacent to China. They stress Ho's attempts in 1945 and 1946 to obtain Western backing, and point out that antipathy to China is a pillar of Viet nationalism. Many concede that the Tito analogy is not wholly appropriate. Unlike Tito, Ho came to power after the war without the aid of another communist state. More basically, there was no analogy to be made until late 1948, when the experiment with Tito seemed like it would work. Nonetheless, these authors point out that if the U.S. found it advantageous to set aside its repugnance to Tito's communism in the interest of stemming Russian expansion in Europe, it should have been willing to accommodate Ho Chi Minh's communism for similar ends in Asia. This critique generally ends with the accusation that the U.S. purpose in Southeast Asia is simply and solely to stop communism.

An examination of Ho Chi Minh's political development through 1950 may provide a basis to narrow the range of speculation concerning Ho and U.S. policy. From such a review, it is evident that the man who in 1945 became President of the Democratic Republic of Vietnam was a mature, extraordinarily dedicated revolutionary who had undergone severe hardships serving the cause of Vietnam's freedom from France. Fifty-five years of age in 1945, he had been a communist for twenty-five years—one of the founding members of the French Communist Party—and a Comintern agent in Asia for fifteen years before World War II. He was originally of Nghe-An, a province traditionally a spawning ground of revolutionists; of a father imprisoned by the French for nationalist activism; and of a Hue school known for radical nationalism among its students. Exiled from Vietnam from 1910 to 1940, imprisoned in Hong Kong and in China, deprived of home, family, fame, fortune and companionship outside the Comintern's conspiratorial circles, he apparently devoted himself selflessly all those years to revolution in Vietnam. Ruth Fischer, a well-known German former communist who knew Ho during this period, has written, "It was Ho Chi Minh's nationalism which impressed us European Communists born and bred in a rather grey kind of abstract internationalism."

For Ho, now back in Asia, World War II opened new avenues to the attainment of his life-long goals. France discredited itself in Vietnam through Vichy's collaboration with the Japanese, and then in 1945 was toppled from power altogether by Japanese arms. In the meantime, Ho had built the Viet Minh into the only Vietnam-wide political organization capable of effective resistance to either the Japanese or the French. Ho was the only Vietnamese wartime leader with a national following, and he assured himself wider fealty among the Vietnamese people when in August–September, 1945, he overthrew the Japanese, obtained the abdication of Bao Dai, established the DRV, and staged receptions for in-coming allied occupation forces—in which the DRV acted as the incumbent Vietnamese government. For a few weeks in September 1945, Vietnam was —for the first and only time in its modern history—free of foreign domination, and united from north to south under Ho Chi Minh.

Ho became the focus of the nationalist fervor evoked by these and subsequent events. Leaders of the rival Vietnamese Nationalist Party (VNQDD) and the Revolutionary League (Dong Minh Hoi), although admitted to the DRV government, commanded no grass-roots organizations, and since they were closely associated with the Chinese Nationalists, shared in full measure in the anti-Chinese odium among the people of North Vietnam. In South Vietnam, French intrigue, and Vietnamese disunity precluded the emergence of a competitor to Ho. When France resorted to force to restore its control over Vietnam, Ho again became the head of Viet resistance, and the Viet Minh became the primary nationalist protagonists. Hence, Ho Chi Minh, both on his own merits and out of lack of competition, became the personification of Vietnamese nationalism.

Ho, nonetheless, found himself, his movement, and his government under intense pressure. From within the nation, the Chinese-backed Viet parties attacked communist domination of his government. For the sake of national unity, Ho dissolved the Communist Party, avoided communist cant, announced general elections, and assured the contending factions representation in the government well out of proportion to their popular support. External pressures from France and from China proved more difficult. The French capitalized on the relative weakness of the Viet Minh in South Vietnam, and the dissension among the Vietnamese there to overthrow the DRV government in Saigon, and to force the Viet Minh to resort to guerrilla warfare. In famine-wracked North Vietnam, Chinese hordes under booty-minded warlords descended on the DRV, supplanting its local government with committees of their own sponsoring and systematically looting. Ho vainly sought aid abroad; not even the Soviet Union proved helpful. Ho eventually (March, 1946) negotiated with the French, accepting a French military presence in North Vietnam for a period of five years in return for vague French assurances to the DRV as a "Free State within the French Union." When Ho was attacked for this by the pro-Chinese elements within the DRV, he declared:

> You fools! Don't you realize what it means if the Chinese stay? Don't you remember your history? The last time the Chinese came, they stayed one thousand years!
>
> The French are foreigners. They are weak. Colonialism is dying out. Nothing will be able to withstand world pressure for independence. They may stay for a while, but they will have to go because the white man is finished in Asia. But if the Chinese stay now, they will never leave.

As for me, I prefer to smell French shit for five years, rather than Chinese shit for the rest of my life.

The unresolved historic problem, of course, is to what extent Ho's nationalist goals over-rode his communist convictions in these maneuvers. Ho seemed to place the former above the latter not solely as a matter of dissemblance, as he might have done in the dissolution of the Party and the simultaneous formation of a "Marxist Association," but possibly as a result of doubts about communism as a political form suitable for Vietnam. Bao Dai is reputed to have said that: "I saw Ho Chi Minh suffer. He was fighting a battle within himself. Ho had his own struggle. He realized communism was not best for his country, but it was too late. Ultimately, he could not overcome his allegiance to communism." During negotiations for a *modus vivendi* with the French in Paris in autumn, 1946, Ho appealed to the French to "save him from the extremists" within the Viet Minh by some meaningful concession to Vietnamese independence, and he told the U.S. Ambassador that he was not a communist. He is reputed to have asserted at that time that Vietnam was not ready for communism, and described himself as a Marxist. In reply to a journalist's inquiry, Ho claimed that he could remain neutral, "like Switzerland" in the developing world power struggle between communism and the West. But these and other such statements could have come either from a proper Leninist or a dedicated nationalist. Ho's statements and actions after 1949, and his eventual close alignment with the Sino–Soviet Bloc, support the Leninist construction. But, then, U.S. insistence on Ho's being a doctrinaire communist may have been a self-fulfilling prophesy.

There remains, however, the matter of Ho's direct appeals for U.S. intervention in Vietnam, at which even a Leninist might have scrupled. These occurred (late 1945, early 1946) just after France has reasserted itself militarily in South Vietnam, while Chinese Nationalist warlords were ensconced in Hanoi, and before the 6 March 1946 Accord with France. Desperately, Ho turned to the United States, among other powers, asking for "immediate interference" in Vietnam.

There were, at least, eight communications from Ho to the President of the United States, or to the Secretary of State, from October, 1945, to February, 1946. Ho had conveyed earlier, in August and September, 1945, *via* O.S.S. channels, proposals that Vietnam be accorded "the same status as the Philippines," for an undetermined period of tutelage preliminary to independence. With the outbreak of hostilities in South Vietnam, September–October 1945, he added formal requests for U.S. and U.N. intervention against French aggression, citing the Atlantic Charter, the U.N. Charter, and a foreign policy address of President Truman in October, 1945, endorsing national self-determination. Ho's last direct communication with the U.S. was in September, 1946, when he visited the U.S. Ambassador in Paris to ask vaguely for U.S. assistance in obtaining independence for Vietnam within the French Union.

There is no record of U.S. reply to any of Ho's appeals for aid. Extant instructions to a U.S. diplomat in contact with Ho in December, 1946, reveal U.S. preoccupation with his known communist background, and apprehension that he might establish a "communist-dominated, Moscow-oriented state." Two months later, when the Franco–Viet Minh war in North Vietnam was underway, Secretary of State Marshall emphasized that "we do not lose sight [of the] fact that Ho Chi Minh has direct Communist connections and it should be obvious that we are not interested in seeing colonial empire administrations supplanted by philosophy and political organizations emanating from and controlled by the

Kremlin." In May, 1949, Secretary of State Acheson admitted that as a "theoretical possibility" the establishment of a "National Communist state on pattern Yugoslavia in any area beyond reach [of the] Soviet Army," but pointed out that:

> Question whether Ho as much nationalist as Commie is irrelevant. All Stalinists in colonial areas are nationalists. With achievement national aims (i.e., independence) their objective necessarily becomes subordination state to Commie purposes and ruthless extermination not only opposition groups but all elements suspected even slightest deviation. . . .

When, in early 1950, Ho's DRV lay within reach of Mao's Chinese Army, and Ho had openly embraced communism, Secretary Acheson declared that bloc recognition of the DRV "should remove any illusion as to the nationalist character of Ho Chi Minh's aims and reveals Ho in his true colors as the mortal enemy of native independence in Vietnam."

But Ho's behavior in 1949–1950, however convincingly it endorsed U.S. policy at that juncture, does not necessarily explain away his earlier eagerness for U.S. and U.N. intervention in Vietnam, nor otherwise gainsay the "Tito" hypothesis as applied to the 1945–1947 period. Of that period, it can be said that the U.S. offered Ho only narrow options. He received no replies to his appeals. After 1946, not only were Ho's direct communications with the U.S. cut, but also the signals he received from the U.S. were hardly encouraging. By the time the Indochina war began in earnest in late 1946, U.S. military equipment had already been used by French forces against the Vietnamese, and the U.S. had arranged credit for France to purchase $160 million worth of vehicles and miscellaneous industrial equipment for use in Indochina. Secretary of State George C. Marshall's public comment on the outbreak of war in January, 1947, was limited to a hope that "a pacific basis for adjustment of the difficulties could be found," and within six months the Marshall Plan threw even greater U.S. resources behind France.

The simple truth seems to be that the U.S. knew little of what was transpiring inside Vietnam, and certainly cared less about Vietnam than about France. Knowing little and caring less meant that real problems and variety of choices were perceived but dimly. For example, the U.S. could have asked itself—"Did we really have to support France in Southeast Asia in order to support a noncommunist France internally and in Europe?" Another question we could have asked ourselves was—"If the U.S. choice in Vietnam really came down to either French colonialism or Ho Chi Minh, should Ho automatically be excluded?" Again, "If the U.S. choice was to be France, did France have any real chance of succeeding, and if so, at what cost?"

Even before World War II was over, Washington had placed the decision on Ho's fate in the hands of France. It can be argued, nonetheless, that the U.S. could have insisted that Paris buy Ho and provide Indochinese independence without endangering the more basic relationship between the U.S. and France in Europe. Just as the U.S. came to recognize the prime importance of Europe over any policy it pursued elsewhere, so the French government would have soon realized (if it had not already done so) that nothing should be done to impair seriously U.S. acceptance of common interests in European recovery and collective security. Moreover, it was not as if there were not sizable segments of the French community which would not have supported graceful U.S. attempts to extricate France from Indochina. It may well be, however, that the "Tito hypothesis" assumes a compliance from France of which France was demonstrably incapable. No French government is likely to have survived a genuinely liberal policy toward Ho in 1945 or 1946; even French communists then favored redemption of control in Indochina. From '46 on, however, bloodshed hardened policy in France. As before, the Ho alternative was never seriously contemplated.

French representations to the contrary notwithstanding, Ho Chi Minh possessed real political strength among the people of Vietnam. While calling Ho another George Washington may be stretching the point, there is no doubt about his being the only popularly-recognized wartime leader of the Vietnamese resistance, and the head of the strongest and only Vietnam-wide political movement. There can be no doubt either that in a test by ballot only Ho's Viet Minh could have delivered votes at the hamlet level. Washington and Paris, however, did not focus on the fact of Ho's strength, only on the consequences of his rule. Paris viewed Ho as a threat to its regaining French economic, cultural and political prerogatives in Indochina. The U.S., wary of Ho's known communist background, was apprehensive that Ho would lead Vietnam into the Soviet, and later Chinese, orbit. President Eisenhower's later remark about Ho's winning a free election in Vietnam with an 80% vote shone through the darkness of our vision about Vietnam; but U.S. policy remained unillumined.

In the last speculation, U.S. support for Ho Chi Minh would have involved perspicacity and risk. As clear as national or independent or neutral communism may seem today, it was a blurred vision in 1945–1948. Even with the benefit of seeing Tito successfully assert his independence, it would have been hard for Washington to make the leap from there to an analogy in Asia. Recourse to "national communism" in Vietnam as an eventual bulwark against China, indeed, would have called for a perspicacity unique in U.S. history. The risk was there, too. The reality of Ho's strength in Vietnam could have worked seriously against U.S. interests as well as against Chinese Communist interests. Ho's well-known leadership and drive, the iron discipline and effectiveness of the Viet Minh, the demonstrated fighting capability of his armies, a dynamic Vietnamese people under Ho's control, could have produced a dangerous period of Vietnamese expansionism. Laos and Cambodia would have been easy pickings for such a Vietnam. Ho, in fact, always considered his leadership to extend to Indochina as a whole, and his party was originally called the Indochinese Communist Party. Thailand, Malaya, Singapore, and even Indonesia, could have been next. It could have been the "domino theory" with Ho instead of Mao. And, it could have been the dominoes with Mao. This may seem implausible, but it is only slightly less of a bad dream than what has happened to Vietnam since. The path of prudence rather than the path of risk seemed the wiser choice.

[Supporting text not available]

2.   U.S. Involvement in the Franco–Viet Minh War, 1950–1954

Foreword

This portion of the study treats U.S. policy towards the war in Indochina from the U.S. decision to recognize the Vietnamese Nationalist regime of the Emperor Bao Dai in February, 1950, through the U.S. deliberations on military intervention in late 1953 and early 1954.

Summary

It has been argued that even as the U.S. began supporting the French in Indochina, the U.S. missed opportunities to bring peace, stability and independence to Vietnam. The issues arise from the belief on the part of some critics that (a) the U.S. made no attempt to seek out and support a democratic-nationalist alternative in Vietnam; and (b) the U.S. commanded, but did not use, leverage to move the French toward granting genuine Vietnamese independence.

U.S. POLICY AND THE BAO DAI REGIME

The record shows that through 1953, the French pursued a policy which was based on military victory and excluded meaningful negotiations with Ho Chi Minh. The French did, however, recognize the requirement for an alternative focus for Vietnamese nationalist aspirations, and from 1947 forward, advanced the "Bao Dai solution." The record shows that the U.S. was hesitant through 1949 to endorse the "Bao Dai solution" until Vietnam was in fact unified and granted autonomy and did consistently support the creation of a genuinely independent, noncommunist Vietnamese government to supplant French rule. Nonetheless, the fall of China and the deteriorating French military position in Indochina caused both France and the U.S. to press the "Bao Dai solution." In early 1950, after French ratification of the Elysee Agreement granting "Vietnam's independence," the U.S. recognized Bao Dai and initiated military and economic aid, even before transfer of governmental power actually occurred. Thereafter, the French yielded control only *pro forma*, while the Emperor Bao Dai adopted a retiring, passive role, and turned his government over to discreditable politicians. The Bao Dai regime was neither popular nor efficient, and its army, dependent on French leadership, was powerless. The impotence of the Bao Dai regime, the lack of any perceptible alternatives (except for the communists), the fact of continued French authority and control over the GVN, the fact that the French alone seemed able to contain communism in Indochina—all these constrained U.S. promptings for a democratic-nationalist government in Vietnam.

LEVERAGE: FRANCE HAD MORE THAN THE UNITED STATES

The U.S.–French ties in Europe (NATO, Marshall Plan, Mutual Defense Assistance Program) only marginally strengthened U.S. urgings that France make concessions to Vietnamese nationalism. Any leverage from these sources was severely limited by the broader considerations of U.S. policy for the containment of communism in Europe and Asia. NATO and the Marshall Plan were of themselves judged to be essential to our European interests. To threaten France with economic and military sanctions in Europe in order to have it alter its policy·in Indochina was, therefore, not plausible. Similarly, to reduce the level of military assistance to the French effort in Indochina would have been counter-productive, since it would have led to a further deterioration in the French military position there. In other words, there was a basic incompatibility in the two strands of U.S. policy: (1) Washington wanted France to fight the anti-communist war and win, preferably with U.S. guidance and advice; and (2) Washington expected the French, when battlefield victory was assured, to magnanimously withdraw from Indochina. For France, which was probably fighting more a colonial than an anti-communist war, and which had to consider the effects of withdrawal on colonial holdings in Algeria, Tunisia and Morocco, magnanimous withdrawal was not too likely.

France, having no such policy incompatibilities, could and did pursue a consistent course with the stronger bargaining hand. Thus, the French were able to resist pressures from Washington and through the MAAG in Saigon to create a truly Vietnamese army, to grant the Vietnamese more local autonomy and to wage the war more effectively. MAAG was relegated to a supply function and its occasional admonitions to the French were interpreted by them as interference in their internal affairs. Even though by 1954, the U.S. was financing 78% of the costs of the war, the French retained full control of the dispensation of military assistance and of the intelligence and planning aspects of the military struggle. The expectation of French victory over the Viet Minh encouraged the U.S. to "go along" with Paris until the conclusion of the war. Moreover, the U.S. was reluctant to antagonize the French because of the high priority given in Washington's planning to French participation in the European Defense Community. France, therefore, had considerable leverage and, unless the U.S. supported Paris on its own terms, the French could, and indeed did, threaten not to join the EDC and to stop fighting in Indochina.

PERCEPTIONS OF THE COMMUNIST THREAT TO SOUTHEAST ASIA AND TO BASIC U.S. INTERESTS

American thinking and policy-making was dominated by the tendency to view communism in monolithic terms. The Viet Minh was, therefore, seen as part of the Southeast Asia manifestation of the world-wide communist expansionary movement. French resistance to Ho Chi Minh, in turn, was thought to be a crucial link in the containment of communism. This strategic perception of the communist threat was supported by the espousal of the domino principle: the loss of a single nation in Southeast Asia to communism would inexorably lead to the other nations of the area falling under communist control. The domino principle, which probably had its origin at the time of the Nationalist withdrawal from mainland China, was at the root of U.S. policy. Although elements of a domino-like theory could be found in NSC papers before the start of the Korean War, the Chinese intervention in Korea was thought to be an ominous confirmation of its validity. The possibility of a large-scale Chinese intervention in Indochina, similar to that in Korea, was feared, especially after the armistice in Korea.

The Eisenhower Administration followed the basic policy of its predecessor, but also deepened the American commitment to containment in Asia. Secretary Dulles pursued a forthright, anti-communist policy and made it clear that he would not permit the "loss" of Indochina, in the manner the Democrats had allegedly allowed the "loss" of China. Dulles warned China not to intervene, and urged the French to drive toward a military victory. Dulles was opposed to a cease-fire and tried to dissuade the French from negotiations with the Viet Minh until they had markedly improved their bargaining position through action on the battlefield. The NSC in early 1954 was persuaded that a non-communist coalition regime would eventually turn the country over to the Viet Minh. In consequence of this more militant policy, the U.S. Government tended to focus on the military rather than the political aspects of the French–Viet Minh struggle.

Among the more frequently cited misapprehensions concerning U.S. policy in Vietnam is the view that the Eisenhower Administration flatly rejected intervention in the First Indochina War. The record shows plainly that the U.S. did seriously consider intervention, and advocated it to the U.K. and other allies. With the intensification of the French–Viet Minh war and the deterioration of the French military position, the United States was forced to take a position on: first, a possible U.S. military intervention in order to avert a Viet Minh victory; second, the increasingly likely contingency of negotiations between Paris and Ho Chi Minh to end the war through a political settlement. In order to avoid a French sell-out, and as an alternative to unilateral U.S. intervention, the U.S. proposed in 1954 to broaden the war by involving a number of allies in a collective defense effort through "united action."

THE INTERAGENCY DEBATE OVER U.S. INTERVENTION IN INDOCHINA

The U.S. Government internal debate on the question of intervention centered essentially on the desirability and feasibility of U.S. military action. Indochina's importance to U.S. security interests in the Far East was taken for granted. The Eisenhower Administration followed in general terms the rationale for American interest in Indochina that was expressed by the Truman Administration. With respect to intervention, the Truman Administration's NSC 124 of February 1952 recognized that the U.S. might be forced to take some military action in order to prevent the subversion of Southeast Asia. In late 1953–early 1954, as the fall of Indochina seemed imminent, the question of intervention came to the fore. The Defense Department pressed for a determination by highest authority of the size and nature of the forces the U.S. was willing to commit in Indochina. Some in DOD questioned the then operating assumption that U.S. air and naval forces would suffice as aid for the French. The Army was particularly concerned about contingency planning that assumed that U.S. air and naval action alone could bring military victory, and argued for realistic estimates of requisite land forces, including the degree of mobilization that would be necessary. The State Department thought that Indochina was so critical from a foreign policy viewpoint that intervention might be necessary. But DOD and the JCS, estimating that air-naval action alone could not stem the surging Viet Minh, recommended that rather than intervening directly, the U.S. should concentrate on urging Paris to train an expanded indigenous army, and should exert all possible pressures—in Europe as well as in Asia—to motivate the French to fight hard for a military victory. Many in the U.S. Government (the Ridgway Report stands out in this group) were wary that U.S. intervention might provoke Chinese Communist intervention. In the latter case, even a considerable U.S. deployment of ground forces would not be able to stem the tide in Indochina. A number of special high-level studies were unable to bridge the evident disparity between those who held that vital U.S. interests were at stake in Indochina, and those who were unwilling to make a firm decision to intervene with U.S. ground forces to assure those interests. Consequently, when the French began pressing for U.S. intervention at Dien Bien Phu, the Eisenhower Administration took the position that the U.S. would not intervene unilaterally, but only in concert with a number of European and Far Eastern allies as part of a combined force.

THE ATTEMPT TO ORGANIZE "UNITED ACTION"

This "united action" proposal, announced publicly by Secretary Dulles on March 29, 1954, was also designed to offer the French an alternative to surrender at the negotiating table. Negotiations for a political settlement of the Franco–Viet Minh war, however, were assured when the Big Four Foreign Ministers meeting in February at Berlin placed Indochina on the agenda of the impending Geneva Conference. Foreign Minister Bidault insisted upon this, over U.S. objections, because of the mounting pressure in France for an end to the seemingly interminable and costly war. The "peace faction" in Paris became stronger in proportion to the "peace feelers" let out by Ho Chi Minh, and the lack of French success on the battlefield. U.S. policy was to steer the French away from negotiations because of the fear that Indochina would thereby be handed over to the communist "empire."

Secretary Dulles envisaged a ten-nation collective defense force to take "united action" to prevent a French defeat—if necessary before the Geneva Conference. Dulles and Admiral Radford were, at first, inclined towards an early unilateral intervention at Dien Bien Phu, as requested by the French (the so-called "Operation Vulture"). But Congressional leaders indicated they would not support U.S. military action without active allied participation, and President Eisenhower decided that he would not intervene without Congressional approval. In addition to allied participation, Congressional approval was deemed dependent upon a public declaration by France that it was speeding up the timetable for independence for the Associated States.

The U.S. was unable to gather much support for "united action" except in Thailand and the Philippines. The British response was one of hesitation in general, and flat opposition to undertaking military action before the Geneva Conference. Eden feared that it would lead to an expansion of the war with a high risk of Chinese intervention. Moreover, the British questioned both the U.S. domino principle, and the belief that Indochina would be totally lost at Dien Bien Phu and through negotiations at Geneva. As for the French, they were less interested in "united action" than in immediate U.S. military assistance at Dien Bien Phu. Paris feared that united action would lead to the internationalization of the war, and take control out of its hands. In addition, it would impede or delay the very negotiations leading towards a settlement which the French increasingly desired. But repeated French requests for direct U.S. intervention during the final agony of Dien Bien Phu failed to alter President Eisenhower's conviction that it would be an error for the U.S. to act alone.

Following the fall of Dien Bien Phu during the Geneva Conference, the "domino theory" underwent a reappraisal. On a May 11 press conference, Secretary Dulles observed that "Southeast Asia could be secured even without, perhaps, Vietnam, Laos and Cambodia." In a further remark that was deleted from the official transcript, Dulles said that Laos and Cambodia were "important but by no means essential" because they were poor countries with meager populations.

(End of Summary)

I. U.S. POLICY AND THE BAO DAI REGIME

A. THE BAO DAI SOLUTION

1. The French Predicament

French perceptions of the conflict which broke out in December, 1946, between their forces in Indochina and the Viet Minh forces of the Democratic Republic of Vietnam (DRV) began to alternate between boundless optimism and unbridled gloom. In May, 1947, Minister of War Coste-Floret announced in Paris that: "There is no military problem any longer in Indochina . . . the success of French arms is complete." Within six months, though ambitious armored, amphibious, and airborne drives had plunged into the northern mountains and along the Annam coast, Viet Minh sabotage and raids along lines of communication had mounted steadily, and Paris had come to realize that France had lost the military initiative. In the meantime, the French launched political forays similarly ambitious and equally unproductive. Leon Pignon, political adviser to the French Commander in Indochina, and later High Commissioner, wrote in January, 1947, that:

> Our objective is clear: to transpose to the field of Vietnamese domestic politics the quarrel we have with the Viet Minh, and to involve ourselves as little as possible in the campaigns and reprisals which ought to be the work of the native adversaries of that party.

Within a month, an emissary journeyed into the jungle to deliver to Ho Chi Minh's government demands tantamount to unconditional surrender. About the same time, French representatives approached Bao Dai, the former Emperor of Annam, with proposals that he undertake to form a Vietnamese government as an alternate to Ho Chi Minh's. Being unable to force a military resolution, and having foreclosed meaningful negotiations with Ho, the French turned to Bao Dai as their sole prospect for extrication from the growing dilemma in Vietnam.

2. The Ha Long Bay Agreement, 1948

Bao Dai's mandarinal court in Hue, Annam, had been little more than an instrument of French colonial policy, and—after the occupation by Japan—of Japanese policy. Bao Dai had become Emperor at the age of 12, in 1925, but did not actually ascend the throne until 1932, after education in France. In August, 1945, when the Viet Minh arrived in Hue, he abdicated in favor of Ho's Democratic Republic of Vietnam, and accepted the post of "Supreme Adviser" to the new state. In 1946, he left Vietnam, and went to Hong Kong. There, he found himself solicited not only by French representatives, but by the DRV, who sought him to act on their behalf with the French.

Bao Dai attempted at first to maintain a central position between the two protagonists, but was soon persuaded to decline the Viet Minh overtures by non-Communist nationalists. A group of these, including members of the Cao Dai, Hoa Hao, Dong Minh Hoi, Dai Vet, and the VNQDD formed a National Union, and declared support for Bao Dai. One authority termed the National Union "a fragile coalition of discredited collaborators, ambitious masters of intrigue, incompetent sectarians, and a smattering of honest leaders without a following."

Among the latter were Ngo Dinh Diem, who "for the first and only time, joined a party of which he was not the founder," and pledged to back the Emperor so long as he pursued independence for Vietnam. Now, having eliminated the Viet Minh support option, Bao Dai became more compliant in his discussions with the French, and the French became correspondingly stiffer in their attitude toward the Viet Minh. Yet, little came of the talks. On December 7, 1947, aboard a French warship in Ha Long Bay, Bao Dai signed an accord with the French, committing the French to Vietnamese political independence so minimally that it was promptly condemned not only by Diem, but also by more opportunistic colleagues in the National Union. Bao Dai, in what might have been a political withdrawal, removed himself from the developing intrigue, and fled to European pleasure centers for a four month jaunt which earned him the sobriquet "night club emperor."

The French, despite lack of cooperation from their elusive Vietnamese principal, sent diplomats to pursue Bao Dai and publicized their resolve "to carry on, outside the Ho Chi Minh Government, all activities and negotiations necessary for the restoration of peace and freedom in the Vietnamese countries"—in effect, committing themselves to military victory and Bao Dai. French persistence eventually persuaded Bao Dai to return to Hong Kong, to endorse the formation of a Vietnamese national government prior to independence, and finally, to return to Vietnam as the Head of State. French negotiating pressures on him and the National Union included both spurious "leaks" of Franco–Viet Minh settlement talks, and further assurances of intentions to grant Vietnamese autonomy. On June 5, 1948, Bao Dai witnessed the signing of another Bay of Ha Long Agreement. Thereby, France publicly and "solemnly" recognized the independence of Vietnam—but specifically retained control over foreign relations and the Army, and deferred transfer of other governmental functions to future negotiations; no authority was in fact transferred to the Vietnamese. Again Bao Dai retired to Europe, while in Hanoi the French assembled a transparently impotent semblance of native government. A second summer of war passed in 1948 without dispelling the military miasma over Indochina, and without making the "Bao Dai solution" any less repugnant among Vietnamese patriots. Opposition to it began to mount among French Leftists. This disenchantment, combined with a spreading acceptance of the strategic view that the Franco–Viet Minh war was a key anti-Communist struggle, influenced French leaders to liberalize their approach to the "Bao Dai solution."

3. Elysee Agreement, 1949

On March 8, 1949, after months of negotiations, French President Auriol, in an exchange of letters with Bao Dai, reconfirmed independence for Vietnam as an Associated State of the French Union and detailed procedures for unifying Vietnam and placing it under Vietnamese administration. Nonetheless, in the Elysee Agreement, France yielded control of neither Vietnam's army nor its foreign relations, and again postponed arrangements for virtually all other aspects of autonomy. However, Bao Dai, apparently convinced that France was now sufficiently desperate in Indochina that it would have to honor the Agreements, declared that:

> . . . An era of reconstruction and renovation will open in Vietnam. The country will be given democratic institutions that will be called on primarily to approve the present agreement. . . . Profound economic and social re-

forms will be instituted to raise the general standard of living and to promote social justice, which is the condition and guarantee of order . . . [I look for] the union of all Vietnamese regardless of their political and religious tendencies, and the generous support of France on which I can count . . .

His public stance notwithstanding, Bao Dai delayed his return to Vietnam until a Cochinchinese Assembly had been elected (albeit in a farce of an election), and did not proceed to Saigon until the French Assembly had approved Cochinchina's joining the rest of Vietnam. In late June, 1949, Vietnam was legally united under Bao Dai, but the related alteration of administrative functions was slow, and usually only *pro forma;* no genuine power or authority was turned over to the Vietnamese. The State of Vietnam became a camouflage for continued French rule in Indochina. As Bao Dai himself characterized the situation in 1950, "What they call a Bao Dai solution turned out to be just a French solution. . . . The situation in Indochina is getting worse every day . . ."

4. Bao Dai's Governments

The unsavory elements of the coalition supporting Bao Dai dominated his regime. Ngo Dinh Diem and a few other upright nationalists refused high government posts, and withdrew their support from Bao Dai when their expectations of autonomy were disappointed. Diem's public statement criticized the probity of those who did accept office:

> The national aspirations of the Vietnamese people will be satisfied only on the day when our nation obtains the same political regime which India and Pakistan enjoy . . . I believe it is only just to reserve the best posts in the new Vietnam for those who have deserved best of the country; I speak of those who resist . . .

However, far from looking to the "resistance," Bao Dai chose his leaders from among men with strong identification with France, often men of great and dubious wealth, or with ties with the sub-worlds of French neo-mercantilism and Viet vice. None commanded a popular following. General Georges Revers, Chief of Staff of the French Army, who was sent to Vietnam to appraise the situation in May and June, 1949, wrote that:

> If Ho Chi Minh has been able to hold off French intervention for so long, it is because the Viet Minh leader has surrounded himself with a group of men of incontestable worth . . . [Bao Dai, by contrast, had] a government composed of twenty representatives of phantom parties, the best organized of which would have difficulty in rallying twenty-five adherents . . .

Bao Dai himself did next to nothing to make his government either more representative or more efficient. He divided his time among the pleasures of the resort towns of Dalat, Nha Trang, and Banmethuout, and for all practical purposes, remained outside the process of government.

An American diplomat serving in Vietnam at the time who knew Bao Dai well, characterized him in these terms:

> Bao Dai, above all, was an intelligent man. Intellectually, he could discuss the complex details of the various agreements and of the whole involved

relationship with France as well as or better than anyone I knew. But he was a man who was crippled by his French upbringing. His manner was too impassive. He allowed himself to be sold by the French on an erroneous instead of a valid evolutionary concept, and this suited his own termperament. He was too congenial, and he was almost pathologically shy, which was one reason he always liked to wear dark glasses. He would go through depressive cycles, and when he was depressed, he would dress himself in Vietnamese clothes instead of European ones, and would mince no words about the French. His policy, he said to me on one of these dour occasions, was one of "grignotage," or "nibbling," and he was painfully aware of it. The French, of course, were never happy that we Americans had good relations with Bao Dai, and they told him so. Unfortunately, they also had some blackmail on him, about his relationship with gambling enterprises in Saigon and his love of the fleshpots.

Whatever his virtues, Bao Dai was not a man who could earn the fealty of the Vietnamese peasants. He could not even hold the loyalty of honest nationalists, one of whom, for example, was Dr. Phan Quang Dan—a prominent and able non-Communist leader and early supporter of the "solution," and a personal friend of Bao Dai—(Dr. Dan later was the opposition leader of the Diem era). Dr. Dan reported a touching conversation with Bao Dai's mother in which she described her son at a loss to know whom to trust, and heartsick at the atmosphere of hostility which surrounded him. Yet Dr. Dan resigned as Bao Dai's Minister of Information over the Elysee Agreement, and, though he remained close to the Emperor, would not reassume public office for him. Bao Dai himself furnished an apt description of his political philosophy which may explain why he failed to capture the hearts of either beleaguered farmers or serious political leaders—neither of whom could stomach "nibbling" when revolution was required. Said Bao Dai:

> To practice politics is like playing a game, and I have always considered life a game.

5.   *The Pau Negotiations, 1950*

Yet Bao Dai did work at pressing the French. French officials in fact complained to an American writer that Bao Dai spent too much of his time on such pursuits:

> He has concentrated too much on getting what he can from us instead of building up his support among the people of the country . . . History will judge if he did right in putting so much stress on that . . .

From late June, 1950, until the end of November, Bao Dai stayed close to the series of conferences in Pau, France, designed to arrange the transfer to the Vietnamese of the services of immigration, communications, foreign trade, customs, and finances. The issue of the finance service was a particularly thorny one, involving as it did lucrative foreign exchange controls. While the French did eventually grant significant concessions to the Vietnamese, Laotians, and Cambodians in each area discussed, they preserved "rights of observation" and "intervention" in matters that "concerned the French Union as a whole." Indeed, the French assured themselves full access to government information, license to participate in all government decisions, and little reduction in economic benefits. Some French commentators viewed Pau as an unmitigated disaster and the assurance of an early French demise in Indochina. As one writer put it:

> By accepting the eventual restriction of trade within the French Union, by losing all effective authority over the issuance of money, by renouncing control over foreign trade, by permitting a system of controlled prices for exports and imports, we have given the Associated States all the power they need if they wish to assure the ruin of our enterprises and compel their withdrawal without in any way molesting our compatriots.

But a contemporary Vietnamese critic took a quite different view:

> All these conventions conserve in Indochina a privileged position for French capital, supported by the presence of a powerful fleet and army. Even if no one talks any more of an Indochinese Federation, it is still a federalism both administrative and economic (Monetary Union, Customs Union, Communications Union, etc.) which co-ordinates the various activities of the three Associated States. France always exercises control through the representatives she has in all the organs of planning or of federal surveillance, and through what is in effect the right of veto, because the president or the secretary general of these committees is always elected by joint decision of the four governments and, further, because most of the decisions of the committees are made by unanimous agreement.

Bao Dai's delegates were, however, generally pleased with the outcome of Pau. His Prime Minister, Tran Van Huu declared as he signed the conventions that "our independence is now perfect." But to the ordinary Vietnamese, to honest Frenchmen, and to the Americans, Tran Van Huu was proved dramatically wrong.

B.   U.S. POLICY TOWARDS BAO DAI

1.   *Qualified Approval, 1947–1950*

The "Bao Dai solution" depended on American support. During the 1950 negotiations in Pau, France, Bao Dai's Prime Minister Tran Van Huu was called back to Indochina by a series of French military reverses in Tonkin. Tran Van Huu seized the occasion to appeal to the United States "as the leading democratic nation," and hoped that the U.S. would:

> . . . bring pressure to bear on France in order to achieve democratic freedom. We want the right to decide our own affairs for ourselves.

Tran demanded the Elysee Agreement be superseded by genuine autonomy for Vietnam:

> It is not necessary for young men to die so that a French engineer can be director of the port of Saigon. Many people are dying every day because Viet Nam is not given independence. If we had independence the people would have no more reason to fight.

Tran's addressing the U.S. thus was realistic, if not judicious, for the U.S. had already become involved in Indochina as one part of a troubled triangle with France and Bao Dai's regime. Indeed, there had been an American role in the "Bao Dai solution" from its inception. Just before the Ha Long Bay Agreements, the French initiative had received some support from a December, 1947, *Life* magazine article by William C. Bullitt, former U.S. Ambassador to France. Bullitt argued for a policy aimed at ending "the saddest war" by winning the majority of Vietnamese nationalists away from Ho Chi Minh and from the Communists through a movement built around Bao Dai. Bullitt's views were widely accepted in France as a statement of U.S. policy, and a direct endorsement, and promise of U.S. aid, for Bao Dai. Bao Dai, whether he accepted the Bullitt canard or not, seemed to sense that the U.S. would inevitably be drawn into Southeast Asia, and apparently expected American involvement to be accompanied by U.S. pressure on France on behalf of Vietnamese nationalism. But the U.S., though it appreciated France's dilemma, was reluctant initially to endorse the Bao Dai solution until it became a reality. The following State Department messages indicate the U.S. position:

July 10, 1948 (Paris 3621 to State):
    . . . France is faced with alternatives of unequivocally and promptly approving principle [of] Viet independence within French union and [the] union [of the] three parts of Vietnam or losing Indochina.

July 14, 1948 (State 2637 to Paris):
    . . . Once [Bay of Ha Long] Agreement together with change in status [of] Cochinchina [is] approved, Department would be disposed [to] consider lending its support to extent of publicly approving French Government's action as forward looking step toward settlement of troubled situation [in] Indochina and toward realization of aspirations Vietnamese people. It appears to Department that above stated U.S. approval would materially assist in strengthening hands of nationalists as opposed to communists in Indochina . . .

August 30, 1948 (State 3368 to Paris):
    Department appreciates difficulties facing any French Government taking decisive action vis-a-vis Indochina, but can only see steadily deteriorating situation unless [there is] more positive approval [Bay of Ha Long] Agreement, enactment legislation or action permitting change Cochinchina status, and immediate commencement formal negotiations envisaged that Agreement. Department believes [that] nothing should be left undone which will strengthen truly nationalist groups [in] Indochina and induce present supporters [of the] Viet Minh [to] come to [the] side [of] that group. No such inducement possible unless that group can show concrete evidence [that] French [are] prepared [to] implement promptly creation Vietnamese free state [which is] associated [with the] French Union and with all attributes free state . . .

January 17, 1949 (State 145 to Paris):
    While Department desirous French coming to terms with Bao Dai or any truly nationalist group which has reasonable chance winning over preponderance of Vietnamese, we cannot at this time irretrevably [sic] commit U.S. to support of native government which by failing develop appeal among Vietnamese might become virtually puppet government, separated from people, and existing only by presence French military forces . . .

The Elysee Agreement took place in March, 1949. At this juncture, the fall of China obtruded, and the U.S. began to view the "Bao Dai solution" with a greater sense of urgency:

> May 10, 1949 (State 77 to Saigon):
> Assumption . . . Department desires [the] success Bao Dai experiment entirely correct. Since [there] appears [to] be no other alternative to [established] Commie pattern [in] Vietnam, Department considers no effort should be spared by France, other Western powers, and non-Commie Asian nations to assure experiment best chance succeeding.
>
> At proper time and under proper circumstances Department will be prepared [to] do its part by extending recognition [to the] Bao Dai Government and by exploring [the] possibility of complying with any request by such a Government for U.S. arms and economic assistance. [It] must be understood, however, [that] aid program this nature would require Congressional approval. Since U.S. could scarcely afford backing [a] government which would have color [of], and be likely [to suffer the] fate of, [a] puppet regime, it must first be clear that France will offer all necessary concessions to make Bao Dai solution attractive to nationalists.
>
> This is [a] step of which French themselves must see urgency [and] necessity [in] view possibly short time remaining before Commie successes [in] China are felt [in] Indochina. Moreover, Bao Dai Government must through own efforts demonstrate capacity [to] organize and conduct affairs wisely so as to ensure maximum opportunity of obtaining requisite popular support, inasmuch as [any] government created in Indochina analogous [to the] Kuomintang would be foredoomed failure.
>
> Assuming essential French concessions are forthcoming, best chance [of] success [for] Bao Dai would appear to be in persuading Vietnamese nationalists:
> (1) their patriotic aims may be realized promptly through French–Bao Dai agreement
> (2) Bao Dai government will be truly representative even to the extent of including outstanding non-Commie leaders now supporting Ho, and
> (3) Bao Dai solution [is the] only means [of] safeguarding Vietnam from aggressive designs [of the] Commie Chinese.

Through 1949, the southward march of Mao's legions continued, and the Viet Minh were obviously preparing to establish relations with them.

2. *Recognition, 1950*

The Elysee Agreements were eleven months old before the U.S. considered that France had taken the concrete steps toward Vietnamese autonomy which the U.S. had set as conditions for recognizing Bao Dai. In late January, 1950, events moved swiftly. Ho Chi Minh announced that his was the "only legal government of the Vietnam people" and indicated DRV willingness to cooperate with any nation willing to recognize it on the basis of "equality and mutual respect of national sovereignty and territory." Mao responded promptly with recognition, followed by Stalin. In France there was an acrimonious debate in the National Assembly between leftist advocates of immediate truce with the

Viet Minh and government supporters of the Elysee Agreement to proceed with the Bao Dai solution. René Pleven, Minister of National Defense, declared that:

> It is necessary that the French people know that at the present time the only true enemy of peace in Viet Nam is the Communist Party. Because members of the Communist Party know that peace in Indochina will be established by the policy of independence that we are following.
> ("Peace with Viet Nam! Peace with Viet Nam!" shouted the Communists.)

Jean Letourneau arose to assert that:

> It is not at all a question of approving or disapproving a government; we are very far beyond the transitory life of a government in an affair of this gravity. It is necessary that, on the international level, the vote that takes place tonight reveals truly the major importance that this event should have in the eyes of the entire world.

Frédéric Dupont said:

> The Indochina war has always been a test of the French Union before international Communism. But since the arrival of the Chinese Communists on the frontier of Tonkin, Indochina has become the frontier of Western civilization and the war in Indochina is integrated into the cold war.

Premier Georges Bidault was the last speaker:

> The choice is simple. Moreover there is no choice.

The National Assembly vote on January 29, 1950, was 396 to 193. From the extreme left there were cries of "Down with the war!" and Paul Coste-Floret replied: "Long live peace." On February 2, 1950, France's formal ratification of the independence of Vietnam was announced.

The U.S. assessment of the situation, and its action, is indicated in the following:

DEPARTMENT OF STATE
Washington
February 2, 1950

MEMORANDUM FOR THE PRESIDENT

Subject: U.S. Recognition of Vietnam, Laos and Cambodia

1. The French Assembly (Lower House) ratified on 29 January by a large majority (396 - 193) the bill which, in effect, established Vietnam, Laos and Cambodia as autonomous states within the French Union. The opposition consisted of 181 Communist votes with only 12 joining in from other parties. The Council of the Republic (Senate) is expected to pass the bills by the same approximate majority on or about February 3. President Auriol's signature is expected to follow shortly thereafter.

2. The French legislative and political steps thus taken will transform areas which were formerly governed as Protectorates or Colonies into states within the French Union, with considerably more freedom than they enjoyed under their

prior status. The French Government has indicated that it hopes to grant greater degrees of independence to the three states as the security position in Indochina allows, and as the newly formed governments become more able to administer the areas following withdrawal of the French.

3. Within Laos and Cambodia there are no powerful movements directed against the governments which are relatively stable. However, Vietnam has been the battleground since the end of World War II of conflicting political parties and military forces. Ho Chi Minh, who under various aliases, has been a communist agent in various parts of the world since 1925 and was able to take over the anti-French nationalist movement in 1945. After failing to reach agreement with the French regarding the establishment of an autonomous state of Vietnam, he withdrew his forces to the jungle and hill areas of Vietnam and has harassed the French ever since. His followers who are estimated at approximately 75,000 armed men, with probably the same number unarmed. His headquarters are unknown.

The French counter efforts have included, on the military side, the deployment of approximately 130,000 troops, of whom the approximately 50,000 are local natives serving voluntarily, African colonials, and a hard core made up of French troops and Foreign Legion units. Ho Chi Minh's guerrilla tactics have been aimed at denying the French control of Vietnam. On March 8, 1949 the French President signed an agreement with Bao Dai as the Head of State, granting independence within the French Union to the Government of Vietnam. Similar agreements were signed with the King of Laos and the King of Cambodia.

Recent developments have included Chinese Communist victories bringing those troops to the Indochina border; recognition of Ho Chi Minh as the head of the legal Government of Vietnam by Communist China (18 January) and by Soviet Russia (30 January).

4. Recognition by the United States of the three legally constituted governments of Vietnam, Laos and Cambodia appears desirable and in accordance with United States foreign policy for several reasons. Among them are: encouragement to national aspirations under non-Communist leadership for peoples of colonial areas in Southeast Asia; the establishment of stable non-Communist governments in areas adjacent to Communist China; support to a friendly country which is also a signatory to the North Atlantic Treaty; and as a demonstration of displeasure with Communist tactics which are obviously aimed at eventual domination of Asia, working under the guise of indigenous nationalism.

Subject to your approval, the Department of State recommends that the United States of America extend recognition to Vietnam, Laos and Cambodia, following ratification by the French Government.

(signed) DEAN ACHESON

Approved
(signed)
Harry S. Truman
February 3, 1950

---

3. *U.S. Aid to Indochina*

On February 16, 1950, France requested U.S. military and economic assistance in prosecuting the Indochina War. The Secretary of Defense in a Memorandum for the President on March 6 stated that:

The choice confronting the United States is to support the legal governments in Indochina or to face the extension of Communism over the remainder of the continental area of Southeast Asia and possibly westward . . .

The same month, the State Department dispatched an aid survey mission under R. Allen Griffin to Indochina (and to Burma, Indonesia, Thailand, and Malaya). The Griffin Mission proposed (inter alia) aid for the Bao Dai government, since the State of Vietnam was considered:

. . . not secure against internal subversion, political infiltration, or military aggression.

The objective of each program is to assist as much as possible in building strength, and in so doing . . . to assure the several peoples that support of their governments and resistance to communist subversion will bring them direct and tangible benefits and well-founded hope for an increase in living standards. Accordingly, the programs are of two main types: (1) technical and material aid to essential services and (2) economic rehabilitation and development, focused primarily on the provision of technical assistance and material aid in developing agricultural and industrial output. . . . These activities are to be carried on in a way best calculated to demonstrate that the local national governments are able to bring benefits to their own people and thereby build political support, especially among the rural population. . . .

The aims of economic assistance to Southeast Asia . . . are to reinforce the non-Communist national governments in that region by quickly strengthening and expanding the economic life of the area, improve the conditions under which its people live, and demonstrate concretely the genuine interest of the United States in the welfare of the people of Southeast Asia.

In a strategic assessment of Southeast Asia in April, 1950, the JCS recommended military assistance for Indochina, provided:

. . . that United States military aid not be granted unconditionally; rather that it be carefully controlled and that the aid program be integrated with political and economic programs . . . [Doc. 3]

On May 1, 1950, Presiden Truman approved $10 million for urgently needed military assistance items for Indochina. The President's decision was taken in the context of the successful amphibious invasion of Nationalist-defended Hainan by a Communist Chinese army under General Lin Piao—with obvious implications for Indochina, and for Taiwan. One week later, on May 8, the Secretary of State announced U.S. aid for "the Associated States of Indochina and to France in order to assist them in restoring stability and permitting these states to pursue their peaceful and democratic development." Sixteen days later, Bao Dai's government and France were notified on May 24 of the U.S. intention to establish an economic aid mission to the Associated States. [Doc. 6] As the North Korean Army moved southward on June 27, 1950, President Truman announced that he had directed "acceleration in the furnishing of military assistance to the forces of France and the Associated States in Indochina . . ." [Doc. 8]

The crucial issue presented by the American decision to provide aid to Indochina was who should be the recipient—Bao Dai or France—and, hence, whose policies would U.S. aid support?

4. *French Intransigence*

While the U.S. was deliberating over whether to provide economic and military assistance to Indochina in early 1950, negotiations opened at Pau, France, among France and the Associated States to set the timing and extent of granting autonomy. Had these talks led to genuine independence for Bao Dai's regime, the subsequent U.S.–French relationship would probably have been much less complex and significantly less acerbic. As it was, however, the Pau accords led to little more independence than had the Ha Long Bay or Elysee Agreements. Moreover, France's reluctance to yield political or economic authority to Bao Dai was reinforced by its proclivity to field strong-willed commanders, suspicious of the U.S., determined on a military victory, and scornful of the Bao Dai solution. General Marcel Carpentier, Commander in Chief when the French applied for aid, was quoted in the *New York Times* on March 9, 1950, as follows:

> I will never agree to equipment being given directly to the Vietnamese. If this should be done I would resign within twenty-four hours. The Vietnamese have no generals, no colonels, no military organization that could effectively utilize the equipment. It would be wasted, and in China, the United States has had enough of that.

a. *1950–1951: De Lattre and "Dynamisme"*

Carpentier's successor, High Commissioner-Commander in Chief General Jean de Lattre de Tassigny, arrived in December, 1950, following the severe setback of the autumn. De Lattre electrified the discouraged French forces like General Ridgway later enheartened U.S. forces in Korea. De Lattre saw himself as leading an anti-communist crusade. He calculated that he could win a decisive victory within fifteen months in Vietnam, and "save it from Peking and Moscow." He deprecated the idea that the French were still motivated by colonialism, and even told one U.S. newsman that France fought for the West alone:

> We have no more interest here . . . We have abandoned all our colonial positions completely. There is little rubber or coal or rice we can any longer obtain. And what does it amount to compared to the blood of our sons we are losing and the three hundred and fifty million francs we spend a day in Indochina? The work we are doing is for the salvation of the Vietnamese people. And the propaganda you Americans make that we are still colonialists is doing us tremendous harm, all of us—the Vietnamese, yourselves, and us.

Moreover, De Lattre was convinced that the Vietnamese had to be brought into the fight. In a speech—"A Call to Vietnamese Youth"—he declared:

> This war, whether you like it or not, is the war of Vietnam for Vietnam. And France will carry it on for you only if you carry it on with her. . . . Certain people pretend that Vietnam cannot be independent because it is part of the French Union. Not true! In our universe, and especially in our world of today, there can be no nations absolutely independent. There are

only fruitful interdependencies and harmful dependencies. . . . Young men of Vietnam, to whom I feel as close as I do to the youth of my native land, the moment has come for you to defend your country.

Yet, General De Lattre regarded U.S. policy vis-a-vis Bao Dai with grave misgivings. Americans, he held, afflicted with "missionary zeal," were "fanning the fires of extreme nationalism . . . French traditionalism is vital here. You cannot, you must not destroy it. No one can simply make a new nation overnight by giving out economic aid and arms alone." As adamantly as Carpentier, De Lattre opposed direct U.S. aid for Vietnamese forces, and allowed the Vietnamese military little real independence.

Edmund A. Gullion, U.S. Minister Counselor in Saigon from 1950 on, faulted De Lattre on his inability to stimulate in the Vietnamese National Army either the *elan vital* or *dynamisme* he communicated to the rest of the French Expeditionary Corps:

> . . . It remained difficult to inculcate nationalist ardor in a native army whose officers and non-coms were primarily white Frenchmen . . . The Vietnamese units that went into action were rarely unsupported by the French. American contact with them was mainly through the French, who retained exclusive responsibility for their training. We felt we needed much more documentation than we had to assess the army's true potential. We needed battalion-by-battalion reports on the performance of the Vietnamese in training as well as in battle and a close contact with intelligence and command echelons, and we never got this. Perhaps the most significant and saddest manifestation of the French failure to create a really independent Vietnamese Army that would fight in the way de Lattre meant was the absence, at Dienbienphu, of any Vietnamese fighting elements. It was a French show.

Gullion is not altogether correct with respect to Dien Bien Phu; nonetheless, statistics on the ethnic composition of the defending garrison do reveal the nature of the problem. The 5th Vietnamese Parachute Battalion was dropped to reinforce the garrison so that as of May 6, 1954, the troops at Dien Bien Phu included:

GARRISON OF DIEN BIEN PHU

	Officers	NCO's	EM's	Totals
Vietnamese	11	270	5,119	5,480
Total	393	1,666	13,026	15,105
Viet % of Total	2.8	16.2	39.2	36.2

Thus, the Vietnamese comprised more than a third of the fighting forces (and nearly 40% of the enlisted troops); but among the leaders, they provided one-sixth of the non-commissioned officers and less than 3% of the officers.

The paucity of Viet officers at Dien Bien Phu reflected the general condition of the National Army: as of 1953, there were 2,600 native officers, of whom only a handful held rank above major, compared to 7,000 French officers in a force of 150,000 Vietnamese troops.

b. *1951–1953: Letourneau and "Dictatorship"*

De Lattre's successor as High Commissioner, Jean Letourneau, was also the French Cabinet Minister for the Associated States. Letourneau was sent to Indochina to assume the same power and privilege in the "independent" State of Vietnam that any of France's Governor Generals had ever exercised from Saigon's Norodom Palace. In May, 1953, a French Parliamentary Mission of Inquiry accused the Minister-High Commissioner of "veritable dictatorship, without limitation or control":

> The artificial life of Saigon, the temptations of power without control, the security of a judgment which disdains realities, have isolated the Minister and his entourage and have made them insensible to the daily tragedy of the war . . .
>
> It is no longer up to us to govern, but to advise. The big thing was not to draw up plans irresponsibly, but to carry on daily a subtle diplomacy. In Saigon our representatives have allowed themselves to be inveigled into the tempting game of power and intrigue.
>
> Instead of seeing the most important things and acting on them, instead of making on the spot investigations, of looking for inspiration in the village and in the ricefield, instead of informing themselves and winning the confidence of the most humble people, in order to deprive the rebels of their best weapon, the Norodom Palace clique has allowed itself the luxury of administering à la francaise and of reigning over a country where revolution is smouldering . . .
>
> The press has not the right of criticism. To tell the truth, it has become official, and the principal newspaper in Saigon is at the disposition of the High Commissariat. Letters are censored. Propaganda seems to be issued just to defend the High Commissariat. Such a regime cannot last, unless we are to appear as people who are determined not to keep their promises.

The Parliamentary Mission described Saigon: "where gambling, depravity, love of money and of power finish by corrupting the morale and destroying will-power . . ."; and the Vietnamese government: "The Ministers [of the Bao Dai regime] appear in the eyes of their compatriots to be French officials . . ." The report did not hesitate to blame the French for Vietnamese corruption:

> It is grave that after eight years of *laisser-aller* and of anarchy, the presence in Indochina of a resident Minister has not been able to put an end to these daily scandals in the life in regard to the granting of licenses, the transfer of piastres, war damages, or commercial transactions. Even if our administration is not entirely responsible for these abuses, it is deplorable that one can affirm that it either ignores them or tolerates them.

Commenting on this report, an influential French editor blamed the "natural tendency of the military proconsulate to perpetuate itself" and "certain French political groups who have found in the war a principal source of their revenues . . . through exchange operations, supplies to the expeditionary corps and war damages . . . He concluded that:

> The generally accepted theory is that the prolongation of the war in Indochina is a fatality imposed by events, one of those dramas in history which

has no solution. The theory of the skeptics is that the impotence or the errors of the men responsible for our policy in Indochina have prevented us from finding a way out of this catastrophic enterprise. The truth is that the facts now known seem to add up to a lucid plan worked out step by step to eliminate any possibility of negotiation in Indochina in order to assure the prolongation without limit of the hostilities and of the military occupation.

5. Bao Dai, Attentiste

Despite U.S. recognition of the grave imperfections of the French administration in Vietnam, the U.S. was constrained to deal with the Indochina situation through France both by the overriding importance of its European policy and by the impotence and ineptitude of the Bao Dai regime. The U.S. attempted to persuade Bao Dai to exercise more vigorous leadership, but the Emperor chose differently. For example, immediately after the Pau negotiations, the Department of State sent these instructions to Edmund Gullion:

OUTGOING TELEGRAM

DEPARTMENT OF STATE

OCT 18 1950

PRIORITY

AMLEGATION
SAIGON
384

DEPT wishes to have FOL MSG delivered to Bao Dai personally by MIN IMMED after Chief of State's arrival in Saigon. It SHLD be delivered informally without submission written text with sufficient emphasis to leave no doubt in Emperor's mind that it represents DEPTS studied opinion in matter now receiving ATTN highest auths US GOVT. Begin MSG:

Bao Dai will arrive in Saigon at moment when Vietnam is facing grave crisis outcome of which may decide whether country will be permitted develop independence status or pass in near future to one of Sino-Soviet dominated satellite, a new form of colony immeasurably worse than the old from which Vietnam has so recently separated herself.

The US GOVT is at present moment taking steps to increase the AMT of aid to FR Union and ASSOC States in their effort to defend the territorial integrity of IC and prevent the incorporation of the ASSOC States within the COMMIE-dominated bloc of slave states but even the resources of US are strained by our present UN commitments in Korea, the need for aid in the defense of Western Europe and our own rearmament program. We sometimes find it impossible to furnish aid as we WLD wish in a given AMT at a given time and in a given place.

Leadership of Vietnam GOVT during this crucial period is a factor of preponderant importance in deciding ultimate outcome. GOVT must display unusually aggressive leadership and courage before a discouraged people, distraught and floundering in the wake of years of civil war. Lesser considerations concerning the modalities of relations between the States of the FR Union and the REP of FR must, for instance, be at least temporarily laid aside in face of serious threat to very existence of Vietnam as autonomous state, within FR Union or otherwise.

We are aware (as in Bao Dai) that present Vietnamese GOVT is so linked with person of Chief of State that leadership and example provided by latter takes on extraordinary importance in determining degree of efficiency in functioning of GOVT. Through circumstances of absence in FR of Bao Dai and other Vietnamese leaders for prolonged period, opportunity for progress in assumption of responsibilities from FR and extension authority and influence of GOVT with people was neglected. Many people, including great number AMERS, have been unable understand reasons for Emperor's GTE prolonged holiday UNQTE on Riviera and have misinterpreted it as an indication of lack of patriotic attachment to his role of Chief of State. DEPT is at least of opinion that his absence did not enhance the authority and prestige of his GOVT at home.

Therefore, DEPT considers it imperative Bao Dai give Vietnamese people evidence his determination personally take up reins of state and lead his country into IMMED and energetic opposition COMMIE menace. Specifically he SHLD embark upon IMMED program of visits to all parts Vietnam making numerous speeches and public appearances in the process. Chief of State SHLD declare his determination plunge into job of rallying people to support of GOVT and opposition to VM IMMED upon arrival Saigon. He SHLD announce US, FR support for formation NATL armies and his own intention assume role Commander in Chief. He SHLD take full advantage of FR official declaration of intention to form NATL armies (confirmed yesterday by MIN ASSC States Letourneau) and set up precise plan for such formation IMMED.

Finally, it SHLD be tactfully suggested that any further display procrastination in facing realities in the form prolonged periods of seclusion at Dalat or otherwise WLD confirm impressions of those not as convinced of Emperor's seriousness of purpose as DEPT and LEG are and raise questions of the wisdom of continuing to support a Vietnamese GOVT which proves itself incapable of exercising the autonomy acquired by it at such a high price. End of MSG.

Endeavor obtain private interview soonest possible after arrival for DEPT regards timing as of prime importance. Simultaneously or IMMED FOL inform Letourneau and Pignon of action. Saigon advise Paris in advance to synchronize informing FONOFF

ACHESON

Whatever Bao Dai's response—probably polite and obscure—he did not act on the U.S. advice. He subsequently told Dr. Phan Quang Dan, aboard his imperial yacht, that his successive governments had been of little use, and added that it would be dangerous to expand the Vietnamese Army because it might defect en masse and go to the Viet Minh:

> I could not inspire the troops with the necessary enthusiasm and fighting spirit, nor could Prime Minister Huu . . . Even if we had an able man, the present political conditions would make it impossible for him to convince the people and the troops that they have something worth while to fight for . . .

Dr. Dan agreed that the effectiveness of the National Army was a central issue; he pointed out that there were but three Viet generals, non of whom had ever held operational command, and neither they nor the 20 colonels or lieutenant colonels could exercise initiative of any sort. Dr. Dan held that: "The Vietnamese Army is without responsible Vietnamese leaders, without ideology, without objective, without enthusiasm, without fighting spirit, and without popular backing." But it was very clear that Bao Dai did not propose to alter the conditions of his army except by the long, slow process of "nibbling" at French military prerogative. On other vital issues Bao Dai was no more aggressive. For all practical purposes, the Emperor, in his own fashion, like Dr. Dan and Ngo Dinh Diem, assumed the posture of the *attentiste*—a spectator as the French and Americans tested their strength against each other, and against the Viet Minh.

6. *The American Predicament*

Among the American leaders who understood the vacuity of the Bao Dai solution, and recognized the pitfalls in French intransigence on genuine independence was the then Senator John F. Kennedy. Kennedy visited Vietnam in 1951 and evidently weighed Gullion's views heavily. In November, 1951, Kennedy declared that:

> In Indochina we have allied ourselves to the desperate effort of the French regime to hang on to the remnants of an empire. There is no broad general support of the native Vietnam Government among the people of that area.

In a speech to the U.S. Senate in June, 1953, he pointed out that:

> Genuine independence as we understand it is lacking in Indochina . . . local government is circumscribed in its functions . . . the government of Vietnam, the state which is of the greatest importance in this area, lacks popular support, that the degree of military, civil, political, and economic control maintained by the French goes well beyond what is necessary to fight a war . . . It is because we want the war to be brought to a successful conclusion that we should insist on genuine independence . . . Regardless of our united effort, it is a truism that the war can never be successful unless large numbers of the people of Vietnam are won over from their sullen neutrality and open hostility to it and fully support its successful conclusion . . . I strongly believe that the French cannot succeed in Indochina without giving concessions necessary to make the native army a reliable and crusading force.

Later, Kennedy criticized the French:

> Every year we are given three sets of assurances: first, that the independence of the Associated States is now complete; second, that the independence of the Associated States will soon be completed under steps "now" being taken; and third, that military victory for the French Union forces is assured, or is just around the corner.

Another American knowledgeable concerning the U.S.–French difficulties and with the Bao Dai solution was Robert Blum, who headed the economic aid program extended to the Bao Dai regime in 1950. General De Lattre viewed U.S. economic aid as especially pernicious, and told Blum that: "Mr. Blum, you are the most dangerous man in Indochina." De Lattre resented the American intrusion. "As a student of history, I can understand it, but as a Frenchman I don't like it." In 1952, Blum analyzed the Bao Dai-French-American triangle as follows:

> The attitude of the French is difficult to define. On the one hand are the repeated official affirmations that France has no selfish interests in Indochina and desires only to promote the independence of the Associated States and be relieved of the terrible drain of France's resources. On the other hand are the numerous examples of the deliberate continuation of French controls, the interference in major policy matters, the profiteering and the constant bickering and ill-feeling over the transfer of powers and the issues of independence . . . There is unquestionably a contradiction in French actions between the natural desire to be rid of this unpopular, costly and apparently fruitless war and the determination to see it through with honor while satisfying French pride and defending interests in the process. This distinction is typified by the sharp difference between the attitude toward General de Lattre in Indochina, where he is heralded as the political genius and military savior . . . and in France, where he is suspected as a person who for personal glory is drawing off France's resources on a perilous adventure . . .
>
> It is difficult to measure what have been the results of almost two years of active American participation in the affairs of Indochina. Although we embarked upon a course of uneasy association with the "colonialist"-tainted but indispensable French, on the one hand, and the indigenous, weak and divided Vietnamese, on the other hand, we have not been able fully to reconcile these two allies in the interest of a single-minded fight against Communism. Of the purposes which we hoped to serve by our actions in Indochina, the one that has been most successful has been the strengthening of the French military position. On the other hand, the Vietnamese, many of whom thought that magical solutions to their advantage would result from our appearance on the scene, are chastened but disappointed at the evidence that America is not omnipotent and not prepared to make an undiluted effort to support their point of view . . . Our direct influence on political and economic matters has not been great. We have been reluctant to become directly embroiled and, though the degree of our contribution has been steadily increasing, we have been content, if not eager, to have the French continue to have primary responsibility, and to give little, if any, advice.

Blum concluded that:

> The situation in Indochina is not satisfactory and shows no substantial prospect of improving, that no decisive military victory can be achieved, that the Bao Dai government gives little promise of developing competence and winning the loyalty of the population . . . and that the attainment of American objectives is remote.

Shortly before his death in 1965, Blum held that a clash of French and U.S. interests was inevitable:

> We wanted to strengthen the ability of the French to protect the area against Communist infiltration and invasion, and we wanted to capture the

nationalist movement from the Communists by encouraging the national aspirations of the local populations and increasing popular support of their governments. We knew that the French were unpopular, that the war that had been going on since 1946 was not only a nationalist revolt against them but was an example of the awakening self-consciousness of the peoples of Asia who were trying to break loose from domination by the Western world. We recognized right away that two-pronged policy was beset with great difficulties. Because of the prevailing anti-French feeling, we knew that any bolstering by us of the French position would be resented by the local people. And because of the traditional French position, and French sensitivity at seeing any increase of American influence, we know they would look with suspicion upon the development of direct American relations with local administrations and peoples. Nevertheless, we were determined that our aid program would not be used as a means of forcing co-ordination upon unwilling governments, and we were equally determined that our emphasis would be on types of aid that would appeal to the masses of the population and not on aid that, while economically more sophisticated, would be less readily understood. Ours was a political program that worked with the people and it would obviously have lost most of its effectiveness if it had been reduced to a role of French-protected anonymity . . . [The program was] greatly handicapped and its beneficial psychological results were largely negated because the United States at the same time was pursuing a program of [military] support to the French . . . on balance, we came to be looked upon more as a supporter of colonialism than as a friend of the new nation.

In 1965, Edmund Gullion, who was also very close to the Bao Dai problem, took this retrospect:

We really should have pushed the French right after the Elysee agreements of March, 1949. We did not consider the exchange of letters carefully enough at the time. It was understandable. We obviously felt it was going to be a continuing process, and we hoped to be able to have some influence over it. But then we got involved in Korea, and since the French were in trouble in Indochina, we pulled our punches . . . The French could have said unequivocally, as we did with regard to the Philippines, that in such-and-such a number of years Vietnam would be totally free, and that it could thereupon join the French Union or stay out, as it desired . . . An evolutionary solution was the obvious one, and it should have been confronted openly and honestly without all the impossible, protracted preliminary negotiations involving efforts to bring the three Associated States together, to get them to agree among each other, and with France, separately and collectively. The French, in arguing against any kind of bilateral agreements, claimed that their attempt at federation in Indochina was like our effort to build some sort of federated system in Europe. But their involvement and interest in Indochina was obviously different, and they used the formula they devised to avoid any real agreement on Vietnam. The problem grew more complex as the military and political aspects of the situation became unavoidably tied together, and the Korean War, of course, complicated it further. From the outset, the French sought to regard the war in Korea and the war in Indochina as related parts of one big fight against Communism, but it wasn't that simple. Actually, what the Korean War did do was make it more difficult for us to urge an evolutionary settlement in Vietnam. By 1951, it may have been too late for us to do anything about this, but we could still have tried much harder than we did. The trouble was the world by then had begun to close in on us. The E.D.C. formula in Europe was being rejected by the French, just as in 1965 they were rejecting the North Atlantic Treaty Organization concept. Our degree of leverage was being drastically reduced.

Had Bao Dai been willing or capable of more effective leadership, the U.S. role in the war might not have fallen into what Edmund Gullion called the "pattern of prediction and disappointment":

> It can be timed almost to the month to coincide with the rainy season and the campaign season. Thus, in May or June, we usually get French estimates of success in the coming campaign season, based partly on an assessment of losses the Vietminh are supposed to have suffered in the preceding fall, which are typically claimed as the bright spot in an otherwise gloomy fighting season. The new set of estimates soon proves equally disappointing; by October, French Union troops are found bottled up in mountain defiles far from their bases . . . There are rumblings about late or lacking American aid and lack of American understanding. Some time around the first of the new year, special high-level United States–French conferences are called. We ask some questions about the military situation but only a few about the political situation. There is widespread speculation that the French may pull out of Indochina if we press them for explanations of their political and economic program. We promise the French more aid. The French make a stand: they claim great casualties inflicted on the enemy. They give us new estimates for the following campaign season—and the round begins once more.

In that bleak pattern, Bao Dai played only a passive role; the "Bao Dai solution" ultimately solved nothing. The outcome rested rather on France's military struggle with the Viet Minh, and its contest of leverage with the United States.

II. LEVERAGE: FRANCE HAD MORE THAN THE UNITED STATES

It is sometimes asserted that France could not have continued the war in Indochina without American aid, but that the United States failed to use its considerable leverage on the French to force them to take more positive steps towards granting complete independence to the Associated States. An examination of Franco–American relations between 1950–1954 suggests, however, that American leverage was severely limited and that, given the primacy accorded in U.S. policy to the containment of communism in Southeast Asia, French leverage on the United States was the stronger of the two.

A. AMERICAN LEVERAGE ON FRANCE

1. *NATO and Marshall Plan*

In the first postwar decade, France was relatively weak and depended upon the United States through NATO and the Marshall Plan for its military security and economic revival. But neither NATO nor the Marshall Plan offered usable fulcrums for influencing French policy on Indochina. Both were judged by the U.S. Government and public to be strongly in the American national interest at a time when the Soviet threat to Western Europe, either through overt aggression or internal subversion, was clearly recognizable. A communist take-over in France was a real possibility. (The French Communist Party was the largest political party in the nation, and, at the time, quite militant in character.) Thus, an American threat to withdraw military and economic support to metropolitan France if it did not alter its policies in Indochina was not plausible. To threaten France with sanctions in NATO or through the Marshall Plan would have jeopardized a U.S. interest in Europe more important than any in Indochina.

2. *Military Assistance Program*

The chief remaining source of influence was the military assistance program to the French in Indochina. Announced by President Truman on May 8, 1950, in response to an urgent French request of February 16, 1950, for military and economic assistance, the purpose of the aid was to help the French in the prosecution of the war against the Viet Minh. The American Ambassador in Paris was called to the Quay d'Orsay, following a determination by the French Government that "it should set forth to the United States Government fully and frankly the extreme gravity of the situation in Indochina from French point of view as a result of recent developments and the expectation that at least increased military aid will be furnished to Ho Chi Minh from Communist China." He was told:

> . . . that the effort in Indochina was such a drain on France that a long-term program of assistance was necessary and it was only from the United States that it could come. Otherwise . . . it was very likely that France might be forced to reconsider her entire policy with the possible view to cutting her losses and withdrawing from Indochina . . . looking into the future it was obvious . . . that France could not continue indefinitely to bear this burden alone if the expected developments in regard to increased assistance to Ho Chi Minh came about. . . .

Although the decision to extend aid to the French military effort in Indochina was taken before the outbreak of the Korean War, it clearly was heavily influenced by the fall of Nationalist China and the arrival of Communist Chinese troops on the Indochina border in December, 1949. The Ho Chi Minh regime was recognized as the legal government of Vietnam by the Chinese Communists on January 18, 1950, and twelve days later the Soviet Government similarly announced its recognition. The NSC was thereupon asked "to undertake a determination of all practicable United States measures to protect its security in Indochina and to prevent the expansion of communist aggression in that area." In NSC 64 (February 27, 1950) it concluded that:

> It is important to United States security interests that all practicable measures be taken to prevent further communist expansion in Southeast Asia. Indochina is a key area of Southeast Asia and is under immediate threat.
>
> The neighboring countries of Thailand and Burma could be expected to fall under Communist domination if Indochina were controlled by a

Communist-dominated government. The balance of Southeast Asia would then be in grave hazard. [Doc. 1]

The Joint Chiefs of Staff, referring on April 5, 1950, to intelligence estimates indicating that the situation in Southeast Asia had deteriorated, noted that "without United States assistance, this deterioration will be accelerated." Therefore, the rationale for the decision to aid the French was to avert Indochina's sliding into the communist camp, rather than aid for France as a colonial power or a fellow NATO ally.

U.S. assistance, which began modestly with $10 million in 1950, reached $1,063 million in fiscal year 1954, at which time it accounted for 78% of the cost of the French war burden. The major portion of the increase came in the last year of the war, following the presentation in 1953 of the Navarre Plan, which called for the enlargement of Franco–Vietnamese forces and a dynamic strategy to recapture the initiative and pave the way for victory by 1955. The optimistic endorsement of the Navarre Plan by Lt. General John W. O'Daniel, head of the MAAG in Indochina, as being capable of turning the tide and leading to a decisive victory over the Viet Minh contributed to Washington's agreement to substantially raise the level of assistance. But equally important, the Navarre Plan, by being a concrete proposal which held out the promise of ending the long war, put France in a position to pressure the United States for more funds to underwrite the training and equipping of nine additional French battalions and a number of new Vietnamese units.

3.   U.S. Supports Independence for Associated States

Throughout the period of assistance to the French military effort, American policy makers kept in mind the necessity of encouraging the French to grant the Associated States full independence and to take practical measures in this direction, such as the training of Vietnamese officers and civil servants. Such active persuasion was delicate and difficult because of the high sensitivity of the French to any "interference" in their "internal" affairs.

A reading of the NSC memorandum and the France–American diplomatic dialogue of the time indicates that Washington kept its eyes on the ultimate goal of the de-colonialization of Indochina. Indeed, it was uncomfortable in finding itself—forced by the greater necessity of resisting Viet Minh communism—in the same bed as the French. American pressure may well have helped account for the public declaration of Premier Joseph Laniel of July 3, 1953, that the independence and sovereignty of the Associated States would be "perfected" by transferring to them various functions which had remained under French control, even though no final date was set for complete independence. At an NSC meeting on August 6, 1953 President Eisenhower stated that assistance to the French would be determined by three conditions:

(1) A public French commitment to "a program which will insure the support and cooperation of the native Indochina";

(2) A French invitation for "close [U.S.] military advice";

(3) Renewed assurances on the passage of the EDC.

Consistent with these, Washington's decision of September 9, 1953, to grant $385 million towards implementation of the Navarre Plan was made dependent upon a number of conditions. The American Ambassador was instructed to inform Prime Minister Laniel and Foreign Minister Bidault that the United States Government would expect France to:

. . . continue pursue policy of perfecting independence of Associated States in conformity with July 3 declaration;

facilitate exchange information with American military authorities and take into account their views in developing and carrying out French military plans Indochina;

assure that no basic or permanent alteration of plans and programs for NATO forces will be made as result of additional effort Indochina; . . . .

4.   *Limitation on American Leverage*

The United States attempted to use its military assistance program to gain leverage over French policies, but was severely constrained in what it could do. The U.S. military mission (MAAG) in Saigon was small and limited by the French in its functions to a supply-support group. Allocation of all U.S. aid to the Associated States had to be made, by agreement, solely through the French. Thus, MAAG was not allowed to control the dispensing of supplies once they arrived in Vietnam. MAAG officers were not given the necessary freedom to develop intelligence information on the course of the war; information supplied by the French was limited, and often unreliable or deliberately misleading. The French resisted repeated U.S. admonitions that the native armies of the Associated States be built up and consequently they did not create a true national Vietnamese army. With some minor exceptions, the French excluded American advisors from participating in the training for the use of the materials being furnished by the U.S.

General Navarre viewed any function of MAAG in Saigon beyond bookkeeping to be an intrusion upon internal French affairs. Even though it would have been difficult beyond 1952 to continue the war without American aid, the French never permitted participation by U.S. officials in strategic planning or policy making. Moreover, the French suspected the economic aid mission of being oversympathetic to Vienamese nationalism. The director of the economic aid program, Robert Blum, and the DCM of the American Embassy, Edmund Gullion, were subjected to French criticisms of their pro-Vietnamese views, although the American Ambassador, Donald Heath, remained staunchly pro-French. Thus, French officials insisted that American assistance be furnished with "no strings attached" and with virtually no control over its use. Underlying this attitude was a deepseated suspicion that the United States desired to totally supplant the French, economically as well as politically, in Indochina.

B.   FRENCH LEVERAGE ON THE UNITED STATES

French leverage over the United States was made possible by the conviction, apparently firmly held in Washington, that the maintenance of a non-Communist Indochina was vital to Western—and specifically American—interests.

1.   *Primarily It Was France's War*

The most fundamental fact was that the French were carrying on a war which the United States considered, rightly or wrongly, to be essential. Thus, the French were always able to threaten simply to end the war by pulling out of Indochina. By the early 1950's, with the French nation tired of the "la sale guerre," this would not have been an unpopular decision within France. Paris was thereby able to hint—which it did—that if U.S. assistance was not forthcoming, it would simply withdraw from Indochina, leaving to the United States alone the task of the containment of communism in Southeast Asia. When the Laniel Government requested in the fall of 1953 a massive increase in American assistance, the State Department representative at an NSC meeting asserted that "if this French Government, which proposes reinforcing Indochina with our aid, is not supported by us at this time, it may be the last such government prepared to make a real effort to win in Indochina." In effect, then, because of the overriding importance given by Washington to holding the communist line in Indochina, the French in being able to threaten to withdraw possessed an important instrument of blackmail.

The upshot of this was that U.S. leverage was quite minimal. Since the French were, in a way, fighting a U.S. battle as well as their own to prevent communist control of Indochina, any ham-fisted U.S. pressure was bound to weaken the French resolve and capability. Consequently, the leverage which the U.S. attained through its aid could be used for little more than to urge greater efficiency and determination on France. In other words, Washington could move Paris to formulate a Navarre type plan, but could not influence the way France conducted the war, nor could it move France on political issues in dispute.

2. *Expectation of French Success*

The temptation to "go along" with the French until the Viet Minh was defeated was all the more attractive because of the *expectation* of victory which pervaded official Washington. Before Dien Bien Phu, General O'Daniel consistently reported that victory was within reach if the United States continued its support. In November, 1953, General O'Daniel submitted a progress report on the Navarre Plan which summarized what the French had been doing and what remained to be accomplished. The report said that French Union forces held the initiative and would begin offensives in mid-January, 1954 in the Mekong Delta and in the region between Cape Varella and Da Nang. Meanwhile, a relatively small force would attempt to keep the Viet Minh off balance in the Tonkin Delta until October, 1954, when the French would begin a major offensive North of the 19th parallel. The report concluded by assessing that the Navarre Plan was basically sound and should be supported since it would bring a decisive victory.

O'Daniel's optimism was not duplicated by other observers. CINCPAC, for one, considered the report over-optimistic, stating that political and psychological factors were of such crucial importance that no victory would be possible until the Vietnamese were able to capture villages and until psychological warfare operations could be undertaken to win over the people. The Army attaché in Saigon was even less sanguine. He flatly stated that the French, after six months of the Navarre Plan, were still on the defensive and showed no sign of being able to win the war in the future. The attaché's views were, moreover, concurred in by the Assistant Chief of Staff for Intelligence, who observed that other high U.S. military officers in Indochina agreed with the attaché and found O'Daniel's report unwarrantedly optimistic.

3. *American Policy in Europe: The EDC*

An important source of French leverage was to be found outside of Far Eastern affairs. A primary objective of American foreign policy in 1953–1954 was the creation of a European Defense Community (E.D.C.). The purpose of the EDC was to "envelope" a new West German Army into an integrated six nation army which would go a long way towards providing for the defense of Western Europe. Washington officials expected that the EDC would permit a reduction (but not complete elimination) of American ground forces in Europe. The membership of France in the EDC—as a counter-weight to the proposed re-arming of Germany—was essential to its adoption by the five other European nations. Because of the high priority given to EDC in American planning, there was a strong reluctance to antagonize the French in Indochina. This was reinforced by knowledge that the French placed a far lower priority on EDC, in part because of the traditional French fear of an armed Germany, in part because the French estimate of Soviet intentions in Western Europe differed from that of the United States in that it placed a low probability on a direct Soviet intervention.

Apparently unnoticed at the time was an implicit contradiction in the American policy of pushing the French simultaneously on both adopting the EDC and on making a greater effort in Indochina. The latter required increased French forces in the Far East. But the French National Assembly would not adopt the EDC unless, at a minimum, it was assured that French forces in Europe would be on parity with those of Germany. Thus, the French argued that the possible coming into effect of the EDC prevented them from putting larger forces into Indochina. After the loss of North Vietnam and the French rejection of EDC, the Chairman of an Interdepartmental Working Group set up to formulate a new American policy on Indochina for the post-Geneva period observed that "our policies thus far have failed because we tried to hit two birds with one stone and missed both."

4.   *French Desire for Negotiations*

French leverage was also demonstrated by their ability to have the Indochina problem placed on the agenda for the Geneva Conference at the time of the Quadripartite Foreign Minister's meeting in February 1954 in Berlin. The Geneva Conference had been called to work out a political settlement for the Korean War. Dulles did not wish to negotiate on Indochina until there was a marked improvement in the military situation of the French and they could negotiate from a position of far greater strength. But the Laniel Government was under mounting pressure from French public opinion to end the Indochinese war. At Berlin the French delegation insisted, despite American objections, that Indochina be inscribed on the Geneva agenda. Foreign Minister Bidault reportedly warned that if the United States did not acquiesce on this point, EDC would doubtlessly be scuttled.

Dulles did succeed in opposing Soviet efforts to gain for Communist China the status of a sponsoring power at Geneva and forced the acceptance in the Berlin communiqué of a statement that no diplomatic recognition would be implied in the Chinese invitation to the conference. In return for this concession, however, the French were able to give highly visible evidence of their interest in ending the war soon through negotiations. Ironically, this had a double-edged effect: in Paris the "peace faction" was mollified; but in Hanoi plans were made to step up the intensity of the war so as to make a show of strength prior to the beginning of the Geneva Conference. Thus, the coming battle of Dien Bien Phu came to have a crucial significance in large measure because of the very inclusion of the Indochina item for the Geneva Conference. As Ellen Hammer has written:

> This was the last opportunity before the Geneva Conference for the Viet Minh to show its military strength, its determination to fight until victory.

And there were those who thought that General Giap was resolved on victory, no matter the cost, not only to impress the enemy but also to convince his Communist allies that the Viet Minh by its own efforts had earned a seat at the conference table and the right to a voice in its own future. For the French . . . upon the outcome of the battle depended much of the spirit in which they would send their representatives to Geneva.

5. Conclusion: Incompatibility of American and French Objectives

In summary, one must take notice of the paradox of U.S. policy vis-à-vis the French with respect to Indochina, 1950–1954. American interests and objectives were basically different from those of the French. The United States was concerned with the containment of communism and restricting the spread of Chinese influence in Southeast Asia. The immediate U.S. objective was supporting a domino. France, on the other hand, was fighting primarily a colonial war designed to maintain the French presence in Southeast Asia and avoid the crumbling of the French Union. Despite occasional pledges to the "perfectionment" of independence for the Associated States—pledges which were usually given under circumstances which were forcing France to "justify" the war, in part to receive further American assistance—France was *not* fighting a long and costly war in order to thereafter completely pull out.

The fact that the American and French means—pushing for military victory—converged in 1950–1954 obscured the fact that the ends of the two nations were inherently incompatible. This further led to a basic incompatibility in the two strands of American policy: (1) Washington wanted France to fight the war and win, preferably with American guidance and advice; and (2) having achieved success at great cost in what the French viewed at least initially as more a "colonial" than "anti-communist" war, Washington expected the French to withdraw magnanimously. (A Frenchman might have asked how France, even if it wished to, could have left Indochina without creating similar pressures for withdrawal from Algeria, Tunisia, and Morocco, where over one million Frenchmen lived.) In this inherent inconsistency can be found much of the explanation for the lack of American leverage over France during the pre-Geneva years.

III. PERCEPTIONS OF THE COMMUNIST THREAT TO SOUTHEAST ASIA AND TO BASIC U.S. INTERESTS

Three major perceptions dominated U.S. thinking and policy-making on Indochina during the years 1950–1954. The first was the growing importance of Asia in world politics. The process of devotion from colonial empires to independent states, it was thought, would create power vacuums and conditions of instability which would make Asia susceptible to becoming a battleground in the growing East-West cold war conflict. Second, there was an undeniable tendency to view the worldwide "communist threat" in monolithic terms. This was perhaps understandable given the relatively extensive influence then exerted by the Soviet Union over other communist nations, and the communist parties in non-communist states. Moreover, the West, and especially the U.S., was challenged by the expansionist policies openly proclaimed by leaders of virtually all the communist movements. Third, the attempt of the patently Communist Ho Chi Minh regime to evict the French from Indochina was seen as part of the Southeast Asian manifestation of the communist world-wide aggressive intent. The resistance of France to Ho, therefore, was seen as a crucial stand on the line along which the West would contain communism.

A. "DOMINO PRINCIPLE" BEFORE KOREA

These three perceptions help explain the widely held assumption in official Washington that if Indochina was "lost" to communism, the remaining nations of Southeast Asia would inexorably succumb to communist infiltration and be taken over in a chain reaction. This strategic conception of the communist threat to Southeast Asia pre-dated the outbreak in June 1950 of the Korean War. It probably had its period of gestation at the time of the Nationalist withdrawal from mainland China. NSC 48/1 was the key document in framing this conception. Drawn up in June 1949, after Secretary of Defense Louis Johnson had expressed concern at the course of events in Asia and had suggested a widening of the previous country-by-country memorandum approach to a regional plan, NSC 48/1 included the statements that "the extension of communist authority in China represents a grievous political defeat for us . . . If Southeast Asia is also swept by communism, we shall have suffered a major political rout the repercussions of which will be felt throughout the rest of the world, especially in the Middle East and in a then critically exposed Australia."

It was Russia rather than China that was seen in 1949 as being the principal source of the communist threat in Asia. Although it was conceded that in the course of time China (or Japan or India) may attempt to dominate Asia:

> now and for the foreseeable future it is the USSR which threatens to dominate Asia through the complementary instruments of communist conspiracy and diplomatic pressure supported by military strength. For the foreseeable future, therefore, our immediate objective must be to contain and where feasible to reduce the power and influence of the USSR in Asia to such a degree that the Soviet Union is not capable of threatening the security of the United States from that area and that the Soviet Union would encounter serious obstacles should it attempt to threaten the peace, national independence or stability of the Asiatic nations.

NSC 48/1 also recognized that "the colonial-nationalist conflict provides a fertile field for subversive communist movements, and it is now clear that Southeast Asia is the target for a coordinated offensive directed by the Kremlin."

At this time, the NSC believed that the United States, as a Western power in any area where the bulk of the population had long been suspicious of Western influence, should insofar as possible refrain from taking any lead in Southeast Asia. The United States should instead "encourage the peoples of India, Pakistan, the Philippines and other Asian states to take the leadership in meeting the common problems of the area," recognizing "that the non-communist governments of South Asia already constitute a bulwark against communist expansion in Asia." NSC 48/2 pointed out that particular attention should be given to the problem of Indochina where "action should be taken to bring home to the French the urgency of removing the barriers to the obtaining by Bao Dai or other non-communist nationalist leaders of the support of a substantial proportion of the Vietnamese."

B. IMPORTANCE OF INDOCHINA

Indochina was of special importance because it was the only area adjacent to China which contained a large European army which was in armed conflict with "communist" forces. The Chinese Communists were believed to be furnishing the Viet Minh with substantial material assistance. Official French sources reported that there were some Chinese troops in Tonkin, as well as large numbers ready for action against the French on the Chinese side of the border. The first NSC memorandum dealing solely with Indochina (NSC 64) [Doc. 1] was adopted as policy on February 27, 1950. This paper took note of Chinese assistance to the Viet Minh and estimated that it was doubtful that the French Expeditionary forces, combined with Indochinese troops, could successfully contain Ho Chi Minh's forces should they be strengthened by either Chinese troops crossing the border, or by communist-supplied arms and material in quantity.

NSC 64—written, it should be noted, by the Truman Administration and before the outbreak of the Korean War—observed that "the threat of Communist aggression against Indochina is only one phase of anticipated communist plans to seize all of Southeast Asia." It concluded with a statement of what came to be known as the "domino principle":

> It is important to United States security interests that all practicable measures be taken to prevent further communist expansion in Southeast Asia. Indochina is a key area of Southeast Asia and is under immediate threat.
>
> The neighboring countries of Thailand and Burma could be expected to fall under Communist domination if Indochina were controlled by a Communist-dominated government. The balance of Southeast Asia would then be in grave hazard.

C. IMPACT OF START OF KOREAN WAR

The outbreak of the Korean War, and the American decision to resist North Korean aggression, sharpened overnight our thoughts and actions with respect to Southeast Asia. The American military response symbolized in the most concrete manner possible the basic belief that holding the line in Southeast Asia was essential to American security interests. The French struggle in Indochina came far more than before to be seen as an integral part of the containment of communism in that region of the world. Accordingly, the United States intensified and enlarged its programs of aid in Indochina. Military aid shipments to Indochina acquired in 1951 the second highest priority, just behind the Korean war program.

A consequence of the Korean War, and particularly the Chinese intervention, was that China replaced the Soviet Union as the principal source of the perceived communist threat in Southeast Asia. This was made explicit in NSC 124/2 (June 1952) [Doc. 13] which stated that "the danger of an overt military attack against Southeast Asia is inherent in the existence of a hostile and aggressive Communist China."

The "domino principle" in its purest form was written into the "General Considerations" section of NSC 124/2. It linked the loss of any single state of Southeast Asia to the stability of Europe and the security of the United States:

> 2. Communist domination, by whatever means, of all Southeast Asia would seriously endanger in the short term, and critically endanger in the longer term, United States security interests.
>
> a. The loss of any of the countries of Southeast Asia to communist control as a consequence of overt or covert Chinese Communist aggression would have critical psychological, political and economic consequences. In the absence of effective and timely counteraction, the loss of any single

country would probably lead to relatively swift submission to or an alignment with communism by the remaining countries of this group. Furthermore, an alignment with communism of the rest of Southeast Asia and India, and in the longer term, of the Middle East (with the probable exceptions of at least Pakistan and Turkey) would in all probability progressively follow. Such widespread alignment would endanger the stability and security of Europe.

b. Communist control of all of Southeast Asia would render the U.S. position in the Pacific offshore island chain precarious and would seriously jeopardize fundamental U.S. security interests in the Far East.

c. Southeast Asia, especially Malaya and Indonesia, is the principal world source of natural rubber and tin, and a producer of petroleum and other strategically important commodities. The rice exports of Burma and Thailand are critically important to Malaya, Ceylon and Hong Kong and are of considerable significance to Japan and India, all important areas of free Asia.

d. The loss of Southeast Asia, especially of Malaya and Indonesia, could result in such economic and political pressures in Japan as to make it extremely difficult to prevent Japan's eventual accommodation to communism.

The possibility of a large-scale Chinese intervention in Indochina, similar to the Chinese intervention in Korea, came to dominate the thinking of American policy-makers after the start of the Korean War. Such an intervention would not have been surprising given the larger numbers of Chinese troops massed along the Tonkin border and the material assistance being given to the Viet Minh. The NIE of December 1950 considered direct Chinese intervention to be "impending." The following year it was estimated that after an armistice in Korea the Chinese would be capable of intervention in considerable strength, but would be inhibited from acting overtly by a number of factors, including the risk of American retaliation and the disadvantages attendant upon involvement in another protracted campaign. By early 1952, as the French position showed signs of deterioration, intelligence authorities believed that the Chinese would be content to continue aiding the Viet Minh without undertaking direct involvement (except for material aid) unless provoked into it. Thus, the intelligence community, after estimating a high risk of Chinese intervention at the start of the Korean War, gradually reduced its estimate of Indochina being broadened into a wider war as the Viet Minh showed signs of doing well enough on their own.

Nevertheless, the NSC undertook in 1952 to list a course of action for the "resolute defense" of Indochina in case of a large-scale Chinese intervention. It included the provision of air and naval forces; the interdiction of Chinese communication lines, including those in China proper; and a naval blockade of the China coast. If these "minimum courses of action" did not prove to be sufficient, the U.S. should take air and naval action "against all suitable military targets in China," when possible in conjunction with British and French forces.

In prescribing these recommended actions, the NSC focused on the less likely contingency of a Chinese intervention rather than the more likely contingency of the continued deterioration of the French position in Indochina itself. It did so despite the fact that NSC 124/2 conceded that the "primary threat" was the situation in Indochina itself (increasing subversive efforts by indigenous communist forces, increased guerrilla activity, and increased Viet Minh civil control over population and territory). Apparently, the NSC wanted to make clear that direct U.S. involvement in Indochina was to be limited to dealing with direct Chinese involvement. In the absence of this contingency, however, and to meet the existing situation in Indochina, the NSC recommended that the United States increase its level of aid to French Union forces but "without relieving the French authorities of their basic military responsibility for the defense of the Associated States."

D.   REPUBLICAN ADMINISTRATION AND FAR EAST

Two events in 1953 served to deepen the American commitment in Indochina. The first was the arrival of a Republican Administration following a long period in which the G.O.P. had persistently accused the Truman Administration of being responsible for the "loss" of China to communism. The writings and speeches of John Foster Dulles before the election left no doubt that he regarded Southeast Asia as a key region in the conflict with communist "imperialism," and that it was important to draw the line of containment north of the Rice Bowl of Asia—the Indochina peninsula. In his first State of the Union Message on February 3, 1953, President Eisenhower promised a "new, positive foreign policy." He went on to link the communist aggression in Korea and Malaya with Indochina. Dulles subsequently spoke of Korea and Indochina as two flanks, with the principal enemy—Red China—in the center. A special study mission headed by Representative Walter Judd, a recognized Republican spokesman on Asia, surveyed the Far East and reported on its view of the high stakes involved:

> The area of Indochina is immensely wealthy in rice, rubber, coal, and iron ore. Its position makes it a strategic key to the rest of Southeast Asia. If Indochina should fall, Thailand and Burma would be in extreme danger, Malaya, Singapore and even Indonesia would become more vulnerable to the Communist power drive. . . . Communism would then be in an exceptional position to complete its perversion of the political and social revolution that is spreading through Asia. . . . The Communists must be prevented from achieving their objectives in Indochina.

The Republican Administration clearly intended to prevent the loss of Indochina by taking a more forthright, anti-communist stand.

E.   IMPACT OF KOREAN ARMISTICE

Second, the armistice in Korea created apprehension that the Chinese Communists would now turn their attention to Indochina. President Eisenhower warned in a speech on April 16, 1953, that any armistice in Korea that merely released armed forces to pursue an attack elsewhere would be a fraud. Secretary Dulles continued this theme afer the Korean armistice in a speech on September 2, 1953, on the war in Indochina. After noting that "a single Communist aggressive front extends from Korea on the north to Indochina in the south" he said:

> Communist China has been and now is training, equipping and supplying the Communist forces in Indochina. There is the risk that, as in Korea, Red China might send its own Army into Indochina. The Chinese Communist regime should realize that such a second aggression could not

occur without grave consequences which might not be confined to Indochina. I say this soberly . . . in the hope of preventing another aggressor miscalculation.

Underlying these warnings to China was the belief that the difference between success or failure in avoiding a takeover of all Vietnam by Ho Chi Minh probably depended upon the extent of Chinese assistance or direct participation. Signaling a warning to China was probably designed to deter further Chinese involvement. Implicit in the signals was the threat that if China came into the war, the United States would be forced to follow suit, preferably with allies but, if necessary, alone. Furthermore, the Eisenhower Administration implied that in keeping with its policy of massive retaliation the United States would administer a punishing nuclear blow to China without necessarily involving its land forces in an Asian war.

F.   DEEPENING OF U.S. COMMITMENT TO CONTAINMENT

In addition to the new mood in Washington created by the strategic perceptions of a new Administration and the Korean armistice, the Viet Minh invasion of Laos in the spring of 1953 and the deepening war weariness in France served to strengthen those who favored a more assertive policy in Indochina. The United States rushed supplies to Laos and Thailand in May 1953 and provided six C-119's with civilian crews for the airlift into Laos. It increased substantially the volume and tempo of American military assistance to French Union forces. For fiscal year 1954, $460 million in military assistance was planned. Congress only appropriated $400 million, but following the presentation by the French of the Navarre Plan an additional $385 million was decided upon by the NSC. No objection was raised when France asked our views in August, 1953, on the transfer of its battalion in Korea to Indochina and subsequently took this action. The Navarre Plan, by offering a format for victory which promised success without the direct involvement of American military forces, tended, because of its very attractiveness, to have the effect of enlarging our commitment to assist the French towards achieving a military solution.

In the last NSC paper approved before the Indochina situation was totally transformed by the French defeat at Dien Bien Phu and the Geneva Conference, the "successful defense of Tonkin" was said to be the "keystone of the defense of mainland Southeast Asia except possibly Malaya." NSC 5405 [Doc. 20] took some, but probably not sufficient, account of the deterioration in the French position which had occurred since NSC 124/2 was approved eighteen months earlier. It, nevertheless, repeated the domino principle in detail, including the admonition that "such is the interrelation of the countries of the area that effective counteraction would be immediately necessary to prevent the loss of any single country from leading to submission to, or an alignment with, communism by the remaining countries of Southeast Asia and Indonesia." The document also noted that:

In the conflict in Indochina, the Communists and non-Communists worlds clearly confront one another in the field of battle: The loss of the struggle in Indochina, in addition to its impact in Southeast Asia and South Asia, would therefore have the most serious repercussions on U.S. and free world interests in Europe and elsewhere.

The subject of possible negotiations was broached in NSC 5405, following the observation that political pressures in France may impel the French Government to seek a negotiated rather than a military settlement. It was noted (before Dien Bien Phu) that if the Navarre Plan failed or appeared doomed to failure, the French might seek to negotiate simply for the best possible terms, irrespective of whether these offered any assurance of preserving a non-communist Indochina.

In this regard the NSC decided the U.S. should employ every feasible means to influence the French Government against concluding the struggle on terms "inconsistent" with the basic U.S. objectives. The French should be told that: (1) in the absence of a marked improvement in the military situation, there was no basis for negotiation on acceptable terms; (2) the U.S. would "flatly oppose any idea" of a cease-fire as a preliminary to negotiations, because such a cease-fire would result in an irretrievable deterioration of the Franco–Vietnamese military position in Indochina; (3) *a nominally non-communist coalition regime would eventually turn the country over to Ho Chi Minh with no opportunity for the replacement of the French by the United States or the United Kingdom.* [Emphasis Added]

G. CONCLUSION

In conclusion, two comments can be made:

a. With the growing perception of a Chinese threat to Indochina, and, therefore, to all of Southeast Asia, the U.S. Government tended to concentrate on the military rather than the political aspects of the French–Viet Minh struggle. In consequence, American attention focused on (1) deterring external intervention from China, and (2) assisting the French in successfully prosecuting the war through the implementation of the Navarre Plan. The result of this was that the encouragement and support of the non-communist nationalist governments in the Associated States was almost inadvertently given lower priority. The United States was reluctant to press the French too strongly on taking measures to foster Vietnam nationalism because of its overriding interest in halting the potential sweep of communism through Southeast Asia. Moreover, it was easier to develop a policy for dealing with the external threat of intervention than to meet the internal threat of subversion, or the even more difficult process of finding and sustaining a genuine nationalist alternative to the Viet Minh.

b. The "domino theory" and the assumptions behind it were never questioned. The homogeneity of the nations of Southeast Asia was taken as a given, as was the linkage in their ability to remain democratic, or at an acceptable minimum, non-communist, nations. Undoubtedly, in the first decade of the cold war there existed an unfortunate stereotype of a monolithic communist expansionary bloc. It was reinforced by a somewhat emotional approach on the part of many Americans to communism in China and Asia. This "syndrome" was, in part, the result of the "fall" of China, which some felt could have been averted, and a few hoped would still be reversed.

Accordingly, not sufficient cognizance was taken of the individuality of the states of Southeast Asia and the separateness of their societies. Probably there was some lack of knowledge in depth on the part of Washington policy-makers about the area. No one before World War II had expected that the United States would be called upon to take a position of leadership in these remote colonial territories of our European allies. In hindsight, these shortcomings may have led to the fallacious belief that a neutralist or communist Indochina would inevitably draw the other states of Asia into the communist bloc or into neutralism. But the "fallacy" was neither evident then, nor is it demonstrable now in retrospect.

IV. THE INTERAGENCY DEBATE OVER U.S. INTERVENTION IN INDOCHINA

A. *THE GENERAL POLICY CONTEXT*

The debate over the wisdom and manner of American intervention in Indochina was based primarily on the desirability of military involvement, not on questions concerning Indochina's value to United States security interests in the Far East. The Eisenhower Administration was in general agreement with the rationale for American interest in Indochina expressed by the Truman Administration. The United States Government first came to full grips with the question of intervention in late 1953–early 1954 as the fall of Indochina seemed to become imminent.

1. *The Final Truman Program (NSC 124)*

NSC 124 (February, 1952) considered imperative the prevention of a Communist take-over in Indochina. It recognized that even in the absence of "identifiable aggression" by Communist China, the U.S. might be forced to take some action in order to prevent the subversion of Southeast Asia. In case of overt Chinese intervention, NSC 124 recommended: (1) naval, air and logistical support of French Union forces; (2) naval blockade of Communist China; (3) attacks by land and carrier-based aircraft on military targets in Mainland China. It stopped short of recommending the commitment of U.S. ground forces in Indochina.

2. *Eisenhower Administration's "Basic National Security Policy"*

NSC 162/2 [Doc. 18], adopted in October, 1953, ten months after the Republican Administration took office, was the basic document of the "New Look." After commenting on U.S. and Soviet defense capabilities, the prospect of nuclear parity and the need to balance domestic economic policy with military expenditures, it urged a military posture based on the ability "to inflict massive retaliatory damage" on the enemy. Indochina was listed as an area of "strategic importance" to the U.S. An attack on such important areas "probably would compel the United States to react with military force either locally at the point of attack or generally against the military power of the aggressor." The use of tactical nuclear weapons in conventional war situations was recommended, but they were not specifically suggested for use in Indochina.

B. *THE QUESTION OF INTERVENTION WITH GROUND FORCES*

1. *The Problem Is Presented*

In late 1953, the Army questioned prevalent assumptions that ground forces would not be required in Indochina if the area was as important to U.S. security interests as the NSC papers stated. The Army urged that the issue be faced squarely in order to provide the best possible preparation for whatever courses of action might be undertaken. The Plans Division of the Army General Staff pointed out that under current programs the Army did not have the capability of providing divisional forces for operations in Indochina while maintaining its existing commitments in Europe and the Far East. Army also suggested a "re-evaluation of the importance of Indochina and Southeast Asia in relation to the possible cost of saving it."

With the deterioration of the French military situation in Indochina, the first serious attention came to be given to the manner and size of a U.S. intervention. The question to be faced was: how far was the U.S. prepared to go in terms of force commitments to ensure that Indochina stayed out of Communist hands? The Defense Department, though not of a single mind on this question, pressed for an early determination of the forces the U.S. would be willing to dispatch in an emergency situation. The Chief of Naval Operations, Admiral Robert Anderson, proposed to Secretary of Defense Wilson on January 6, 1954, that the U.S. decide immediately to employ combat forces in Indochina on the "reasonable assurance of strong indigenous support of our forces," whether or not the French Government approved. But Vice Admiral A. C. Davis, Director of the Office of Foreign Military Affairs in OSD, wrote:

> . . . Involvement of U.S. forces in the Indochina war should be avoided at all practical costs. If, then, National Policy determines no other alternative, the U.S. should not be self-duped into believing the possibility of partial involvement—such as "Naval and Air units only." One cannot go over Niagara Falls in a barrel only slightly.

Admiral Davis then went on:

> Comment: If it is determined *desirable* to introduce air and naval forces in combat in Indochina it is difficult to understand how involvement of ground forces could be avoided. Air strength sufficient to be of worth in such an effort would require bases in Indochina of considerable magnitude. Protection of those bases and port facilities would certainly require U.S. ground force personnel, and the force once committed would need ground combat units to support any threatened evacuation. It must be understood that there is no cheap way to fight a war, once committed.

2. NSC: State and Defense Views

The evident disparity between, on the one hand, our high strategic valuation of Indochina, and on the other, our unwillingness to reach a firm decision on the forces required to defend the area became the subject of the NSC's 179th meeting on January 8, 1954. At this meeting the Council discussed NSC 177 on Southeast Asia, but it decided not to take up the Special Annex to NSC 177 which laid out a series of choices which might face the United States if the French military position in Indochina continued to deteriorate. Nevertheless, the NSC at that time did make some headway on the problem it had posed for itself.

According to summary notes taken of the meeting, State and Defense were at considerable variance on what should be done in either of two contingencies: first, French abandonment of the struggle; second, a French demand for substantial U.S. forces (ground, sea, and air). The State view considered the French position so critical already as (in the rapporteur's words) to "force the U.S. to decide now to utilize U.S. forces in the fighting in Southeast Asia." The Defense representative refused to underwrite U.S. involvement. He reportedly stated that the French could win by the spring of 1955 given U.S. aid and given "improved French political relations with the Vietnamese . . . The commitment of U.S. forces in a 'civil war' in Indochina will be an admission of the bankruptcy of our political policies re Southeast Asia and France and should be resorted to only in extremity." He urged that every step be taken to avoid a direct American commitment.

The Council meeting reached two important conclusions, both fully in keeping with the Defense position. First, it decided that a discussion of contingencies for U.S. involvement missed the essential point that the French were capable of winning *provided* they gained native political and military cooperation. Second, NSC 177 was, as Defense suggested, inadequate in that the study failed to come to grips with the fact that eventual success in Indochina depended upon French ability to solve the problem of *how* to obtain Vietnamese support for the war effort.

3.   The JCS View

The NSC meeting of January 8 still left open the question of U.S. action in the event troops were indisputably necessary to prevent the "loss" of Indochina. In this regard, the Joint Chiefs of Staff kept their options open. The Chiefs thought that the Navarre Plan was fundamentally sound, but was being steadily undercut by the gulf separating the French from the Vietnamese, by General Navarre's failure to implement U.S. recommendations, and by hesitancy in Paris over the necessary political concessions to the Bao Dai government. Yet JCS refused either to rule out the use of U.S. combat forces or to back unequivocally their employment.

4.   Formation of Special Working Group on Indochina

Dissatisfaction with NSC 177 and the NSC's subsequent failure in NSC 5405 to resolve the ground force commitment issue led to the formation of a working group to evaluate the French military effort, to make recommendations concerning future U.S. contributions to it, and to devote attention to the various contingencies under which the U.S. might be called upon to intervene directly in the war. The working group, under the chairmanship of General G. B. Erskine (USMC, Ret.), was composed of representatives from the Departments of State and Defense, the Joint Chiefs, and CIA. The group was responsible to NSC through General W. Bedell Smith, Under Secretary of State, who had been appointed by the Council to head the Special Committee on the U.S. and Indochina.

5.   The Erskine Report, Part I: Motivate the French

The first section of Erskine's two-part report, dated February 6, 1954, was based on the assumption that U.S. policy toward Indochina would *not* require resort to overt combat operations by U.S. forces. Within that framework, the report adhered closely to the Defense Department position that the French, if properly motivated, could win in Indochina, but that their failure to carry through on needed reforms would require U.S. consideration of active involvement. The report noted that:

There is in Indo-China, or programmed for Indo-China . . . , a sufficient amount of equipment and supplies and a potential manpower pool sufficient eventually to defeat the Communists decisively if properly utilized and maintained and *if* the situation continues to permit this manpower to be converted into military effectiveness. Success will ultimately be dependent upon the inspiration of the local population to fight for their own freedom from Communist domination and the willingness of the French both to take the measures to stimulate that inspiration and to more fully utilize the native potential.

The Erskine Report (Part I) recommended: (1) augmentation of the French air force, but not using American personnel; (2) additional U.S. military assistance support of $124 million (supplementing FY 1954 commitments of $1.115 billion); (3) elevation of MAAG's status to that of Military Mission, with expanded personnel and advisory authority over training and planning; (4) assignment of additional U.S. personnel with the mission of acting as instructors and performing other key duties within the French forces; (5) Presidential letters to the Heads of State of the Associated States reaffirming our support of their independence and explaining our motivations in assisting them through the French; (6) an effort be undertaken to persuade Bao Dai to take a more active part in the anti-Viet Minh struggle. The report concluded that the program of recommended changes could bring about victory over the Viet Minh if it received full French approval and barring Chinese intervention.

6. The Erskine Report, Part II: Intervention Only After Geneva?

The second part of the Erskine Report [Doc. 24] did not appear until March 17, 1954, and unlike the first, was the responsibility only of the Defense Department and the Joint Chiefs, with the State Department position "reserved." The report confirmed previous determinations that the loss of Indochina would be a major military and political setback for the United States. It recommended that prior to the start of the Geneva Conference, the U.S. should inform Britain and France that it was interested only in military victory in Indochina and would not associate ourselves with any settlement which falls short of that objective. It further recommended that in the event of an unsatisfactory outcome at Geneva, the U.S. should pursue ways of continuing the struggle in concert with the Associated States, the United Kingdom, and other allies. The National Security Council was therefore requested to determine the extent of American willingness to commit combat forces to the region with or without French cooperation. But with the Dien Bien Phu siege just beginning, and the Geneva Conference six weeks away, the Erskine Report suggested that the United States influence and observe developments at the Geneva Conference before deciding on active involvement.

7. NSC 177 Annex Raises Intervention Question Anew

Following the second part of the Erskine Report, the President evidently decided that the Special Annex to NSC 177, which had been withdrawn in January 1954, should be redistributed for consideration by the Council's Planning Board. The Annex to NSC 177 posed the fundamental choice between (a) acceptance of the loss of Indochina, which would be *followed* by U.S. efforts to prevent further deterioration of our security position in Southeast Asia, or (b) direct military action to save Indochina *before* the French and Vietnamese became committed to an unacceptable political settlement at Geneva.

Among the alternative courses of action outlined in the Annex, two in particular—both geared to direct U.S. action *prior* to a Geneva settlement—were discussed. Under the first, based on French consent to continue fighting, the U.S. was urged to (1) seek a Franco–Vietnamese settlement of the independence issue, (2) insist upon a build-up of indigenous forces with U.S. advisory and material support, (3) demand the maintenance of French forces in the field at their then present level, and (4) prepare to provide sufficient U.S. forces to make possible the success of a joint effort. Full internationalization of the war would be discussed with the French later, thereby discounting immediate action in concert with the British or Asian nations.

The second alternative assumed a French pull-out. In such a case the United States could either accept the loss of Indochina, or adopt an active policy while France gradually withdrew its troops. Should we accept the latter course, our "most positive" step offering "the greatest assurance of success" would be, NSC estimated, to join with indigenous forces in combatting the Viet Minh until they were reduced "to the status of scattered guerrilla bands." U.S. land, sea, and air forces would be involved.

The Annex was based upon assumptions that U.S. involvement against the Viet Minh would not provoke massive Chinese intervention, would not lead to direct Soviet involvement, and that there would be no resumption of hostilities in Korea. It acknowledged that any change in these assumptions would seriously jeopardize the success of the alternatives proposed. In particular, it noted that U.S. participation heightened the risk of Chinese intervention, and Chinese entry would alter radically both the immediate military situation and U.S. force requirements.

8.   *Army Questions Feasibility of Air-Naval Intervention and Outlines Ground Forces Requirements*

The principal result of the discussions on the NSC 177 Special Annex was to bring into the open the issue of the costs in manpower and materiel of a U.S. involvement. The Army was critical of contingency planning that was based on the assumption that U.S. air and naval forces could be used in Indochina without the commitment of ground combat forces. General Matthew B. Ridgway, Army Chief of Staff, later wrote in his *Memoirs* that he was quite disturbed at talk in high government circles about employing air-naval power alone in Indochina. An Army position paper [Doc. 31] submitted to the NSC in the first week of April, 1954, argued as follows:

1. U.S. intervention with combat forces in Indochina is not militarily desirable . . .
2. A victory in Indochina cannot be assured by U.S. intervention with air and naval forces alone.
3. The use of atomic weapons in Indochina would not reduce the number of ground forces required to achieve a victory in Indochina.
4. Seven U.S. divisions or their equivalent, with appropriate naval and air support, would be required to win a victory in Indochina if the French withdraw and the Chinese Communists do not intervene. However, U.S. intervention plans cannot be based on the assumption that the Chinese Communists will not intervene.

5. The equivalent of 12 U.S. divisions would be required to win a victory in Indochina, if the French withdraw and the Chinese Communists intervene.

6. The equivalent of 7 U.S. divisions would be required to win a victory in Indochina if the French remain and the Chinese Communists intervene.

7. Requirements for air and naval support for ground force operations are:

a. Five hundred fighter-bomber sorties per day exclusive of interdiction and counter-air operations.

b. An airlift capability of a one division drop.

c. A division amphibious lift.

8. Two U.S. divisions can be placed in Indochina in 30 days, and an additional 5 divisions in the following 120 days. This could be accomplished without reducing U.S. ground strength in the Far East to an unacceptable degree, but the U.S. ability to meet its NATO commitment would be seriously affected for a considerable period. The amount of time required to place 12 divisions in Indochina would depend upon the industrial and personnel mobilization measures taken by the government . . .

9. *Defense-JCS "Solution": Rectify French Deficiencies*

Faced with estimates that U.S. air-naval action could not turn the tide, and that U.S. ground forces of appropriate size would impinge upon other commitments, DoD and the JCS took the position that an alternative military solution existed within the reach of the French which required no U.S. intervention. DoD argued that the three reasons for France's deteriorating position were (1) lack of the will to win; (2) reluctance to meet Indochinese demands for true independence; (3) refusal to train indigenous personnel for military leadership. Defense believed that premature U.S. involvement would therefore beg the basic question of whether the U.S. was prepared to apply the strongest pressure on France, primarily in the European context, to attempt to force the French in Paris and in Indochina to take appropriate measures to rectify these deficiencies. Only if these measures were forthcoming, DoD held, should the U.S. seriously consider committing ground forces in defense of the interests of France and the Associated States. The net effect of the Defense-JCS position was to challenge the notion that a quick U.S. military action in Indochina would be either feasible or necessary.

C. THE NEW APPROACH: "UNITED ACTION"

At this juncture the Eisenhower Administration began giving serious consideration to broadening any American military intervention in Indochina by making it part of a collective venture along with its European and Asian allies. Secretary of State Dulles in a speech on March 29 warned the public of the alarming situation in Indochina and called for "united action"—without defining it further—in these words:

Under the conditions of today, the imposition on Southeast Asia of the political system of Communist Russia and its Chinese Communist ally, by whatever means, would be a grave threat to the whole free community. The United States feels that the possibility should not be passively accepted but should be met by united action. This might involve serious risks. But these risks are far less than those that will face us a few years from now if we dare not be resolute today.

Under Secretary of State W. Bedell Smith's Special Committee on the U.S. and Indochina, to which the Erskine working group had reported, issued a study on April 2. This report went beyond the question of holding Indochina and agreed that whatever that area's fate, the U.S. should begin developing a system of mutual defense for Southeast Asia. For the short term, the Smith Committee favored American sponsorship of a mutual defense treaty directed against Communist aggression in Indochina and Thailand. In the long run, it recommended promotion of a "regional and Asian mutual defense arrangement subscribed and underwritten by the major European powers with interests in the Pacific."

The State Department's thinking in early April 1954 was not greatly at variance from that of Defense and the Smith Committee. Perhaps more so than Defense, State was concerned about the Chinese reaction to a U.S. military intervention. It urged caution and suggested that in any type of "united action" the U.S. make clear to both the Chinese and the allies that the intervention would not be aimed at the overthrow or destruction of the Peking regime. State recommended: (1) no U.S. military intervention for the moment, nor should it be promised to the French; (2) planning for military intervention continue; (3) discussions with potential allies on possibility of forming a regional grouping in the event of an unacceptable settlement at Geneva.

1. *Presidential Decision to Support Only "United Action"*

Meanwhile, the President decided, following a meeting of Secretary Dulles and Admiral Radford, Chairman of the Joint Chiefs, with Congressional leaders on April 3, that the U.S. would not undertake a unilateral intervention. Any U.S. military involvement in Indochina would be contingent upon (1) formation of a coalition force with U.S. allies to pursue "united action"; (2) declaration of French intent to accelerate independence of Associated States; (3) Congressional approval of U.S. involvement (which was throught to be dependent upon (1) and (2)).

These policy guidelines undoubtedly influenced the NSC which, at a meeting on April 6, developed the somewhat incompatible objectives that the U.S. (a) "intervene if necessary to avoid the loss of Indochina, but advocate that no steps be left untaken to get the French to achieve a successful conclusion of the war on their own" and (b) support as the best alternative to U.S. intervention a regional grouping with maximum Asian participation.

The President accepted the NSC recommendations but decided that henceforth the Administration's primary efforts would be devoted toward: (1) organizing regional collective defense against Communist expansion; (2) gaining British support for U.S. objectives in Southeast Asia; (3) pressing France to accelerate its timetable for Indochinese independence. The President would seek Congressional approval for U.S. participation in a regional arrangement, if it could be put together, and meanwhile contingency planning for mobilization would commence.

2. *Rejection of Unilateral Intervention*

Thus, as the curtain began to fall on the French effort at Dien Bien Phu, and the question of what the U.S. would do became critical, the U.S. Government backed away from unilateral intervention. The Defense Department was reluctant to intervene following the Army's presentation of the view that air-naval action alone would not do the job and ground forces would be needed. The very recent experience of the Korean War mitigated strongly against another American involvement in an Asian land war. Furthermore, the President was not willing to enter into such a venture unless it was cloaked with Congressional approval. Such approval, in turn, depended upon the participation of the allies. Hence, Secretary Dulles undertook the task of persuading Britain, France and the Asian allies to participate in a coalition for "united action" in Indochina.

V.   THE ATTEMPT TO ORGANIZE "UNITED ACTION"

A.   *THE BERLIN CONFERENCE OF 1954*

Negotiations for a political settlement of the French–Viet Minh war were practically assured when it was decided at the Big Four meeting in Berlin in February 1954 that the Indochina question would be added to the agenda of an upcoming international conference at Geneva which was to discuss primarily a settlement of the Korean War. The period between the Berlin and Geneva conferences (i.e., between February and May 1954) unexpectedly witnessed a denouement of the Indochina drama with the siege and fall of Dien Bien Phu, the U.S. decision not to intervene, and the unsuccessful U.S. attempt to rally its allies together in order to form a collective force in pursuance of "united action."

1.   *Viet Minh Strategy and French Attitudes*

The half-year before the Berlin Foreign Ministers conference of February 1954 saw both a marked step up of Viet Minh military activity and the presentation of a peace feeler from Ho Chi Minh. The Vietnam Peoples Army (VPA) began to change its strategy against the French from guerrilla activities to conventional battle deployments. This was accompanied by an increase in the amount of Chinese military assistance, no doubt facilitated by the end of armed conflict in Korea. Thus, the Viet Minh appeared to be showing a newly found strength and confidence, although at the time the French refused to recognize this either publicly or to themselves.

Meanwhile, Ho Chi Minh put out a peace feeler in late November 1953 in reply to a questionnaire submitted by a correspondent for the Swedish newspaper *Expressen.* The one pre-condition set by Ho for negotiations was French recognition of Vietnamese independence. In subsequent weeks, the peace feeler was repeated on several occasions, but each time it failed to indicate the place at which talks might be held, nor did it propose a scope for the talks.

Nothing resulted directly from these peace feelers, but indirectly they added to the mounting public and political sentiment in France for an end to the seemingly interminable and costly war. The armistice agreement negotiated at Panmunjom in July 1953 served as an example which many Frenchmen hoped could be followed in the negotiation of a cease-fire with the DRV. A widespread disenchantment with the Indochina war pervaded France. This was reflected in public statements by Prime Minister Laniel that Paris would be satisfied with an "honorable solution" to the war.

The French then adopted a policy toward the war of "keep fighting—seek talking." There was an increase in French military activity and confidence stimulated by the Navarre Plan, but this was offset by a growth in the size and influence of the peace faction in France, as indicated by the "dovish" votes of the National Assembly favoring an early settlement of the protracted war. Premier Laniel and French officials told the U.S. Embassy that they considered the Ho Chi Minh offer pure propaganda, but said also that Ho's move had produced the intended impact on public and military circles in France and Indochina. Laniel mentioned that President Vincent Auriol had become so excited by Ho's proposal that he told Laniel "to consult representatives of three Associated States immediately with view to seeking earliest possible opening of negotiations with representatives of Ho Chi Minh. Laniel had flatly refused . . ." But American officials were skeptical. The U.S. Embassy reported that a Laniel speech of November 24, 1953, "left considerable latitude for negotiations," and that Ho's offers had increased the pressure for a settlement.

2. *Early U.S. Opposition to Negotiations*

The consistent U.S. policy was to attempt to steer the French clear of the negotiating table pending substantial military gains on the battlefield. In bilateral U.S.–French talks in July, 1953, while the Korean armistice was being discussed at Panmunjom, Foreign Minister Bidault told Secretary Dulles that parallel talks should be pursued on Indochina. Bidault explained that the French public would never understand why negotiations were fit and honorable for Korea but were not for Indochina. A cease-fire in Korea, with nothing similar in prospect for Indochina, would make his government's position "absolutely impossible."

Secretary Dulles in reply stressed that "negotiations with no other alternative usually end in capitulation." In the Korean case, Dulles said, the alternative was the U.S. threat of "other and unpleasant measures" which the Communists realized we possessed. He urged the French to adopt the Navarre Plan, not only for military reasons, but because it would improve the French negotiating position. Dulles made it clear that the U.S. felt it was inadvisable to have the Indochina war inscribed on the agenda of a post-armistice political conference on Korea. The U.S. position at this time foreclosed negotiating on Indochina until after a Chinese decision to eliminate or cut down aid to the Viet Minh. In general, the U.S. sought to convince the French that military victory was the only guarantee of diplomatic success.

Dulles wished the French to continue the war because of his deep conviction that Indochina was a principal link in the line of the containment of Communism. In addition, Washington was undoubtedly influenced by optimistic reports on the progress of the war. General O'Daniel reported from Saigon that a French victory was likely if U.S. material support was forthcoming. On February 6, 1954, it was announced that forty B-26 bombers and 200 U.S. technicians to service them would be sent to Indochina. Admiral Radford told a House Foreign Relations Subcommittee, a month before the siege of Dien Bien Phu began (March, 1954), that the Navarre Plan was "a broad strategic concept which within a few months should insure a favorable turn in the course of the war."

At the Berlin Quadripartite Foreign Ministers meeting in February, however, Secretary Dulles was forced to give in on the French demand that Indochina be placed on the Geneva agenda. Bidault pressured the U.S. by threatening to scuttle the project for the European Defense Community which then was at the top of U.S. priorities. Dulles could not block Paris' determination to discuss Indochina at Geneva for it was, in the last analysis, France's war. He must have realized that the Laniel Government could not completely avoid negotiations without alienating itself from popular opinion and bringing about its downfall at the hands of the anti-war opposition parties.

The United States successfully opposed Soviet efforts at Berlin to gain for Communist China the status of a sponsoring power, and successfully held out, furthermore, for the inclusion in the Berlin communiqué of a statement that no diplomatic recognition, not already accorded, would be implied either in the invitation to, or the holding of, the Geneva Conference.

B. THE ELY MISSION (MARCH 20–24)

1. Dien Bien Phu Begins

On March 13, 1954, the VPA, under the direct command of General Giap, began its assault upon Dien Bien Phu. This fortress in Northern Vietnam was to take on a political and psychological importance far out of proportion to its actual strategic value because of the upcoming Geneva Conference. The Viet Minh correctly foresaw that a show of decisive force, not to mention a victory, would markedly strengthen their hand at the conference. Further, a defeat of the French Union forces would sap the will of the French nation to continue the struggle. The Viet Minh were greatly helped by a substantial increase in the level of Chinese military aid including artillery and radar. As the battle developed, the optimism which had pervaded Washington statements, public and private, on the war was replaced with the conviction that unless new steps were taken to deal with Chinese aid, the French were bound to go under.

General Paul Ely, French Chief of Staff, arrived in Washington on March 20 to confer with U.S. officials on the war situation. Ely's principal aims were to obtain American assurance of air intervention in the event of Chinese aerial attack, and to obtain further U.S. material assistance, especially B-26 bombers. Dulles told Ely that he could not then answer regarding U.S. response to Chinese air intervention. Ely subsequently contended in his *Mémoires* that he received a promise from Admiral Radford, Chairman of the Joint Chiefs of Staff, to push for prompt American approval of interdiction should the contingency arise. As to the supply of bombers, twenty-five additional B-26's were promised.

2. Operation Vulture (Vautour)

According to subsequent French reports, General Ely was asked to stay 24 hours longer than planned in Washington, during which time Admiral Radford made an informal but major proposal to him. Radford is said to have suggested a nighttime raid against the perimeter of Dien Bien Phu by aircraft of the U.S. Air Force and U.S. Navy. The plan, named Operation Vulture, called for about sixty B-29's to take off from Clark Field near Manila, under escort of 150 fighters of the U.S. Seventh Fleet, to conduct a massive strike against VPA positions on the perimeter of Dien Bien Phu.

Operation Vulture, according to French sources, was conceived by a joint American–French military staff in Saigon. It is admitted to have been an informal proposal which had not as yet received full U.S. Government backing as policy. No record of Operation Vulture has been found in files examined. In an interview in 1965, Admiral Radford stated that no plans for "Operation Vulture" existed, since planning to aid Dien Bien Phu by an air strike never proceeded beyond the conceptual stage. Nevertheless, such an operation probably was the subject of informal discussions both in Vietnam, and between Radford and Ely.

C. "UNITED ACTION" AS AN ALTERNATIVE TO EITHER NEGOTIATIONS OR TO UNILATERAL U.S. INTERVENTION

1. Formulation of U.S. Policy

By late March the internal debate within the Eisenhower Administration had reached the point where it was recognized that: (a) unilateral U.S. intervention in the Indochina War would not be effective without ground forces; (b) the involvement of U.S. ground forces was logistically and politically undesirable; (c) preferably, "free world" intervention in Indochina to save the area from communism would take the form of a collective operation by allied forces. This was the import of the NSC deliberations, the Ridgway Report, the Report of Under Secretary of State W. Bedell Smith's Special Committee on the U.S. and Indochina, and President Eisenhower's general train of thought.

Accordingly, Secretary Dulles in his discussions with General Ely went beyond the question of immediate assistance to the French garrison at Dien Bien Phu and broached the possible establishment of a regional defense arrangement for Southeast Asia.

This proposal was given public exposure in Secretary Dulles' speech of March 29 before the Overseas Press Club. Dulles described the importance of resisting communist aggression in Indochina in these words:

> If the Communist forces were to win uncontested control over Indo-China or any substantial part thereof, they would surely resume the same pattern of aggression against the other free peoples in that area.
>
> The propagandists of Red China and of Soviet Russia make it perfectly apparent that the purpose is to dominate all of Southeast Asia.
>
> Now Southeast Asia is an important part of the world. It is the so-called "rice bowl" . . . It is an area that is rich in many raw materials . . .
>
> And in addition to these tremendous economic values, the area has great strategic value . . . Communist control of Southeast Asia would carry a grave threat to the Philippines, Australia and New Zealand . . . The entire western Pacific area, including the so-called "offshore island chain," would be strategically endangered.

He then went on call for "united action," and after noting Chinese assistance to the Viet Minh, prophesied that aggression would "lead to action in places by means of the free world's choosing, so that the aggression would surely cost more than it would gain."

In the following weeks the aim of U.S. diplomacy was to escure allied agreement to a collective defense pact consisting of ten nations: the U.S., France, Britain, Australia, New Zealand, Philippines, Thailand, and the three Associated States. Secretary Dulles presented his proposal in discussions with British Ambassador Sir Roger Makins and French Ambassador Henri Bonnet. President Eisenhower addressed a personal message to Prime Minister Churchill explaining the proposed coalition. The President noted that:

> Geneva is less than four weeks away. There the possibility of the Communists driving a wedge between us will, given the state of mind in France,

be infinitely greater than at Berlin. I can understand the very natural desire of the French to seek an end to this war which has been bleeding them for eight years. But our painstaking search for a way out of the impasse has reluctantly forced us to the conclusion that there is no negotiated solution of the Indochina problem which in its essence would not be either a face-saving device to cover a French surrender or a face-saving device to cover a Communist retirement. The first alternative is too serious in its broad strategic implications for us and for you to be acceptable. . . .

Somehow we must contrive to bring about the second alternative.

President Eisenhower went on to outline the need for a coalition willing to fight the Communists, if this proved necessary. He concluded with a historical question certain to appeal to Churchill:

If I may refer again to history; we failed to halt Hirohito, Mussolini and Hitler by not acting in unit and in time. That marked the beginning of many years of stark tragedy and desperate peril. May it not be that our nations have learned something from that lesson? . . .

In these discussions the United States sought generally to stiffen the will of the free nations in the Indochina crisis. It emphasized both the avowed intention of France to grant real independence to the Associated States, and the condition accepted by the French at Berlin for the United States' agreeing to discuss Indochina at Geneva. That condition was that France would not agree to any arrangement which would directly or indirectly result in the turnover of Indochina to the Communists. The United States sought solid support for this position, especially from the United Kingdom, Australia, and New Zealand. Although the possibility was held out of future involvement of the United Nations in the Indochina problem, there was no thought of immediate UN action.

2. Initial Allied Reaction to "United Action"

Thailand and the Philippines gave a favorable response to the call for united action. The British response was one of caution and hesitancy. Churchill accepted Eisenhower's suggestion that Secretary Dulles go to London for further talks, but the British saw dangers in pressing for a defensive coalition *before* the Geneva conference. Eden was determined not to be "hustled into injudicious military decisions." As Eden later wrote:

I welcomed the American proposal for the organization of collective defence in South-East Asia, since this would contribute to the security of Malaya and Hong Kong and would remove the anomaly of our exclusion from the A.N.Z.U.S. Pact, to which the United States, Australia and New Zealand were party. But I felt that to form and proclaim a defensive coalition, before we went to the conference table, would be unlikely to help us militarily and would harm us politically, by frightening off important potential allies. By the beginning of May, the rains would be starting in Indo-China and extensive campaigning by either side would be impossible for several months. Since the complete collapse of the French military effort before then was improbable, I did not think that concern for the immediate military situation should be the guiding factor in our policy.

3. *French Call for U.S. Intervention at Dien Bien Phu* (*April 4–5*)

The French response to the proposal for united action was overtaken by military events at Dien Bien Phu. Foreign Minister Bidault contended on April 5 that the time for a coalition approach had passed and that the fate of Dien Bien Phu would be decided in the next ten days. The previous day Ambassador Douglas Dillon was called to an emergency Sunday cabinet meeting and was informed by Bidault, in the company of Laniel, that "immediate armed intervention of U.S. carrier aircraft at Dien Bien Phu is now necessary to save the situation." Bidault, reporting Navarre's desperate state in the field and the extent of Chinese intervention in support of General Giap's forces, asked the Ambassador point-blank for U.S. action, saying that "the fate of Southeast Asia now rested on Dien Bien Phu," and that "Geneva would be won or lost depending on outcome" of the battle. The United States was now being called upon to act quickly and unilaterally to save a local situation, rather than, as Dulles desired, in concert with Asian and Western Allies.

4. *U.S. Decision Not to Intervene Unilaterally*

In the first week of April it became clear that the question of U.S. intervention was now crucial. Fighting at Dien Bien Phu reached major proportions as Chinese-supplied artillery pounded the French and drove them backwards. Without an early intervention by an external power, or group of powers, the French position at Dien Bien Phu was likely to be overrun. In anticipation of the French request for intervention, the Eisenhower Administration decided to consult with Congressional leaders. The President appears to have thought that Congressional support was vital for whatever active role the U.S. might now take in Indochina.

Available Government documents do not provide details of the two meetings to be described below. However, on the basis of seemingly reliable published sources, it appears that on April 3 Secretary Dulles and Admiral Radford met with eight Congressmen (three Republicans and five Democrats) at the State Department. Radford apparently outlined a plan for an air strike on the Vietnam People's Army (VPA) at Dien Bien Phu using 200 planes from the aircraft carriers *Essex* and *Boxer,* stationed on maneuvers in the South China Sea. An unsuccessful air strike might need to be followed by a second air strike, but ground forces were not envisaged at this stage. It has been averred that there were atomic bombs on the aircraft carriers which could be delivered by the planes, but there is no indication that there was any serious consideration given to using nuclear weapons at Dien Bien Phu or elsewhere in Indochina. In the event of a massive Chinese troop intervention, however, it is quite possible that the U.S. would have retaliated with strategic nuclear weapons against targets in China.

The Congressional leaders raised questions about the amount of allied support for such an action, about the position of the other Joint Chiefs, about the need for ground forces if a second air strike also failed, and about the danger of a mammoth Chinese intervention which could transform Indochina into another Korean-type war. Radford apparently was forced to admit that he was the only one of the Joint Chiefs who favored the intervention plan. Dulles conceded that the allies had not as yet been consulted. In consequence, Dulles, who had been thinking of a joint Congressional resolution authorizing Presidential use of U.S. air-naval power in Indochina (which it is alleged he had ready in his pocket) left the meeting without the vital support he needed. The Congressional leaders laid down three conditions necessary for their support: (a) formation of an allied "coalition"-type force; (b) a French declaration indicating an intent to accelerate independence for the Associated States; (c) French agreement to continue their Expeditionary Corps in Indochina. Thus Congressional opposition put the brake on a possible unilateral U.S. intervention. According to a subsequent State Department Summary:

> It was the sense of the meeting that the U.S. should not intervene alone but should attempt to secure the cooperation of other free nations concerned in Southeast Asia, and that if such cooperation could be assured, it was probable that the U.S. Congress would authorize U.S. participation in such "United Action."

The following day, April 4, Dulles and Radford met with the President at the White House. The President reached the decision to intervene only upon the satisfaction of the three conditions necessary for the U.S. "to commit belligerent acts" in Indochina. There would have to be a coalition "with active British Commonwealth participation"; a "full political understanding with France and other countries," and Congressional approval.

President Eisenhower clearly did not want the U.S. to intervene alone. He also was very concerned with having broad Congressional support for any step which might involve the U.S. in a war. As Sherman Adams later observed:

> Having avoided one total war with Red China the year before in Korea when he had United Nations support, he [Eisenhower] was in no mood to provoke another one in Indo-China by going it alone in a military action without the British and other Western Allies. He was also determined not to become involved militarily in any foreign conflict without the approval of Congress. He had had trouble enough convincing some Senators that it was even necessary to send small groups of noncombatant Air Force technicians to Indo-China.

5. British Oppose "United Action"

From April 11 to 14, Secretary Dulles visited London and Paris to attempt to obtain British and French commitments to support his proposal for "United Action." According to President Eisenhower, Dulles felt that he had been given assurance of Congressional support for "United Action" if the allies approved his plan.

Dulles found the British opposed to any type of collective military action prior to the Geneva Conference. Dulles explained, according to Eden's account, that the U.S. had concluded that the French could no longer deal with the situation in Indochina, militarily or politically, alone. If the French position in Indochina collapsed, the consequences in the rest of Southeast Asia would be grave. U.S. air and naval forces were ready to intervene and some aircraft carriers had already been moved from Manila to the Indochina coast. On reflection, said Dulles, he had thought that the U.S. should not act alone in this matter and that an *ad hoc* coalition might be formed which might develop later into a Southeast Asia defense organization. This in itself would deter China from further interference in Indochina and would strengthen the western position at Geneva by giving evidence of solidarity.

Eden was not convinced. He drew a distinction between the long term issue of collective security in Southeast Asia—which might well be guaranteed by treaty after Geneva—and the more immediate question of "united action" in Indochina. He was opposed to any military action or warning announcement before Geneva. The British were willing to provide the French with full diplomatic support at Geneva, either as a guarantor of the final settlement or as a participant in multilateral talks if a settlement failed to materialize. In the latter case, the British were prepared to discuss a collective defense formula that would comprehend any non-Communist portion of Indochina formed as the result of the Geneva deliberations. But they would not, prior to Geneva, commit themselves to united action.

Britain's distinction between the appropriateness of a united approach after, as opposed to before, the Conference was founded on serious doubts about the true import of united action. As Dulles correctly judged, behind Britain's push for a settlement was the "fear that if fighting continues, we will in one way or another become involved, thereby enhancing risk of Chinese intervention and possibility further expansion of war." Eden charged that action prior to the Conference would not only destroy chances for a peaceful settlement, but would critically raise the risk of a wider war. American planning admitted the strong possibility of direct Chinese intervention, and his own intelligence staff had concluded that Western involvement would bring on the Chinese by land and air once the Viet Minh effort became "seriously endangered."

Thus, while Dulles was angered at the way he felt the British were writing off Indochina, Eden was highly pessimistic about Dulles' militancy in an area of uncertain value for which the United States had ambiguous, high-risk plans. There was considerable difference, in Eden's mind, between warnings to Communist China against direct intervention before the fact (which the British went along with in mid-1953) and united action, which would, despite any allied assurances to Peking, be interpreted by the Chinese as provocatory.

British suspicions, furthermore, were an extension of the belief that Indochina need not be entirely lost at Geneva in the absence of united action. London was apparently puzzled by American talk of the "loss" of Indochina, for to 10 Downing Street, "French cannot lose the war between now [April 1954] and the coming of the rainy season however badly they may conduct it." [Doc. 35] While Dulles kept telling the British that only united action through the formation of a coalition could ensure against a complete Communist diplomatic triumph at Geneva, Eden was equally convinced that the best way to assure continuation of the war would be united action, and that the French, even after Dien Bien Phu, were still strong enough to prevent the Communists from gaining all Indochina.

Even before Dulles' April flight to London to sound out the British on united action, the Churchill government was closely questioning American evaluations of Indochina. In an April 1 cable, for instance, Dulles vented his disturbance at Britain's refusal to accept the view that the loss of Indochina would ultimately affect their security interests in Malaya, Australia, and New Zealand. This was indeed the case, as Dulles discovered for himself once he talked to Eden in London and later at Geneva. Eden steadfastly refused to buy Dulles' analogy between Indochina and Malaya, retorting that the situation in Malaya was "well in hand" while that in Indochina was clearly not. Admiral Radford concluded in late April from talks with the British chiefs of staff that the U.K. policy seemed "to be on a very narrow basis strictly in terms of local U.K. interest without regard to other areas of the Far East such as Japan."

The British simply could not accept the domino principle even as they admitted Southeast Asia's security value to the free world. By the opening of the Geneva Conference, the U.S.–U.K. relations had reached a low point: Dulles was insisting that the British were the major roadblock to implementation of united action, while Eden was clinging to the notion that a negotiated settlement leading to partition would be the best outcome of an impossibly complex politico-military situation in Indochina.

6. *French Oppose "United Action"*

Secretary Dulles fared little better in selling "united action" in Paris than he did in London, but for somewhat different reasons. The French were seeking a quick action to avoid an imminent military defeat at Dien Bien Phu. Dulles, however, refused to be torn from a collective allied approach to the Indochina War. The French feared that a coalition arrangement would lead to an internationalization of the war and take control of it out of their hands. They, therefore, only desired local assistance at Dien Bien Phu along the lines of Operation Vulture.

Furthermore, another objection to "united action" from the French viewpoint was that it would only delay or impede the very negotiations leading towards a settlement which the French increasingly desired. The U.S. objective was to keep alive the French determination to continue the war. Dulles feared that the French would use Geneva to find a face-saving formula for a French surrender. Premier Laniel reaffirmed to Dulles in Paris that his government would take no action which directly or indirectly turned Indochina over to the Communists. But he also called attention to the increasing desire on the part of many in France to get out of Indochina at any cost. The French stressed that it was necessary to await the results of the Geneva Conference and that they could not give the impression in advance that they believed Geneva would fail.

7. *Aborted Working Group on Collective Defense in Southeast Asia (April 20)*

Immediately upon returning to Washington on April 15 Secretary Dulles invited representatives of the United Kingdom, France, the Associated States, Australia, New Zealand, the Philippines, and Thailand to attend a meeting on the 20th to set up an ad hoc defense group for the Southeast Asia region. The delegates were to work on a draft for a future organization. The Secretary had been under the impression from his talk in London with Eden that the U.K., while rejecting immediate "united action" in Indochina, would have no objection to such a preliminary meeting.

On April 18, just two days before the scheduled meeting, the British Ambassador informed Dulles that there would be no British participation. The reasons: no understanding on the part of the British Foreign Secretary that the working group would go forward at once, and no agreement concerning membership. The Department expressed amazement, but in view of the British attitude the April 20 meeting was transformed into a general briefing for the nations comprising the allied side at the Geneva Conference. In a later explanation of the shift in British attitude, Foreign Secretary Eden said that in agreeing to informal working group talks he had overlooked the pending Colombo Conference and that he felt that it would have been most undesirable to give any public indication of membership in a program for united action before the end of the Colombo discussions. It is now clear that the British were restrained by India and by a fear that British attendance at the meeting would be construed as assent to "united action." Moreover, London could not have been reassured by a "trial balloon" speech of Vice President Nixon on April 17 in which he suggested that the U.S. might have to "take the risk by putting our boys in" in order to avoid "further Communist expansion in Asia and Indochina."

8. Continued French Prodding for U.S. Intervention (April 21–25)

In preparation for the Indochina phase of the Geneva Conference, tripartite discussions (U.S., U.K., France) took place in Paris in mid-April. In these discussions, the French contended that a successful Geneva settlement was dependent on a favorable outcome of the battle at Dien Bien Phu and that their participation in a Southeast Asian coalition might not be possible if Dien Bien Phu fell. There could be no guarantee what position France would take in the event of a collapse at Dien Bien Phu. The French argued that only large-scale United States air and naval intervention could retrieve the situation in Indochina. They made no formal request for intervention in the tripartite discussions, but on several occasions suggested or implied to the Americans that such action was necessary.

On April 21, Marc Jacquet, French Secretary of State for the Associated States, told the American Ambassador to Indochina, Donald Heath, then in Paris, that no French military authority still believed a victory was possible in Indochina without United States air and naval intervention, and that such action should be indicated after the impending failure of the Indochina phase of the Geneva Conference.

On April 22, Foreign Minister Bidault, with General Ely, suggested to Secretary Dulles that there should be emergency consultation between General Navarre and American military commanders in Indochina. The Foreign Minister indicated that, although he had been opposed to internationalizing the war, he would now favor it with United States participation if that would save Dien Bien Phu.

On April 23 the French Under Secretary of State, André Bougenot, in the presence of Premier Laniel, suggested to Douglas MacArthur II, Counselor of the Department of State, that the United States could commit its naval aircraft to the battle at Dien Bien Phu without risking American prestige or committing an act of belligerency by placing such aircraft, painted with French insignia and construed as part of the French Foreign Legion, under nominal French command for an isolated action consisting of air strikes lasting two or three days.

On the same day Foreign Minister Bidault showed the Secretary a message from General Navarre in which the French commander said that the situation at Dien Bien Phu was desperate and that he believed that the only alternatives were (1) Operation VAUTOUR, massive B-29 bombing (which Secretary Dulles understood would be a United States operation from bases outside Indochina), or (2) a French Union request for a cease-fire (which the Secretary assumed would be at Dien Bien Phu only, but which General Navarre, as it turned out, meant should apply to all of Indochina).

D. FINAL U.S. POSITION BEFORE GENEVA

1. Exchanges with the French

The American response to these various suggestions was to reiterate to the French the necessary preconditions for American intervention: (1) complete independence for the Associated States; (2) Congressional authorization; (3) a coalition that would include the United Kingdom. In relation to the need for a coalition, Secretary Dulles in Paris and Under Secretary W. Bedell Smith in Washington suggested to French officials that France, in the same way as it had asked for American air intervention in Indochina, should appeal for British intervention there.

Before leaving Paris for Geneva, Secretary Dulles gave Foreign Minister Bidault a letter replying to General Navarre's suggestion that United States air intervention at Dien Bien Phu was the sole alternative to a cease-fire. In this letter, the Secretary stated again the necessary preconditions for United States intervention, and contended that if Dien Bien Phu fell there was no reason that this should make it necessary to plead for a cease-fire. The French Foreign Minister, in a letter limited to the military consequences of United States intervention, replied that in the opinion of French military experts "a massive intervention of American aviation would still be able to save the garrison."

2. *Exchanges with the U.K.*

In the discussions with the British, meanwhile, the United States had tried both to induce the United Kingdom to participate in a joint Anglo–American air and naval intervention at Dien Bien Phu and to persuade the United Kingdom that the prompt organization of a collective defense in Southeast Asia was necessary to bolster the French in Indochina.

But the British indicated that they would make no commitment to intervene militarily in Indochina and wished to postpone conversations on collective defense arrangements until after the Geneva Conference. Foreign Secretary Eden told Secretary Dulles on April 24 that the British did not want at this juncture to intervene in the Indochina War. Immediately afterward Eden returned to London for a special Cabinet meeting on the Indochina crisis which was held on April 25. Prime Minister Churchill reported to the House of Commons two days later that the British Government was "not prepared to give any undertakings about United Kingdom military action in Indochina in advance of the results of Geneva," and had "not entered into any new political or military commitments." Before addressing the Commons, Churchill had rejected a plea from French Ambassador René Massigli, made on behalf of Premier Laniel, for a statement that Great Britain would join the United States and France in defense of Dien Bien Phu.

The United Kingdom was willing, however, to participate in early military discussions to consider measures which might be taken in Southeast Asia if Indochina were lost. Along these lines, Foreign Secretary Eden and Secretary Dulles had discussed tentatively on April 22 the possibility of a secret military appraisal—by the United States, the United Kingdom, Australia, New Zealand, and Thailand—of what could be done to bolster Thailand in the event of a French collapse in Indochina. The Foreign Secretary had returned to this proposition in another conversation with Secretary Dulles the next day.

On April 30, indicating that the British were prepared to defend the area outside Indochina, and possibly the free part of a partitioned Indochina, Eden proposed to Secretary Dulles "an immediate and secret joint examination of the political and military problems in creating a collective defense for Southeast Asia, namely: (a) nature and purpose; (b) membership; (c) commitments." He added that this examination should also cover immediate measures to strengthen Thailand.

Secretary Dulles raised the question of early military talks that might strengthen the French position at the Geneva Conference at a meeting in Geneva on May 2 with the Foreign Ministers of Australia and New Zealand, partners of the United States in the ANZUS organization. The three agreed at this meeting that there should be five-power military talks in Washington among the ANZUS powers, the United Kingdom, and France, with the possible participation of Thailand.

3. The Washington Viewpoint

In Washington in the meantime, the President on April 26, the opening date of the Geneva Conference, told a group of Republican leaders that it would be a "tragic error" for the United States to intervene unilaterally as a partner of France in the Indochina struggle. Two days later, in a discussion with Under Secretary W. Bedell Smith, Presidential Assistant Robert Cutler, and Admiral Radford (who had just been to London and had talked with the British Chiefs of Staff and Prime Minister Churchill), the President expressed disappointment over the British attitude of refraining from active participation in discussions on a Southeast Asian collective security arrangement before the end of the Geneva Conference. President Eisenhower, in this discussion, reiterated his firm decision that there would be no United States military intervention in Indochina by executive action. He urged his aides to provide help to the French in repairing three airfields in Indochina but to avoid any undue risk of involving the United States in combat operations.

The feasibility of American intervention at Dien Bien Phu was finally removed with the fall of that fortress on May 7. President Eisenhower sent messages to the President of France, René Coty, and to the Chief of State of Vietnam, Bao Dai, praising the defenders of Dien Bien Phu and stressing the determination of the free world to remain "faithful to the causes for which they fought."

E. REAPPRAISAL OF DOMINO THEORY AFTER DIEN BIEN PHU

The fall of Dien Bien Phu, and the failure to organize an intervention through "united action" prior to the opening of the Geneva Conference in late April, 1954, led to a reappraisal of the "domino theory" which had been at the center of U.S. policy in Southeast Asia since the late 1940's. The loss of Tonkin, or Vietnam, or perhaps even all of Indochina, was no longer considered to lead inexorably to the loss to Communism of all of Southeast Asia.

Accordingly, Secretary Dulles in a press conference on May 11 (four days after the French surrender at Dien Bien Phu) observed that "Southeast Asia could be secured even without perhaps Vietnam, Laos and Cambodia." He went on to note that although he would not want to underestimate the importance of these countries he would not want either to give the impression that "if events that we could not control, and which we do not anticipate, should lead to their being lost that we would consider the whole situation hopeless and we would give up in despair . . ." In a remark at the press conference that was later deleted from the official transcript, Dulles said that Laos and Cambodia were "important but by no means essential" because they were poor countries with meager populations.

Later, as the U.S. became reconciled to a political settlement at Geneva which would yield northern Vietnam to the Ho Chi Minh regime, the concept of "united action" was given a new twist. It now was transformed into an attempt to organize a *long-range* collective defense alliance which would offset the setback in Indochina and prevent further losses. That long-feared setback was now perceived to be less serious than had once been envisaged. The loss of Tonkin was no longer seen as leading necessarily to a Communist take-over of other territory between China and the American shore. Eventually, in SEATO, the U.S. sought to create an alliance which would be strong enough to withstand the fall of one such domino.

3.   The Geneva Conference, May–July, 1954

I.   BACKGROUND TO THE CONFERENCE

On February 18, 1954, a joint communiqué from Berlin issued by the United States, Great Britain, the Soviet Union, and France announced that in late April the Big Four and other parties concerned would meet at Geneva to seek a peaceful solution of the eight-year-old war in Indochina. Between those dates, the Western allies engaged in a series of discussions centered around American proposals for direct intervention, while the Communist side—the USSR, Communist China (CPR), and the Viet Minh—worked to ensure that they would enter the forthcoming Geneva Conference from a position of strength.

The Eisenhower Administration found as much difficulty in persuading France and Great Britain that fundamental changes in the war were necessary before the start of the conference as in accepting the notion of a negotiated solution in Indochina. The troubles with France had begun in mid-1953 when the U.S. Government gave its conditional approval to the Navarre Plan, which provided for radically new French field tactics and a buildup of the Vietnamese National Army (VNA). American hopes that assistance in money and war matériel would elicit a French commitment to a program to attract native Indochinese into close military and political collaboration with the colonial governments, especially in Vietnam, were not fulfilled. Nor was France hospitable to American suggestions for greater involvement of the Military Advisory Assistance Group (MAAG) in French planning. As was to be the case almost throughout the Indochina crisis, France capitalized on American fears of National Assembly rejection of the European Defense Community (EDC) treaty and of a French pull-out from Indochina to gain U.S. aid without having to make commensurate concessions on Vietnamese independence or tactical planning. American attempts to tie aid to such concessions were never followed through, and whatever leverage on French policy-making in Indochina the United States possessed was left largely unexploited.

For the most part, France's rejection of American conditions and suggestions was based on the Laniel government's conviction, implemented zealously by French civil and military authorities in Indochina, that the United States would be intruding in France's domain. A policy of systematic restrictions on American officials in the field prevented the United States from making independent evaluations of the war's progress, with the result that the Government was for many months badly informed and unwarrantedly optimistic about the French Union army's chances against the Viet Minh. In late March and April 1954, when it became clear to Washington that the Navarre Plan had failed and that (in Secretary of State Dulles' words) "united action" was necessary to prevent Indochina from falling to the Communists, the French revealed that their distrust of American "interference" extended to any plans for overt American air-naval involvement. The Laniel government was perfectly amenable to localized American intervention at Dienbienphu to save the besieged French army from disaster; but it stood firmly opposed to Dulles' concept of collective (Western–Asian) defense in a security organization that would, if necessary, intervene to prevent the "loss" of Indochina. France's requests for assistance at Dienbienphu were entirely consistent with long-standing policy in Paris that looked to a negotiated settlement of the war on "honorable" terms at the same time as it hoped to be in the best possible military position at the time negotiations began.

Opposition to "united action" was no less stubborn in London. The British, like the French, were suspicious of American intentions in calling for that alternative, though for different reasons. To the Churchill government, the United States, even while proclaiming a strong desire to avoid open conflict with Communist China, was tending precisely in that direction by insisting on the formation of a collective security pact prior to the start of the Geneva Conference. Eisenhower's letter to Churchill on April 4, 1954, could only have reinforced those suspicions, for the President described united action as an attempt to make China stop supporting the Viet Minh rather than face the prospect of large-scale allied involvement in Vietnam. Although the British were not asked to make substantial ground troop commitments to a united action, they felt that their approval would ultimately condone a widening of the war that would risk bringing in the Chinese who, the British argued, could not possibly be expected to cease assistance they had been providing since 1950. London therefore told Dulles it would not approve united action and preferred to await the outcome of the negotiations before deciding whether the Indochina situation warranted resort to military alternatives. The British were perfectly willing to talk about regional defense in the Far East, but only after the results were in on the negotiations. Until then, they said, they would limit themselves to providing full diplomatic support to the French in search of a peaceful solution.

Differences among the allies were therefore acute as the conference opened. The French had cleverly exploited the American assistance program without having brought in the Americans in full force, yet had also been unable to save Dienbienphu from being overrun on May 7. The British were felt in Washington to have been the primary obstacle to united action; they were accused of having been so blinded by their own self-interest in other areas of Southeast Asia that they failed to appreciate the vast strategic importance to the Free World of saving Indochina.

Contrasting Communist unity on the eve of the conference was more a matter of Sino-Soviet agreement on the desirability of negotiations than of complete accord among the three parties. In the aftermath of Stalin's death, Soviet foreign policy under Malenkov had altered considerably. Domestic priorities no doubt influenced the regime's proclaimed hopes for a reduction in international tension. Peking, more intimately involved in the Viet Minh cause, stepped up its assistance to General Giap's forces between February and April 1954, but also agreed with Moscow on the desirability of convening an international conference, which China would attend, to end the fighting. The limited available evidence suggests that the Democratic Republic of Vietnam (DRV) alone among the three Communist parties considered the call for negotiations premature and urged that they be preceded by intensified military efforts. Ho's much-publicized offer in late November 1953 to talk with the French was intended more to influence French domestic and official opinion and to demoralize Franco–Vietnamese troops than to evince sincere interest in arriving at an equitable settlement. In ensuing months, DRV broadcasts showed a far greater interest in first achieving a clear-cut military victory in the Tonkin Delta and parts of Laos than in engaging in discussions while French forces remained scattered throughout Indochina.

These developments, in very broad outline, provided the backdrop to the Geneva Conference. Strength and weakness seemed to be the respective characteristics of the Communist and Western positions. Yet these terms are, as we shall see, not entirely accurate, for the interaction between and within the two sides was to make clear that the Geneva Conference would not be the setting for a victor's peace.

II. THE CONDUCT AND STRUCTURE OF DIPLOMACY

One of the first agreements reached at the Geneva Conference occurred in the course of a conversation between V. M. Molotov and Anthony Eden on May 5, when the Soviet foreign minister endorsed the foreign secretary's assertion that this negotiation was the most difficult he had ever encountered.* Indeed, it seems at first glance somewhat paradoxical that the Indochina phase of the Geneva Conference (May 8–July 21) should have resulted in a settlement within less than a dozen weeks, given the unusual difficulties facing the negotiators on both sides. (See Table 1) Key issues were postponed until the eleventh hour while debate wore endlessly on over relatively insignificant matters; contact among the delegations was limited by ideological prejudices and political antagonisms, forcing some delegates to act as mediators no less than as representatives of national interests; and major agreements were reached outside the special framework for discussions that the conferees had taken a month to build.

TABLE 1

CHIEF NEGOTIATORS AT THE GENEVA CONFERENCE ON INDOCHINA

United Kingdom Anthony Eden	*USSR* Vyacheslav Molotov
United States General Walter Bedell Smith U. Alexis Johnson	*France* Georges Bidault Jean Chauvel Pierre Mendès-France
Chinese People's Republic Chou En-lai Chang Wen-t'ien Li K'e-nung	*Vietnam* Dac Khe Tran Van Do
Cambodia Tep Phan Sam Sary	*Laos* Phoui Sananikone
Viet Minh Pham Van Dong	

* A valuable source is Anthony Eden, *Memoirs: Full Circle,* Houghton-Mifflin, Boston, 1960.

A. THE REPRESENTATION QUESTION

The first major roadblock in the negotiations was the Communist claims concerning the representation of parties not present at the conference. Since the conference had already begun when these claims were forwarded, the chances of expanding the list of invited parties were very limited. Nevertheless, through fourteen restricted and seven plenary sessions,* bitter controversy raged over Communist insistence that the Viet Minh-led Free Cambodian (Khmer Issarak) and Free Laotian (Pathet Lao) forces were entitled to be seated beside representatives of the Royal Governments of Cambodia and Laos. Not until June 16, when Premier Chou En-lai, China's foreign minister and chief delegate, indicated to Eden that Viet Minh forces would be withdrawn from Cambodia and Laos, was the debate resolved and the way opened for serious efforts to bring about cease-fires throughout Indochina.

The time-consuming exchanges over the authenticity of Communist "resistance forces" in Laos and Cambodia were, interestingly enough, not duplicated when it came to determining the status of the DRV. The Berlin Conference final communiqué had specified that the Indochina deliberations would be attended by the United States, Great Britain, Communist China, the Soviet Union, France, "and other states concerned." Invitations to the participants would, it was further agreed, be issued only by the Berlin conferees, i.e., by the Big Four but not by Peking. Yet, as Molotov admitted at the first plenary session (May 8), Peking as well as Moscow invited the DRV, a move vigorously assailed by France and the United States. [Doc. 45] No attempt was made, however, to block the DRV's *participation*. Despite the antagonism of the Vietnamese government nominally headed by Bao Dai, (Bao Dai's consistent position, supported by Ngo Dinh Diem when he took over the premiership on June 18, was that his was the only legitimate government in Vietnam, while the Viet Minh were not political competitors but merely armed rebels.) the DRV was generally considered one of the principal combatants whose consent to a cease-fire, being indispensable, required its participation. Moreover, the Soviet Union indicated to the French that it would not accept the presence of delegates from the Associated States of Indochina (Vietnam, Cambodia, and Laos) unless the DRV was admitted to the conference. By the time of Dienbienphu's fall (May 7), all parties were agreed that there would be nine delegations (though not States) discussing Indochina; and on May 8 the first session got underway.

B. THE COMMUNICATION GAPS

Nine delegations seated at a roundtable to exchange views, about every second day, obscured the fact that true bargaining was not taking place. Proposals were, of course, tabled and debated; but actual give-and-take was reserved for private discussions, usually in the absence of the pro-Western Indochinese parties. Even then, the Geneva talks on Indochina were hardly dominated by

---

* In all, the Geneva Conference comprised eight plenary and twenty-two restricted sessions. These were quite apart from the Franco-Viet Minh military command conferences held after June 2, as well as from Viet Minh military staff talks with Laotian and Cambodian representatives that begain in late June. Finally, during the latter half of the conference, French and Viet Minh delegation heads met secretly in so-called "underground" negotiations, the results of which were closely held, at least by the French.

Big Power cabals; political and ideological differences were so intense, particularly between the American and Chinese representatives, that diplomacy had to be conducted circuitously, with Eden and Molotov frequently acting as mediators and messengers for delegates unwilling to be found together. (As one example of the American attitude, Dulles told reporters just prior to the first session that the only way he could possibly meet with Chou En-lai was if their cars collided.)

Anthony Eden, whose persistence in the face of adverse developments throughout the conference was rewarded in the end, has provided this description of personal tribulation:

> I was conscious that time was not on our side. Since neither the Americans nor the French had established any contacts with the Communist representatives [in mid-June], I had been compelled to adopt the role of intermediary between the Western powers and the Communists. My activities in this respect were open to every kind of misrepresentation. I was concerned about their effect on Anglo-American relations. On the other hand, I was encouraged by the close accord maintained throughout the conference between ourselves and the other members of the Commonwealth, including those, like Mr. Nehru, who were not represented at Geneva. They sent me messages of thanks and encouragement. I needed them, for I began to feel that we should never make effective headway. I had never known a conference of this kind. The parties would not make direct contact and we were in constant danger of one or another backing out of the door.

Not until the latter half of June did high-ranking French and Viet Minh delegates meet face-to-face, did Viet Minh military officials confer with Cambodian and Laotian representatives, and did French and Chinese heads-of-delegation privately exchange views. Communist and non-Communist Vietnamese, meanwhile, refused to talk to one another until July, when finally Tran Van Do and Pham Van Dong were persuaded to have private discussions. Most importantly, the American delegation (USDEL), under strict instructions to avoid contact with the Chinese, had to rely on second-hand information provided by the British, French, and Soviet representatives, a procedure that was repeated with respect to the Viet Minh.

The problem of contact was no more acutely felt than by the delegation of the State of Vietnam. Although finally granted complete independence by France under treaties initialed in Paris April 28 and approved by both governments June 4, Vietnam did not gain the concurrent power to negotiate its own fate. The French, clearly anxious lest the Vietnamese upset the delicate state of private talks with the Viet Minh, avoided Bao Dai's representatives whenever possible and sought to exploit close Vietnamese-American relations in informing the Vietnamese only after agreements had been reached. During June, for instance, Jean Chauvel, head of the French delegation, on several occasions approached the Americans with information on the "underground" negotiations with the Viet Minh and with the hope that, once partition had been fixed, the United States would "sell" that solution to Saigon. [Doc. 60] In the same month, Chauvel, evincing complete understanding of American determination to avoid approving or acquiescing in a partition settlement, nevertheless asked if the United States would soften Vietnamese opposition to it by indicating it was the best solution obtainable. Chauvel described Diem and his predecessor, Buu Loc, as difficult, unrealistic, and unreasonable on the subject. [Doc. 66]

In an aide-memoire delivered to Dulles and Eden on June 26 by Henri Bonnet, the French ambassador to Washington, Paris urged Washington not to encourage an adverse Vietnamese reaction to partition. The United States was also asked "to intervene with the Vietnamese to counsel upon them wisdom and self-control and to dissuade them from refusing an agreement which, if it is reached, is dictated not by the spirit of abandoning them, but on the contrary by the desire to save in Indochina all that can possibly be saved, and to give the Vietnamese state, under peaceful conditions, opportunities which have not always been possible heretofore because of the war." To these approaches, the United States consistently reacted negatively in the undoubtedly correct belief that the French were merely attempting to identify the United States in Vietnamese eyes with the partition concept. By refusing to act as intermediaries for the French, the American delegation kept free of association with a "French solution" to the Vietnam problem.

French aloofness from the Vietnamese continued into July. Despite American requests of the French delegation that the Vietnamese be kept informed of developments, the French demurred. Chauvel informed U. Alexis Johnson, chief deputy to the head of the USDEL, General Walter Bedell Smith, that "he was handling this [liaison with the Vietnamese] through members of his staff and was avoiding direct contact with Vietnamese in order not to have to answer their questions." When Offroy, another member of the French delegation, suggested that the United States placate the Vietnamese with assurance of Free World political, economic, and military support after the settlement, Johnson replied that this was a matter for the French to handle. Not until late in the Conference did the Vietnamese government become aware of the strong possibility that partition would become part of the settlement; on this and other developments, as we shall see, the Vietnamese were kept in the dark, a circumstance that was to solidify Vietnamese hostility to and dissociation from the final terms.

But the Vietnamese loyal to Bao Dai were not alone in being denied important information, although they suffered worst from it. The United States delegation itself several times suspected that it was not receiving all the news the French were in a position to provide. The fault, however, lay as much with the ambiguous status under which the delegation operated as with the French who were to act as messengers. On the one hand, the Americans wanted to use their influence to ensure that the French not sell out Western interests for the sake of a quick settlement; on the other, they were determined not to become so involved in the bargaining process as to link the Administration to the final terms. The resolution of these apparently conflicting aims was offered by Dulles on the eve of the conference in a background briefing to newsmen at Geneva. He said that primary responsibility for decisions taken at the conference belonged to the French and Vietnamese on one side, and to the Viet Minh on the other. The United States "would be inclined not to try to interpose [its] veto in any sense as against what they might want to do." As to whether this attitude applied equally to substantive provisions of any settlement, the Secretary indicated that the United States would, if necessary, refuse to acknowledge results contrary to American "interests":

> I would think that [nonapplication of a veto] would be true up to the point at least where we felt that the issues involved had a pretty demonstrable interest to the United States itself. The United States does have pretty considerable interests in the Western Pacific, and there are some solutions there which we would regard as so disadvantageous that we would

seek to prevent them. And if we failed in that respect, we would probably want to disassociate ourselves from it [the final settlement].

Thus, the United States would apply the tactic of "disassociation" should its influence not be sufficient to make the final terms compatible with American "interests." Yet the French, against whom the tactic was primarily directed, were probably (and quite naturally) averse to keeping their American colleagues so well informed of developments in the talks with the Viet Minh that the United States would have occasion to resort to "disassociation." Throughout the conference, in fact, the French aimed at exploiting the American presence for the strength they believed it provided their negotiators, and this policy meant pressuring Washington to retain a high-ranking delegation at the conference right up to the moment of the settlement.

Whatever the rationale for French behavior, the USDEL complained to Washington that it was not being kept fully informed of developments in the "underground" Franco-Viet Minh talks. The change in government in Paris during June from Laniel to Pierre Mendès-France helped matters somewhat. But though it was conceded that Mendès-France's representatives had done better than their predecessors in keeping the United States apprised, the United States still felt, as Dulles put it, that while Paris was not willfully concealing information, there remained a "certain lack of any intimacy. . . ." [Doc. 65]

The British also felt locked out of news that vitally affected them. Particularly during May, when Washington and Paris were frequently in touch about possible military intervention, the British were highly disturbed to find newspapers their best source of information on the intentions of their foremost allies. Since London was no longer considered essential to "united action" (see Section IV), the Americans and the French had evidently agreed that their negotiations should be kept under wraps until such time as a decision was made. Only after Eden confronted Under Secretary Smith with the newspaper stories (which may have been deliberate "leaks" to influence the Geneva deliberations) did Dulles direct that the British, Australian, and New Zealand ambassadors be informed "in general terms" regarding U.S.–French talks. Diplomay among the Western Big Three clearly reflected the rifts that had developed in the alliance over intervention before the Dienbienphu disaster; as a result, secrecy and bilateral discussions tended to be the rule, thereby complicating the already mammoth task of presenting a united Western front against the Communist negotiators.

Thus far we have been dealing with diplomacy as it was conducted by the non-Communist delegations. What of the Communists? The available documentation limits the comments we may make, but still permits some remarks, both definite and speculative. First, the Chinese, Soviet, and Viet Minh delegations were in constant touch, as reported by their news agencies. Moreover, Chou En-lai was able to make three stopovers in Moscow during the conference that very likely heightened Sino-Soviet coordination. Finally, during a recess for heads of delegation, Chou and Ho Chi Minh held a three-day meeting in early July that may have provided the turning point in the Viet Minh's more conciliatory attitude thereafter. In brief, the Communists apparently were not plagued by the kinds of communication problems that hampered the Americans, British, and Vietnamese.

As will be argued in greater detail subsequently, the frequent meetings of the Communist delegations did not result in a uniformity of views. The Chinese and Soviets evidently worked independent of the Viet Minh whenever their separate interests dictated the need for advancement of progress in the negotiations. At times when the Viet Minh were intransigent, Chou and Molotov frequently took the initiative to break log jams that threatened to plunge the conference into irresolvable deadlock. Much like Eden, Chou and Molotov sometimes found themselves playing the role of mediator, a role which they, and particularly Chou, relished for what Fred Iklé has called the "side-effects" of negotiations—benefits deriving from, but incidental to, negotiations, such as enhanced prestige. In the end, the Viet Minh advantage of close rapport with Moscow and Peking did not prevent the Viet Minh from sharing with their non-Communist compatriots the ignominious distinction of having been undercut by allies.

III. THE DEVELOPMENT OF BARGAINING POSITIONS

A. *THE UNITED STATES AND THE NEGOTIATIONS*

In underwriting the Navarre Plan and proceeding with utmost caution in urging France to improve its relationship with the non-Communist Vietnamese nationalists, the United States hoped to influence Paris to postpone a commitment to negotiations until French forces were at least on the threshold of military victory. While aware of the strong pressures on the Laniel government from the National Assembly and the French public for a peaceful settlement, the United States, clearly influenced by the experience at Panmunjom, sought to persuade the premier not to let the clamor for peace drive him to the bargaining table. As late as December 1953 Laniel agreed that Washington's aversion to premature negotiations was well-advised; but two months later, at Berlin, his government joined with the Soviet Union in calling for an international conference to end the Indochina conflict. The French government found it could no longer ignore anti-war sentiment at home without jeopardizing its survival, while the Americans, however strongly opposed to bringing the war to the conference table with victory nowhere in sight and with Communist China as a negotiating opponent, felt compelled to approve the Berlin decision if only to blunt the French threat of scuttling EDC.

Forced to go along with French preference for negotiating with the Communists, the United States remained unalterably pessimistic about the probable results. This attitude was first set out fully by the Joint Chiefs of Staff in March 1954. [Doc. 23] The Chiefs examined the alternatives to military victory and found them all infeasible or unacceptable to the United States. A ceasefire prior to a political settlement, the JCS paper states, "would, in all probability, lead to a political stalemate attended by a concurrent and irretrievable deterioration of the Franco-Vietnamese military position." A coalition government would lead to Communist control by keeping any outside assistance from preventing a seizure of power from within. Partition, on the other hand, would mean recognizing Communist success by force of arms, ceding the key Tonkin Delta to the Communists, and, even if confined to only one of the three Indochinese states, undercutting our containment policy in Asia.

The Chiefs also commented at some length on the difficult question of elections in Vietnam. They took the position that even if elections could be held along democratic lines (which they doubted), a Communist victory would almost certainly result because of Communist territorial control, popular support, and superior tactics:

Such factors as the prevalence of illiteracy, the lack of suitable educational media, and the absence of adequate communications in the outlying areas would render the holding of a truly representative plebiscite of doubtful feasibility. The Communists, by virtue of their superior capability in the field of propaganda, could readily pervert the issue as being a choice between national independence and French Colonial rule. Furthermore, it would be militarily infeasible to prevent widespread intimidation of voters by Communist partisans. While it is obviously impossible to make a dependable forecast as to the outcome of a free election, current intelligence leads the Joint Chiefs to the belief that a settlement based upon free elections would be attended by almost certain loss of the Associated States to Communist control.

The JCS views, together with the recommendation that the United States not associate itself with any settlement that "would fail to provide reasonably adequate assurance of the future political and territorial integrity of Indochina . . . ," were approved by the Secretary of Defense on March 23.

The JCS position reflected Government policy, for in the remaining months before the Conference the United States privately stood opposed to any course of action other than full prosecution of the war. Dulles, speaking with French Ambassador Henri Bonnet on April 3, reasoned that' a negotiated settlement would lead *only* to face-saving formulae for either a French or a Viet Minh surrender. The Secretary termed a division of Indochina "impractical" and a coalition government the "beginning of disaster"; neither arrangement could prevent a French surrender. [Doc. 27] The President himself echoed this either-or approach. Writing to Churchill April 4, Eisenhower proposed: "There is no negotiated solution of the Indochina problem which in essence would not be either a face-saving device to cover a French surrender or a face-saving device to cover a Communist retirement." And, as already observed, it was precisely to bring about the latter—China's "discreet disengagement" from support of the Viet Minh—that the President wanted British cooperation in united action.

Concomitantly, the United States was concerned that a disaster at Dienbienphu would propel the French into acceptance of an immediate, unsupervised cease-fire even before the conference was to begin. Dulles obtained assurances from Bidault that the French would not agree to such a cease-fire. But the Secretary found the British less inflexible, with Eden doubting the American view that a sudden cease-fire would lead either to a massacre of the French by the native people or to large-scale infiltration of French-held terrain by Viet Minh forces. [Doc. 37]

Thus assured by the French but mindful of both French and British preference for trying to bargain with the Communists before resorting to further military steps, Washington, in late April and early May, sought to develop guidelines for the American delegation. The National Security Council, less than a week before the opening conference session, carefully examined American alternatives. Disturbed by what it regarded as peace-at-any-price thinking in Paris, the NSC urged the President to decide not to join the Geneva deliberations without assurance from France that it was not preparing to negotiate the surrender of Indochina. Again, the Korean example was foremost: Communist tactics at Geneva, the NSC forecast, would likely resemble those at Panmunjom; a cease-fire might be announced that the Communists would not comply with for lack of effective supervision; the French would wilt before the Communists' predictable dilatory tactics and end by accepting almost any terms.

The NSC therefore decided that the French had to be pressured into adopting a strong posture in the face of probable Communist intransigence. The President was urged to inform Paris that French acquiescence in a Communist takeover of Indochina would bear not only on France's future position in the Far East, but also on its status as one of the Big Three; that abandonment of Indochina would grievously affect both France's position in North Africa and Franco-U.S. relations in that region; that U.S. aid to France would automatically cease upon Paris' conclusion of an unsatisfactory settlement; and, finally, that Communist domination of Indochina would be of such serious strategic harm to U.S. interests as to produce "consequences in Europe as well as elsewhere [without] . . . apparent limitation." In addition, the NSC recomended that the United States determine immediately whether the Associated States should be approached with a view to continuing the anti-Viet Minh struggle in some other form, including unilateral American involvement "if necessary." The NSC clearly viewed the Indochina situation with extreme anxiety, and its action program amounted to unprecedented proposals to threaten France with the serious repercussions of a sell-out in Southeast Asia.

Pessimism over the prospects for any meaningful progress in talks with the Communists was shared by Secretary Dulles. In a background briefing for newsmen at Geneva, Dulles gave the first official indication for public consumption that the United States would dissociate itself from any settlement rather than be party to unacceptable terms. As to the acceptability of partition, the Secretary, in views that would change later, said he did not see how partition could be arranged with the fighting not confined to any single area. He as much as ruled out a territorial division when he commented that the United States would only agree to an arrangement in which all the Viet Minh troops would be placed in a small regroupment area out of harm's way. But that arrangement "might not be acceptable to them," Dulles said coyly.

American opinions on the likely ramifications of a settlement were also made known, and with greater precision, in private. On May 7, for instance, Livingston Merchant of the State Department presented the American view to the Ministers of New Zealand and Australia. Predicting that the French would finally settle for part of Vietnam and manage to salvage Cambodia and Laos, Merchant said the United States could not accept such a surrender of territory. While we could not prevent the French from making concessions, neither did we have to associate ourselves with the results. Thus, both publicly and privately, Administration leaders indicated at the outset of the conference that the United States would divorce itself from any settlement that resulted in less than a complete French-Vietnamese victory.

The first test of U.S. policy came May 5 when the French informed Washington of the proposals they intended to make in the opening round of the Geneva talks on May 8. The proposals included a separation of the "civil war" in Vietnam from the Communist aggressions in Cambodia and Laos; a cease-fire, supervised by a well-staffed international authority (but not the UN) and followed by political discussions leading to free elections; the regrouping of regular forces of the belligerents into defined zones (as Laniel had proposed in a speech on March 5) upon signature of a cease-fire agreement; the disarming of all irregular forces (i.e., the Viet Minh guerrillas); and a guarantee of the agreements by "the States participating in the Geneva Conference."

The JCS were first to react to the French plan. The Chiefs strongly felt that even if the Communists unexpectedly agreed to it, the likely outcomes would still be either rapid French capitulation in the wake of the cease-fire or virtual

French surrender in the course of protracted political discussions. Once more, the Chiefs fell back on the Korean experience, which they said demonstrated the certainty that the Communists would violate any armistice controls, including those supervised by an international body. An agreement to refrain from new military activities during armistice negotiations would be a strong obstacle to Communist violations; but the Communists, the JCS concluded, would never agree to such an arrangement. On the contrary, they were far more likely to intensify military operations so as to enhance their bargaining position, precisely at the time the French would seek to reduce operations to avoid taking casualties. The Chiefs therefore urged that the United States not get trapped into backing a French armistice proposal that the Communists, by voicing approval, could use to bind us to a cease-fire while they themselves ignored it. The only way to get satisfactory results was through military success, and since the Navarre Plan was no longer tenable, the next best alternative was not to associate the United States with any cease-fire in advance of a satisfactory political settlement. The first step, the Chiefs believed, should be the conclusion of a settlement that would "reasonably assure the political and territorial integrity of the Associated States . . . "; only thereafter should a cease-fire be entertained.

As previously, the Joint Chiefs' position became U.S. policy with only minor emendations. The President, reviewing the Chiefs' paper, agreed that the Government could not back the French proposal with its call for a supervised cease-fire that the Communists would never respect. Eisenhower further concurred with the Chiefs' insistence on priority to a political settlement, with the stipulation that French forces continue fighting while negotiations were in progress. He added that the United States would continue aiding the French during that period and would, in addition, work toward a coalition "for the purpose of preventing further expansion of Communist power in Southeast Asia."

These statements of position paved the way for a National Security Council meeting on May 8, which set forth the guidelines of U.S. policy on negotiations for the delegation at Geneva. The decision taken at the meeting simply underscored what the President and the Chiefs had already stated:

> The United States will not associate itself with any proposal from any source directed toward a cease-fire in advance of an acceptable armistice agreement, including international controls. The United States could concur in the initiation of negotiations for such an armistice agreement. During the course of such negotiations, the French and the Associated States should continue to oppose the forces of the Viet Minh with all the means at their disposal. In the meantime, as a means of strengthening the hands of the French and the Associated States during the course of such negotiations, the United States will continue its program of aid and its efforts to organize and promptly activate a Southeast Asian regional grouping for the purpose of preventing further expansion of Communist power in Southeast Asia.

B. THE COMMUNIST PROPOSALS

Official American perspectives on the likely pattern of the Geneva negotiations were confirmed when the Viet Minh forwarded their first proposal "package" at the second plenary session on May 10. Pham Van Dong, then the DRV's vice-minister for foreign affairs and already a seasoned negotiator with the French, introduced his case with the argument that the Viet Minh were the "stronger" force in "more than three-fourths of the country." He went on to describe the successful administration of this territory by his government, which he said "represents the will of the entire Vietnamese nation. . . ." The opposition, the Bao Dai regime, characterized as "the government of the temporarily occupied zone," did not enjoy popular support and was merely the tool of the French.

Pham Van Dong did not, however, demand that France concede control of all Vietnam to the DRV. Instead, Dong urged that France recognize "the sovereignty and independence of Vietnam throughout the territory of Vietnam," a statement which amounted to a rejection of the Franco-Vietnamese treaties approved April 28 in Paris by Laniel and Premier Nguyen Trung Vinh. The main points of Dong's proposal for a cease-fire and political settlement in Vietnam were as follows:

(1) Conclusion of an agreement on the withdrawal of all "foreign" (i.e., French) troops from the Associated States, to be preceded by the relocation of those troops to regroupment areas

(2) Convening of advisory conferences, to be composed of representatives of the "governments of both sides," in each country of Indochina, with the objective of holding general elections leading to the establishment of unified governments

(3) Supervision of elections by local commissions

(4) Prior to the establishment of unified governments, the carrying out by the opposing parties of "the administrative functions in the districts which will be [temporarily] under their administration . . ."

(5) Cease-fire in all Indochina supervised by mixed commissions composed of the belligerents, *the cease-fire to take effect upon implementation of all other measures*. No new forces or military equipment to be introduced into Indochina during the armistice

To placate the French, Dong asserted the DRV's readiness "to examine the question of the entry of the Democratic Republic of Vietnam into the French Union. . . ."

The meaning of Dong's proposal was clear. A political settlement would precede a military agreement to a cease-fire rather than the reverse, which the French preferred. Somewhat ironically, the Viet Minh position was in line with the American preference for giving priority to a political settlement; but the Viet Minh in effect proposed to stop fighting only when French troops had left Vietnam and a political process favorable to the Communists had been set up. By first getting rid of the French, and then substituting all-Vietnamese consultations for strict control and supervision of the cease-fire, the regroupment, and the general elections, the Viet Minh could legitimately expect a quick takeover of power from the relatively weak Vietnamese National Army, by then bereft of its French command structure. As Dong well knew, the relocation of French forces in the Tonkin Delta to a tighter perimeter was having, and would continue to have, major repercussions on VNA morale. Once the French could be persuaded to withdraw, the VNA would undoubtedly collapse under Viet Minh military pressure. Moreover, inasmuch as Dong's plan made no allowance for the disarming, much less the regrouping, of indigenous forces on either side, the Viet Minh would be militarily in a virtually unassailable position to control any general election that might be held. Dong's proposal, then, amounted to a request that the French abandon Vietnam to a certain fate.

In the same speech, Dong made clear that the DRV's concern extended beyond Vietnam to Cambodia and Laos. By 1954, Viet Minh coordination with the Pathet Lao and Free Khmer "resistance forces" had been going on for at least three years, or since the formal announcement on March 11, 1951, of formation of a Viet Minh–Free Khmer–Pathet Lao "National United Front." Viet Minh soldiers and cadres were active participants in the fighting there, where they provided the hard core of the "resistance." In addition, forces under General Vo Nguyen Giap had invaded Laos in April and December 1953, and Cambodia in April 1954 (a move which prompted a formal protest by the Royal Khmer Government to the Secretary General of the UN on April 23). Viet Minh battalions were still active in both countries during May and June, with greater priority given operations in Laos. Thus, Dong's proposals on a settlement in Laos and Cambodia reflected not simply the DRV's assumption of the role of spokesman for the unrepresented Free Khmer and Pathet Lao movements, but also direct Viet Minh interests in those neighboring kingdoms.

Dong argued that the Pathet Lao and Free Khmer forces enjoyed widespread popular support and controlled most of the territory of their respective countries. With considerable distortion of history (subsequently corrected by the Laotian and Cambodian delegates), Dong sought to demonstrate that the Pathet Lao and Free Khmer were *de facto* governments carrying out "democratic reforms" in the areas their armies had "liberated." France was therefore advised to recognize the "sovereignty and independence" of those movements no less than of the DRV. French forces alone were to withdraw from Cambodia and Laos; the Pathet Lao and Free Khmer were not "foreign" troops. The same election procedure offered for Vietnam, without neutral or international supervision, would, Dong proposed, take place in Cambodia and Laos, thereby granting the Pathet Lao and Free Khmer a status equal to that of the lawful governments. And during the electoral process, Dong insisted on "conditions securing freedom of activity for patriotic parties, groups, and social organizations . . . ," agreement to which would have permitted various Communist fronts to function with impunity. The inclusion of the Pathet Lao and Free Khmer in the DRV's settlement plan—in particular, the demand that they merited political and territorial recognition—very quickly brought the conference to a standstill and, much later, compelled the Soviets and Chinese to work against Viet Minh ambitions.

C. THE AMERICAN REACTION

Pham Van Dong's opening gambit was clearly anathema to the Western delegations. Certainly, from the American standpoint, his proposals met none of the criteria for acceptability outlined by the National Security Council on May 8. Smith said as much at Geneva when he spoke on May 10 and again at the third plenary session May 12. Accordingly, Smith did not wholeheartedly embrace Bidault's proposals, for despite giving a general endorsement of the French plan, he departed from it at two important junctures. First, he declined to commit the United States in advance to a guarantee of the settlement despite Bidault's call for all the participants to make such a guarantee; second, he proposed that national elections in Vietnam be supervised specifically by an international commission "under United Nations auspices." As his speeches made clear, the United States believed the UN should have two separate functions—overseeing not only the cease-fire but the elections as well. Both these points in Smith's remarks were to remain cardinal elements of American policy throughout the negotiations despite French (and Communist) efforts to induce their alteration.

Entirely in keeping with Smith's position at the conference, as well as with the tenor of the Viet Minh proposals, Secretary Dulles, on May 12, sent Smith instructions intended to make the United States an influential, but unentangled and unobligated, participant. As Dulles phrased it, the United States was to be "an interested nation which, however, is neither a belligerent nor a principal in the negotiation." Its primary aim would be to:

help the nations of that area [Indochina] peacefully to enjoy *territorial integrity and political independence* under *stable and free governments* with the opportunity to expand their economies, to realize their legitimate national aspirations, and to develop security through individual and collective defense against aggression, from within and without. This implies that these people *should not be amalgamated* into the Communist bloc of imperialistic dictatorship.

Accordingly, Smith was told, the United States should not give its approval to any settlement or cease-fire "which would have the effect of *subverting* the existing lawful governments of the three aforementioned states or of *perma nently impairing their territorial integrity* or of placing in jeopardy the forces of the French Union of Indochina, or which otherwise contravened the principles stated . . . above." [Doc. 47]

The NSC decision of May 8, Smith's comments at the second and third plenary sessions, and Dulles' instructions on May 12 reveal the rigidity of the American position on a Geneva settlement. The United States would not associate itself with any arrangement that failed to provide adequately for an internationally supervised cease-fire and national elections, that resulted in the partitioning of any of the Associated States, or that compromised the independence and territorial integrity of those States in any way. It would not interfere with French efforts to reach an agreement, but neither would it guarantee or otherwise be placed in the position of seeming to support it if contrary to policy. Bedell Smith was left free, in fact, to withdraw from the conference or to restrict the American role to that of observer. [Doc. 47] The rationale for this approach was clear enough: the United States, foreseeing inevitable protraction of negotiations by the Communists in the manner of Korea, would not be party to a French cession of territory that would be the end result of the Communists' waiting game already begun by Pham Van Dong. Rather than passively accept that result, the United States would withdraw from active involvement in the proceedings, thereby leaving it with at least the freedom to take steps to recapture the initiative (as by rolling back the Viet Minh at some future date) and the moral purity of having refused to condone the enslavement of more people behind the Iron Curtain. American policy toward negotiations at Geneva was therefore in perfect harmony with the Eisenhower-Dulles global approach to dealing with the Communist bloc.

Gloomy American conclusions about the conference, and no doubt the extravagant opening Communist demands, were intimately connected with events on the battlefield. After the debacle at Dienbienphu on May 7, the French gradually shifted their forces from Laos and Cambodia into the Tonkin Delta, leaving behind weak Laotian and Cambodian national armies to cope with veteran Viet Minh battalions. As the French sought to consolidate in northern Vietnam, the Viet Minh pressed the attack, moving several battalions eastward from Dienbienphu. U.S. Army intelligence reported in late May, on the basis of French evaluations, that the Viet Minh were redeploying much faster than anticipated, to the point where of 35,000 troops originally in northwestern

Tonkin only 2,000 remained. At the same time, two Viet Minh battalions stayed behind in Cambodia and another ten in Laos; and in both those countries, American intelligence concluded that the Viet Minh position was so strong as to jeopardize the political no less than the military stability of the royal governments.

To thwart the Communist military threat in Vietnam, the French chief of staff, General Paul Ely, told General J. H. Trapnell, the MAAG chief (on May 30), that French forces were forming a new defensive perimeter along the Hanoi-Haiphong axis; but Ely made no effort to hide the touch-and-go nature of French defensive capabilities during the rainy season already underway. This precarious situation was confirmed by General Valluy of the French command staff. In a report in early June to U.S., British, Australian, and New Zealand chiefs of staff assembled in Washington, Valluy held that the Delta was in danger of falling to the Communists, that neither Frenchmen nor Vietnamese would fight on in the south in that eventuality, and that only prompt allied intervention could save the situation. [Doc. 53] American assessments merely echoed those provided by the French. A National Intelligence Estimate published June 15 determined that French Union forces, despite a numerical advantage, faced defections on a mounting scale that could become very large if the Viet Minh scored major victories or if the French were believed (and Vietnamese suspicions were rife on this score in Hanoi and Saigon) about to abandon Hanoi and portions of the Delta. In sum, the tenor of intelligence reports by French and American sources during this period (from early May through mid-June) was that the Viet Minh armies were solidly entrenched in portions of Cambodia and Laos, were preparing for further advances in the Tonkin Delta, and, if the war were to continue beyond the rainy season, had the capability to destroy positions then being fortified by French Union forces throughout northern Vietnam.

The upshot of this military deterioration throughout much of Indochina was to reinforce the American conviction that the Communists, while making proposals at Geneva they knew would be unacceptable to the West, would drive hard for important battlefield gains that would thoroughly demoralize French Union troops and set the stage for their withdrawal southward, perhaps precipitating a general crisis of confidence in Indochina and a Viet Minh takeover by default. More clearly than earlier in the year, American officials now saw just how desperate the French really were, in part because French field commanders were being far more sincere about and open with information on the actual military situation. But the thickening gloom in Indochina no less than at Geneva did not give way to counsels of despair in Washington. The Government concluded *not* that the goals it had set for a settlement were unrealistic, but rather that the only way to attain them, as the President and the JCS had been saying, was through decisive military victory in conformity with the original united action proposal of March 29. While therefore maintaining its delegation at Geneva throughout the indecisive sessions of May and June, the United States once again alerted France to the possibility of a military alternative to defeat under the pressure of Communist talk-fight tactics.

IV. THE UNITED STATES AT GENEVA: THE STAGE OF FORCE AND DIPLOMACY, MAY TO MID-JUNE

In keeping open the option of united action, the Administration, no less during May and the first half of June than in April, carefully made direct involvement conditional on a range of French concessions and promises. This second

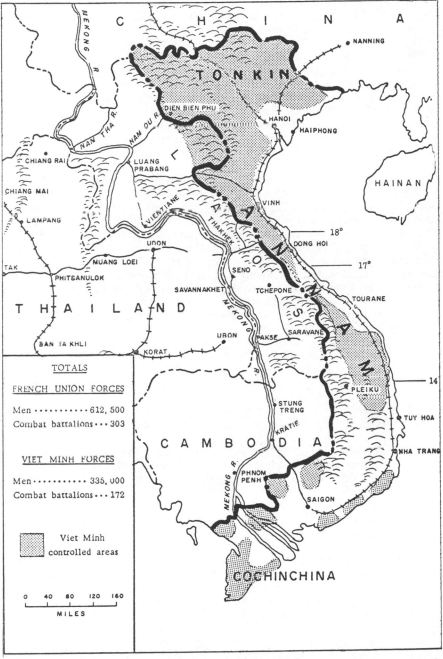

Indochina, July 1954

go-'round on united action was not designed to make further negotiations at Geneva impossible; rather, it was intended to provide an alternative to which the French might turn once they, and hopefully the British as well, conceded that negotiations were a wasteful exercise.

The issue of united action arose again in early May when Premier Laniel, in a talk with Ambassador Dillon, expressed the view that the Chinese were the real masters of the negotiations at Geneva. This being the case, Laniel reasoned, the Chinese would probably seek to drag out the talks over any number of peripheral issues while the Viet Minh pushed on for a military decision. The French position in the field, with a major redeployment on the order of 15 battalions to the Tonkin Delta probably very soon, would be desperate, Laniel said, unless the United States decided to give its active military cooperation. In the interim, the premier requested that an American general be dispatched to Paris to assist in military planning.

Laniel's views failed to make an impression in Washington. Although the Administration agreed to dispatch a general (Trapnell), Dulles proposed, and Eisenhower accepted, a series of "indispensable" conditions to American involvement that would have to be met by Paris. Even after those conditions were met, American intervention would not follow automatically; Laniel would have to request further U.S.-French consultations. The conditions were: (In forwarding these conditions to the Embassy for transmittal to the French, Dulles noted that a prompt, favorable decision would be premature inasmuch as it might internationalize the war in a way offensive to the British, leaving the French with the difficult choice of internationalization or capitulation.)

(1) Formal requests for U.S. involvement from France and the Associated States

(2) An immediate, favorable response to those invitations from Thailand, the Philippines, Australia, and New Zealand, as well as the assurance that Britain "would either participate or be acquiescent"

(3) Presentation of "some aspect of matter" to the UN by one of the involved Asian states

(4) A French guarantee of complete independence to the Associated States, "including unqualified option to withdraw from French Union at any time. . . ."

(5) A French undertaking not to withdraw the Expeditionary Corps from Indochina during the period of united action in order to ensure that the United States would be providing air and sea, but not combat-troop, support

(6) Franco-American agreement on the training of native forces and a new command structure during united action (Admiral Radford was reported to be thinking in terms of a French supreme command with a U.S. air command)

(7) Full endorsement by the French cabinet and Assembly of these conditions to ensure a firm French commitment even in the event of a change in government in Paris

It was further agreed that *in the course of* united action, the United States would pursue efforts to broaden the coalition and to formalize it as a regional defense pact.

During the same conference in which the conditions were drawn up, top American officials went deeper into them. Eisenhower was insistent on collective action, but recognized that the British might not commit themselves initially and that the Australians, facing a general election later in May, could only give "evidence" of their willingness to participate. A second major problem was Indochinese independence. Dulles posed the American dilemma on this score: on the one hand, the United States had to avoid giving Asians reason to believe we were intervening on behalf of colonialism; on the other, the Associated States lacked the administrative personnel and leadership necessary to carrying on alone. "In a sense," said Dulles, "if the Associated States were turned loose, it would be like putting a baby in a cage of hungry lions. The baby would rapidly be devoured." His solution was that the Associated States be granted (evidently, orally) the right to withdraw from the French Union after passage of a suitable time period, perhaps five or ten years.

A final point concerned Executive-Congressional relations once a French request, backed by Parliamentary assent, reached Washington. The President felt he should appear before a joint session of Congress and seek a Congressional resolution to use the armed forces in Indo-China [words missing] act on the formal invitation of France and the Associated States, and with the cooperation of friends and allies in the region. At Eisenhower's request, Dulles directed that the State Department begin working up a first draft of a Presidential message.

The American response to Laniel's requests set the stage for an extended series of discussions over the ensuing five weeks. In Paris, Dillon communicated the American conditions to Laniel and Maurice Schumann, the Deputy Minister for Foreign Affairs; in a talk with the Ambassador May 14, they accepted the conditions, but with important reservations. First, Laniel indicated his dismay at the American insistence on the right of the Associated States to withdraw from the French Union. The premier predicted that the French public would never accept this condition inasmuch as the Associated States had themselves never made it and since even the Viet Minh envisioned joining the Union. The obvious American reluctance to go beyond air and naval forces also disturbed the premier. He requested that the United States additionally provide artillery forces and a token contingent of ground troops. But he indicated pleasure that UK participation was no longer a prerequisite to American involvement.

Laniel's qualified approval of the preconditions was accompanied by a request for a response to two other questions: could the United States in some way guarantee the borders and independence of Laos and Cambodia following a French withdrawal from those countries? Could the United States provide written assurance of prompt air intervention to meet a possible Chinese Communist air attack on French forces in the Tonkin Delta?

The American response to Laniel's demurrers and requests was for the most part negative. On the French-Associated States relationship, which Ambassador Dillon had said was the chief barrier to a French request for intervention,*

* Dillon commented: "I am certain that unless we can find some way to get around this requirement [that the Vietnamese have the option of leaving the French Union], French will never ask for outside assistance."

Dillon proposed that the real objection among Asians to the position of the Associated States rested not on the "purely juridical" problem of the right to leave the Union, but on Indochina's lack of powerful national armies. The Ambassador recommended that American training and equipping of the VNA, coupled with a French statement of intention to withdraw the Expeditionary Corps after the establishment of peace and a national army, would significantly dampen Asian antagonism to the Bao Dai regime. It is difficult to understand why Dillon assumed Asians would significantly change their attitude toward French Indochina when, even with an American takeover of the training and equipping of the VNA, French forces would still be on Vietnamese territory for a lengthy period.

Dulles replied (through Dillon) that the United States might have some flexibility on the matter, but had to remain adamant on complete independence if it ever hoped to gain Thai and Filipino support. Next, on the question of the extent of American involvement, the Government was more flexible: It would not exclude antiaircraft "and limited U.S. ground forces for protection of bases which might be used by U.S. naval and air forces." As to Laniel's questions, Washington answered that it saw no way, in view of the military and legal impracticalities, to guarantee the security of Laos and Cambodia; the alternative was that Laos and Cambodia join with Thailand in requesting the stationing of a UN Peace Observation Commission (POC) on their territories. The possibility of Chinese MIG intervention, considered extremely remote by the Defense Department, ruled out the need for a written commitment. The French were to be assured, however, that a collective defense arrangement would include protection against that contingency, and that prior to the formation of the organization, Chinese air involvement would prompt a Presidential request for Congressional authorization to respond with U.S. aircraft.

Although the setting up of several preconditions to involvement and the qualifications of the French reply by no means made intervention an immediate possibility, the Administration moved ahead on contingency planning. The State Department's Bureau of Far Eastern Affairs took the lead by producing a hypothetical timetable based on the assumption of U.S.–French agreement in principle to the proposed conditions by May 21. FEA also outlined a full slate of urgent priority studies, including U.S. strategy under differing circumstances of Chinese involvement in the war. By May 24, FEA had forwarded a contingency study from the Operations Planning Board that proposed, among other things, public and private communications to Peking to prevent, or at least reduce the effectiveness of, direct Chinese intervention.

The initiation of planning for intervention extended to more far-ranging discussions of the purposes, requirements, and make-up of a Southeast Asia collective defense organization. The framework of the discussions evidenced the Government's intention that united action be undertaken only *after* the Geneva Conference had reached a stalemate or, far less likely, a settlement. Three regional formulations were envisaged: the first would be designed for direct action, probably (it was felt) without British participation, either to defeat the Viet Minh or to prevent them from gaining control of Indochina; the second, formed after a settlement, would comprise the present SEATO members and functions, in particular active assistance to the participating Asian states resisting external attack or "Communist insurrection"; the third would have have a broad Asian membership, but would be functionally limited to social and economic cooperation.

An important input to contingency planning on intervention came from the Joint Chiefs of Staff. On May 20, the JCS sent a memorandum to the Secretary of Defense entitled "U.S. Military Participation in Indochina." In the paper, the Chiefs requested formulation of a Defense Department position on the size of any American contributions and the nature of the command structure once united action began. They noted the "limited availability of U.S. forces for military action in Indochina" and the "current numerical advantage of the French Union forces over the enemy, i.e., approximately 5 to 3." Pointing out the disadvantages of either stationing large numbers of U.S. troops in Indochina or of basing U.S. aircraft on Indochina's limited facilities, the Chiefs considered "the current greatest need" to be an expanded, intensified training program for indigenous troops. They observed, moreover, that they were guided in their comments by the likely reaction of the CPR to U.S. involvement, as well as by the prescription: "Atomic weapons will be used whenever it is to our military advantage."

In view of these problems and prospects, the JCS urged the limitation of United States involvement to strategic planning and the training of indigenous forces through an increase in MAAG from less than 150 to 2250 men. Its force commitment should be restricted, they advised, primarily to air-naval support directed from outside Indochina; even here, the Chiefs cautioned against making a "substantial" air force commitment. The Chiefs were also mindful of the Chinese. Since Viet Minh supplies came mainly from China, "the destruction or neutralization of those outside sources supporting the Viet Minh would materially reduce the French military problems in Indochina."

The Chiefs were simply taking their traditional position that any major U.S. force commitment in the Far East should be reserved for a war against China in the event the President decided that such a conflict was necessary for the preservation of vital American interests. Recognizing the limitations of the "New Look" defense establishment for large-scale involvement in "brushfire" wars, the Chiefs were extremely hesitant, as had consistently been the case during the Indochina crisis, to favor action along the periphery of China when the strategic advantages of American power lay in decisive direct blows against the major enemy. Thus, the JCS closed their memorandum with the admonition that air-naval commitments beyond those specified:

> will involve maldeployment of forces and reduce readiness to meet probable Chinese Communist reaction elsewhere in the Far East. From the point of view of the United States, with reference to the Far East as a whole, Indochina is devoid of decisive military objectives and the allocation of more than token U.S. armed forces to that area would be a serious diversion of limited U.S. capabilities.*

The JCS evidently also decided to call a meeting of military representatives from the United States, France, the UK, Australia, and New Zealand. At first, the Chiefs suggested the downgrading of the representatives to below chief-of-staff level; but apparently on the strong protest of Under Secretary Smith at Geneva, and of the British too, the Chiefs acquiesced in a meeting at chief-of-staff

---

* These conclusions were *subsequently* confirmed when, at the direction of General Matthew B. Ridgway, Army Chief of Staff, a technical team of seven officers representing the Engineer, Transportation, and Signal Corps went to Indochina on a covert mission to determine military and military-related resources available there in the event U.S. intervention were implemented. The team spent the period May 31–June 22 in the field. Their conclusions were, in brief, that Indochina was devoid of the logistical, geographic, and related resources necessary to a substantial American ground effort. The group's findings are in a report from Col. David W. Heiman, its leader, to Ridgway, July 12, 1954.

The Chiefs' conclusions were disputed, however, by Everett Drumright of State (FEA) (in a memorandum to MacArthur, May 24, 1954). He argued that if, as everyone agreed, Indochina was vital to American security, the United States should not consider more than a token group troop commitment to be a serious diversion of our capabilities. While not arguing *for* a substantial troop commitment, Drumright suggested that the United States *plan* for *that* eventuality rather than count on defense with atomic weapons or non-nuclear strikes on Chinese territory. Somehow, however, Drumright's concern about the Chinese did not extend to the consideration that a massive troop commitment, which he stated elsewhere in the memorandum *might* prove necessary should token forces fail to do the job, also risked bringing in the Chinese.

level. But prior to the meeting, which began the first week of June, important developments occurred in the U.S.–France discussions of intervention.

The ticklish problem of bringing France to concede the critical importance of granting full independence to the Associated States occupied center stage once more. On May 27, the State Department, acknowledging France's hesitancy to go too far on this score, still insisted on certain "minimum measures," the most important of which was that France, during or immediately after formal approval of the April 28 draft treaties, announce its willingness to withdraw all its forces from Indochina unless invited by the governments of the Associated States to maintain them or to establish bases. (The United States, the Department added, would be prepared to make a similar declaration if it committed forces.) Beyond that step, the French were also asked to permit Indochinese participation in the programming of economic aid and their direct receipt of all military aid, to find ways to broaden participation of the Vietnamese defense ministry and armed forces in national defense, and to push for the establishment of "representative and authentic nationalist governments" at the earliest possible date.

Transmitting these new proposals to the French, Dillon (incorrectly as it turned out) found them so well received that he reported on May 29, following a conversation with Laniel, that the two partners "had now reached accord in principle on political side." Laniel, he cabled Dulles, urged immediate military talks to complete arrangements on training of the Vietnamese, a new command structure, and war plans. Inasmuch as Ely and General John W. O'Daniel in Indochina had reached general agreement on American assumption of responsibility for training the VNA, [Doc. 52] the way was apparently cleared for bilateral military talks in Washington to take place simultaneously with, and therefore disguised by, the five-power staff negotiations.

Dillon's optimistic assessment proved premature, however, on several grounds. When he reported May 28 on talks with Schumann, he had added Schumann's and Defense Minister René Pleven's concern about Chinese air intervention, which they felt would be so damaging as to warrant a deterrent action in the form of a Presidential request to the Congress for discretionary authority to defend the Delta in case of CCAF attack. The French wanted a virtually instantaneous U.S. response, one that would be assured by a Presidential request *before* rather than after overt Chinese aerial intervention. The State Department's retort was that the French first had to satisfy the previously reported conditions before any such move by the President could be considered.

Dillon was no less disappointed by Washington's reply than the French. He cabled back that there apparently was an "extremely serious misunderstanding between U.S. and French":

> French draw sharp distinction between (1) U.S. intervention in present circumstances with Viet Minh bolstered by Chinese Communist materiel, technicians and possibly scattered troops and (2) U.S. reaction against full-scale air attack mounted from Communist Chinese bases.

Dillon said that, for the French, Washington's preconditions *applied in the first case but not the second,* wherein only Congressional authorization was understood to stand in the way of direct American action. Ely, the Ambassador reported, had all along believed he had Radford's personal assurance of an American countermove against Chinese air attack in the Delta. Now, the French wanted to know if they could count on instant U.S. interdiction of a CCAF strike. The Ambassador closed by reminding the Department of the incalculable harm to

NATO, to the whole U.S. role in Western Europe, and to the U.S. position against the Communists' world strategy if a Chinese attack was not met.

Despite Dillon's protestations, the Department stuck by its initial position of May 15, namely, that Chinese air attack was unlikely and that the United States would meet that problem when it arose. Clearly, the Administration was unwilling to make any advance commitments which the French could seize upon for political advantage at Geneva without having to give a *quid pro quo* in their Indochina policy. Eisenhower affirmed this view and went beyond it: The conditions for united action, he said, applied equally to Chinese direct and indirect involvement in Indochina. *The United States would make no unilateral commitment against any contingency, including overt, unprovoked Chinese aggression, without firm, broad allied support.**

There were other obstacles to U.S.–French agreement, as brought into the open with a memorandum to the President from Foreign Minister Georges Bidault on June 1. One was the question of timing involved in American insistence on French Assembly approval of a government request for U.S. intervention. The French cabinet considered that to present a program of allied involvement to the Assembly except under the circumstance of "a complete failure of the Geneva Conference" attributable to the Communists "would be literally to wish to overthrow the [French] Government." A second area of continuing disagreement concerned the maintenance of French forces in the field and the nature of a U.S. commitment. The French held that the United States could bypass Congress by committing perhaps one division of Marines without a declaration of war. Although assured by Washington that the Marines would not be excluded from a U.S. air-naval commitment, the French were not satisfied. In his memorandum, Bidault asked that the United States take account of

---

* Eisenhower's unwavering attitude toward action in Asia only in concert with allies put him at odds with Dulles, who was prepared to act unilaterally in cases of overt aggression. When the issue of possible CPR air intervention came before the President, he is reported to have reacted sharply. Evidently supposing that conflict in the air would mean a Sino-American war, the President:

> said the United States would not intervene in China on any basis except united action. He would not be responsible for going into China alone unless a joint Congressional resolution ordered him to do so. The United States should in no event undertake alone to support French colonialism. Unilateral action by the United States in cases of this kind would destroy us. If we intervened alone in this case we would be expected to intervene alone in other parts of the world. He made very plain that the need for united action as a condition of U.S. intervention was not related merely to the regional grouping for the defense of Southeast Asia but was also a necessity for U.S. intervention in response to Chinese communist overt aggression.

See memorandum of conversation between Eisenhower and Robert Cutler, the President's special assistant, June 1, 1954.

The rationale for the President's difference of view with his Secretary was laid out more fully the next day. Eisenhower said that since direct Chinese aggression would force him to go all the way with naval and air power (including "new weapons") in reply, he would need to have much more than Congressional authorization. Thai, Filipino, French, and Indochinese support would be important but not sufficient; other nations, such as Australia, would have to give their approval, for otherwise he could not be certain the public would back a war against China. (Memorandum of conversation in the President's office, June 2, 1954, involving also Dulles, Anderson, Radford, MacArthur, and Cutler.) At its 200th meeting on June 3, the NSC received, considered, and agreed upon the President's views.

France's defense obligations elsewhere, an indirect way of asking that Washington go beyond a token ground-troop commitment. Confronted by a war-weary Parliament on one side and opponents of EDC on the other, Bidault doubtless believed that the retention of French soldiers in Indochina without relief from American GIs was neither militarily nor politically acceptable.

A final but by no means negligible French objection to the American proposals concerned the independence issue. Far from having been settled, as Dillon supposed, the French were still unhappy about American pressure for concessions even after the State Department's May 27 revisions. The French were particularly disturbed (as Bidault implied) at the notion that the Associated States could leave the Union at any time, even while French fighting men were in the field on Indochina's behalf. "Such a formula," Bidault wrote, "is unacceptable to the French Government, first because it is incompatible with the French Constitution, and also because it would be extremely difficult to explain to French opinion that the forces of the French Union were continuing the war in Indochina for the benefit of States that might at any moment leave the Union." France was perfectly willing, Bidault remarked, to sign new treaties of association with the three Indochinese States, to allow them a larger voice in defense matters, and to work with them toward formation of truly national governments; but, to judge from his commentary, Paris would not go the whole route by committing itself in advance to Indochina's full freedom of action in the French Union. And while this and other issues remained unresolved, as Dulles observed June 4, Laniel's reported belief that the United States and France were politically agreed was a "serious overstatement."

By early June the unsettled issues separating the United States from France began to lose their relevance to the war. Even if they could be resolved, it was questionable whether American involvement could any longer be useful, much less decisive. On the matter of training the VNA, for instance, the United States was no longer certain that time would permit its training methods to take effect even if the French promptly removed themselves from responsibility in that area. The State Department now held that the Vietnam situation had deteriorated "to point where any commitment at this time to send over U.S. instructors in near future might expose us to being faced with situation in which it would be contrary to our interests to have to fulfill such commitment. Our position accordingly is that we do not wish to consider U.S. training mission or program separately from over-all operational plan on assumption conditions fulfilled for U.S. participation war Indochina." Morale of the Franco-Vietnamese forces, moreover, had dropped sharply, the whole Tonkin Delta was endangered, and the political situation in Saigon was reported to be dangerously unstable. Faced with this uniformly black picture, the Administration determined that the grave but still retrievable military situation prevailing at the time united action was proposed and pursued had, in June, altered radically, to the point where united action might have to be withdrawn from consideration by the French.

By mid-June American diplomacy was therefore in an unenviable position. At Geneva, very little progress had been made of a kind that could lead any of the Allies to expect a satisfactory outcome. Yet the alternative which the United States had reopened no longer seemed viable either. As Dulles told Smith, any "final agreement" with the French would be "quite impossible," for Paris was moving farther than ever from a determination that united action was necessary. "They want, and in effect have, an option on our intervention," Dulles wrote, "but they do not want to exercise it and the date of expiry of our option is fast running out." [Doc. 57] From Paris, in fact, Ambassador Dillon urged the

Secretary that "the time limit be now" on U.S. intervention. [Doc. 56] And Dulles was fast concluding that Dillon was correct.

In view of France's feeling that, because of strong Assembly pressure for a settlement, no request could be made of the United States until every effort to reach agreement at Geneva had been exhausted, Dulles in effect decided, on June 15, that united action was no longer tenable. In a conversation with Bonnet, in which the French Ambassador read a message from Bidault which indicated that the French no longer considered the United States bound to intervene on satisfaction of the seven conditions, the Secretary put forth the difficulty of the American position. He stated that the United States stood willing to respond to a French request under the conditions of May 11, but that time and circumstance might make future intervention "impracticable or so burdensome as to be out of proportion to the results obtainable." While this offer would be unsatisfactory to Bidault, especially in his dealings with the Communists at Geneva, Dulles "could not conceive that it would be expected that the United States would give a third power the option to put it into war at times and under conditions wholly of the other's choosing." With this, united action was shelved, and it never appeared again in the form and with the purpose originally proposed.

As a break with France on united action became likely, American interest focused on a collective defense arrangement after a Geneva settlement with British participation. The French and British roles in U.S. planning were in effect reversed; Paris, it was felt, could no longer be counted on as an active participant in regional security. As their delegate to Geneva, Jean Chauvel, told Smith, Bidault was still hopeful of getting "something" from the conference. [Doc. 54] On the other hand, Eden told Smith on June 9 of his extreme pessimism over the course of the negotiations. Eden believed a recess in the talks was likely within a few days (it came, in fact, ten days later), and proposed that the Cambodian and Laotian cases be brought before the United Nations immediately after the end of the conference, even if France opposed the move. Smith drew from the conversation the strong impression that Eden believed negotiations to have failed and would now follow the American lead on a coalition to guarantee Cambodia and Laos "under umbrella of some UN action" (Smith's words). [Doc. 54] Days later, Dulles likewise anticipated a British shift when he observed sardonically that events at Geneva had probably "been such as to satisfy the British insistence that they did not want to discuss collective action until either Geneva was over or at least the results of Geneva were known. I would assume," Dulles went on, "that the departure of Eden [from Geneva] would be evidence that there was no adequate reason for further delaying collective talks on Southeast Asia defense." But whether the United States and Great Britain would see eye-to-eye on their post-settlement security obligations in the region, and whether joint diplomatic initiatives to influence the nature of the settlement could be decided upon, remained outstanding questions.

The rebirth and demise of united action was a rare case of history repeated almost immediately after it had been made. The United States, having failed to interest Britain and France in united action prior to the start of the Geneva Conference, refused to be relegated to an uninfluential role and determined instead to plunge ahead without British participation. But the conditions for intervention which had been given the French before the fall of Dienbienphu were now stiffened, most importantly by a greater detailing of the process the French government would have to go through before the United States would consider direct involvement.

Even while the French pondered the conditions, urged their refinement and redefinition to suit French policies, and insisted in the end that they saw no political obstacles separating the United States and France, Washington anticipated that the French were very unlikely to forward a request for U.S. involvement. Having learned something of French government priorities from the futile diplomatic bargaining in April, Department of State representatives in Paris and Washington saw that what the French wanted above all was not the military advantages of active U.S. intervention but the *political* benefits that might be derived from bringing into the open the fact that the two allies were *negotiating* American participation in the fighting. Thus, Dillon correctly assessed in mid-May that French inquiries about American conditions for intervention represented a "wish to use possibility of our intervention primarily to strengthen their hand at Geneva." The French hoped they would not have to call on the United States for direct support; they *did* hope the Communists would sense the dangers of proposing unacceptable terms for a settlement. Dillon's sensitivity to the French position was proven accurate by Bidault's memorandum to the President: France would, in reality, only call on the United States if an "honorable" settlement could clearly not be obtained at Geneva, for only under that circumstance could the National Assembly be persuaded that the Laniel government had done everything possible to achieve peace.

Recognition of the game the French were playing did not keep the United States from posing intervention as an alternative for them; but by adhering tenaciously to the seven conditions, it ruled out either precipitous American action or an open-ended commitment to be accepted or rejected by Paris. The State Department, guided on the military side by strong JCS objections to promising the French American combat troops in advance of a new and satisfactory command structure and strategic plan, became increasingly distraught with and suspicious of French motivations. "We cannot grant French an indefinite option on us without regard to intervening deterioration" of the military situation, Dulles wrote on June 8. As much as the Administration wanted to avoid a sell-out at Geneva, it was aware that events in Indochina might preclude effective U.S. action even if the French suddenly decided they wanted American support. Put another way, one of the primary differences between American diplomacy before and after the fall of Dienbienphu was its ability to project ahead—to weigh the factors of time and circumstance against the distasteful possibility that Vietnam, by French default at the negotiating table or defeat on the battlefield, might be lost. As the scales tipped against united action, American security planning began to focus on the future possibilities of collective defense in Southeast Asia, while the pattern of diplomacy shifted from disenchantment with the Geneva Conference to attempts to bring about the best possible settlement terms.

V. THE MAJOR ISSUES AT THE CONFERENCE, MAY–JUNE

Washington's sense that the conference had essentially gotten nowhere—a view which Smith and Dulles believed was shared by Eden, as already noted—was not entirely accurate; nor was it precisely the thinking of other delegations. Following the initial French and Viet Minh proposals of May 8 and 10, respectively, some progress had in fact been made, although certainly not of an order that could have led any of the chief negotiators to expect a quick settlement. As the conference moved ahead, three major areas of contention emerged: the separation of belligerent forces, the establishment of a framework for political settlements in the three Indochinese states, and provision for effective control and supervision of the cease-fire.

A. SEPARATION OF THE BELLIGERENTS

The question how best to disentangle the opposing armies was most acute in Vietnam, but was also hotly debated as it applied to Cambodia and Laos. In Vietnam, Viet Minh forces were concentrated in the Tonkin Delta, though large numbers had long been active in Annam (central Vietnam) and Cochinchina (the south). The original French and Viet Minh proposals sought to take account of this situation by dismissing (although for separate reasons) the concept of single regroupment areas and forwarding instead the idea of perhaps several concentration points to facilitate a cease-fire. To this point, the Vietnamese delegation was in agreement: regroupment of the belligerents should in no way have the effect of dividing the country into makeshift military zones that could have lasting political implications.

It was an entirely different matter where the regroupment areas should be located; whether "foreign" (i.e., French) troops should be withdrawn, and if so, from what areas and during what period; whether irregular troops (i.e., Viet Minh guerrillas) should be disarmed and disbanded, and if so, whether they and their comrades in the regular forces should be integrated (as the Bao Dai delegation proposed) into the VNA; and, of crucial importance, whether a cease-fire should be dependent upon success in the regroupment process or, as Pham Van Dong proposed, upon an overall political settlement.

This last question was tackled first by the negotiators. On Eden's initiative, the conference had moved in mid-May from plenary to restricted sessions, where fewer delegates were present, no verbatim record was systematically kept, and the press was barred. Eden's expectation that the opportunities for greater intimacy among the delegates would enhance the possibility of making some headway was partially fulfilled. At the first restricted session on May 17, Molotov responded to Bidault's implication that one cause of continuing irresolution in the negotiations was the Viet Minh's insistence on coupling a military with a political settlement, whereas the French proposal had been geared to dealing only with the military portion before going on to discuss the political side. The Soviet delegate argued that while military and political matters were obviously closely linked, the conference might do best to address the military settlement first, since it was a point common to the French and Viet Minh proposals. Dong objected that military and political matters were so closely knit that they could not be separated; however, he agreed (although, we may surmise, with some reluctance) that the two problems could be dealt with in that order.

With a basic procedural obstacle removed, it was finally agreed that a cease-fire should have priority in the conference's order of business.* Toward that goal, the problem of regroupment and disarmament of certain forces was taken up. At the fifth restricted session on May 24, Foreign Minister Bidault proposed, among other things, that a distinction be admitted between "regular" and "irregular" forces. Regular troops, he said, included all permanently organized

---

* On May 20, Chou En-lai told Eden that military and political matters should indeed be dealt with separately, and that priority should be given to the attainment of a cease-fire. (Smith tel. SECTO 267 from Geneva, May 20, 1954.) The Communists were quick to point out thereafter, though, that a political settlement should not be dropped from consideration. In fact, at the fifth restricted session, Molotov returned to the issue of military versus political settlements by proposing that they be considered at alternate meetings. The Western side held fast to concentrating on the cease-fire and turning to political matters only when agreement had been reached on the military side; this position was tacitly adopted.

forces, which for the Viet Minh meant regional as well as regular units. These, he suggested, should be regrouped into demilitarized zones, whereas loosely organized irregulars should be disarmed under some form of control. Pham Van Dong, in his reply, agreed on the urgency of a cease-fire and on the importance of disarming irregulars; but, in contrast to Bidault's proposal, Dong asserted that inasmuch as each side would have responsibility for all forces in areas under its control *after* the cease-fire, disarmament would take place naturally. Dong implicitly rejected the idea of controlled disarmament, therefore, by placing the problem in the post- rather than pre-cease-fire period.

The issues of regroupment and disarmament might have brought the conference to a standstill had not Pham Van Dong, at the sixth restricted session (May 25), suddenly reversed his position on regroupment and proposed what amounted to the partitioning of Indochina. Following only moments after the Vietnamese delegate, Nguyen Quoc Dinh, had offered a plan based on the maintenance of his country's territorial integrity,* Dong suggested that in the course of the regroupment, specific territorial jurisdictions be established such that each side would have complete economic and administrative, no less than military, control. So as not to be misunderstood, Dong further urged that a temporary line of demarcation be drawn that would be topographically suitable and appropriate for transportation and communication within each zone thus created. The American delegate, General Smith, immediately dismissed Dong's proposal and advised that the conferees return to discussion of the original cease-fire issues. But, as was to become clear very soon, Dong's new move struck a responsive chord among the French even as it confirmed to the Bao Dai delegation its worst fears.

What had prompted Dong to introduce a partition arrangement when, at previous sessions, the Viet Minh had pushed repeatedly for a settlement procedure that would facilitate their consolidation of control over the entire country? What evidence we have is circumstantial, but it suggests that the Viet Minh delegation may have come under Sino-Soviet pressure to produce an alternative to cease-fire proposals that were consistently being rejected by the West. The partition alternative, specifically at the 16th parallel, had been intimated to American officials as early as March 4 by a member of the Soviet Embassy in London, apparently out of awareness of Franco-American objections to a coalition arrangement for Vietnam. On the opening day of the conference, moreover, Soviet officials had again approached American officials on the subject, this time at Geneva, averring that the establishment of a buffer state to China's south would be sufficient satisfaction of China's security needs. While these events do not demonstrate that Dong's partition proposal† was the direct outgrowth of Sino-Soviet disposition toward a territorial division, they do reveal that partition was a solution, albeit temporary, which Moscow, at least, early found agreeable.

---

* The GVN's position called for the disbandment and disarming of Viet Minh forces and their later integration into a national army under international control; international supervision of elections to be conducted by the Bao Dai government at an unspecified future date; and recognition of the integrity of the Vietnamese state. The GVN also insisted that the withdrawal of foreign forces come after all other issues had been resolved.

† The DRV, it should be added, refused to call its proposal one for partition. As the official newspaper, *Nhan Dan* (The People) put it, the proposal amounted merely to "zonal readjustment" necessary to achieving a cease-fire. The readjustment "is only a stage in preparation for free general elections with a view toward the realization of national unity." Vietnam News Agency (VNA) broadcast in English to Southeast Asia, June 7, 1954.

Whatever lay behind Dong's gambit, the French were put in the position of being challenged on their prior commitments to the Vietnamese. At the time the conference began, Bao Dai's government, perhaps mindful of past instances of partition-type solutions in Korea and Germany, and almost certainly suspicious of ultimate French intentions in the face of Viet Minh territorial demands, urged Paris to provide written assurance it would neither seek nor accept a division of Vietnam at Geneva. To make his own position perfectly clear, Bao Dai, through his representatives in the French capital, issued a communique (in the name of the GVN cabinet) which took note of various plans in the air for partition. The communique stated that partition "would be in defiance of Vietnamese national sentiment which has asserted itself with so much strength for the unity as well as for the independence of the country. Neither the Chief of State nor the national government of Vietnam admits that the unity of the country can be severed legally. . . ." The cabinet warned that an agreement compromising that unity would never receive Vietnam's approval:

> . . . neither the Chief of State, nor the Vietnamese Government will consider themselves [*sic*] as bound by decisions running counter to the interests, i.e., independence and unity, of their country that would, at the same time, violate the rights of the peoples and offer a reward to aggression in opposition to the principles of the Charter of the United Nations and democratic ideals.

In response to this clear-cut statement, the French came forward with both oral and written promises. On May 3, Maurice Dejean, the Commissioner General for Indochina, said in Saigon:

> The French Government does not intend to seek a settlement of the Indochina problem on the basis of a partition of Vietnamese territory. . . . Formal assurances were given on this subject last April 25 by the French minister for foreign affairs to the minister for foreign affairs of Vietnam, and they were confirmed to him on May 1.

Written assurance came from Bidault on May 6 when he wrote Bao Dai that the task of the French government was to establish peace in Indochina, not "to seek here [at Geneva] a definitive political solution." Therefore, the French goal would be, said Bidault, to obtain a cease-fire with guarantees for the Associated States, hopefully with general elections in the future. Bidault continued:

> As of now, I am however in a position to confirm to Your Majesty that nothing would be more contrary to the intentions of the French government than to prepare for the establishment, at the expense of the unity of Vietnam, two States having each an international calling (*vocation*).

Bidault's support of Vietnam's opposition to partition, which he repeated privately before Eden and Smith at Geneva, collapsed once the new government of Pierre Mendès-France took over in mid-June. Mendès-France, keenly aware of the tenor of French public opinion, was far more disposed than the Laniel-Bidault administration to making every effort toward achieving a reasonable settlement. While by no means prepared for a sell-out, Mendès-France quickly foresaw that agreement with the Viet Minh was unlikely unless he accepted the concept of partition. His delegate at Geneva, who remained Chauvel, and the new Commissioner General for Indochina, General Ely, reached the same conclusion. At a high-level meeting in Paris on June 24, the new government thoroughly revised the French negotiating position. The objectives for subsequent talks, it was decided, would be: (1) the regroupment of forces of both sides, and their separation by a line about at the 18th parallel;* (2) the establishment of enclaves under neutral control in the two zones, one for the French in the area of the Catholic bishoprics at Phat Diem and Bui Chu, one for the Viet Minh at an area to be determined; (3) the maintenance of Haiphong in French hands in order to assist in the regroupment. The meeting also decided that, for the purpose of psychological pressure on the Viet Minh if not military preparedness for future contingencies, France should break with past practice and announce plans to send a contingent of conscripts (later determined as two divisions) to Indochina. Thus, by late June, the French had come around to acceptance of the need to explore a territorial settlement without, as we have already observed, informing the Vietnamese that Bidault's and Dejean's assurances had been superseded. On June 26, Paris formally notified Washington and London that Chauvel would soon begin direct talks with Pham Van Dong on a partition arrangement that would provide the GVN with the firmest possible territorial base. [Doc. 66]

While ground had been broken on the cease-fire for Vietnam, debate continued on Laos and Cambodia. Prior to and after Dong's proposal of May 25, the delegates argued back and forth without progress over the relationship between the conflict in Vietnam and that in Cambodia and Laos. The Khmer and Laotian delegates insisted they represented free and independent governments which were being challenged by a handful of indigenous renegades assisted by the invading Viet Minh. Thus, the delegates reasoned, their situations were quite different from the "civil war" in Vietnam, and therefore cease-fires could readily be established in Laos and Cambodia by the simple expedient of removing the aggressors. These delegates saw no reason—and they received solid support from the American, French and British representatives—for acceding to the Viet Minh demand that cease-fires in their two countries be contingent upon, and hence forced to occur simultaneously with, one in Vietnam.

The Communists' retorts left little room for compromise. Pham Van Dong held, as before, that he spoke for "governments" which were being refused admission to the conference. The Pathet Lao and the Free Khmer were separate, genuine "national liberation movements" whose stake in their respective countries, Dong implied, would have to be acknowledged before a cease-fire could be arranged anywhere in Indochina. Molotov buttressed this argument with the claim that Laos and Cambodia were no more "independent" than Vietnam. Using a common negotiating tactic, he excerpted from a public statement by Dulles to point out how France was still being urged by the United States in May to grant real independence to all three Indochinese states, not just Vietnam.

* French insistence on the 18th parallel originated in the recommendation of General Navarre, who was asked several questions by the French delegation at Geneva regarding the likely impact of the then-existing military situation on the French negotiatory position. Navarre's responses were sent April 21. On the demarcation line, Navarre said that the 18th parallel would leave "us" the ancient political capital of Hue as well as Tourane (Da Nang), and permit the retention of militarily valuable terrain. (See General Ely's *Mémoires: l'Indochine dans la Tourmente* [Paris: Plon, 1964], p. 112, and Lacouture and Devillers, *La fin d'une guerre,* p. 126.) Thus, the choice of the 18th parallel was based on military considerations, and apparently assumed a continuing French role in southern Vietnam after partition.

Molotov's only retreat was on the extent of Pathet Lao and Free Khmer territorial control. He admitted that while the Viet Minh were dominant in Vietnam, the Khmer-Laotian resistance movements controlled some lesser amount of territory.

For a while it seemed that the conference would become inextricably bogged down on the question whether the Pathet Lao and Free Khmer were creatures of the Viet Minh or genuine nationalist forces. Certainly the Viet Minh delegation remained steadfast. At the fourth restricted session (May 21), Pham Van Dong made his implication of the previous sessions clearer when he said he had always understood the French cease-fire proposal to have applied to all Indochina (an outright fabrication) inasmuch as the problems in the three states were different only in degree, not in nature. If Cambodia and Laos were detached from Vietnam in the discussions, Dong said, the cease-fire issue would be attacked in the wrong way and a satisfactory solution would not be reached. The warning of no cease-fire settlement for Cambodia and Laos without one for Vietnam was clear.

These last remarks by Dong, however, were no longer wholly in accord with what the Chinese were privately indicating. Chou En-lai, in the same conversation with Eden on May 20 in which Chou had agreed to separate military from political matters, also admitted that *political* settlements might be different for the three Indochinese states. Chou thus moved one step closer to the Western position, which held that the Laotian and Cambodian cases were substantially different from that in Vietnam and hence should be decided separately. The concession, however small, paved the way for agreement to Eden's proposal on May 25 that the problem of a cease-fire in Vietnam be dealt with separately and directly by having the Viet Minh and French military commands meet in Geneva and on the spot in Vietnam (later determined as Trung Gia) to discuss technical aspects of the regroupment. The military staffs would report their findings to the conferees. On June 2 formal agreement was reached between the commands to begin work; but it was not until June 10, apparently, that the Viet Minh actually consented that their *secret* talks with the French, like the discussions of the military commands, should be concerned only with Vietnam to the exclusion of Laotian and Cambodian problems. Thus, it would seem that the Viet Minh position on the indivisibility of the three Indochinese states for purposes of a settlement was undercut by the Chinese (doubtless with Soviet support); yet for about three weeks following Chou's talk with Eden, the Viet Minh had privately refused to deal with the French on Vietnam alone.

B. POLITICAL SETTLEMENTS

Communist agreement to treat Laos and Cambodia separately as well as to consider a territorial division did not, however, signal imminent progress on the substance of military or political settlements for those countries any more than for Vietnam. Several additional plenary and restricted sessions made no headway at all during late May and the first weeks of June. Eden's disappointment led him to state to his fellow delegates:

In respect . . . to the arrangements for supervision and to the future of Laos and Cambodia, the divergencies are at present wide and deep. Unless we can narrow them now without further delay, we shall have failed in our task. We have exhausted every expedient procedure which we could devise to assist us in our work. We all know now what the differences are.

We have no choice but to resolve them or to admit our failure. For our part, the United Kingdom Delegation is still willing to attempt to resolve them here or in restricted session or by any other method which our colleagues may prefer.

But, gentlemen, if the positions remain as they are today, I think it is our clear-cut duty to say so to the world and to admit that we have failed.

Days later, his pessimism ran even deeper as the conference indeed seemed close to a breakdown. The Americans did not help matters, either: "Bedell Smith," Eden has since divulged, "showed me a telegram from President Eisenhower advising him to do everything in his power to bring the conference to an end as rapidly as possible, on the grounds that the Communists were only spinning things out to suit their own military purposes."

For reasons which will be speculated on subsequently, the Soviets and Chinese were not prepared to admit that the conference had failed and were willing to forestall that prospect by making concessions sufficient to justify its continuation. While the Americans may have wished to see a breakdown, Eden was not yet convinced that was inevitable. Again, his patience was rewarded. On June 16, Chou told the foreign secretary that the Cambodian resistance forces were small, making a political settlement with the Royal Government "easily" obtainable. In Laos, where those forces were larger, regroupment areas along the border with Vietnam (in Sam Neua and Phong Saly provinces) would be required, Chou thought. Asked by Eden whether there might not be difficulty in gaining Viet Minh agreement to the withdrawal of their troops from the two countries, Chou replied it would "not be difficult" in the context of a withdrawal of all foreign forces. The CPR would even be willing to consider the royal governments as heading independent states that could maintain their ties to the French Union, provided no American bases were established in their territories. China's preeminent concern, Eden deduced, was that the United States might use Laos and Cambodia as jump-off points for an attack on the mainland.

From the conversation, Eden "received a strong impression that he [Chou] wanted a settlement and I accordingly urged Georges Bidault to have a talk with him and to discuss this *new offer*." On the next day (June 17), Bidault met with Chou for the first time, as well as with Molotov, and reported the Communists' great concern over a break-up of the conference. Two days later a French redraft of a Chinese proposal to broaden the military staff conferences to include separate talks on Laos and Cambodia was accepted.

This first major breakthrough in the negotiations, with the Chinese making an overture that evidently had full Soviet backing,* seems not to have had Viet Minh approval. At the same time as the Chinese were saying, for example in a New China News Agency (NCNA) broadcast of June 17, that all three Communist delegations had "all along maintained that the conditions in each

---

* When Molotov met with Smith on June 19, the Soviet representative said he saw the possibility of agreement on Laos and Cambodia so long as neither side (i.e., the French and Viet Minh) "adopted one-sided views or put forward extreme pretensions." Molotov said about 50 percent of Laotian territory was not controlled by the royal government (putting the Pathet Lao case in the negative), with a much smaller movement in Cambodia. The tone of Smith's report on this conversation suggests that Molotov saw no obstacles to Viet Minh withdrawal of its "volunteers." Smith tel. DULTE 202 from Geneva, June 19, 1954.

of the three Indochinese countries are not exactly alike," and hence that "conditions peculiar to each of these countries should be taken into consideration," the Viet Minh were claiming that "the indivisibility of the three questions of Vietnam, Khmer, and Pathet Lao" was one of several "fundamental questions" which the conference had failed to resolve. In fact, of course, that question *had* been resolved; yet the Viet Minh continued to proclaim the close unity of the Viet Minh, Pathet Lao, and Free Khmer under the banner of their tri-national united front alliance formed in 1951. No doubt the Viet Minh were seeking to assure their cadres and soldiers in Cambodia and Laos that Pham Van Dong would not bargain away their fate at the conference table, but it may also be that the broadcasts were meant to imply Viet Minh exceptions to objectionable Sino-Soviet concessions.

Those concessions, first on the separability of Laos and Cambodia from Vietnam and subsequently on Viet Minh involvement there, compelled the DRV delegation to take a new tack. On the former question, Viet Minh representatives indicated on June 16 during "underground" discussions with the French that insofar as Vietnam was concerned, their minimum terms were absolute control of the Tonkin Delta, including Hanoi and Haiphong. While the French were reluctant to yield both cities, which they still controlled, a bargaining point had been established inasmuch as the Viet Minh were now willing to discuss specific geographic objectives. On the second question, the Viet Minh, apparently responding to Chou En-lai's "offer" of their withdrawal from Cambodia and Laos, indicated flexibility at least toward the latter country. A Laotian delegate reported June 23, following a meeting with Pham Van Dong in the garden of the Chinese delegation's villa, that the Viet Minh were in apparent accord on the withdrawal of their "volunteers" and even on Laos' retention of French treaty bases. The Viet Minh's principal demand was that French military personel in Laos be reduced to a minimum. Less clearly, Dong alluded to the creation in Laos of a government of "national union," Pathet Lao participation in 1955 elections for the national assembly, and a "temporary arrangement" governing areas dominated by Pathet Lao military forces. But these latter points were interpreted as being suggestive; Dong had come around to the Western view shared (now by the Soviets and Chinese) that the Pathet Lao not be accorded either military or political weight equal to that of the royal government. Later in the conference, Dong would make a similar retreat on Cambodia.

C. CONTROL AND SUPERVISION

Painstakingly slow progress toward cease-fires and political settlements for the Indochinese states also characterized the work of devising supervisory organs to oversee the implementation and preservation of the cease-fire. Yet here again, the Communist side was not so intransigent as to make agreement impossible.

Three separate but interrelated issues dominated the discussions of control and supervision at this stage of the conference and afterward. First, there was sharp disagreement over the structure of the supervisory organ: Should it consist solely of joint commissions composed of the belligerents, or should it have superimposed above an international authority possessing decisionmaking power? Second, the composition of any supervisory organ other than the joint commissions was also hotly disputed: Given agreement to have "neutral" nations observe the truce, which nations might be considered "neutral"? Finally, if it were agreed that there should be a neutral control body, how would it discharge its duties?

In the original Viet Minh proposals, implementation of the cease-fire was left to joint indigenous commissions, with no provision for higher, international supervision. Vehement French objections led to a second line of defense from the Communist side. At the fourth plenary session (May 14), Molotov suggested the setting up of a Neutral Nations Supervisory Commission (NNSC) such as existed in Korea, and said he did not foresee any insurmountable problem in reaching agreement on its membership. But Molotov's revision left much to be determined and, from the Western standpoint, much to be desired too. Serious debate on the control and supervision problem did not get underway until early June. At that time, Molotov expressly rejected the American plan, supported by the Indochinese delegations and Great Britain, to have the United Nations supervise a cease-fire. He argued that the UN had nothing to do with the Geneva Conference, especially as most of the conferees were not UN members. Returning to his plan for an NNSC, Molotov reiterated his view that Communist countries could be as neutral as capitalist countries; hence, he said, the problem was simply one of choosing which countries should comprise the supervisory organ, and suggested that the yardstick be those having diplomatic and political relations with both France and the Viet Minh. As to that body's relationship to the joint commissions, Molotov shied away from the Western proposal to make them subordinate to the neutral commission. "It would be in the interest of our work to recognize," Molotov said, "that these commissions should act in coordination and in agreement between each other, but should not be subordinate to each other." No such hierarchical relationship had existed in Korea, so why one in Indochina? Finally, the foreign minister saw no reason why an NNSC could not reach decisions by unanimous vote on "important" questions. Disputes among or within the commissions, Molotov concluded, would be referred to the states guaranteeing the settlement, which would, if necessary, take "collective measures" to resolve them.

The Western position was stated succinctly by Bidault. Again insisting on having "an authority remote from the heat of the fighting and which would have a final word to say in disputes," Bidault said the neutral control commission should have absolute responsibility for the armistice. It would have such functions as regrouping the regular forces, supervising any demilitarized zones, conducting the exchange of prisoners, and implementing measures for the nonintroduction of war materiel into Indochina. While the joint commission would have an important role to play in these control processes, such as in working out agreement for the safe passage of opposing armies from one zone to another or for POW exchange, its functions would have to be subordinate to the undisputed authority of a neutral mechanism. Bidault did not specify which nations fitted his definition of "neutrality" and whether they would decide by majority or unanimous vote. These omissions were corrected by Eden a few days later when he suggested the Colombo Powers (India, Pakistan, Ceylon, Burma, and Indonesia), which he argued were all Asian, had all been actively discussing Indochina outside the conference, were five in number and hence impervious to obstruction by a two-to-two vote (as on the NNSC) or requirement for unanimity, and were truly impartial.

The basis for agreement on the vital question of supervising a cease-fire seemed at this stage nonexistent. The Communists had revised their position by admitting the feasibility of a neutral nations' control organ in addition to joint commissions of the belligerents. But they clearly hoped to duplicate in Indochina the ineffective machinery they had foisted on the United Nations command at Panmunjom, one in which effective peacekeeping action was basically proscribed by the built-in veto of a four-power authority evenly divided among Communist and non-Communist representatives. The West, on the other hand, absolutely refused to experiment again with an NNSC; a neutral organ was vital, but it could not include Communist representatives, who did not know the meaning of neutrality. If the United Nations was not acceptable to the Communists, the Colombo Powers should be.

However remote these positions, various kinds of trade-offs must have been apparent to the negotiators. Despite differing standards of "neutrality" and "impartiality," for instance, compromise on the membership problem seemed possible. The real dilemma was the authority of a neutral body. Unless superior to the joint commissions, it would never be able to resolve disputes, and unless it had the power to enforce its own decisions, it would never be more than an advisory organ. Whether some new formula could be found somewhere between the Communists' insistence on parallel authority and the West's preference for a hierarchical arrangement remained to be seen.

On June 19 the Korea phase of the conference ended without reaching a political settlement. The conferees at that point agreed to a prolonged recess by the delegation leaders on the understanding that the military committees would continue to meet at Geneva and in the field. Eden wrote to the Asian Commonwealth prime ministers that "if the work of the committees is sufficiently advanced, the Heads of Delegations will come back." Until that time, the work of the conference would go on in restricted session. Chauvel and Pham Van Dong remained at their posts; Molotov returned to Moscow; Chou En-lai, en route to Peking, made important stopovers in New Delhi, Rangoon, and Nanning that were to have important bearing on the conference. Smith remained in Geneva, but turned the delegation over to Johnson. It was questionable whether the Under Secretary would take over again; gloom was so thick in Washington over the perceived lack of progress in the talks and the conviction that the new Mendès-France government would reach a settlement as soon as the conference reconvened, that Dulles cabled Smith: "Our thinking at present is that our role at Geneva should soon be restricted to that of observer. . . ." [Doc. 65] As for Eden, he prepared to accompany Churchill on a trip to Washington for talks relating to the conference and prospects for a Southeast Asia defense pact.

VI. THE ANGLO-AMERICAN RAPPROCHEMENT

With its preconceptions of Communist negotiating strategy confirmed by the harshness of the first Viet Minh proposals, which Washington did not regard as significantly watered down by subsequent Sino-Soviet alterations, and with its military alternatives no longer considered relevant to the war, the United States began to move in the direction of becoming an influential actor at the negotiations. This move was not dictated by a sudden conviction that Western capacity for inducing concessions from the Communist side had increased; nor was the shift premised on the hope that we might be able to drive a wedge between the Viet Minh and their Soviet and Chinese friends. Rather, Washington believed that inasmuch as a settlement was certain to come about, and even though there was near-equal certainty it could not support the final terms, basic American and Western interests in Southeast Asia might still be preserved if France could be persuaded to toughen its stand. Were concessions still not forthcoming— were the Communists, in other words, to stiffen in response to French firmness

—the Allies would be able to consult on their next moves with the confidence every reasonable effort to reestablish peace had been attempted.

As already observed, the American decision to play a more decisive role at the conference depended on gaining British support. The changing war situation now made alignment with the British necessary for future regional defense, especially as Washington was informed of the probability that a partition settlement (which London had foreseen months before) would place all Indochina in or within reach of Communist hands. The questions remained how much territory the Communists could be granted without compromising non-Communist Indochina's security, what measures were needed to guarantee that security, and what other military and political principles were vital to any settlement which the French would also be willing to adopt in the negotiations. When the chief ministers of the United States and Great Britain met in Washington in late June, these were the issues they had to confront.

The British and American representatives—Eden, Churchill, Dulles, and Eisenhower—brought to the talks positions on partition and regional security that, for all the differences, left considerable room for a harmonization of viewpoints. The UK, as the Americans well knew, was never convinced either that Indochina's security was inextricably linked to the security of all Asia, or that the Franco–Viet Minh war would ever bring into question the surrender of all Indochina to the Communists. London considered partition a feasible solution, but was already looking beyond that to some more basic East-West understanding that would have the effect of producing a laissez-faire coexistence between the Communist and Western powers in the region. As Eden recalled his thinking at the time, the best way of keeping Communism out of Southeast Asia while still providing the necessary security within which free societies might evolve was to build a belt of neutral states assisted by the West. The Communists might not see any advantage to this arrangement, he admitted. But:

> If we could bring about a situation where the Communists believed that there was a balance of advantage to them in arranging a girdle of neutral states, we might have the ingredients of a settlement.

Once the settlement was achieved, a system for guaranteeing the security of the neutral states thus formed would be required, Eden held. Collective defense, of the kind that would ensure action without unanimity among the contracting parties—a system "of the Locarno type"—seemed most reasonable to him. These points, in broad outline, were those presented by him and Churchill.

The United States had from the beginning dismissed the viability of a partition solution. Dulles' public position in his major speech of March 29 that Communist control even of part of Indochina would merely be the prelude to total domination was fully supported in private by both State and Defense. Nevertheless, the Government early recognized the possibility that partition, however distasteful, might be agreed to among the French and Communist negotiators. As a result, on May 5, the Defense Department drew up a settlement plan that included provision for a territorial division. As little of Vietnam as possible should be yielded, Defense argued, with the demarcation line fixed in the north and "defined by some defensible geographic boundary (i.e., the Red or Black Rivers, or the Annamite Mountains). . . . ." In accord with the French position that evolved from the meeting of Mendès-France's cabinet on June 24, Defense urged provision for a Vietnamese enclave in the Hanoi–Haiphong area or, alternatively, internationalization of the port facilities there. Fairly well convinced, however, that partition would be fragile, Defense also called for "sanctions" against any form of Communist aggression in Laos, Cambodia, or Thailand, and for allied agreement to united action in the event the Communists violated a cease-fire by conducting subversive activities in the non-Communist area of Vietnam.

The Defense proposal amounted to containing the Communist forces above the 20th parallel while denying them sovereign access to the sea. This position went much further than that of the French, who also favored a demarcation line geared to military requirements but were willing to settle on roughly the 18th parallel. Moreover, when the five-power military staff conference met in Washington in early June, it reported (on the 9th) that a line midway between the 17th and 18th parallels (from Thakhek in Laos westward to Dong Hoi on the north Vietnam seacoast) would be defensible in the event partition came about. [Doc. 61] Undercutting the Defense plan still further was the French disposition to yield on an enclave in the Hanoi–Haiphong area were the Viet Minh to press for their own enclave in southern Vietnam. As Chauvel told U. Alexis Johnson, should the choice come to a trade-off of enclaves or a straight territorial division, the French preferred the latter. [Doc. 62] Thus, by mid-June, a combination of circumstances made it evident to the Administration that some more flexible position on the location of the partition line would have to be, and could be, adopted.

American acceptance of partition as a workable arrangement put Washington and London on even terms. Similarly, on the matter of an overall security "umbrella" for Southeast Asia, the two allies also found common ground. While the United States found "Locarno" an unfortunate term, the Government did not dispute the need to establish a vigorous defense mechanism capable of acting despite objections by one or more members. It will be recalled that the NSC Planning Board, on May 19, had outlined three possible regional groupings dependent upon the nature and timing of a settlement at Geneva. Now, in late June, circumstances dictated the advisability of concentrating on the "Group 2" formula, in which the UK, the United States, Pakistan, Thailand, the Philippines, Australia, and New Zealand would participate but not France (unless it was decided that the pact would apply to Indochina). The concerned states would exchange information, act as a united front against Communism, provide actual assistance to Asian members against external attack or "Communist insurrection," and make use of Asian facilities and/or forces in their defense assistance program.

American planning for what was to become SEATO evinced concern, however, about the commitment of American forces in cases of Communist infiltration and subversion. As the Planning Board's paper notes, the role of the United States and other countries should be limited to support of the country requesting assistance; *Asian* member nations would be expected to "contribute facilities and, if possible, at least token military contingents." The Board's paper did not represent a final policy statement; but it did reflect American reluctance, particularly on the part of the President and the Joint Chiefs, to have American forces drawn into the kind of local conflict the Administration had steered clear of in Vietnam. On this question of limiting the Western commitment, the British, to judge from their hostility toward involvement against the Viet Minh, were also in general agreement.

Aside from partition and regional security, a basis also existed for agreement to assisting the French in their diplomatic work by the device of some carefully

worded warning to the Communists. The British, before as well as after Dienbienphu, were firmly against issuing threats to the Communists that involved
military consequences. When united action had first been broached, London rejected raising the threat of a naval blockade and carrying it out if the Chinese
continued to assist the Viet Minh. Again, when united action came up in private
U.S.–French discussions during May, the British saw no useful purpose in seeking to influence discussions at Geneva by making it known to the Communists
that united action would follow a breakdown in negotiations. The situation was
different now. Instead of threatening direct military action, London and Washington apparently agreed, the West could profit from an open-ended warning
tied to a lack of progress at Geneva. When Eden addressed the House of Commons on June 23 prior to emplaning for Washington, he said: "It should be
clear to all that the hopes of agreement [at Geneva] would be jeopardized if
active military operations in Indochina were to be intensified while negotiations
for an armistice are proceeding at Geneva. If this reminder is needed, I hope
that it may be heeded." Eden was specifically thinking of a renewed Viet Minh
offensive in the Delta, but was not saying what might happen once negotiations
were placed in jeopardy.

This type of warning was sounded again at the conclusion of the Anglo-
American talks, and encouragement for it came from Paris. In the same aide-
memoire of June 26 in which the French Government had requested that the
United States counsel Saigon against a violent reaction to partition, Washington
was also urged to join with London in a declaration. The declaration would
"state in some fashion or other that, if it is not possible to reach a reasonable
settlement at the Geneva Conference, a serious aggravation of international relations would result. . . ." [Doc. 66] The French suggestion was acted upon.
Eisenhower and Churchill issued a statement on June 29 that "if at Geneva
the French Government is confronted with demands which prevent an acceptable agreement regarding Indochina, the international situation will be seriously
aggravated." In retrospect, the statement may have had an important bearing on
the Communists' negotiating position—a point to which we shall return subsequently.

The joint statement referred to "an acceptable agreement," and indeed the
ramifications of that phrase constituted the main subject of the U.S.–UK talks.
In an unpublicized agreement, the two governments concurred on a common
set of principles which, if worked into the settlement terms, would enable both
to "respect" the armistice. These principles, known subsequently as the Seven
Points, were communicated to the French. As reported by Eden, they were:

(1) Preservation of the integrity and independence of Laos and Cambodia,
and assurance of Viet Minh withdrawal from those countries

(2) Preservation of at least the southern half of Vietnam, and if possible an
enclave in the Delta, with the line of demarcation no further south than
one running generally west from Dong Hoi

(3) No restrictions on Laos, Cambodia, or retained Vietnam "materially impairing their capacity to maintain stable non-Communist regimes; and
especially restrictions impairing their right to maintain adequate forces
for internal security, to import arms and to employ foreign advisers"

(4) No "political provisions which would risk loss of the retained area to
Communist control"

(5) No provision that would "exclude the possibility of the ultimate reunification of Vietnam by peaceful means"

(6) Provision for "the peaceful and humane transfer, under international supervision, of those people desiring to be moved from one zone to another of Vietnam"

(7) Provision for "effective machinery for international supervision of the agreement."

The Seven Points represented something of an American diplomatic victory when viewed in the context of the changed Administration position on partition. While any loss of territory to the Communists predetermined the official American attitude toward the settlement—Eden was told the United States would almost certainly be unable to guarantee it—the terms agreed upon with the British were sufficiently hard that, if pushed through by the French, they would bring about a tolerable arrangement for Indochina. The sticking point for Washington lay not in the terms but in the unlikelihood that the British, any more than the French, would actually stand by them against the Communists. Thus, Dulles wrote: ". . . we have the distinct impression that the British look upon this [memorandum of the Seven Points] merely as an optimum solution and that they would not encourage the French to hold out for a solution as good as this." The Secretary observed that the British, during the talks, were unhappy about finding Washington ready only to "respect" the final terms reached at Geneva. They had preferred a stronger word, yet they "wanted to express these 7 points merely as a 'hope' without any indication of firmness on our part." The United States, quite aside from what was said in the Seven Points, "would not want to be associated in any way with a settlement which fell materially short of the 7 point memorandum." [Doc. 70] Thus, the seven points, while having finally bound the United States and Great Britain to a common position on the conference, did not allay Washington's anxiety over British and French readiness to conclude a less-than-satisfactory settlement. The possibility of a unilateral American withdrawal from the conference was still being "given consideration," Dulles reported, even as the Seven Points were agreed upon.

Despite reservations about our Allies' adherence to the Seven Points, the United States still hoped to get French approval of them. On July 6, Dillon telegraphed the French reaction as given him by Parodi, the secretary-general of the cabinet. With the exception of Point 5, denoting national elections, the French were in agreement. They were confused about an apparent conflict between the elections provision and Point 4, under which political provisions, which would include elections, were not to risk loss of retained Vietnam. In addition, they, too, felt American agreement merely to "respect" any agreement was too weak a term, and requested clarification of its meaning.

Dulles responded the next day (July 7) to both matters. Points 4 and 5 were not in conflict, he said. It was quite possible that an agreement in line with the Seven Points might still not prevent Indochina from going Communist. The important thing, therefore, was to arrange for national elections in a way that would give the South Vietnamese a liberal breathing spell:

. . . since undoubtedly true that elections might eventually mean unification Vietnam under Ho Chi Minh this makes it all more important they should be only held as long after cease-fire agreement as possible and in conditions free from intimidation to give democratic elements [in South Vietnam] best chance. We believe important that no date should be set now and especially that no conditions should be accepted by French which would have direct or indirect effect of preventing effective international supervision of agreement ensuring political as well as military guarantees.

And so far as "respect" of that agreement was concerned, the United States and Britain meant they "would not oppose a settlement which conformed to Seven Points. . . . It does not of course mean we would guarantee such settlement or that we would necessarily support it publicly. We consider 'respect' as strong a word as we can possibly employ in the circumstances. . . . 'Respect' would also mean that we would not seek directly or indirectly to upset settlement by force." *

Dulles' clarification of the American position on elections in Vietnam, together with his delimitation of the nation's obligation towards a settlement, did not satisfy the French completely but served the important purpose of enlightening them as to American intentions. Placed beside the discussions with Eden and Churchill, the thrust of American diplomacy at this time clearly was to leave no question in the minds of our allies as to what we considered the elements in a reasonable Indochina settlement and what we would likely do once a settlement were achieved.

VII.   TOWARD A SETTLEMENT: THE LAST THIRTY DAYS

A.   THE BARGAINING CONTINUES

While the French and British pondered the implications of the Seven Points, bargaining continued behind the scenes against a background of further military advance by the Viet Minh. At about the same time the Viet Minh made their first specific partition proposal, their forces in the field completed their deployment from the Dienbienphu area. By mid-June, according to American intelligence, the Viet Minh were believed prepared for a massive attack in the Delta. Another report spoke of their renewed attention to southern Annam and of an apparent buildup of military strength there. Not surprisingly in light of these developments, the Viet Minh, in late June, responded to the French proposal of a division at the 18th parallel with a plan for a line in southern Annam running northwest from the 13th to the 14th parallel, i.e., from Tuy Hoa on the coast through Pleiku to the Cambodian border. Moreover, in secret talks with the French, the Viet Minh's vice-minister for national defense, Ta Quang Buu, also insisted on French withdrawal from the Delta within two months of a cease-fire, in contrast to French demands for a four-month interval. [Doc. 69] As suggested by Lacouture and Devillers, the Viet Minh may have been seeking to capitalize not only on their improved military position in the Delta, where French Union forces were still in retreat, but also on Mendès-France's reputation as a man of peace obviously desirous of a settlement.

This resurgence of Viet Minh toughness on terms for a cessation of hostilities applied also to Laos and Cambodia. In the military staff conferences that had begun separately on those two countries in late June, no progress was made. The Viet Minh indicated, in the Laotian case, that they had already withdrawn; if forces opposing the royal government remained (as in fact some 15,000 did), negotiations with the resistance groups would have to be undertaken. Thus, de-

---

* Dulles to American Embassy, Paris, tel. No. 77, July 7. 1954 (Secret). [Doc. 64] Regarding the U.S. view of a Ho Chi Minh electoral victory, we not only have the well-known comment of Eisenhower that Ho, at least in early 1954, would have garnered 80 percent of the vote. (See *Mandate for Change* [Garden City, New York: Doubleday], pp. 337–38.) In addition, there is a Department of State memorandum of conversation of May 31, 1954, in which Livingston Merchant reportedly "recognized the possibility that in Viet Nam Ho might win a plebiscite, if held today."

spite Chou En-lai's claim that Viet Minh withdrawal from Laos and Cambodia could easily be accomplished, the Viet Minh were hardly ready to move out unless they received substantial guarantees (such as a permanent regroupment area), which the royal governments refused to give.

Whether because of or in spite of Viet Minh intransigence, the Chinese forcefully made known their earnest desire to keep the conference moving. In an important encounter at Bern on June 23, Chou En-lai several times emphasized to Mendès-France that the main thing was a cease-fire, on which he hoped progress could be made before all the heads of delegation returned to Geneva. Regarding Laos and Cambodia, Chou thought regroupment areas for the insurgents would be necessary, but reiterated that national unity was the affair of the royal governments; he hoped the resistance elements might find a place in the national life of their respective countries. Chou told the French premier, as he had told Eden previously, that no American bases could be permitted in those countries; yet Chou spoke sympathetically of the French Union. Turning finally to the Viet Minh, Chou urged that direct contact be established between them and the Vietnamese. He promised that for his part, he would see that the Viet Minh were thoroughly prepared for serious discussions on a military settlement. Clearly, the Chinese were far more interested in moving forward toward a cease-fire than were their Viet Minh counterparts.

Even though the Viet Minh were making demands that the French, Cambodians, and Laotians could not accept, the debate was narrowing to specifics. The question when national elections in Vietnam should be held is illustrative. The Viet Minh did not budge from their insistence that elections occur six months after the cease-fire. But the French, attempting to make some headway in the talks, retreated from insistence on setting no date (a position the Vietnamese had supported) and offered to hold elections 18 months after completion of the regroupment process, or between 22 and 23 months after the cessation of hostilities. [Doc. 69] The French now admitted that while they still looked forward to retaining Haiphong and the Catholic bishoprics as long as possible, perhaps in some neutral environment, total withdrawal from the north would probably be necessary to avoid cutting up Vietnam into enclaves. [Doc. 66] But partition in any manner faced the French with hostile Vietnamese, and it was for this reason that Chauvel not only suggested American intervention to induce Vietnamese self-control, but also received Pham Van Dong's approval, in a conversation July 6, to having the military commands rather than governments sign the final armistice so as to avoid having to win Vietnamese consent. As Ngo Dinh Diem, who became prime minister June 18, suspected, the French were prepared to pull out of Tonkin as part of the cease-fire arrangements.

On the matter of control and supervision, the debate also became more focused even as the gulf between opposing views remained wide. The chief points of contention were, as before, the composition and authority of the neutral supervisory body; but the outlines of an acceptable arrangement were beginning to form. Thus, on composition, the Communist delegations, in early July, began speaking in terms of an odd-numbered (three or five) neutral commission chaired by India, with pro-Communist and pro-Western governments equally sharing the remaining two or four places. Second, on the powers of that body, dispute persisted as to whether it would have separate but parallel authority with the joint commissions or supreme authority; whether and on what questions it would make judgments by unanimous vote; and whether it would (as the French proposed) be empowered to issue majority and minority reports in case of disagreement. These were all fundamental issues, but the important point is that the

Communist side refused to consider them irremovable obstacles to agreement. As Molotov's understudy, Kuznetsov (the deputy foreign minister), put it, the Soviet and French proposals on control and supervision revealed "rapprochement in the points of view on certain questions. It is true with respect to the relationships between the mixed commission and the international supervisory commission. This rapprochement exists also in regard to the question of the examination of the functions and duties of the commission. . . ." In fact, a "rapprochement" did not exist; but the Soviets, interestingly, persisted in their optimism that a solution could be found.

B.   CHINESE DIPLOMACY

While the negotiations went on among the second-string diplomats, a different kind of diplomacy was being carried on elsewhere. Chou En-lai, en route to Peking, advanced Communist China's effort, actually begun in late 1952, to woo its Asian neighbors with talk of peaceful coexistence. This diplomatic offensive, which was to have an important bearing on the outcome at Geneva, had borne its first fruit in April 1954, when Chou reached agreement with Nehru over Tibet. At that time, the Chinese first introduced the "five principles" they vowed to follow in their relations with other nations. The five principles are: mutual respect for territorial integrity and sovereignty, nonaggression, noninterference in internal affairs, equality and mutual benefit, and peaceful coexistence.

Chou's first stopover was in New Delhi, the scene of his initial success. On June 28 he and Nehru reaffirmed the five principles and expressed the hope that a peaceful settlement in Indochina would be concluded in conformity with them. Similar sentiments appeared in a joint statement from Rangoon, scene of talks with Prime Minister U Nu. Promises were exchanged, moreover, for the maintenance of close contact between China and Burma, and support was voiced for the right of countries having different social systems to coexist without interference from outside. "Revolution cannot be exported," the joint statement proclaimed; "at the same time outside interference with the common will expressed by the people of any nation should not be permitted."

Peking made full use of these diplomatic achievements by contrasting them with the American policy of ruthless expansionism, which Peking said was carried out by Washington under the label of opposing Communism. Peking proclaimed that the era of colonialism which the United States was seeking to perpetuate in Indochina had come to en end. "A new era has dawned in which Asian countries can coexist peacefully and establish friendly relations on the basis of respect for each other's territorial integrity and sovereignty and mutual nonaggression," said *Jen-min jih-pao.* Another newspaper, *Kuang-ming jih-pao,* offered similar testimony to the inspirational effect of the Sino-Indian and Sino-Burmese agreements, considering them to conform to the interests of all Asian peoples. The daily castigated the American "policy of strength" as being totally incompatible with the five principles. Clearly, China was exploiting its gains through diplomacy not simply to acquire Asian support (and thus detract from pro-Westernism in the region), but more broadly to muster recognition for China as the leading Asian power in the fight against "imperialism" and "colonialism."

Chou's diplomatic efforts took a different turn, it seems, when he met with Ho Chi Minh at Nanning, on the Sino-Vietnamese frontier, from July 3–5. Although the final communique merely stated that the two leaders "had a full exchange of views on the Geneva Conference with respect to the question of the restoration of peace in Indochina and related questions," it subsequently appeared that much more may have taken place. According to observers in Hong Kong, Chou pressed for the meeting out of fear that the Viet Minh might engage in intensified military action that would destroy chances for an armistice and upset China's budding role as an Asian peacemaker. Conceivably, Chou sought to persuade Ho that his territorial gains were about as much as he could expect at that juncture without risking an end to negotiations and renewed American attempts to forge a military alliance for intervention. To judge from the Viet Minh reaction to the talks, Ho was not completely satisfied with Chou's proposed tactics.

Momentarily leaving aside Chou's motivations, it is vital to note the impact of the talks on the Geneva negotiations. On July 9, Chauvel dined with Li K'e-nung and Chang Wen-t'ien, a vice-minister for foreign affairs and CPR ambassador to the Soviet Union. Chauvel opened the conversation—as he later recounted to Johnson—by complaining that discussions with the Viet Minh were not going well, that Viet Minh demands were exorbitant and well beyond Chou En-lai's stated position. The Chinese delegates evinced surprise but said nothing in direct reply. However, Chang did report that Chou had had a "very good meeting" with Ho Chi Minh, the results of which "would be helpful to French." Chauvel received the impression—one which seems, in retrospect, to have been accurate—that the Viet Minh had been given a free hand by the Soviets and Chinese up to the point where their demands were unacceptable to the French, at which time the Soviets and/or Chinese felt compelled to intervene. [Doc. 66] If such was the case, Chou's talk with Ho, coming after Mendès-France and his negotiators showed no sign of being more compromising than their predecessors, Laniel and Bidault, may have been intended to inform the Viet Minh that the "point" had been reached and that they had to soften their demands if a settlement were ever to be attained.

C.   THE FRANCO-AMERICAN UNDERSTANDING

Precisely how Chou's stopover in Nanning would be "helpful" to the French did not become apparent until four days after Chauvel's conversation with Li and Chang. By that time, the French had been engaged in intensive conversations with the Americans, the aim of which was to convince Washington that the United States, to be truly influential at the conference—to realize, in other words, a settlement in line with the Seven Points—had to back the French with a high-level representative in Geneva. Unless the United States did more than offer its views from afar on an acceptable settlement, Mendès-France argued, France could not be expected to present a strong front when Molotov and Chou resumed their places. As though to prove his determination to stand fast against Communist demands, Mendès-France told Ambassador Dillon in Paris that if a cease-fire was not agreed to by July 20, the premier would approve the dispatch of conscripts to Indochina and would introduce a law into Parliament to that effect on July 21. His government would not resign until that law passed; the ships would be prepared to transport the conscripts to Indochina beginning July 25. [Doc. 62]

Despite Mendès-France's willingness to establish a deadline and, for the first time in the history of French involvement in Indochina, to conscript soldiers for service there, Washington remained opposed to upgrading its Geneva delegation. Sensitive as much to any proposal that might implicate the United States in the final settlement terms as to Mendès-France's difficulties at the conference table, Dulles believed the French would end by accepting a settlement unsatisfactory to the United States whether or not the USDEL were upgraded. As he explained to Dillon, were he (the Secretary) or Smith to return to Geneva only to find the French compelled to negotiate an unacceptable agreement anyway, the United States would be required to dissociate itself in a manner "which would be deeply resented by the French as an effort on our part to block at the last minute a peace which they ardently desire," with possible "irreparable injury to Franco-American relations. . . ." The least embarrassing alternative, Dulles felt, was to avoid the probability of having to make a "spectacular disassociation" by staying away from the conference altogether. [Doc. 65]

When Dulles' position was reported to Mendès-France, the premier said he understood the Americans' reluctance but considered it misplaced. The American fear of in some way becoming committed to the settlement, he said, was precisely his dilemma, for he had no idea what the Communists would propose in the crucial days ahead. The French negotiating position *was* the Seven Points, he went on, and would not deviate substantially from them. With great feeling, Mendès-France told a member of the American Embassy that the presence of Dulles or Smith was "absolutely essential and necessary"; without either of them, the Communists would sense and seek to capitalize on a lack of unity in the allied camp. "Mendès indicated that our high-level presence at Geneva had direct bearing on where Communists would insist on placing line of demarcation or partition in Vietnam."

These arguments did not prove convincing to Washington. On July 10, Dulles wrote Mendès-France a personal message reiterating that his or General Smith's presence would serve no useful purpose. And Dulles again raised doubts that France, Britain, and the United States were really agreed on a single negotiating position:

> What now concerns us is that we are very doubtful as to whether there is a united front in relation to Indochina, and we do not believe that the mere fact that the high representatives of the three nations physically reappear together at Geneva will serve as a substitute for a clear agreement on a joint position which includes agreement as to what will happen if that position is not accepted by the Communists. We fear that unless there is the reality of such a united front, the events at Geneva will expose differences under conditions which will only serve to accentuate them with consequent strain upon the relations between our two countries greater than if the US does not reappear at Geneva, in the person of General Smith or myself. [Doc. 67]

The Secretary questioned whether the Seven Points truly represented a common "minimum acceptable solution" which the three Allies were willing to fight for in the event the Communists rejected them. Charging that the Seven Points were actually "merely an optimum solution" for Paris no less than for London, Dulles sought to demonstrate that the French were already moving away from the Seven Points. He cited apparent French willingness to permit Communist forces to remain in northern Laos, to accept a demarcation line "considerably south of Donghoi," to neutralize and demilitarize Laos and Cambodia, and to permit "elections so early and so ill-prepared and ill-supervised as to risk the loss of the entire area to Communism" as evidences of a "whittling-away process" which, cumulatively, could destroy the intent of the Seven Points. [Doc. 67] Unquestionably, the Secretary's firm opposition to restoring to the American delegation its high rank was grounded in intense suspicion of an ultimate French sell-out, yet suspicion based on apparent misinformation concerning both the actual French position and the degree of French willingness to stand firm.

Thus believing that the French had already gone far toward deflating some of the major provisions of the U.S.–UK memorandum, Dulles reiterated the Administration's position that it had the right "not to endorse a solution which would seem to us to impair seriously certain principles which the US believes must, as far as it is concerned, be kept unimpaired, if our own struggle against Communism is to be successfully pursued." Perhaps seeking to rationalize the impact of his rejection, Dulles wrote in closing that the American decision might actually assist the French: "If our conduct creates a certain uncertainty in the minds of the Communists, this might strengthen your hand more than our presence at Geneva. . . ." [Doc. 67] Mendès-France had been rebuffed, however, and while Dulles left the door slightly ajar for his or Smith's return if "circumstances" should change, it seemed more probable that France would have to work for a settlement with only the British along side.

The Dulles–Mendès-France exchanges were essentially an exercise in credibility, with the French premier desperately seeking to persuade the Secretary that Paris really did support and really would abide by the Seven Points. When Mendès-France read Dulles' letter, he protested that France would accept nothing unacceptable to the United States, and went so far as to say that Dulles' presence at the conference would give him a veto power, in effect, on the decisions taken. Beyond that, Mendès-France warned of the catastrophic impact of an American withdrawal on the American position in Europe no less than in the Far East; withdrawal, he said, was sure to be interpreted as a step toward isolationism. Asked what alternative his government had in mind if the conference failed even with an American high-level presence, Mendès-France replied there would have to be full internationalization of the war.*

Mendès-France's persistence was sufficiently persuasive to move Dulles, on July 13, to fly to Paris to document the premier's support of the Seven Points. On the 14th, the Secretary and the premier signed a memorandum which duplicated that agreed to by the United States and Great Britain. In addition, a position paper was drawn up the same day reiterating that the United States was at the conference as "a friendly nation" whose role was subordinate to that of the primary non-Communist parties, the Associated States and France. The Seven Points were described, as they had been some two weeks earlier, as those acceptable to the "primarily interested nations" and which the United States could "respect." However, should terms ultimately be concluded which differed markedly from the Seven Points, France agreed that the United States would neither be asked nor expected to accept them, and "may publicly disassociate itself from such differing terms" by a unilateral or multilateral statement.

One of Dulles' objections had been that a true united front did not exist so long as agreement was lacking on allied action in the event of no settlement. On this point, too, the French were persuaded to adopt the American position. In the event of a settlement, it was agreed in the position paper that the United States would "seek, with other interested nations, a collective defense association

---

* Dillon from Paris priority tel. No. 134, July 11, 1954. [Doc. 68] The same day, Mendès-France had told Dillon again of France's intention to send conscripts, with parliamentary approval, by July 25, with two divisions ready for action by about September 15. The premier said that while he could not predict how the Assembly would react, he personally saw the need for direct American involvement in the war once negotiations broke down and the conscripts were sent. Dillon from Paris priority tel. No. 133, July 11, 1954.

designed to preserve, against direct and indirect aggression, the integrity of the non-Communist areas of Southeast Asia. . . ." Should no settlement be forth-coming, U.S.–France consultations would take place; but these would not pre-clude the United States from bringing "the matter" before the UN as a threat to the peace. Previous obstacles to French objections to UN involvement were nonexistent, for France reaffirmed in the position paper its commitment under the June 4 treaty of independence with Vietnam that Saigon, as well as Vientiane and Phnom Penh, was an "equal and voluntary" partner in the French Union, and hence no longer subject in its foreign policy to French *diktat*.

On all but one matter, now, the United States and France were in complete accord on a negotiating strategy. That matter was, of course, the American delegation. Mendès-France had formally subscribed to the Seven Points and had agreed to American plans for dealing with the aftermath of the conference; yet he had gained nothing for the French delegation. Writing to the Secretary, the premier pointed out again:

> In effect, I have every reason to think that your absence would be precisely interpreted as demonstrating, before the fact, that you disapproved of the conference and of everything which might be accomplished. Not only would those who are against us find therein the confirmation of the ill will which they attribute to your government concerning the reestablishment of peace in Indochina; but many others would read in it a sure sign of a divi-sion of the western powers. [Doc. 70]

Once more, Mendès-France was putting forth the view that a high-level Ameri-can representation at the conference would do more to ensure a settlement in conformity with the Seven Points than private U.S.–French agreement to them.

For reasons not entirely clear, but perhaps the consequence of Eisenhower's personal intervention, Mendès-France's appeal was now favorably received in Washington. Dulles was able to inform the premier on July 14: "In the light of what you say and after consultation with President Eisenhower, I am glad to be able to inform you that the President and I are asking the Under Secretary of State, General Walter Bedell Smith, to prepare to return at his earliest con-venience to Geneva to share in the work of the conference on the basis of the understanding which we have arrived at." [Doc. 70] For the first time since late 1953, the United States and France were solidly joined in a common front on Indochina policy.

In accordance with the understandings reached with France, Smith was sent new instructions on July 16 based upon the Seven Points. After reiterating the passive formal role the United States was to play at the conference, Dulles in-formed his Under Secretary he was to issue a unilateral (or, if possible, multi-lateral) statement should a settlement be reached that "conforms substantially" to the Seven Points. "The United States will not, however, become cosignatory with the Communists in any Declaration," Dulles wrote with reference to the procedure then being discussed at Geneva of drafting military accords and a final declaration on a political settlement. Nor should the United States, Smith's in-structions went on, be put in a position where it could be held responsible for guaranteeing the results of the conference. Smith's efforts should be directed, Dulles summed up, toward forwarding ideas to the "active negotiators," France, Cambodia, Laos, and Vietnam.

This last point of guidance referred to the possibility of a breakdown in the negotiations. Should no settlement be reached, the United States delegation was to avoid permitting the French to believe that outcome was the result of American advice or pressure, and that in some way the United States was morally obligated to intervene militarily in Indochina. The United States, Dulles wrote, was "not prepared at the present time to give any commitment that it will intervene in the war if the Geneva Conference fails. . . ." While this stricture almost certainly reflected the President's and the Joint Chiefs' extreme reluctance to become committed, in advance, to a war already past the point of return, it was also doubtless a reaction to Mendès-France's intimations to Dillon of French willingness to reconsider active American involvement if the conference failed.

With French and British adherence to the Seven Points promised by written agreement, the United States had gone about as far as it could toward ensuring an acceptable settlement without becoming tied to it. The Administration still apparently believed that the final terms would violate the Seven Points in several significant respects;* but by making clear in advance that *any* settlement would be met with a unilateral American declaration rather than Bedell Smith's signature, the United States had at least guaranteed its retention of a moral advantage, useful particularly in placating domestic public opinion. In the event of an unsatisfactory settlement, Washington would be in a position to say that it had stood steadfastly by principle only to be undercut by "soft" Allies and Communist territorial ambitions.

D. THE FINAL WEEK OF BARGAINING

Prior to Smith's return, positions had tended to harden rather than change at Geneva, although the Viet Minh had yielded a trifle on partition. Chang Wen-t'ien's encouraging remark to Chauvel of July 9 had been fulfilled four days later, as already indicated. The final signal was Chou's comment to Mendès-France on the 13th that both sides, French and Viet Minh, had to make concessions on the demarcation problem, but that this "does not signify that each must take the same number of steps." That same day, Pham Van Dong told the French premier the Viet Minh were willing to settle on the 16th parallel.

Dong's territorial concession meant little to the French, however, and, as the negotiations continued, it became plain that the Viet Minh were not concerned about Mendès-France's July 20 deadline. Yet the Chinese remained optimistic, at least publicly. *Jen-min jih-pao*'s Geneva reporter, for instance, wrote July 12 that while no solution had yet been worked out on the control and supervision problem, "there seems no reason why agreement cannot be reached." As for defining the regroupment areas, the correspondent asserted that "speedy agreement would seem probable after the return of the Foreign Ministers of the Big Powers. . . ." So long as all parties were "sincere," he wrote, agreement would indeed come about.

The minuscule progress made on settling the Vietnam problem loomed large in

---

* Thus, on July 15 (one day *after* the Franco-American agreements), the National Security Council, after being briefed on the Geneva situation, decided that the likely settlement would go against the Seven Points. The NSC was told the Communists would: (1) seek partition of Vietnam somewhere between the 14th and 18th parallels; (2) demand control of some part of Laos, neutralization of the remainder, and agreement on the formation of a coalition government; (3) ask neutralization of Cambodia and some form of recognition for the Free Khmer movement. Were the Communists to accept the Dong Hoi line for Vietnam, they would then demand an enclave in southern Vietnam plus part of Laos, or simply extend the Dong Hoi line through Laos.

comparison with the seemingly unbreakable log jam that had developed over Laos and Cambodia. Since the major Communist concessions of mid-June, which had at least paved the way for separating Laos and Cambodia from Vietnam for discussion purposes, virtually nothing had been accomplished toward cease-fires. Debate on Laos and Cambodia occupied the spotlight again on July 9 when, from the remarks of the Chinese delegate (Li K'e-nung), it quickly became apparent that for all their willingness to discuss the withdrawal of Viet Minh troops, the Chinese remained greatly concerned about possible Laotian and Cambodian rearmament and alignment. Simply put, the Chinese were negotiating for their own security, not for Viet Minh territorial advantage.

As Chou had pointed out to Eden in June, the CPR's major concern was that Cambodia and Laos might, after a settlement, be left free to negotiate for a permanent American military presence. In his presentation, therefore, Li K'e-nung insisted that the two countries not be permitted to acquire fresh troops, military personnel, arms, and ammunition except as might be strictly required for self-defense; nor should they, he held, allow foreign military bases to be established. Li formalized Chou's passing remark to Eden that China was not much disturbed by French Union (as opposed to American) technicians. Li allowed that French military personnel to assist the training of the Laotian and Cambodian armies was a matter that "can be studied."

The Cambodian case, presented by Foreign Minister Sam Sary, revealed a stubborn independence that was to assist the country greatly in the closing days of the conference. Sam Sary said that foreign bases would indeed not be authorized on Khmer soil "only as far as there is no menace against Cambodia. . . . If our security is imperiled, Cambodia will keep its legitimate right to defend itself by all means." As for foreign instructors and technicians, his government wished to retain those Frenchmen then in Cambodia; he was pleased to note Li K'e-nung's apparent acceptance of this arrangement. Finally, with regard to the importation of arms, Sam Sary differentiated between a limitation on quantity (which his government accepted) and on quality (which his government wished to have a free hand in determining).

While the Chinese publicly castigated the Cambodians for working with the Americans to threaten "the security of Cambodia's neighboring countries under the pretext of self-defense," the Americans gave the Cambodians encouragement. In Washington, Phnom Penh's ambassador, Nong Kimny, met with Dulles on July 10. Nong Kimny said his Government would oppose the neutralization and demilitarization of the country; Dulles replied that hopefully Cambodia would become a member of the collective security arrangement envisaged in American-British plans. Cambodia, the Secretary said, possessed a kind of independence superior to that in Vietnam and Laos, and as such should indeed oppose Communist plans to neutralize and demilitarize her. As an independent state, Cambodia was entitled to seek outside military and economic assistance.

The Laotian delegation was also experiencing difficulties, though with the Viet Minh rather than the Chinese. The Viet Minh negotiators, in the military command conferences, insisted on making extraneous demands concerning the Pathet Lao. The Laotians were concerned not so much with the demands as with the possibility of a private French deal with the Viet Minh that would subvert the Laotian position. A member of the royal government's delegation went to Johnson to be assured that a behind-the-scenes deal would not occur. The delegate said Laos hoped to be covered by and to participate in a Southeast Asia collective security pact. Johnson did not guarantee that this arrangement could be worked out; but as the conference drew to a close, as we shall see, the United

States made it clear to the Cambodians and Laotians that their security would in some fashion be taken care of under the SEATO treaty.

Irresolution over Cambodia and Laos, a continuing wide gap between French and Viet Minh positions on the partition line, and no progress on the control and supervision dilemma were the highlights of the generally dismal scene that greeted General Smith on his return July 16 to the negotiating wars. Smith apparently took heart, however, in the steadfastness of Mendès-France, although the Under Secretary also observed that the Communists had reacted to this by themselves becoming unmoving. Smith attributed Communist intransigence to the probability that "Mendès-France has been a great disappointment to the Communists both as regards the relatively firm position he has taken on Indochina and his attitude toward EDC. They may therefore wish to force him out of the government by making settlement here impossible."

Actually, what had disturbed the Communists most was not so much Mendès-France's firmness as Smith's return. That became clear following a private meeting requested by a member of the CPR delegation, Huang Hua, with Seymour Topping, the *New York Times* correspondent at Geneva. Topping, as the Chinese must have expected, reported the conversation to the American delegation. He said Huang Hua, speaking in deadly earnest and without propagandistic overtones, had interpreted Smith's return as an American attempt to prevent a settlement. Indeed, according to Huang Hua, the Paris talks between Dulles and Mendès-France on July 13 and 14 had been primarily responsible for Mendès-France's stubbornness; the French premier had obviously concluded a deal with the United States in which he agreed to raise the price for a settlement. [Doc. 78]

Overt Chinese statements in this period lent credence to Topping's report. First, Peking was far from convinced that continued discussions on the restoration of peace in Indochina removed the possibility of dramatic new military moves by the United States. Washington was accused, as before the conference, of desiring to intervene in Indochina so as to extend the war there into "a new military venture on China's southern borders. In support of this contention, Peking cited such provocative moves as trips during April and June by General James A. Van Fleet ("the notorious butcher of the Korean War") to Korea, Japan, and Taiwan, for the purpose of establishing a North Pacific military alliance; American intentions of concluding a mutual defense treaty with Taiwan as the first step in Chiang Kai-shek's invasion plans; American efforts, through the five-power and later Eisenhower-Churchill talks, to create a Southeast Asia alliance for a military thrust into Indochina; and stepped-up U.S. military assistance, including training, for the Thai armed forces.

Second, Peking was clearly disturbed that the French were still heeding American advice when the path to a settlement lay before them. In a *People's Daily* editorial of July 14, for instance, the French people and National Assembly were said to be strongly desirous of peace. Thus: "A policy running counter to French interests cannot work. France is a major world power. She should have her own independent and honorable path. This means following an independent foreign policy consistent with French national interests and the interests of world peace." The American alternative—a Southeast Asia coalition with French participation—should be rejected, the editorial intoned, and a settlement conforming to the five principles achieved instead. In keeping with its line of previous months, Peking was attempting to demonstrate—for Asian no less than for French ears —that it had a keen interest in resolving the Indochina problem rather than seeing the conference give way to new American military pressures and a possibly wider war.

Finally, Peking paid considerable attention to Dulles' stay in Paris and to his dispatch of Smith to Geneva. Dulles' sudden trip to the French capital was said to reveal American determination to obstruct progress in the negotiations by pressuring Mendès-France not to grasp the settlement that lay just around the corner. Dulles originally had no intention of upgrading the American delegation, according to Peking. "But Bedell Smith had to be sent back to Geneva because of strong criticism in the Western press, and Washington was fearful lest agreement could be reached quickly despite American boycotting of the conference." Yet China's optimism over a settlement did not diminish: "Chinese delegation circles," NCNA reported, "see no reason whatsoever why the Geneva Conference should play up to the U.S. policy and make no efforts towards achieving an agreement which is acceptable and satisfactory to all parties concerned and which is honorable for the two belligerent sides." If Smith's return, then, was viewed from Peking as a challenge to its diplomatic ingenuity, the Chinese (and, we may surmise, the Soviets) were prepared to accept it.

In doing so, however, the Chinese evidently were not about to sacrifice in those areas of dispute where they had a special interest, namely, Laos and Cambodia. On July 14, Chou called on Nong Kimny to state China's position. The premier said first that, in accord with his recent talks with Nehru, U Nu, and Ho Chi Minh, he could report a unanimous desire for peace in Indochina, for the unity of each of the three Associated States, and for their future cordial relationship with the Colombo Powers. Chou then asked about the status of Cambodian talks with the Viet Minh. When Nong Kimny replied that Pham Van Dong, in two recent get-togethers, had insisted on interjecting political problems into discussions of a military settlement—as by requesting Cambodia's retention of certain provincial officials appointed by the Free Khmers, and by suggesting the royal government's preservation of a Free Khmer youth movement—Chou is said to have laughed off these claims and to have replied that these were indeed matters for Cambodia to handle by herself.

Chou had his own views on what Cambodia should and should not do; however, Khmer sovereignty should not mean discrimination against the resistance elements, the establishment of foreign military bases in Cambodia, Laos, and Vietnam, or the conclusion of military alliances with other states. Chou was less adamant only on the subject of Cambodia's importation of arms and military personnel; when Nong Kimny flatly stated that Phnom Penh would absolutely reject any limitations inasmuch as these would be incompatible with Cambodian sovereignty, Chou did not contradict him. Instead, he promised to study the matter further and asked to know precisely what quantities of arms and personnel the royal government had in mind. Later on, he became a bit more flexible by saying that a prohibition on arms and personnel should apply only to the armistice period, not permanently. Only in Vietnam, Chou said, would there be a flat proscription against military equipment and troops.

Chou and Nong Kimny met again three days later, on July 17. On this occasion, Chou was obviously less conciliatory (as Nong Kimny reported), stating China's position more in terms of demands than suggestions. He urged the Cambodian government to incorporate resistance elements into the army, police, and civil service. But he reserved his emphasis for Cambodia's future security position. In a thinly-veiled warning, Chou said that should Cambodia join the pact, permit foreign bases on its territory, or accept American military instructors, "the consequences would be very serious and would aggravate the situation with unfortunate consequences for Cambodian independence and territorial integrity" (Smith's paraphrase). Cambodia could have French or British instructors, Chou said. But his three-fold limitation, obviously directed at assuring against future Cambodia–U.S. defense ties, remained—and, he added, it applied to Laos and Vietnam as well.

The Chinese were clearly out to get from the conference what they could, without Russian assistance, before a settlement was concluded. Chou did not stop at warning Nong Kimny, either. On July 17 he took his case to Eden, telling the foreign secretary that while the CPR stood ready to join in guaranteeing the freedom and independence of all three Indochinese states, membership in a Southeast Asia pact would change everything. Evidently intent on removing what he may have sensed was a possible last-minute obstacle, Eden implied that he knew of no proposal for including the United States in the pact, although he did not deny American interest in forming a defense organization for Southeast Asia. Chou said he had no objections to ANZUS (it was directed against Japan, he thought), but he went into a lengthy discourse on the danger to China of having foreign bases in Indochina.

Eden's assurances evidently did not [words illegible] Chou deeply. On July 18 Chou met with the Laotian foreign minister and presented "unofficial" but extravagant demands which the latter found totally unacceptable. Laos was willing to provide the resistance elements with [words illegible] zones in the northern provinces of Phong Saly and Sam Neua; Chou proposed, additionally, portions of Luang Prabang and Xien Khouang provinces. The royal government was further willing to concede the insurgents freedom of movement in those zones, but Chou demanded administration by joint royal-insurgent committees and a supervisory joint committee in Vientiane until the general elections of August 1955. Finally, where the Laotians thought the issue of French Union bases had been resolved in their favor, Chou now said the bases should be completely eliminated even though established by Franco-Laotian treaty.

Chou's obsession with foreign military bases and related issues led to an effort to make a settlement contingent upon Western acceptance of Chinese neutralization plans. A Chinese informant (probably Huang Hua) told Seymour Topping that Western willingness to bar foreign military bases from Indochina and to deny the Associated States admission to any military blocs would assure agreement by July 20. More than that, the informant said, the United States had also to subscribe to and guarantee the final settlement, evidently in the belief that America's signature would make Indochinese participation in SEATO illegal. [Doc. 74] A more direct statement was made by NCNA's "special correspondent" in Geneva, who drew a harsh characterization of a cease-fire agreement that left the door open to Indochinese involvement in a military alliance:

> If efforts are made at the same time negotiations for peace are taking place to drag the three Indochinese countries into an aggressive military bloc whose purpose is to unleash war, then the cease-fire would mean nothing other than a respite for adjusting battle lines and dispositions of strength in order to start the fighting again on an even larger scale. In such circumstances, the armistice agreement would become no more than a scrap of paper.

Whether the Chinese seriously believed that the United States would sign the accords in order to achieve a settlement, or that Laos and Cambodia [words missing] out of the Southeast Asia collective defense is at best debatable. There seems little doubt, however, that Peking sincerely considered a written prohibition on the accords against Indochinese alliances or foreign bases as a major step toward the neutralization of Southeast Asia and the area's eventual dissociation from the American defense system.

General Smith felt that Topping's report dovetailed with growing Communist intransigence in the past few days, particularly on the part of Molotov. He believed that Molotov, who had urgently requested a restricted session for the 18th, would likewise raise the question of explicit American acquiescence in a final settlement. [Doc. 74] When the meeting came, however, Molotov did not reiterate Huang Hua's implication that American failure to sign the accords might scuttle the conference. Perhaps aware that a warning of that kind would not work, Molotov instead limited himself to talking of the conference's achievements to date. He complimented those who had been engaged in private negotiations, and went so far as to voice confidence that a settlement of outstanding problems relating to Laos and Cambodia could be achieved. He closed by pointing out that two drafts were before the conference relating to the cessation of hostilities in Vietnam and Laos, two on Cambodia, and two on a final declaration dealing with political matters. That ended Molotov's contribution, leaving the Americans, and probably others, wondering why the Soviet foreign minister had hastily summoned the meeting. [Doc. 76]

E. AGREEMENT

If Molotov's refusal at the July 18 restricted session to warn the conference of failure signaled renewed Communist efforts toward agreement, his subsequent actions proved the point. Between July 18 and 21, the conferees were able to iron out their differences sufficiently to produce agreements now commonly referred to as the Geneva "accords." In fact, the accords consist of military agreements for Vietnam, Cambodia, and Laos to fulfill the conference's primary task of restoring peace to Indochina, and a Final Declaration designed to establish the conditions for future political settlements throughout Indochina. The nature of the eleventh-hour compromises reached, and a broad outline of the settlement, are treated below.

Vietnam

The Geneva accords temporarily established two zones of Vietnam separated by a line running roughly along the 17th parallel and further divided by a demilitarized zone. Agreement to the demarcation line was apparently the work of Molotov, who gained French acceptance of the 17th parallel when he found the French flatly opposed to the 16th, a late Viet Minh compromise perhaps prompted by Molotov himself. [Doc. 72] Precisely what motivated Molotov to make his proposal is not clear. Speculatively, he may simply have traded considerable territorial advantage which the Viet Minh enjoyed for a specific election date he, Chou, and Pham Van Dong wanted from the outset. The Western negotiators certainly recognized the trade-off possibility: Eden considered a line between the 17th and 18th parallels worth exchanging for a mutually acceptable position on elections; and Mendès-France observed in a conversation with Molotov that the election and demarcation questions might be linked in the sense that each side could yield on one of the questions. [Doc. 72]

Whether or not a trade-off actually took place, the fact remains that the French came off much better in the matter of partition than on elections, which they had insisted not be given a specific date. On July 16, Molotov had proposed holding elections in 1955, with the exact date to be decided between Vietnamese and Viet Minh authorities. [Doc. 72] The Chinese were more flexible. In a talk with a member of the British delegation, Li K'e-nung argued for a specific date, but said his government was willing to set it within two or three years of the cease-fire. [Doc. 76] The compromise formula was reportedly worked out by Molotov, who, at a meeting July 19 attended also by Eden, Mendès-France, Chou, and Dong, drew the line at two years. It was agreed in the Final Declaration that the Vietnamese of the two zones would consult together in July 1955 and reunify Vietnam by national plebiscite one year later. Importantly for the Viet Minh, the demarcation line was said to be "provisional and should not in any way be interpreted as constituting a political or territorial boundary." Representatives of the member states on the ICC would act as a commission to supervise the national elections, which were to be freely conducted by secret ballot. As shall be pointed out later, however, the evident intention of all the conferees (including the United States and the Government of South Vietnam) to see Vietnam reunified was to a large extent undercut by the nature of the military and political settlements.

The military accords on Vietnam also stipulated that the Joint Commission, which was to take over the work of the military commission that had met at Trung Gia, would have general responsibility for working out the disengagement of forces and implementation of the cease-fire. French Union soldiers were to be removed from North Vietnam in stages within 300 days (article 15), a lengthy period in keeping with French demands. Thereafter, the introduction into the two zones of fresh arms, equipment, and personnel was prohibited with the exception of normal troop rotation and replacement of damaged or destroyed matériel (articles 16 and 17). The establishment of new military bases in Vietnam, and the adherence of either zone to military alliances, were also proscribed under articles 18 and 19.

The membership and powers of the International Control Commission were finally resolved (Chapter VI of the accords). Apparently through Chou En-lai's efforts, agreement was reached that India, Poland, and Canada should be the member states of the ICC. The ICC was empowered to form fixed and mobile inspection teams and to have full freedom of movement in both zones of Vietnam. In the performance of these tasks, the ICC was to expect complete cooperation from local civil and military officials. Its functions extended to control of the movement of armed forces and the release of prisoners of war, and to supervision of the demarcation line, frontiers, ports, and airfields.

Less clearly decided was the delicate question of the ICC's relationship to the Joint Commission. Generally, the plan adopted was close to that originally submitted by the French in early July, wherein the ICC's supremacy was tacitly admitted. The ICC was to be informed by the Joint Commission of disputes arising out of differences of interpretation, either of a provision or of fact, that the Joint Commission could not resolve. The ICC would then (article 40) have the power of recommendation; but, quite aside from the limited effectiveness of a recommendation, there remained the problem of majority or unanimous voting by the ICC in reaching agreement to recommend. Under article 42, the rule of unanimity was to apply to "questions concerning violations, or threats of violations, which might lead to a resumption of hostilities," namely, a refusal to regroup is provided in the accords, or an armed violation by one party of the territory of the other. The West, which had pushed hard for majority rule, had to settle for its application to those less volatile questions that would not be considered threats to the peace. Furthermore, under article 43, recognition was taken of possible splits among the three members by providing for majority and minority reports; but these, like ICC decisions, could be no more than suggestive, and as such wholly dependent upon the cooperativeness of the conference members who had created it.

Cambodia and Laos

In conflict with the wishes of the Cambodian and Laotian delegations, cease-fires in their countries occurred simultaneously with the cessation of hostilities in Vietnam. Nevertheless, in most other respects, their persistence was largely responsible for settlements highly favorable to their respective interests.

In the first place, the Agreement on the Cessation of Hostilities in Cambodia called for the removal of nonnative Free Khmer troops, whether Communist Vietnamese or Cambodians, ninety days from the cease-fire date (July 20). (French Union units, but not instructors, were also scheduled for departure.) As the Cambodian delegation had promised, those insurgents still in the country would be guaranteed the right to rejoin the national community and to participate, as electors or candidates, in elections scheduled under the constitution for 1955; but the agreement assured their demobilization within one month of the cease-fire. Separate joint and international supervisory commissions for Cambodia were established, as Phnom Penh had demanded. Finally, a declaration issued July 21 by the Cambodian delegation was incorporated into the accord proclaiming, in effect, Phnom Penh's inherent right of self-defense. The royal government vowed not to enter into military alliances "not in conformity with the principles of the Charter of the United Nations"; nor, so long as its security was not threatened, would Cambodia permit the establishment of foreign military bases. As for war matériel and military personnel, the delegation made clear that these would not be solicited during the period July 20, 1954, to the election date in 1955 "except for the purpose of the effective defence of the territory." Thus, *after* the elections, Cambodia proclaimed itself free to take any steps it considered necessary for its security, whether or not such steps were absolutely necessary for self-defense.

Cambodia's acquisition of considerable latitude was entirely in keeping with the royal government's expressed insistence on not being either neutralized or demilitarized. On this point, the Cambodians received indirect assurance from the United States that their security would in some way be covered by the Southeast Asian pact despite their unilateral declaration. Toward the end of the conference, Philip Bonsal of the State Department and the American delegation, told Sam Sary that he (Bonsal) "was confident U.S. and other interested countries looked forward to discussing with Cambodian government" the security problem upon implementation of a cease-fire. When Sam Sary called a few days later on Smith in the company of Nong Kimny, the Under Secretary recommended that Phnom Penh, at the conference, state its intention not to have foreign bases on its territory and not to enter into military alliances. At the same time, though, Cambodia would be free to import arms and to employ French military instructors and technicians. Cambodia might not be able to join SEATO under this arrangement, Smith said, but it could still benefit from it. Smith:

> assured the Cambodian Foreign Minister that, in our view, any aggression overt or covert against Cambodian territory would bring pact into operation even though Cambodia not a member. I took position that French Union

membership afforded Cambodia adequate desirable means of securing through France necessary arms some of which would be American as well as necessary instructors and technicians some of which might well be American trained.

Nong Kimny replied that Cambodia relied heavily on the United States for protection against future aggression. The way was thus cleared for the subsequent inclusion of Cambodia in the Protocol to the SEATO treaty.

The cease-fire agreement on Laos followed lines similar to those drawn for Cambodia. A separate joint commission was set up to supervise the withdrawal of Pathet Lao units, although provision was made for their prior regroupment in the provinces of Phong Saly and Sam Neua.* Although Laos was prohibited from seeking to augment its military establishment, the royal government was specifically permitted a maximum of 1,500 French training instructors. Moreover, the prohibition against the establishment of foreign military bases on Laotian territory did not apply to two French bases in operation under a 1949 treaty, and employing 3,500 Frenchmen. Laos, like Cambodia, was allowed to import arms and other military equipment essential for self-defense; but Vientiane also issued a unilateral declaration on July 21 making clear, in terms that nearly duplicated those used in Cambodia's declaration, that its refrainment from alliances and foreign military bases was limited to situations in which Laotian security was not threatened. In view of Vientiane's expressed hope for American protection, its delegates had succeeded admirably in getting a settlement containing terms that restricted, but did not eliminate, Laotian control over their security requirements.

F. DISSENTING VIEWS: THE AMERICAN AND VIETNAMESE POSITIONS

No delegate at the final plenary session on Indochina July 21 should have been surprised when Under Secretary Smith issued a unilateral statement of the American position. The United States had frequently indicated, publicly and privately, directly and indirectly, that it would not be cosignatory with the Communist powers to any agreement and that, at best, it would agree only to "respect" the final settlement. At the restricted session of July 18, Smith had, moreover, indicated the points which were to become basic features of his final statement. Despite the fact that the accords were in line with the Seven Points in nearly every particular, it would have been presumptuous of any delegation to believe that the United States, given the implacable hostility of Administration leaders to Communist China and to any agreement that would imply American approval of a territorial cession to the Communists, would formally sign the Geneva accords.

Bedell Smith, revealing a considerably more pliant approach to dealing with the Communist world, was able to exact from Washington agreement to partial American acceptance of the Final Declaration. On July 19 he had been approached by Mendès-France, who from the beginning had sought to identify the United States as closely as possible with the final terms, with the proposal that

---

* The Laotian delegation also issued a declaration averring the government's willingness to integrate former insurgents into the national community without reprisal. Elections in Laos were scheduled for September 1955, and former Pathet Lao were promised the right to participate in the balloting as electors or candidates.

Washington not simply respect any military agreements reached, but in addition take note of them and the political statements that comprised the first nine paragraphs of the proposed conference declaration. Mendès-France indicated the French would be sharply disappointed if the United States could not at least take note of those portions of the declaration. Smith, apparently swayed by the premier's views, recommended to Washington that his instructions be amended to provide for taking note in the event the Final Declaration was substantially as the French had indicated. [Doc. 80] Dulles gave his approval, demurring only on the second part of paragraph 9 (in the final version, paragraph 13), which the Secretary said "seems to imply a multilateral engagement with Communists which would be inconsistent with our basic approach and which subsequently might enable Communist China to charge us with alleged violations of agreement to which it might claim both governments became parties." [Doc. 81] When Smith, therefore, issued his unilateral statement, note was taken only of the first twelve paragraphs of the Final Declaration; but this was much more than had been called for in his revised instructions of July 16.

In line with his instructions, Smith declared on behalf of the Government that the United States would "refrain from the threat or the use of force to disturb" the accords. Moreover, the United States "would view any renewal of the aggression in violation of the aforesaid agreements with grave concern and as seriously threatening international peace and security." Finally, Smith reiterated a U.S. policy declaration of June 29, made during the visit of Eden and Churchill, that registered Washington's support of UN supervision of free elections to reunify countries "now divided against their will. . . ." Smith mentioned on this point that the United States could not associate itself with any arrangement that would hinder "its traditional position that peoples are entitled to determine their own future. . . ."

Smith's caution against "any renewal of aggression" deserves additional comment inasmuch as it was cited by President Kennedy (in a letter to President Ngo Dinh Diem on December 14, 1961) as the basis for the American commitment to South Vietnam's defense. Viewed in the context of the conference, the statement does not seem to have been intended as an open-ended American commitment to South Vietnam against possible aggression from the North. Rather, the Administration apparently intended the statement as a warning to the Viet Minh that should they, *within the two-year interval* before general elections, "renew" what Washington and Saigon regarded as their "aggression" since 1946, the United States would be gravely concerned. Smith's statement, in short, seems to have been limited to the period July 1954 to July 1956.

That part of Smith's unilateral statement dealing with United Nations supervision of elections is also noteworthy. Coming in the wake of Dulles' expressed concern over provision in the accords for ICC supervision, [Doc. 81] Smith's reference to the UN may have forecast American unwillingness to back an electoral process not supervised by the Organization. Inasmuch as the United States delegation had consistently pushed at Geneva for United Nations rather than any other form of international machinery, Smith may have meant to give an advance signal of American displeasure with free Vietnamese elections that the UN would be prevented from overseeing.

American qualifications to the Geneva accords paled beside those made by the South Vietnam delegation. However naively, the "South" Vietnamese refused to accept a divided country and believed, to the end of the conference, that the French had brazenly and illegally sold out Vietnamese interests. Vietnam's anger at French manipulation of its political future was reflected in a note handed to the French delegation on July 17 by Nguyen Huu Chau. [Doc. 73] The note maintained that not until the day before (an exaggeration by about three weeks, it would appear) did Vietnam learn that at the very time the French High Command had ordered the evacuation of troops from important areas in the Tonkin Delta, the French had also "accepted abandoning to the Viet Minh all of that part situated north of the eighteenth parallel and that the delegation of the Viet Minh might claim an even more advantageous demarcation line." The Vietnamese delegation protested against having been left "in complete ignorance" of French proposals, which were said not to "take any account of the unanimous will for national unity of the Vietnamese people."

While it may have been absurd for the Vietnamese to believe that partition was avoidable given Viet Minh strength, their rationale for keeping the country united was, as matters developed, eminently clear-sighted. In speeches during June and July, their leaders had warned that partition would be merely a temporary interlude before the renewal of fighting. When the Viet Minh first proposed a temporary division of territory, the Defense Minister, Phan Huy Quat, said in Saigon on June 2 that partition would "risk reviving the drama of the struggle between the North and the South." Diem, in his investiture speech of early July, warned against a cease-fire that would mean partition, for that arrangement "can only be the preparation for another more deadly war. . . ." And General Nguyen Van Hinh, head of the Vietnamese National Army, declared:

> To realize a cease-fire by partition of Vietnamese territory can be only a temporary measure to stop the bloodshed but not to end the war. And it is possible that we shall have to face a cold war as in Korea where both sides' troops have their fingers on the triggers of their guns all the time, and people are thinking only of recovering what has been given up under the pressure of the circumstances.

Although their struggle against partition, which reached a climax in the aftermath of the signing of the accords with huge rallies in the major cities, proved futile, the Vietnamese early gave notice that they would accept neither partition nor a fixed date for national elections. We need only recall the statements by Bao Dai's cabinet in Paris on the eve of the conference to find evidence of Vietnam's early determination that it would not be party to a sell-out of its own territory. When partition became certain in July with the circulation of draft final declarations, the Vietnamese delegation became more vocal. At the final plenary session, Tran Van Do said: ". . . the Government of the State of Viet-Nam wishes the Conference to take note of the fact that it reserves its full freedom of action in order to safeguard the sacred right of the Vietnamese people to its territorial unity, national independence, and freedom." When asked to consent to the military accords and the Final Declaration, Do requested insertion of the following text into the Declaration:

> The conference takes note of the Declaration of the Government of the State of Viet-Nam undertaking:
>   to make and support every effort to reestablish a real and lasting peace in Viet-Nam;
>   not to use force to resist the procedures for carrying the ceasefire into effect, in spite of the objections and reservations that the State of Viet-Nam has expressed, especially in its final statement.

The request was denied.

As for elections, the Vietnamese believed that the war situation compelled the postponement of elections until the country had achieved a measure of internal stability. As early as May, Diem indicated his opposition to elections for a National Assembly, much less to national elections for the presidency. In its note to the French delegation, moreover, the Vietnamese asserted that a cease-fire without disarmament was incompatible with elections; the regroupment of the armed forces of the belligerents into separate zones was said to compromise their freedom in advance. In Vietnam's view, elections could only be considered after security and peace had been established, thereby excluding a set time interval of two years. [Doc. 73]

Having taken these positions, the Vietnamese could hardly adhere to the Final Declaration. At the same time, they protested against the "hasty conclusion of the Armistice Agreement by the French and Vietminh High Commanders only . . ." (as Tran Van Do put it at the July 21 session). Inasmuch as the military accords, by prearrangement, were signed by French and Viet Minh commanders precisely to avoid seeking Vietnamese consent, there was nothing Saigon could do but protest. Nevertheless, by having protested, they were asserting that the treaties with France of June 4 had indeed made Vietnam a sovereign state, that the interests of non-Communist Vietnamese were deeply involved in the settlement, and that France's by-passing of the Bao Dai government only made the settlement possible, not legal. Despite article 27 of the agreement on Vietnam, which bound "successors" (such as Vietnam) to the signatories to respect and enforce the agreement, Vietnam was in a legally persuasive position to argue that France could not assume liabilities in its behalf, least of all to the political provisions contained in the Final Declaration, which was an unsigned document.*

G. SUMMARY

Throughout the rapid series of compromises in the last thirty days of the Geneva Conference, American diplomacy revealed a constancy of purpose fully in line with the Eisenhower Administration's global foreign policy. Based largely on the unfortunate experiences at Panmunjom, the Administration could not reconcile itself to the notion that Sino-Soviet negotiating tactics in the post-Stalin period of peaceful coexistence had changed. Consequently, even as the realization dawned that the Communists could not be expelled from Indochina and that some compromise with them by France was inevitable, the Administration stuck fast to the position that the United States delegation to the conference would only assist, but not take an active part, in bringing about an acceptable settlement. From June on, the delegation was under instructions to remain clear of any involvement in the negotiations such as might implicate or commit the United States to the final terms reached, yet simultaneously was to maintain an influential role in making the best of difficult circumstances. British and French agreement to the Seven Points proved a diplomatic victory, not because their acceptance of them assured a reasonable settlement but because, quite contrary to American expectations, they returned to Geneva prepared to hold the line against exorbitant

---

* Article 27, which is frequently cited to demonstrate that Vietnam was bound to abide by the accords, and particularly the elections provision, refers to "signatories of the present [*military*] Agreement. . . ." Hence, the article would seem not to obligate France's "successor" with respect to any provisions of the Final Declaration, a document to which South Vietnam did not adhere.

Communist demands. Allied agreement to future discussions of a regional defense system for Southeast Asia was really a hedge against a French sell-out at Geneva; in the event Vietnam, and parts of Cambodia and Laos, were ceded to the Communist insurgents, the United States would at least have Anglo-French consent to protect the security of what remained of Indochina and its neighbors.

The Seven Points represented principles, not American objectives. They constituted not a statement of goals to be achieved by the United States, but of principles to be adopted by the British and French negotiators toward concluding a satisfactory settlement. In this manner, the Administration could preserve its dignity before anticipated Vietnamese outrage at partition and domestic displeasure at further Communist inroads in the Far East without losing its ability to influence the terms. Under Secretary Smith's final statement taking note of the agreements and vowing not to disturb them thus culminated a careful policy that rejected an American commitment to the accords such as might identify the Administration with a cession of territory and people to the Communist bloc.

The Geneva Conference left much work undone, especially on a political settlement for Vietnam. The State of Vietnam, like the United States, had refused to adhere to the Final Declaration and was not signatory to the military accord that partitioned the country. In the next section, the focus is therefore on the practical effect of the Geneva accords, the expectations of the conferees concerning them, and the extent to which the major powers, in reaching a settlement, achieved the objectives they had set for themselves.

VIII. THE MEANING OF GENEVA

Much of the controversy surrounding the American involvement in Vietnam relates to the post-Geneva period, in particular to the two-year interval before national elections were to bring about Vietnam's reunification. To address the question whether the United States instigated or colluded with the Government of Vietnam to defy the Final Declaration's stipulation for national elections would broaden this paper beyond its intended scope. What is relevant, however, are the documented or presumed expectations and objectives of the major participants concerning Vietnam, as well as Cambodia and Laos, at the time the conference closed. How had the accords met the aims of the participants, and to what extent were objectives intertwined with, or perhaps divorced from, expectations? To anticipate, the present argument over the failure to hold elections in July 1956 overlooks the relative unimportance of them, for a variety of reasons, to the five major powers at the Geneva Conference; *their* objectives only secondarily took into account the expectations of the Vietnamese, north and south.

An assessment of the hopes and goals of the Geneva conferees in the immediate aftermath of the conference should, in the first place, be differentiated from the practical effect of the accords they drew up. The distinction not often made, yet highly important to an understanding of the conference and its achievements, is between the intent of the parties regarding Vietnam and the seemingly contradictory consequences of their agreement.

A. THE PRACTICAL NATURE OF THE ACCORDS

With the exception of South Vietnam, every nation represented at the conference came to believe that partition was the only way to separate the combatants, settle the widely disparate military and political demands of the French and Viet Minh, and conclude an armistice. It might further be argued (although the evidence available does not actually permit a definitive statement one way or the other) that these eight delegations intended the partition line to be temporary inasmuch as they all desired Vietnamese elections in 1956. But what needs to be pointed out is that the accords themselves did not further that intent. By creating two regimes responsible for "civil administration" (article 14-a of the Vietnam armistice agreement), by providing for the regroupment of forces to two zones and for the movement of persons to the zone of their choice, and by putting off national elections for two years, the conferees had actually made a future political settlement for Vietnam extremely unlikely. Certainly, the separation of Vietnam at the 17th parallel was designed to facilitate the armistice, not to create political subdivisions; but its unintended effect was to allow time for the development of two *governments,* headed by totally divergent personalities and committed to antithetical political philosophies, foreign policies, and socio-economic systems. Thus, the call for elections in the Final Declaration had as little chance of implementation in Vietnam as previously in Korea and Germany, a point brought home by Vietnamese officials and reinforced by the failure of the same Geneva conferees to agree on a political settlement in Korea. "Elections," Victor Bator has commented "can, indeed, decide secondary problems of co-existence in circumstances where some measurable minimum basis for political agreement exists. But they are incapable of acceptance by two opposing states, or parts of a state, when diametrically opposite philosophies are involved." If the intent of the Geneva accords was subverted, the subverters were the conferees themselves, who aspired to an ideal political settlement incompatible with the physical and psychological dismemberment of Vietnam on July 21, 1954.

B.   OBJECTIVES OF THE PARTICIPANTS: THE COMMUNIST SIDE

Whether or not one accepts the view offered here that the central political provision of the Final Declaration was decisively undercut by provisions of the military accords and the Declaration itself, an examination of the objectives of the Soviet Union and Communist China can go far toward determining, albeit by surmisal, the importance they, as distinct from the DRV, attached to Vietnamese unity. For it is the conclusion here that Vietnamese unity, whether achieved by free elections or the disintegration of South Vietnam, was *not a priority objective* of Moscow or Peking even though both powers may well have *anticipated* an all-Communist Vietnam by July 1956. If this is so, we may ask, what were the primary aims of Moscow and Peking in supporting a settlement? Why did the Communists apparently strive for a settlement, and why did Molotov in particular, who was not personally identified in Western eyes at the time as a vigorous proponent of *détente,* play such a key role in keeping the conference from the brink of failure?

Although it would appear that, on the major issues at least, the Soviet Union coordinated its actions with Communist China, the two Communist powers were clearly pursuing separate national interests in working toward a settlement of the war. The reconciliation of those interests seems to have been achieved not so much through Soviet ability (which did exist) to compel Chinese acquiescence as through a common desire for a settlement.

Soviet Objectives at the Conference

In retrospect, the Soviet Union seems to have had four major objectives at the conference: (1) to avert a major war crisis over Indochina that would stimulate Western unity, enable the United States to gain support it previously lacked for "united action," and conceivably force Moscow into a commitment to defend the Chinese; (2) to reduce the prospects for successful passage of EDC in the French National Assembly; (3) to heighten the prestige of the Soviet Union as a world peacemaker; (4) to bolster the prestige of Communist China, probably more as an adjunct to the Soviet drive for leadership of the "peaceful coexistence" movement than as a means of supporting any Chinese claim to unrivaled leadership in Asia.

On the first point, the Soviets were surely aware that the United States, under certain conditions, was prepared to consider active involvement in the war. While united action was a dead issue in Washington by mid-June, the Soviets (and the Chinese as well) could not have known this. Moreover, newspaper reports of the time added both credence and uncertainty to American military plans. In the course of private discussions at Geneva, Molotov indicated his concern that a breakdown of the conference might lead to continued fighting right up to the point of World War III. The French and British did nothing to dispel those fears. Chauvel, for instance, told the Russian delegate, Kuznetsov, that France's proposed division of Vietnam at the 18th parallel would be more acceptable to the other conferees than the unreasonable Viet Minh demand for the 13th parallel, and that a settlement along the French line would thereby avert the risk of an internationalization of the conflict. And Mendès-France vowed to back his call for conscripts by informing Molotov he "did not intend Geneva would turn into a Panmunjom."

The possibility of renewed fighting leading to a wider war was particularly influential on the Soviets, it would seem, as a consequence of Moscow's inner debate during 1953 and 1954 over American strategic intentions and their meaning for the Soviet defense system. The views of the so-called Khrushchev wing apparently won out in the spring of 1954: The United States was considered fully capable of initiating a nuclear exchange and a new world war. Free-wheeling discussion in the Western press on the foreign policy implications of Eisenhower's "New Look" and Dulles' "massive retaliation" speech of January 12, 1954, was closely followed by the Soviets, who may have been persuaded in their pessimistic assumptions regarding American strategy by the very ambiguity of American "reliance" on nuclear weapons to combat Communist aggression. In fact, it can be argued that even though the United States and its allies went to the conference table from a position of diplomatic weakness, their hands were considerably strengthened because of Soviet uncertainty over what the West might do in the event the conference failed. Inasmuch as Soviet analyses by no means excluded American recklessness with nuclear weapons, Moscow might have been highly reluctant to press too vigorously for the West's acceptance of exorbitant Viet Minh demands. Soviet awareness that the United States had seriously considered active involvement in Indochina prior to the fall of Dienbienphu may therefore have been a significant lever for the West in the Geneva negotiations. Had the opposite perception been true—had the Soviets, that is, been confident that the American Administration would be highly sober, conservative, and cautious in responding to war situations—Molotov might have been instructed to play a far more audacious game while the Viet Minh intensified their military operations. Dulles' reputation as a militant anti-Communist with tremendous influence on Eisenhower probably served the Western cause well at Geneva.

As a result, to conclude on this point, one of the Soviets' principal aims at the conference was to diminish the possibility of American unilateral or multilateral intervention in the likely belief that intervention would have built up tremendous pressure on Moscow to make new commitments in Southeast Asia. While this outlook did not prevent the Soviets from at first seeking to capitalize on the change in government in Paris from Laniel to Mendès-France, it did work in the general direction of a reasonable settlement that would be honorable for the French and still valuable to the Viet Minh. The Russians evidently believed that so long as the French (and the British) were kept interested in a settlement, the Americans would be hard-pressed to disregard their allies and intervene.

That Moscow may have been anxious about a wider war does not, however, address the *incentives* it may have had in concluding the cease-fire. Here, the European Defense Community treaty must have been uppermost in Molotov's mind. No evidence has been found to support the contention that Molotov explicitly baited Mendès-France with a lenient Indochina settlement in return for Assembly rejection of EDC. But Molotov need not have been that obtrusive. Throughout 1953 and into 1954, Soviet propaganda was dominated by comments on EDC and the danger of a rearmed Germany. It was certainly in Soviet interests to pressure the Viet Minh for concessions to the French, since removal of the French command from Indochina would restore French force levels on the Continent and thereby probably offset their need for an EDC. Soviet interests thus dictated the sacrifice of Viet Minh goals if necessary to prevent German remilitarization. Given Moscow's belated attention to the Indochina war, it appears that the consolidation of Viet Minh gains short of complete reunification of Vietnam was more than sufficient to justify termination of the struggle in Soviet eyes —and this perception, it might be added, dovetailed with what seems to have been the Chinese outlook.

Thirdly, the worldwide Soviet peace offensive which gained priority in the aftermath of Stalin's death could be given added impetus through vigorous Soviet support of an Indochina settlement. This point, in fact, was the theme of Molotov's closing remarks to the conference on July 21. He called the accords "a major victory for the forces of peace and a major step towards a reduction of international tensions." Considering that the conference had demonstrated the value of international negotiations to settle dangerous disputes, Molotov said: "The results of the Geneva Conference have confirmed the rightness of the principle which is fundamental to the whole foreign policy of the Soviet Union, namely, that there are no issues in the contemporary international situation which cannot be solved and settled through negotiations and by agreements designed to consolidate peace." At a time when the United States was alleged to be jeopardizing world peace with its "policy of strength," the Soviet Union could lay claim to sparing no effort in the struggle for ways to avoid a nuclear holocaust.

In this light, Communist China was important to the USSR as a partner in the peace offensive. While Moscow could not have wished to see China so gain in prestige as to rival the Soviet Union in Asia or elsewhere, the Russians do seem, in 1954, to have considered a gain in Chinese influence highly desirable if only because the United States would be bound to suffer a corresponding loss. As Molotov phrased it on July 21:

> . . . the Geneva Conference indicated the great positive importance that the participation of the People's Republic of China has in the settlement of urgent international problems. The course of work at this Conference has shown that any artificial obstacles on the road to China's participation in the settlement of international affairs, which are still being put up by aggressive circles of some countries, are being swept away by life itself.

Noteworthy is Molotov's omission of the additional claim made at the time by Peking that China's participation was absolutely essential to the solution of Asian problems. While the Soviet foreign minister was perhaps thinking in terms of CPR admission to the United Nations, the Chinese apparently were looking beyond the UN to the kind of full-scale diplomatic effort that would earn them Asia's respect as founders of what was later termed the "Bandung spirit." Nor did Molotov assert that China's work at the conference had earned it a status equivalent to one of the major powers. The Soviets were willing to admit that Peking had gained a new importance as a result of the conference, but they refused to go as far as the Chinese in asserting China's first-rank status either in Asia or worldwide.

The Soviets, then, had much to gain from an honorable settlement of the Indochina war and much to risk in permitting the talks to drag on inconclusively. The Viet Minh had proven their strength as a national liberation movement and had been amply rewarded with a firm territorial base assured by international agreement. With overriding interests in Western Europe, Moscow no doubt found great appeal in giving the French a face-saving "out" from Indochina. That EDC was eventually defeated in the National Assembly (in August) was testimony not to the cleverness of any Soviet "deal" with Mendès-France, but simply to a low-cost Soviet diplomatic gamble that paid off handsomely.

Chinese Objectives

For Peking, a negotiated settlement of the Indochina war represented an important opportunity to propel China forward as a major Asian power whose voice in Asian councils could not be ignored. When the Berlin Conference decided in February 1954 to hold an international conference on Indochina, the Chinese applauded the move and prophesied then that the People's Republic, as an invitee, would thereby gain recognition of its major role in Asian affairs. With the Geneva Conference coming at a time of vigorous Chinese diplomatic activity in India and Burma, Peking probably considered a settlement short of a complete Viet Minh victory acceptable, since it would prove China's sincere commitment to peace. Had the CPR spurred the Viet Minh on, it not only would have been in conflict with the Soviets, whose aid was vital to China's economic recovery plans, but would also have lost considerable ground in the support Chou En-lai's travels had earned. The war in Indochina had become, for China, a demonstration test of its sincerity in promoting peaceful coexistence. From the tactical standpoint, devotion to peaceful coexistence may also have been seen as reducing the prospects of widespread Asian support of, or participation in, the American plan for a regional alliance. With the conference ended, China was in a position to offer Asian nations an alternative to alliance with the United States—the concept of "collective peace and security," sustained by mutual agreement to foster the five principles.

The motive force behind China's drive for Asian leadership during the period of the Geneva Conference was the theme that negotiated solutions were possible for all outstanding world problems. By the time of Geneva, Peking had already been party to the armistice in Korea, to agreement with India over Tibet, and to statements of mutual respect issued bilaterally with India and Burma. Moreover, China had joined with Moscow in supporting negotiations of the Indochina war as early as September 1953, while the Sino-Indian and Sino-Burmese statements also contained calls for an early settlement. The major role played by Chou En-lai at Geneva therefore not simply affirmed China's interest in peace, but as importantly established China's reputation as a flexible bargainer willing to negotiate disputes and make concessions to resolve them. Indeed, once the conference ended, Peking declared that the conference had proved that negotiations could resolve such other East-West problems as a final Korea settlement, arms control, nuclear weapons proliferation, German unification, and European security.

Relatedly, China urged that the Geneva Conference was a benchmark in the rise of the People's Republic to new prominence on the international scene. "The great significance of the convening of the Geneva Conference," the *People's Daily* proclaimed before its close, "lies in the fact that the Chinese People's Republic is participating in the settlement of Asian questions as one of the Great Powers, thus putting an end to the era when the Asian peoples were denied their say in their own problems." China stood not only for a resurgent, decolonialized Asia, but also as a Great Power. As stated by the authoritative *World Culture*:

> The contributions of the CPR at the Geneva Conference to the search for peace, and its efforts to establish collective security in Asia, have received the universal recognition and trust of the world's peace-loving peoples and nations. Because of this, the position of the CPR as one of the world's great nations has been even more affirmed and its international prestige greatly elevated. The Chinese people feel extraordinary glory because of this.

The fact that China had, in Indochina and as was not the case in Korea, been invited to join with the Big Four in discussing measures for the restoration of peace was considered by Peking to have given the CPR still more international authority.

Augmentation of Chinese prestige in Asia and throughout the world was a benefit due to the conference; but it does not fully explain why China apparently pressed for a settlement when she did rather than prolong the talks until better terms were available. Having negotiated at Panmunjom for two years, why did she take less than three months to conclude a cease-fire in Indochina? There seem to have been three reasons for China's reluctance to engage in extended discussions: (1) agreement with the Soviets that the United States could intervene to spark a wider war; (2) consideration that Laos and Cambodia had been effectively neutralized; (3) satisfaction that a communist state had been established on China's southern flank.

In the first place, Peking was convinced, to judge from its published comments on the war, that influential men in Washington, including Secretary Dulles and the Joint Chiefs of Staff, were quite prepared to move directly against China if circumstances permitted. Washington's warnings to Peking in 1953 left room for the continuation of Chinese aid to the Viet Minh, but Peking could never be certain when that aid might become the pretext for active American intervention. By 1954, moreover, the Chinese had evinced greater concern than before over the military effectiveness of nuclear weapons. Having been through a costly war in Korea, and having decided as early as the fall of 1952 to give priority to "socialist reconstruction" at home, Peking had nothing to gain from provoking the United States. Were the Viet Minh encouraged to strive for the maximum territorial advantage, the United States—Peking may have calculated—might withdraw from the conference and change the nature of the war. Once those events occurred, the Chinese advocacy of peace through diplomacy would have been irreparably undercut.

Peking, moreover, was made clearly aware of the dangers inherent in continued fighting. At the conference, Eden used the implied threat of American involvement against Chou in much the same way as Chauvel had used it against Kuznetsov. During late May, for example, Eden warned Chou "again" of the dangers in the Indochina situation; unpredictable and serious results could come about. When Chou said he was counting on Britain to prevent these from happening, the foreign secretary replied Chou was mistaken, since Britain would stand by the United States in a showdown. Furthermore, with the Eisenhower-Churchill warning of June 28 that unacceptable demands made against France would "seriously aggravate" the international situation, with Dulles' perceived pressure on Mendès-France at the Paris meeting of mid-July, and with the return of Smith to the conference table, the Chinese were given unmistakable signs that Western unity had finally been achieved and some kind of coordination worked out on the settlement. At that juncture, the outstanding issue for Peking was not how much territory the DRV would ultimately obtain, but how far Cambodia and Laos could be pressed before the July 20 deadline passed.

By the deadline, as we have seen, Chou En-lai's hardened attitude in conversations with the Cambodian and Laotian delegates had not swayed them from their hope of eventual security coverage by the United States. From China's standpoint, however, the vital agreement had been secured: None of the Indochinese states was permitted to join a military alliance or to allow the establishment of foreign military bases on their soil. Whether the Chinese recognized the alternative for the three states of obtaining protection through a device such as the SEATO Protocol is not known. When the accords were signed, Peking greeted them with the remark that the restrictions upon Indochina's military ties to the West had dealt a severe blow to American regional security ambitions. So long as the United States was not permitted to establish bases in the three countries and to introduce military personnel there, China's security requirements were fulfilled even though, in their internal political make-up, the three states might take a strong anti-Communist line. It was perhaps because the CPR had emerged with these advantages that a Chinese journalist confided on July 23: "We have won the first campaign for the neutralization of all Southeast Asia."

The supposed "neutralization" of Cambodia and Laos was coupled with the securance of a solid territory for the DRV along China's southern frontier. Further territorial gains by the Viet Minh would augment DRV resources, but would not significantly enhance China's security. With agreement by the conference to stabilize the military assets of both zones of Vietnam and to forbid their military alignment with other nations, China could feel some confidence that a divided Vietnam would not present an immediate threat. Thus, the agreements on Cambodia and Laos complemented the Vietnam accord in bolstering China's security from the south even as it also meant a sacrifice of the Viet Minh's capability for overrunning all Vietnam.

The argument here is, in summary, that the Soviet Union and Communist China were less concerned with the specific terms of the settlement than with attaining it once their basic objectives had been achieved. A settlement along lines that would satisfy the Viet Minh need for territory, give France the satisfaction that it had not sold out, go far toward fulfilling Chinese security requirements and political ambitions in Southeast Asia, and reduce the possibility of a precipitate American withdrawal from the conference was, to Moscow and Peking, acceptable and even desirable. They saw advantages to themselves in an early equitable agreement that clearly conflicted with Viet Minh terms, but not with their own objectives.

Precisely how Chou and Molotov reasoned with Ho Chi Minh—by threat, persuasion, or a combination of the two—will likely never be known; but it seems reasonable to suppose that, given the precarious political situation in South Vietnam, the multitude of armed sects and other groups hostile to the Saigon government, the continued exacerbating presence of the French, and the economic and social vulnerabilities of a society wracked by war, Peking and Moscow could argue convincingly that South Vietnam would never cohere sufficiently to pose a viable alternative to the DRV. It may thus have been the Communists' expectation that the DRV would as likely assume control of the entire country by default as by an election victory in 1956. The Chinese, to be sure, accepted the notion that the Geneva accords had, temporarily at least, created two Vietnamese governments rather than simply divided the country administratively. [Doc. 64] But it is improbable that either they or the Soviets anticipated that even an American-supported South Vietnam could survive. Put another way, the possibility of a prospering, anti-Communist South Vietnam may simply not have been a serious, and certainly was not an immediate, concern for either Communist power. The Geneva Conference had created French goodwill for Moscow and added security for Peking; what might happen in South Vietnam may, in 1954, have seemed inconsequential.

Viet Minh Objectives

The Viet Minh did not emerge as "losers" in the negotiations. They received the territorial benefits of the settlement without having to cede the French or any neutral body control of enclaves in northern Vietnam. In addition, the DRV was promised an opportunity within two years to gain full control of the country through a ballot box victory, although it appears that Viet Minh leaders put more stock in a collapse of the southern regime before the election date as the path to complete control of the country. In Laos, the Pathet Lao had not been disarmed immediately; instead, they were permitted to regroup over a wide expanse of terrain that would make disarmament difficult to accomplish. And in both Laos and Cambodia, the resistance elements were to be accorded full political rights to participate, as individuals, in the 1955 elections.

In their public commentaries on the Geneva accords, Viet Minh leaders displayed full satisfaction. Military victories had gained political recognition, they said, thanks to the support rendered by the Soviet and Chinese delegations. Vietnam's independence and territorial integrity were admitted by Paris, Ho Chi Minh proclaimed. Moreover, the regroupment to two zones in Vietnam was, as he put it, "a temporary action, a transitional step in the realization of a cease-fire, toward restoring peace and attaining the unification of our country by means of general elections." No "administrative partition" was intended; nor would the "zonal arrangements" be permitted to interfere with Vietnam's future unification:

> . . . North, Central and South Viet Nam are territories of ours. Our country will certainly be unified, our entire people will surely be liberated. Our compatriots in the South were the first to wage the war of Resistance. They possess a high political consciousness. I am confident that they will place national interests above local interests, permanent interests above temporary interests, and join their efforts with the entire people in strengthening peace, achieving unity, independence and democracy all over the country . . . . our people, armymen and cadres from North to South must unite closely. They must be at one in thought and deed.

And Ton Duc Thang vowed: "The Vietnam State will undoubtedly be unified through general elections."

Despite these protestations of satisfaction and confidence, Tillman Durdin's report from Geneva that members of the Viet Minh delegation were sharply disappointed by the results and vexed at pressure applied by their Chinese and Russian comrades seems on the mark. The Viet Minh command evidently believed—and no French authority on the spot doubted this—that they could eliminate the French from Tonkin with one major offensive and proceed from there against a weakened, demoralized Franco-Vietnamese army in Annam. Surely Ho Chi Minh must have considered the possibility of American intervention—although this concern does not emerge as clearly from Viet Minh public commentaries as it does from the official Moscow and Peking organs. But the Viet Minh looked to the Korea experience as having demonstrated that fighting and talking simultaneously was, as put by a mid-May VNA broadcast, a tactic they could pursue for two years (like the Chinese during the Panmunjom talks) in order to maximize territorial gains. Whether the Viet Minh ultimately envisaged the conquest of all Vietnam before reaching agreement with the French to cease fire is debatable; at the least, they, like the French, probably regarded maximum control of population and territory as insurance against future elections. Thus, to the Viet Minh, a settlement at the 17th parallel could only have been regarded as a tactical blunder in violation of the guerrilla war theory and practice they had mastered.

Forfeiture of considerable territory in Vietnam was undoubtedly not the only ground for the Viet Minh's displeasure. Their frequent pronouncements on the "indivisibility" of the Viet Minh, Free Khmer, and Pathet Lao were largely ignored by Chou and Molotov, whose agreement on Laos and Cambodia seems to have given priority to Chinese interests. Account had been taken, as Chou insisted, of the desirability of integrating the resistance forces into the national Khmer and Laotian communities, but those forces were eventually to be disarmed and disbanded, or withdrawn. Conceivably, the Viet Minh leaders never intended to leave Laos, or were assured by the Chinese and Soviets that the agreements reached regarding the Pathet Lao were not meant to exclude future North Vietnamese support. Nevertheless, any future Viet Minh contacts with the rebels would be a clear violation of the Geneva accords and provide the occasion for intensified Laotian ties to the West.

The Viet Minh also yielded ground on national elections. Their hopes for an all-Vietnamese political settlement soon after the cease-fire were quashed by the Soviets and Chinese, who were disposed to accept a longer waiting period. Furthermore, the political settlement itself was not given the priority the Viet Minh had originally demanded; it would be achieved, as phrased in the Final Declaration, "in the near future," as the result of rather than as the precondition to a military (cease-fire) settlement. Finally, when the time for a political settlement was at hand, the Declaration specified that an international body would supervise it rather than the Viet Minh and "South" Vietnamese alone. The overriding interests of the Soviets and Chinese had taken the heart out of the initial Viet Minh proposals of May 10 and, in addition, had considerably undercut their "fallback" positions expressed in late May and June. Jean Chauvel was apparently correct when he perceived, after private talks with the Chinese, that the Viet Minh were really on the end of a string being manipulated from Moscow and Peking. When they moved forward too quickly, Chou and Molotov were always at hand to pull them back to a more accommodating position. Briefly put, the Viet Minh very likely felt they had been compelled to give away much of what they had earned even as they acquired the attributes of sovereignty for which they had fought.

C. OBJECTIVES OF THE PARTICIPANTS: THE WESTERN BIG THREE

The British

For Great Britain, the accords signalled the end of a war that more than once threatened to involve the United States and risk a regional conflagration. Had the point of direct American intervention been reached, the Churchill government would have been faced with an extraordinarily difficult decision: whether to join with an old ally in a war venture that Britain considered politically wrong and militarily foolish, or to break with Washington and thereby throw into question the Anglo-American alliance. Britain's consistent advice to delay irreversible military steps, including formation of a Southeast Asia defense organization, until the Communists had been given an opportunity to make good on their proclaimed devotion to a peaceful solution over Indochina had been grudgingly accepted by the United States; the choice of following or ignoring American leadership was averted.

A diplomatic untangling of the Indochina problem, as Britain's first hope, also became in large measure its responsibility. If the allies were not to be pressed into a military response, it was as much up to Eden as to Bidault (and, later, Mendès-France), to establish the grounds for a settlement. Although final agreement at the conference required Soviet and Chinese preparedness to offer equitable terms, Eden's own contributions cannot be exaggerated. Working closely with Molotov and Chou, Eden apparently earned their respect as a forthright, flexible, but firm negotiator. That the accords were drawn up testified to Eden's persistence. They were a triumph of British diplomacy to the extent that the Chinese and Soviets, in press commentaries immediately following the close of the Conference, accorded the UK delegation the unusual accolade of having, along with their delegations, rendered the most important services in the agonizing process of reaching agreement.

At the same time as the British successfully pushed through a settlement by diplomatic rather than military means, they also reserved the right to join with the United States in a regional security arrangement immediately after the conference. As Eden had told Chou, the formation of a SEATO would not be put off, even though the Associated States would not become members. British membership in SEATO represented another significant *diplomatic* victory. They had on several occasions informed the United States that a Southeast Asia pact formed in advance of or during the Geneva deliberations might be interpreted as provocatory by the Chinese and reduce, if not eliminate, chances for a settlement. The British never opposed the concept of SEATO, but they cautioned against poor timing. SEATO's establishment in September 1954 was thus doubly welcomed by London: It satisfied Britain's conviction that a much-needed regional organization should be formed to preserve what remained of Indochina, not to take action to recover it all from the Viet Minh.

Britain's opposition to forming SEATO before or during the conference so as, in part, not to provoke the Chinese fitted with London's aspirations for better Sino-British relations. Quite unlike the dominant voices in Washington, Churchill and Eden were amenable to attempting to achieve some kind of working relationship with Peking, particularly in view of the ongoing guerrilla war in Malaya. The conference, as Eden noted in his June 23 speech to the Commons, had resulted in an improvement of Sino-British relations, demonstrated by Peking's agreement on June 17, after four years of silence, to exchange chargés d'affaires. In the remaining month of the conference, moreover, British youth delegations traveled to China, and there were hopeful comments from both countries on the possibilities for stepped up trade and the exchange of cultural delegations. Thus, in sharp contrast to the United States, Great Britain fully exploited this period of harmony through diplomacy to change, rather than preserve, its pattern of contact with Peking.

The French

France probably had as much cause for satisfaction with the outcome at Geneva as any other party to the conference. Paris had extricated itself from *la sale guerre* with honor, yet had also retained a foothold in South Vietnam and a close relationship with Cambodia and Laos. The French Union lost much of its strength, but not all of its appeal, in Indochina. At least in mid-1954, it appeared that French cultural and economic interests in all three former colonies would be substantially preserved; and even the DRV had indicated, at the close as well as at the beginning of the negotiations, that it aspired to membership in the Union. French military power would have to be surrendered, of course;* but French influence could (and did) remain in all three countries.

While the British were ready to join with the United States and other interested nations in SEATO, the French clearly intended, as evidenced by their concern over the location of the demarcation line, that South Vietnam have a defensible territory within which to establish a stable regime competitive with the DRV.** As already observed, Paris was not motivated by altruism alone; a substantial territorial base was as much for the preservation of French economic holdings in the South as for the future security of the Saigon government. To judge from the French attitude, the Paris government, no less than the American administration, looked forward to participating fully in the consolidation and rehabilitation of the GVN at least in the two years before nationwide elections.

The Americans

The United States viewed the conference results with mixed emotions. On the one hand, the terms of the settlement conformed surprisingly well to those the Administration had agreed with the French and British would be acceptable. Even as the Administration could not do more than agree to "respect" and "take note" of the Geneva accords, it had to concede that they represented a reasonable outcome given the chaotic state of Allied relations before the conference, the rejection by France of a possible military alternative, and the undeniable military superiority of the Viet Minh beyond as well as within Vietnam. On the other hand, the settlement, viewed through the special lenses of the Eisenhower-Dulles Administration, also contained the elements of defeat. Part

---

* Even as most French troops were withdrawn, a French military *presence* remained for some time. The last troops did not leave Vietnam until February 1956 while, under the military accords, French instructors remained in Laos and Cambodia and two bases continued to function in Laos.
** French interest was not confined to South Vietnam after July 21, 1954. Soon thereafter, Paris dispatched Jean Sainteny, its former chief negotiator with the Viet Minh at Fontainebleau and Dalat in 1946, to Hanoi to represent French interests without conferring recognition on the DRV. France recognized only one Vietnam but in fact dealt with two.

of the Free World's "assets" in the Far East had been "lost" to the Sino-Soviet bloc (much as China had been "lost" to Mao Tse-tung's forces); our allies had begged off when offered a chance to deal with the Communists by force of arms and, later, by an Asian–Western anti-Communist alliance ready for action; and the United States had been compelled to attend an international conference which not only confirmed to the Communists by diplomacy what they had gained by force, but also enhanced their image elsewhere in Asia and worldwide as standard-bearers of peace.

The view that Geneva had come out better than could have been expected was the one offered publicly. The President, at a July 21 news conference, declined to criticize the accords. He said they contained "features which we do not like, but a great deal depends on how they work in practice." He announced the Government's intention to establish permanent missions in Laos and Cambodia, and said the United States was actively "pursuing discussions with other free nations with a view to the rapid organization of a collective defense in Southeast Asia in order to prevent further direct or indirect Communist aggression in that general area."

Under Secretary Smith likewise was very guarded in remarks two days later. Denying that Geneva was another "Munich," Smith said: "I am . . . convinced that the results are the best that we could possibly have obtained in the circumstances," adding that "diplomacy has rarely been able to gain at the conference table what cannot be gained or held on the battlefield." When Dulles spoke (also on July 23), he was much less interested in the past than in the future. Referring to "the loss in Northern Vietnam," the Secretary expressed the hope that much would be learned from the experience toward preventing further Communist inroads in Asia. Two lessons could be culled, he observed. First, popular support was essential against Communist subversion; "the people should feel that they are defending their own national institutions." Second, collective defense should precede rather than come during the aggression—a pointed criticism of British policy during the crisis. A collective security system now in Southeast Asia, he concluded, would check both outright aggression and subversion.

A point-by-point comparison of the Seven Points with the provisions of the accords indicates that quite apart from what had happened to American interests in Southeast Asia as a consequence of the conference, American diplomacy had, on balance, succeeded:

(1) The integrity and independence of Laos and Cambodia were preserved, and Viet Minh forces were to be withdrawn or disarmed and disbanded.

(2) Southern Vietnam was retained, although without an enclave in the North and with the partition line somewhat south of Dong Hoi.

(3) Laos, Cambodia, and "retained" Vietnam were not prevented from forming "non-Communist regimes" (in the case of Vietnam, within the two-year pre-election period); nor were they expressly forbidden "to maintain adequate forces for internal security." Vietnam's right to import arms and other war materiel was, however, restricted to piece-by-piece replacement, and its employment of foreign advisers to the number in the country at the war's close.

(4–5) Recalling Dulles' interpretation of July 7 that elections should "be only held as long after cease-fire agreement as possible and in conditions free from intimidation to give democratic elements best chance," the accords did not "contain political provisions which would risk loss of the retained area to Communist control"; nor did they "exclude the possibility of the ultimate reunification of Vietnam by peaceful means." Although Dulles and Mendès-France preferred that no date be set for the elections, the compromise two-year hiatus gave the Americans, the French, and the South Vietnamese a considerable breathing spell. The first priority, therefore, was to "give democratic elements best chance"; as was subsequently determined by Washington, this meant providing South Vietnam with economic assistance and political support. Elections, as Dulles indicated then, and as the OCB concurred in August, were agreeable to the United States; but they were two years away, and *the immediate, primary task* was "to maintain a friendly non-Communist South Vietnam. . . ." Thus, the corollary objective (stated by the NSC in August and approved by the President) "to prevent a Communist victory through all-Vietnam elections" did *not* connote American intention to subvert the accords; read in context, the phrase meant that American influence would aim at assuring that the Communists not gain an electoral victory through deceitful, undemocratic methods in violation of the Final Declaration's stipulation that they be "free."

(6) The accords expressly provided for the transfer of individuals desiring to move from one zone to another.

(7) The accords did seem, *at the time,* to have basically fulfilled the precondition of providing "effective machinery for international supervision of the agreement." Although the machinery would be the ICC's rather than the UN's, Under Secretary Smith noted that the ICC would have a veto power on important questions (referring, evidently, to the unanimity rule); would be composed of one genuine neutral (India) and one pro-Western government (Canada); and would be permitted full freedom of movement into demilitarized zones and frontier and coastal areas. Smith gave this assessment:

> Taking everything into consideration, I strongly feel this [the control and supervision arrangement] is satisfactory and much better than we were able to obtain in Korea. French feel, and Eden and I agree, that with such composition built-in veto will work to our advantage. This setup is best French or anybody else could get, and I feel it is within spirit of point 7. [Doc. 79]

Despite the overall concordance of major provisions of the accords with the Seven Points, the fact that another piece of territory had been formally ceded to the Communists obviously weighed heavily on the Administration. When, in August, papers were drawn up for the National Security Council, the Geneva Conference was evaluated as a major defeat for United States diplomacy and a potential disaster for United States security interests in the Far East. The Operations Control Board, in its progress report on the then-current NSC paper 5405, stated that the Final Declaration of the conference "completed a major forward stride of communism which may lead to the loss of Southeast Asia. It therefore recorded a drastic defeat of key policies in NSC 5405 and a serious loss for the free world, the psychological and political effects of which will be felt throughout the Far East and around the globe." In a separate report, the NSC was somewhat more specific concerning the extent of the damage, but no less restrained. The Communists had acquired "an advance salient" in Vietnam for use in military and nonmilitary ways; the United States had lost prestige as a leader in Asia capable of stemming Communist expansion; the Communist peace line had gained at America's expense; and Communist military and political prestige had been enhanced as the result of their proven ability to exploit unstable situations in Southeast Asian countries without resort to armed attack.

The conclusion that emerges from the obvious contrast between the public and private comments of Administration officials and organs is that where

American diplomacy fell down was not at the conference but during the Indo-china crisis as a whole. Nearly all the revised American negotiatory *principles* had emerged unscathed; but American *objectives* in Indochina—the elimination of the Viet Minh threat, preservation of the strategically vital Tonkin Delta, and obstruction of Communist political and military expansionist policies in the region (all of which were enumerated in NSC 5405—had still been defeated. The United States had admirably maneuvered at Geneva in its self-limited role of interested party; but the Administration, convinced that any attrition of what had been regarded as "Free World" territory and resources was inimical to American global interests, could only view the settlement as the acceptance of terms from the Communist victors. The task in Vietnam in the two years ahead was therefore to work with what had been "retained" in the hope, by no means great, that the Diem government could pull the country up by its bootstraps in time to present a meaningful alternative to Ho Chi Minh's DRV.

4. U.S. and France in Indochina, 1950–1956

Summary

AID FOR FRANCE IN INDOCHINA, 1950–1954

The United States decision to provide military assistance to France and the Associated States of Indochina was reached informally in February/March 1950, funded by the President on May 1, 1950, and was announced on May 8 of that year. The decision was taken in spite of the U.S. desire to avoid direct involvement in a colonial war, and in spite of a sensing that France's political-military situation in Indochina was bad and was deteriorating. Moreover, predictions that U.S. aid would achieve a marked difference in the course of the Indochina War were heavily qualified.

The situation in which the decision was made was completely dominated by the take-over of and consolidation of power in China by the communists. Nationalist Chinese forces had been withdrawn from mainland China and Communist Chinese troops had arrived on the border of Indochina in late 1949. This period was the high water mark of U.S. fears of direct Chinese Communist intervention in Indochina. NIE 5 of 29 December 1950 stated: "Direct intervention by Chinese Communist troops may occur at any time . . . it is almost certain to occur in strength whenever there is danger either that the Viet Minh will fail to maintain its military objective of driving the French out of Indochina, or that the Bao-Dai Government is succeeding in undermining the support of the Viet Minh."

The rationale of the decision was provided by the U.S. view that the Soviet-controlled expansion of communism both in Asia and in Europe required, in the interests of U.S. national security, a counter in Indochina. The domino thesis was quite prominent. On 6 March 1950, the Secretary of Defense wrote the President as follows: "The choice confronting the United States is to support the legal government in Indochina or to face the extension of communism over the remainder of the continental area of Southeast Asia and possibly westward . . ." Despite this statement, it was a generally accepted proposition that "regardless of current U.S. commitments for certain military assistance to China, the U.S. will not commit any of its armed forces to the defense of Indochina against overt, foreign aggression, under present circumstances."

The decision to begin military assistance to France and the Associated States of Indochina was not made under the illusion of great expectations. In April 1950, the Joint Chiefs would go no further than to say that prompt delivery of the aid would do no more than create the "possibility of success." In July 1950, General Erskine, after completing his Presidential mission to Indochina, reported that "the amount of aid and the scope of the assistance thus far requested by the French were inadequate to the needs of the situation." All U.S. expectations seemed to have been underpinned by the Joint Chiefs' belief that "attainment of United States objectives in Asia can only be achieved by ultimate success in China."

Results of the decision were mixed. Although implementation of the decision was partially successful in that it enabled the French to continue the military campaign in Indochina to the time of the Geneva Accords, military assistance was by and large a failure as an instrument of U.S. policy: the U.S. neither assured the French a military success, influenced the political situation to advantage, nor prevented the loss of North Vietnam to the communists at Geneva.

The U.S. MAAG Indochina was unable to perform even the limited functions assigned it. The French, never eager for U.S. advice, succeeded in limiting the function of MAAG to order-taking in the commercial sense.

Contributing to the initial U.S. decision to aid the French, and to limiting the effectiveness of the U.S. program of assistance, were (1) setting impracticable preconditions for assistance upon the French, (2) the U.S. proclivity to accept a slender chance of success without weighing alternatives, (3) the suppression of alternatives leading to decisional circularity and reinforcement of existing policies, (4) repeated failures of the U.S. to bargain effectively with the French, and (5) the vulnerability of the U.S. policy-making machinery to spoofing, particularly as regards U.S. credulity in accepting French information at face value and in being susceptible to "red" scares.

The decision to provide assistance to France and the Associated States is the focus of this discussion; it was but one issue among hundreds preoccupying the United States Government in the time period under consideration—the fall of China and the Korean War—and it was probably not regarded by those who made policy as among their critical decisions. There is no evidence of any high U.S. official arguing that any significant *commitment threshold* was being crossed. There were, however, those who maintained that the important anti-colonial stand of the U.S. was being undermined. These voices (and they were basically from the public domain) were drowned out by those who advocated immediate security needs. The importance of the decision was that when the U.S. was faced with an unambiguous choice between a policy of anti-colonialism and a policy of anti-communism, it chose the latter. And, although the decision was not *perceived* as getting the U.S. more deeply "involved" in Indochina, it did mark a tangible first step in that direction.

THE U.S. AND FRANCE'S WITHDRAWAL FROM VIETNAM, 1954–1956

Vietnam was the crucible of contemporary France. Military defeat by the Viet Minh—unprecedented victory of Asian over European—was but one political reagent: there was also intense frustration and disappointment among French of Rightist-colon convictions that sneaker-shod Asian peasants could undo a century of costly labor at France's "civilizing mission," and jeopardize the largest investment of French capital in the Far East. The Tonkin Delta region represented in a special way all that Vietnam meant to France. Tonkin, of all Vietnam, was where French economic stakes were highest, where the culture of France most completely overglossed indigenous ways, where stood educational focus of Vietnam—the University of Hanoi, with its French faculty—and where Catholicism flourished among the rural folk. Thus, evacuation of Tonkin per the dictates of the Geneva Settlement stung less from a sense of humiliation over Dien Bien Phu than from a sense of abandonment: an epoch had closed, France was demeaned.

Had the Geneva Settlement been fulfilled, France might have retained a presence and influence in Vietnam that would have mollified both the Right and Left. After all, no significant body of opinion in France held the French should continue to mold Vietnamese politics or that the French Expeditionary Corps should remain there undiminished—the reality of the DRV and the exigencies of North Africa rendered such a position untenable. The Left and the Center were quite willing for France to withdraw under the Geneva formula; even the "Indochina" clique within the army recognized the priority of Algeria. But France in the end, at American instance, had to accept withdrawal without the cover of general elections, and to accede to a second, further, more final abandoment.

The supplanting of France by the U.S. in South Vietnam, and the failure of the Geneva Settlement, both well advanced by mid-1956, denied the French Left its prospects for cooperation with Ho Chi Minh in a precedent-setting experiment in coexistence. It disappointed moderates who had hoped to preserve French cultural influence and salvage French capital. It enraged Rightists who interpreted American policies in Vietnam invidiously. None of these factions was prepared to take a stand for France's staying, but all attempted to draw political sustenance from acerbic treatment of the U.S.

The whole episode of French withdrawal from Vietnam, in fact, soured the Western alliance. It is possible that France's rejection of the European Defense Community on August 30, 1954, may have been in part payment for Soviet good offices on behalf of France at Geneva. But it is certain that many French were persuaded that the U.S. and the UK furnished inadequate support to France during the latter phases of the war, and at the Conference. And it is equally certain that American policy in the aftermath of Geneva widely alienated affection for the U.S. in France, and created that lack of confidence which the Suez crisis of summer, 1956, translated into outright distrust.

After the Geneva Conference, all the governments involved in the Accords, with one significant exception, anticipated that France would remain in Vietnam. The exception was the State of Vietnam, whose Premier, Ngo Dinh Diem, was determined to uproot French influence as a concomitant to the establishment of a genuinely independent nationalist government. The policy of the United States was initially directed toward a partnership with France, a joint sponsorship of Diem and the newly independent nation he headed.

Almost at once, however, U.S. policy began to respond to military urgency, and this in turn caused the U.S. to move beyond partnership to primacy. In September of 1954, SEATO was brought into being, its protection extended to Vietnam by a protocol to the Manila Pact. The U.S. resolved through SEATO to balk further expansion of communist dominion, and looked to transforming Vietnam into a key redoubt in the line of containment. The U.S. was determined that Vietnam would become politically sound, economically self-sufficient, and militarily capable of providing for its own internal security, coping with invasion from North Vietnam, and contributing to the deterrent strength of the SEATO coalition. France, then beset with internal political divisions, and plagued with Algeria, evidenced doubt, indecision, and occasional reluctance in aiding Vietnam toward the foregoing objectives. The U.S. was not prepared to wait. In late September 1954, the U.S. cut out the French as middle-men in all its assistance for Vietnam, and began to deal directly with Diem, his government, and his armed forces.

France did not readily accept this enlarged American role, nor was there complete agreement with the U.S. Government that the United States should pursue a further shouldering aside of France. Through the fall of 1954, France–U.S. relations worsened, and a policy debate developed in Washington. Once again, military considerations emerged as paramount. The JCS were originally opposed to the United States assuming responsibility for training the Army of Vietnam. They took the position, however, that if political considerations dictated such a U.S. involvement "the Joint Chiefs of Staff would agree to the assignment of a training mission to MAAG Saigon, with safeguards against French interference with the U.S. training mission." On October 26, 1954, the Secretary of Defense, acting on behalf of the President, instructed the JCS to prepare a "long-range program for the organization and training of a minimum number of free Vietnam forces necessary for internal security." The development of this plan and an appropriate working relationship with the French continued into 1955, and necessitated the dispatch to Vietnam of General J. Lawton Collins, with Ambassadorial status, to obtain a tri-partite agreement acceptable in Saigon, in Paris, and in Washington. During November 1954, the JCS expressed serious reservations about the success of such a combined undertaking. Nevertheless, the NSC considered the policy sound, and this judgment was confirmed from the field by General Collins. Collins reported that:

> It would be disastrous if the French Expeditionary Corps would be withdrawn prematurely since otherwise Vietnam would be overrun by an enemy attack before the Manila Pact Powers could be enacted.

Collins recommended that the United States continue military aid to France to "encourage the French to retain sufficient forces." In the meantime, events in Vietnam seemed to support those who, like the JCS, continued to entertain strong reservations about the future of Ngo Dinh Diem and his government. Diem managed to survive attempted coups by army leaders, and succeeded in maintaining an unhappy peace with the several armed factions of Cochinchina. But his political future remained questionable at best. At the same time, the French mission in Hanoi pressed hard to preserve French economic and cultural prerogatives in North Vietnam, and certain French political leaders in Paris spoke grandiloquently of a cooperative *modus vivendi* with the DRV becoming a model for east-west relations—a disquieting message for the U.S. Secretary of State and those who shared his convictions within the Administration. Finally, parallel to these developments, the Emperor Bao Dai, retaliating for Diem's vituperative political campaign against him, actively sought to supplant Diem.

All the foregoing tension resolved to two central issues between the United States and France. The first was the question of how and by whom Vietnam's armed forces were to be trained. The second, and more far-reaching, was whether Ngo Dinh Diem was to remain at the head of Vietnam's government, or whether he was to be replaced by another nationalist leader more sympathetic to Bao Dai and France. The first issue was resolved relatively quickly. General Collins struck an agreement with General Ely in Vietnam by which, despite serious misgivings in Paris, France agreed to turn over the training of the Vietnamese army to the U.S. and to withdraw French cadres. On February 12, 1955, the U.S. assumed responsibility for training Vietnamese forces, and the French disassociation began.

But the political controversy over Diem was less easily resolved. Diem exacerbated matters with increasingly vehement stricture against the French and Bao Dai. The United States on its part was insensitive to the impact within France of Diem's militant anti-communism—frequently directed at the French Left—and of the rancor aroused by U.S. statements portraying America as the only friend of Vietnamese nationalism. The U.S. did alert, however, to French statements that Diem was categorically incapable of unifying Vietnamese nationalists. French advice to the U.S. that Diem should, therefore, be replaced was seconded by Ambassador Collins from Vietnam. Throughout the winter and spring, Secretary Dulles and the Department of State in general seemed disposed to consider favorably suggestions that an alternative leader for the Vietnamese be placed in power. However, despite an ostensibly thorough search, no nationalist leader with qualities competitive with Diem's was identified.

Both the U.S. and France were then caught up in the sweep of events. The armed sects directly challenged Diem's authority, and he responded with force. An uneasy truce ended the first clash in March, and amid the mounting tension in April 1955, the U.S., France, and amid the mounting tension in April 1955, the U.S., France, and Bao Dai all sought actively to bring about a change in the GVN. On 28 April, Diem, against U.S. advice, against French advice, and against the advice of his cabinet, moved again against the sects. When Binh Xuyen resisted in Saigon, he committed the Vietnamese army to battle. Diem's forces won an immediate military victory, and simultaneously Diem's brother, Nhu, co-opted a committee of nationalist figures who called for Bao Dai's removal, and transfer of civil and military power to Diem.

Encouraged by Diem's success, the U.S. declared its unequivocal support for him as opposed to Bao Dai. The U.S. choice presented acute difficulties for France. The French Government was convinced that Nhu's "Revolutionary Committee" was under Viet Minh influence, and was strongly resentful of a renewed GVN campaign against French presence. In May 1955, France, the U.S., and Britain met in Paris to discuss European defense, but France promptly made Vietnam the principal agenda item. France maintained that the U.S., in backing Diem, forced upon France the necessity for withdrawing altogether from Vietnam. The French Foreign Minister Faure held that Diem was "not only incapable but mad . . . France can no longer take risks with him." Secretary Dulles in reply indicated that the U.S. was aware of Diem's weaknesses, but stressed Diem's recent successes as indicating redeeming qualities. But, Dulles pointed out "Vietnam is not worth a quarrel with France," and offered U.S. withdrawal in preference to allied disunity. No decision was taken immediately, and during a recess Secretary Dulles received advice from the JCS that Diem seemed the most promising avenue to achievement of U.S. objectives, and that while withdrawal of the French Expeditionary Corps is "ultimately to be desired," a precipitate withdrawal was to be prevented since it would "result in an increasingly unstable and precarious situation" and the eventual loss of South Vietnam to communism. Secretary Dulles then proposed to the French that they continue to support Diem until a national assembly were elected. British support for Diem seems to have swayed Faure, and he accepted Dulles' proposal. The tri-partite meeting ended on a note of harmony, but the undertones were distinct: the days of joint U.S.–French policy were over; thereafter, the U.S. would act independently of France in Vietnam.

Backed by the United States, Diem refused to open consultation with the North Vietnamese concerning general elections when the date for these fell due in July 1955. Pressing his military advantage against the sects, he moved to consolidate his position politically within South Vietnam. In October, he won a resounding victory in a popular referendum in which voters were given a choice between Diem and Bao Dai. As Diem's political strength grew, his relations with Paris deteriorated. In December 1955, Diem suddenly terminated the existing economic and financial agreements with France, and called upon France to denounce the Geneva agreements and break relations with Hanoi. Soon thereafter, he withdrew South Vietnamese representatives from the French Union Assembly.

On January 2, 1956, general elections in France produced a government under Socialist Guy Mollet, a third of the members of which were communists or avowed neutralists. In early March, Mollet's Foreign Minister, Pineau, declared in a speech to the Anglo-American Press Association in Paris that France would actively seek policy position bridging East and West, and that there was no unanimity of policy among the U.S., UK, and France. He cited UK Middle East policy and U.S. support for Diem as contrary to French interests, and condemned both powers for stirring up the Moslem world to France's distinct disadvantage in North Africa. A few days later, at a SEATO Council meeting in Karachi, Pineau proclaimed the end of the "era of aggression," and called for a "policy of coexistence."

Action followed Pineau's line. On March 22, 1956, France agreed with Diem to withdraw the FEC altogether. On April 26, 1956, the French High Command in Saigon was disestablished. On the due date for the general elections agreed to at Geneva, France possessed no military forces in Vietnam. And the date for the fulfillment of the political portions of the Settlement, July 1956, coincided with the inception of the Suez crisis.

End of Summary

I. AID FOR FRANCE IN INDOCHINA, 1950–1954

A. THE AMERICAN PERSPECTIVE DEVELOPS

1. *The U.S. and the French Colonial War*

Because the early phase (1946–1949) of the Indochina war was an overt attempt by the French to reassert authority and control over their Indochinese colonies, the United States, although aware that European Recovery Program (ERP) funds were indirectly used to finance the war, refused to support that war directly. However, American actions taken to assure a neutral position—refusal to sell armaments to the French for use in Indochina; refusal to transport troops, arms, or ammunition "to or from Netherlands East Indies or French Indochina" —accompanied by public and private statements of anti-colonialist sentiments, did constitute, at least in French eyes, a policy hostile to the French interest in Indochina. Therefore, early in 1947, the Department of State attempted to reassure the French Government, and to make U.S. policies and actions more palatable to them:

> . . . In spite any misunderstanding which might have arisen in minds French in regard to our position concerning Indochina they must appreciate that we have fully recognized France's sovereign position in that area and we do not wish to have it appear that we are in any way endeavoring undermine that position, and French should know it is our desire to be helpful and we stand ready assist any appropriate way we can to find solution for Indochinese problem. At same time we cannot shut our eyes to fact that there are two sides this problem and that our reports indicate both a lack French understanding of other side (more in Saigon than in Paris) and continued existence dangerously outmoded colonial outlook and methods in area. . . .

Neither direct nor indirect assistance to the French effort in Indochina was deemed "appropriate," however, until the French took concrete steps to grant autonomy to Laos, Cambodia, and Vietnam. The U.S. was prepared to support the "Bao Dai solution" for Vietnam when and if Bao Dai acquired genuine independence. The U.S. warned France against settling for a "native government [headed by Bao Dai] which by failing to develop appeal among Vietnamese might become virtually [a] puppet government, separated from [the] people and existing only by [the] presence [of] French military forces."

In March, 1949, in the so-called Elysee Agreement, France contracted with Bao Dai to grant "independence within the French Union" to Vietnam, Cambodia, and Laos. Despite U.S. urgings, the Elysee Agreement remained a potentially empty and ill-defined French promise for eleven months. In that period, the Nationalist forces of Chiang Kai-shek were driven from the China mainland, and in November, Mao's legions arrived at the Indochina border. In January, 1950, Ho Chi Minh declared that his was the "only legal government of the Vietnamese people" and indicated his willingness to cooperate with any nation willing to recognize it on the basis of "equality and mutual respect of national sovereignty and territory." The Communist Chinese promptly responded with *recognition*, followed by the Soviets. In France, there was a sharp debate in the National Assembly between Leftist advocates of an immediate truce with the Viet Minh, and Government supporters of ratification for the Elysee Agreement. On 2 February 1950, the French Government prevailed, and the Elysee Agreement was formally ratified. Under the circumstances, the United States determined that this action met its minimum requirements for tangible French progress towards Vietnamese autonomy. On 3 February, President Truman approved recognition of the States of Vietnam, Laos, and Cambodia. Within three months the United States decided to extend economic and military aid to the new States. On 8 May 1950, the Secretary of State announced that:

> The United States Government, convinced that neither national independence nor democratic evolution exist in any area dominated by Soviet imperialism, considers the situation to be such as to warrant its according economic aid and military equipment to the Associated States of Indochina and to France in order to assist them in restoring stability and permitting these states to pursue their peaceful and democratic development.

The U.S. involvement in the Vietnam war originated with its decision to provide assistance to France and the Associated States, and to form MAAG Indochina. Therefore, it is of particular importance to understand the reasons for the decision, the form of its execution, and its effects.

2. *The Containment of Communism*

U.S. chagrin and increasing concern over the post-World War II expansion of the Soviet Union in Europe, together with fear of further gains by communism, set the tone of U.S. policy toward Asian communist nations in the 1948–1950 period. As the Secretary of State's statement above indicates, these were the days of the "monolithic Communist bloc," dominated by the Soviet Union. A National Security Council policy paper of 1949 stated that:

> The USSR is now an Asiatic power of the first magnitude with expanding influence and interest extending throughout continental Asia and into the Pacific. Since the defeat of Japan . . . the Soviet Union has been able to consolidate its strategic position until the base of Soviet power in Asia comprises not only the Soviet Far East, but also China north of the Great Wall, Northern Korea, Sakahalin, and the Kuriles.

The question of how best to oppose the expansion of communism in Asia was raised to crisis proportions by the "loss" of China. An extensive and acrimonious national debate on foreign policy was stirred, conducted in the midst of growing public apprehension over communist penetration, espionage, and subversion in Europe and within the United States. Many advocated increased aid to the Chinese Nationalists, who were regarded by many, even at this late date, as the bulwark containing communism in Asia. Although no major emphasis was given Indochina in 1949, NSC papers did discuss the importance of the Franco-Viet Minh struggle, and link the future of Indochina with that of the rest of the world:

> In any event, colonial-nationalist conflict provides a fertile field for subversive communist activities, and it is now clear that Southeast Asia is the target of a coordinated offensive directed by the Kremlin. In seeking to gain control of Southeast Asia, the Kremlin is motivated in part by a desire to acquire Southeast Asia's resources and communication lines, and to deny them to us. But the political gains which would accrue to the USSR from communist capture of Southeast Asia are equally significant. The extension of communist authority in China represents a grievous political defeat for us: if Southeast Asia also is swept by communism we shall have suffered a major political rout the repercussions of which will be felt throughout the rest of the world, especially in the Middle East and in a then critically exposed Australia.

It was precisely the extension of communist authority over China referred to above that led to increased emphasis in U.S. policy on Indochina in late 1949 and 1950.

Following the Chinese Communist victories of 1949 and the movement of Chinese Communist troops to the border of Indochina in November of that year, NSC 64 (February 27, 1950) [Doc. 1] concluded that "the Departments of State and Defense should prepare, as a matter of priority, a program of all practicable measures designed to protect U.S. security interests in Indochina." On the same day, following the Communist Chinese (January 18) and the Soviet (January 30) recognition of the Ho Chi Minh regime, the United States announced its recognition of the Bao Dai Government. Theretofore, the U.S. had remained neutral, hesitating to choose between supporting France, a friendly colonial power engaged in re-establishing its authority, or supporting the Viet Minh, a communist-dominated independence movement in opposition to that European ally. This dilemma had been resolved by the victory of the Chinese Communists over the Nationalists, and by the threat posed to Indochina. The United States policy of support for the French and the Associated States was adjudged one befitting an anti-colonial democracy: support of nationalism and independence; opposition to attempted encroachments thereon by international communism.

3. *"The Line of Containment" and "The Domino Theory"*

The logic of this shift in U.S. policy is found not only in the direct threat to Southeast Asia posed by Communist China (and the Soviet Union), but also in the broader strategic concept of a line of containment, and in the early articulation of what later became known as the "domino theory." Discussion of the line of containment centered about *where* that line was to be drawn: Indochina, and, later, Korea, fell on the free side of that line. The domino notion had been advanced by General Claire Chennault, among others, in the reference to Nationalist China; the domino theory as applied to Indochina reinforced the decision of where to draw the line of containment. Both ideas were embodied by the Joint

Chiefs of Staff in a 1950 memorandum to the Secretary of Defense evaluating "the strategic importance, from the military point of view, of Southeast Asia":

> c. Southeast Asia is a vital segment in the line of containment of Communism stretching from Japan southward and around to the Indian Peninsula . . . The security of the three major non-Communist base areas in this quarter of the world—Japan, India, and Australia—depends in a large measure on the denial of Southeast Asia to the Communists. If Southeast Asia is lost, these three base areas will tend to be isolated from one another;
>
> d. The fall of Indochina would undoubtedly lead to the fall of the other mainland states of Southeast Asia . . .
>
> e. The fall of Southeast Asia would result in the virtually complete denial to the United States of the Pacific Littoral of Asia . . .
>
> f. . . . Soviet control of all the major components of Asia's war potential might become a decisive factor affecting the balance of power between the United States and the USSR . . .
>
> g. A Soviet position of dominance over the Far East would also threaten the United States position in Japan . . . The feasibility of retention by the United States of its offshore island bases could thus be jeopardized. [Doc. 3]

This theory, whether more or less completely articulated, appears in the relevant NSC papers of the Indochina War period, and underlies all major U.S. policy decisions taken relevant to the area.

4. *U.S. Perception of the Chinese Communist Threat*

In the words of NSC 64 (February, 1950), "The presence of Chinese Communist troops along the border of Indochina makes it possible for arms, material and troops to move freely from Communist China to the northern Tonkin area now controlled by Ho Chi Minh. There is already evidence of movement of arms." NIE 5 maintained somewhat later, as the decision to help the French was being re-examined, that: "The Communist Chinese regime is already furnishing the Viet Minh materiel, training, and technical assistance. Official French sources report that Chinese Communist troops are already present in Tonkin in some strength . . . Direct intervention by Chinese Communist troops may occur at any time . . . It is almost certain to occur in strength whenever there is danger either that the Viet Minh will fail to attain its military objective of driving the French out of Indochina, or that the Bao Dai Government is succeeding in undermining the support of the Viet Minh." NIE 5 appeared on December 29, 1950.

Although the threat of intervention to be expected from Communist China did not again reach this intensity or certainty during the remainder of the war—the estimated probability of intervention declined consistently after the publication of NIE 5—estimates throughout the period indicate continuing Communist Chinese provision of military arms, materiel, and training to the Viet Minh, and the existence of Communist Chinese *potential* for direct intervention. No direct reference was made to possible Viet Minh resentment toward, or resistance to, direct Chinese intervention.

In sum, the U.S. perceived a major Chinese threat at the time the decision to support France and the Associated States was made; a high probability was assigned direct Chinese Communist intervention at the time this decision was being confirmed; this assigned probability declined rapidly, and it remained low through the post-Korean war period. It was believed that the Chinese were providing assistance to the Viet Minh throughout the period late 1949–1954.

5.   *U.S. Perceptions of the Situation Within Vietnam*

On April 5, 1950, the Joint Chiefs of Staff, referring to intelligence estimates, indicated to the Secretary of Defense their view that "the situation in Southeast Asia has deteriorated," and that, further, "without United States assistance, this deterioration will be accelerated." (The implication that U.S. assistance would result in improvement over and above the present situation cannot be detected in this carefully worded statement.) The Joint Chiefs of Staff went on to state that: "In general, the basic conditions of political and economic stability in this area, as well as the military and internal security conditions, are unsatisfactory. These factors are closely interrelated, and it is probable that, from the long-term point of view, political and economic stability is the controlling factor. On the other hand, the military situation in some areas, particularly Indochina, is of pressing urgency."

NIE 5 was the over-all U.S. assessment of the situation in Vietnam closest in time to the U.S. decision to support the French and the Associated States. It estimated the French position as "critically endangered by the Viet Minh," and as "precarious." Combining the more detailed estimates of this document with statements and estimates contained in other U.S. documents contemporary with NIE 5, the following picture emerges:

a.   *The Military Situation*

  (1) *French-Viet Minh areas of control*—see Figures 1-5
  (2) *Force ratio*—French between 1.5 and 1.6 to 1 Viet Minh; vis-a-vis regular forces in the Tonkin Delta, the ratio was reversed—approximately 1.15 Viet Minh to 1 French (NIE 5).
  (3) *Equipment status*—French superiority, but Viet Minh improving due to Chinese aid.
  (4) *Mobility*—Viet Minh superior; French roadbound.
  (5) *Strategy*—French strategy lacking in aggressiveness, defensive, of doubtful value.
  (6) *Status of Vietnamese National Army*—essentially none; "only a slight chance that the French can maintain their military position long enough" to build such an army.
  (7) *Relative capabilities*—danger of a major military defeat of the French by the Viet Minh in Tonkin within six to nine months, which would jeopardize the French position in the remainder of Vietnam, Laos, and Cambodia.

b.   *The Economic and Political Situation*

French resources badly strained; little or no real nationalist Vietnamese leadership, government; little popular support of Bao Dai regime; political and economic situation generally poor.

c.   *French Objectives in Vietnam*

French slowness and obstruction over the years in creating a Vietnamese national government and national army (March 8, 1949, agreements were not ratified by France until February 2, 1950), and continued slowness in giving con-

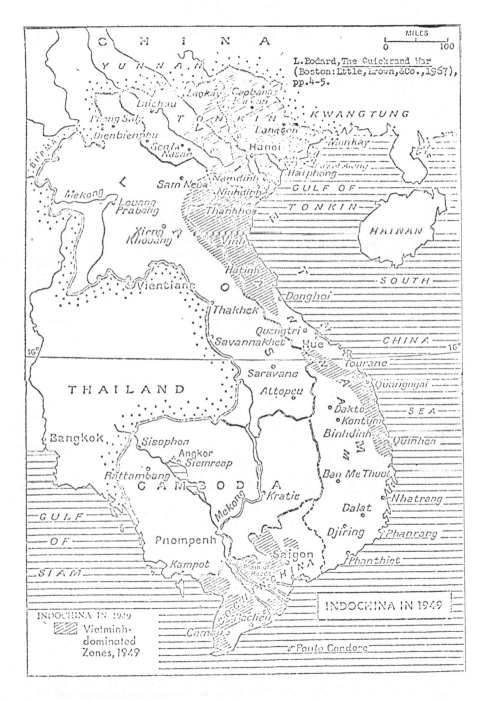

L. Bodard, The Quicksand War (Boston: Little, Brown, & Co., 1967), pp. 4-5.

INDOCHINA IN 1949

INDOCHINA IN 1949
Vietminh-dominated Zones, 1949

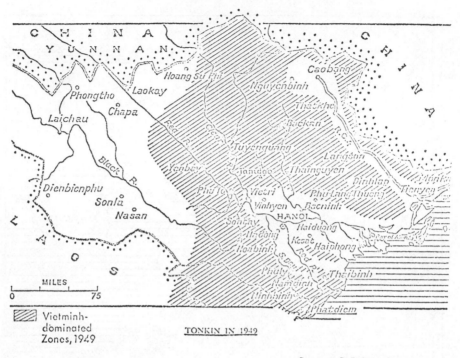

TONKIN IN 1949

Vietminh-
dominated
Zones, 1949

Source: L. Bodard, *The Quicksand War* (Boston: Little, Brown &Co., 1967).??

trol of the bureaucracy to the Vietnamese, indicate a reluctant departure, if any departure, from colonial objectives.

d. *French Resolve to Remain in Vietnam*

". . . there are grounds for questioning the French will to remain in Indochina."

Thus, the American perception of the situation in Vietnam in 1950 was generally one of gloom, with little light at the end of the tunnel; in retrospect, it seems reasonably accurate.

B. *THE BEGINNING OF AMERICAN AID*

1. *The Decision to Assist France and the Associated States*

a. *French Request Aid*

United States involvement in the bleak Indochinese situation was hastened when, on February 16, 1950, the French requested U.S. military and economic assistance for the prosecution of the Indochinese war. The French forwarded

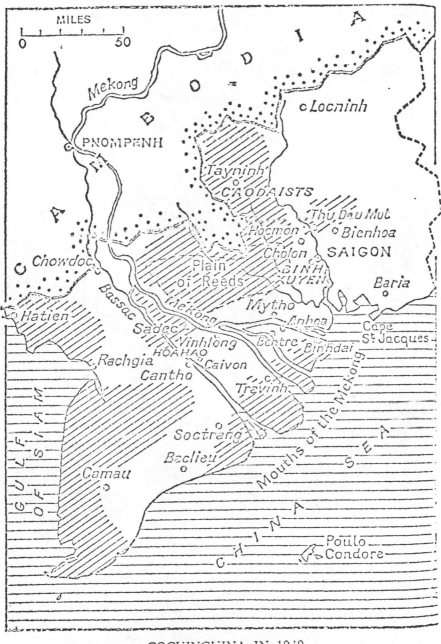

COCHINCHINA IN 1949

Vietminh-
dominated
Zones, 1949

Source: L. Bodard,
The Quicksand War
(Boston: Little, Brown&Co.
1967),30.

DISSIDENT ACTIVITIES IN INDOCHINA

(3 November 1950)

SOURCE: CIA,NIE-5
        Map Supplement
        5 January 1951

Source: V.J.Croizat,trans.,A Translation from the French:
Lessons of the War in Indochina(Santa Monica: RAND Corp.,
RM-5271-PR, May 1967),107.

VIET MINH TROOP STRENGTH
(Thousands)
Popular(guerrilla).. 100
Regional............. 70
Regular............. 160
330
In North Vietnam:80%

DMZ

LEGEND

○ Infantry battalion (regular)

◯ Regional battalion

△ Artillery or anticircraft or engineer battalion

Viet Minh deployment
September 30, 1953

their request after deciding "to set forth to the United States Government fully and frankly the extreme gravity of the situation in Indochina . . ."

> . . . the truth of the matter was that the effort in Indochina was such of a drain on France that a long-term program of assistance was necessary and it was only from the United States that it could come. Otherwise . . . it was very likely that France might be forced to reconsider her entire policy with the possible view to cutting her losses and withdrawing from Indochina . . . looking into the future it was obvious . . . that France could not continue indefinitely to bear this burden alone if the expected developments in regard to increased assistance to Ho Chi Minh came about . . . In any event the French Government was confronted with necessity of reducing the present French forces in Indochina by at least 25,000 not only for budgetary reasons, but because additional men were urgently needed in connection with French national military program.

Yet this appeal for aid, its thinly-veiled reinforcing arguments referring to withdrawal and the defense of Europe (on the day following the severing of U.S.–Bulgarian relations), was unaccompanied by a willingness to satisfy a U.S. request for France to announce the "evolutionary nature" of the governments of the Associated States, or to clarify otherwise the French intentions toward Indochina.

On February 27, a Department of State report on the position of the United States with respect to Indochina was submitted for the NSC's consideration. Issued on February 27 as NSC 64, the report concluded that:

> 10. It is important to United States security interests that all practicable measures be taken to prevent further Communist expansion in Southeast Asia. Indochina is a key area of Southeast Asia and is under immediate threat.
>
> 11. The neighboring countries of Thailand and Burma could be expected to fall under Communist domination if Indochina were controlled by a Communist-dominated government. The balance of Southeast Asia would then be in grave hazard.
>
> 12. Accordingly, the Departments of State and Defense should prepare as a matter of priority a program of all practicable measures designed to protect United States security interests in Indochina. [Doc. 1]

To "facilitate" Department of Defense consideration of NSC 64, then Deputy Under Secretary of State Dean Rusk provided Major General James H. Burns of OSD a brief statement of Department of State policy in Indochina and Southeast Asia:

> The Department of State believes that within the limitations imposed by existing commitments and strategic priorities, the resources of the United States should be deployed to reserve Indochina and Southeast Asia from further Communist encroachment. The Department of State has accordingly already engaged all its political resources to the end that this object be secured. The Department is now engaged in the process of urgently examining what additional economic resources can effectively be engaged in the same operation.

It is now, in the opinion of the Department, a matter of the greatest urgency that the Department of Defense assess the strategic aspects of the situation and consider, from the military point of view, how the United States can best contribute to the prevention of further Communist encroachment in that area.

In a memorandum for the President of March 6, 1950, the Secretary of Defense described U.S. options as follows:

The French are irrevocably committed in Indochina and are supporting the three states as a move aimed at achieving non-Communist political stability . . . The choice confronting the United States is to support the legal governments in Indochina or to face the extension of Communism over the remainder of the continental area of Southeast Asia and possibly westward . . .

b. *The Griffin Mission*

While the choice among alternatives awaited provision of the views of the Joint Chiefs of Staff and the military departments, the Secretary of State sent to the Far East "the Griffin Mission," which was given the task of surveying "the kinds and approximate value of assistance needed" in Indochina (among other countries). Departing when it did, some five months following the fall of Nationalist China, and headed by the former Deputy Chief of the Aid Mission to Mainland China, the Griffin Mission was probably intended to avoid further attacks on the State Department's Asia policy as well as to determine how U.S. economic resources might effectively be employed in Southeast Asia.

On March 22, the Griffin Mission report recommended U.S. aid for a program of rural rehabilitation, the provision of limited amounts of commodities and industrial equipment, and a program of technical assistance. These measures were estimated to cost $23.5 million for the period through June, 1951. The mission also recommended the "psychological shock of ships with military aid material in the immediate future," as a measure to dramatize the U.S. commitment to those on the scene.

c. *JCS Views*

On April 5, the Joint Chiefs of Staff responded to a request by the Secretary of Defense with recommendations for measures which, from the United States military point of view, might prevent communist expansion in Southeast Asia. The six most important points made by the Chiefs are these:

(1) A recommendation for early implementation of military aid programs for Indochina and the other states of Southeast Asia, with funds already allocated to the states of Southeast Asia, to be delivered at the earliest practicable date and to be augmented as a matter of urgency with funds from the unallocated portion of the President's emergency fund. For the next fiscal year, an estimated $100 mllion will be required for the military portion of this program.

(2) "In view of the history of military aid in China, the Joint Chiefs of Staff urge that these aid programs be subject, in any event, to the following conditions:

"*a.* That United States military aid not be granted unconditionally; rather that it be carefully controlled and that the aid program be integrated with political and economic programs; and "*b*. That requests for military equipment be screened first by an officer designated by the Department of Defense and on duty in the recipient state. These requests should be subject to his determination as to the feasibility and satisfactory coordination of specific military operations. It should be understood that military aid will only be considered in connection with such coordinated operational plans as are approved by the representative of the Department of Defense on duty in the recipient country. Further, in conformity with current procedures, the final approval of all programs for military materiel will be subject to the concurrence of the Joint Chiefs of Staff."

(3) "Formation of a Southeast Asia Aid Committee is recommended.

(4) "The Joint Chiefs of Staff recognize the political implications involved in military aid to Indochina. It must be appreciated, however, that French armed forces . . . are in the field and that if these were to be withdrawn this year because of political considerations, the Bao Dai regime probably could not survive even with United States aid. If the United States were now to insist upon independence for Vietnam and a phased French withdrawal from that country, this might improve the political situation. The French could be expected to interpose objections to, and certainly delays in such a program. Conditions in Indochina, however, are unstable and the situation is apparently deteriorating rapidly so that the urgent need for at least an initial increment of military and economic aid is psychologically overriding. The Joint Chiefs of Staff, therefore, recommend the provision of military aid to Indochina at the earliest practicable date under a program to implement the President's action approving the allocation of $15 million for Idochina and that corresponding increments of political and economic aid be programmed on an interim basis without prejudice to the pattern of the policy for additional military, political and economic aid that may be developed later."

(5) ". . . the Joint Chiefs of Staff recommend the immediate establishment of a small United States military aid group in Indochina . . . The Joint Chiefs of Staff would expect the senior member of this group to sit in consultation with military representatives of France and Vietnam and possibly of Laos and Cambodia. In addition to screening requests for materiel, he would be expected to insure full coordination of military plans and efforts between the French and Vietnamese forces and to supervise the allocation of materiel."

(6) "The Joint Chiefs of Staff believe in the possibility of success of a prompt coordinated United States program of military, political, and economic aid to Southeast Asia and feel that such a success might well lead to the gaining of the initiative in the struggle in that general area."

The last of these points is clearly fundamental to the undertaking of any program of assistance; yet in the Chiefs' memorandum it appears only as the concluding portion of the paragraph (paragraph 15) recommending establishment of a military aid group in Indochina, and is subsequently subjected to the qualification that "attainment of United States objectives in Asia can only be achieved by ultimate success in China." More remarkable, however, is the rarity with which even such equivocal predictions of success appear in the available documents relating directly to the decision to provide assistance to Indochina. Direct statements on the probable effectiveness of such United States programs of the period are typically absent; indirect statements are typically of the implied-imperative ("we must do X *if* Asia is to be saved."), or the negative-imperative (if we do *not* do X, Asia will be lost"). There was no assurance of military success given; and the calculus of the decision-making process relating to the weighing of the probability of success against the costs of failure of U.S. programs in the 1950 period is not evident, unfortunately, in available documents.

d. *Presidential Approval*

On May 1, 1950, President Truman approved the allocation of $10 million to the Department of Defense to cover the early shipment of urgently needed military assistance items to Indochina, thus taking the first crucial decision regarding U.S. military involvement in Vietnam. On May 8, the Secretary of State, in a statement at the ministerial level meeting in Paris, announced United States assistance to the Associated States and France. And on May 24, the governments of France and the Associated States were notified of the United States intention to establish an economic aid mission to the Associated States, thus marking the implementation of the recommendations of the Griffin Mission.

On June 27, 1950, President Truman, in announcing the onset of the Korean war, also stated that he had "directed acceleration in the furnishing of military assistance to the forces of France and the Associated States in Indochina and the dispatch of a military mission to provide close working relations with those forces." [Doc. 8] The concept of a military assistance advisory group had also been approved, although the President did not refer to MAAG in his public statement. Also, in June, following the recommendation of the Joint Chiefs of Staff, the Southeast Asia Aid Policy Committee was established.

e. *Erskine Mission*

The military mission dispatched by the President and headed by Major General Graves B. Erskine, USMC, arrived in Saigon on July 15, and reported its findings on August 5. General Erskine reported that a permanent solution of the Indochina crisis went beyond military action alone, the core of the problem being a deep-seated hatred and distrust of the French by the population that precluded their cooperation in the prosecution of the war. The mission also reported that the amount of aid and the scope of the assistance thus far requested by the French were inadequate to the needs of the situation.

The first elements of the U.S. MAAG were assigned to Indochina on August 3, 1950; Brigadier General Francis G. Brink, USA, assumed command as the first Chief of MAAG on October 10. The mission of the MAAG was limited to provision of material assistance to the French forces and indirect provision of military aid to the forces of the Associated States; General Brink was directed not to assume any training or advisory responsibilities toward the indigenous armies. But from the outset, the French rigorously limited end-use inspections of MAAG to a small number of carefully prescribed visits.

f. *JCS Reevaluation*

After the initial decision to provide assistance to France and the Associated States had been taken, the formation of an economic mission had been announced, the first shipment of arms and equipment had arrived in Indochina, and the MAAG had been approved and was in the process of formation, concern mounted over the soundness of these moves. The Joint Chiefs of Staff were again asked by the Secretary of Defense to formulate a position on future U.S. actions with respect to Indochina, and the Southeast Asia Aid Policy Committee (SEAAPC) published, on October 11, 1950, a draft "Proposed Statement of U.S. Policy on Indochina." The SEAAPC statement proposed adding another dimension to U.S. assistance policy: "Regardless of current U.S. commitments for provision of certain military assistance to Indochina, the U.S. will not commit any of its armed forces to the defense of Indochina against overt, foreign aggression, under present circumstances." The paper also recommended that the U.S. support the "prompt acceleration of the formation of new national armies of the three Associated States," and a covering memorandum to the Secretaries of State and Defense recommended that if negotiations were conducted with the French, U.S. representatives should:

> . . . secure French acceptance of the following conditions which shall attach to the extension of U.S. assistance in the formation of national armies in Indochina: (1) French Union Forces would not be withdrawn from Indochina until such Associated States armies are fully trained and ready to act effectively in replacement; (2) France would not decrease its outlays for Indochina below the 1950 rate during the period of the American military aid requested; (3) the national armies project would have the approval of the three Associated States governments; (4) the High Commissioner for Indochina, the French Command, and the three Associated States would maintain full consultative relations with the Legation and MAAG during the period of the formation of the armies.

The Joint Chiefs of Staff reevaluation appeared on October 27: military aid should be continued on an expedited basis. Again the judgment was offered that genuine autonomy and self-government had to be extended to the people of Indochina to ameliorate the basic cause of the deterioration of security in Indochina: lack of popular support for the authorities. But the most clearly articulated and complete expression of the Joint Chiefs' over-all position at year end is found in NSC 64/1, a November 28 paper by the Chiefs which takes account of a report from General Brink and the Southeast Asia Aid Policy Committee's draft of October 11; in fact, this statement of short- and long-run objectives contained in NSC 64/1 was to remain the basis of United States policy toward Indochina for the duration of the French-Indochina war:

SHORT TERM OBJECTIVES

a. The United States should take action, as a matter of urgency, by all means practicable short of the actual employment of United States military forces, to deny Indochina to Communism.

b. As long as the present situation exists, the United States should continue to insure that the primary responsibility for the restoration of peace and security in Indochina rests with the French.

c. The United States should seek to develop its military assistance program for Indochina based on an over-all military plan prepared by the French, concurred in by the Associated States of Indochina, and acceptable to the United States.

(1) Both the plan and the program should be developed and implemented as a matter of urgency. It should be clearly understood, however, that United States acceptance of the plan is limited to the logistical support which the United States may agree to furnish. The aid provided under the program should be furnished to the French in Indochina and to the Associated States. The allocation of United States military assistance as between the French and the national armies of Indochina should be approved by the French and United States authorities in Indochina.

(2) Popular support of the Government by the Indochinese people is essential to a favorable settlement of the security problem of Indochina. Therefore, as a condition to the provision of those further increases in military assistance to Indochina necessary for the implementation of an agreed over-all military plan, the United States Government should obtain assurances from the French Government that:

(a) A program providing for the eventual self-government of Indochina either within or outside of the French Union will be developed, made public, and implementation initiated at once in order to strengthen the national spirit of the Indochinese in opposition to Communism.

(b) National armies of the Associated States of Indochina will be organized as a matter of urgency. While it is doubtful that the buildup of these armies can be accomplished in time to contribute significantly to the present military situation, the direct political and psychological benefits to be derived from this course would be great and would thus result in immediate, although indirect, military benefits.

(c) Pending the formation and training of Indochinese national armies as effective units, and as an interim emergency measure, France will dispatch sufficient additional armed forces to Indochina to insure that the restoration of peace and internal security in that country will be accomplished in accordance with the timetable of the over-all military plan for Indochina.

(d) France will change its political and military concepts in Indochina to:

i. Eliminate its policy of "colonialism."

ii. Provide proper tutelage to the Associated States.

iii. Insure that a suitable military command structure, unhampered by political interference, is established to conduct effective and appropriate military operations. . .

(3) At an appropriate time the United States should institute checks to satisfy itself that the conditions set forth in subparagraph *c.*(2) above are being fulfilled.

d. The United Sttates should exert all practicable political and diplomatic measures required to obtain the recognition of the Associated States by the other non-Communist states of Southeast and South Asia.

e. In the event of overt attack by organized Chinese Communist forces against Indochina, the United States should not permit itself to become engaged in a general war with Communist China but should, in concert with the United Kingdom, support France and the Associated States by all means short of the actual employment of United States military forces. This support should include appropriate expansion of the present military assistance program and endeavors to induce States in the neighborhood of Indochina to commit armed forces to resist the aggression.

f. The United States should immediately reconsider its policy toward Indochina whenever it appears that the French Government may abandon its military position in that country or plans to refer the problem of Indochina to the United Nations. Unless the situation throughout the world generally, and Indochina specifically, changes materially, the United States should seek to dissuade the French from referring the Indochina question to the United Nations.

g. Inasmuch as the United States-sponsored resolution, "Uniting for Peace," has been adopted by the General Assembly of the United Nations, and should a situation develop in Indochina in a manner similar to that in Korea in which United Nations forces were required, the United States would then probably be morally obligated to contribute its armed forces designated for service on behalf of the United Nations. It is, therefore, in the interests of the United States to take such action in Indochina as would forestall the need for the General Assembly to invoke the provisions of the resolution, "Uniting for Peace." . . .

The JCS also proposed long-term objectives, urging the development of an underground guerrilla warfare capability, a psychological warfare program ("to demonstrate the evils of Communism. . . . and to warn . . . of renewed Chinese imperialism"), and encouragement of an appropriate regional security arrangement. These concepts formed the heart of an NSC Staff Study of December 28. The initial decision to give assistance was confirmed after nearly one year's continual re-examination, and remained basic to U.S. policy for the remainder of the war.

2. *MAP for Indochina*

a. *Magnitude*

The U.S. military assistance program to the French and Associated States was implemented rapidly, considering the major U.S. commitment to the Korean war. In a somewhat premature judgment of outcomes, a progress report on the implementation of NSC 64 (March 15, 1951) stated that "American military aid furnished the States' forces and the Army of the French Union may have been the decisive factor in the preservation of the area against Communist aggression." Through 1952 and into 1954 the MDAP shipments to Indochina increased steadily: by February 3, 1953, the United States had shipped 137,200 long tons of material (224 ships' cargoes); by July 1954, approximately 150,000 long tons had been sent, including 1,800 combat vehicles, 30,887 motor transport vehicles, 361,522 small arms and machine guns, 438 naval craft, 2 World War II aircraft carriers, and about 500 aircraft. By the conclusion of the Geneva agreements in July, 1954, the U.S. had delivered aid to Indochina at an original cost of $2,600 million. Nonetheless, protests of the French at the slowness of deliveries and the "interference" of MAAG with French requests were recurrent, and peaked, during the crisis days of 1954. Yet these complaints probably reflected less genuine U.S. shortcomings than French resentment of American efforts to advise, screen, inspect, and verify, and sheer frustration. Moreover, the vagaries of the French logistic system not only made the MAAG job more difficult, but further impeded combat supplies.

b. *Effectiveness*

In spite of the conditions under which U.S. assistance to France and the Associated States was given, the MAAG during the period of the Indochina war was little more than a small (70 in 1950, 342 in 1954) supply-support group which exerted far more influence upon U.S. decisions than on the French. The French, never eager for American advice, not only succeeded in limiting the function of MAAG to order-taking in the commercial sense, but in fact—through adroit pressuring of officials above the MAAG—sometimes reduced MAAG to the position of taking their military orders. Available data do not permit detailed evaluation of the efficiency of MAP, but it seems clear that French restrictions on the U.S. MAAG reduced it to virtual impotence.

If it would be an eror to evaluate the effectiveness of the U.S. program in terms of war outcome, and if the efficiency of MAP and MAAG cannot meaningfully be analyzed, it remains to evaluate the degree to which France met the conditions under which assistance was tendered, which presumably impinged directly on U.S. political objectives:

(1) The United States objective of insuring "that the primary responsibility for the restoration of peace and security in Indochina rests with the French" was fulfilled; in fact, it was insisted on by the French. On the one hand, U.S. military forces were never directly engaged in the Indochina war. On the other hand, the French, in retaining this primary responsibility, preserved the prerogative to determine policy and the freedom to reject U.S. advice. U.S. "leverage" was minimal.

(2) The condition of basing the assistance program on "an urgently prepared French plan acceptable to the Associated States and to the U.S." was frustrated in several ways. At the outset no overall plan was presented, and those portions of existing plans to which U.S. authorities were privy (*e.g.*, Allessandri's pacification plan for the Tonkin Delta) were not acceptable to U.S. thinking. Second, when the Letourneau-Allard and Navarre plans were finally prepared (in 1953, three years after the U.S. decided that a plan was a necessary precondition for aid), some U.S. observers realized that these were more concepts than plans. U.S. acceptance of the plans was more reluctant than the granting of $385 million in additional assistance might indicate. Finally, the plans, once "accepted," were not vigorously carried out.

(3) The French met *pro forma* the condition that they provide the U.S. assurances that they would grant self-government for Indochina, and form national armies for the Associated States. But it was clear throughout the war that, regardless of the amounts of U.S. assistance rendered, France's declarations of intent were grudgingly issued, and were seldom followed by action. The French Indochina war had to be lost before Vietnam was granted genuine independence.

(4) Although France did expand its forces in Indochina, these forces were never sufficient to the task. French draftees were never employed in Indochina. France continually pointed to its European defense posture in explanation. In at least one case, U.S. personnel were requested (*e.g.*, as aircraft mechanics), and 200 were provided, when a pool of suitable personnel existed in Metropolitan France.

(5) Statements to the contrary notwithstanding, the French did not ameliorate neo-mercantilism or other colonial policies, or provide "proper tutelage" to the Associated States; nor did it develop a command structure suitable to the United States.

(6) The U.S. "checks to satisfy itself that the conditions" imposed were being satisfied, were, by and large, few and far between, and were conducted at the pleasure and within the specifications of the French.

(7) The French chose not to refer Indochina to the United Nations. Certainly the U.S. assistance program bore on this decision; whether or not it was the deciding factor is unclear.

The effectiveness of the United States assistance program as an instrument of United States policy—quite aside from the outcome of the war—was thus quite low.

3. *Critique*

As earlier sections of this paper have suggested, the U.S. was persuaded to involve itself in the Indochina war by the perceived need, following the fall of Nationalist China, to hold a line against communists. This strategic drawing of the line at the Chinese-Indochina border was reinforced by the belief that the fall of Indochina would undoubtedly lead to the fall of the other mainland states of Southeast Asia, and that the fall of Southeast Asia would eventuate in the virtually complete denial to the United States of the Pacific Littoral of Asia. Prospects for a French victory in Indochina were assessed in contemporary U.S. intelligence documents as poor; nonetheless, the U.S. provided military and economic assistance to the French and the Associated States in the belief that a prompt, co-ordinated United States program of military, political, and economic aid offered some prospect that France might succeed in gaining the initiative in the struggle in that area. Six major points of critique of U.S. policy follow:

a. *The U.S. Misestimated France*

U.S. policymakers apparently realized that the conditions they imposed upon the French were impracticable to some degree. Nonetheless, they believed that pre-conditions were necessary and could assist in convincing the French to mend their colonial ways and to pursue the war with American methods, diligence, and aggressiveness. The French, long noted for proficiency and precision in logic, required no Descartes to realize that the United States was thus asking France (1) to regain full responsibility for the Indochina War, and in particular for fighting and taking casualties in that war; (2) to follow the "guidance" and "advice" of the United States on the exercise of this French responsibility; and (3) having fought the war, presumably to a successful conclusion, to relinquish control over Indochina. In view of the French willingness to retain responsibility for the war, it is not surprising that they were reluctant, at best, to accept propositions (2) and (3). Despite French pronouncements on their role in fighting communism, there is little reason to believe that they regarded the Indochina war in the same light as the U.S. viewed the Korean War. Rather, their behavior resembled that of other colonial powers who had fought to retain profitable colonies.

b. *Slim Chance Accepted by the U.S.*

Had U.S. policymakers recognized the slimness of the chance of persuading France to accept the three propositions specified above, they might have sought alternative courses of action in Indochina. As it was, the possibility (as opposed to the probability) of success was their prime consideration, and, overestimating U.S. leverage for influencing a favorable outcome, alternatives were not considered.

c. *Circular U.S. Policy*

Suppression of alternatives, both on the general and the particular level (see Note 48 for an example of the latter), led to a circularity in and reinforcement of existing policies—constant forced choices between "bad" and "worse."

d. *Poor Bargaining*

Having taken a hard policy line toward the French, the United States failed to bargain effectively. Thus, in circumstances not totally dissimilar from those prevailing in Vietnam in subsequent time periods, the U.S. continued to provide assistance disregarding infractions of pre-conditions; moreover, the pre-conditions for aid were not modified. Without modification, the conditions became worse than meaningless: standing testaments to U.S. impotence, to be recognized only when and how the French chose. The U.S. became virtually a prisoner of its own policy. Containment of communism, concern for the French in relation to the postwar Europe of NATO, EDC, and the Soviet threat in the West, combined with a fear, based on World War II strategy, that a French withdrawal from Indochina would leave exposed the U.S. flank in Korea, all compelled the U.S. to continue aid. Yet none of these considerations should have precluded modification of the U.S. bargaining strategy.

e. *Misinformation*

The U.S. policymaking machinery was highly vulnerable to spoofing, on at least three counts: (1) the very strength of the U.S. position regarding communism must have been a constant temptation, not always resisted, for other parties to cry "red" and thus to manipulate the U.S.; (2) dependence on official French sources for intelligence and other information was potentially misleading; (3) reliance on the high-level mission technique for gathering information to be used as a direct input to policy decisions proved unsatisfactory.

f. *Costs Not Weighed*

Finally, there is little indication that U.S. policymakers, their thoughts dominated by the objective of containing the monolithic communist bloc, faced up to the costs of winning the Indochina war, even while direct U.S. intervention was being considered. Nor does the evidence suggest that consideration was given to the tangible and intangible costs of providing U.S. military assistance to a power losing a war, including the potential impact on the U.S. position in Asia. And, finally, available documents fail to reveal any consideration given to the notion of sunk costs. There were, of course, voices in the wilderness. An unsigned, undated memorandum posed eight key questions to be answered by the NSC *during the spring of 1954.* Comment on the following four questions, in relation to the time at which they were raised, is unnecessary:

—Just how important is Southeast Asia to the security interests of the U.S.? Is the analysis in NSC 5405 still valid? Is the area important enough to fight for?

—How important is Indochina in the defense of Southeast Asia? Is the "domino theory" valid? Is Indochina important enough to fight for? If not, what are the strategic consequences of the loss of all or part of Indochina?

—If the U.S. intervenes in Indochina, can we count on the support of the natives? Can we fight as allies of the French and avoid the stigma of colonialism?

—Is there a strategic concept for the conduct of a war in Indochina which offers promise of early success. . . ?

The decision of the United States to provide assistance to France and the Associated States during the Indochina War is usually treated lightly, if at all, in current histories. Yet, both the taking of the decision and its implementation were significant for and remarkably similar to subsequent U.S. experiences in Vietnam.

II.   THE U.S. AND FRANCE'S WITHDRAWAL FROM VIETNAM, 1954–1956

CHRONOLOGY

7 July 54   *Diem appointed Premier of South Vietnam*
Urged by America and France, Emperor Bao Dai named Ngo Dinh Diem premier of South (Free) Vietnam. Bao Dai remained legal, constitutionally recognized Chief of State.

21 July 54   *Geneva Accords signed*
France became guarantor of Vietnamese sovereignty, unity, territorial integrity (Conference Final Declaration, Article 7); with the PAVN, guarantor of armistice agreements (Geneva Agreements, Articles 22, 23), and all-Vietnam elections (Conference Final Declaration, Article 7) France agreed to withdraw the French Expeditionary Corps at the request of local governments (Conference Final Declaration, Article 10, Unilateral Declaration, France)

8, 12 Aug 54;   *National Security Council meetings; NSC 5429/2*
20 Aug 54   US policies toward post-Geneva Vietnam.
Economic: disassociate France from levers of command, integrate land reform with refugee resettlement, work with the French but "encourage" them to turn over financial, administrative, economic controls to the Vietnamese. Give aid directly to the Vietnamese— not through France.
Military: work with France only insofar as necessary to build up indigenous military forces able to provide internal security.
Political: France must grant total independence (including right to withdraw from French Union) to South Vietnam and support a strong indigenous government. Diem must broaden the governmental base, elect an assembly, draft a constitution and legally dethrone Bao Dai. French support and cooperation for these policies was necessary; retention of the FEC was essential to South Vietnamese security.

Aug 54   *Sainteny Mission*
Jean Sainteny was sent to Hanoi to find ways to protect French economic and cultural interests in the DRV. Political overtones of the mission annoyed the US and General Paul Ely, High Commissioner in the South. Ely received firm assurance from Mendes-France that France was not playing a "double game," has not sent Sainteny for political bridge-building purposes. Mendes-France reaffirmed French support for an independent, strong South Vietnam.

8 Sep 54   *Manila Pact Signed*
Dulles' anti-communist military alliance was realized in SEATO. The Associated States of Indochina were covered by separate protocol ensuring collective defense by SEATO nations in case of subversion or aggression.

27–29 Sep 54 *Washington Conference*
France agreed to support Diem (against the French belief that Diem would prove unable to unify or stabilize the country); agreed to keep the FEC in South Vietnam but received no indication of possible US financial aid for the French forces. France knew economic and military aid would be given directly to Vietnam but was led to believe she would have a hand in its distribution by ambiguous US-drafted statements. The US military role in Vietnam was not discussed because of a State-JCS split (Dulles wanted to assume training responsibilities; JCS did not because of political instability, presence of French troops and Geneva restrictions).

22 Oct 54   *NSC Action Program*
The U.S. decided to take firmer steps to strengthen Diem, to tell Paris that French support had been inadequate. An earlier JCS concession to consider a training program for the NVA opened the way for the decision to inaugurate a "limited" U.S. role in military affairs.

24 Oct 54   *Eisenhower letter to Diem*
Announced direct economic aid and military assistance from the U.S.; demanded no Vietnamese moves as reciprocation for aid. France called it a carte americaine, said it violated the principle of joint action adopted in September.

8 Nov 54   *Collins Mission*
General J. Lawton Collins, given broad authority to coordinate all U.S. programs and—with French support—get things moving, arrived in Vietnam.

13 Dec 54   *Collins-Ely Minute of Understanding*
France will grant full autonomy to the VNA by July 1955, the U.S. will assume training responsibilities, the U.S. MAAG, Indochina, will direct the training program—under General Ely's overall authority. French and U.S. instructors will be phased out as VNA efficiency increases. Washington approved the Minute; Paris objected, particularly to the phase-out of French trainers. France did not relent and consent until 11 February 1955.

16 Dec 54   *Collins recommends Diem be replaced*
Diem's failure to include Dr. Quat in the cabinet as Defense Minister confirmed Collins' doubts about Diem's capacity to stabilize the government, or rally support for his regime. He recommended Bao Dai's return be considered, but if this were unacceptable, recommended the U.S. withdraw from Vietnam.

19 Dec 54   *Trilateral Meetings, Paris (U.K., U.S., France)*
Mendes-France insisted the time had come to consider an alterna-

tive to Diem. Recommended Collins and Ely study the problem and come up with suggestions for a change by mid-January. France felt Bao Dai should be involved in an alternative plan. Dulles: Diem is the only suitable leader but we will consider alternatives and will allow Collins and Ely to consider the matter. But Dulles made it clear that Congress would probably not appropriate funds to a Vietnam without Diem. U.S. study of alternatives was cursory, however; Dulles was sure Diem could succeed, with proper direction; he was more sure that no other possible leader existed.

20 Jan 55   Collins' report to NSC
December's despair over Diem had dissipated; Diem's had acted well on a few matters. Collins recommended continued support for Diem because without it South Vietnam will surely fall to communism and the rest of other Southeast Asia will soon follow. The NSC approved Collins' report.

12 Feb 55   Training Relations and Instruction Mission (TRIM) opens
General O'Daniel, under Ely's general supervision, took charge of programs to train and reorganize the VNA along American lines. Despite friction between French and Americans in Saigon and despite Paris-Washington disputes, officers in TRIM seemed able to rise above differences and initiate sound programs for the VNA.

22 Feb 55   United Front announced
French subsidies to the Cao Dai and Hoa Hao sect armies—about 40,000 men—ended in February. When Diem refused to meet sect requests for financial aid, integration of forces into the VNA and recognition of spheres of influence, previous sect cooperation with Diem ceased. Representatives of the Cao Dai, Hoa Hao, Dan Xa (Ba Cut), Lien Minh (Thinh Minh Thé) and Binh Xuyen (Bay Vien) forces met at Tay Ninh, agreed to work together against Diem. Cao Dai Pope Tac headed the group.

21 Mar 55   United Front "ultimatum"
Claiming to speak for the popular will, the United Front asked that Diem form a government of national union and make other political, economic, military reforms. Diem called this an ultimatum and refused to consider the request. The Front then sent an emissary to Bao Dai asking him to intervene on its behalf. Bao Dai refused.

29–30 Mar 55 Diem attacks central police headquarters
Brewing for months, the fight finally broke between Diem and the Binh Xuyen (a coalition of gangsters and river pirates which ran gambling and prostitution in Cholon, and the Saigon-Cholon police, paid Bao Dai for his protection and enjoyed some French support). A company of paratroopers took over the central police station, driving the Binh Xuyen back into Cholon. Diem then wanted to go after Police Commissioner Sang and end Binh Xuyen control. Defense Minister Minh resigned when Diem refused to consult the cabinet over this. However, French representations dissuaded Diem from taking on Bay Vien's 600-man force at this

time, and the French then negotiated a truce between Diem and the Binh Xuyen.

7 Apr 55   *Collins and Ely agree Diem must go*
Collins says Diem has proved himself incapable of inspiring unity, and must be replaced. Dulles demurs, then agrees to consider a change if Collins will fly to Washington for consultations.

23 Apr 55   *Diem proposes to broaden the government*
Diem calls for a national referendum and elections for a national assembly within six months. The Front scores the proposal.

26 Apr 55   *Diem fires Sang*
(Collins had left Saigon for Washington.) Diem replaces Sang with a man loyal to his regime but Sang refuses to resign saying only Bao Dai had the legal authority to remove him.

27 Apr 55   *Dulles agrees to a change in Saigon*
Collins met with Dulles in Washington. Dulles agreed to consider an alternate to Diem but was determined to keep this from the French until their purposes were clear and their promise to unequivocally support a new regime firm. Saigon was informed of this new policy.

28 Apr 55   *Diem hits the Binh Xuyen*
Diem struck at the Sureté—and Sang—after fighting erupted between the VNA and Binh Xuyen forces in Cholon. The French said Diem instigated the fight; Americans supported Diem's version that the Binh Xuyen began firing first. Whatever its origin, the fight ended with a VNA victory. The Binh Xuyen were driven out of Cholon into the Rung Sat swamps.

30 Apr 55   *Revolutionary Congress Announced*
Diem's brother Nhu had a hand in organizing this broad amalgam of political interests behind a program calling for support of Diem against the Binh Xuyen sects and Bao Dai, in favor of broad representation in the government. Generals Thé and Phuong, tired of the "weak" Revolutionary Congress, formed a Revolutionary Committee whose outlook was more anti-Bao Dai and anti-French than the Congress. Present and former Vietminh supporters were members of the Congress and Committee.

1 May 55   *Bao Dai's ultimatum*
Bao Dai summoned Diem to replace the Army Chief of Staff with his own man. Diem ignored the summons and orders.

1 May 55   *The U.S.: back on the track behind Diem*
Because of Diem's victory—superficial though it may have been —over the Binh Xuyen, because of VNA support for Diem, Dulles canceled the cable of 28 April: again, the U.S. will support Diem.

8 May 55   *A National Campaign launched*
Diem announced a national campaign to regain "wayward" provinces and unify the country. Or: he declared war on the sects. The VNA fought over a year against Hoa Hao and Binh Xuyen

forces, but finally established control over them, over areas of sect influence and control.

8–11 May 55   *Tripartite Talks, Paris*
Faure: We cannot support Diem—but Vietnam is not worth a split in Franco-American relations. Therefore, France offers to withdraw from Vietnam. Dulles: We must support Diem. But if a U.S. withdrawal would prevent discord, the U.S. will consider it. Then, after hearing JCS and Collins' arguments against either precipitate French withdrawal or a U.S. withdrawal, Dulles urged Faure to [words missing] Diem a while longer on the grounds that he will broaden the government and call for elections. Faure agreed— against his own wishes and against strong popular pressure and on several conditions (most of which required action from Diem and which Dulles coud not guarantee). Dulles then suggested France and the U.S. apprise each other of policy and actions but pursue them more independently than in the past. The days of joint policy—of togetherness in Vietnam—were over.

July 1955   *Diem refuses to meet with the DRV about elections*
France and Britain urged Diem to hold consultations with Hanoi for all-Vietnam elections, as stipulated in the Geneva Accords. The U.S. suggested consultations but also suggested Diem request firm guarantees (for secret ballot, UN or international supervision) which the DRV was expected to reject. But Diem refused to meet with the North Vietnamese. He had not signed the Geneva Accords and denied being bound by them in any way.

24 Oct 55   *National Referendum*
With 98 percent of the vote, Diem became President of the Republic of Vietnam—and Bao Dai was dethroned.

Aug–Dec   *Franco-Vietnamese Conferences*
1955   Diem wanted renegotiation of economic and financial accords reached in 1954; transfer of Vietnamese affairs from the ministry of the associated states to the Foreign Office; abolition of Ely's former post of High Commissioner; termination of the military High Command and Vietnamese authority over remaining French troops in Vietnam. (The FEC now numbered about 35,000—*vice* the 150,000-man force which France spoke of retaining in Vietnam during the September 1954 Washington Conference.) France could not accept Diem's last demand; had difficulty satisfying the others, but finally made major concessions. Diem's response was to withdraw Vietnamese representatives from the French Union Assembly.

26 Apr 56   *French High Command abolished*
Only about 5,000 French troops remained in Vietnam; most French instructors had left TRIM. A French liaison mission with the ICC still functioned, however, and France still served on the Joint Armistice Commission with DRV military representatives.

July, 1956   *All-Vietnam elections*
Diem had refused to consult with the DRV about elections in

1955; he refused to hold them in 1956. Diem did agree to take over the French responsibility to support the ICC; France would continue to finance ICC operations. The Joint Armistice Commission gradually died of inactivity.

KEY AMERICAN PERSONALITIES: 1954–1956
20 Jan 53–20 Jan 61
President: Dwight D. Eisenhower
Secretary of State: John Foster Dulles
Secretary of Defense: Charles E. Wilson
Ambassador to Vietnam: Donald R. Heath (25 Jun 52–20 Apr 55);
   Gen. J. Lawton Collins, Special Mission (8 Nov 54–6 May 55);
   G. Frederick Reinhart (20 Apr 55–14 Mar 57)
Chairman, JCS: Arthur W. Radford, Adm., USN (14 Aug 53–15 Aug 57)
Chief MAAG, Indochina:
   John W. O'Daniel, Lt. Gen., USA (31 Mar 54–23 Oct 55);
   Samuel T. Williams, Lt. Gen., was 1st Chief of MAAG to Vietnam (24 Oct 55–31 Aug 60)

KEY FRENCH PERSONALITIES: 1954–1956
Jun 54–Feb 55
Prime Minister: Pierre Mendes-France
Foreign Minister: Georges Bidault
Minister for Associated States: Guy La Chambre
Minister for National Defense: Rene Pleven
High Commissioner, Vietnam: General Paul Ely

23 Feb 55–31 Jan 56
Prime Minister: Edgar Faure
Foreign Minister: Antoine Pinay
Minister for Associated States: M. La Forest
Minister for National Defense: General Pierre Koenig
High Commissioner, Vietnam: General Ely's post abolished after his departure, June 1955. (Gen. Jacquot assumed military responsibilities until April, 1956)
Ambassador, Vietnam: Henri Hoppenot (July, 1955)

31 Jan 56–16 Apr 57
Prime Minister: Guy Mollet
Foreign Minister: Christian Pineau
Minister for National Defense: Maurice Bourges-Maunouvy
High Commissioner, Vietnam: (General Jacquot—military responsibilities until April 1956)
Ambassador, Vietnam: M. Payart (November, 1956)

KEY SOUTH VIETNAMESE PERSONALITIES: 1954–1956
Mar 49–26 Oct 55
Head of State: Bao Dai, Emperor

12 Jan 54–16 Jun 54
Head of State: Bao Dai
Premier: Prince Buu Loc
Minister for Foreign Affairs: Nguyen Quoc Dinh

7 Jul 54–1 Nov 63
Head of State: Ngo Dinh Diem (President: 23 Oct 55)
Premier: Ngo Dinh Diem
Minister for Foreign Affairs: Tran Van Do (Jul 54–May 55)
                              Vu Van Mau (Jul 55–Nov 63)
Minister for National Defense: Ngo Dinh Diem (General Minh served temporarily, early 1955).

A. INTRODUCTION: POST-GENEVA EXPECTATIONS

1. France Will Stay in Vietnam

After 100 years of investment, interest and influence, France got out of Vietnam in less than a year after the Geneva Conference of July 1954. And France did not want to leave. On July 25, three days after signing the Geneva Accords, Prime Minister Mendes-France said France would maintain cultural and economic ties with North Vietnam and would assist the development of Free (South) Vietnam. The predecessor Laniel Government had recognized "Vietnam as a fully independent and sovereign state in possession of all qualifications and powers known in international law" on June 4, 1954; Mendes-France pledged to uphold and further that treaty. In August he announced a three-phase formula to implement it. Economic, administrative and financial ties with the Associated States would be terminated as fast as possible. By December 1954, the last vestiges of the French colonial apparatus had been eliminated. However, Mendes-France's formula viewed membership in the French Union as compulsory—indicative of French desire to stay in Vietnam but inimical to demands lodged by Diem and the United States for independence which included the right to withdraw from the French Union.

Also in August, General Paul Ely, French High Commissioner in Vietnam, reaffirmed French support of Vietnamese independence and French readiness to further Vietnamese development. That the French had a role to play was clear: French economic investment, cultural institutions, military, political and administrative operations were already part of South Vietnamese life. That France must play a role was also clear. Under the Geneva Accords, France had pledged to guarantee all-Vietnam elections in 1956, guarantee execution of the armistice agreement, guarantee Vietnamese sovereignty, unity and territorial integrity, pledged to maintain the French Expeditionary Corps until Vietnam requested its removal. General Ely had been delegated extensive political and military authority to enable him to meet these obligations. He worked sincerely to persuade both Vietnamese and French that mutual cooperation would be mutually beneficial, to erase the colonialist tinge of French presence, to both speed and smooth the French transition from master to equal partner of Vietnam.

2. Diem: France Will Leave South Vietnam

In this endeavor, Ely received qualified support from French officials, "colons" and military officers in Vietnam. He received sporadic support from Paris. He received almost no support from the Vietnamese. France was not welcome in Vietnam for many reasons, a major one being Premier Ngo Dinh Diem. A Francophobe of the first order, Diem wanted full independence for South Vietnam and wanted France out of the country as soon as possible. Many shared Diem's sentiments. France had just lost a long, devastating and demoralizing war against Vietnamese communists as well as Vietnamese nationalists. French colonial rule had been tight, previous French promises of independence had been broken. Why believe professions of French good intentions in 1954 were any different from those of the past? Added to this was the problematical relationship of France *vis-a-vis* South Vietnam and the Democratic Republic of North Vietnam. Some South Vietnamese expected France to actively work toward accommodation with the Viet Minh and reunification of North and South under Viet Minh direction. Many more felt the fact of continued French presence alone compromised South Vietnamese independence. "To convince the people of Vietnam that the administration was independent, it became a political necessity to be anti-colonial and specifically anti-French."

3.   The U.S. Will "Join" France in South Vietnam

Finally, France was not alone in Vietnam. More than Diem, more than the psychological damage done by colonial years, the United States made life in Vietnam difficult for France. The U.S. was eager to strengthen Vietnam, needed and demanded French cooperation, but offered little in return. U.S. policy insisted upon an immediate and dramatic transformation of French policy. But the U.S. little understood what this meant to France, what problems it created for French domestic and foreign policy or what U.S. concessions might help effect the transformation.

Although remnants of the French Expeditionary Corps remained until 1956, France was out of Vietnam to all intents and purposes by May 1955, ten months after Geneva. These months are characterized by professions of Franco–American cooperation but demonstrations of Franco–American division, characterized by conflict of word and action on several levels. Paris said one thing but did another, Paris said one thing and French officials in Saigon did the opposite; Washington activities were not always in line with Washington pronouncements and the gulf between the thought and deed of Ngo Dinh Diem only compounded an already sensitive situation. It is during this period that Diem established his rule, against French advice and best interests but with almost unwavering support from Secretary of State John Foster Dulles. And it is the period during which the anti-communist moralism of Dulles and Diem rejected any rapprochement with the North, ultimately ensuring that the temporary military demarkation line would become a permanent division of Vietnam.

B.   INITIAL U.S. POLICY TOWARD INDOCHINA

The U.S. began revising policy toward Indochina as the Geneva Conference closed. The exercise was marked by urgency dictated by the belief that Geneva had been a disaster for the free world. Geneva gave Communist China and North Vietnam a new base for exploitation of Southeast Asia; it enhanced Peking's prestige to Washington's dismay and detriment; it restricted free world room to maneuver in Southeast Asia. And its grant of Vietnamese territory above the seventeenth parallel to the communist Ho Chi Minh was a painful reminder of the scarifying French defeat by the Viet Minh, the first defeat of a European power by Asians (Asian communists at that), a defeat shared by the United States to the tune of more than $1.5 billion in economic and military assistance granted France and the Associated States of Indochina.

1. *SEATO: The New Initiative?*

The first step toward countering this disaster had been discussed with Britain and France since the spring of 1954, and Walter Bedell Smith's comment as Geneva closed, "We must get that pact!," heralded its inauguration. The Southeast Asian Collective Defense Treaty was to be a "new initiative in Southeast Asia" to protect the U.S. position in the Far East and stabilize "the present chaotic situation . . . to prevent further losses to communism" through subversion or overt aggression. But the Manila Pact, signed on September 8, 1954, proved to be neither the new initiative nor the strong anti-communist shield called for by Secretary Dulles. Vice Admiral A. C. Davis, deputy assistant secretary and Defense Department representative at Manila, reported the Pact left Southeast Asia "no better prepared than before to cope with Communist aggression." The failure was largely of American making. While Dulles wanted to put the communists on notice that aggression would be opposed, the Joint Chiefs of Staff insisted the United States must not be committed financially, militarily or economically to unilateral action in the Far East and that U.S. freedom of action must not be restricted. The two objectives conflicted and one cancelled out the other. Thus, Article IV of the treaty, the mechanism for collective action in case of enemy threat, did not pledge automatic response with force to force. Instead, each signatory promised to "act to meet the common danger in accordance with its constitutional processes." The United States, particularly Mr. Dulles, tried to put teeth into SEATO through unilateral declarations of U.S. readiness to act. Dulles defined the obligations under Article IV as "a clear and definite agreement on the part of the signatories, including the United States, to come to the aid of any member of the Pact who under the terms of this treaty is subjected to aggression." However, Dulles failed to instill the same dedication to instant intervention in the other SEATO members.

The obligation assumed at Manila emphasized the importance attached to Southeast Asia by the U.S. Government. U.S. refusal to pledge unqualified support to Indochina emphasized the need for indigenous strength and stability in the area to counter communist power, to make infiltration and aggression less appetizing to the enemy. Of the three Indochina states, most important yet least stable and least strong was South Vietnam. Thus, the second step in policy development was to decide what the U.S. could do to change the situation, a decision which turned on what France could or would do in South Vietnam.

2. *Alternative French Policies*

That France and the United States would eventually part company over Vietnam might have been predicted in August 1954, when U.S. policy toward Vietnam was drawn. Formulae for economic, military and especially political courses of action were different from—often antithetical to—French objectives and interests.

The U.S. intelligence community felt if France "acted swiftly to insure Vietnam full independence and to encourage strong nationalist leadership . . . anti-French nationalist activity might be lessened (and) with French military and economic assistance—backed by U.S. aid—the Vietnamese could proceed to develop gradually an effective security force, local government organization and a long range program for economic and social reform." But there were three other routes or combinations of routes open to France in post-Geneva Vietnam. France could work to maintain French Union ties, indirect French political control and economic domination rather than grant full independence to Vietnam. Or, France could try to reach an agreement with the Viet Minh, expedite elections and achieve a unified country in which French cultural, economic and political interests could be maintained. A fourth possibility, thought likely only if the situation deteriorated to the point of hopelessness, was a French decision to withdraw all military, economic and administrative support from Indochina.

Of the four courses of action open to France, three were rejected by the Eisenhower Administration. Continuation of French Union ties plus indirect French controls would be impossible under Diem, whose anti-French feeling ran deep, who had not in the past and would not now accept anything less than complete freedom from France. And Diem had American backing. Dulles believed "the kind of thing he stands for" is the "necessary ingredient of success" and called the Diem government the "nucleus for future efforts." Accommodation with the Viet Minh was anathema to both Diem and the U.S. Although American policy spoke of taking steps to prevent the complete absorption of the DRV into the Soviet bloc, those steps amounted to nothing more than maintenance of a U.S. consulate in Hanoi. Dulles in particular could not see Ho Chi Minh as Asia's Tito and refused to deal with him, thereby crushing Mendes-France's hope that Vietnam could become an experiment in peaceful coexistence. The U.S. was equally determined to prevent the quick withdrawal of the French Expeditionary Corps from Vietnam. It was believed:

> in the last analysis, Vietnamese security will be determined by the degree of French protection and assistance in the development of a national army,

plus Vietnamese energies and the will of other powers to guarantee Vietnamese security.

Thus, United States policy required France to grant full Vietnamese independence quickly and to support a strong indigenous political regime, to maintain French military presence but reduce military, economic and political controls. Basic guidance determined at National Security Council meetings on August 8 and 12 became NSC 5429/2, issued on August 20.

3. *U.S. Objectives in Vietnam: Political, Economic, Military*

The American formula for government in free Vietnam rested on three legs. Independence was first and more important. France must treat South Vietnam as an independent sovereign nation and the U.S. would deal with it on that basis. Full independence was the only way to win nationalist support away from the Viet Minh, and nationalist support was thought to be essential to successful government in South Vietnam. Secondly, the U.S. would urge Ngo Dinh Diem to establish a government of national union representative of dominant elements on the political scene. After bringing some stability to the nation, a Constituent Assembly would be called and a constitution drafted to herald the legal dethroning of Emperor Bao Dai and inauguration of democracy. Finally, the formula demanded firm French and U.S. support for Diem. Despite his rigidity, his penchant for a one-man show and his inability to communicate or deal with people, Diem was a nationalist untainted by past association with either Viet Minh or French. This quality, plus full independence, plus Franco–American backing and encouragement for broad reform ultimately would result in a strong anti-communist South Vietnam. Or so the U.S. thought.

U.S. determination to back Diem was made with the knowledge that French support for him was hardly enthusiastic. Guy La Chambre, Minister for the Associated States, faulted Diem on three essential points: Diem would oppose a representative government, oppose agrarian reform and refuse to depose Bao Dai and create a republic. La Chambre expected a new government would be necessary to give South Vietnam a chance of winning the 1956 elections.

American's economic policy for South Vietnam was designed to yield immediate political advantage, cope with the staggering distortion of Vietnamese economic life and ease France out of economic affairs. U.S. planners believed integration of land reform measures with refugee resettlement would fill a triple bill: surplus land distributed among the thousands of refugees would invite their political support, facilitate assimilation of Tonkinese with Cochin–Chinese and bring the land to full productivity. Aid would be given directly to Vietnam as befitting its independence and as a means to accelerate the "disassociation of France from (economic) levers of command." French domination in this area, it was thought, stifled Vietnamese efforts and contradicted Vietnamese independence. It also inhibited American economic interests. Militarily, the U.S. would build up "indigenous military forces necessary for internal security . . . working through the French only insofar as necessary." Exactly how indigenous forces would be developed was not decided until December 1954, because France had some ideas about what to do and the Joint Chiefs of Staff differed with State Department opinions as to the kind of U.S. involvement required.

4. The U.S. "Chooses" Policy for France

In effect, these policy decisions of August 1954 asked Mendes-France to overcome "French traditional interests and emotions which have in the past governed the implementation of policy in Indochina." They asked for—or demanded—a "dramatic transformation in French policy" because policy makers believed this was necessary to "win the active loyalty and support of the population for a South Vietnamese Government." The U.S. asked France to stay in Vietnam militarily, to get out of Vietnamese economic and political life, but at the same time Washington asked for French support and cooperation in implementing U.S. programs. This was probably asking too much.

By December, the U.S. no longer asked for French support but demanded it. By December, the qualified U.S. commitment to Diem had hardened, U.S. involvement in Vietnam had deepened and U.S. activities there either dominated or simply excluded the French. Several forces converged to produce this change in U.S. policy. Resolution of differences within the Eisenhower Administration on military issues opened the way for U.S. assumption of responsibilities in what had been an exclusively French preserve. The belief that Diem for all his failings and weaknesses was the only available leader for South Vietnam, and that he needed stronger U.S. and French support to quell opponents and speed development led to the creation of programs designed to provide that strong support.

Finally, the U.S. believed France had not done enough for Diem, believed the schizophrenic French policy of professing support while acting to undermine Diem's regime was largely to blame for Vietnamese difficulties. This resulted in demands that France live up to her promises. It made unilateral American efforts more attractive—French assistance might not be available in any case—and it inspired a feeling that Americans had to do more because the French were doing so little.

C. TENTATIVE U.S. INVOLVEMENT
BECOMES DEEPER, FIRMER

1. Adoption of Military Responsibilities

Authorization for General John (Iron Mike) O'Daniel, Chief of the Military Assistance and Advisory Group (MAAG), Indochina, to take up the task of training the Vietnamese National Army (VNA) was long in coming. General O'Daniel and French General Ely had discussed U.S. participation in training in June 1954; O'Daniel drew up a comprehensive plan for advisory assistance at all levels of the military establishment and in July begged the U.S. to beef up the MAAG staff before August 11, when the Geneva prohibition against introduction of new military personnel went into effect. But the Joint Chiefs of Staff objected.

a. The JCS Arguments Against U.S. Training the VNA

Early in August, the JCS listed four preconditions essential to the success of a U.S. training effort in Indochina, preconditions which should be met before training obligations were assumed. First:

> It is absolutely essential that there be a reasonably strong, stable civil government in control. It is hopeless to expect a US military training mission to achieve success unless the nation concerned is able effectively to perform those governmental functions essential to the successful raising and maintenance of armed forces.

Secondly, that government "should formally request that the United States assume responsibility for training . . . forces and providing the military equipment, financial assistance and political advice necessary to insure internal stability." The Chiefs saw no role in training for the French; the third precondition called for complete French withdrawal from the country:

> Arrangements should be made with the French granting full independence to the Associated States and providing for the phased, orderly withdrawal of French forces, French officials and French advisors from Indochina in order to provide motivation and a sound basis for the establishment of national armed forces. The United States from the beginning should insist on dealing directly with the governments of the respective Associated States, completely independent of French participation or control.

Finally, both "local military requirements and the over-all U.S. interests should dictate the size and composition of indigenous forces."

b. Dulles' Views

Of the four preconditions, only the second presented no problem. The State Department, notably Secretary Dulles, Walter F. Robertson, Assistant Secretary of State for the Far East, and Kenneth T. Young, head of an interdepartmental Vietnam Task Force, objected to the other three stipulations. Dulles outlined his thinking in a letter of August 18 to Defense Secretary Charles Wilson. Agreeing that the Diem government "is far from strong or stable" Dulles pointed out that reorganization and retraining of the army was "one of the most efficient means of enabling the Vietnamese Government to become strong." Calling this "the familiar hen-and-egg argument as to which comes first," Dulles made his preference clear. He saw two courses of action open to the United States:

> one, to strengthen the government by means of a political and economic nature and the other, to bolster that government by strengthening the army which supports it.

Dulles wished to adopt both courses.

As for the question of French presence or absence, Dulles said:

> It would be militarily disastrous to demand the withdrawal of French forces from Vietnam before the creation of a new National Army. However . . . there would seem to be no insuperable objection to the U.S. undertaking a training program . . . while at the same time the French Forces commence a gradual phasing out from that theater.

c. *The NSC Backs Dulles*

Adoption of NSC 5429/2 indicates the U.S. Government found Dulles' views more persuasive that those of the Joint Chiefs of Staff. But while it was agreed to "work through the French only insofar as necessary" to build up indigenous forces, the program for bolstering the Vietnamese army was not developed for several months.

d. *JCS-State Split on Force Level, Mission for VNA*

On September 22, in a memorandum recommending establishment of a MAAG, Cambodia (if "all French advisors ultimately" are withdrawn, if the U.S. deals directly with Phnom Penh and if these caveats are written into a bilateral agreement with Cambodia), the JCS recommended against assignment of training responsibilities to the Saigon MAAG because of the "unstable political situation" in South Vietnam. Instability was noted "with concern" by the JCS in a second September 22 memorandum dealing with development of forces in Indochina, as was the cease-fire agreement (called "a major obstacle to the introduction of adequate U.S. MAAG personnel and of additional arms and equipment"). Because of these factors, the Chiefs considered "this is not a propitious time to further indicate United States intentions with respect to the support and training of Vietnamese forces."

But the JCS had been directed by the NSC to address the question of Vietnamese force levels; against their best wishes, one supposes, this memorandum forwarded their views. A 234,00-man army was proposed for Vietnam; the annual cost of training and maintaining this force—assuming France turned over to the VNA arms and equipment furnished under the U.S. Military Development Assistance Program since 1950—was put at $420 million. Another $23.5 million would be needed to train and equip the Navy and Air Forces. Further, the JCS wanted speedy relinquishment of French over-all command of the VNA and speedy withdrawal of French forces as the Vietnamese "are capable of exercising command of an effective force." Finally, the JCS requested "a definite agreement . . . be obtained from the French Government with respect to the timing of their programmed phased withdrawal" before U.S. assumption of training responsibilities.

Dulles objected to these proposals:

> It seems to me that the mission of the Vietnamese National Armed Forces should be to provide internal security. The manpower and cost estimates (of the JCS) would seem to be excessive in the above context.

The Secretary called a French request of $330 million to support the French Expeditionary Corps, then expected to number 150,000 men through 1955, and the Vietnamese plan to keep 230,000 men under arms ". . . beyond what the United States should consider feasible to support for maintaining the security of free Indochina at this time." Instead, he called it "imperative" that the U.S. Government—e.g., the JCS—"prepare a firm position on the size of the forces we consider a minimum level to assure the internal security of Indochina."

A week later the Chiefs in turn objected. The idea of training the VNA for internal security contradicted NSC 162/2 which "envisages reliance on indigenous ground forces to the maximum extent possible" in territorial defense. Citing the threat from "considerable numbers of Viet Minh guerrillas and sympathizers . . . known to be or suspected of being within the territory of free Vietnam" and the GVN "intention of requesting the phased withdrawal of the French forces by 1956" the Chiefs said:

> This would result in a complete military vacuum unless the Vietnamese are adequately prepared to take over progressively as the French withdraw.

The force levels recommended on September 22 were reaffirmed as "the minimum required ultimately to carry out the . . . objectives" of the VNA, which should be "to attain and maintain internal security and to deter Viet Minh aggression by a limited defense of the Geneva Armistice demarcation line." The JCS pointed again to the unstable political situation in Vietnam, the 342-man MAAG ceiling and concluded:

> Under these conditions, U.S. participation in training not only would probably have but limited beneficial effect but also would assume responsibility for any failure of the program. In light of the foregoing and from a military point of view, the Joint Chiefs of Staff consider that the United States should not participate in the training of Vietnamese forces in Indochina. However, if it is considered that political considerations are overriding, the Joint Chiefs of Staff would agree to the assignment of a training mission to MAAG, Saigon, with safeguards against French interference with the U.S. training effort.

e. *Again, the NSC Backs Dulles, Recommends a U.S. Military Program in South Vietnam*

Political considerations were overriding. The JCS concession to consider training the Vietnamese for internal security alone coincided with deliberations in the Operations Coordinating Board over possible ways in which to strengthen the Diem regime. A crash program had been outlined by State, part of which was a limited interim training program recommended by the OCB. Admiral

Radford, Chairman of the Joint Chiefs of Staff, believed this would set in motion the long-range training program proposed by General O'Daniel in June; he still believed that program should not be adopted. But before the JCS could consider or suggest revisions to the OCB proposal, the National Security Council met on October 22 and approved a joint State-Defense message to Saigon authorizing Ambassador Donald Heath and O'Daniel to "collaborate in setting in motion a crash program designed to bring about an improvement in the loyalty and effectiveness of the Free Vietnamese Forces." The JCS were directed to recommend force levels necessary to "accomplish the military objective merely of the maintenance of internal security."

Responding on November 17, the JCS proposed a force of 89,085 at an estimated cost of $193.1 million for Fiscal Year 1956 and approximately $100 million for the remainder of FY 1955. To provide internal security and "in an attempt to stabilize the Diem government" the JCS suggested prompt reduction in force and prompt reassigment of selected personnel and units to maintain "the security of the legal government in Saigon and other major population centers," execute "regional security operations in each province" and perform "territorial pacification missions." Later, military centers·would be established for reorganization and training of the military.

The Chiefs expressed serious reservations about the probability of Vietnamese —and American—success. First,

> the chaotic internal political situation within Vietnam is such that there is no assurance that the security forces visualized herein can be developed into loyal and effective support for the Diem Government, or, if developed, that these forces will result in political and military stability within South Vietnam. Unless the Vietnamese themselves show an inclination to make individual and collective sacrifices required to resist communism, which they have not done to date, no amount of external pressure and assistance can long delay complete Communist victory in South Vietnam.

Secondly, "the cooperation and collaboration of the French MAAG" is vital to effective execution of the program—and the JCS doubted that support would be readily offered. Finally, the Chiefs cautioned,

> the above program does not provide adequate security for the Associated States against external aggression after the withdrawal of the French forces. With the Viet Minh increasing the size and effectiveness of their forces and with no forces in being committed to mutual defense under the Southeast Asia Collective Defense Treaty, the above long-range program would be insufficient to provide more than limited initial resistance to an organized military assault by the Viet Minh.

f.   *Collins Agrees with the NSC*

Another memorandum of November 17 indicated how quickly the United States had moved to inaugurate the crash program approved at the October 22 NSC meeting. Secretary Dulles outlined for President Eisenhower the recommendations of General J. Lawton Collins, special envoy sent to Vietnam to over-see all U.S. operations, coordinate them with French programs and get things moving. Collins recommended the "Vietnamese National Army . . . be reduced by July 1955 to 77,000. It should be placed under Vietnamese command and control by that date. . . . The cost to the U.S. would be two hundred million dollars annually. . . . The United States should assume training responsibility . . . by January 1, 1955, with French cooperation and utilizing French trainers."

Collins insisted that French forces be retained in Vietnam:

> It would be disastrous if the French Expeditionary Corps were withdrawn prematurely since otherwise Vietnam would be overrun by an enemy attack before the Manila Pact Powers could act.

To "encourage the French to retain sufficient forces," Collins urged U.S. financial support of at least $100 million through December 1955. General Ely concurred.

2. *Conditions in Vietnam Invite Firmer Action*

The situation in Vietnam during the autumn of 1954 invited an action program of some kind—any kind. Premier Diem barely controlled Saigon; he was opposed by his army's chief of staff, by powerful sect politicians guarding significant special interests with powerful sect armies; he was at least tacitly opposed by many French in Vietnam. The countryside had been devastated by the war; communications, administration and financial operations were stalled; an already prostrate economy was threatened by the deluge of some 860,000 refugees from the north. Over all hung "an atmosphere of frustration and disillusionment" created by the Geneva Accords and imposed partition, "compounded by widespread uncertainty as to French and U.S. intentions." U.S. policy in August set out to correct the uncertainty.

a. *The Military Threatens Diem*

General Nguyen Van Hinh, Chief of Staff of the Vietnamese National Army, was the first coup-plotter to rise and first to fall. September threats of a military revolt were first staved off by the mediation of U.S. Ambassador Donald Heath and General Ely (who doubted Diem's capacity to lead but worked to prevent his violent downfall.) Then Diem uncovered a coup plot, arrested some Hinh supporters, removed the general from command and ordered him out of the country. Hinh refused to leave and continued his machinations against the government. Plans for one coup in October were dropped when Hinh was told revolt would mean automatic termination of U.S. aid. Another scheduled for October 26 was foiled when Colonel E. G. Lansdale, head of the Saigon Military Mission and chief CIA man on the scene, lured two key subordinates out of the country. Lansdale invited Hinh and staff to visit the Philippines. Hinh unhappily declined but his supporters—one of whom allegedly was a French agent —could not resist the chance to see the inner workings of the Magsaysay-led, U.S.-supported operation against Huk insurgents. Finally, in November, Bao Dai was persuaded by America and France to intervene on Diem's behalf. He did, ordered Hinh to report to Cannes, and on November 19, the general left the country. General Hinh enjoyed some French support in his anti-Diem activity. Ambassador Heath reported he received "quiet encouragement if not unofficial support" from many French officers and officials in Saigon and "at the working level in Paris." Hinh was also aided initially by the sects, later by the Binh Xuyen.

b. *The Sects Threaten Diem*

The Cao Dai and Hoa Hao sects, basically religious groups with important political controls and interests as well as private, French-subsidized armies, worked with Hinh through early September. Then, spurred by the knowledge that precipitate action would jeopardize American aid, the sects agreed to work with Diem. Last minute threats and "heavy pressure" from French officials against coalition left sect leaders "dizzy" but they recovered sufficiently to accept cabinet positions on September 24. Shaky to begin with, the coalition never worked: Diem refused to delegate responsibility to his eight new ministers and they soon tired of trying to work through the government.

c. *And the Binh Xuyen Oppose Diem*

The Binh Xuyen, too, considered joining the coalition but pulled out when Diem refused to name Binh Xuyen leader, "a colorful brigand named Le Van (Bay) Vien" Minister of the Interior. Bay Vien had forged a motley group of small-time gangsters into a fairly sophisticated organization of 6000 big-time gangsters and river pirates, and had been helped in this endeavor by Bao Dai and French colonial administrators. The Binh Xuyen controlled prostitution and gambling in Cholon and the Saigon–Cholon police force—reportedly because Bay Vien paid Bao Dai some 40 million piasters for these privileges. Still-dissident sect leaders such as Ba Cut, whose 5000 Hoa Hao adherents denounced Geneva and refused cooperation with Diem, and Frenchmen opposed to Diem abetted Binh Xuyen intrigues against the government.

3. *French Laxity Demands Strong U.S. Programs*

More than the Vietnamese power struggles and Diem's inability to consolidate his rule, French activities during the autumn of 1954 galvanized the United States. From acquiescence to U.S. demands in September, American policy makers felt France had moved toward opposition to U.S. demands by November. That this assessment of French actions was either objective or fair is questionable.

a. *The Washington Conference, September, 1954*

After Franco-American discussions in Washington in late September—the first in a progression of monthly meetings on Vietnam—the United States seemed to have scored highest. France promised to support Diem, to grant independence to Vietnam quickly. The transfer of financial, administrative, economic and other functions to the Vietnamese had begun and would be completed by December 1954. That France balked at U.S. demands for an immediate grant of independence outside of the French Union is not surprising: French cultural, economic and political interests in Vietnam were still strong; the Frenchman's belief in the validity of the French Union was deep. No French government dared defy public opinion by seeming to hasten the end of the French Union. France felt the U.S. had an "almost psychological attachment to 'independence' without giving sufficient thought and attention to the practical problems and risks involved."

Secondly, the U.S. had been able to defer a commitment to finance the French Expeditionary Corps in Vietnam although an indication that aid would be resumed, if not resumption itself, had been the first order of French business at the Washington Conference. France agreed to maintain the Corps in Vietnam but was told no aid figures would be available until December.

Both France and the U.S. thought their respective economic aims had been won. France objected strongly to the idea of direct American aid to Vietnam on the grounds that it violated the Geneva Accords, would needlessly provoke Communist China, promote graft and corruption in Vietnam, and intensify the political struggle. Plus, "past (French) sacrifices on behalf of Vietnam and their obligation as a member of the French Union" made French supervision of aid essential. To France, a compromise agreement drafted by Walter Bedell Smith meant the U.S. accepted these arguments and was willing to give France a hand in disbursing aid to the Associated States. The U.S. chose not to interpret the agreement this way. The State Department said the U.S. merely indicated willingmess to consult on such matters. On 29 October, Dulles told Mendes-France that the U.S. alone would disperse aid; by late November Mendes-France finally tired of arguing an obviously lost cause and dropped the matter.

h   *The U.S. Faults French Support for Diem*

Despite apparent agreement at Washington to back Diem, Secretary Dulles met with Mendes-France three weeks later in Paris about the same subject. "For . . . ready reference" Acting Secretary of State Herbert Hoover quoted for Dulles part of the 29 September Minute of Understanding in which the

> . . . representatives of France and the United States agree that their respective governments support Ngo Dinh Diem in the establishment and maintenance of a strong, anti-Communist and nationalist government. To this end France and the United States will urge all anti-Communist elements in Vietnam to cooperate fully with the Government of Ngo Dinh Diem in order to counter vigorously the Viet Minh and build a strong free Vietnam. . . . While Ely seems to have attempted honestly to carry out this agreement, the fact that many French elements have never accepted Diem solution must have weakened Ely's efforts and encouraged Hinh camarilla in its recalcitrance. . . . Unless Diem receives unreserved U.S. and French support, his chances of success appear slight. With such support, his chances are probably better than even, repeat even.

c.   *Accommodation Between Paris and Hanoi?*

Apart from the quiet backing given Diem's opponents by French officers and officials in Saigon and persistent Paris proposals for a change in government (Prince Buu Hoi, whose "political ideologies" were repugnant to Dulles, was a French favorite at this time), the U.S. found in French accommodative gestures toward Hanoi ample proof that French backing for Diem was reserved at best. Ambassador Dillon felt Mendes-France found in Vietnam a "situation ideally designed to test (the) bases of his fundamental political philosophy of 'peaceful coexistence' " and that his government grew more and more "disposed to explore and consider a policy looking toward an eventual peaceful North–South rapprochement." French insistence on strict legal interpretation of the Geneva Accords was one example of accommodation thinking. France objected to anything which could possibly delay or destroy elections in 1956; Dillon predicted Paris would accept the results of elections "however academic that exercise may eventually prove to be." But the most worrisome example to those at the State

Department who lined up against any kind of accommodation was the Sainteny Mission to Hanoi.

d. *Sainteny or Ely?*

Jean Sainteny, credited with reaching short-lived independence accords with Ho Chi Minh in March 1946, was sent back to Hanoi in August 1954 to find ways to protect French business and cultural interests in Tonkin. Sainteny's past success at rapprochement gave the mission definite political overtones. General Ely wished Paris had sent a "stupid type of consular official" not a man of Sainteny's "active stripe"; he was disturbed enough to fly to Paris to tell Mendes-France he would resign if French policy was to play a "double game" in North and South Vietnam aimed at backing whichever side ultimately won. Mendes-France assured Ely that French policy was to give maximum support to the anti-Communist elements in South Vietnam and do everything possible to assure their victory in 1956. Ely was placated and returned to Saigon. But Sainteny remained in Hanoi and maximum support for Diem did not materialize.

From another source came word that Ely was not "au courant" with French policy. French Union Counsellor Jacque Raphael-Leygues, reportedly a member of the Mendes-France "brain trust" on Indochina, told Ambassador Dillon that Sainteny had convinced Paris that South Vietnam was doomed and the "only possible means of salvaging anything was to play the Viet Minh game and woo the Viet Minh away from Communist ties in the hope of creating a Titoist Vietnam which would cooperate with France and might even adhere to the French Union." Raphael-Leygues said France deferred to U.S. wishes over which government to support in Saigon to get money for the French Expeditionary Corps and to fix responsibility for the eventual loss of South Vietnam on the U.S.

In December 1954, Sainteny won Ho Chi Minh's agreement to permit French enterprises to carry on without discrimination. But if the contract pleased Paris it did not assure French businessmen in Tonkin. Viet Minh legislation would regulate their operations; profits could not be transferred outside the Communist orbit. Most French concerns decided potential benefit was not worth the risk of doing business with the DRV and despite Sainteny's efforts to establish mixed government-private corporations, most withdrew from the North. Sainteny remained as a "general delegate" to the DRV.

e. *The Mansfield Report*

A final spur to U.S. action was the Mansfield Report. After a fact-finding trip to South Vietnam, Senator Mansfield concluded his old acquaintance Diem was the only man for the job in Saigon. He said the issue "is not Diem as an individual but rather the program for which he stands." That program "represents genuine nationalism, . . . is prepared to deal effectively with corruption and . . . demonstrates a concern in advancing the welfare of the Vietnamese people." The Senator felt it "improbable" that any other leadership "dedicated to these principles" could be found and recommended the Government "consider an immediate suspension of all aid to Vietnam and the French Union Forces there, except that of a humanitarian nature, preliminary to a complete reappraisal of our present policies in Free Vietnam" if Diem fell.

The Mansfield Report elated Diem (who proceeded to react with even more intransigent self-righteousness to suggestions of change), subdued the French and annoyed Paris. For those Frenchmen who favored conciliation with the Viet Minh, Mansfield's analysis proved the validity of their policy. Obviously, they said, if Diem falls the U.S. will heed Mansfield and withdraw from Vietnam. Equally obviously, they said, Diem will fall. *Ergo,* France should start "betting on Viet Minh to win war." To French officials willing to back Diem the Report and Washington's endorsement of it was a violation of the Franco–American agreement to support another government if Diem fell. When Mendes-France reminded Dulles of this and spoke of the need to lay plans for "another structure of government" which both France and the U.S. could support, Dulles was noncommittal.

4. *NSC Action Program of October and Eisenhower Letter to Diem*

President Eisenhower's letter to Diem of 24 October (written August and shown to the French at that time; held up until the political situation in South Vietnam setled somewhat; finally approved for transmission at the October 22 NSC meeting) was called a direct violation of the principle of cooperative action agreed upon in September by Minister La Chambre. French Ambassador Bonnet told Secretary Dulles that "it was felt (the letter) had given Diem full rein without requiring of him as a preliminary condition that he should first succeed in forming a strong and stable government, even though this preliminary condition had been a part of the basis of the Washington agreements." Bonnet added that the letter might be a violation of the armistice and the Viet Minh might take advantage of it. Then, when Ambassador Dillon suggested to the Quai d'Orsay that French support for Diem had not been all that it might have been, La Chambre was inflamed. Not only was this a false allegation, it was a direct slur on General Ely, the government in Paris and the glory of France. M. La Chambre said he was personally convinced Diem was leading South Vietnam to disaster but would still support him:

> We prefer to lose in Vietnam with the U.S. rather than to win without them . . . we would rather support Diem knowing he is going to lose and thus keep Franco–U.S. solidarity than to pick someone who could retain Vietnam for the free world if this meant breaking Franco–U.S. solidarity.

In response, Secretary Dulles formally told Mendes-France that both the Eisenhower letter and the stronger U.S. action were "in furtherance of the understandings reached at Washington." The U.S. had not "the slightest idea of questioning the good faith of the French government" but "many French officials have not concealed their belief that Diem has failed . . . and . . . should be replaced." This attitude produced an "impasse in Saigon" necessitating firmer action. La Chambre received this with "little comment" other than to suggest appointment of Nguyen Van Tam (General Hinh's father, Premier during 1952–1953 and a strong-even oppressive-administrator) to the Interior Ministry. La Chambre called this a "way out of the mess . . . (for) here is a man who knows how to fight Communists." As in the past, the U.S. rejected the proposal.

5. *More Action: The Collins Mission*

The initial U.S. action program rested on three assumptions: that Diem could be persuaded to accept U.S. proposals, that Hinh would obey the government, that the French at all levels would cooperate. None proved immediately valid.

So the U.S. adopted yet another tactic. General J. Lawton Collins, U.S. Representative to the NATO Military Committee, was dispatched to Vietnam on November 8 with the personal rank of Ambassador (Heath returned to the State Department). As President Eisenhower described it, Collins' mission was:

> to coordinate and direct a program in support of (Diem's) government to enable it to: (a) promote internal security and political and economic stability; (b) establish and maintain control throughout the territory; and (c) effectively counteract Viet Minh infiltration and paramilitary activities south of the demarkation line.

After initial resistance to the Collins mission (seen as a precursor to complete U.S. take-over of Indochina), General Ely established a close working relationship with Collins. A seven-point program for political, military and economic action was quickly designed. On December 13, Ely and Collins signed a Minute of Understanding agreeing that France would grant full autonomy to the VNA by July 1, 1955 and that the U.S. would assume training duties in January. They agreed the French Expeditionary Corps must remain in Vietnam and the level of financial assistance suggested by Collins ($100 million through December 1955 after which assistance was not contemplated) was adopted by the Foreign Operations Administration and subsequently announced to Paris. Aid was contingent upon consultation with Congress and "subject to Ely and Collins and the two governments mutually agreeing on what is to be done in Indochina."

6. *France Objects to Collins–Ely Agreements*

Paris was unhappy about the aid figure—a third of what France requested. Consequently, withdrawal of French forces was speeded: of the 150,000 troops scheduled to remain in Vietnam through 1955 all but 35,000 were phased out. Monetary reasons were said to be paramount but political and psychological pressures for the pull-out were probably more important. There was strong sentiment in France for sending the FEC to North Africa where it could serve the interests of France and the French Union. In Vietnam, French soldiers served the free world but were hated by the Vietnamese and ignored by the very powers they aided, powers which did not care enough to properly defray French expenses.

Paris was more upset by the Minute of Understanding. During November discussion with Dulles, Mendes-France had said he doubted full autonomy could be assumed by the Vietnamese by July 1955 and believed a readjustment of MAAG personnel for the new training mission might violate the Geneva Accords. These arguments were reiterated at December Trilateral meetings. But Mendes-France's real trouble was agreeing to phase out French instructors. Neither the French people nor French soldiers would understand why France was denied influence while required to support such a heavy burden in Vietnam. Mendes-France and General Ely insisted that if French instructors were eliminated the U.S. automatically would have assumed primary responsibility for free world policy toward Indochina. (Dulles and General Collins rejected that line of reasoning but convinced neither the French nor others that it was fallacious.)

Collins compromised in the Minute of Understanding by agreeing to softer language (both French and American instructors would be removed as Vietnamese efficiency increased), hoping to assuage Paris. He failed. When the

Minute was forwarded for final approval Mendes-France stalled. First he had to study it closely to ensure no conflict with Geneva was involved. Then on January 7, the French submitted a redraft of the Minute which omitted reference to General O'Daniel's authority over French personnel.

Collins was already annoyed by hedging in December, tantamount to a slap in the face of Ely to whom full authority to negotiate the agreement had been delegated. He refused to "agree to (the redraft) unless specifically instructed by higher authority" because lines of authority were not spelled out. Yet Ely thought Paris had approved the original agreement. He urged Collins to continue negotiations with the Vietnamese on the basis of the first Minute, advice Collins followed despite the Paris–Washington snafu. On January 19 and 20 a formal exchange of letters finalized the agreement for U.S. assumption of training duties and financial support ($214.5 million) for the Vietnamese forces. The forces would be scaled down to 100,00 by December 1955. Both cost and force levels were raised from Collins' November recommendations in deference to Vietnamese arguments. The U.S. and France remained deadlocked until February 11, 1955, when the terms—but not the form—of the original agreement were finally accepted. The next day, General O'Daniel assumed responsibility for training Vietnamese forces and the Training Relations and Instruction Mission (TRIM) went into operation.

D. FRANCO–AMERICAN IMPASSE OVER DIEM

Resolution of military problems within the U.S. Government and between the U.S. and France was a fairly major accomplishment. Political differences were not similarly resolved. To support or not to support Ngo Dinh Diem was the issue over which France and America split.

1. Paris: Diem Is Ill-Suited for Rule

As noted above, France acquiesced in the retention of Diem as Prime Minister in deference to U.S. insistence and French concern for U.S. financial assistance for the FEC during the September Washington conference. In mid-November, Mendes-France reaffirmed the 29 September agreement but said an alternative form of government had to be considered unless Diem implemented an energetic program within the next two months. By December, when Mendes-France Dulles and Eden met in Paris, the French Premier made it clear he thought the time had come for a change. Two ways to accomplish change were suggested. Bao Dai could name a Viceroy and give him full authority to use the powers of Chief of State to unify the warring political factions. Tran Van Huu, Nguyen Van Tam or Dr. Phan Huy Quat were possible candidates for this job. Or, Bao Dai himself could return to Saigon and form a government with Huu as Premier, Tam as Interior Minister, Quat in Defense.

France wanted Diem out of power for several reasons. U.S. policymakers did not seem to fully appreciate how galling Diem's Franco-phobia must have been, nor did the U.S. seem to understand—or allow for—the divisive effect Diem's militant anti-communist stance had within the French Government. Little consideration was given to charges that the U.S. was undermining France by portraying itself as the only friend of Vietnamese nationalism. But the U.S. could appreciate the validity of French arguments that Diem had not been and perhaps would not be able to unify and stabilize South Vietnam.

2.   *Collins: Diem Cannot Lead South Vietnam*

General Collins had been skeptical about Diem from the outset; by December he was convinced an alternative to his government should be urgently considered. Diem's refusal to name Dr. Quat as Defense Minister triggered Collins' recommendation. Both Collins and Colonel Lansdale had urged Diem to accept Quat, agreeing Quat alone was strong enough to unify the Vietnamese armed forces behind the Saigon government. On December 13, Collins suggested five reasons for Diem's adverse decision:

> (1) unwillingness to delegate control of Vietnam armed forces to any strong man; (2) fear of Quat as potential successor; (3) opposition of sects (who also feared a strong man in the defense post); (4) influence of brothers Luyen and Nhu (anxious to neutralize the power of any potential successor); (5) desire [material missing]

According to Collins,

> Whatever the reasons, the failure to utilize Quat epitomizes lack of unity among Vietnamese and lack of decisive leadership on part of Diem. . . . Acceptance of status quo with Minh elevated to Defense Ministry and sects reinforced in veto power over government is simply postponing evil day of reckoning as to when, if ever, Diem will assert type of leadership that can unify this country and give it chance of competing with hard, effective, unified control of Ho Chi Minh.

Three days later, General Collins communicated his "final judgment" on the situation. He made four recommendations:

> A. Continue to support Diem along present lines for short while longer but without committing U.S. to specific aid programs;
> B. Consider urgently, as possible alternative, the early return of Bao Dai;
> C. If after short period of further test Diem Government fails to achieve substantial progressive action and if return to Bao Dai is acceptable to U.S. Government, to support his prompt return;
> D. If return of Bao Dai is not acceptable to U.S. Government, assuming Diem Government continues to demonstrate inability to unite free Vietnam behind an aggressive program, I recommend re-evaluation of our plans for assisting Southeast Asia with special attention (to an) earlier proposal.

The earlier proposal, made by General Collins on December 13, was that the U.S. gradually withdraw from Vietnam. Collins said this was the "least desirable (but) in all honesty and in view of what I have observed here to date this may be the only sound solution."

3.   *State Department: Diem Is the Only Available Leader*

The State Department went along with Collins' suggestion to avoid specific assistance commitments at the present time but could not see salvation in Bao Dai. A memorandum from Ambassador Heath, then working in the Far East Bureau is indicative of State Department thinking. Heath first called attention to "massive opposition" faced by Diem and French unwillingness to firmly support him—implying that all Diem's problems were not Diem's fault. He then spoke of General Collins' "attempt to achieve a rapid solution," said Collins' "recommendations are now based on the circumstances of a satisfactory settlement prior to January 1"—thereby suggesting that one not looking for a rapid solution might not arrive at similar conclusions.

The memorandum closed with Heath's interpretation of Secretary Dulles' policy and his own thoughts as to what ought to be done:

> In our view, General Collins' recommendations ignore the basic factor that we would assist a Communist takeover by a withholding of our aid, even if it must necessarily be given to a government which is less than perfect. The Secretary has analyzed the situation as one in which we are conducting a time buying operation. If we withhold our support to Vietnam, it will be taken over sooner than if we extend smaller aid, at a figure of about a third of last year. In the meantime, we will proceed to do what we can to strengthen Cambodia, Laos and Thailand. This is my understanding of the Secretary's policy.

> I recommend we inform the Secretary and General Collins that we recognize the dangers posed by the above policy, but that in the lack of more useful alternatives that we will continue to support Diem, because there is no one to take his place who would serve U.S. objectives any better. This includes the Bao Dai solution which is opposed by the facts of Bao Dai's lack of support in Vietnam and his past demonstrations of inability to govern. The fear that a fiscal commitment of over $300 million plus our national prestige would be lost in a gamble on the retention of Free Vietnam is a legitimate one, but the withholding of our support at this juncture would almost inevitably have a far worse effect."

The substance of the memorandum was cabled to Secretary Dulles, then in Paris for the Tripartite French, U.S. and British discussions.

4. December Tripartite Talks

a. France Proposes Alternative to Diem, Dulles Seems to Acquiesce

On 19 December, Mendes-France opened the Indochina talks by calling Diem's approach "wholly negative," said "not a single reform suggested (by Franco–American working groups advising the government on all matters) had been accepted by Diem," that the "French Government now considered . . . a strong approach would have to be made to Diem." Reaffirming his past agreement with Dulles' "thesis that we must do our maximum to permit Diem Government to succeed" Mendes-France added:

> now . . . he was no longer sure that even maximum would help. He said we must now have alternate formula in mind. Without varying from our stated purpose of supporting Diem Government as long as it exists we must now prepare in our minds [material missing]

Dulles agreed the

> task in South Vietnam was difficult (but) regarded basic factors as favorable. People were opposed to communism and had great natural resources

. . . they received greater aid from abroad than North . . . situation was much improved now that there was full cooperation between French and American authorities. The problem must not be approached in spirit of defeatism. Only serious problem we have not yet solved is that of indigenous leadership. We cannot expect it to be solved ideally because there is no tradition among indigenous people for self-government. We must get along with something less good than best. . . . (The U.S. was) not repeat not committed to Diem in any irrevocable sense. We have accepted him because we knew of no one better. Developments have confirmed our fears as to his limitations but no substitute for him has yet been proposed. Those suggested in past varied from month to month. Now it is claimed that only Bao Dai can save situation. If that is case, then we must indeed be desperate. . . . We should continue to back Diem but exert more pressure on him to make changes we consider necessary.

Mendes-France suggested the U.S. and France approach Bao Dai and mentioned the French Viceroy plan to replace Diem. Dulles countered by saying the U.S. and French might use Bao Dai but "we must go to him prepared with our own ideas and not . . . simply accept his." Dulles did not expect any Viceroy to be able "to decide on alternate to Diem and to set up machinery to implement our ideas . . . our job (is) to create this machinery." He added,

> We must exhaust all our pressures on Diem to get things done before considering alternate solutions. . . . He asked Mendes not to think we had obstinately closed our minds to possible alternate solution. We had not repeat not, but our investigation of alternate must be done on careful basis and we must for present support Diem.

Mendes-France agreed. He summarized his position as follows:

> First, to support Diem; second, to study alternatives. Collins and Ely should be instructed to explore further possibilities including Bao Dai with great discretion . . . third point was that Ely and Collins should be requested to investigate matter of timing. How much further delay can be tolerated? . . . We must set deadline. . . .

Then Dulles agreed—but added a fourth point:

> If the US should decide that there is no repeat no good alternative to Diem we will have to consider how much more investment we will be prepared to make in Indochina. Our policy would have to be reappraised. Congressional committees . . . would have to be consulted. Mansfield believes in Diem. . . . Even slight chance of success in Vietnam was worth considerable investment. US had also to think of what happened in adjacent countries—in Cambodia, Laos, Thailand and Malaya. US situation was different from that of French. French had an investment in lives and property in Vietnam while ours involved effect that fate of Vietnam would have on rest of Southeast Asia.

b. *But Dulles Reports, No Other Suitable Leader Can Be Seen*

After the Tripartite meetings, Dulles reported his assessment of their outcome to Saigon. He said he had agreed with Mendes-France on four points concerning

Diem but had not agreed to a deadline for Diem's replacement. Rather, "Collins and Ely would report late January on overall situation."

Dulles called the "investment in Vietnam justified even if only to buy time to build up strength elsewhere in area" and concluded:

> We are going to have to maintain flexible policy and proceed carefully by stages in Vietnam. . . . Under present circumstances and unless situation (in Vietnam) clearly appears hopeless and rapidly disintegrating, we have no choice but continue our aid Vietnam and support of Diem. There no other suitable leader known to us.

France believed Dulles had in fact committed the United States to consider a change with which Bao Dai would be associated by mid-January. Washington denied it and Paris protests were unable to budge the State Department. The U.S. and France did agree that the Tripartite talks had given Collins and Ely a mandate to study alternatives, however.

c. *The U.S. Looks at Alternatives*

Having told Paris the U.S. was not committed to either a deadline or an alternative involving Bao Dai, the U.S. proceeded to study alternatives. Secretary of Defense Wilson asked the Joint Staff to assess the impact on military commitments to Southeast Asia of the loss of South Vietnam, of continued but reduced assistance to that nation and of a range of actions in between. The JCS responded by calling Wilson's alternate options incomplete, that consideration of increased aid, and institution of a unilateral program of direct guidance to the GVN through an "advisory system" should be among U.S. considerations.

[material missing]

As a result of Collins' recommendations the NSC endorsed a strong policy in Vietnam: the U.S. would continue to support the Diem government and continue to press France to carry out its commitments under the Smith–LaChambre agreement. The NSC approved in principle the programs of military and economic aid to implement Collins' recommendations (about $500 million) and determined to seek reaffirmation of the Manila powers' determination to react under the SEATO treaty if hostilities were resumed. Dulles decided to "take the plunge" and begin direct aid to Vietnam on January 1, 1955. The aid program was to be flexible and fluid, adjusted according to circumstances and subject to discontinuance at any time, as at present.

E. CRISIS OF THE SPRING, 1955

With strong United States backing, Diem went into the sect crisis of the spring, 1955. Different from the military coup crisis of Autumn 1954 and the Quat cabinet crisis of December, the sect crisis was resolved by Diem's taking firm action and was not followed by another. It was followed by the end of any real French presence in Vietnam.

1. *The Problem of the Sect Armies*

The sects had been quiescent but not quiet since Cao Dai and Hoa Hao ministers had joined the cabinet in September 1954. The end of French subsidies for sect armies in February shook them out of complacency. Diem agreed to pay a part of what the armies had received from the French to ease the transition of some 40,000 soldiers to civilian life. But transition it was to be: he would not tolerate armed bands separate from VNA command and separate from Saigon's political guidance. Sect leaders had different objectives, however. They wanted to preserve their military forces by integrating, intact, as many units as possible into the National Army. (With a VNA force level of 100,000, few could be accommodated; in January only 6,000 sect troops had been absorbed.) Secondly, the sects wanted substantial government assistance for soldiers forced to leave the military. Most important, they wanted recognition of their areas of influence and Diem's assurance that he would not encroach on their territories. Diem would countenance no part of this third request.

Since December, a Franco-American group headed by Col. Lansdale and directed to "come up with a peaceful solution" to the problem had worked furiously, found a solution and urged its prompt adoption. Generals Collins and Ely decided to give the matter further study. Lansdale's reaction:

> We warned them that time was extremely short, that the sects were about to take action by arms and that a peaceful solution would have to be introduced immediately or the opportunity would be lost. The opportunity was lost.

2. The United Front Challenges Diem

Lost because Cao Dai and Hoa Hao sect leaders joined with Bay Vien in February, put down hostilities among themselves and joined in a United Front of Nationalist Forces. In March, the United Front demanded Diem form a government of large national union. The eight sect cabinet members resigned (although Cao Dai Generals Thé and Phuong soon changed their minds). A United Front delegate tried to convince Bao Dai to withdraw Diem's powers as premier but the timely arrival of a personal letter from President Eisenhower outlining US objectives and progress in Vietnam proved more persuasive. The letter either reassured Bao Dai that the US had not written him out of the political picture or made him think twice about joining with the sects and thereby incurring US wrath. Whatever the reason, he refused to intervene on behalf of the Front. Diem called the Front Program an ultimatum and would not budge.

France wanted Bao Dai to mediate between Diem and the United Front. The US wanted to issue a joint declaration telling the sects both America and France opposed violence and warning them that the French Expeditionary Corps would block any movement of Hoa Hao troops into Saigon to reinforce the Binh Xuyen. Ely and Paris refused the warning clause: French troops would act only in protection of the lives and property of French and foreign nationals.

3. Diem Challenges the Binh Xuyen

During this time, Lansdale was meeting almost nightly with Diem. He reports Diem

> was desperately trying to get French and US help to remove the Sureté from the control of the Binh Xuyen. French and US reactions to the problem were in the form of advice to proceed slowly, to act with caution. Events would not permit this.

Before dawn on the 28th of March, a paratrooper company loyal to Diem attacked and overcame the Binh Xuyen-controlled central police headquarters. The next day, Diem told Defense Minister Minh he planned to oust Binh Xuyen

Police Commissioner Lai Van Sang that afternoon—March 29—and replace him with someone loyal to his regime. Minh insisted Diem at least consult the cabinet before taking action. Diem refused and Minh resigned. Representatives of General Ely were able to persuade Diem to defer any move against the Sureté, however.

On the night of March 29–30 the Binh Xuyen struck back. Mortar shells fell on the palace grounds and Binh Xuyen trooys tried to regain the prefecture. They were repulsed by National Army troops. The VNA then moved to attack the Sureté itself in retaliation but French officers apparently cut off their gas and ammunition supplies temporarily to keep the National Army on the defensive. Fighting ended by 3:30 in the morning of March 30.

General Ely opposed a VNA offensive against the Sureté headquarters, not because it might fail but because it was irrelevant. Relevant was Diem's inability to defeat the sects rapidly and decisively throughout the country. If force were used to prove a minor point, a long, bloody and major civil war would surely ensue. Ely was outraged at Diem's attitude. He felt the premier verged on megalomania and was ready to "put the city to sword and flame to establish his authority. Collins sympathized with Ely, but also felt if Diem did not prove he could control Saigon he would be forced to accede to sect demands.

4. *Truce—But No Calm*

On March 31, a 48-hour cease-fire was won by General Jean Gambiez, trusted by both the National Army and the Binh Xuyen. The truce was extended into April but failed to cool tempers or ease tensions. (Cao Dai forces which had broken with the United Front were integrated into the National Army on March 31, however—one happy note for Diem.)

a. *Lansdale Version*

Lansdale, whose account of this and later developments is not at all flattering to the French, says Ely decided to impose a cease-fire and won Collins' concurrence. French officers then moved in and stopped the fighting. Lansdale "saw Ambassador Collins . . . explaining that only the Binh Xuyen would gain by the cease-fire." But it continued:

> Ambassador Collins was sincerely convinced that the Binh Xuyen could be induced by French negotiations to withdraw from the Sureté and police control of the metropolis. . . .

Lansdale reports the French had long been working against Diem through the Vietnamese National Army (they used its G–6 as an arm of French intelligence) and that French soldiers under his command in the National Security Division of TRIM tried to sabotage the Diem regime and US programs designed to strengthen it.

> The French had daily fed us the latest French propaganda line (Diem was weak, Diem was bloodthirsty, the VNA had low morale . . . was unable to fight, Americans didn't understand the Vietnamese, all whites must encourage only selected Vietnamese loyal to the French because the remainder would turn against all whites in another "night of the long knives" similar to that of 1946.)

Now the French had been insistent that the National Army was a hollow shell, that its officers would refuse to fight . . . that morale was so bad the troops would desert rather than follow "bloody Diem."

Lansdale implies Collins fell for this "propaganda" but he, Lansdale, did not. On the cease-fire, Lansdale reports:

The French told Diem that if he tried to take over Sureté headquarters which was now included in the French zone, French troops would open fire on the Vietnamese Army. The US advised Diem to be patient, that the French were really being helpful by negotiating with the Binh Xuyen. The cease-fire limit was extended . . . Sizeable sums were being offered (by French) to Army officers and to sect leaders who were remaining loyal to Diem and to entice them into being at least neutral. Those who refused were subjected to character assassination attacks . . .

b. *Ely and Collins' Decision: Diem Must Go*

On April 7, Collins and Ely discussed Diem. Ely said Diem could be maintained only by overcoming enormous difficulties. After a full day of "soul-searching," Ely had been forced to conclude Diem had to go to preserve Vietnam for the free world. He would accept anyone but Diem as premier. Collins had been nearing a similar conclusion. On March 31 he told the State Department it was necessary to consider alternatives to Diem. A week later Collins cabled Dulles to insist Diem be removed. He recommended Tran Van Do (Diem's foreign minister who also resigned from the cabinet in March) or Dr. Quat as replacements.

c. *Dulles' Indecision*

Dulles replied as he had in December: he could not see how Diem's replacement would solve the sect problem for any successor worthy of US assistance would still have to contend with them. A change in premiers would damage US prestige throughout the Far East: the US would be charged with paying lip service to the cause of Asian nationalism, then abandoning a nationalist leader when pressured by "colonial interests." Plus pro-Diem Congressional sentiment was a problem. The Mutual Security bill was under debate and Mansfield had made it clear that Congress would be reluctant to appropriate funds to a Vietnam without Diem. Despite these difficulties, Dulles eventually agreed to consider a change if Collins would personally come to Washington for consultation.

d. *Paris: Diem's Time Is Up*

At the same time Paris was fast losing patience. The time has come to form a government responsive to dominant political forces in Vietnam, to abandon the unrealistic U.S. policy of maintaining and strengthening Diem, said France. Formation of a Conseil Superieur was proposed, representative of Diem and his supporters, the sects, intellectuals, politicians and the army. The Conseil would decide policy and a cabinet of non-political technicians headed by Diem would implement it. But the U.S. rejected this plan saying Diem should be allowed to strike back at the Binh Xuyen with force and France and America should support him—morally and logistically.

Then Washington asked the Quai d'Orsay to answer a set of questions designed to elicit specific French plans for the change in Vietnamese government. Paris' rejoinder: the questions should be answered jointly or the united Franco-American effort in Vietnam would be over and France would have to say publicly that the U.S. had assumed sole responsibility for developments in Vietnam. But in mid-April, France filled-in part of the questionnaire—leaving blank a successor to Diem (only joint consultation could decide this). Paris proposed Collins and Ely draw up a slate of acceptable candidates for major positions. The U.S. and French governments would agree on a final list, ask Bao Dai to summon representatives of various factions to Cannes and on the basis of French–U.S. recommendations, negotiate a solution to the sect–Binh Xuyen–Diem impasse. Sect support would be assured by their membership in a high council and a program of honors, indemnification and integration of sect troops into the National Army.

e. *Bao Dai's Plan*

On April 21, Bao Dai announced his own plan for resolving the crisis, remarkably similar to that submitted by Paris. Bao Dai wanted to summon various representatives to Cannes, name Dr. Quat as premier, ask him to form a cabinet of technicians and a high council of notables. On April 26, Bao Dai said he would implement the scheme unilaterally unless the U.S. made some response by the following day.

Meanwhile, Collins had left Saigon for consultations with Dulles. Lansdale reports a meeting held just before his departure:

> He (Collins) told Lansdale not to be worried by newspaper rumors that the US would stop supporting Diem. Lansdale asked then if his orders were to continue supporting Diem; Collins said yes. Members of the country team privately felt that Diem should be supported by us, that the National Army was ready to support him and had the capability of defeating the Binh Xuyen.

f. *Dulles' Decision: U.S. Will Consider a Change in Regime*

General Collins and Secretary Dulles met on April 27. Dulles agreed to consider shifting support to either Quat or Do and a message to this effect was sent to Saigon. But Dulles determined not to discuss this with France until a full and frank statement of her intentions had been received. That statement was to include an unequivocal assurance to back whole-heartedly any new political arrangements in Saigon and to resolve "certain ambiguities" in French policy toward North Vietnam. Until this declaration appeared the US would reveal no change of heart over Diem.

5. *Diem Acts Against the Binh Xuyen*

Then the truce exploded. On 28 April, Diem told Lansdale:

> The Army and people laid the blame (for the crisis between the government and the Binh Xuyen) on the French because they could see French armored vehicles and troops in the streets evidently ready for action against the Vietnamese. We (Lansdale and an assistant) told him that it looked as the Vietnamese still needed a leader, that Diem was still President, that the US was still supporting him.

That afternoon, Diem's private secretary called Lansdale. He said the palace was

> under heavy mortar fire, that the President was on another line talking to General Ely, that Ely stated that he couldn't hear any explosions and the President was holding the mouthpiece out towards the explosions so Ely could hear them. Hai (the secretary) started to ask what should be done, interrupted himself to say that the President had just ordered the National Army to start returning the fire and had so informed Ely. He hung up.

Against the advice of French, US and most cabinet advisors, Diem had issued a decree charging Police Commissioner Lai Van Sang with "very grave official misconduct" and named Col. Nguyen Ngoc Le to replace him. Sang refused to resign, saying only Bao Dai had authority to remove him. Binh Xuyen troops in Cholon apparently opened fire on National Army units and Binh Xuyen shells fell again on the palace. But within nine hours after Diem's order to take the offensive, the National Army had driven the Binh Xuyen back into Cholon. Fires raged (set by the Binh Xuyen, according to Lansdale); hundreds were killed or wounded.

6.   *Washington Acts: U.S. Will (Again) Support Diem*

Washington responded with alacrity to Diem's success, superficial though it was. Saigon was told to forget Dulles' earlier message about US willingness to see a change in government. Policy had not changed after all: the US supported Diem. The Saigon Embassy burned the first message.

7.   *Diem and Others Defy Bao Dai*

Buoyed by his showing against Bay Vien, Diem ignored the summons from Bao Dai which appeared on April 28. The Emperor ordered Diem and General Ty to Cannes, placed Binh Xuyen sympathizer General Vy in charge of the army and dispatched General Hinh to Saigon with personal instructions from Bao Dai. Diem refused to leave Saigon, refused to allow General Vy to assume command, refused to allow General Hinh into the country.

On April 30 a new development surfaced. The National Revolutionary Congress of the Vietnamese people was announced. Backed by Cao Dai Generals Phuong and Thè, Hoa Hao General Ngo, other *attentiste* politicians, it claimed to represent almost all political parties in South Vietnam. The Congress declaration repudiated Bao Dai, dissolved the present government and called on Diem to form a new government and elect a national assembly to draft a constitution.

Diem was receptive to the program of the Revolutionary Congress, particularly since his brother Nhu had a hand in drafting it. He was probably not as receptive to some of the activist members of the Congress, however, most of whom joined in a Revolutionary Committee. Generals Trinh Minh Thè and Phuong confided to Lansdale:

> The Revolutionary Committee had grown out of the Revolutionary Congress Front organization which Diem's brother Nhu had tried to organize some days earlier; they had followed (SMM's) advice and had joined with Nhu in the Front but were dissatisfied with some of the weak organizations they felt Nhu was depending on, so had organized something more dynamic to

meet the threat of Vy and Bao Dai and called themselves the Revolutionary Committee. They wanted Bao Dai dethroned and wanted the French to stop interfering in Vietnamese affairs.

Support, backhanded though it may have been, helped Diem politically in Vietnam and with the United States. Militarily he was never really threatened by Bao Dai or Generals Vy or Hinh (who was never able to deliver Bao Dai's special orders). The National Army was stronger than French and Americans thought and it refused to obey General Vy. The following episode, related to Lansdale by General Ty and Colonel Tran Van Don after their temporary arrest by Vy, illustrates this. General Vy bragged about being able to get anything he wanted from the French. Ty and Don asked him to prove it. "(They) . . . asked him to call up the French and request the armored vehicles which the French had been holding at Bien Hoa so long without delivering to the Vietnamese Army. The French rushed these vehicles to Hinh's house (Vy's headquarters), evidently having been holding them just outside town for this emergency, where Army men took them over and drove them into the fight against the Binh Xuyen. Don said the French still hadn't caught on, still thought that Vy would use this armor to bring the Army into line to stop fighting the Binh Xuyen and be loyal to Bao Dai. Don added that the Army felt the same as the Revolutionary Committee: Bao Dai was finished." General Vy retreated to Dalat (and Bao Dai's Imperial Guards), then left the country.

During these days, General Ely had grown more convinced that Diem was not only irresponsible, he was quite mad. Ely feared fighting would spread to the European sector but was unable to win American or British support for an attempt to reimpose the cease-fire. American Charge d'Affairs Kidder felt Ely himself was approaching hysteria and that his emotional involvement compromised his usefulness to either France or the United States. Ely's premonitions of violence between Vietnamese and French forces proved unfounded. But violence did accompany Diem's final offensive against the Binh Xuyen which opened on May 2 when the VNA crossed the Chinese Arroyo and attacked Bay Vien's forces in Cholon. By the following day, most of the Binh Xuyen had been driven out into the Rung Sat swamps.

When Collins returned to Saigon he urged Diem to hold the Revolutionary Committee in check (Collins, most of the French and French intelligence thought Vietminh had infiltrated the front organization; they feared Diem would become its prisoner if he backed it too strongly). Collins wanted Diem to reconstitute the government and get on with reforms, leaving the problem of Bao Dai to an elected national assembly. Diem followed this advice. He invited some 700 elected counselors from 39 provinces to consider Bao Dai's legality. An Estates General composed of 50 counselors drew up a program demanding Bao Dai transfer all civilian and military powers to Diem who would exercise them until the assembly met—within six months—to draw up a constitution.

8. *May Trilateral Meetings*

a. *Dulles Backs Diem*

At this same time, France, the United States and Britain met once again in Paris. The Tripartite session had been called to discuss problems of European Defense but Vietnam was the real subject. The positions of both Secretary Dulles and French Prime Minister Edgar Faure (who succeeded Mendes-France in February 1955) toward Diem had hardened. Dulles insisted he be upheld:

> Diem is only means US sees to save South Vietnam and counteract (the) revolutionary movement underway in Vietnam. US sees no one else who can. Whatever US view has been in past, today US must support Diem whole-heartedly. US must not permit Diem to become another Karensky.
>
> . . . Bao Dai . . . had irretrievably lost capacity to be anything but titular head of government. . . . Cao Dai and Hoa Hao could be used but not Binh Xuyen. . . . With support (of France and US) Diem could sit on top of revolution. Diem is only force of moderation. FEC is certain stabilizing influence. US was giving funds to support Vietnamese army and could not see anyone else to give funds to but Diem for that purpose.
>
> . . . In US view present revolution is not yet dominated or influenced by Communists to any appreciable degree. . . . Support of Diem did not indicate US non-recognition of his weaknesses. US . . . had been and remained ready to support any other man who might be presented by orderly process of law. (Dulles) remarked that just before outbreak of fighting US was prepared to consider alternatives but he was not sure now that it would have been practical. . . . If there is a better man US is ready to consider him but . . . no one has been suggested. Although Collins had reached agreement with Ely in early April to change Diem he now believes we must support him.

b.   *The French Position*

French Minister La Forest had opened the meeting by pointing to consultations (scheduled for July) between North and South Vietnam about elections. He said France felt South Vietnam could win the contest if a "nationalist, stable and broadly based government" were in control and that France wanted South Vietnam to win.

> There is no ambiguity in French policy between North and South Vietnam. Presence of France in North could not be erased by stroke of pen. It is French duty to protect her cultural and economic presence there. Sainteny mission is designed for only that purpose. France had given up thought of mixed companies as result (US) objections and had now surrendered coal mines. . .

LaForest presented the French analysis of events over the past four months. While the US could not argue his facts, the US could not accept LaForest's interpretation of them. Differences between the two nations were more fundamental than at any time in the past.

> . . . France had loyally supported government of Diem from beginning. Any allegation to contrary is untrue . . . France reached agreement with US last December to persuade "or compel" Diem to enlarge government. It was agreed to give him until January at which time, if he had failed, we would look into matter of alternate discreetly. This was not done. Last March present government broke into open conflict with sects. United Front of sects was formed against Diem. Both December agreement and common sense told us at that time that something (had) to be done to avoid civil war. . . . For this reason, joint Ely-Collins approach was tried. It was

hoped they would arrive at joint plan for solution. Washington appeared first to welcome this concept then changed its mind. Collins left Saigon when civil war was about to break out. Untenable truces were declared. When they were about to expire Bao Dai submitted his own plan . . . in order to try to reconcile US and French failure to act. US failed to reply to Bao Dai. In absence of Collins from Saigon, Bao Dai acted.

La Forest continued

. . . that new Revolutionary Committee appeared to have control. Committee is strongly under Viet Minh influence. . . . There is violent campaign against French and French Expeditionary Control. Viet Minh agents make good use of it and certain Americans do not seem sufficiently aware of this. French Government does not wish to have its army act as platform for Vietminh propaganda. Army will not be maintained at any cost . . .

c. *Faure: We Will Withdraw to Save the U.S.–France Alliance*

Then M. Faure took the floor, stating France was not in agreement with the United States and that it was time to speak frankly. He said Diem is "not only incapable but mad," he took advantage of Collins' absence to effect a "coup de force which won primary victory but which has not contributed to any lasting solution" and "France can no longer take risks with him." Diem will "bring on a Viet Minh victory, focus the hostility of everyone on French" and force a break between France and the US.

Faure concluded with this significant statement.

Diem is a bad choice, impossible solution, with no chance to succeed and no chance to improve the situation. Without him some solution might be possible, but with him there is none. However, I cannot guarantee any other solution would work nor is it possible to clarify the situation. There seems to be fundamental disagreement between us. I could have claimed that since French position is predominant in Vietnam, you should accommodate your views more to ours, but I have rejected this. What should be done under the circumstances? What would you say if we were to retire entirely from Indochina and call back the FEC as soon as possible. I fully realize this would be a grave solution, as it would leave French civilians and French interests in a difficult position. . . . If you think this might be a possible solution, I think I might be able to orient myself towards it if you say so. It would have advantage of avoiding all further reproach to France of "colonialism" while at same time giving response to Diem's request that France should go. Since it contemplates the liquidation of the situation and the repatriation of the FEC, would the United States be disposed to help protect French civilians and the refugees?

Secretary Dulles repeated his awareness of Diem's weaknesses but did not agree with Faure's opinion. Diem "showed so much ability that US fails to see how he can be got rid of now . . . Diem is stronger now than when Bao Dai first withdrew his powers." Dulles said the worst aspect of the problem was the differences between France and the US: "Vietnam is not worth quarrel with France." Then he matched Faure's offer by saying the US would withdraw from Vietnam if that would solve the problem.

Choice open to us is to have Diem supported or to withdraw . . . US interest in Vietnam is simply to withhold area from communists. US will give consideration to any suggestion French make but must warn that US financial support may not be expected to any solution which (Dulles) can think of as alternative to Diem.

Foreign Secretary MacMillan, calling British interests "more indirect but nonetheless vital because (1) interest in area itself and (2) interest in Communist threat from any area in world," made the obvious statement that a decision on Vietnam was too grave to be taken that evening. Faure and Dulles agreed.

d. Dulles: Continue with Diem—but Independently of France

By May 11, when the three ministers reconvened, Dulles had received counsel from the JCS and General Collins. As was their wont, the Joint Chiefs of Staff offered no opinion about whether Diem should or should not be continued (a matter for "resolution at the governmental level") but then stated his government showed the "greatest promise of achieving the internal stability essential for the future security of Vietnam." Addressing the military aspects of the problem, the Chiefs found neither withdrawal of the French Expeditionary Corps nor withdrawal of US military support acceptable. The Vietnamese National Army was considered incapable of maintaining internal security, even less able to resist outside aggression without outside military assistance. The US was barred by Geneva from increasing its forces either to defend Vietnam or to defend French civilians, other foreign nationals or refugees. Thus, although withdrawal of the French Expeditionary Corps is "ultimately to be desired," precipitate withdrawal at this time was not: it would "result in an increasingly unstable and precarious situation" and the eventual fall of South Vietnam to communism. The Chiefs felt France alone would be unable to stabilize the situation, that the VNA would fall apart without "US moral and materiel support," and that the "best interest of France as well as the United States" warranted energetic action to restore internal order and prevent South Vietnam's loss to the free world.

General Collins also opposed French withdrawal for three reasons: first, the FEC was responsible under the Manila Pact for the defense of Indochina and neither the US nor Britain were prepared to take over that responsibility. Secondly, French military assistance (logistical support and training) was essential to the development of the Vietnamese forces. Third, although the presence of French troops was a source of bitterness to the Vietnamese, General Collins believed the FEC was a stabilizing influence on Vietnamese politics.

Dulles' proposal to Faure on May 11 reflected these judgments. Emphasizing that Indochina, for all its importance, must not be allowed to damage Franco-American relations, that US support for Diem must not be allowed to split the alliance, Dulles proposed that France continue to support Diem until a National Assembly could be elected to determine the ultimate political structure of South Vietnam, a structure which might or might not include Diem.

Against his own views, against French public opinion and on certain conditions, Faure accepted the proposal. The Prime Minister insisted the Diem government be enlarged, elections be held as soon as possible, the sect problem be resolved, anti-French propaganda cease, Bao Dai be retained as chief of state, French and American officials deemed disturbing to Franco–US harmony be removed from Vietnam (Lansdale, for one) and that the US assure him French economic, cultural and financial relations with South Vietnam would be nurtured. Agreeing to these stipulations, Dulles added Diem was not a US puppet and he could not guarantee conditions involving Vietnamese action would be met. Then, saying the problem in Vietnam did not lend itself to a contractual agreement between France and the United States, Dulles suggested each should state its policy and proceed accordingly. In effect, said Dulles, the days of joint policy are over; the US will act (more) independently of France in the future.

F. THE TWILIGHT OF FRENCH PRESENCE IN VIETNAM

Back in Vietnam, Diem was doing well. He had dealt the Binh Xuyen a coup de grace; the Army was pleased with its success against Bay Vien, supported Diem and rather relished the chance to continue the fight against remaining sect armies. Diem launched a campaign against the sect armies on May 8, to regain control of wayward provinces and solidify Saigon's control through-out the country. The US, again, gave Diem unqualified support and the French, again, reluctantly backed him. Bao Dai was a minor threat; trying to overthrow Diem had been a blunder and his popularity was very low. On May 10, a relatively unknown group of "technicians" was named as Diem's cabinet, to function until elections for a national assembly (held on March 4, 1956). General Collins left Vietnam on May 14; Ambassador G. Frederick Reinhardt replaced him later in the month. And on June 2, General Ely's mission terminated. General Jacquot assumed military duties as Commissioner-General, duties which consisted primarily of supervising the increasingly rapid pace of the French military pull-out.

1. *All-Vietnam Elections*

Although political concessions made to the United States in May and economic and military actions taken before and after that time had reduced—almost eliminated—French presence and influence in Vietnam France still was obligated to carry out the provisions of the Geneva Accords. Under increasing pressure from French public opinion to give Hanoi no pretext for renewing hostilities as long as the French Expeditionary Corps remained in South Vietnam, the French Government urgently sought to persuade Diem to accept consultations about the elections scheduled to begin in July 1955. Britain wanted to prevent any public repudiation of the Accords and joined France in urging Diem to talk to the Vietminh. But Diem had not changed his view of the Accords: he had refused to sign them and continued to insist he was not bound by them.

The United States stood between these extremes. A draft policy toward all-Vietnam elections—finally produced in May 1955—held that to give no impression of blocking elections while avoiding the possibility of losing them, Diem should insist on free elections by secret ballot with strict supervision. Communists in Korea and Germany had rejected these conditions; hopefully the Vietminh would follow suit.

Diem could not bring himself to sit down with the Vietminh. Consultations would give the appearance of having accepted the Geneva settlement; consultation with the Vietminh without the kind of Western backing given Rhee and Adenauer would be futile. On July 16, Diem said South Vietnam could "not consider any proposal from the Communists" without proof that they had mended their ways and were prepared to hold genuinely free elections. But another reason was Diem's belief that he could not represent a sovereign nation —or be free of Vietminh propaganda charges of being a colonialist puppet— until the French High Command and the French Expeditionary Corps were gone. Minister Nguyen Huu Chau was dispatched to Paris to negotiate the withdrawal of the FEC from Vietnam (except naval and air forces which Diem wanted under VNA command) and revision of economic, cultural and financial accords. Diem also wanted Vietnamese affairs transferred from the Ministry of Associated States to the French Foreign office; he insisted the post of High Commissioner be abolished and that Ely's successor (Henri Hoppenot) be credited as Ambassador.

2. *Franco-Vietnamese Differences, Autumn 1955*

France was anxious to get the FEC out of Vietnam (and into North Africa); the matter of turning the High Command over to the VNA was not a problem. Placing French units under Vietnamese command was a definite problem, however and domestic politics would not allow any immediate change of Vietnam's status within the French Union. Talks stalled until July. Diem accepted Ambassador Hoppenot (whose duties, if not title, were that of High Commissioner) and things moved a bit, then stopped when Diem arrested two French officers suspected of bombing electric power stations in Saigon and said they would be tried by Vietnamese courts. In October, France refused to talk unless the officers were released. The deadlock was finally broken by the French in December. Paris agreed the Quai d'Orsay would handle Vietnamese affairs, refused to accept the assignment of a diplomatic representative from the DRV to France and made it clear the Sainteny mission was in Hanoi solely for economic and cultural reasons. France had already recognized Vietnam as a Republic after Diem's resounding—too resounding—victory of 98 percent of the vote in an October popular referendum. Diem finally released the officers into French custody.

But these concessions produced no improvement in French-Vietnam relations. In December, Diem suddenly terminated the economic and financial accords worked out at the Paris conference of 1954; mounting US activity fast drove the former colony from franc to dollar area and stringent commerical regulations applied to French businesses in South Vietnam forced already outraged entrepreneurs out of the country in increasing numbers. Diem laid down these conditions on which he would consider renewed relations with France. France had to

> denounce the Geneva Agreements, to renounce to speak about the general elections in 1956; to approve openly and without reservation the policy of Mr. Diem, to break all relations with the Vietminh and of course to call home the Sainteny Mission.

Soon after this, Diem withdrew South Vietnamese representatives from the French Union Assembly.

There was little France could do. Diem spoke for a government no longer dependent on French support, no longer near collapse. By February 1956, only 15,000 French troops remained in Vietnam and 10,000 of these were to be evacuated by the end of March. The High Command was abolished on April 26, 1956. The next month, the US Temporary Equipment Recovery Mission (TERM) entered Vietnam and another 350 military personnel were added to the US advisory effort. Few French instructors remained at the TRIM.

3. *What of French Obligations Under the Geneva Accords?*

But an important question remained. Under the Geneva agreements France was responsible for protection and support of the International Control Commission; representatives of the People's Army of North Vietnam and France sat on the Joint Armistice Commission charged with ensuring provisions of the armistice agreement were met. France could not lightly cast off these obligations nor could France transfer them to South Vietnam: Diem denounced the Geneva accords and refused to be bound by them in any way.

In February, French Foreign Minister Pineau described the difficult French position as a result of certain conditions:

> These are the independence granted to South Vietnam and the Geneva accords some provisions of which have up to date demanded and justified our presence in this country.

Particularly difficult was the question of ICC support. Diem refused to associate South Vietnam openly with the ICC but did agree to assume responsibility for its servicing if France would leave a small mission in Vietnam to fulfill French obligations. Dulles liked this idea. His view was: "while we should certainly take no positive step to speed up present process of decay of Geneva Accords, neither should we make the slightest effort to infuse life into them."

Eight months later, Diem finally relaxed his uncompromising stand against Geneva, agreed to respect the armistice and provide security for the ICC. In July 1956, Vietnam promised to replace the French liaison mission to the ICC. France maintained membership on the Joint Armistice Commission and continued to bear ICC expenses. But France was never able to meet Geneva obligations concerning the elections of 1956, for Diem matched his refusal to consult with the Vietminh about elections with an adamant refusal to ever hold them. Neither Britain nor the Soviet Union pressed the matter; the United States backed Diem's position.

5. Origins of the Insurgency in South Vietnam, 1954–1960

Summary

From the perspective of the United States, the origins of the insurgency in South Vietnam raise four principal questions:

1. Was the breakdown of the peace of 1954 the fault of the U.S., or of the ambiguities and loopholes of the Geneva Accords?
2. Was the insurgency in essence an indigenous rebellion against Ngo Dinh Diem's oppressive government, transformed by the intervention of first the U.S., and then the DRV?
3. Or was it, rather, instigated, controlled, and supported from its inception by Hanoi?
4. When did the U.S. become aware of the Viet Cong threat to South Vietnam's internal security, and did it attempt to counter it with its aid?

The analysis which follows rests on study of three corpora of evidence:

(a) Intelligence reports and analyses, including the most carefully guarded finished intelligence, and pertinent National Intelligence Estimates.

(b) Unfinished governmental intelligence, field reports, and memoranda such as interrogations of prisoners and translated captured documents, as well as contract studies based on similar evidence.

(c) Open sources, including the works of former U.S. officials, Vietnam correspondents, and the like.

The U.S. has attempted to amplify (c) by publishing White Papers in 1961 and 1965, in which substantial citations were made from (b) and interpretations offered consistent with (a). This study has benefited from further effort during 1967 and early 1968 to identify in (b) evidence which could be publicly released. But, based on the survey of (a), (b), and (c) reported on below, the U.S. can now present no conclusive answers to the questions advanced above.

Tentative answers are possible, and form a continuum: By 1956, peace in Vietnam was plainly less dependent upon the Geneva Settlement than upon power relationships in Southeast Asia—principally upon the role the U.S. elected to play in unfolding events. In 1957 and 1958, a structured rebellion against the government of Ngo Dinh Diem began. While the North Vietnamese played an ill-defined part, most of those who took up arms were South Vietnamese, and the causes for which they fought were by no means contrived in North Vietnam. In 1959 and 1960, Hanoi's involvement in the developing strife became evident. Not until 1960, however, did the U.S. perceive that Diem was in serious danger of being overthrown and devise a Counterinsurgency Plan.

It can be established that there was endemic insurgency in South Vietnam throughout the period 1954–1960. It can also be established—but less surely—that the Diem regime alienated itself from one after another of those elements within Vietnam which might have offered it political support, and was grievously at fault in its rural programs. That these conditions engendered animosity toward the GVN seems almost certain, and they could have underwritten a major resistance movement even without North Vietnamese help.

It is equally clear that North Vietnamese communists operated some form of subordinate apparatus in the South in the years 1954–1960. Nonetheless, the Viet Minh "stay-behinds" were not directed originally to structure an insurgency, and there is no coherent picture of the extent or effectiveness of communist activities in the period 1956–1959. From all indications, this was a period of reorganization and recruiting by the communist party. No direct links have been established between Hanoi and perpetrators of rural violence. Statements have been found in captured party histories that the communists plotted and controlled the entire insurgency, but these are difficult to take at face value. Bernard Fall ingeniously correlated DRV complaints to the ICC of incidents in South Vietnam in 1957 with GVN reports of the same incidents, and found Hanoi suspiciously well informed. He also perceived a pattern in the terrorism of 1957–1959, deducing that a broad, centrally directed strategy was being implemented. However, there is little other corroborative evidence that Hanoi instigated the incidents, much less orchestrated them.

Three interpretations of the available evidence are possible:

Option A—That the DRV intervened in the South in reaction to U.S. escalation, particularly that of President Kennedy in early 1961. Those who advance this argument rest their case principally on open sources to establish the reprehensible character of the Diem regime, on examples of forceful resistance to Diem independent of Hanoi, and upon the formation of the National Liberation Front (NLF) alleged to have come into being in South Vietnam in early 1960. These also rely heavily upon DRV official statements of 1960–1961 indicating that the DRV only then proposed to support the NLF.

Option B—The DRV manipulated the entire war. This is the official U.S. position, and can be supported. Nonetheless, the case is not wholly compelling, especially for the years 1955–1959.

Option C—The DRV seized an opportunity to enter an ongoing internal war in 1959 prior to, and independent of, U.S. escalation. This interpretation is more tenable than the previous; still, much of the evidence is circumstantial.

The judgment offered here is that the truth lies somewhere between Option B and C. That is, there was some form of DRV apparatus functioning in the South throughout the years, but it can only be inferred that this apparatus originated and controlled the insurgency which by 1959 posed a serious challenge to the Diem government. Moreover, up until 1958, neither the DRV domestic situation nor its international support was conducive to foreign adventure; by 1959, its prospects were bright in both respects, and it is possible to demonstrate its moving forcefully abroad thereafter. Given the paucity of evidence now, well after the events, U.S. intelligence served policy makers of the day surprisingly well in warning of the developments described below:

FAILURE OF THE GENEVA SETTLEMENT

The Geneva Settlement of 1954 was inherently flawed as a durable peace for Indochina, since it depended upon France, and since both the U.S. and the Republic of South Vietnam excepted themselves. The common ground from which the nations negotiated at the Geneva Conference was a mutual desire to halt the hostilities between France and the Viet Minh, and to prevent any widening of the war. To achieve concord, they had to override objections of the Saigon government, countenance the disassociation of the U.S. from the Settlement, and accept France as one executor. Even so, Geneva might have wrought an enduring peace for Vietnam *if* France had remained as a major power in Indochina, *if*

Ngo Dinh Diem had cooperated with the terms of the settlement, *if* the U.S. had abstained from further influencing the outcome. No one of these conditions was likely, given France's travail in Algeria, Diem's implacable anti-communism, and the U.S.' determination to block further expansion of the DRV in Southeast Asia.

Therefore, the tragedy staged: partition of Vietnam, the sole negotiable basis found at Geneva for military disengagement, became the prime *casus belli*. To assuage those parties to Geneva who were reluctant to condone the handing over of territory and people to a communist government, and to reassure the Viet Minh that their southern followers could be preserved *en bloc*, the Accords provided for regrouping forces to North and South Vietnam and for Vietnamese freely electing residence in either the North or the South; the transmigrations severely disrupted the polity of Vietnam, heated the controversy over reunification, and made it possible for North Vietnam to contemplate subversive aggression. Both sides were fearful that the armistice would be used to conceal construction of military bases or other preparations for aggression; but these provisions depended on a credible international supervision which never materialized. Partition and regroupment pitted North against South Vietnam, and arms control failed patently and soon. Geneva traded on long-run risks to achieve short-run disengagement. France withdrew from Vietnam, leaving the Accords in the hands of Saigon. Lasting peace came between France and the Viet Minh, but the deeper struggle for an independent, united Vietnam remained, its international implications more grave, its dangers heightened.

The Southeast Asia policy of the U.S. in the aftermath of the Geneva Conference was conservative, focused on organizing collective defense against further inroads of communism, not on altering *status quo*. *Status quo* was the two Vietnams set up at Geneva, facing each other across a demilitarized zone. Hanoi, more than other powers, had gambled: hedged by the remaining Viet Minh, it waited for either Geneva's general elections or the voracious political forces in the South to topple the Saigon government. In South Vietnam, Diem had begun his attempt to gain control over his people, constantly decried DRV subversion and handling of would-be migrants as violations of the Geneva Accords, and pursued an international and domestic policy of anti-communism. Both Vietnams took the view that partition was, as the Conference Final Declaration stated, only temporary. But statements could not gainsay the practical import of the Accords. The separation of Vietnam at the 17th parallel facilitated military disengagement, but by establishing the principle that two regimes were separately responsible for "civil administration" each in distinct zones; by providing for the regroupment of military forces to the two zones, and for the movement of civilians to the zone of their choice; and by postponing national elections for at least two years, permitting the regimes in Hanoi and Saigon to consolidate power, the Geneva conferees in fact fostered two governments under inimical political philosophies, foreign policies, and socio-economic systems.

The Geneva powers were imprecise—probably deliberately indefinite—concerning who was to carry out the election provisions. France, which was charged with civil administration in the "regrouping zone" of South Vietnam, had granted the State of Vietnam its independence in June 1954, six weeks before the Accords were drawn up. Throughout 1954 and the first half of 1955, France further divested itself of authority in South Vietnam: police, local government, and then the Army of Vietnam were freed of French control, and turned over to the Saigon government. Concurrently, the U.S. began to channel aid directly to South Vietnam, rather than through France. The convolution of French policy then thrust upon the U.S. a choice between supporting Diem or the French presence in Indochina. The U.S. opted for Diem. By the time the deadlines for election consultations fell due in July 1955, South Vietnam was sovereign *de facto* as well as *de jure,* waxing strong with U.S. aid, and France was no longer in a position to exert strong influence on Diem's political actions.

As early as January 1955, President Diem was stating publicly that he was unlikely to proceed with the Geneva elections:

> Southern Viet-Nam, since it protested the Geneva Agreement when it was made, does not consider itself a party to that Agreement, nor bound by it.
>
> In any event, the clauses providing for the 1956 elections are extremely vague. But at one point they are clear—in stipulating that the elections are to be free. Everything will now depend on how free elections are defined. The President said he would wait to see whether the conditions of freedom would exist in North Viet-Nam at the time scheduled for the elections. He asked what would be the good of an impartial counting of votes if the voting has been preceded in North Viet-Nam by a campaign of ruthless propaganda and terrorism on the part of a police state.

As the deadline for consultations approached (20 July 1955), Diem was increasingly explicit that he did not consider free elections possible in North Vietnam, and had no intention of consulting with the DRV concerning them. The U.S. did not—as is often alleged—connive with Diem to ignore the elections. U.S. State Department records indicate that Diem's refusal to be bound by the Geneva Accords and his opposition to pre-election consultations were at his own initiative. However, the U.S., which had expected elections to be held, and up until May 1955 had fully supported them, shifted its position in the face of Diem's opposition, and of the evidence then accumulated about the oppressive nature of the regime in North Vietnam. "In essence," a State Department historical study found, "our position would be that the whole subject of consultations and elections in Viet-Nam should be left up to the Vietnamese themselves and not dictated by external arrangements which one of the parties never accepted and still rejects." Secretary of State Dulles explained publicly that:

> Neither the United States Government nor the Government of Viet-Nam is, of course, a party to the Geneva armistice agreements. We did not sign them, and the Government of Viet-Nam did not sign them and, indeed, protested against them. On the other hand, the United States believes, broadly speaking, in the unification of countries which have a historic unity, where the people are akin. We also believe that, if there are conditions of really free elections, there is no serious risk that the Communists would win. . . .

Thus, backed by the U.S., Diem obdurately refused to open talks with the Hanoi government. He continued to maintain that the Government of South Vietnam had not signed the Geneva Agreements and thus was not bound by them.

> Our policy is a policy for peace. But nothing will lead us astray of our goal, the unity of our country, a unity in freedom and not in slavery. Serving the cause of our nation, more than ever we will struggle for the reunification of our homeland.

We do not reject the principle of free elections as peaceful and democratic means to achieve that unity. However, if elections constitute one of the bases of true democracy, they will be meaningful only on the condition that they be absolutely free.

Now, faced with a regime of oppression as practiced by the Viet Minh, we remain skeptical concerning the possibility of fulfilling the conditions of free elections in the North.

On 1 June 1956, the Assistant Secretary of State for Far Eastern Affairs, Walter Robertson, stated:

President Diem and the Government of Free Viet-Nam reaffirmed on April 6 of this year and on other occasions their desire to seek the reunification of Viet-Nam by peaceful means. In this goal, we support them fully. We hope and pray that the partition of Viet-Nam, imposed against the will of the Vietnamese people, will speedily come to an end. For our part we believe in free elections, and we support President Diem fully in his position that if elections are to be held, there first must be conditions which preclude intimidation or coercion of the electorate. Unless such conditions exist there can be no free choice.

President Eisenhower is widely quoted to the effect that in 1954 as many as 80% of the Vietnamese people would have voted for Ho Chi Minh, as the popular hero of their liberation, in an election against Bao Dai. In October 1955, Diem ran against Bao Dai in a referendum and won—by a dubiously overwhelming vote, but he plainly won nevertheless. It is almost certain that by 1956 the proportion which might have voted for Ho—in a free election against Diem—would have been much smaller than 80%. Diem's success in the South had been far greater than anyone could have foreseen, while the North Vietnamese regime had been suffering from food scarcity, and low public morale stemming from inept imitation of Chinese Communism—including a harsh agrarian program that reportedly led to the killing of over 50,000 small-scale "landlords." The North Vietnamese themselves furnished damning descriptions of conditions within the DRV in 1955 and 1956. Vo Nguyen Giap, in a public statement to his communist party colleagues, admitted in autumn, 1956, that:

We made too many deviations and executed too many honest people. We attacked on too large a front and, seeing enemies everywhere, resorted to terror, which became far too widespread. . . . Whilst carrying out our land reform program we failed to respect the principles of freedom of faith and worship in many areas . . . in regions inhabited by minority tribes we have attacked tribal chiefs too strongly, thus injuring, instead of respecting, local customs and manners. . . . When reorganizing the party, we paid too much importance to the notion of social class instead of adhering firmly to political qualifications alone. Instead of recognizing education to be the first essential, we resorted exclusively to organizational measures such as disciplinary punishments, expulsion from the party, executions, dissolution of party branches and calls. Worse still, torture came to be regarded as a normal practice during party reorganization.

That circumstances in North Vietnam were serious enough to warrant Giap's *confiteor* was proved by insurrection among Catholic peasants in November 1956, within two weeks of his speech, in which thousands more lives were lost. But the uprisings, though then and since used to validate the U.S.-backed GVN stand, were not foreseen in 1955 or 1956; the basis for the policy of both nations in rejecting the Geneva elections was, rather, convictions that Hanoi would not permit "free general elections by secret ballot," and that the ICC would be impotent in supervising the elections in any case.

The deadlines for the consultations in July 1955, and the date set for elections in July 1956, passed without international action. The DRV repeatedly tried to engage the Geneva machinery, forwarding messages to the Government of South Vietnam in July 1955, May and June 1956, March 1958, July 1959, and July 1960, proposing consultations to negotiate "free general elections by secret ballot," and to liberalize North–South relations in general. Each time the GVN replied with disdain, or with silence. The 17th parallel, with its demilitarized zone on either side, became *de facto* an international boundary, and—since Ngo Dinh Diem's rigid refusal to traffic with the North excluded all economic exchanges and even an interstate postal agreement—one of the most restricted boundaries in the world. The DRV appealed to the UK and the USSR as co-chairmen of the Geneva Conference to no avail. In January 1956, on DRV urging, Communist China requested another Geneva Conference to deal with the situation. But the Geneva Co-Chairmen, the USSR and the UK, responded only by extending the functions of the International Control Commission beyond its 1956 expiration date. By early 1957, partitioned Vietnam was a generally accepted *modus vivendi* throughout the international community. For instance, in January 1957, the Soviet Union proposed the admission of both the GVN and the DRV to the United Nations, the USSR delegate to the Security Council declaring that "in Vietnam two separate States existed, which differed from one another in political and economic structure. . . ." Thus, reunification through elections became as remote a prospect in Vietnam as in Korea or Germany. If the political mechanism for reunifying Vietnam in 1956 proved impractical, the blame lies at least in part with the Geneva conferees themselves, who postulated an ideal political settlement incompatible with the physical and psychological dismemberment of Vietnam they themselves undertook in July 1954.

But partition was not, as the examples of Korea and Germany demonstrate, necessarily tantamount to renewed hostilities. The difference was that in Korea and Germany international forces guarded the boundaries. In Vietnam, the withdrawal of the French Expeditionary Corps prior to the date set for elections in 1956 left South Vietnam defenseless except for such forces as it could train and equip with U.S. assistance. The vague extending of the SEATO aegis over Vietnam did not exert the same stabilizing influence as did NATO's Central Army Group in Germany, or the United Nations Command in Korea. Moreover, neither East Germany nor North Korea enjoyed the advantage of a politico-military substructure within the object of its irredentism, as the Viet Minh residue provided North Vietnam. The absence of deterrent force in South Vietnam invited forceful reunification; the southern Viet Minh regroupees in the North and their comrades in the South made it possible.

Pursuant to the "regroupment" provisions of the Geneva Accords, some 190,-000 troops of the French Expeditionary Corps, and 900,000 civilians moved from North Vietnam to South Vietnam; more than 100,000 Viet Minh soldiers and civilians moved from South to North. Both nations thereby acquired minorities with vital interests in the outcome of the Geneva Settlement. In both nations, the regroupees exerted an influence over subsequent events well out of proportion to their numbers.

In North Vietnam, the DRV treated the southern regroupees from the outset as strategic assets—the young afforded special schooling, the able assigned to separate military units.

The southerners in the North, and their relatives in the South, formed, with the remnants of the Viet Minh's covert network in South Vietnam, a means through which the DRV might "struggle" toward reunification regardless of Diem's obduracy or U.S. aid for South Vietnam. These people kept open the DRV's option to launch aggression without transcending a "civil war" of southerners against southerners—no doubt an important consideration with the United States as a potential antagonist. The evidence indicates that, at least through 1956, Hanoi did not expect to have to resort to force; thereafter, the regroupees occupied increasing prominence in DRV plans.

For Diem's government, refugees from the North were important for three reasons: firstly, they provided the world the earliest convincing evidence of the undemocratic and oppressive nature of North Vietnam's regime. Though no doubt many migrants fled North Vietnam for vague or spurious reasons, it was plain that Ho's Viet Minh were widely and genuinely feared, and many refugees took flight in understandable terror. There were indications that the DRV forcefully obstructed the migration of other thousands who might also have left the North. In 1955 and 1956, the refugees were the most convincing support for Diem's argument that free elections were impossible in the DRV.

Secondly, the refugees engaged the sympathies of the American people as few developments in Vietnam have before or since, and solidly underwrote the U.S. decision for unstinting support of Diem. The poignancy of hundreds of thousands of people fleeing their homes and fortunes to escape communist tyranny, well journalized, evoked an outpouring of U.S. aid, governmental and private. The U.S. Navy was committed to succor the migrants, lifting over 300,-000 persons in "Operation EXODUS" (in which Dr. Tom Dooley—then a naval officer—won fame). U.S. government-to-government aid, amounting to $100 per refugee, more than South Vietnam's annual income per capita, enabled Diem's government to provide homes and food for hundreds of thousands of the destitute, and American charities provided millions of dollars more for their relief. U.S. officials defending American aid programs could point with pride to the refugee episode to demonstrate the special eligibility of the Vietnamese for U.S. help, including an early, convincing demonstration that Diem's government could mount an effective program with U.S. aid.

Thirdly, the predominantly Catholic Tonkinese refugees provided Diem with a claque: a politically malleable, culturally distinct group, wholly distrustful of Ho Chi Minh and the DRV, dependent for subsistence on Diem's government, and attracted to Diem as a co-religionist. Under Diem's mandarinal regime, they were less important as dependable votes than as a source of reliable political and military cadres. Most were kept unassimilated in their own communities, and became prime subjects for Diem's experiments with strategic population relocation. One heritage of Geneva is the present dominance of South Vietnam's government and army by northerners. The refugees catalyzed Diem's domestic political rigidity, his high-handedness with the U.S., and his unyielding rejection of the DRV and the Geneva Accords.

The Geneva Settlement was further penalized by the early failure of the "International Supervisory Commission" established by the Agreement (Article 34) and cited in the Conference Declaration (Article 7). While a Joint Commission of French and Viet Minh military officers was set up to deal with the cease-fire and force regroupment, the International Commission for Supervision and Control (ICC), furnished by Poland, India, and Canada, was to oversee the Accords in general. Its inability to cope with violations of the Armistice in the handling of would-be migrants, vociferously proclaimed in both Saigon and Hanoi, impugned its competence to overwatch the general free elections, for which it was also to be responsible.

Equally serious for the Settlement, the ICC was expected to control arms and guarantee against aggression. The armistice agreement signed by the French and the Viet Minh, and affirmed in the several declarations of the Geneva Conference, included four main provisions for arms control: (1) arms, bases, and armed forces were to be fixed at the level existing in Vietnam in July 1954, with allowance for replacement of worn or damaged equipment, and rotation of personnel; (2) further foreign influences were to be excluded, either in the form of alliances, or foreign military bases established in either North or South Vietnam; (3) neither party was to allow its zone to be used for the renewal of aggression; and, (4) all the foregoing were to be overseen by the ICC. As was the case of the regroupment provisions, these arrangements operated in practice to the detriment of the political solution embodied in the Accords, for the ICC, the election guardian, was soon demonstrated to be impotent.

The level of arms in Vietnam in 1954 was unascertainable. The Viet Minh had been surreptitiously armed, principally by the Chinese, from 1950 onward. That Viet Minh forces were acquiring large amount of relatively advanced weaponry was fully evident at Dien Bien Phu, but neither the DRV nor its allies owned to this military assistance. After the 1954 armistice, French, U.S., and British intelligence indicated that the flow of arms into North Vietnam from China continued on a scale far in excess of "replacement" needs. Similarly, while U.S. military materiel had been provided to the French more openly, no one— neither the French, the Vietnamese, the U.S., nor certainly the ICC—knew how much of this equipment was on hand and serviceable after 1954. The issue of arms levels was further complicated by regroupment, French withdrawals, and the revamping of the national army in South Vietnam. The ICC could determine to no one's satisfaction whether the DRV was within its rights to upgrade the armament of the irregulars it brought out of South Vietnam. Similarly, though the DRV charged repeatedly that the U.S. had no right to be in South Vietnam at all, the ICC had to face the fact that U.S. military advisors and trainers had been present in Vietnam since 1950 under a pentilateral agreement with Laos, Cambodia, Vietnam, and France. If France withdrew its cadres in Vietnamese units, could they not be "replaced" by Americans? And if the French were withdrawing both men and equipment in large quantities, did not Vietnam have a right under the Accords to replace them in kind with its own, American-equipped formations? To DRV charges and GVN countercharges, it could reply with legalistic interpretations, but it found it virtually impossible to collect facts, or exercise more than vague influence over U.S., GVN, or DRV policy. The only major example of U.S.' ignoring the ICC was the instance of the U.S. Training and Equipment Recovery Mission (TERM), 350 men ostensibly deployed to Vietnam in 1956 to aid the Vietnamese in recovering equipment left by the French, but also directed to act as an extension of the existing MAAG by training Vietnamese in logistics. TERM was introduced without ICC sanction, although subsequently the ICC accepted its presence.

The question of military bases was similarly occluded. The DRV protested repeatedly that the U.S. was transforming South Vietnam into a military base for the prosecution of aggression in Southeast Asia. In fact, as ICC investigation subsequently established, there was no wholly U.S. base anywhere in South

Vietnam. It was evident, however, that the South Vietnamese government had made available to the U.S. some portions of existing air and naval facilities—e.g., at Tan Son Nhut, Bien Hoa, and Nha Be—for the use of MAAG and TERM. ICC access to these facilities was restricted, and the ICC was never able to determine what the U.S. was shipping through them, either personnel or materiel. By the same token, ICC access to DRV airports, rail terminals, and seaports was severely limited, and its ability to confirm or deny allegations concerning the rearming of the People's Army of Vietnam correspondingly circumscribed. International apprehensions over arms levels and potential bases for aggression were heightened by statements anticipating South Vietnam's active participation in SEATO, or pronouncements of DRV solidarity with China and Russia.

Not until 1959 and 1961 did the ICC publish reports attempting to answer directly DRV charges that the U.S. and South Vietnam were flagrantly violating the arms control provisions of the Geneva Accords. Similarly, though in its Tenth and Eleventh Interim Reports (1960 and 1961) the ICC noted "the concern which the Republic of Vietnam has been expressing over the problem of subversion in South Vietnam," it did not mention that those expressions of concern had been continuous since 1954, or attempt to publish a factual study of that problem until June 1962. In both cases, the ICC was overtaken by events: by late 1960, international tensions were beyond any ability of the ICC to provide reassurances, and the U.S. was faced with the decision whether to commit major resources to the conflict in South Vietnam.

The Geneva Settlement thus failed to provide lasting peace because it was, as U.S. National Security Council papers of 1956 and 1958 aptly termed it, "only a truce." It failed to settle the role of the U.S. or of the Saigon government, or, indeed, of France in Vietnam. It failed because it created two antagonist Vietnamese nations. It failed because the Geneva powers were unwilling or unable to concert follow-up action in Vietnam to supervise effectively observance of the Accords, or to dampen the mounting tension. Mutual distrust led to incremental violations by both sides, but on balance, though neither the United States nor South Vietnam was fully cooperative, and though both acted as they felt necessary to protect their interests, both considered themselves constrained by the Accords. There is no evidence that either deliberately undertook to breach the peace. In contrast, the DRV proceeded to mobilize its total societal resources scarcely without pause from the day the peace was signed, as though to substantiate the declaration of its Deputy Premier, Pham Van Dong, at the closing session of the Geneva Conference:

> We shall achieve unity. We shall achieve it just as we have won the war. No force in the world, internal or external, can make us deviate from our path . . .

Diem's rejection of elections meant that reunification could be achieved in the foreseeable future only by resort to force. Diem's policy, and U.S. support of it, led inevitably to a test of strength with the DRV to determine whether the GVN's cohesiveness, with U.S. support, could offset North Vietnam's drive to satisfy its unrequited nationalism and expansionism.

REVOLT AGAINST MY-DIEM

By the time President Kennedy came to office in 1961, it was plain that support for the Saigon government among South Vietnam's peasants—90% of the population—was weak and waning. The Manifesto of the National Liberation Front, published in December 1960, trumpeted the existence of a revolutionary organization which could channel popular discontent into a political program. Increasingly Diem's government proved inept in dealing either through its public administration with the sources of popular discontent, or through its security apparatus with the Viet Cong. Diem's government and his party were by that time manifestly out of touch with the people, and into the gap between the government and the populace the Viet Cong had successfully driven. When and why this gap developed is crucial to an understanding of who the Viet Cong were, and to what extent they represented South as opposed to North Vietnamese interests.

The U.S. Government, in its White Papers on Vietnam of 1961 and 1965, has blamed the insurgency on aggression by Hanoi, holding that the Viet Cong were always tools of the DRV. Critics of U.S. policy in Vietnam usually hold, to the contrary, that the war was started by South Vietnamese; their counter-arguments rest on two propositions: (1) that the insurgency began as a rebellion against the oppressive and clumsy government of Ngo Dinh Diem; and (2) that only after it became clear, in late 1960, that the U.S. would commit massive resources to succor Diem in his internal war, was the DRV impelled to unleash the South Vietnamese Viet Minh veterans evacuated to North Vietnam after Geneva. French analysts have long been advancing such interpretations; American protagonists for them often quote, for example, Philippe Devillers, who wrote in 1962 that:

> . . . In 1959, responsible elements of the Communist Resistance in Indo-China came to the conclusion that they had to act, whether Hanoi wanted them to or no. They could no longer continue to stand by while their supporters were arrested, thrown into prison and tortured, without attempting to do anything about it as an organization, without giving some lead to the people in the struggle in which it was to be involved. Hanoi preferred diplomatic notes, but it was to find that its hand had been forced.

Devillers related how in March 1960 the "Nambo Veterans of the Resistance Association" issued a declaration appealing for "struggle" to "liberate themselves from submission to America, eliminate all U.S. bases in South Vietnam, expel American military advisors . . ." and to end "the colonial regime and the fascist dictatorship of the Ngo family." Shortly thereafter, according to Devillers, a People's Liberation Army appeared in Cochinchina and:

> From this time forward it carried on incessant guerrilla operations against Diem's forces.

It was thus by its *home* policy that the government of the South finally destroyed the confidence of the population, which it had won during the early years, and practically drove them into revolt and desperation. The non-Communist (and even the anti-Communist) opposition had long been aware of the turn events were taking. But at the beginning of 1960 very many elements, both civilian and military, in the Nationalist camp came to a clear realization that things were moving from bad to worse, and that if nothing were done to put an end to the absolute power of Diem, then Communism would end up by gaining power with the aid, or at least with the consent, of the population. If they did not want to allow the Communists to make capital out of the revolt, then they would have to oppose Diem actively. . . .

Based on a similar analysis, Arthur Schlesinger, Jr., held that:

Diem's authoritarianism, which increasingly involved manhunts, political reeducation camps, and the "regroupment" of population, caused spreading discontent and then armed resistance on the countryside. It is not easy to disentangle the events of these murky years; but few scholars believe that the growing resistance was at the start organized or directed by Hanoi. Indeed, there is some indication that the Communists at first hung back . . . it was not until September, 1960 that the Communist Party of North Vietnam bestowed its formal blessing and called for the liberation of the south from American imperialism.

Events in Vietnam in the years 1954 to 1960 were indeed murky. The Diem government controlled the press tightly, and discouraged realism in reports from its provincial bureaucracy. Even official U.S. estimates were handicapped by reliance upon GVN sources for inputs from the grass roots of Vietnamese society, the rural villages, since the U.S. advisory effort was then largely confined to top levels of the GVN and its armed forces. But enough evidence has now accumulated to establish that peasant resentment against Diem was extensive and well founded. Moreover, it is clear that dislike of the Diem government was coupled with resentment toward Americans. For many Vietnamese peasants, the War of Resistance against French–Bao Dai rule never ended; France was merely replaced by the U.S., and Bao Dai's mantle was transferred to Ngo Dinh Diem. The Viet Cong's opprobrious catchword *"My-Diem"* (American–Diem) thus recaptured the nationalist mystique of the First Indochina War, and combined the natural xenophobia of the rural Vietnamese with their mounting dislike of Diem. But Viet Cong slogans aside, in the eyes of many Vietnamese of no particular political persuasion, the United States was reprehensible as a modernizing force in a thoroughly traditional society, as the provider of arms and money for a detested government, and as an alien, disruptive influence upon hopes they held for the Geneva Settlement. As far as attitudes toward Diem were concerned, the prevalence of his picture throughout Vietnam virtually assured his being accepted as the sponsor of the frequently corrupt and cruel local officials of the GVN, and the perpetrator of unpopular GVN programs, especially the population relocation schemes, and the "Communist Denunciation Campaign." Altogether, Diem promised the farmers much, delivered little, and raised not only their expectations, but their fears.

It should be recognized, however, that whatever his people thought of him, Ngo Dinh Diem really did accomplish miracles, just as his American boosters said he did. He took power in 1954 amid political chaos, and within ten months surmounted attempted coups d'etat from within his army and rebellions by disparate irregulars. He consolidated his regime while providing creditably for an influx of nearly one million destitute refugees from North Vietnam; and he did all of this despite active French opposition and vacillating American support. Under his leadership South Vietnam became well established as a sovereign state, by 1955 recognized *de jure* by 36 other nations. Moreover, by mid-1955 Diem secured the strong backing of the U.S. He conducted a plebiscite in late 1955, in which an overwhelming vote was recorded for him in preference to Bao Dai; during 1956, he installed a government—representative in form, at least—drafted a new constitution, and extended GVN control to regions that had been under sect or Viet Minh rule for a decade; and he pledged to initiate extensive reforms in land holding, public health, and education. With American help, he established a truly national, modern army, and formed rural security forces to police the countryside. In accomplishing all the foregoing, he confounded those Vietnamese of North and South, and those French, who had looked for his imminent downfall.

While it is true that his reforms entailed oppressive measures—e.g., his "political reeducation centers" were in fact little more than concentration camps for potential foes of the government—his regime compared favorably with other Asian governments of the same period in its respect for the person and property of citizens. There is much that can be offered in mitigation of Diem's authoritarianism. He began as the most singularly disadvantaged head of state of his era. His political legacy was endemic violence and virulent anti-colonialism. He took office at a time when the government of Vietnam controlled only a few blocks of downtown Saigon; the rest of the capital was the feudal fief of the Binh Xuyen gangster fraternity. Beyond the environs of Saigon, South Vietnam lay divided among the Viet Minh enclaves and the theocratic dominions of the Cao Dai and the Hoa Hao sects. All these powers would have opposed any Saigon government, whatever its composition; in fact, their existence accounts for much of the confidence the DRV then exhibited toward the outcome of the Geneva Settlement. For Diem to have erected any central government in South Vietnam without reckoning resolutely with their several armed forces and clandestine organizations would have been impossible: they were the very stuff of South Vietnam's politics.

Diem's initial political tests reinforced his propensity to inflexibility. The lessons of his first 10 months of rule must have underscored to Diem the value of swift, tough action against dissent, and of demanding absolute personal loyalty of top officials. Also, by May 1955, Ngo Dinh Diem had demonstrated to his satisfaction that the U.S. was sufficiently committed to South Vietnam that he could afford on occasion to resist American pressure, and even to ignore American advice. Diem knew, as surely as did the United States, that he himself represented the only alternative to a communist South Vietnam.

Diem was handicapped in all his attempts to build a nation by his political concepts. He had the extravagant expectations of a Rousseau, and he acted with the zeal of a Spanish Inquisitor. Despite extensive travel and education in the West, and despite his revolutionary mien, he remained what he had been raised: a mandarin of Imperial Hue, steeped in filial piety, devoted to Vietnam's past, modern only to the extent of an intense, conservative Catholicism. The political apparatus he created to extend his power and implement his programs reflected his background, personality, and experience: a rigidly organized, over-centralized familial oligarchy. Though his brothers, Ngo Dinh Nhu and Ngo Dinh Can, created extensive personal political organizations of considerable power—Nhu's semi-covert *Can Lao* party borrowed heavily from communist doctrine and technique—and though a third brother, Ngo Dinh Thuc, was the ranking Catholic bishop, in no sense did they or Diem ever acquire a broad popular base for his government. Diem's personality and his political methods practically assured that he would remain distant, virtually isolated from the peasantry. They also seem to have predetermined that Diem's political history over the long-run would be a chronicle of disaffection: Diem alienated one after another of the key groups within South Vietnam's society until, by late 1960, his regime rested on the narrow and disintegrating base of its own bureaucracy and the northern refugees.

Such need not have been the case. At least through 1957, Diem and his government enjoyed marked success with fairly sophisticated pacification programs in the countryside. In fact, Diem at first was warmly welcomed in some former Viet Minh domains, and it is probable that a more sensitive and adroit leader could have captured and held a significant rural following. Even the failure of the Geneva Accords to eventuate in general elections in 1956 at first had little impact upon GVN pacification. The strident declamations of the DRV notwithstanding, reunification of partitioned Vietnam was not at first a vital political issue for South Vietnam's peasants. By and large, as late as 1961 as Devillers pointed out:

> For the people of the South reunification is not an essential problem. Peace, security, freedom, their standard of living, the agrarian question— these are far more important questions to them. The stronghold of the sects over certain regions remains one of the factors of the situation, as is also, in a general fashion, the distrustful attitude of the Southerner towards the Northerner, who is suspected of a tendency to want to take charge of affairs.

The initial GVN pacification effort combined promises of governmental level reforms with "civic action" in the hamlets and villages. The latter was carried out by "cadre" clad in black pajamas, implementing the Maoist "three-withs" doctrine (eat with, sleep with, work with the people) to initiate rudimentary improvements in public health, education, and local government, and to propagandize the promises of the central government. Unfortunately for Diem, his civic action teams had to be drawn from the northern refugees, and encountered Cochinchinese–Tonkinese tensions. More importantly, however, they incurred the enmity of the several Saigon ministries upon whose field responsibilities they impinged. Moreover, they became preoccupied with Diem's anti-communist campaign to the detriment of their social service. By the end of 1956, the civic action component of the GVN pacification program had been cut back severely.

But the salesmen were less at fault than their product. Diem's reform package compared unfavorably even in theory with what the Viet Minh had done by way of rural reform. Diem undertook to: (1) resettle refugees and other land destitute Vietnamese on uncultivated land beginning in 1955; (2) expropriate all rice land holdings over 247 acres and redistribute these to tenant farmers beginning in 1956; and (3) regulate landlord-tenant relations beginning in 1957 to fix rents within the range 15–25% of crop yield, and to guarantee tenant land tenure for 3–5 years. Despite invidious comparison with Viet Minh rent-free land, had these programs been honestly and efficiently implemented, they might have satisfied the land-hunger of the peasants. But they suffered, as one American expert put it from "lack of serious, interested administrators and top side command." Government officials, beginning with the Minister for Agrarian Reform, had divided loyalties, being themselves land holders. Moreover, the programs often operated to replace paternalistic landlords with competitive bidding, and thus increased, rather than decreased, tenant insecurity. And even if all Diem's goals had been honestly fulfilled—which they were not— only 20% of the rice land would have passed from large to small farmers. As it turned out, only 10% of all tenant farmers benefited in any sense. By 1959, the land reform program was virtually inoperative. As of 1960, 45% of the land remained concentrated in the hands of 2% of landowners, and 15% of the landlords owned 75% of all the land. Those relatively few farmers who did benefit from the program were more often than not northerners, refugees, Catholics, or Annamese—so that land reform added to the GVN's aura of favoritism which deepened peasant alienation in Cochinchina. Farmer–GVN tensions were further aggravated by rumors of corruption, and the widespread allegation that the Diem family itself had become enriched through the manipulation of land transfers.

Diem's whole rural policy furnishes one example after another of political maladroitness. In June 1956, Diem abolished elections for village councils, apparently out of concern that large numbers of Viet Minh might win office. By replacing the village notables with GVN appointed officials, Diem swept away the traditional administrative autonomy of the village officials, and took upon himself and his government the onus for whatever corruption and injustice subsequently developed at that level. Again, the GVN appointees to village office were outsiders—northerners, Catholics, or other "dependable" persons—and their alien presence in the midst of the close-knit rural communities encouraged revival of the conspiratorial, underground politics to which the villages had become accustomed during the resistance against the French.

But conspiracy was almost a natural defense after Diem launched his Denunciation of Communists Campaign, which included a scheme for classifying the populace into lettered political groups according to their connections with the Viet Minh. This campaign, which featured public confessions reminiscent of the "people's courts" of China and North Vietnam, invited neighbors to inform on each other, and raised further the premium on clandestine political activity. In 1956, the GVN disclosed that some 15–20,000 communists had been detained in its "political reeducation centers," while Devillers put the figure at 50,000. By GVN figures in 1960, nearly 50,000 had been detained. A British expert on Vietnam, P. J. Honey, who was invited by Diem to investigate the reeducation centers in 1959, concluded that, after interviewing a number of rural Vietnamese, "the consensus of the opinion expressed by these peoples is that . . . the majority of the detainees are neither communists nor pro-communists." Between 1956 and 1960, the GVN claimed that over 100,000 former communist cadres rallied to the GVN, and thousands of other communist agents had surrendered or had been captured. The campaign also allegedly netted over 100,000 weapons and 3,000 arms caches. Whatever it contributed to GVN internal security, however, the Communist Denunciation Campaign thoroughly terrified the Vietnamese peasants, and detracted significantly from the regime's popularity.

Diem's nearly paranoid preoccupation with security influenced his population relocation schemes. Even the refugee relief programs had been executed with an eye to building a "living wall" between the lowland centers of population and the jungle and mountain redoubts of dissidents. Between April 1957 and late 1961, the GVN reported that over 200,000 persons—refugees and landless families from coastal Annam—were resettled in 147 centers carved from 220,000 acres of wilderness. These "strategic" settlements were expensive: although they affected only 2% of South Vietnam's people, they absorbed 50% of U.S. aid for agriculture. They also precipitated unexpected political reactions from the Montagnard peoples of the Highlands. In the long run, by introducing ethnic Vietnamese into traditionally Montagnard areas, and then by concentrating Montagnards into defensible communities, the GVN provided the tribes with a cause and focused their discontent against Diem. The GVN thus facilitated rather than hindered the subsequent subversion of the tribes by the Viet Cong. But of all Diem's relocation experiments, that which occasioned the most widespread and vehement anti-GVN sentiment was the "agroville" program begun in mid-1959. At first, the GVN tried to establish rural communities which segregated families with known Viet Cong or Viet Minh connections from other citizens, but the public outcry caused this approach to be dropped. A few months later, the GVN announced its intent to build 80 "prosperity and density centers" along a "strategic route system." By the end of 1963, each of these 80 agrovilles was to hold some 400 families, and each would have a group of satellite agrovilles of 120 families each. In theory, the agroville master plan was attractive: there were provisions for community defense, schools, dispensary, market center, public garden, and even electricity. Despite these advantages, however, the whole program incurred the wrath of the peasants. They resented the corvee labor the GVN resorted to for agroville construction, and they abhorred abandoning their cherished ancestral homes, tombs, and developed gardens and fields for a strange and desolate community. Passive peasant resistance, and then insurgent attacks on the agrovilles, caused abandonment of the program in early 1961 when it was less than 25% complete.

Yet, for all Diem's preoccupation with rural security, he poorly provided for police and intelligence in the countryside. Most of the American aid the GVN received was used for security, and the bulk of it was lavished on the Army of Vietnam. Security in the villages was relegated to the Self-Defense Corps (SDC) and the Civil Guard (CG)—poorly trained and equipped, miserably led. They could scarcely defend themselves, much less secure the farmers. Indeed, they proved to be an asset to insurgents in two ways: they served as a source of weapons; and their brutality, petty thievery, and disorderliness induced innumerable villagers to join in open revolt against the GVN. The Army of Vietnam, after 1956, was withdrawn from the rural regions to undergo reorganization and modernization under its American advisors. Its interaction with the rural populace through 1959 was relatively slight. The SDC and CG, placed at the disposal of the provincial administrators, were often no more venal nor offensive to the peasants than the local officials themselves, but the corrupt, arrogant and overbearing men the people knew as the GVN were among the greatest disadvantages Diem faced in his rural efforts.

Nor was Ngo Dinh Diem successful in exercising effective leadership over the Vietnamese urban population or its intellectuals. Just as Diem and his brothers made the mistake of considering all former Viet Minh communists, they erred in condemning all non-Diemist nationalists as tools of Bao Dai or the French. The Diem family acted to circumscribe all political activity and even criticism not sanctioned by the oligarchy. In late 1957, newspapers critical of the regime began to be harassed, and in March 1958, after a caustic editorial, the GVN closed down the largest newspaper in Saigon. Attempts to form opposition political parties for participation in the national assembly met vague threats and bureaucratic impediments. In 1958, opposition politicians risked arrest for assaying to form parties unauthorized by Nhu or Can, and by 1959 all opposition political activity had come to a halt. In the spring of 1960, however, a group of non-communist nationalist leaders came together—with more courage than prudence—to issue the Caravelle Manifesto, a recital of grievances against the Diem regime. Eleven of the 18 signers had been cabinet members under Diem or Bao Dai; 4 had been in other high government positions, and others represented religious groups. Their manifesto lauded Diem for the progress that he had made in the aftermath of Geneva, but pointed out that his repressions in recent years had "provoked the discouragement and resentment of the people." They noted that "the size of the territory has shrunk, but the number of civil servants has increased and still the work doesn't get done"; they applauded the fact that "the French Expeditionary Corps has left the country and a Republican Army has been constituted, thanks to American aid," but deplored the fact that the Diem influence "divides the men of one and the same unit, sows distrust between friends of the same rank, and uses as a criterion for promotion fidelity to the party in blind submission to its leaders"; they described, despairingly, "a rich and fertile country enjoying food surpluses" where "at the present time many people are out of work, have no roof over their heads, and no money." They went on to "beseech the government to urgently modify its policies." While the Caravelle Manifesto thoroughly frightened Diem, coming, as it did, three days after Syngman Rhee was overthrown in Korea, it prompted him only to further measures to quell the loyal opposition. By the fall of 1960, the intellectual elite of South Vietnam was politically mute; labor unions were impotent; loyal opposition in the form of organized parties did not exist. In brief, Diem's policies virtually assured that political challenges to him would have to be extra-legal. Ultimately, these emerged from the traditional sources of power in South Vietnam—the armed forces, the religious sects, and the armed peasantry.

Through 1960, the only serious threats to Diem from inside the GVN were attempted military coups d'etat. In his first 10 months in office, Diem had identified loyalty in his top army commanders as a *sine qua non* for his survival. Thereafter he took a personal interest in the positioning and promoting of officers, and even in matters of military strategy and tactics. Many of Vietnam's soldiers found Diem's attentions a means to political power, wealth, and social prominence. Many others, however, resented those who rose by favoritism, and objected to Diem's interference in military matters. In November 1960, a serious coup attempt was supported by three elite paratroop battalions in Saigon, but otherwise failed to attract support. In the wake of the coup, mass arrests took place in which the Caravelle Group, among others, were jailed. In February 1962, two Vietnamese air force planes bombed the presidential palace in an unsuccessful assassination attempt on Diem and the Nhus. Again, there was little apparent willingness among military officers for concerted action against Diem. But the abortive attempts of 1960 and 1962 had the effect of dramatizing the choices open to those military officers who recognized the insolvency of Diem's political and military policies.

Diem's handling of his military impinged in two ways on his rural policy. Diem involved himself with the equipping of his military forces showing a distinct proclivity toward heavy military forces of the conventional type. He wanted the Civil Guard equipped very much like his regular army—possibly with a view to assuring himself a check on army power. There were a few soldiers, like General Duong Van Minh, who sharply disagreed with the President on this point. Nonetheless, Diem persisted. His increasing concern for the loyalty of key officials, moreover, led him to draw upon the military officer corps for civil administrators. From 1956 on his police apparatus was under military officers, and year by year, more of the provincial governments were also placed under military men. By 1958, about ⅓ of the province chiefs were military officers; by 1960, that fraction had increased to nearly ⅔; by 1962, ⅞ of all provinces were headed by soldiers.

Diem's bete noire was communism, and he appealed to threats from communists to justify his concentration on internal security. In August 1956, GVN Ordinance 47 defined being a communist, or working for them, as a capital crime. In May 1959, by GVN Law 10/59, the enforcement of Ordinance 47 was charged to special military tribunals from whose decisions there was no appeal. But "communist" was a term not used by members of the Marxist–Leninist Party headed by Ho Chi Minh, or its southern arms. Beginning in 1956, the Saigon press began to refer to "Viet Cong," a fairly precise and not necessarily disparaging rendition of "Vietnamese Communist." There is little doubt that Diem and his government applied the term Viet Cong somewhat loosely within South Vietnam to mean all persons or groups who resorted to clandestine political activity or armed opposition against his government; and the GVN meant by the term North as well as South Vietnamese communists, who they presumed acted in concert. At the close of the Franco–Viet Minh War in 1954, some 60,000 men were serving in organized Viet Minh units in South Vietnam. For the regroupments to North Vietnam, these units were augmented with large numbers of young recruits; a reported 90,000 armed men were taken to North Vietnam in the regroupment, while the U.S. and the GVN estimated that from 5–10,000 trained men were left behind as "cadre." If French estimates are correct that in 1954 the Viet Minh controlled over 60–90% of rural South Vietnam outside the sect domains, these 5–10,000 stay-behinds must have represented only a fraction of the Viet Minh residue, to which GVN figures on recanting and detained communists in the years through 1960 attest.

From studies of defectors, prisoners of war, and captured documents, it is now possible to assess armed resistance against Diem much better than the facts available at the time permitted. Three distinct periods are discernible. From 1954 through 1957, there was a substantial amount of random dissidence in the countryside, which Diem succeeded in quelling. In early 1957, Vietnam seemed to be enjoying the first peace it had known in over a decade. Beginning, however, in mid-1957 and intensifying through mid-1959, incidents of violence attributed to Viet Cong began to occur in the countryside. While much of this violence appeared to have a political motive, and while there is some evidence that it was part of a concerted strategy of guerrilla base development in accordance with sound Mao-Giap doctrine, the GVN did not construe it as a campaign, considering the disorders too diffuse to warrant committing major GVN resources. In early 1959, however, Diem perceived that he was under serious attack and reacted strongly. Population relocation was revivified. The Army of Vietnam was committed against the dissidents, and the Communist Denunciation Campaign was reinvigorated. By autumn 1959, however, the VC were in a position to field units of battalion size against regular army formations. By 1960, VC could operate in sufficient strength to seize provincial capitals for periods ranging up to 24 hours, overrun ARVN posts, and cut off entire districts from communication with the GVN-controlled towns. Diem's countermeasures increasingly met with peasant obstructionism and outright hostility. A U.S. Embassy estimate of the situation in January 1960 noted that:

> While the GVN has made an effort to meet the economic and social needs of the rural populations . . . these projects appear to have enjoyed only a measure of success in creating support for the government and, in fact, in many instances have resulted in resentment . . . the situation may be summed up in the fact that the government has tended to treat the population with suspicion or to coerce it and has been rewarded with an attitude of apathy or resentment.

In December 1960, the National Liberation Front of SVN (NLF) was formally organized. From its inception it was designed to encompass all anti-

GVN activists, including communists, and it formulated and articulated objectives for all those opposed to "My-Diem." The NLF placed heavy emphasis on the withdrawal of American advisors and influence, on land reform and liberalization of the GVN, on coalition government and the neutralization of Vietnam; but through 1963, the NLF soft-pedalled references to reunification of Vietnam. The NLF leadership was a shadowy crew of relatively obscure South Vietnamese. Despite their apparent lack of experience and competence, however, the NLF rapidly took on organizational reality from its central committee, down through a web of subordinate and associated groups, to villages all over South Vietnam. Within a few months of its founding, its membership doubled, doubled again by fall 1961, and then redoubled by early 1962. At that time an estimated 300,000 were on its rolls. Numerous administrative and functional "liberation associations" sprang into being, and each member of the NLF normally belong simultaneously to several such organizations.

The key operational components of the NLF were, however, the Liberation Army and the People's Revolutionary Party. The former had a lien on the services of every NLF member, man, woman, or child, although functionally its missions were usually carried out by formally organized military units. The People's Revolutionary Party was explicitly the "Marxist–Leninist Party of South Vietnam" and claimed to be the "vanguard of the NLF, the paramount member." It denied official links with the communist party of North Vietnam beyond "fraternal ties of communism." Although the PRP did not come into existence until 1962, it is evident that communists played a paramount role in forming the NLF, and in its rapid initial growth. The official U.S. view has been that the PRP is merely the southern arm of the DRV's communist party, and a principal instrument through which Hanoi instigated and controlled the revolt against "My-Diem." The organizational genius evident in the NLF, as well as the testimony of Vietnamese communists in interrogations and captured documents supports this interpretation.

But significant doubt remains. Viet Minh stay-behinds testified in 1955 and 1956 that their mission was political agitation for the holding of the general elections promised at Geneva. Captured documents and prisoner interrogations indicate that in 1957 and 1958, although there was some "wildcat" activity by local communists, party efforts appeared to be devoted to the careful construction of an underground apparatus which, though it used assassinations and kidnapping, circumspectly avoided military operations. All evidence points to fall of 1959 as the period in which the Viet Cong made their transition from a clandestine political movement to a more overt military operation. Moreover, throughout the years 1954–1960, a "front" seems to have been active in Vietnam. For example, the periodic report submitted by USMAAG, Vietnam, on 15 July 1957—a time of ostensible internal peace—noted that:

> The Viet Cong guerrillas and propagandists, however, are still waging a grim battle for survival. In addition to an accelerated propaganda campaign, the Communists have been forming "front" organizations to influence portions of anti-government minorities. Some of these organizations are militant, some are political. An example of the former is the "Vietnamese Peoples' Liberation Movement Forces," a military unit composed of ex-Cao Dai, ex-Hoa Hao, ex-Binh Xuyen, escaped political prisoners, and Viet Cong cadres. An example of the latter is the "Vietnam–Cambodian Buddhist Association," one of several organizations seeking to spread the theory of "Peace and Co-existence."

Whether early references to the "front" were to the organizations which subsequently matured as the NLF cannot be determined. Indeed, to shed further light on the truth or falsehood of the proposition that the DRV did not intervene in South Vietnam until after the NLF came into existence, it is necessary to turn to the events in North Vietnam during the years 1954–1960.

HANOI AND THE INSURGENCY IN SOUTH VIETNAM

The primary question concerning Hanoi's role in the origins of the insurgency is not so much *whether* it played a role or not—the evidence of direct North Vietnamese participation in subversion against the Government of South Vietnam is now extensive—but *when* Hanoi intervened in a systematic way. Most attacks on U.S. policy have been based on the proposition that the DRV move on the South came with manifest reluctance, and after massive U.S. intervention in 1961. For example, George McTurnin Kahin and John W. Lewis, in their book *The United States in Vietnam,* state that:

> Contrary to United States policy assumptions, all available evidence shows that the revival of the civil war in the South in 1958 was undertaken by Southerners at their own—not Hanoi's—initiative. . . . Insurgency activity against the Saigon government began in the South under Southern leadership not as a consequence of any dictate from Hanoi, but contrary to Hanoi's injunctions.

As discussed above, so much of this argument as rests on the existence in South Vietnam of genuine rebellion is probably valid. The South Vietnamese had both the means, the Viet Minh residue, and motive to take up arms against Ngo Dinh Diem. Moreover, there were indications that some DRV leaders did attempt to hold back southern rebels on the grounds that "conditions" were not ripe for an uprising. Further, there was apparently division within the Lao Dong Party hierarchy over the question of strategy and tactics in South Vietnam. However, the evidence indicates that the principal strategic debate over this issue took place between 1956 and 1958; all information now available (spring, 1968) points to a decision taken by the DRV leaders not later than spring, 1959, actively to seek the overthrow of Diem. Thereafter, the DRV pressed toward that goal by military force and by subversive aggression, both in Laos and in South Vietnam.

But few Administration critics have had access to the classified information upon which the foregoing judgments are based. Such intelligence as the U.S. has been able to make available to the public bearing on the period 1954–1960 has been sketchy and not very convincing: a few captured documents, and a few prisoner interrogations. Indeed, up until 1961 the Administration itself publicly held that Ngo Dinh Diem was firmly in control in South Vietnam, and that the United States aid programs were succeeding in meeting such threat to GVN security as existed both within South Vietnam and from the North. Too, the vigorous publicizing of "wars of national liberation" by N. S. Khrushchev and the "discovery" of counterinsurgency by the Kennedy Administration in early 1961 tended to reinforce the overall public impression that North Vietnam's aggression was news in that year. Khrushchev's speech of 6 January 1961, made, according to Kennedy biographer Arthur Schlesinger, Jr., "a conspicuous impression on the new President, who took it as an authoritative exposition of Soviet intentions, discussed it with his staff and read excerpts from it aloud to the National Security Council." Thereafter, Administration leaders, by their frequently identifying that Khrushchev declamation as a milestone in the development of communist world strategy, lent credence to the supposition that the Soviet Union had approved aggression by its satellite in North Vietnam only in December 1960—the month the NLF was formed.

American Kremlinologists had been preoccupied, since Khrushchev's "de-Stalinization" speech at the 20th Congress of the Communist Party of the Soviet Union in February 1956, with the possibilities of a genuine detente with the USSR. They were also bemused by the prospect of a deep strategic division with the "Communist Bloc" between the Soviets and the Chinese. Yet, despite evidences of disunity in the Bloc—in Yugoslavia, Albania, Hungary, Poland, and East Germany—virtually all experts regarded North Vietnamese national strategy, to the extent that they considered it at all, as a simple derivative of that of either the USSR or the CPR. P. J. Honey, the British authority on North Vietnam, tends to the view that Hanoi remained subservient to the dictates of Moscow from 1956 through 1961, albeit carefully paying lip service to continue solidarity with Peking. More recently, a differing interpretation has been offered, which holds that the Hanoi leaders were in those years motivated primarily by their concern for internal development, and that they, therefore, turned to the Soviet Union as the only nation willing and able to furnish the wherewithal for rapid economic advancement. Both interpretations assume that through 1960 the DRV followed the Soviet line, accepted "peaceful coexistence," concentrated on internal development, and took action in South Vietnam only after Moscow gave the go-ahead in late 1960.

But it is also possible that the colloquy over strategy among the communist nations in the late 1950's followed a pattern almost exactly the reverse of that usually depicted: that North Vietnam persuaded the Soviets and the Chinese to accept its strategic view, and to support simultaneous drives for economic advancement and forceful reunification. Ho Chi Minh was an old Stalinist, trained in Russia in the early '20's, Comintern colleague of Borodin in Canton, and for three decades leading exponent of the Marxist–Leninist canon on anti-colonial war. Presumably, Ho spoke with authority within the upper echelons of the communist party of the Soviet Union. What he said to them privately was, no doubt, quite similar to what he proclaimed publicly from 1956 onward: the circumstances of North Vietnam were not comparable to those of the Soviet Union, or even those of the CPR, and North Vietnam's policy had to reflect the differences.

Khrushchev's de-Stalinization bombshell burst in February 1956 at a dramatically bad time for the DRV. It overrode the Chinese call for reconvening of the Geneva Conference on Vietnam, and it interfered with the concerting of communist policy on what to do about Diem regime's refusal to proceed toward the general elections. Although the Soviets issued in March 1956 a demand for GVN observance of the Accords, its diplomacy not only failed to bring about any action on behalf of the DRV, but elicited, in April 1956, a sharp British note condemning Hanoi for grave violations of the Accords. Hanoi received the British note about the time that Khrushchev proclaimed that the Soviet was committed to a policy of "peaceful coexistence." At the Ninth Plenum of the Central Committee of the Lao Dong Party, held in Hanoi that month, Ho Chi Minh lauded "de-Stalinization," but unequivocally rejected "peaceful coexistence" as irrelevant to the DRV. In November 1957, after more than a year of upheavals and evident internal political distress in North Vietnam, Ho Chi Minh and Le Duan journeyed to Moscow for the Conference of Communist and Workers' Parties of Socialist Countries. That conference issued a declaration admitting the possibility of "non-peaceful transition to socialism" remarkably similar in thrust to Ho's 1956 speech. Further, Khrushchev's famous January 1961 speech was simply a precis of the Declaration of the November 1960 Conference of Communist and Workers' Parties of Socialist Countries. That 1960 Declaration, which formed the basis for Khrushchev's pronouncements on wars of national liberation in turn explicitly reaffirmed the 1957 Declaration.

Other evidence supports the foregoing hypothesis. The DRV was, in 1960, an orthodoxically constituted communist state. Both the government and the society were dominated by the Lao Dong (Communist) Party, and power within the party concentrated in a small elite—Ho Chi Minh and his lieutenants from the old-time Indochinese Communist Party. This group of leaders were unique in the communist world for their homogeneity and for their harmony—there has been little evidence of the kind of turbulence which has splintered the leadership of most communist parties. While experts have detected disputes within the Lao Dong hierarchy—1957 appears to be a critical year in that regard—the facts are that there has been no blood-purge of the Lao Dong leadership, and except for changes occasioned by apparently natural deaths, the leadership in 1960 was virtually identical to what it had been in 1954 or 1946. This remarkably dedicated and purposeful group of men apparently agreed among themselves as to what the national interests of the DRV required, what goals should be set for the nation, and what strategy they should pursue in attaining them.

These leaders have been explicit in setting forth DRV national goals in their public statements and official documents. For example, Ho Chi Minh and his colleagues placed a premium on "land reform"—by which they meant a communization of rural society along Maoist lines. Moreover, they clearly considered a disciplined society essential for victory in war and success in peace. It was also evident that they were committed to bring about an independent, reunified Vietnam capable of exerting significant influence throughout Southeast Asia, and particularly over the neighboring states of Laos and Cambodia. What is not known with certainty is how they determined the relative priority among these objectives.

In the immediate aftermath of Geneva, the DRV deferred to the Geneva Accords for the achievement of reunification, and turned inward, concentrating its energies on land reform and rehabilitation of the war-torn economy. By the summer of 1956, this strategy was bankrupt: the Geneva Settlement manifestly would not eventuate in reunification, and the land reform campaign foundered from such serious abuses by Lao Dong cadre that popular disaffection imperiled DRV internal security. In August 1956, the Lao Dong leadership was compelled to "rectify" its programs, to postpone land reform, and to purge low echelon cadre to mollify popular resentment. Even these measures, however, proved insufficient to forestall insurrection; in November 1956, the peasant rebellions broke out, followed by urban unrest. Nonetheless, the DRV leadership survived these internal crises intact, and by 1958 appears to have solved most of the problems of economic efficiency and political organization which occasioned the 1956–1957 outbursts.

But domestic difficulty was not the only crisis to confront the Lao Dong leaders in early 1957. In January, when the Soviet Union proposed to the United Nations the admitting of North and South Vietnam as separate states, it signalled that the USSR might be prepared in the interests of "peaceful coexistence," to make a great power deal which would have lent permanency to the partition of Vietnam. Ho Chi Minh, in evident surprise, violently dissented. When in February 1957 Khrushchev went further in affirming his intention to "coexist" with the United States, the DRV quickly moved to realign its own and Soviet policies. In May 1957, the Soviet head of state, Voroshilov, visited Hanoi, and in July and August 1957, Ho Chi Minh traveled extensively in Eastern Europe, spending several days in Moscow. The Voroshilov visit was given top billing by the Hanoi Press and Ho, upon his return from Moscow, indicated that important decisions had been reached. Thereafter, Hanoi and Moscow marched more in step.

In the meantime, the needs and desires of communist rebels in South Vietnam had been communicated directly to Hanoi in the person of Le Duan, who is known to have been in South Vietnam in 1955 and 1956, and to have returned to Hanoi sometime before the fall of 1957. In September of that year, upon Ho's return from Europe, Le Duan surfaced as one of the members of the Lao Dong Politburo, it is possible that he was already at that time *de facto* the First Secretary of the Lao Dong Party, to which position he was formally promoted in September 1960. In 1955 and 1956, Le Doan, from the testimony of prisoners and captured documents, had been expressing conviction that Diem would stamp out the communist movement in South Vietnam unless the DRV were to reinforce the party there. Presumably, he carried these views into the inner councils of the DRV. In November 1957, Le Duan and Ho traveled to Moscow to attend the Conference of Communist and Workers' Parties of Socialist Countries. The Declaration of that conference, quoted above, has since been cited repeatedly by both North and South Vietnamese communists, as one of the strategic turning points in their modern history. Le Duan, upon his return to Hanoi from Moscow, issued a statement to the effect that the DRV's way was now clear. Taking Le Duan literally, it could be construed that the DRV deemed the Moscow Declaration of 1957 the "go ahead" signal from Moscow and Peking for forceful pursuit of its objectives.

There is some sparse evidence that the DRV actually did begin moving in 1958 to set up a mechanism for supporting the insurgency in South Vietnam. But even had the decision been taken, as suggested above, in late 1957, it is unlikely that there would have been much manifestation of it in 1958. The Lao Dong leadership had for years stressed the lessons that they had learned from experience on the essentiality of carefully preparing a party infrastructure and building guerrilla bases before proceeding with an insurgency. Viet Minh doctrine would have dictated priority concern to refurbishing the communist party apparatus in South Vietnam, and it is possible that such a process was set in motion during 1958. Orders were captured from Hanoi which directed guerrilla bases be prepared in South Vietnam in early 1959.

There is, however, other evidence that questioning among the DRV hierarchy concerning strategy and tactics for South Vietnam continued throughout 1958 and into 1959. Captured reports from party headquarters in South Vietnam betrayed doubt and indecisions among party leaders there and reflected the absence of clear guidance from Hanoi. Moreover, in 1958, and in 1959, the DRV did concentrate much of its resources on agricultural and industrial improvement; extensive loans were obtained from the Soviet Union and from the Chinese Peoples Republic, and ambitious uplift programs were launched in both sectors. It is possible, therefore, to accept the view that through 1958 the DRV still accorded priority to butter over guns, as part of its base development strategy.

In the larger sense, domestic progress, "consolidation of the North," was fundamental to that strategy. As General Vo Nguyen Giap put it in the Lao Dong Party journal *Hoc Tap* of January 1960:

The North has become a large rear echelon of our army . . . The North is the revolutionary base for the whole country.

Up until 1959, the economy of North Vietnam was scarcely providing subsistence for its people, let alone support for foreign military undertakings; by that year, substantial progress in both agriculture and industry was evident:

NORTH VIETNAM
FOOD GRAIN PER CAPITA

	1955	1956	1957	1958	1959	1960
Kilograms	260	310	283	315	358	304
%	100	119	109	121	138	117

Due mainly, however, to industrial growth, the Gross National Product reached a growth rate of 6% per annum in 1958, and sustained that rate thereafter. Both 1958 and 1959 were extraordinarily good years in both industry and agriculture. A long-range development plan launched in 1958 achieved an annual industrial expansion of 21% per year through 1960, chiefly in heavy industry. Foreign aid—both Chinese and Soviet—was readily obtained, the USSR supplanting the CPR as prime donor. Foreign trade stepped up markedly. Compared with 1955, the DRV's foreign commerce doubled by 1959, and nearly tripled by 1960.

By 1959, it seems likely that the DRV had elected to pursue a "guns *and* butter" strategy, and obtained requisite Soviet *and* Chinese aid. While pressing forward with its economic improvement programs—which were showing definite progress—the DRV prepared with word and deed for large-scale intervention in South Vietnam. In May 1959, at the Fifteenth Plenum of the Central Committee of the Lao Dong Party, a Resolution was adopted identifying the United States as the main obstacle to the realization of the hopes of the Vietnamese people, and as an enemy of peace. The Resolution of the Fifteenth Plenum called for a strong North Vietnam as a base for helping the South Vietnamese to overthrow Diem and eject the United States. A Communist Party history captured in South Vietnam in 1966, and the testimony of high-ranking captives, indicate that South Vietnamese communists still regard the resolution of the Fifteenth Plenum as the point of departure for DRV intervention.

Within a month of the Fifteenth Plenum, the DRV began to commit its armed forces in Laos, and steadily escalated its aid to the Pathet Lao. By the time the National Liberation Front issued its manifesto in December 1960, the conflict in Laos had matured to the point that Pathet Lao–NVA troops controlled most of NE Laos and the Laotian panhandle; moreover, by that time, the Soviet Union had entered the fray, and was participating in airlift operations from North Vietnam direct to Pathet Lao–NVA units in Laos. Also, by fall of 1959, the insurgency in South Vietnam took a definite upsurge. Viet Cong units for the first time offered a direct challenge to the Army of Vietnam. Large VC formations seized and held district and province capitals for short periods of time, and assassinations and kidnappings proliferated markedly. The Preamble of the Constitution of the DRV, promulgated on 1 January 1960, was distinctly bellicose, condemning the United States, and establishing the reunification of Vietnam as a DRV national objective. During 1959 and 1960, the relatively undeveloped intelligence apparatus of the U.S. and the GVN confirmed that over 4,000 infiltrators were sent from North Vietnam southward—most of them military or political cadre, trained to raise and lead insurgent forces.

In September 1960, the Lao Dong Party convened its Third National Congress. There Ho Chi Minh, Le Duan, Giap, and others presented speeches further committing the DRV to support of the insurgency in the South, demanding the U.S. stop its aid to Diem, and calling for the formation of a unified front to lead the struggle against "My-Diem." The Resolution of the Third Congress, reflecting these statements, is another of those historic benchmarks referred to in captured party documents and prisoner interrogations.

In November 1960, the Moscow Conference of Communist and Workers' Parties of Socialist Countries once again declared its support of the sort of "just" war the DRV intended to prosecute. The United States was identified as the principal colonial power, and the right and obligation of communist parties to lead struggles against colonial powers was detailed. By the time Khrushchev cited that Declaration in his "wars of national liberation" speech, the "liberation war" for South Vietnam was nearly a year and a half old.

The evidence supports the conclusion, therefore, that whether or not the rebellion against Diem in South Vietnam proceeded independently of, or even contrary to directions from Hanoi through 1958, Hanoi moved thereafter to capture the revolution. There is little doubt that Hanoi exerted some influence over certain insurgents in the South throughout the years following Geneva, and there is evidence which points to its preparing for active support of large-scale insurgency as early as 1958. Whatever differences in strategy may have existed among Moscow, Peking, and Hanoi, it appears that at each critical juncture Hanoi obtained concurrence in Moscow with an aggressive course of action. Accordingly, it was not "peaceful coexistence," or concern over leadership of the "socialist camp" which governed Hanoi's policy. What appeared to matter to Hanoi was its abiding national interests: domestic consolidation in independence, reunification, and Vietnamese hegemony in Southeast Asia. Both Soviet and Chinese policy seems to have bent to these ends rather than the contrary. If Hanoi applied brakes to eager insurgents in South Vietnam, it did so not from lack of purpose or because of Soviet restraints, but from concern over launching one more premature uprising in the South. Ngo Dinh Diem was entirely correct when he stated that his was a nation at war in early 1959; South Vietnam was at war with both the Viet Cong insurgents and with the DRV, in that the latter then undertook to provide strategic direction and leadership cadres to build systematically a base system in Laos and South Vietnam for subsequent, large-scale guerrilla warfare. Persuasive evidence exists that by 1960 DRV support of the insurgency in South Vietnam included materiel as well as personnel. In any event, by late 1959, it seems clear that Hanoi considered the time ripe to take the military offensive in South Vietnam, and that by 1960 circumstances were propitious for more overt political action. A recently captured high-ranking member of the National Liberation Front has confirmed that in mid-1960 he and other Lao Dong Party leaders in South Vietnam were instructed by Hanoi to begin organizing the National Liberation Front, which was formally founded upon the issuance of its Manifesto on 20 December 1960. The rapid growth of the NLF thereafter—it quadrupled its strength in about one year—is a further indication that the Hanoi-directed communist party apparatus had been engaged to the fullest in the initial organization and subsequent development of the NLF.

U.S. PERCEPTIONS OF THE INSURGENCY, 1954–1960

Much of what the U.S. knows about the origins of the insurgency in South Vietnam rests on information it has acquired since 1963, approximately the span of time that an extensive and effective American intelligence apparatus had been functioning in Vietnam. Before then, our intelligence was drawn from a significantly more narrow and less reliable range of sources, chiefly Vietnamese, and could not have supported analysis in depth of insurgent organization and intentions. The U.S. was particularly deprived of dependable information concerning events in South Vietnam's countryside in the years 1954 through 1959. Nonetheless, U.S. intelligence estimates through 1960 correctly and consistently estimated that the threat to GVN internal security was greater than the danger from overt invasion. The intelligence estimates provided to policy makers in Washington pegged the Viet Cong military offensive as beginning in late 1959, with preparations noted as early as 1957, and a definite campaign perceived as of early 1959. Throughout the years, they were critical *of* Diem, consistently expressing skepticism that he could deal successfully with his internal political problems. These same estimates miscalculated the numerical and political strength of the Viet Cong, misjudged the extent of rural disaffection, and overrated the military capabilities of the GVN. But as strategic intelligence they were remarkably sound.

Indeed, given the generally bleak appraisals of Diem's prospects, they who made U.S. policy could only have done so by assuming a significant measure of risk. For example, on 3 August 1954, an NIE took the position that:

> Although it is possible that the French and Vietnamese, even with firm support from the U.S. and other powers, may be able to establish a strong regime in South Vietnam, we believe that the chances for this development are poor and, moreover, that the situation is more likely to continue to deteriorate progressively over the next year . . .

This estimate notwithstanding, the U.S. moved promptly to convene the Manila Conference, bring SEATO into being with its protocol aegis over Vietnam, and eliminate France as the recipient of U.S. aid for Vietnam. Again on 26 April 1955, an NIE charged that:

> Even if the present empasse [with the sects] were resolved, we believe that that it would be extremely difficult, at best, for a Vietnamese government, regardless of its composition, to make progress towards developing a strong, stable, anti-Communist government capable of resolving the basic social, economic, and political problems of Vietnam, the special problems arising from the Geneva Agreement and capable of meeting the long-range challenge of the Communists . . .

Within a matter of weeks, however, the U.S. firmly and finally committed itself to unstinting support of Ngo Dinh Diem, accepted his refusal to comply with the political settlement of Geneva, and acceded to withdrawal of French military power and political influence from South Vietnam. Even at the zenith of Diem's success, an NIE noted adverse political trends stemming from Diem's "authoritarian role" and predicted that, while no short-term opposition was in prospect:

> Over a longer period, the accumulation of grievances among various groups and individuals may lead to development of a national opposition movement . . .

There was no NIE published between 1956 and 1959 on South Vietnam: an NIE of May 1959 took the position that Diem had a serious military problem on his hands:

> The [GVN] internal security forces will not be able to eradicate DRV supported guerrilla or subversive activity in the foreseeable future. Army

units will probably have to be diverted to special internal security assignments . . .

The same NIE noted a waning of popular enthusiasm for Diem, the existence of some disillusionment, "particularly among the educated elite," some "dissatisfaction among military officers," but detected little "identifiable public unrest":

> The growth of dissatisfaction is inhibited by South Vietnam's continuing high standard of living relative to that of its neighbors, the paternalistic attitude of Diem's government towards the people, and the lack of any feasible alternative to the present regime.

The 1959 NIE again expressed serious reservations about Diem's leadership and flatly stated that:

> The prospects for continued political stability in South Vietnam hang heavily upon President Diem and his ability to mantain firm control of the army and police. The regime's efforts to assure internal security and its belief that an authoritarian government is necessary to handle the country's problems will result in a continued repression of potential opposition elements. This policy of repression will inhibit the growth of popularity of the regime and we believe that dissatisfaction will grow, particularly among those who are politically conscious . . .

Despite these reservations, U.S. policy remained staunchly and fairly uncritically behind Diem through 1959.

The National Intelligence Estimates reservations *re* Diem do not appear to have restrained the National Security Council in its two major reviews of U.S. policy between 1954 and 1960. In 1956, the NSC (in policy directive NSC 5612) directed that U.S. agencies

> Assist Free Vietnam to develop a strong, stable, and constitutional government to enable Free Vietnam to assert an increasingly attractive contrast to conditions in the present Communist zone . . . [and] work toward the weakening of the Communists in North and South Vietnam in order to bring about the eventual peaceful reunification of a free and independent Vietnam under anti-Communist leadership.

In 1958 (in NSC 5809) this policy, with its "roll-back" overtones, was reiterated, although revisions were proposed indicating an awareness of the necessity to adapt the army of Vietnam for anti-guerrilla warfare. Operations Coordinating Board Progress Reports on the implementation of the policies laid out in NSC 5612 and 5809 revealed awareness that Vietnam was under internal attack, and that "in spite of substantial U.S. assistance, economic development, though progressing, is below that which is politically desirable."

While classified policy papers through 1959 thus dealt with risks, public statements of U.S. officials did not refer to the jeopardy. To the contrary, the picture presented the public and Congress by Ambassador Durbrow, General Williams, and other Administration spokesmen was of continuing progress, virtually miraculous improvement, year-in and year-out. Diem was depicted as a strong and capable leader, firmly in command of his own house, leading his people into modern nationhood at a remarkable pace. As late as the summer of 1959, Ambassador Durbrow and General Williams assured the Senate Foreign Relations Committee that Vietnam's internal security was in no serious danger, and that Vietnam was in a better position to cope with invasion from the North than it had ever been. In the fall of 1959, in fact, General Williams expressed the opinion that by 1961 GVN defense budgets could be reduced, and in the spring of 1960, he wrote to Senator Mansfield that American military advisors could begin a phased withdrawal from MAAG, Vietnam the following year.

Whatever adverse judgment may be deserved by such statements or by the quality of U.S. assistance to Vietnam on behalf of its internal security, the American aid program cannot be faulted for failing to provide Diem funds in plenty. The U.S. aid program—economic and military—for South Vietnam was among the largest in the world. From FY 1946 through FY 1961, Vietnam was the third ranking non-Nato recipient of aid, and the seventh worldwide. In FY 1961, the last program of President Eisenhower's Administration, South Vietnam was the fifth ranking recipient overall. MAAG, Vietnam, was the only military aid mission anywhere in the world commanded by a lieutenant general, and the economic aid mission there was by 1958 the largest anywhere.

Security was the focus of U.S. aid; more than 75% of the economic aid the U.S. provided in the same period went into the GVN military budget; thus at least $8 out of every $10 of aid provided Vietnam went directly toward security. In addition, other amounts of nominally economic aid (e.g., that for public administration) went toward security forces, and aid for agriculture and transportation principally funded projects with strategic purposes and with an explicit military rationale. For example, a 20-mile stretch of highway from Saigon to Bien Hoa, built at Gen. Williams' instance for specifically military purposes, received more U.S. economic aid than all funds provided for labor, community development, social welfare, health, and education in the years 1954–1961.

In March 1960, Washington became aware that despite this impressive outpouring of treasure, material, and advice, the Viet Cong were making significant headway against Diem, and that U.S. aid programs ought to be reconfigured. In March, the JCS initiated action to devise a Counter-insurgency Plan (CIP), intended to coordinate the several U.S. agencies providing assistance to the GVN, and rationalize the GVN's own rural programs. The CIP was worked out among the several U.S. agencies in Washington and Saigon during the summer and fall of 1960.

The heightened awareness of problems in Vietnam did not, however, precipitate changes in NSC policy statements on Vietnam. Objectives set forth in NSC 6012 (25 July 1960) were virtually identical to those of NSC 5809.

Planning proceeded against a background of developing divergence of view between the Departments of State and Defense. As Ambassador Durbrow and his colleagues of State saw the problem on the one hand, Diem's security problems stemmed from his political insolvency. They argued that the main line of U.S. action should take the form of pressures on Diem to reform his government and his party, liberalizing his handling of political dissenters and the rural populace. Department of Defense officials, on the other hand, usually deprecated the significance of non-communist political dissent in South Vietnam, and regarded Diem's difficulties as proceeding from military inadequacy. In this view, what was needed was a more efficient internal defense, and, therefore, the Pentagon tended to oppose U.S. leverage on Diem because it might jeopardize his confidence in the U.S., and his cooperation in improving his military posture. Communist machination, as Defense saw it, had created the crisis; the U.S. response should be "unswerving support" for Diem.

While the CIP was being developed, Department of Defense moved to adapt the U.S. military assistance program to the exigencies of the situation. On 30 March 1960 the JCS took the position that the Army of Vietnam should develop an anti-guerrilla capability within the regular force structure, thus reversing an antithetical position taken by General Williams. During 1959 Diem had attempted to form a number of special "commando" units from his regular forces, and the MAAG had opposed him on the grounds that these would deplete his conventional strength. In May, MAAG was authorized to place advisers down to battalion level. In June, 1960, additional U.S. Army special forces arrived in Vietnam, and during the summer a number of Ranger battalions, with the express mission of counter-guerrilla operations, were activated. In September, General Williams was replaced by General McGarr who, consistent with the directives of the JCS, promptly began to press the training of RVNAF to produce the "anti-guerrilla guerrilla." General McGarr's desire for an RVNAF capable of meeting and defeating the Viet Cong at their own game was evident in the CIP when it was forwarded to Washington, in January, 1961, just before John F. Kennedy took office.

The CIP had been well coordinated within the U.S. mission in Vietnam, but only partially with the Vietnamese. The plan, as forwarded, incorporated one major point of difference between the Embassy and MAAG. General McGarr desired to increase the RVNAF force level by some 20,000 troops, while Ambassador Durbrow maintained reservations concerning the necessity or the wisdom of additional forces. The Ambassador's position rested on the premise that Diem wanted the force level increase, and that the United States should not provide funds for that purpose until Diem was patently prepared to take those unpalatable political measures the Ambassador had proposed aimed at liberalizing the GVN. The Ambassador held out little hope that either the political or even military portions of the CIP could be successfully accomplished without some such leverage: "Consideration should, therefore, be given to what actions we are prepared to take to encourage, or if necessary to force, acceptance of all essential elements of the plan." In the staff reviews of the CIP in Washington, the divergence between State and Defense noted above came once more to the fore. Those (chiefly within DOD) who considered the VC threat as most important, and who therefore regarded military measures against this threat as most urgent, advocated approval and any other measures which would induce Diem's acceptance of the CIP, and his cooperation with MAAG. They were impatient with Ambassador Durbrow's proposed "pressure tactics" since they saw in them the possibility of GVN delay on vital military matters, and the prospect of little profit other than minor concessions from Diem in political areas they deemed peripheral or trivial in countering the VC. Tipping the scales toward what might be called the Diem/MAAG/DOD priorities was the coincident and increasing need to "reassure" Diem of U.S. support for the GVN and for him personally. The fall of President Syngman Rhee of Korea in April, the abortive November 1960 coup d'etat in Saigon, Ambassador Durbrow's persistent overtures for reform, and above all, uncertainties over U.S. support for the Royal Laotian Government. This requirement to reassure Diem was plainly at cross purposes with the use of pressure tactics.

Ten days after President Kennedy came to office, he authorized a $41 million increase in aid for Vietnam to underwrite a level increase and improvements in the Civil Guard—a complete buy of the CIP. In March, Ambassador Durbrow was replaced by Frederick E. Nolting. Ambassador Durbrow's closing interview with Diem in mid-March was not reassuring. While Diem stated that he was prepared to carry out the military aspects of the CIP, he dodged Durbrow's questions on the political action prescribed. It was on this disquieting note that the Kennedy Administration began its efforts to counter the insurgency in South Vietnam.

End of Summary

MAJOR PROVISIONS OF THE 1954 GENEVA ACCORDS

Three Agreements on the Cessation of Hostilities for Vietnam, Laos, Cambodia

Provisions	Vietnam	Laos	Cambodia
A. Disengagement, Partition, and Military Regroupment			
Disengagement of combatants, including concentration of forces into provisional assembly areas (and provisional withdrawal of other party's forces from such areas in Vietnam)	To be completed 15 days after effective date of cease-fire in each area. Provisional assembly areas for French Union forces; perimeter of Hanoi, perimeter of Haiduong, perimeter of Haiphong Provisional assembly areas for Vietnam People's Army: Quang Ngai-Binh Dinh perimeter (Central Vietnam), Xuyen-Moc, Ham Tan perimeter (South Vietnam), Plaine des Jones perimeter, and Cape Camau perimeter (both South Vietnam) [Art. 15]	To be completed 15 days after effective date of cease-fire (Aug. 22, 1954) [Art. 11] Provisional assembly areas: 5 areas for reception Vietnamese People's Volunteer forces; 5 areas for reception French forces, 12 areas, one per province, for reception "fighting units Pathet Lao" [Art. 12]	No provision
Withdrawals of forces, supplies and equipment	French Union forces to withdraw from provisional assembly areas to regrouping zones south of demarcation line within 300 days (May 19, 1955), according to following schedule: From Hanoi perimeter—80 days (October 11, 1954) From Haiduong perimeter—100 days (November 1, 1954) From Haiphong perimeter—300 days (May 19, 1955	French forces to withdraw, except from bases at Seno and in MeKong Valley near or downstream from Vientiane, in 120 days (Nov. 20, 1954) [Art. 4, 12] Vietnames People's Volunteers, except those settled in Laos before hostilities	French armed forces and military combatant personnel, combatant formations of all types which have entered Cambodia from other countries or regions, and non-native Cambodians holding supervisory functions in bodies

	People's Army of Vietnam to withdraw from provisional assembly areas to regrouping zone north of demarcation line within 300 days (May 19, 1955), according to following schedule: From Xuyen-Moc, Ham Tan—80 days (October 11, 1954) From Central Vietnam I—80 days (October 11, 1954) From Plaine des Jones—100 days (November 1, 1954) From Central Vietnam II—100 days (November 1, 1954) From Cape Camau—200 days (February 8, 1955) From Central Vietnam III—300 days (May 19, 1955) [Art. 15]	(special convention), to withdraw by provinces in 120 days (Nov. 20, 1954 [Art. 4, 13]	connected with Vietnamese (DRV) activities in Cambodia to withdraw within 90 days (Oct. 21, 1954) [Art. 4]
Plans for movements into regrouping zones	To be communicated between the parties within 25 days (August 17, 1954) [Art. 11]	No provision	No provision
Provisional military demarcation line	Vicinity of 17° N latitude from the mouth of the Song Ben Hat (Cua Tung River) and the course of that river (known as the Rao Tkanh in the mountain) to the village of Bo Ho Su, then the parallel of Bo Ho Su to the Laos–Viet–Nam frontier [Art. 1–4, Annex]	No provision	No provision
Demilitarized zone	On either side of demarcation line to width of not more than 5 kms. to act as a buffer zone [Art. 1]	No provision	No provision

Provisions	Vietnam	Laos	Cambodia
Withdrawal of all forces, supplies, and equipment from demilitarized zone	To be completed within 25 days (August 14, 1954) [Art. 5]	No provision	No provision
Withdrawal for assembly or regrouping through territory of the other party	Forces of the other party to withdraw provisionally 3 kms. on each side of route of withdrawal [Art. 12]	No provision	No provision
On-the-spot demobilization	No provision	Any military personnel of the fighting units of "Pathet Lao," who so wish, may be demobilized on the spot [Art. 14]	Khmer Resistance Forces to be demobilized on the spot within 30 days (August 22, 1954) [Art. 5]
Concentration areas	No provision	Pending political settlement, fighting units of "Pathet Lao" to move into provinces of Phong Saly and Sam-Neus and to move between these two provinces in defined corridor along Laos–Vietnam border Concentration to be completed within 120 days (Nov. 20, 1954) [Art. 14]	No provision

B. Civil Regroupment and Administration

Movement across demarcation line or into demilitarized zones	Prohibited except by specific permission of the Joint Commission; fully authorized for the Joint Commission, its organs, the International Supervisory Commission and its organs [Art. 6, 7, 9]	No provision	No provision
Civil administration and relief in demilitarized zones	Responsibility of the Commanders in Chief of the two parties in their respective zones on either side of the demarcation line [Art. 14]	No provision	No provision
Civil and administrative measures pending general elections	In each regrouping zone, a) civil administration to be in hands of party whose forces to be regrouped in that zone, b) civil administration in a territory to be transferred to continue in hands of present controlling force until the withdrawing troops have completely left, c) from July 25 through completion of troop regroupment (May 19, 1955) any civilians so desiring may be permitted and helped to move to other zone, d) from July 23 through completion of troop regroupment, any civilians so desiring may be permitted and helped to move to other zone [Art. 14]	Each party to refrain from any reprisals or discrimination against persons or organizations for their activities during hostilities and to guarantee their democratic freedoms [Art. 15]	No reprisals to be taken against any nationals or their families, each being entitled, without any discrimination, to all constitutional guarantees concerning protection of person and property and democratic freedoms [Art. 5, 6]

Provisions	Vietnam	Laos	Cambodia
Liberation and repatriation of POW's and civilian internees	All POW's and civilian internees (latter term covering all persons who have been detained by reason of contributing in any way to the "political and armed struggle" between the parties) held by both sides to be liberated within 30 days after the cease-fire in each theater and to be surrendered to appropriate authorities of other party who shall assist them in proceeding to their country of origin, place of habitual residence, or zone of their choice [Art. 21]	Same as for Vietnam, except that only foreign POW's captured by either party are to be surrendered to appropriate authorities of other party [Art. 16]	Same as for Vietnam, except that no time period is given, and that only foreign POW's captured by either party are to be surrendered to appropriate authorities of other party [Art. 8]

C. Arms Control

Provisions	Vietnam	Laos	Cambodia
Introduction of troop reinforcements and additional military personnel, including instructors	Prohibited from July 23, 1954, except for: rotation of units, admittance of individual personnel on a temporary duty basis, and return to Vietnam of individual personnel from leave or temporary duty abroad, which are allowed under defined and controlled conditions [Art. 16]	Prohibited after proclamation of cease-fire, but French may leave maximum of 1,500 officers and NCO's to train Laotian National Army [Art. 6]	Prohibited after date of cease-fire in Vietnam and until final political settlement in Vietnam, except for purpose of "effective defense of its territory" [Art. 7]

	Vietnam	Laos	Cambodia
Introduction of all types of arms, munitions, and other war materiels, including aircraft	Prohibited from July 23, 1954, except for piece-for-piece replacement of war materiel, arms, munitions destroyed, damaged, worn out, or used up after cessation hostilities (exception does not apply to French Union forces north of demarcation line during 300 day withdrawal period) Admission of any materials on excepted basis to be under defined and controlled conditions [Art. 17]	Prohibited after July 23, except for specified quantities of arms in categories specified as necessary for defense of Laos [Art. 9]	Prohibited after date of cease-fire in Vietname and until final political settlement in Vietnam, except for purpose of "effective defense of its territory" [Art. 7]
Specified points of entry for excepted personnel and re-placement material	1) North of Line: Laokay, Langson, Tien-Yen, Haiphong, Vinh, Dong-Hoi, Muong-Sen 2) South of Line: Tourane, Quinhon, Nhatrang, Bangoi, Saigon, Cap St. Jacques, Tranchau [Art. 20]	Luang-Prabang, Xieng-Khouang, Vientiane, Seno, Paksé, Savannakhet, Tchépone [Art. 10]	No provision
Establishment of new military bases in Vietnam and Laos and military bases of foreign powers in Vietnam, Laos, Cambodia	Prohibited after July 23, 1954 throughout Vietnam [Art. 18, 19]	Prohibited after July 23, except for 1) French base at Seno, 2) French base in Mekong Valley, either in Vientiane Province or downstream from Vientiane. Effectives in these two French bases may not exceed 3,500 men. Bases of foreign powers prohibited "so long as its security is not threatened" [Art. 7, 8]	Military bases of foreign powers prohibited after July 23 "so long as its security is not threatened" [Art. 7]

Provisions	Vietnam	Laos	Cambodia
Adherence to military alliances	Prohibited for both zones from July 23, 1954 [Art. 19]	No provision	May not join agreements carrying the the obligation to enter into military alliance "not in conformity with the principles of the Charter of the UN or with the principles of the agreements on the cessation of hostilities or, so long as its security is not threatened, to establish bases on Cambodian territory for the military forces of foreign powers" [Art. 7]
Use of zones to resume hostilities or to further aggressive policy	Prohibited from July 23, 1954 [Art. 19]	No provision	No provision

D. International Supervision and Control

Provisions	Vietnam	Laos	Cambodia
Responsibility for ensuring observance and enforcement of terms and provisions of the agreements	Rests with the French and People's Army Commanders [Art. 22]	Rests with the parties [Art. 24]	Rests with the parties [Art. 10]

International Control Commission	To be composed of India, Canada, Poland, with India as chairman, and to be set up at time of cessation of hostilities "to ensure control and supervision." Headquarters not given [Art. 29, 34, 36]	Same as for Vietnam; Headquarters, Vientiane [Art. 25]	Same as for Vietnam; Headquarters, Phnom-Penh [Art. 12]
Fixed inspection teams (of International Control Commission)	At Laokay, Langson, Tien-Yen, Haiphong, Vinh, Dong-Hoi, Muong-Sen, Tourane, Quinhon, Nhatrang, Bangoi, Saigon, Cap St. Jacques, Tranchau [Art. 35]	At Paksé, Seno, Tchépone, Vientiane, Xieng-Khouang, Phong-Saly, Sophao (Sam-Neua) [Art. 26]	At Phnom Penh, Kompong-Cham, Kratié, Svay-Rieng, Kampot [Art. 12]
Mobile inspection teams (of International Control Commission)	Zones of action: Regions bordering land and sea frontiers of Vietnam, demarcation lines between regrouping zones, and demilitarized zones [Art. 35]	Zones of action: Land frontiers of Laos [Art. 26]	Zones of action: Land and sea frontiers of Cambodia [Art. 12]
Joint Commission of the parties	Established by the parties to facilitate execution of provisions concerning joint actions by the two parties (equal number of representatives of the commands of both parties) [Art. 33]	Set up to facilitate implementation of the agreement (equal number of representatives of commands of parties concerned) [Art. 28]	
Joint Commission teams or groups	To be set up by Joint Commission and governed by the parties [Art. 32]	Formed by Joint Commission [Art. 28]	Formed by Joint Commission [Art. 14]

Provisions	*Vietnam*	*Laos*	*Cambodia*
International Control Commission recommendations	1) Adopted by majority, except when dealing with questions concerning violations, threats of violations, or problems which might lead to resumption of hostilities, in which cases unanimity applies; 2) Sent directly to the parties and Joint Commission is notified; 3) Recommendation concerning amendments and additions to provisions of the agreement may be formulated with unanimous participation [Art. 40, 41]	[Art. 34, 35]	[Art. 19, 20]
Appeal to members of the Geneva Conference	If one party refuses to put into effect a recommendation of the International Control Commission, the parties concerned or the Commission itself shall inform the members of the Geneva Conference. If unanimity is not reached by the Commission in cases where it applies, a majority and one or more minority reports shall be submitted. The Commission shall inform members of the conference in all cases where its activity is being hindered. [Art. 43]	[Art. 36]	[Art. 22]

E. Procedural Matters

Provisions	*Vietnam*	*Laos*	*Cambodia*
Parties and signatories to agreements	For the Commander in Chief of the People's Army of Vietnam, Ta-Quang Buu, Vice-Minister of National Defense of the DRV; For the Commander in Chief of the French Union Forces in Indochina, Brig. Gen. Delteil [Art. 47]	For the Commander in Chief of the fighting units of "Pathet Lao" and for the Commander in Chief of the People's Army of Vietnam, Ta-Quang Buu; For the Commander in Chief of the French Union Forces in Indochina, Brig. Gen. Delteil [Art. 41]	For the Commander of the units of the Khmer Resistance Forces and for the Commander in Chief of the Vietnamese (DRV) military units, Ta-Quang Buu; For the Commander in Chief of the Khmer National armed forces, General Nhiek Tioulong [Art. 33]
Entry into force of agreements	Except as provided, 2400 hours, July 22, 1954 (Geneva time) [Art. 47]	2400 hours, July 22, 1954 (Geneva time) [Art. 40]	00 hours, July 23, 1954 (Geneva time) [Art. 33]

MAJOR PROVISIONS OF THE 1954 GENEVA ACCORDS

Conference Final Declaration*
and
Unilateral Declarations**

Provisions	Vietnam	Laos	Cambodia
Effective date of cessation of hostilities	North Vietnam: 0800 (local), July 27, 1954 Central Vietnam: 0800 (local), August 1, 1954 Southern Vietnam: 0800 (local), August 11, 1954 [Art. 11]	0800 (local), August 6, 1954 [Art. 40]	0800 (local), August 7, 1954 [Art. 2]
Principles of political settlement	Respect for "independence, unity, territorial integrity," and enjoyment of "fundamental freedoms guaranteed by democratic institutions established as a result of free general elections by secret ballot" [CFD Art. 7]	All citizens of Laos and Cambodia to be integrated without discrimination into the national community and to be guaranteed enjoyment of rights and freedoms provided by the constitution [UD Laos and Cambodia; CFD Art. 3]	

* Abbreviated "CFD" in table.
** Abbreviated "UD" in table. Laos, Cambodia, and France each made two unilateral declarations referring to the CFD.

Provisions	Vietnam	Laos	Cambodia
Method of political settlement	"General elections to be held in July 1956, under supervision of an international commission composed of representatives of the Member States of the International Supervisory Commission referred to in the agreement on cessation of hostilities. Consultations will be held on this subject between the competent, representative authorities of the two zones from 20 July 1955 onwards." [CFD Art. 7]	All Laotian and Cambodian citizens to participate freely as electors or candidates in general elections by secret ballot; in conformity with the constitution, next general elections to take place in the course of 1955 by secret ballot and in conditions of respect for fundamental freedoms [UD Laos and Cambodia; CFD Art. 3]	
Withdrawal of French forces	At the request of the government and within a period to be fixed by agreement between the parties, except in cases where, by agreement between the two parties, a certain number of French troops shall remain at specified points and for a specified time [UD France; CFD Art. 10]		
Reprisals against persons who have collaborated with one of parties during war, or their families	Must not be permitted [CFD Art. 9]	Must not be permitted [CFD Art. 9]	Must not be permitted [CFD Art. 9]
Protection of individuals and property	Provisions of agreements on cessation hostilities must be most strictly applied [CFD Art. 8]		
Free choice of zone of residence	Everyone must be allowed to decide freely in which zone he wishes to live [CFD Art. 8]	No provision	No provision
Principle of relations with Vietnam, Laos and Cambodia	The French Government and each member of the Geneva Conference undertakes to respect the independence, sovereignty, unity, and territorial integrity of Vietnam, Laos and Cambodia and to refrain from any interference in their internal affairs [UD France; CFD Art. 11, 12]		

	Vietnam	Laos	Cambodia
Special representation for dissident elements	No provision	Government of Laos will promulgate measures to provide for special representation, in the Royal Administration of Phong-Saly and Sam-Neua Provinces during interval between cessation hostilities and general elections, of the interests of Laotian Nationals who did not support royal forces during hostilities [UD Laos]	No provision
Introduction of arms and force, adherence to military alliances, or establishment of foreign bases	Clauses in Agreement on Cessation of Hostilities Vietnam noted [CFD Art. 4, 5]	Government of Laos will not join in any agreement with other states if it includes the obligation to participate in a military alliance not in conformity with the principles of the UN Charter or with the principles of the agreement on the cessation of hostilities or, unless its security is threatened, the obligation to establish bases on Laotian territory for military forces of foreign powers. [UD Laos; CFD Art. 4, 5]	"The Royal Government of Cambodia will not join in any agreement with other States, if this agreement carries for Cambodia the obligation to enter a military alliance not in conformity with the principles of the Charter of the United Nations, or, as long as its security is not threatened, the obligation to establish bases on Cambodian territory for the military forces of foreign powers." [UD Cambodia; CFD Art. 4, 5]

Provisions	Vietnam	Laos	Cambodia
Use of territory to further aggression	Clauses in Agreement on Cessation of Hostilities in Vietnam noted [CFD Art. 5]	The Government of Laos undertook "never to permit the territory of Laos to be used in furtherance of a policy of aggression." [UD Laos]	The Government of Cambodia "resolved never to take part in an aggressive policy and never to permit the territory of Cambodia to be utilized in service of such a policy." [UD Cambodia]

I. FAILURE OF THE GENEVA SETTLEMENT

A. INTRODUCTION: THE FLAWED PEACE

The Geneva Conference of 1954 brought only transitory peace to Indochina. Nonetheless, except for the United States, the major powers were, at the time of the Conference, satisfied that with their handiwork: the truce averted a further U.S. military involvement on the Asian mainland, and dampened a heightening crisis between East and West which might readily have led to conflict outside Southeast Asia. So long as these conditions obtained, neither France, the U.K., the U.S.S.R. nor Communist China were seriously disposed to disturb the *modus vivendi* in Vietnam. U.S. leaders publicly put the best face possible on the Geneva Settlement—about all that might possibly have been obtained from a seriously disadvantaged negotiating position, and no serious impairment to freedom of United States action. But the U.S., within its inner councils immediately after Geneva, viewed the Settlement's provisions for Vietnam as "disaster," and determined to prevent, if it could, the further extension of communist government over the Vietnamese people and territory. U.S. policy adopted in 1954 to this end did not constitute an irrevocable nor "open-ended" commitment to the government of Ngo Dinh Diem. But it did entail a progressively deepening U.S. involvement in the snarl of violence and intrigue within Vietnam, and therefore a direct role in the ultimate breakdown of the Geneva Settlement.

The Settlement of Geneva, though it provided respite from years of political violence, bitterly disappointed Vietnamese of North and South alike who had looked toward a unified and independent Vietnam. For the Viet Minh, the Settlement was a series of disappointing compromises to which they had agreed at the urging of the Soviet Union and China, compromises beyond what hard won military advantage over the French had led them to expect. For the State of Vietnam in the South, granted independence by France while the Geneva Conference was in progress, the Settlement was an arrangement to which it had not been party, and to which it could not subscribe. The truce of 1954, in fact, embodied three serious deficiencies as a basis for stable peace among the Vietnamese:

—It relied upon France as its executor.
—It ignored the opposition of the State of Vietnam.
—It countenanced the disassociation of the United States.

These weaknesses turned partitioned Vietnam into two hostile states, and given the absence of a stabilizing international force and the impotence of the ICC, brought about an environment in which war was likely, perhaps inevitable. A nominally temporary "line of demarcation" between North and South at the 17th parallel was transformed into one of the more forbidding frontiers of the world. A mass displacement of nearly 5% of the population disrupted the polity and heightened tensions in both North and South. And both the Democratic Government of Vietnam (DRV) in the North, and the Government of Vietnam (GVN) in the South armed, with foreign aid, for what each perceived as a coming struggle over reunification. Some of the main roots of the present conflict run to these failures of Geneva.

B. THE PARTITION OF VIETNAM

1. *Provisions for Unifying Vietnam*

The sole formal instrument of the Geneva Conference was the document signed by the military commanders of the two hostile forces termed "Agreement on the Cessation of Hostilities in Viet-Nam," dealing largely with the disengagement and regroupment of military forces. Article 14 of the Agreement contained one brief—but fateful allusion—to a future political solution:

> Article 14a. Pending the general elections which will bring about the unification of Vietnam, the conduct of civil administration in each regrouping zone shall be in the hands of the party whose forces are to be regrouped there in virtue of the present agreement. . . .

A more general expression of the intent of the conferees was the unsigned "Final Declaration of the Geneva Conference," by which the Conference "takes note" of the aforementioned Agreement and several declarations by represented nations and:

> . . . recognizes that the essential purpose of the agreement relating to Vietnam is to settle military questions with a view to ending hostilities and that the military demarcation line is provisional and should not in any way be interpreted as constituting a political or territorial boundary . . . declares that, so far as Vietnam is concerned, the settlement of political problems, effected on the basis of respect for the principles of independence, unity, and territorial integrity, shall permit the Vietnamese people to enjoy the fundamental freedoms, guaranteed by democratic institutions established as a result of free general elections by secret ballot. In order to insure that sufficient progress in the restoration of peace has been made, and that all the necessary conditions obtain for free expression of the national will, general elections shall be held in July, 1956, under the supervision of an international commission composed of representatives of the member States of the International Supervisory Commission, referred to in the agreement on the cessation of hostilities. Consultations will be held on this subject between the competent representative authorities of the two zones from 20 July 1955 onwards. . . .

The DRV approved the Final Declaration, and, having failed in its attempts to bring about immediate elections on unification, no doubt did so reluctantly. There has been some authoritative speculation that the Viet Minh accepted this aspect of the Settlement with deep cynicism; Pham Van Dong, the DRV delegate at Geneva is supposed to have expressed conviction that the elections would never be held. But it seems more likely that the communist powers fully expected the nascent GVN, already badly shaken from internal stresses, to collapse, and unification to follow with elections or not. In any event, the public stance of the DRV stressed their expectations that the election would be held. Ho Chi Minh stated unequivocally on 22 July 1954 that: "North, Central and South Vietnam are territories of ours. Our country will surely be unified, our entire people will surely be liberated."

The Saigon Government was no less assertive in calling for unification of

Vietnam. In a note to the French of 17 July 1954, the GVN delegate at Geneva protested having been left until then "in complete ignorance" of French intentions regarding the division of the country, which he felt failed to "take any account of the unanimous will for national unity of the Vietnamese people"; he proposed, futilely, United Nations trusteeship of all Vietnam in preference to a nation "dismembered and condemned to slavery." At the final session of the Conference, when called upon to join in the Final Declaration, the GVN delegate announced that his government "reserves its full freedom of action in order to safeguard the sacred right of the Vietnamese people to its territorial unity, national independence and freedom." Thus the Geneva truce confronted from the outset the anomaly of two sovereign Vietnamese states, each calling for unification, but only one, the DRV, committed to achieving it via the terms of the Settlement.

2. *France Withdraws, 1954–1956*

France, as the third party in Vietnam, then became pivotal to any political settlement, its executor for the West. But France had agreed to full independence for the GVN on June 4, 1954, nearly six weeks before the end of the Geneva Conference. By the terms of that June agreement, the GVN assumed responsibility for international contracts previously made on its behalf by France; but, there having been no reference to subsequent contracts, it was technically free of the Geneva Agreements. It has been argued to the contrary that the GVN was bound by Geneva because it possessed at the time few of the attributes of full sovereignty, and especially because it was dependent on France for defense. But such debates turn on tenuous points of international law regarding the prerogatives of newly independent or partitioned states. France speedily divested itself of responsibilities for "civil administration" in South Vietnam. In February, 1956, the GVN requested France to withdraw its military forces, and on April 26, 1956, the French military command in Vietnam, the signatory of the Geneva Agreement, was dissolved. France, torn by domestic political turbulence in which past disappointments and continued frustrations in Vietnam figured prominently, and tested anew in Algeria, abandoned its position in Southeast Asia. No doubt, an increasingly acerbic relation between its representatives and those of the United States in South Vietnam hastened its departure, where American policy clashed with French over the arming and training of a national army for the GVN, over French military assistance for the religious sects, over French economic policy on repatriating investments, and over general French opposition to Diem. But more fundamentally, France felt itself shouldered aside in South Vietnam by the United States over:

(1) *Policy toward the DRV*. The French averred initially that Ho was a potential Tito, and that they could through an accommodation with him preserve their economic and cultural interests in Vietnam—in their view, a "coexistence experiment" of world wide significance in the Cold War. As of December, 1954, they were determined to carry out the Geneva elections. Eventually, however, they were obliged to choose between the U.S. and the DRV, so firmly did the U.S. foreclose any adjustment to the DRV's objectives.

(2) *Policy toward Diem*. France opposed Diem not solely because he was a vocally Francophobe Annamite, but because he threatened directly their position in Vietnam. His nationalism, his strictures against "feudalists," his notions of moral regeneration all conjoined in an enmity against the French nearly as heated as that he harbored against the communists—but to greater effect, for it was far easier for him to muster his countrymen's opinion against the French

than against the Viet Minh. By the spring of 1955, the Diem–France controversy acquired military dimensions when French supported sect forces took up
arms against the GVN. At that time, while the U.S. construed its policy as
aiding "Free Vietnam," the French saw Diem as playing Kerensky's role in
Vietnam, with the People's Revolutionary Committee as the Bolsheviks, and
Ho, the Viet Minh Lenin, waiting off stage.

(3) *Military Policy*. By the end of 1954, the French were persuaded that
SEATO could never offer security for their citizens and other. interests in
Vietnam, and had despaired of receiving U.S. military aid for a French Expeditionary corps of sufficient size to meet the threat. U.S. insistence that it
should train RVNAF increased their insecurity. Within the combined U.S.–
French headquarters in Saigon thereafter, officers of both nations worked side
by side launching countervailing intrigues among the Vietnamese, and among
each other. In March of 1956, as France prepared to accede to the GVN request
for withdrawal of its remaining military forces, Foreign Minister Pineau, in a
Paris speech, took the U.K. and the U.S. to task for disrupting Western unity.
While Pineau selected U.S. support of French-hating Diem for particular rancor,
he did so in the context of decrying France's isolation in dealing with nationalist
rebels in North Africa—and thus generally indicated two powers who had
threatened the French empire since the U.K. intervened in Syria in 1941, and
President Roosevelt assured the Sultan of Morocco that his sympathies lay with
the colonial peoples struggling for independence.

Ultimately, France had to place preservation of its European position ahead of
empire, and, hence, cooperation with the U.S. before opposition in Indochina.
France's vacating Vietnam in 1956 eased U.S. problems there over the short
run, and smoothed Diem's path. But the DRV's hope for a national plebescite
were thereby dashed. On January 1, 1955, as the waning of France's power in
Vietnam became apparent, Pham Van Dong, DRV Premier, declared that as
far as Hanoi was concerned: ". . . it was with you, the French, that we signed
the Geneva Agreements, and it is up to you to see that they are respected." Some
thirteen months later the Foreign Minster of France stated that:

> We are not entirely masters of the situation. The Geneva Accords on
> the one hand and the pressure of our allies on the other creates a very
> complex juridical situation. . . . The position in principle is clear: France
> is the guarantor of the Geneva Accords . . . But we do not have the
> means alone of making them respected.

But the GVN remained adamantly opposed to elections, and neither the U.S.
nor any other western power was disposed to support France's fulfillment of its
responsibility to the DRV.

3. *Diem Refuses Consultation, 1955*

Communist expectations that the Diem government would fall victim to the
voracious political forces of South Vietnam were unfulfilled. Diem narrowly
escaped such a fate, but with American support—albeit wavering, and accompanied by advice he often ignored—Diem within a year of the Geneva Conference succeeded in defeating the most powerful of his antagonists, the armed
sects, and in removing from power Francophile elements within his government,
including his disloyal military chiefs. He spoke from comparatively firm political
ground when, on July 16, 1955, before the date set for consulting with the
DRV on the plebescite, he announced in a radio broadcast that:

We did not sign the Geneva Agreements.

We are not bound in any way by these Agreements, signed against the will of the Vietnamese people. . . . We shall not miss any opportunity which would permit the unification of our homeland in freedom, but it is out of the question for us to consider any proposal from the Viet Minh if proof is not given that they put the superior interests of the national community above those of communism.

Moreover, Diem spoke with some assurance of American backing, for the U.S. had never pressed for the elections envisaged by the Settlement. At the final session of Geneva, rather than joining with the Conference delegates in the Final Declaration, the U.S. "observer," Under Secretary of State Walter Bedell Smith, had linked U.S. policy *vis-a-vis* Vietnam to that for Korea, Taiwan and Germany in these terms:

In the case of nations now divided against their will, we shall continue to seek to achieve unity through free elections supervised by the United Nations to insure that they are conducted fairly.

Although the U.S. opposed elections in 1954 because Ho Chi Minh would have then won them handily, the records of the National Security Council and the Operations Coordinating Board of the summer of 1954 establishes that this government then nonetheless expected elections eventually to be held in Vietnam. But, two major misapprehensions were evident: (1) the U.S. planned through "political action" to ameliorate conditions in Southeast Asia to the point that elections would not jeopardize its objective of survival for a "free" Vietnam; and (2) the U.S. estimated that France would usefully remain in Vietnam. By the spring of 1955, although U.S. diplomacy had brought the Southeast Asia Treaty Organization into being, and although Diem had with U.S. aid weathered a number of severe political storms, the U.S. was less sanguine than its "political action" would suffice, and that further French presence would be helpful. Accordingly, it began to look closely at the conditions under which elections might be held, and urged that Vietnamese do the same. One definition of terms acceptable to the U.S. was set forth in a State Department memorandum of 5 May 1955, approved by Secretary Dulles:

The U.S. believes that the conditions for free elections should be those which Sir Anthony Eden put forward and the three Western Powers supported at Berlin in connection with German reunification. The United States believes that the Free Vietnamese should insist that elections be held under conditions of genuine freedom; that safeguards be agreed to assure this freedom before, after, and during elections and that there be adequate guarantees for, among other things, freedom of movement, freedom of presentation of candidates, immunity of candidates, freedom from arbitrary arrest or victimization, freedom of association or political meetings, freedom of expression for all, freedom of the press, radio, and free circulation of newspapers, secrecy of the vote, and security of polling stations and ballot boxes.

Although the U.S. communicated to Diem its conviction that proposing such conditions to the DRV during pre-plebescite consultations would lead promptly to a flat rejection, to Diem's marked advantage in world opinion, Diem found it preferable to refuse outright to talk to the North, and the U.S. indorsed his policy.

4.   *Divided Vietnam: Status Quo Accepted*

The deadline for the consultations in July 1955, and the date set for elections in July 1956, passed without further international action to implement those provisions of the Geneva Settlement. The DRV communicated directly with the GVN in July, 1955, and again in May and June of 1956, proposing not only consultative conference to negotiate "free general elections by secret ballot," but to liberalize North–South relations in general. Each time the GVN replied with disdain, or with silence. The 17th parallel, with its demilitarized zone on either side, became *de facto* an international boundary, and—since Ngo Dinh Diem's rigid refusal to traffic with the North excluded all economic exchanges and even an interstate postal agreement—one of the most restricted boundaries in the world. The DRV appealed to the U.K. and the U.S.S.R. as co-chairmen of the Geneva Conference to no avail. In January, 1956, Communist China requested another Geneva Conference to deal with the situation, but the U.S.S.R. and the U.K. responded only by extending the functions of the International Control Commission beyond its 1956 expiration date. By early 1957 the partition of Vietnam was generally accepted throughout the international community. In January, 1957, the Soviet Union proposed the admission of both the GVN and the DRV to the United Nations, the U.S.S.R. delegate declaring that "in Vietnam two separate States existed, which differed from one another in political and economic structure. . . ."

Professor Hans Morgenthau, writing at the time, and following a visit to South Vietnam, described the political progress of the GVN as a "miracle," but stated that conditions for free elections obtained in neither the North nor the South. He concluded that:

> Actually, the provision for free elections which would solve ultimately the problem of Vietnam was a device to hide the incompatibility of the Communist and Western positions, neither of which can admit the domination of all of Vietnam by the other side. It was a device to disguise the fact that the line of military demarcation was bound to be a line of political division as well. . . .

5.   *The Discontented*

However, there were three governments, at least, for which the *status quo* of a Vietnam divided between communist and non-communist governments was unacceptable. The GNV, while remaining cool to the DRV, pursued an active propaganda campaign prophesying the overturning of communism in the North, and proclaiming its resolve ultimately to reunify the nation in freedom. The United States supported the GVN, having established as national policy in 1956, reaffirmed again in 1958, these guidelines:

> Assist Free Viet Nam to develop a strong, stable and constitutional government to enable Free Viet Nam to assert an increasingly attractive contrast to conditions in the present Communist zone. . . . Work toward the weakening of the Communists in North and South Viet Nam in order to bring about the eventual peaceful reunification of a free and inde-

pendent Viet Nam under anti-Communist leadership. . . . Support the position of the Government of Free Viet Nam that all Viet Nam elections may take place only after it is satisfied that genuinely free elections can be held throughout both zones of Viet Nam. . . . Treat the Viet Minh as not constituting a legitimate government, and discourage other non-Communist states from developing or maintaining relations with the Viet Minh regime. . . .

And the Democratic Republic of Vietnam became increasingly vocal in its calls for "struggle" to end partition. In April, 1956, as the plebescite deadline neared, Ho Chi Minh declared ominously that:

> While recognizing that in certain countries the road to socialism may be a peaceful one, we should be aware of this fact: In countries where the machinery of state, the armed forces, and the police of the bourgeois class are still strong, the proletarian class still has to prepare for armed struggle.
>
> While recognizing the possibility of reunifying Vietnam by peaceful means, we should always remember that our people's principal enemies are the American imperialists and their agents who still occupy half our country and are preparing for war. . . .

In 1956, however, Ho Chi Minh and the DRV faced mounting internal difficulties, and were not yet in a position to translate the partition of Vietnam into *casus belli*.

C. REFUGEES: DISRUPTION OF VIETNAM'S SOCIETY

1. Provisions for Regroupment

Article 14 of the "Agreement on the Cessation of Hostilities in Vietnam," which provided for separate political administrations north and south of the 17th parallel, also stated that:

> 14(d) From the date of entry into force of the present agreement until the movement of troops is completed, any civilians residing in a district controlled by one party who wish to go and live in the zone assigned to the other party shall be permitted and helped to do so by the authorities in that district.

It is probable that none of the conferees foresaw the ramifications of that one sentence, for it put in motion one million Vietnamese refugees, most of them destitute, who became at first heavy burdens on the DRV and the GVN, and ultimately political and military assets for both regimes. For the United States, the plight of these peoples lent humanitarian dimensions to its policy toward Vietnam, and new perspectives to its economic and military assistance.

2. Exodus to South Vietnam

In accordance with Article 1 of the Agreement on Cessation of Hostilities, 190,000 troops of the French Expeditionary Corps were moved from North Vietnam to the South. In addition, some 900,000 civilians exercised their option under Article 14 (d) of the Armistice. While no wholly reliable statistics exist, there is agreement among several authorities that the figures presented by the International Commission for Supervision and Control in Vietnam (ICC), citing chiefly the Saigon Government as its source, are generally correct.

FIGURES OF MOVEMENT OF POPULATION
IN VIETNAM UNDER ARTICLE 14 (d)

North Zone to South Zone   Period Ending

(i)	Total arrivals (Figs. given by the State of Vietnam)	19.5.55	By air	213,635
			By sea	550,824
			Across provisional demarcation line	12,344
			By other means	41,324
			Total	818,127
(ii)	Estimate of arrivals not registered (Figs. given by the State of Vietnam in April)			70,000
			Total	888,127
(iii)	Figs. given by PAVN	19.5.55 20.7.55		4,749
		Up to 20.7.55	TOTAL	892,876

The uncertainty of statistics concerning total numbers of refugees stems not only from DRV reluctance to report departures, but also the turbulent conditions which then obtained throughout Vietnam, where the French were in the process of turning over public administration to Vietnamese, and where Saigon's communications with refugee relief operations in the field were at best tenuous. U.S. Department of State analysis in 1957 estimated the following composition and disposition of the refugees.

CIVILIAN REGROUPEES FROM THE NORTH, 1954–1955

Category	Number (Approximate)
1. Registered with GVN for refugee benefits	640,000 Vietnamese 15,000 Nungs 5,000 Chinese
2. French citizens resettled or repatriated by France	40,000
3. Chinese absorbed into Chinese community in South	45,000
Total	640,000 Vietnamese

(Remainder, 200,000 Vietnamese absorbed without aid, *e.g.,* dependents of military, civil servants.)

The GVN director of refugee programs reported that the refugees were composed, by trade, as follows:

Farmers	76%
Fishermen	10%
Artisans, small businessmen, students, government employees, professionals	14%

But it was religious orientation which ultimately assumed the greatest importance in South Vietnam's political life: an estimated 65% of North Vietnam's Catholics moved to the South, more than 600,000 in all; these, with 2,000 northern Protestants, were settled in their own communities.

3. *Causes of the Exodus*

The flight from North Vietnam reflected apprehension over the coming to power of the Viet Minh. Institutionally, the Viet Minh were further advanced in North Vietnam than the South, and had in areas of the North under their control already conducted several experiments in social revolution.

[Material missing]

II. REBELLION AGAINST MY-DIEM

A. *DIEM'S POLITICAL LEGACY: VIOLENCE AND ANTI-COLONIALISM*

World War II and the First Indochina War left the society of South Vietnam severely torn. The Japanese, during the years of their presence from 1940–1945, had encouraged armed factionalism to weaken the French administration and strengthen their own position. The war between the Viet Minh and the French —which began in South Vietnam in September, 1945—wrought further disunity. Paradoxically, the South suffered political damage compared to the North from having been the secondary theater of both wars. The Japanese had sought during World War II to control it without sizable occupation forces. Similarly, in the First Indochina War, the French had practiced economy of force in the South so that they could concentrate in Tonkin. For conventional forces, both the Japanese and the French substituted irregular warfare and a system of bribes, subversion, arms, military advice, and officially condoned concessions in corruption. From 1945–1954, the fighting in South Vietnam was more sporadic and diffuse than in the North, but in a societal sense, ultimately more destructive. While in Tonkin the Viet Minh flowed in through and behind the French and continued to build a nation and unify the people with surprising efficiency, in the South they were unable to do so. Not only were the Viet Minh centers of power in the North and the China base area too remote to support effectively the southern insurgency, but also the French had imitated the Japanese in arming and supplying certain South Vietnamese factions, fomenting civil war against the southern arm of the Viet Minh. The results approached anarchy: a virtual breakdown in public administration by Franco–Vietnamese central governments and deep cleavages within the Vietnamese body politic. By the summer of 1954, conspiracy had become the primary form of political communication in South Vietnam, and violence the primary mode of political change.

Politically, as well as geographically, South Vietnam consisted of three distinctive regions: the narrow, coastal plan of Annam, thickly settled by Vietnamese, where was located Hue, the ancient Viet capital and cultural center; the Highlands, sparsely populated by Montagnard tribesmen, in which was situated the summer capital of Dalat; and Cochinchina, the fertile, densely peopled river-delta area in which Saigon stood [maps deleted]. Cochinchina had experienced a political development markedly different from that of Annam. The last area of modern Vietnam to be occupied by the Viet people in their expansion southward (8th Century, A.D.), and the first area to fall to French rule (mid-19th Century), Cochinchina had been administered by the French directly as

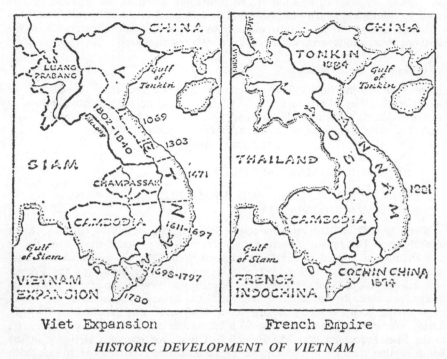

Viet Expansion   French Empire

HISTORIC DEVELOPMENT OF VIETNAM
Dates of Conquest

a colony, while Annam remained under the Emperor as a French protectorate. While the mandarinal rule of the Annamese court was more a matter of form than substance, Annam's public administration preserved a degree of unity among the Vietnamese despite the impress of French culture. In South Vietnam, the French seemed to be a wholly divisive influence. Though Cochinchina was the site of some of the achievements of which French colonialists were most proud —the chief seat of the rubber industry, and focus of major feats of engineering with canals and railroads—the Cochinchinese seem to recall less the triumphs of French civilization than its burdens: the French rubber plantations, abrasive with their labor, high-handed with local peoples; the oppressive taxes, and the French controlled monopolies on salt, alcohol and opium; recurrent *famine* in the midst of one of the earth's richest farming regions; socially restrictive schooling; modernizing challenges to familial piety, village centralism, and other cherished fundaments of Viet culture. While Annam—and Tonkin to the north— developed indigenous political movements opposing French rule, these were mainly foreign-based, foreign-oriented parties, such as the Nationalist Party (VNQDD), a Vietnamese copy of the Kuomintang, or the Indochinese Communist Party (ICP) of the Comintern, headed by Russian-trained Ho Chi Minh. In Cochinchina, however, there emerged a number of nationalist movements peculiar to that region, or principally based on that region. Saigon, for example, developed a range of leftist movements competitive with the ICP, including two Trotskyite parties, as well as a number of VNQDD splinter movements, and a politically active gangster fraternity, the Binh Xuyen. But the important differences were in the countryside, where millions of Vietnamese joined wholly Cochinchinese religious sects which propagated xenophobic nationalism, established theocracies, and fielded armed forces. French and Japanese policy had deliberately fostered conflict among these several factions to the extent that Cochinchina was, in 1954, literally fractioned among the religious sects, the Binh Xuyen, and the Viet Minh. While by 1954 the Viet Minh dominated Annam and the Highlands, control of Cochinchina eluded them, for all their ruthless efficiency.

1. The Binh Xuyen

Saigon itself in 1954 was under the rule of the Binh Xuyen, a secret society of brigands evolved from the Black Flag pirates which had for generations preyed on the city's commerce. The Binh Xuyen ethos included a fierce—albeit eclectic —nationalism. They collaborated with the Japanese during World War II, and in September, 1945, led the savage attack against the French in Saigon which marked the start of the Franco–Viet Minh War. The Binh Xuyen leader, Le Van (Bay) Vien, subsequently contracted an alliance with the Viet Minh, allied his 1300 soldiers with their guerrillas, and served for a time as the Viet Minh deputy commander for Cochinchina and one of its chief sources of funds. Bay Vien's refusal to assassinate certain Viet Minh-condemned Vietnamese intellectuals reputedly stirred Viet Minh misgivings, and called the Binh Xuyen favorably to the attention of the National United Front, an anti-communist, Viet nationalist group then operating out of Shanghai. In 1947, Bay Vien was persuaded to cooperate with the National United Front. Informed, the Viet Minh invited him to the Plain of Reeds in an attempt to capture him. Bay Vien escaped, and thereupon threw in his lot with the French and the State of Vietnam, accepting a commission as the first colonel of the Vietnamese National Army. Bay Vien afterwards paid Bao Dai what Colonel Lansdale termed "a staggering sum" for control of gambling and prostitution in Cholon, and of the Saigon–Cholon police. The French accepted the arrangement because Bay Vien offset the Viet Minh threat to Saigon. By 1954, Bay Vien was operating "Grande Monde," a gambling slum in Cholon; "Cloche d'Or," Saigon's preeminent gambling establishment; the "Noveautes Catinat," Saigon's best department store; a hundred smaller shops; a fleet of river boats; and a brothel, spectacular even by Asian standards, known as the Hall of Mirrors. Besides a feudal fief south of Saigon, he owned an opium factory and distribution system, and held substantial interests in fish, charcoal, hotels, and rubber plantations. Besides the police apparatus and other followers numbering 5000 to 8000, he had some 2500 soldiers at his disposal. He ruled Saigon absolutely; not even Viet Minh terrorists were able to operate there. Moreover, he exercised significant influnce over the Cao Dai and the Hoa Hao leaders.

2. The Cao Dai

The Cao Dai were a religious sect founded by a colonial bureaucrat named Ngo Van Chieu, who with one Pham Cong Tac conducted a series of spiritualist seances from which emerged a new religious faith, and in the early 1920's, a "church" with clerical organization similar to Roman Catholicism. The doctrine of the Cao Dai was syncretic, melding veneration of Christ, Buddha, Confucius, and Lao Tze with a curious occultism which deified such diverse figures as Joan of Arc, Victor Hugo, and Sun Yat Sen. With the dissolution of the authority of the central government during the 1940's and early 1950's, the Cao Dai acquired increasing political and military autonomy. The sect's 1,500,000 to 2,-000,000 faithful comprised a loose theocracy centered in Tay Ninh, the border

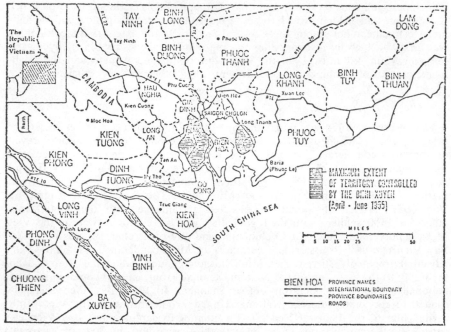

The Binh Xuyen

province northwest of Saigon. The Cao Dai, too, cooperated first with the Japanese, and then with the Viet Minh; and the Cao Dai leadership also found the latter uncomfortable allies. In 1947, the Cao Dai realigned with the French, agreeing to secure with their forces specified rural areas against the Viet Minh in return for military assistance. Although plagued throughout its history by minor heresy and factional disputes, the Cao Dai became the largest political movement in Cochinchina; the Cao Dai shared with the Hoa Hao the distinction of being the only important political forces to originate in the Vietnamese peasantry. When Diem came to power in 1954, Pham Cong Tac, the Cao Dai Pope, had declared for Bao Dai, controlled some 15,000 to 20,000 armed followers, and ruled the region northwest of Saigon.

3. *The Hoa Hao*

Southwest of Saigon there existed the Hoa Hao, a newer sect, similarly endowed with politico-military autonomy, which repeatedly clashed with the Cao Dai and the Binh Xuyen. In 1939, a mystic faith healer named Huynh Phu So, from a village named Hoa Hao, launched a reformed Hinayana Buddhist movement which swiftly acquired a wide following. (Among the Vietnamese whom Huynh Phu So favorably impressed was Ngo Dinh Diem.) Huynh Phu So enjoyed Japanese protection, and with their aid, in 1944 the Hoa Hao formed armed bands, among the leaders of which there was one Tran Van Soai. A Viet Minh attempt to gain the assistance of the Hoa Hao failed, and the Viet Minh on 8 September 1945 massacred hundreds of Hoa Hao faithful in the town of Can Tho. Tran Van Soai replied in kind, and in the ensuing weeks Can Tho became the center of extensive slaughter. French intervention stopped the violence, but turned the Hoa Hao against the French. In April, 1947, the Viet Minh executed Huynh Phu So, which caused Tran Van Soai to rally with 2,000 armed men to the French. He was accepted into the French Expeditionary Corps with the rank of general, and assigned the mission of pacifying his own region. The French from that time forward, until 1955, paid the salaries of the Hoa Hao soldiers. At the time Diem came to office in 1954, the sect had some 1,500,000 believers, controlled most of the Mekong Delta region, and had 10,000 to 15,000 men under arms.

4. *The Viet Minh*

In 1954, the Viet Minh controlled some 60 to 90 percent of South Vietnam's villages (by French estimates) and 30 to 40 percent of its territory (by U.S. estimates). The bulk of organized Viet Minh forces were located in Annam and the Highlands, proximate to Tonkin, and in regions free of competition from the armed sects. In Cochinchina, they were militarily strongest in areas along the Cambodian border and in the Camau peninsula of the extreme south remote from the principal concentrations of people. Nonetheless, their political organization was pervasive, and in some localities, e.g., Quang Ngai province in Annam, the Viet Minh were the only effective government. A hierarchy of Viet Minh committees paralleled the formal government from the village Administrative and Resistance Committee (ARC) through district, province, and what the Viet Minh termed "interzone" or "region." No reliable estimates exist of the numbers of cadres involved in this apparatus, but Viet Minh military forces of all types south of the 17th parallel probably numbered around 100,000. When orders were issued for the Geneva regroupment, the "provisional assembly areas" designated coincided with the areas in which Viet Minh strength had been greatest. During the time allowed for collecting forces for the move north, the Viet Minh evidently undertook to bank the fires of revolution by culling out of their units trained and reliable cadres for "demobilization," "recruiting" youth—forcibly in many instances—to take their place, and caching weapons. Particularly in Annam and the Highlands, then, the Viet Minh posed a significant challenge to Ngo Dinh Diem. His test of strength with the Viet Minh, however, was to be deferred by the Geneva Settlement and DRV policy for some years.

5. *Anti-Colonialism*

The political prospects of Ngo Dinh Diem when he accepted the premiership from Bao Dai were dimmed not only by Viet Minh residue, and by the existence of the armed sects, but by the taint of colonialism. As far as most Cochinchinese peasants were concerned, Diem was linked to Bao Dai, and to the corrupt, French dominated government he headed. Studies of peasant attitudes conducted in recent years have demonstrated that for many, the struggle which began in 1945 against colonialism continued uninterrupted throughout Diem's regime: in 1954, the foes of nationalists were transformed from France and Bao Dai, to Diem and the U.S.—My-Diem, American-Diem, became the universal term of Viet Cong opprobrium—but the issues at stake never changed. There was, moreover, some substance to the belief that Diem represented no change, in that, although Ngo Dinh Diem took office before the Geneva Settlement as prime minister with "full powers civil and military," he did not acquire actual administrative autonomy until September, 1954; proclaim independence until January, 1955; or take command of his army until February, 1955. There was perforce a significant carry-over of civil servants from the pre-Diem days. The national flag and the national anthem remained unchanged. Moreover, the laws remained substantially as they had been: the land-holdings, against which was directed much peasant discontent, were based on pre-Diem law; and old legal proscriptions against nationalist political activities remained on the books during Diem's tenure of office. The onus of colonialism was among the heavy burdens which Ngo Dinh Diem had to shoulder from the outset.

B. NGO DINH DIEM: BASIS OF POWER

1. *Political Origins*

Why amid the military disasters of spring 1954, Bao Dai, head of the State of Vietnam, chose Ngo Dinh Diem from among other Vietnamese nationalists to form a government, has long been debated. Diem was an Annamese Catholic who in his youth had some experience in public administration, first as governor of Phan Thiet province, and then Minister of Interior at Bao Dai's Imperial Court in Hue. In 1933 Diem discovered, after a year in the latter office, that reforms he had been promised were being blocked by high French and Annamite officials. He promptly resigned his office and went into political retirement—an act which earned him modest fame for integrity. Through the years of war and distress in his homeland thereafter, Diem had hewed to *attentisme,* and by refusing public office, had avoided the political discoloration which besmirched more involved Viet nationalists. Bao Dai had sought him for his premier in 1945, Ho Chi Minh for the DRV government in 1946, the French for their "solutions" in 1947 and 1949—all unsuccessfully. Hence, Diem's reputation for incorruptible nationalism, to the extent that he enjoyed one in 1954, was based on an event 20 years old and a long period of political aloofness. He did come from a prominent family; a brother, Ngo Dinh Thuc was a leading Catholic clergyman with countrywide connections, and the family proper retained some considerable influence in Annam. But his personal handicaps were considerable: bachelor, ascetic, shy, inexperienced, he seemed ill-fit for the seething intrigues of Saigon.

One school of conjecture holds that the French pressed him upon Bao Dai in the belief that under him the newly independent State of Vietnam would founder; another that Bao Dai advanced him to power convinced that his inevitable failure would eliminate him as a political competitor. There are those who believe that Diem was foisted upon the Vietnamese and the French by a cabal of prominent American Catholics and a CIA agent. It can be said that Diem was relatively well acquainted among leading Americans, and that Bao Dai might correctly have regarded Diem's contacts in the United States as a possible source of support for Vietnam. Whatever the reasons for his selection, however, at the time he took office there were few who regarded Diem as promising, and fewer still openly willing to back him. Indeed, from the time he took office on 7 July 1954, until the following May, he was virtually alone. Unaided by Bao Dai, opposed by the French, and proferred by Americans mainly advice, criticism, and promises—but scant material assistance—Ngo Dinh Diem in ten months surmounted the partition of his nation by the Geneva powers, two threatened military coups by his Army Chiefs of Staff, frenetic clashes with the Binh Xuyen armed sects, the withdrawal of the Viet Minh, and the influx of 900,000 refugees from North Vietnam.

2. Early U.S.–Diem Relations

Diem's durability was one of those surprises in Vietnam which prompted Americans thereafter to refer to the "miracle in Vietnam." On 7 December 1954, Senator Mansfield judged that U.S. "prospects for helping Diem strengthen and uphold South Vietnam look very dim." U.S. Ambassador Heath reported from Saigon on 17 December 1954 a dim view of Diem's chances since "there is every evidence that the French do not want Diem to succeed." In a January, 1955, report to the National Security Council, General J. Lawton Collins agreed with both analyses. On 7 April 1955, Collins cabled from Saigon that: ". . . it is my considered judgment that the man lacks the personal qualities of leadership and the executive ability successfully to head a government that must compete with the unity of purpose and efficiency of the Viet Minh under Ho Chi Minh." On 19 April, Collins again cabled: "I see no alternative to the early replacement of Diem."

On 26 April 1955, U.S. National Intelligence Estimate 63.1-2-55, "Possible Developments in South Vietnam," took the view that:

> A political impasse exists in Saigon where the legally constituted government of Premier Diem is being challenged by a venal special interest group, the Binh Xuyen, which controls the National Security Police, and is temporarily allied with some elements of the religious sects. . . .
>
> Even if the present impasse were resolved, we believe that it would be extremely difficult, at best, for a Vietnamese government, regardless of its composition, to make progress toward developing a strong, stable anti-Communist government capable of resolving the basic social, economic, and political problems of Vietnam, the special problems arising from the Geneva agreement, and capable of meeting the long-range challenge of the Communists. . . .

But opinion in Washington swung sharply when, in late April, Diem managed to survive a severe test of arms with his army and the sects. Senators Mansfield and Knowland issued strong statements of support for him, and on May 2 Senator Hubert Humphrey told the Senate that:

> Premier Diem is the best hope that we have in South Vietnam. He is the leader of his people. He deserves and must have the wholehearted support of the American Government and our foreign policy. This is no time for uncertainty or half-hearted measures. . . . He is the only man on the political horizon of Vietnam who can rally a substantial degree of support of his people. . . . If we have any comments about the leadership in Vietnam let it be directed against Bao Dai. . . . If the Government of South Vietnam has not room for both these men, it is Bao Dai who must go. . . .

On 9 May 1955, the Joint Chiefs of Staff judged that "the government of Prime Minister Ngo Dinh Diem shows the greatest promise of achieving the internal stability essential for the future security of Vietnam." Five months later, on 11 October, 1955, the National Intelligence Estimate was revised. In NIE 63.1–3–55, "Probable Developments in Vietnam to July 1956," the U.S. Intelligence Advisory Committee found it possible to be more sanguine concerning Diem's prospects:

> . . . Diem has made considerable progress toward establishing the first fully independent Vietnamese government. . . . He faced a basically un-

stable and deteriorating situation. . . . The most significant articulate political sentiments of the bulk of the population was an antipathy for the
French combined with a personal regard for Ho Chi Minh as the symbol
of Vietnamese nationalism. . . .

Diem was forced to move slowly. Although possessing considerable national prestige as a patriot, he was inexperienced in administration and was
confronted at the outset by the intrigues of Bao Dai and other self-inter-
ested individuals and groups, who in many cases benefited from French
support. . . .

Diem concentrated on eliminating or neutralizing the most important
groups and individuals challenging the authority of his government. . . .
By bribery, persuasion, and finally force, Diem virtually eliminated the
Binh Xuyen and the most important elements of the Hoa Hao sects as
threats to his authority. At the same time, he maneuvered the Cao Dai—
the strongest of the sects—into an uneasy alliance. As a result of these
successful actions, Diem gained prestige and increased popularity as a
symbol of Diem's efforts to establish a viable anti-communist government
are still in doubt. . . .

Provided the Communists do not exercise their capabilities to attack
across the 17th Parallel or to initiate large-scale guerrilla warfare in South
Vietnam, Diem will probably make further progress in developing a more
effective government. His position will probably be strengthened as a result of increased popular support, the continued loyalty of the VNA, and
a deterioration in the strength and cohesiveness of his non-Communist opposition. The national government will probably increase the number of
rural communities under its control, particularly in areas now held by the
sects. . . .

It is likely that Diem's stormy first 10 months in office, June, 1954 to May,
1955, strongly conditioned his behavior in later years. He must have been impressed almost at once with the political importance of the army, and the
essentiality of personally loyal ranking officers. He chose openly to oppose the
armed sects against the advice of both his American and French advisers, and
his success no doubt instilled confidence in his own judgments. The same events
probably gave him reason thereafter to value head-on confrontation with a foe
over conciliation or compromise. And in his adamant stand against consultations
with the DRV on plebescite, again contrary to initial American advice, he no
doubt learned that on major issues the U.S. stake in his future was sufficiently
high that he could lead, and American policy would follow. In any event, he
moved with new assurance from mid-1955 forward. In many respects his first
300 days were his finest hours, when he was moving alone, rapidly, and with
determination against great odds.

3.   *Political Concepts: Family Centralism and Personalism*

But Diem's early victories were essentially negative, in eliminating or bypass-
ing obstacles. It remained for him to provide programs for finding homes and
occupations for the refugees, for solving the politically crucial problems of rural
land distribution and taxation, for installing capable and incorrupt public administrators, for stimulating the economy, for improving the education system—in
short, for coping with the whole broad range of problems of governing a developing nation, each rendered especially acute by South Vietnam's war trauma, internal dissention, and partition from North Vietnam. To cite but a few: 600,000

refugees were dependent on his government for subsistence; 85,000 people were jobless as a result of the French troop withdrawal; inter-provincial communications were impaired—700 miles of main road were war-damaged, one third of the railway trackage lay destroyed, 68 concrete bridges on 860 miles of track lay blown. In devising programs to meet these challenges, Diem worked from two primal concepts: family centralism, and "personalism" as a state philosophy.

Diem was raised in a Mandarinal family, born to a tradition of high position in the social hierarchy and governmental bureaucracy. It was also a Catholic family, and Diem received a heritage of obdurate devotion to Christianity under intense persecution—within a century of his birth one hundred relatives had been burned to death by Buddhists in central Annam. His rearing developed his reverence for the past, a capacity for hard work, and a deep seated piety. Two French authors believed that his outlook on life was "born of a profound, of an immense nostalgia for the Vietnamese past, of a desperate filial respect for the society of ancient *Annam*." There was some thought of his becoming a priest, but he elected public administration; his elder brother Thuc, the cleric, is said to have speculated that Diem found himself too inflexible, too willful, too severe for the priesthood. But above all else, Diem's early years impressed upon him the importance of family in performing the duties of station: the family was the first means of extending personal power, the essential mode of political expression. It is possible that Diem resorted to nepotism simply because he lacked a personal political apparatus which would have permitted him to operate otherwise, but nepotism became the style of his rule, and it was quite consistent with his upbringing.

"Society," said Diem, "functions through personal relations among men at the top." One brother, Ngo Dinh Nhu, received the title of Advisor to the President, and controlled the semi-covert Personalist Labor Revolutionary Party. His wife, Madame Nhu, became the President's official hostess, a deputy in the National Assembly, and the founder-chairman of the Woman's Solidarity Movement. Her father became one of Diem's ambassadors, and his wife the GVN observer at the UN. A second brother of Diem, Ngo Dinh Can, became the virtual overlord of Annam, holding no official position, but ruling the region in all respects. A third brother, Ngo Dinh Thuc, the Archbishop of Hue and Primate of Vietnam, also held no office, but functioned as Presidential advisor, and levered Catholic opinion on behalf of Diem. A fourth brother, Ngo Dinh Luyen, became an Ambassador. Three family members—Tran Van Chuong, Tran Van Do, and Tran Van Bac—served in Diem's first cabinet, and two other in-laws, Nguyen Huu Chau and Tran Trung Dung, held the key portfolios of Secretary of State at the Presidency and Assistant Secretary of State for National Defense. One of the reasons General Collins opposed Diem may be a letter he received in April, 1955, from a group of nationalists headed by former Premier Nguyen Phan Long, urging the United States to withdraw its support of Diem on the grounds that his brothers were effectively isolating Diem politically. The observation proved to be correct: Ngo Dinh Nhu and Ngo Dinh Can increasingly gathered power into their own hands, and non-family politicians found themselves quietly shunted aside. Gradually, a concentration of power also occurred within the family circle, again toward Nhu, Mme Nhu and Can, and at the expense of the more remotely related. The President's family thus became an entirely extra-legal elite which in class and geographic origin, as well as religion, was distinct from the South Vietnamese as a whole.

The Diem family circle was promptly targeted by gossipers. In Saigon, rumors were the political medium, and stories were soon rampant that members of the family were looting the government. By 1957, the whispering campaign against the Nhus mounted to such proportions that they issued a public statement denying that they had ever removed money from the country, engaged in financial or commercial speculation, or accepted bribes. But the impression remained, fed by numerous credible reports of official graft at lower levels, that whether or not the Diem family took for personal gain, they took.

Another disadvantage proceeded from the Diem's familial concentration of power: bureaucratic overcentralization; Diem himself seems to have been peculiarly at fault in this instance, reserving for himself the power of decision in minute matters, and refusing to delegate authority to subordinates who might have relieved him of a crushing administrative burden. In part, this may have been simply inexperience in handling a large enterprise, but there seems to have been deeper, philosophical reasons—a passion for perfection, a distrust of other men, a conviction that all subordinates required his paternalistic guidance. The result was an impairment of an administrative system already crippled by the absence of French civil servants. Subordinate officials, incapable of making decisions, fearful of making them, or forbidden to make them, passed upward even minute matters on paper to the brothers Ngo, glutting the communications of government, and imposing long delays on all, even important actions.

Personalism, as Diem called his personal political philosophy, was a melange of Asian and European notions which resembled the French Catholic *personnalisme* of Emmanuel Mounier, or the Encyclicals of Popes Leo XIII and Pius XI. More accurately, it was a blend of Christianity, Marxism, and Confucianism which stressed the development of each individual's moral character as the basis for community progress toward democracy. Diem saw himself as a reformer, even a revolutionary, in the moral realm. His central social message was that each citizen achieved moral fulfillment or harmony only if he applied himself energetically to his civic duties, avoiding on the one hand the selfishness of capitalism, and on the other, the selflessness of Marxist collectivism. "The basis for democracy can only be a spiritual one," said Diem in his Message to the National Assembly on the Constitution of 1956, and in New Delhi in 1957, he took Asians to task for losing sight of the spiritual essence of their political traditions:

> . . . Does not our spirituality of which we are so proud, simply conceal a narrow conservatism and a form of escapism from concrete responsibility? . . . Has not Buddhist compassion become a pretext for not practicing justice . . . And is not tolerance, which so many can mistake for freedom, the result of paternalistic indulgence?

And the same year, in Korea, he spoke of his hopes for restoring the spiritual strength of Vietnam after "the tremendous material and political difficulties which assailed Vietnam after Geneva had plunged even the best of her sons into a state of apprehension colored with despair . . ."

> We pursue two aims.
> First we want to rearm the Vietnamese citizen morally and to make him impervious to all tyranny whatever its origin.
> Second, we want to reinforce the spiritual cohesion of the Vietnamese people, cohesion which accounts for capacity to enjoy a largely decentralized system without falling into anarchy. Yet this cohesion has been largely shaken by the impact of the west.

Yet man does not live only by the idea of liberty. He must be given a minimum of material support which will guarantee that liberty . . .

A GVN approved biography of Diem explained that he recognized in communism the antithesis of true freedom, precisely because communism denied the existence of God and the immortality of the soul. Personalism was the answer therefore to communism, since:

Personalism is a system based on the divine, therefore spiritual law, which . . . extols man's transcendent value . . . The practice of Personalism is symbolic of good citizenship with a highly developed civic spirit . . .

Late in Diem's reign, when his combat with the communists had been fully joined, these vague precepts were elaborated by his brother, Nhu, but hardly clarified:

The personalist conception holds that freedom in an underdeveloped society is not something that is simply given or bestowed. It can only be achieved through militancy and vigilance, by doing away with all pretentions and pretexts for not realistically applying ourselves to our goals. In a situation of underdevelopment, and during a bleeding war of internal division, it may be argued that there is reason enough not to seek to develop democracy, but our personalist approach is precisely militant in denying this. Human rights and human dignity are not static phenomenons. They are only possibilities which men must actively seek and deserve, not just beg for. In this sense, of believing in the process of constantly perfecting of oneself in moral as well as practical ways our personalist approach is similar to Confucianism. Personalism stresses hard work, and it is the working class, the peasants, who are better able to understand the concept than the intellectuals. We must use Personalist methods to realize democracy at the level where people are fighting and working, and in our new scale of values it is those who participate physically and selflessly in the fight against communism who are most privileged, then those who courageously serve the villages without profit, and finally those who engage diligently in productive labor for their own as well as for their villages' benefit . . .

Some American observers found these ideas with their emphasis on "democracy" reassuring. Others, including General Edward Lansdale, urged on Diem a broader ideological strategem of forming a "front" embracing the concepts of the more traditional Viet nationalist parties.

"Personalism," like Diem's Spanish-style Catholicism, harbored little tolerance; merely different political theories were interpreted as competitive, and even dangerous. Personalism thus limited Diem's political horizons, and almost certainly impaired his government's ability to communicate with the peasantry. "Personalism" became the official philosophy of the state, and though government employees were required to attend weekly sessions on its tenets, it never succeeded in becoming much more than the cant of Diem's administration, and the credo of the two political parties organized and directly controlled by his family.

4. Political Parties

The latter were peculiarly Diemist: paternally authoritarian, organized as an extension of family power. The pivotal organization was the Personalist Labor Revolutionary Party (*Can Lao Nhan Vi Cach Mang Dang*), an apparatus devised and controlled by Ngo Dinh Nhu, semi-covert, self-effacing, but with members stationed at all the levers of power within Saigon, and a web of informants everywhere in the country. Nhu envisaged the Can Lao as the vanguard of Diem's undertakings, and it became in fact the backbone of the regime. Drawing intelligence from agents at all echelons of government in the village, in factories, schools, military units, the Can Lao sought to detect the corrupt or disloyal citizen, and was empowered to bring him to arrest and trial. The Can Lao, unfortunately for Diem's political flexibility, concentrated on disloyalty. Ngo Dinh Nhu, who admitted that the Can Lao closely resembled the communists in organization and technique, used it to stifle all political sentiment competitive or opposed to Ngo Dinh Diem.

The other Diemist party was an open, "mass party," the National Revolutionary Movement (*Phong Trao Cach Mang Quoc Gia*). Diem himself was the honorary leader of the Party, and it was the official vehicle for his political movement. The Party claimed to have grown from 10,000 members in 1955 to 1,500,000 in 1959. In that time it acquired a majority in the National Assembly, and amassed strong voting records for Diem and NRM candidates in elections at all levels. The Party claims to have originated in "clandestine struggle for the revolution of national independence and human emancipation" at the time Diem resigned from Bao Dai's government in 1933, but properly it came into being in October, 1954. The NRM was closely associated with the National Revolutionary Civil Servants League (*Lien Doan Cong Chuc Mang Quoc Gia*), and since membership in the latter was a concomitant of government employment, the civil service became the core of the NRM. The relationship also established a NRM-League hierarchy parallel to, and in most instances identical with, the government hierarchy down to the village level. Obviously, too, the arrangement equated a party membership with distinct advantages in dealing with the government. NRM strength figures were probably exaggerated, and its active members —those who attended party functions and political indoctrination sessions— were those in the League; the NRM was, in effect, a party of government employees or dependents.

Diem did not involve himself directly in the managing of either the Can Lao or the NRM. The former, as mentioned, was always the creature of Nhu. Nhu also controlled the southern branches of the NRM, but in Annam and portions of the Central Highlands the NRM was the tightly held instrument of Ngo Dinh Can. Can brooked no opposition whatsoever; Nhu, more confident in the regions where the Can Lao was most efficient, occasionally permitted some political activity by minority groups, such as the Cao Dai and Hoa Hao sects, and the Socialists. But that activity was tolerated only so long as it was pro-Diem and supporting, rather than opposing, GVN policy.

These were the ideas and the political apparatus by which Ngo Dinh Diem sought to weld together a nation in the aftermath of Geneva. Their narrowness, their inappropriateness for most Cochinchinese and Annamites, virtually assured that the history of his regime, after its initial successes, would become an almost unbroken record of alienation of one portion after another of the Vietnamese body politic. This process of alienation accentuated the failures of the Geneva Settlement, and ultimately led to Ngo Dinh Diem's assassination.

C. CONFLICT WITH THE ARMED SECTS

1. Defeat of the Binh Xuyen

At the time he took office, Diem controlled scarcely a few blocks of Saigon, the capital remaining firmly in the control of Bay Vien and the Binh Xuyen. Beginning in September, 1954, Diem tried to divide and conquer the sects. Four leaders from each of the religious sects were brought into his cabinet in an effort to isolate the Binh Xuyen, and with U.S. assistance he sought to integrate the sect forces into the national army. He enjoyed some initial success in rallying Cao Dai forces, and confident from assurances of direct American aid, he shut down, in January, 1955, the Binh Xuyen concessions in Saigon and Cholon. In the ensuing confrontation, the Binh Xuyen swung the Cao Dai and the Hoa Hao into a United Front of Nationalist Forces, and, although French aid for their forces had formally been withdrawn, continued to draw on French funds and advice. On March 29, 1955, fighting broke in Saigon in which sections of the city were burned. Although a truce was struck, the affair polarized relations between Diem and the sects; between Diem and General Collins, whose advice to conciliate he elected not to follow; and between the Americans and the French, over the viability of Diem. Washington apparently decided at that juncture to temporize with the sects, and to find an alternative to Diem. Before the instructions could be sent to Saigon, however, fighting was renewed. Even as the battle was joined, Bao Dai telegraphed orders to Diem to travel to France. Diem disobeyed, and, convinced of his moral grounds in attacking the Binh Xuyen, committed his forces to combat. His brother, Nhu, coopted a "Revolutionary Committee" to confer emergency authority on Diem. They were immediately successful, and by mid-May, 1955, the Binh Xuyen had been driven into the Rung Sat swamp east of Saigon, and their power in Saigon was broken. Bay Vien escaped to Paris.

2. Victory over the Sects

Diem's forces then ranged out after the other armed factions. Tran Van Soai of the Hoa Hao surrendered, and was given asylum. Another Hoa Hao leader, Ba Cut—who had cut off a finger to remind himself to fight the French, and had sworn not to cut his hair until Vietnam was reunited—was captured while negotiating surrender in return for a commission as lieutenant general in the ARVN. Other leaders were bribed, and the remainder fled or rallied to the GVN. By the end of 1955, Diem appeared to have dealt finally with the challenge of the sects.

It was this apparent success which enabled Diem to survive successfully pressures from an even more powerful set of opponents: those among his Western allies who were determined to replace him. The dimensions of his victory in Vietnam were just becoming evident when in May, 1955, the North Atlantic Treaty Organization convened. There promptly developed a sharp division of view between the French and the Americans. Bao Dai made known his opposition to Diem, and the French threatened to pull out of Vietnam unless Diem were removed. From Paris, Secretary Dulles reported that the French held that:

> . . . Time something to be done to avoid civil war. France warned that armed conflict—first civil war, then guerrilla warfare, then terrorism— would result if we failed to take action . . . New Revolutionary Committee . . . is strongly under Viet Minh influence . . . There is violent cam-

paign against French and French Expeditionary Corps. Viet Minh agents make good use of it and certain Americans do not seem sufficiently aware of this. French Govt does not wish to have its army act as platform for Viet Minh propaganda. Army will not be maintained in Vietnam at any cost . . . Continuing with Diem would have three disastrous results:

(1) . . . Viet Minh victory

(2) . . . focus hostility of everyone on the French, and

(3) . . . begin a Franco–U.S. breach . . .

The French then proposed to the U.S. that the French Expeditionary Corps be withdrawn, and asked if the U.S. were willing to guarantee French civilians, and the refugees. From Washington, the following instructions to Dulles were returned promptly:

President's only comment on Vietnam section of (your telegram) was to reiterate position that U.S. could not afford to have forces committed in such undesirable areas as Vietnam. This, of course, is JCS view in past. Am asking Defense and JCS views . . .

Asked, the JCS took the position that the question was fundamentally beyond their purview, that neither the ARVN nor the French Expeditionary Corps seemed capable of preserving the integrity of South Vietnam against a Viet Minh onslaught, and that being debarred from furnishing arms by the Geneva Agreement, the U.S. was in no position to protect French nationals. They suggested that Secretary Dulles be advised that:

a. The government of Prime Minister Ngo Dinh Diem shows the greatest promise of achieving the internal stability essential for the future security of Vietnam.

b. The U.S. could not guarantee the security of the French nationals should the French Expeditionary Corps be withdrawn.

c. Possible United States actions under the Southeast Asia Collective Defense Treaty could ultimately afford security to Vietnam equal to that provided by the continued presence of the French Expeditionary Corps.

In Paris, Secretary Dulles managed to mollify the French. A key development was a message from Malcolm MacDonald, the British representative in Southeast Asia, urging against Diem's replacement at that time. MacDonald, who was among Diem's severest critics—he once remarked of Diem that "He's the worst prime minister I have ever seen"—aligned the British with Dulles, and eventually the French acquiesced in further support of Diem.

The defeat of the sects also opened a domestic political opportunity for Diem. The Popular Revolutionary Committee his brother Nhu had formed during the height of the sect crisis was a "front" of broad political complexion—the membership included prominent nationalists and, as the French had pointed out, two former Viet Minh leaders; it therefore had some substance as what Nhu termed the "democratic revolutionary forces of the nation." The Revolutionary Committee urged the dissolution of the Bao Dai government, and the organizing of general elections for a National Assembly. Nhu acted under its mandate, setting up a popular referendum in which, on October 23, 1955, an overwhelming vote for Diem in preference to Bao Dai was recorded. The Revolutionary Committee dissolved itself on 31 October, apparently under some pressure from Diem and his brother.

3. The Triumph Reappraised

But it is important to note that Diem's military victory over the sects, while impressive, was by no means complete, and was certainly not as decisive as some Americans were led to believe. For example, an NSC report of 1958 mentioned that the Vietnamese Armed Forces were still operating against the sects, and had "succeeded in practically eliminating the Binh Xuyen and Cao Dai forces. . . ." The Deputy Chief, MAAG, Vietnam, stated in April, 1959, that: "The Binh Xuyen group was completely eliminated as a menace. The Cao Dai group was pacified or reoriented. . . . The Hoa Hao had been reduced to a handful of the diehards. . . ." These estimates notwithstanding, Binh Xuyen remnants fought off an ARVN force north of Bien Hoa, in 1956, and marauded along the Saigon River north of Saigon in Binh Duong province throughout 1957 and 1958. In 1958, an insurgent force, among whom Binh Xuyen were identified, sacked the Michelin rubber plantations near Dau Tieng, and in March, 1959, ARVN had a number of encounters with Binh Xuyen elements in the Binh Duong–Bien Hoa area. There is evidence, though scanty, which indicates that the Binh Xuyen survivors joined with "communist" groups for their depredations; for example, in the 1958 Michelin attack the combined gangster–communist strength was reported to be 300–400. ARVN General Nguyen Chanh Thi, who fought these particular forces, has told of capturing a Binh Xuyen soldier who died under torture without admitting more than that his band had been communicating with communist forces from Tay Ninh province. The general also described capturing in March, 1959, in the same operations, flags identical to that raised in late 1960 by the "National Liberation Front."

In 1956, the Cao Dai Pope, Pham Cong Tac, crossed the frontier of Tay Ninh into Cambodia with a number of his followers, thence to remain in opposition to Diem. Bay Dom, who had been the deputy of the captured Hoa Hao leader, Ba Cut, also took his forces to the Cambodian border. In 1956, Diem sent Ba Cut, his hair still uncut, to the guillotine. Bay Dom and another Hoa Hao leader, Muoi Tri, then took an oath to avenge Ba Cut, and opened guerrilla warfare against Diem. Some four Hoa Hao battalions are reported to have conducted operations against the GVN continuously through 1962. Muoi Tri in later years openly embraced the Viet Cong cause.

In brief, while Diem's victory over the sects was impressive, it was not wholly conclusive, and the very obduracy and determination which won him early tactical success seemed to impede his inducing the remaining sect dissidents to perform a constructive role in the nation. Rather, his policy invited a Viet Cong–sect alliance against him. That some of the more startling early defeats of Diem's ARVN forces by Viet Cong in 1959 and 1960 occurred in the regions north of Saigon, where lurked Cao Dai and Binh Xuyen remnants, is more than coincidental.

D. RURAL PACIFICATION

1. Strategy

Americans tended to look at Diem's skein of military and political successes in 1955 with satisfaction, and to regard thereafter Vietnam's internal security with growing complacency. But Ngo Dinh Diem did not. To the contrary, Diem seemed, if anything, over-conscious of the fact that his test with the Viet Minh lay ahead, and that they posed a threat more dangerous than the sects could ever have been, not only because they were politically more pervasive, and not only because they had taught a generation of Vietnamese peasants the techniques of armed conspiracy, but also because their tenets offered competing solutions to the most pressing problems of the Vietnamese people: land and livelihood. Diem's counter is difficult to fault as a broad concept: ARVN forces would reclaim for the GVN regions formerly held by the Viet Minh; political indoctrination teams moving with the troops would carry the message of Diem's revolution to the people; and then a broad follow-up program of Civic Action—political and social development, land reform, and agricultural improvements would be inaugurated to meet fully the aspirations of the people. That these plans miscarried was due in part to the resistance of the farmers they were intended to benefit, reacting sometimes under Viet Cong leadership, sometimes simply out of peasant conservatism. But a principal portion of the blame for failure must be attributed to Diem's inept, overbearing, or corrupt officials, to Diem's own unremitting anti-communist zeal, and to the failure of both he and his American advisers to appreciate the magnitude of the tasks they set for themselves, or the time required to enact meaningful reform.

2.   Reoccupying Viet Minh Territory

The first steps were faltering. In early 1955, ARVN units were sent to establish the GVN in the Camau Peninsula in the southernmost part of the country. Poorly led, ill-trained, and heavy-handed, the troops behaved towards the people very much as the Viet Minh had led the farmers to expect. Accompanying GVN propaganda teams were more effective, assailing communism, colonialism, and feudalism—meaning the rule of Francophile Vietnamese, such as Bao Dai's—and distributing pictures of Diem to replace the omnipresent tattered portraits of Ho. A subsequent operation in Quang Nai and Binh Dinh, Operation *Giai Phong*, reportedly went off more smoothly. Under ARVN Colonel Le Van Kim, the troops behaved well toward the people, and the propagandists exploited Viet Minh errors to the extent that, as the last Viet Minh soldiers marched down toward their ships, the populace jeered them. American advisers were active, and Diem himself visited this operation a week after the last Viet Minh had left, receiving what the Americans present considered a spontaneous welcome by the peasants. Nonetheless, the Cau Mau experience became more typical of the ARVN than the Binh Dinh affair. Foreign observers frequently expressed opinion of the ARVN in terms similar to the 1957 view of correspondent David Hotham, who wrote that "far from giving security, there is every reason to suppose that the army, buttressed by the Civil Guard . . . is regarded by the Southern peasant as a symbol of insecurity and repression."

3.   Civic Action

Nor were the follow-up Civic Action teams significantly more effective. These were patterned after the GAM's (Groupes Administratifs Mobiles) with which the French had experimented, modified to incorporate U.S.–Filipino experience. In theory, they were to have been drawn from the urban elite, to help the government establish communications with the rural folk. Acting on the doctrine of "Three Withs: eat, sleep, and work with the people"—some 1400 to 1800 "cadre" undertook: census and surveys of the physical needs of villages; building schools, maternity hospitals, information halls; repairing and enlarging local roads; digging wells and irrigation canals; teaching personal and public hygiene; distributing medicine; teaching children by day, and anti-illiteracy classes by night; forming village militia; conducting political meetings; and publicizing agrarian reform legislation.

Colonel Lansdale described their origins and operations as follows:

> One of the most promising ideas of this period came from Kieu Cong Cung, who was sponsored by Defense Minister Minh. Cung's idea was to place civil service personnel out among the people, in simple dress, where they would help initially by working alongside the people, getting their hands dirty when necessary. The Vietnamese functionaries were aghast, since they cherished their desk work in Saigon and their dignified white-collar authority, and they fought hard within the government machine to kill the idea. It took some months, with the personal intervention and insistence of President Diem, to get a pilot Civic Action program initiated. It was given administrative support by the Ministry of Defense, at first, simply because no other Ministry would help, although it was established as an entity of the Presidency and its policy decisions were made in Cabinet meetings.
>
> With 80% of the civil service personnel stationed in the national capital, provincial administrators were so under-staffed that few of them could function with even minimum effectiveness. A French colonial administrative system, super-imposed upon the odd Vietnamese imperial system was still the model for government administration. It left many gaps and led to unusually complex bureaucratic practices. There was no uniform legal code, no uniform procedures for the most basic functions of government. The Communists continued their political dominance of many villages, secretly.
>
> Cung established a training center in Saigon and asked for civil service volunteers, for field duty. With none forthcoming, he then selected a small group of young university trained men from among the . . . refugees from Communist North Vietnam after security screening. His training had added realism in the form of rough living quarters, outdoor classes, and students learning to work with their hands by constructing school facilities. All students had to dress in the "calico noir" of farmers and laborers, which became their "uniform" later in the villages. (Provincial authorities originally refused to recognize Civic Action personnel as government officials, due to the plebian dress; Cung, dressed in the same manner, and as a high functionary close to the President, made a rapid tour of the provinces and gained grudging acceptance of this new style of government employee.)
>
> Originally, four-man teams were formed; during training, the members of each team were closely observed, to judge their abilities, with the weak and unwilling being weeded out. After graduation, each team was assigned to a district of a province, with responsibility for a number of villages. When the team finished its work in the first village, it would move to a second village, revisiting the first village periodically to check on local progress. This would continue until all villages in a district were covered, at which time the civic action team directly under the government in the provincial capital would take over district work, now organized and ready for administration.
>
> When a team entered a village, they would call a village meeting, explain their presence and plans. The following morning, they would set to work to build three community buildings with local materials; if they had been successful in winning over the population, the villagers pitched in and helped.

One building was a village hall, for meetings of village officials. Another was a primary school. The third was a combination information hall (news, information about the government, etc.) and dispensary (using the village medical kits developed by ICA). Following up was the building of roads or paths to link the village with provincial roads, if in a remote area, build pit latrines, undertake malaria control, put in drainage, and undertake similar community projects. Villagers were trained to take over these tasks, including primary education and first aid.

The work of Civic Action teams, at the same grass-roots level as that of Communist workers, proved effective. They became the targets of Communist agents, with political attacks (such as stirring up local Cochin-Chinese against Tonkinese Civic Action personnel) and then murders. Even while the field work was in its early development stage, President Diem ordered the teams to start working directly with Army commands in pacification campaigns, as the civil government "troops" in what were essentially combat zones. As Civic Action proved itself, it was extended to all provinces south of the 17th Parallel.

Had the cadres been able to confine themselves to these missions, and had the several Saigon ministries, whose field responsibilities they had assumed, been content to have them continue to represent them, matters might have developed differently. As it happened, the cadres became preoccupied with Diem's Anti-Communist campaign, and their operations came under bureaucratic attack from Saigon agencies unwilling to allow the Civic Action teams to carry their programs to the people. Both influences converted the cadre into exclusively propagandistic and political instruments, and drew them away from economic or social activities; in late 1956, Civic Action was cut back severely. In 1957, Kieu Cong Cung died, and Nhu absorbed the remnants into his organization.

4. Land Reform

But the salesmen were less at fault than the product. Diem had to promise much and deliver well to best the Viet Minh. However, his promises were moderate, his delivery on them both slow and incomplete. The anarchy prevalent in the countryside during the First Indochina War had benefited the peasant by driving off the French and Vietnamese large landlords. When the Viet Minh "liberated" an area, they distributed these lands free to the farmers, and generally won their allegiance thereby. Columnist Joseph Alsop visited one such Viet Minh controlled region in December, 1954, just before they withdrew their military forces, and reported that:

> It was difficult for me, as it is for any Westerner, to conceive of a Communist government's genuinely "serving the people." I could hardly imagine a Communist government that was also a popular government and almost a democratic government. But this was just the sort of government the palm-hut state actually was while the struggle with the French continued. The Viet Minh could not possibly have carried on the resistance for one year, let alone nine years, without the people's strong, untied support.

One of Diem's primary failures lay in his inability similarly to capture loyalties among his 90 percent agricultural people. The core of rural discontent was the large land holdings: in 1954 one quarter of one percent of the population owned forty percent of the rice growing land. The Diem program to ameliorate this situation for the land-hungry peasants took the form of: (1) resettlement of refugees and others on uncultivated land, begun in 1955; (2) expropriation of all rice land holdings above 247 acres, and redistribution of these to tenant farmers, a program announced in 1956, but delayed in starting until 1958; and (3) regulation of landlord-tenant relations, effected in 1957, which fixed rents within the range 15–25 percent of crop yield, and guaranteed tenant tenure for 3 to 5 years. Both the resettlement and redistribution programs guaranteed payments to former owners of the appropriated land; although the land was reasonably priced, and payment allowed over an extended period, the farmers faced payments, and these immediately aroused opposition. Settlers moved into a wilderness, required to clear and irrigate theretofore unused land, could not see why they should pay for their holdings. Tenant farmers were also disaffected, for though rents of 40 percent of crop had been common before the way, many farmers, after eight or so rent-free years, could see no justice in resuming payments to a long absent owner, particularly since the Viet Minh had assured them the land was theirs by right. Nor were many mollified by redistributed land. Land redistribution suffered according to one American expert, from a "lack of serious, interested administrators and topside command. Government officials, beginning with the Minister for Agrarian Reform, had divided loyalties, being themselves landholders." But even if the goals of the program had been honestly fulfilled—which they were not—only 20% of rice land would have passed from large to small farmers. Ultimately only 10% of all tenant farmers benefited. A bolder program, with a maximum holding of 124 acres, could have put 33 percent of rice land up for transfer. As it happened, however, the distribution program was not only of limited scope, but, by 1958 or 1959, it was virtually inoperative. Bernard Fall has reported that despite Diem's land reforms, 45% of the land remained concentrated in the hands of 2% of landowners, and 75% in the hands of 15%. Moreover, since the immediate beneficiaries were more often than not Northerners, refugees, and Catholics, the programs acquired an aura of GVN favoritism, and deepened peasant alienation. In time there were also rumors of corruption, with widespread allegations that the Diem family had enriched itself through the manipulation of the land transfers.

As an example of Diem's rural programs in action at the village level which serves to demonstrate how they fell wide of the mark of meeting rural expectations, that of the village communal land is instructive. After the long period of disrupted public administration during the Franco–Viet Minh War, land records were chaotic. Under Diem, the GVN seized outright nearly half a million acres of land whose title was unclear. Some of this land was rented, the GVN acting as the landlord; some was farmed by ARVN units; and some was converted into communal land and the title passed to village councils. The village councils were then supposed to hold an annual auction of communal land, in which farmers wishing to use certain plots submitted sealed bids. Although this seemed to the casual western observer an equitable system, in actuality it was quite vicious. The bidding farmers were usually seeking to rent land they had been farming free for years. Whether this were the case or not, however, rice growing is a labor intensive process which requires of the farmer a substantial capital investment year by year to build up dikes and ditches. To assure himself that he would not lose this investment, a man farming a plot declared communal land felt compelled to raise his bid each succeeding year to avoid loss of that capital, and to preclude losing his hard work. The consequent competition, however modern, shook the roots of traditional Asian farming communities, for the arrangement had the major disadvantage of creating uncertainty over land from year to year—the antithesis of security for the rice-growing peasant. To cap these disadvantages, village councils were often less than honest, and tended to be considerably less willing than a paternal landlord to tide the farmer over after a bad crop year; if his subsequent bid were low, he lost his land.

There is another chapter in the history of GVN–farmer relationships which illustrates similar clumsiness. In 1956, as the GVN launched its land reform program, Ngo Dinh Nhu enlisted the aid of the Confederation of Vietnamese Labor, which had been organizing tenant farmers in promoting the government's policies through its rural representatives. The GVN then proceeded to form its own, NRM-connected, Farmers' Associations. The latter, interconnected with province officials and with landowners, actively opposed the union organizers, with the result that many of the latter were jailed. Within a year or two, the union was destroyed for all practical purposes. Few of the NRM Farmers' Associations ever did function on behalf of the farmers; of 288 associations reported in-being by the GVN, a USOM study in 1961 could find only 35 which represented peasant interersts in any active sense.

5. *Village Government*

A further example of Diem's maladroitness was his abolishing elections for village councils, a step he took in June, 1956, apparently out of concern that large numbers of former Viet Minh might win office at the village level. The Vietnamese village had traditionally, even under the French, enjoyed administrative autonomy, and the village council was a coterie of prominent residents who were the government in most simple civic matters, adjudicating disputes, collecting taxes, and managing public funds. Under the national regulation of 1956, members of council and the village chief became appointive officials, and their offices subject to scrutiny by the Diemist apparatus. The results were again a thrusting forward of Northern Catholics, city dwellers, or other non-local trustees of the GVN, to assume control at the key political level of South Vietnam, to handle fiscal matters, and to manage the communal lands. For the same reasons that the villagers had mistrusted the Civic Action cadre, they found the GVN officials strange, and not a little incomprehensible. Also, since these officials were the creatures of the province chiefs, corruption at the province level—then, as in recent years, not uncommon—was transmitted directly to the village. Dang Duc Khoi, a young nationalist who rose to become Diem's press officer, and then turned against him, regarded Diem's decision to abolish the village councils his vital error:

> Even if the Viet Minh had won some elections, the danger of doing away with the traditional system of village election was even greater. This was something that was part of the Vietnamese way of life, and the concept should have been retained without interfering with Diem's legitimate desire —indeed, his need—for a strong central government. The security problem existed, but it wouldn't have made much difference if the Viet Minh had elected some village chiefs—they soon established their own underground governments anyway. Diem's mistake was in paralyzing himself. He should have adopted a more intelligent and persuasive policy and concentrated at the outset on obtaining the support of the people. In that way, he could have properly challenged the Viet Minh.

Thus, Ngo Dinh began, in 1956, to place the "security problem" ahead of rural revolution.

6. The Anti-Communist Campaign

Indeed, vocal anti-communism became more central to Diem's rural programs than land reform. Like the Can Lao Party, the GVN borrowed heavily from communist technique in combating the Viet Minh and their residual influence—urged on, in some instances at least, by their American advisers. In the summer of 1955, the government launched an Anti-Communist Denunciation Campaign, which included a scheme for classifying the populace into lettered political groups according to attitude toward the Viet Minh, and village ceremonies similar to community self criticism sessions. Viet Minh cadres and sympathizers would appear before the audience to swear their disavowal of communism. The penitents would tell tales of Viet Minh atrocities, and rip or trample a suitable Viet Minh symbol. In February, 1956, tens of thousands of Saigon citizens assembled to witness the "conversion" of 2,000 former Viet Minh cadres. Tran Chanh Tanh, head of the GVN Department of Information and Youth, announced in May, 1956, that the campaign had "entirely destroyed the predominant communist influence of the previous nine years." According to his figures, 94,041 former communist cadres had rallied to the GVN, 5,613 other cadres had surrendered to government forces, 119,954 weapons had been captured, 75 tons of documents, and 707 underground arms caches had been discovered. One Saigon newspaper boldly referred to Tanh's proceedings as a "puppet show"—for which it was closed down. What relationship GVN statistics bore to reality is not known.

However, for many peasants the Anti-Communist Campaign was considerably more than theatrics. Diem, in a Presidential Ordinance of January 11, 1956, expanded upon an existing system of political re-education centers for communists and active communist supporters. The 1956 order authorized the arrest and detention of anyone deemed dangerous to the safety of the state, and their incarceration in one of several concentration camps. The Secretary of State for Information disclosed in 1956 that 15,000 to 20,000 communists had been in these centers since 1954, a figure probably low at the time, and undoubtedly raised thereafter. On May 6, 1959, the GVN promulgated Law 10/59, which stiffened penalties for communist affiliations, and permitted trial of accused by special military tribunals. That year Anti-Communist Denunciation was also stepped up. In 1960, a GVN Ministry of Information release stated that 48,250 persons had been jailed between 1954 and 1960, but a French observer estimates the numbers in jail at the end of 1956 alone at 50,000. P. J. Honey, who was invited by Diem to investigate certain of the reeducation centers in 1959, reported that on the basis of his talks with former inmates, "the consensus of the opinions expressed by these people is that . . . the majority of the detainees are neither communists nor pro-communists."

The Anti-Communist Campaigns targeted city-dwellers, but it was in the rural areas, where the Viet Minh had been most strong, that it was applied most energetically. For example, in 1959 the Information Chief of An Xuyen Province (Cau Mau region) reported that a five week Anti-Communist Campaign by the National Revolutionary Movement had resulted in the surrender of 8,125 communist agents, and the denunciation of 9,806 other agents and 29,978 sympathizers. To furnish the organization and spark enthusiasm for such undertakings, Ngo Dinh Nhu organized in 1958 the Republican Youth, which with Madame

Nhu's Solidarity Movement, became a vehicle for rural paramilitary training, political, and intelligence activities. Nhu saw the Republican Youth as a means for bringing "controlled liberty" to the countryside, and it seems certainly to have assisted in extending his control.

The GVN also tried to reorganize rural society from the family level up on the communist cellular model. Each family was grouped with two to six others into a Mutual Aid Family Group (*lien gia*), and a like number of *lien gia* comprised a khom. There was an appointed chief for both, serving as a chain of command for the community, empowered to settle petty disputes, and obligated to pass orders and information down from the authorities. Each *lien gia* was held responsible for the political behavior of its members, and was expected to report suspicious behavior (the presence of strangers, unusual departures, and like events). Each house was required to display on a board outside a listing of the number and sex of its inhabitants. These population control measures were combined with improved systems of provincial police identification cards and fingerprinting. The central government thus became visible—and resented—at the village level as it had never been before in Vietnam.

7. *Population Relocation*

Security and control of the populace also figured in GVN resettlement plans. Even the refugee relief programs had been executed with an eye to national security. Diem visualized a "living wall" of settlers between the lowland populace and the jungle and mountain redoubts of dissidents. From flying trips, or from military maps, he personally selected the sites for resettlement projects (*Khu Dinh Dien*)—often in locales deprived of adequate water or fertile soil—to which were moved pioneering communities of Northern refugees, or settlers from the over-crowded Annam coast. Between April 1957 and late 1961, one GVN report showed 210,000 persons resettled in 147 centers carved from 220,-000 acres of wilderness. Some of the resentments over payments for resettled virgin land were mentioned above. More importantly, however, these "strategic" programs drew a disproportionate share of foreign aid for agriculture; by U.S. estimates, the 2% of total population affected by resettlement received 50% of total aid.

The resettlements precipitated unexpected political reactions from the Montagnard peoples of the Central Vietnam Highlands. The tribes were traditionally hostile to the Vietnamese, and proved to be easily mobilized against the GVN. In 1959 the GVN began to regroup and consolidate the tribes into defensible communities to decrease their vulnerability to anti-government agents, and to ease the applying of cultural uplift programs. By late 1961 these relocations were being executed on a large scale. In Kontum Province, for instance, 35,000 tribesmen were regrouped in autumn 1961, about 50 percent of its total Montagnard population. Some of the hill people refused to remain in their new communities, but the majority stayed. In the long run, the relocations probably had the effect of focusing Montagnard discontent against the GVN, and facilitating, rather than hindering, the subversion of the tribes.

But the relocations which catalyzed the most widespread and dangerous anti-GVN sentiment were those attempted among the South Vietnamese farmers beginning in 1959. In February, 1959, a pilot program of political bifurcation was quietly launched in the areas southwest of Saigon which had been controlled by the Viet Minh. Its objective was to resettle peasants out of areas where GVN police or military forces could not operate routinely, into new, policed communities of two distinct political colorations. Into one type of these "rural agglomerations," called *qui khu,* where grouped families with relatives among the Viet Minh or Viet Cong, or suspected of harboring pro-Viet Cong sentiments. Into another type, called *qui ap,* where grouped GVN-oriented families. Security was the primary reason for selecting the sites of these communities, which meant that in many instances the peasants were forced to move some distance from their land. The French had attempted, on a small scale, such peasant relocations in 1953 in Tonkin; Diem encountered in 1959, as had they, stiff resistance from the farmers over separation from their livelihood and ancestral landhold. But Diem's plan also aroused apprehensions during *qui khu* designates over the Anti-Communist Campaign. With a rare sensitivity to rural protest, the GVN suspended the program in March, 1959, after only a month.

In July, 1959, however, Diem announced that the GVN was undertaking to improve rural standards of living through establishing some 80 "prosperity and density centers" (*khu tru mat*). These "agrovilles" were to be located along a "strategic route system"—key roads, protected by the new towns. Some 80 agrovilles were to be built by the end of 1963, each designed for 400 families (2,000 to 3,000 people), and each with a surrounding cluster of smaller agrovilles for 120 families. The GVN master plan provided for each community defense, schools, dispensary, market center, public garden—even electricity. The new communities seemed to offer the farmers many advantages, and the GVN expected warm support. But the peasants objected to the agrovilles even more sharply than they had the earlier experiment. The agrovilles were supposed to be constructed by peasants themselves; *Corvee* labor was resorted to, and thousands of Republican Youth were imported to help. For example, at one site—Vi Thanh near Can Tho—20,000 peasants were assembled from four districts, many more than the number who could expect to profit directly from the undertaking. Moreover, even most of those who were selected to move into agrovilles they had helped build, did so unwillingly, for it often meant abandoning a cherished ancestral home, tombs, and developed gardens and fields for a strange and desolate place. The settler was expected to tear down his old house to obtain materials for the new, and received GVN aid to the extent of a grant of $5.50, and an agricultural loan to assist him in paying for his allotted 1.5 acres of land near the agroville. Peasant resistance, and then insurgent attacks on the agrovilles, caused abandonment of the program, with only 22 out of 80 communities completed.

The agroville program was eventually superseded by the GVN strategic hamlet program, formally launched by President Diem in February, 1962, which avoided the mistake of trying to erect whole new communities from the ground up. Rather, the plan aimed at fortifying existing villages, but did include provisions for destroying indefensible hamlets, and relocation of the inhabitants into more secure communities. The strategic hamlet, *ap chien luoc,* also eschewed elaborate social or economic development schemes, concentrating on civil defense through crude fortifications and organizing the populace to improve its military capability and political cohesiveness. In some exposed sites, "combat hamlets" were established, with a wholly militarized population. High goals were established, the GVN announcing that by 1963 some 11,000 of the country's 16,000–17,000 hamlets would be fortified. In this instance, as before, the GVN encountered opposition from the peasants, and as before, the insurgents attacked it vigorously. Despite its relative sophistication, the strategic hamlet program, like its predecessors, drove a wedge not between the insurgents and the farmers but between the farmers and the GVN, and eventuated in less rather than more security in the countryside.

8. Rural Security Forces

Security was the foremost consideration of the GVN's rural programs, and American aid was lavished on the GVN security apparatus in general. It is surprising, therefore, that the GVN tolerated so ineffective a security apparatus at the village level. The Self-Defense Corps (SDC) and the Civil Guard (CG), charged with rural security, were poorly trained and equipped, miserably led, and incapable of coping with insurgents; they could scarcely defend themselves, much less the peasantry. Indeed, they proved to be an asset to insurgents in two respects: they served as a source of weapons; and their brutality, petty thievery, and disorderliness induced innumerable villagers to join in open revolt against the GVN. Nor was the ARVN much better, although its conduct improved over the years; in any event, the ARVN seldom was afield, and its interaction with the rural populace through 1959 was relatively slight. It should be noted that the SDC and the CG, the security forces at the disposal of the provincial administration, were often no more venal nor offensive to the peasants than the local officials themselves. Corrupt, arrogant, and overbearing, the men the people knew as the GVN were among the greatest disadvantages of the GVN in its rural efforts.

E. URBAN POLITICAL ALIENATION

The rigidity of GVN rural political policy was mirrored in the cities: the regime became preoccupied with security to the exclusion of other concerns, with the result that step by step it narrowed its active or potential supporters, aroused increasing fears among its critics, and drove them toward extremism. In a step similar to that he took on village council elections, Diem abolished elections for municipal councils in 1956. The Anti-Communist Denunciation Campaign had its urban counterpart, but communist strength in the French-occupied cities had been less than in the countryside. Opposition to Diem formed around the old nationalist movements, including the pro-Bao Dai groups Diem labeled "feudalists," around intellectual and individual professional politicians, and eventually around military leaders. Diem's policies successively alienated each.

1. "Feudalists"

The Civic Action teams which Diem projected into the former Viet Minh areas in 1955 trumpeted against "Communism, Colonialism, and Feudalism," the last inveighing against Bao Dai, who was, at the time, still Head of state. "Feudalist" was one epithet applied sweepingly to the religious sects, and to all those whose position or fortune depended upon Bao Dai, from the Binh Xuyen who had purchased its control over Saigon-Cholon from the Emperor, to civil servants and army officers loyal to Bao Dai. The label was virtually as damning as "Communist" in incurring the ungentle attentions of Nhu or Can. In the early years "feudalists" and "communists" were often tarred by the same brush. For example, the Anti-Communist Denunciation Campaign got underway in Quang Tri Province in 1955, under Ngo Dinh Can. But Can was also in pursuit of the anticommunist Dai Viet (Great Vietnam) Party there, which had armed units and, for a time, an anti-government radio station. As with the communists, many Dai Viet were killed, imprisoned, or driven into exile. Diem's defeat of Bao Dai at the polls in October, 1955, strengthened his hand against pro-Bao Dai groups.

With the withdrawal of the French the following spring, it became imprudent for any politician or group who wished to avoid *Can Lao* and NRM scrutiny to maintain ties with "feudalists" in hiding in Vietnam, or operating from abroad. Despite the fact that opposition Vietnamese nationalist parties had been strongly influenced in their organization and methods by the Kuomintang, they had never developed sufficient internal discipline, cohesion or following to admit of challenging Diem after 1956. Such opposition political forces as developed centered around individuals. (Only two non-Diem, non-communist political parties survived the Diem era: the Nationalist Party of Greater Vietnam (*Dai Viet Qhoc Dan Dang,* the Dai Viet) and the Vietnamese Nationalist Party (*Viet Nam Quoc Dan Dang,* the VNQDD)).

2. Dr. Dan

Until November, 1960, Diem's most prominent political opponent was Doctor Phan Quang Dan. Dr. Dan was a northern physician who had been caught up in nationalist politics in 1945, and lived in exile after 1947. He returned to Vietnam in September, 1955, to head up a coalition of opposition to the GVN arrangements for the March, 1956, elections for the National Assembly. He was arrested on the eve of those elections, accused of communist and colonialist activities, and though released, deprived of his position at the University of Saigon Medical School. His subsequent political career underscores the astringent nature of Diem's democracy. In May, 1957 Dr. Dan formed another opposition coalition, the Democratic bloc, which acquired a newspaper called *Thoi Luan. Thoi Luan* became the best-selling newspaper in South Vietnam (all papers were published in Saigon, except Can's government paper in Hue), with a circulation of about 80,000 copies. After a series of statements critical of the GVN, *Thoi Luan* was sacked by a mob in September, 1957. Unheeding of that warning, the paper continued an opposition editorial policy until March, 1958, when the GVN closed the paper, and gave the editor a stiff fine and a suspended prison sentence for an article including the following passage:

> What about your democratic election?
> During the city-council and village council elections under the "medieval and colonialist" Nguyen Van Tam Administration [under Bao-Dai, in 1953], constituents were threatened and compelled to vote; but they were still better than your elections, because nobody brought soldiers into Saigon by the truckload "to help with the voting."
> What about your presidential regime?
> You are proud for having created for Viet-Nam a regime that you think is similar to that of the United States. If those regimes are similar, then they are as related as a skyscraper is to a tin-roofed shack, in that they both are houses to live in.
> In the U.S.A., Congress is a true parliament and Congressmen are legislators, i.e., free and disinterested men who are not afraid of the government, and who know their duties and dare to carry them out. Here the deputies are political functionaries who make laws like an announcer in a radio station, by reading out loud texts that have been prepared [for them] beforehand. . . .

A month later, the Democratic Bloc collapsed. Dr. Dan attempted to obtain GVN recognition for another party, the Free Democratic Party, and permission to publish another paper. No GVN action was ever taken on either application, but a number of Dr. Dan's followers in the new party were arrested. When in March, 1959, the newspaper *Tin Bac* published an article by Dr. Dan, it was closed down. In June, 1959, the newspaper *Nguoi Viet Tu Do* was similarly indiscreet, and met the same fate. In August, 1959, Dr. Dan ran for a seat in the National Assembly, was elected by a six-to-one margin over Diem's candidate unning against him, but was disqualified by court action before he could take his ?at. Dr. Dan's career of opposition to Diem ended in November, 1960, when ..e became the political adviser to the group who attempted a *coup d'etat*. Dan was arrested and jailed, and remained there until the end of the Diem regime three years later.

3.   *The Caravelle Group, 1960*

But Dr. Dan was an exceptionally bold antagonist of Diem. No other politician dared what he did. Even he, however, was unable to bring any unity to the opposition. Such other leaders as there were distrusted Dan, or feared the GVN. There was, however, one occasion in the spring of 1960 when opposition to Diem did coalesce. There was change in the international political winds that year—a students' revolt in Korea, an army revolt in Turkey, demonstrations in Japan which resulted in cancellation of President Eisenhower's planned visit. Diem remembered 1960 well, as a "treasure chest for the communists."

> The United States press and the world press started saying that democracy was needed in the under-developed countries. This came just in time for the communists. Some of the United States press even incited people to rebellion.
>
> That year was the worst we have ever had . . . We had problems on all fronts. On the one hand we had to fight the communists. On the other, we had to deal with the foreign press campaign to incite rebellion vis-a-vis Korea. These were sore anxieties, for some unbalanced people here thought it was time to act. Teachers in the private secondary schools began to incite the students to follow the example of the Korean students. And then there were our amateur politicians who were outdated and thought only of taking revenge. . . .

The last reference was to the Caravelle Group, who issued at the Caravelle Hotel in late April, 1960, a "manifesto" of grievances against the GVN. The eighteen signers were all old-time politicans, leaders of the Cao Dai and Hoa Hao sects, the Dai Viet and the VNQDD parties, and dissenting Catholic groups. Eleven had been Cabinet ministers; four had been in other high government positions. They organized themselves as the Bloc for Liberty and Progress, with a platform of constitutional revision toward greater power for the National Assembly against the Presidency. Dr. Dan could not be induced to join the Caravelle Group, but in the Diem cleanup after the November, 1960 coup attempt, the GVN arrested most of the eighteen, and their Bloc disintegrated. The Caravelle Manifesto is reproduced below:

MANIFESTO OF THE EIGHTEEN

The President of the Republic of Viet-Nam
Saigon

Mr. President:

We the undersigned, representing a group of eminent citizens and personalities, intellectuals of all tendencies, and men of good will, recognize in the face of the gravity of the present political situation that we can no longer remain indifferent to the realities of life in our country.

Therefore, we officially address to you today an appeal with the aim of exposing to you the whole truth in the hope that the government will accord it all the attention necessary so as to urgently modify its policies, so as to remedy the present situation and lead the people out of danger.

Let us look toward the past, at the time when you were abroad. For eight or nine years, the Vietnamese people suffered many trials due to the war: They passed from French domination to Japanese occupation, from revolution to resistance, from the nationalist imposture behind which hid communism to a pseudo-independence covering up for colonialism; from terror to terror, from sacrifice to sacrifice—in short, from promise to promise, until finally hope ended in bitter disillusion.

Thus, when you were on the point of returning to the country, the people as a whole entertained the hope that it would find again under your guidance the peace that is necessary to give meaning to existence, to reconstruct the destroyed homes, put to the plow again the abandoned lands. The people hoped no longer to be compelled to pay homage to one regime in the morning and to another at night, not to be the prey of the cruelties and oppression of one faction; no longer to be treated as coolies; no longer to be at the mercy of the monopolies; no longer to have to endure the depredations of corrupt and despotic civil servants. In one word, the people hoped to live in security at last, under a regime which would give them a little bit of justice and liberty. The whole people thought that you would be the man of the situation and that you would implement its hopes.

That is the way it was when you returned. The Geneva Accords of 1954 put an end to combat and to the devastations of war. The French Expeditionary Corps was progressively withdrawn, and total independence of South Viet Nam had become a reality. Furthermore, the country had benefited from moral encouragement and a substantial increase of foreign aid from the free world. With so many favorable political factors, in addition to the blessed geographic conditions of a fertile and rich soil yielding agricultural, forestry, and fishing surpluses, South Viet Nam should have been able to begin a definitive victory in the historical competition with the North, so as to carry out the will of the people and to lead the country on the way to hope, liberty, and happiness. Today, six years later, having benefited from so many undeniable advantages, what has the government been able to do? Where has it led South Viet Nam? What parts of the popular aspirations have been implemented?

Let us try to draw an objective balance of the situation, without flattery or false accusations, strictly following a constructive line which you yourself have so often indicated, in the hope that the government shall modify its policies so as to extricate itself from a situation that is extremely dangerous to the very existence of the nation.

Policies

In spite of the fact that the bastard regime created and protected by colonialism has been overthrown and that many of the feudal organizations of factions and parties which oppress the population were destroyed, the people do not know a better life or more freedom under the republican regime which you have created. A constitution has been established in form only;

a National Assembly exists whose deliberations always fall into line with the government; antidemocratic elections—all those are methods and "comedies" copied from the dictatorial Communist regimes, which obviously cannot serve as terms of comparison with North Viet Nam.

Continuous arrests fill the jails and prisons to the rafters, as at this precise moment; public opinion and the press are reduced to silence. The same applies to the popular will as translated in certain open elections, in which it is insulted and trampled (as was the case, for example, during the recent elections for the Second Legislature). All these have provoked the discouragement and resentment of the people.

Political parties and religious sects have been eliminated. "Groups" or "movements" have replaced them. But this substitution has only brought about new oppressions against the population without protecting it for that matter against Communist enterprises. Here is one example: the fiefs of religious sects, which hitherto were deadly for the Communists, now not only provide no security whatever but have become favored highways for Viet Minh guerrillas, as is, by the way, the case of the rest of the country.

This is proof that the religious sects, though futile, nevertheless constitute effective anti-Communist elements. Their elimination has opened the way to the Viet Cong and unintentionally has prepared the way for the enemy, whereas a more realistic and more flexible policy could have amalgamated them all with a view to reinforcing the anti-Communist front.

Today the people want freedom. You should, Mr. President, liberalize the regime, promote democracy, guarantee minimum civil rights, recognize the opposition so as to permit the citizens to express themselves without fear, thus removing grievances and resentments, opposition to which now constitutes for the people their sole reason for existence. When this occurs, the people of South Viet Nam, in comparing their position with that of the North, will appreciate the value of true liberty and of authentic democracy. It is only at that time that the people will make all the necessary efforts and sacrifices to defend that liberty and democracy.

Administration

The size of the territory has shrunk, but the number of civil servants has increased, and still the work doesn't get done. This is because the government, like the Communists, lets the political parties control the population, separate the elite from the lower echelons, and sow distrust between those individuals who are "affiliated with the movement" and those who are "outside the group." Effective power, no longer in the hands of those who are usually responsible, is concentrated in fact in the hands of an irresponsible member of the "family," from whom emanates all orders; this slows down the administrative machinery, paralyzes all initiative, discourages good will. At the same time, not a month goes by without the press being full of stories about graft impossible to hide; this becomes an endless parade of illegal transactions involving millions of piastres.

The administrative machinery, already slowed down, is about to become completely paralyzed. It is in urgent need of reorganization. Competent people should be put back in the proper jobs; discipline must be re-established from the top to the bottom of the hierarchy; authority must go hand in hand with responsibility; efficiency, initiative, honesty, and the economy should be the criteria for promotion; professional qualifications should be respected. Favoritism based on family or party connections should be banished; the selling of influence, corruption and abuse of power must be punished.

Thus, everything still can be saved, human dignity can be reestablished; faith in an honest and just government can be restored.

Army

The French Expeditionary Corps has left the country, and a republican army has been constituted, thanks to American aid, which has equipped it with modern materiel. Nevertheless, even in a group of the proud elite of the youth such as the Vietnamese Army—where the sense of honor should be cultivated, whose blood and arms should be devoted to the defense of the country, where there should be no place for clannishness and factions—the spirit of the "national revolutionary movement" or of the "personalist body" divides the men of one and the same unit, sows distrust between friends of the same rank, and uses as a criterion for promotion fidelity toward the party in blind submission to its leaders. This creates extremely dangerous situations, such as the recent incident of Tay-Ninh.*

The purpose of the army, pillar of the defense of the country, is to stop foreign invasions and to eliminate rebel movements. It is at the service of the country only and should not lend itself to the exploitation of any faction or party. Its total reorganization is necessary. Clannishness and party obedience should be eliminated; its moral base strengthened; a noble tradition of national pride created; and fighting spirit, professional conscience, and bravery should become criteria for promotion. The troops should be encouraged to respect their officers, and the officers should be encouraged to love their men. Distrust, jealousy, rancor among colleagues of the same rank should be eliminated.

Then in case of danger, the nation will have at its disposal a valiant army animated by a single spirit and a single aspiration: to defend the most precious possession—our country, Viet Nam.

Economic and Social Affairs

A rich and fertile country enjoying food surpluses; a budget which does not have to face military expenditures,** important war reparations; substantial profits from Treasury bonds; a colossal foreign-aid program; a developing market capable of receiving foreign capital investments—those are the many favorable conditions which could make Viet Nam a productive and prosperous nation. However, at the present time many people are out of work, have no roof over their heads, and no money. Rice is abundant but does not sell; shop windows are well-stocked but the goods do not move. Sources of revenue are in the hands of speculators—who use the [government] party and group to mask monopolies operating for certain private interests. At the same time, thousands of persons are mobilized for exhausting work, compelled to leave their own jobs, homes and families, to participate in the construction of magnificent but useless "agrovilles" which weary them and provoke their disaffection, thus aggravating popular resentment and creating an ideal terrain for enemy propaganda.

* This refers to the penetration of the compound of the 32d ARVN Regiment in January, 1960, when communist forces killed 23 soldiers and captured hundreds of weapons.

** The military expenditures of the Vietnamese budget are paid out of U.S. economic and military aid.

The economy is the very foundation of society, and public opinion ensures the survival of the regime. The government must destroy all the obstacles standing in the way of economic development; must abolish all forms of monopoly and speculation; must create a favorable environment for investments coming from foreign friends as well as from our own citizens; must encourage commercial enterprises, develop industry, and create jobs to reduce unemployment. At the same time, it should put an end to all forms of human exploitation in the work camps of the agrovilles.

Then only the economy will flourish again; the citizen will find again a peaceful life and will enjoy his condition; society will be reconstructed in an atmosphere of freedom and democracy.

Mr. President, this is perhaps the first time that you have heard such severe and disagreeable criticism—so contrary to your own desires. Nevertheless, sir, these words are strictly the truth, a truth that is bitter and hard, that you have never been able to know because, whether this is intended or not, a void has been created around you, and by the very fact of your high position, no one permits you to perceive the critical point at which truth shall burst forth in irresistible waves of hatred on the part of a people subjected for a long time to terrible suffering and a people who shall rise to break the bonds which hold it down. It shall sweep away the ignominy and all the injustices which surround and oppress it.

As we do not wish, in all sincerity, that our Fatherland should have to live through these perilous days, we—without taking into consideration the consequences which our attitude may bring upon us—are ringing today the alarm bell, in view of the imminent danger which threatens the government.

Until now, we have kept silent and preferred to let the Executive act as it wished. But now time is of the essence; we feel that it is our duty—and in the case of a nation in turmoil even the most humble people have their share of responsibility—to speak the truth, to awaken public opinion, to alert the people, and to unify the opposition so as to point the way. We beseech the government to urgently modify its policies so as to remedy the situation, to defend the republican regime, and to safeguard the existence of the nation. We hold firm hope that the Vietnamese people shall know a brilliant future in which it will enjoy peace and prosperity in freedom and progress.

Yours respectfully,

1. TRAN VAN VAN, Diploma of Higher Commercial Studies, former Minister of Economy and Planning
2. PHAN KHAC SUU, Agricultural Engineer, former Minister of Agriculture, former Minister of Labor
3. TRAN VAN HUONG, Professor of Secondary Education, former Prefect of Saigon-Cholon
4. NGUYEN, LUU VIEN, M.D., former Professor at the Medical School, former High Commissioner of Refugees
5. HUYNH-KIM HUU, M.D., former Minister of Public Health
6. PHAN HUY QUAT, M.D., former Minister of National Education, former Minister of Defense
7. TRAN VAN LY, former Governor of Central Viet-Nam
8. NGUYEN TIEN HY, M.D.
9. TRAN VAN DO, M.D., former Minister of Foreign Affairs, Chairman of Vietnamese Delegation to the 1954 Geneva Conference

10. LE NGOC CHAN, Attorney at Law, former Secretary of State for National Defense
11. LE QUANG LUAT, Attorney at Law, former Government Delegate for North Viet-Nam, former Minister of Information and Propaganda
12. LUONG TRONG TUONG, Public Works Engineer, former Secretary of State for National Economy
13. NGUYEN TANG NGUYEN, M.D., former Minister of Labor and Youth
14. PHAM HUU CHUONG, M.D., former Minister of Public Health and Social Action
15. TRAN VAN TUYEN, Attorney at Law, former Secretary of State for Information and Propaganda
16. TA CHUONG PHUNG, former Provincial Governor for Binh-Dinh
17. TRAN LE CHAT, Laureate of the Triennial Mandarin Competition of 1903
18. HO VAN VUI, Reverend, former Parish Priest of Saigon, at present Parish Priest of Tha-La, Province of Tay-Ninh

The November, 1960, coup marked the end of opposition by professional politicians against Diem. In fact, all the Caravelle group were arrested and jailed. Such political activity among them as occurred in 1962 and 1963 was perforce subdued to the point that it captured attention neither from opponents of Diem, nor Diem himself. But 1960 was altogether too late for effective "loyal opposition" to form. By that time the GVN's ability to control the press, to manage demonstrations, to limit travel, and to imprison (and worse) at will, had virtually paralyzed the intellectual elite of Vietnam. Nor were labor unions politically active, despite their power potential. As early as 1956 the GVN had become alarmed over Communist influence in rubber workers' unions in Binh Duong Province, and had arrested union leaders. Farmers' unions were crippled by arrests of union cadre, and the *Can Lao* proved itself quite capable of engineering elections within the unions as effectively as it rigged those for the National Assembly. The threat to Diem, when it came, arose from more traditional sources of power—the religious sects and the armed forces.

4. *Religious Dissenters*

Diem's clash with the armed sects in 1954 and 1955 had the unfortunate political consequence of casting his regime in religious overtones which deepened as the Ngo Dinh Catholicism became more widely known. Together with Diem's obvious U.S. backing, these had the effect of accentuating his Occidental, and especially American, identity. The British Catholic writer and commentator on Vietnam, Graham Greene, observed in 1955 that:

> It is Catholicism which has helped to ruin the government of Mr. Diem, for his genuine piety has been exploited by his American advisers until the Church is in danger of sharing the unpopularity of the United States. An unfortunate visit by Cardinal Spellman . . . has been followed by those of Cardinal Gillroy and the Archbishop of Canberra. Great sums are spent on organized demonstrations for visitors, and an impression is given that the Catholic Church is occidental and an ally of the United States in the cold war. . . .
>
> In the whole of Vietnam the proportion of Catholics to the population is roughly the same as in England—one in ten, a ratio insufficient to justify a Catholic government. Mr. Diem's ministers are not all Catholic, but Mr.

Diem, justifiably suspicious of many of his supporters, has confined the actual government to himself and members of his family. He undertakes personally the granting of exit and entry visas. . . . The south, instead of confronting the totalitarian north with evidences of freedom, had slipped into an inefficient dictatorship: newspapers suppressed, strict censorship, men exiled by administrative order and not by judgment of the courts. It is unfortunate that a government of this kind should be identified with one faith. Mr. Diem may well leave his tolerant country a legacy of anti-Catholicism. . . .

While Vietnam has an ample record of religious intolerance—especially intolerance for Catholics—calling into question Mr. Greene's contrary characterization, his prediction of Diem's impact proved correct. Open opposition to his government by civilians finally manifested itself on the issue of "religous freedom" in Hue and Saigon in 1963, coalescing around militant Buddhists and students—two groups that were, theretofore, for all practical purposes politically mute. There is no doubt, however, that Diem's Catholicism from 1954 on acted to his disadvantage among the non-Catholic masses, and enhanced the My-Diem image of his government's being an instrument of alien power and purpose.

F. TENSIONS WITH THE ARMED FORCES

The soldiers of Vietnam presented Diem with his first, and his last political challenges. Part of the Army's political involvement stemmed from patent military inefficiency in Diem's tight control, for which RVNAF leaders correctly held Diem responsible. Part also correctly can be attributed to vaulting ambition and venality among certain of Diem's officers. And since the United States paid, schooled, and advised the RVNAF, it would also be correct to consider the U.S. involved, if not responsible. The record of Diem's relations with RVNAF, like his relations with other parts of Vietnamese society, is a history of increasing tensions, and of lowering mutual understanding and support.

1. Clashes with Francophiles, 1954–1955

Diem's first interactions with his army were inauspicious. From September to November, 1954, Army Chief of Staff General Nguyen Van Hinh—a French citizen who held a commission in the French Air Force seemed on the verge of overthrowing Diem. Diem ordered Hinh out of the country; Hinh defied him. An apparent *coup d'etat* in late October was blocked by adroit maneuvering by Colonel Landsdale, and by assurance from General Collins to Hinh that American support would be promptly withdrawn from Vietnam were his plot to succeed. As Hinh recalled it:

> I had only to lift my telephone and the *coup d'etat* would have been over. . . . Nothing could have opposed the army. But the Americans let me know that if that happened, dollar help would be cut off. That would not matter to the military. If necessary, we soldiers could go barefoot and eat rice but the country cannot survive without American help.

Diem removed Hinh on 29 November 1954. The Acting Chief of Staff, General Nguyen Van Vy, Diem found "insufficiently submissive," and replaced him on 12 December 1954 with General Le Van Ty, kicking Vy upstairs to be Inspector

General. In April 1955, during the turmoil of the sect rebellion, Bao Dai attempted to appoint Vy as Chief of Staff with full military powers, and to recall Diem to France. As Diem committed his army to battle with the sects, Vy announced that, in the name of Bao Dai, and with the backing of all but ten percent of the Army, he had assumed control of the government. However, General Ty, Diem's Chief of Staff, remained loyal, rallied key local commanders around Diem, and Vy fled. Within weeks both Generals Hinh and Vy were afield against Diem in the Mekong Delta, maneuvering a disparate army of Hoa Hao, French "deserters," and others—Diem's forces again beat them, and both then went into exile.

2. Militarizing Public Administration

What Diem remembered from these experiences was that personal loyalty was the prime requisite for high command. As a result, he took an intense and direct interest in the appointments of military officers, and—as in other endeavors —found it easier to place his trust in Northerners and Catholics. Before long, the upper echelons of the officer corps were preponderantly from these groups, and closely netted to the Diem family web of preferment. As GVN demands for loyal civil servants willing to forego the advantages of Saigon multiplied, Diem was impelled to shift trusted military officers into his civil administration. The head of the General Directorate of Police and Security was a military officer from 1956 forward; his subordinates in the police apparatus included a growing number of military officers—for example, all the Saigon district police chiefs appointed in the year 1960 were soldiers. The government in the provinces reflected similar moves toward militarization:

TRENDS TOWARD MILITARY OFFICERS AS PROVINCE CHIEFS

	No. Provinces	No. Military Chiefs	% Military Chiefs
1958	36	13	36
1960	36	21	58
1962	41	36	88

There was a coextensive militarization of public administration at district and lower levels.

3. Dissatisfaction in the Officer Corps

But if Vietnam's soldiers found the Diem family a way to political power, wealth, and social prominence, they had ample reason to be dissatisfied with Diem's intervention in their professional concerns. The propensity of Ngo Dinh Diem to control his military with a tight rein extended to deciding when and where operations would be conducted, with what forces, and often how they would be used. Moreover, he involved himself with the arming and equipping of the forces, showing a distinct proclivity to heavy military forces of the conventional type, even for the Civil Guard, which reinforced American military leanings in the same direction. There were a few soldiers, like General Duong Van Minh, who sharply disagreed with the President on both points. And there was a growing number of young officers who resented the Catholic–Northern dominant clique within the military, who were dissatisfied with Diem's familial interference in military matters, and who were willing to entertain notions that the GVN had to be substantially modified. Nonetheless, until 1963, there was little apparent willingness to concert action against Diem.

4. *The Early Coup Attempts, 1960 and 1962*

On November 11, 1960, three paratroop battalions stationed in Saigon—considered by Diem among his most faithful—cooperated in an attempted *coup d'etat*. The leadership consisted of a small group of civilians and military officers: Hoang Co Thuy, a Saigon Lawyer; Lt Colonel Nguyen Trieu Hong, Thuy's nephew; Lt Colonel Vuong Van Dong, Hong's brother in law; and Colonel Nguyen Chanh Thi, the commander of the paratroops, who was apparently brought into the cabal at the last moment. The coup failed to arouse significant general pro-coup sentiment, either among the armed forces, or among the populace. Troops marched on Saigon, and rebels surrendered. In February, 1962, two Vietnamese air force planes bombed the Presidential palace in an unsuccessful attempt on President Diem and the Nhus—properly, an assassination attempt rather than a *coup d'etat*.

But the abortive events of 1960 and 1962 had the effect of dramatizing the choices open to those who recognized the insolvency of Diem's political and military policies. When Diem was overthrown in November, 1963, he was attacked by an apparatus that had been months in preparation. Unlike the earlier incident, the 1963 coup was actively supported by virtually all the generals of RVNAF, and was openly condoned by large sectors of the populace.

G. *THE VIET CONG*

1. *Diem and Communists*

Ngo Dinh Diem presided over a state which, for all the lip service it paid to individual freedom and American style government, remained a one party, highly centralized familial oligarchy in which neither operating democracy, nor the prerequisites for such existed. On 11 January, 1956, in GVN Ordinance Number 6, President Diem decreed broad governmental measures providing for "the defense of the state and public order," including authority to detain "individuals considered a danger to the state" or to "national defense and common security" at re-education centers. One month after the date of the scheduled Geneva plebescite, on 21 August 1956, the Government of Vietnam proclaimed Ordinance Number 47, which defined as a breach of law punishable by death any deed performed in or for any organization designated as "Communist." Moreover, the GVN was forced to use violence to establish itself in its own rural areas. In July, 1956, the month the Geneva elections were scheduled to have been held, the U.S. Army attache in Saigon noted in his monthly report that:

> Orders have reportedly been issued to all Viet Minh cadres in Free Viet Nam to increase their efforts to reorganize and revitalize the military units in their zones of responsibility. These cadres have, however, encountered considerable difficulty in motivating their adherents to work for the Communist cause. The military and political cadres are making little progress due to the Communist Denunciation Campaigns promoted by the Government of the Republic of Viet Nam. . . .

The same report submitted an ARVN estimate of 4,300 armed Viet Minh in all of Free Viet Nam, and recorded small ARVN skirmishes with Viet Minh south of Saigon, clashes with 10 Hoa Hao battalions, 8 Cao Dai battalions north and west of Saigon, and incidents of banditry north of Bien Hoa by Binh Xuyen. But, in a relatively short time, the fighting subsided, the Vietnamese Army was withdrawn from the countryside for retraining, reorganization, and modernization under the US MAAG, and South Vietnam ostensibly settled into the first peace it had known in a decade. Peace rested, however, or strong central government. In an article published in the January, 1957, *Foreign Affairs,* an American analyst stated that:

> South Viet Nam is today a quasi-police state characterized by arbitrary arrests and imprisonment, strict censorship of the press and the absence of an effective political opposition. . . . All the techniques of political and psychological warfare, as well as pacification campaigns involving extensive military operations have been brought to bear against the underground.

Police states, efficiently organized and operated, have historically demonstrated much greater ability at countering insurgency than other sorts of governments. South Vietnam in fact succeeded in 1955 and 1956 in quelling rural dissidence through a comprehensive political and military assault on sect forces and other anti-government armed bands using its army, the civic action cadre, the Communist Denunciation campaign, and a broad range of promised reforms. Moreover, at its worst, the Government of South Vietnam compared favorably with other Asian regimes with respect to its degree of repressiveness. Nor did it face endemic violence markedly different from that then prevalent in Burma, Indonesia, South Korea. And its early "counterinsurgency" operations were as sophisticated as any being attempted elsewhere in Asia. In 1957, the Government of Viet Nam claimed that its pacification programs had succeeded:

> We believe that with clear, even clementary ideas based upon facts . . . we can imbue . . . first the youth and ultimately the entire population with the spirit and essential objectives of . . . civic humanism. We believe that this above all is the most effective antidote to Communism (which is but an accident of history). . . .
> . . . We can see that the Viet-Minh authorities have disintegrated and been rendered powerless.

P. J. Honey, the British expert on Vietnam, agreed; his evaluation as of early 1958 was as follows:

> . . . The country has enjoyed three years of relative peace and calm in which it has been able to carry on the very necessary work of national reconstruction. The most destructive feature in the national life of Vietnam throughout recent years has been the lack of security in the countryside, which obliged farmers and peasants to abandon the ricefields and to flee to the large cities for safety. Today it is possible to travel all over South Vietnam without any risk. The army and security forces have mopped up most of the armed bands of political opponents of the Government, of Communists and of common bandits. One still hears of an isolated raid, but the old insecurity is fast vanishing. . . .

After a 1959 trip, however, Honey detected dangerous unease in the countryside:

> For the overwhelming majority of the Vietnamese, heirs to experience of a century of French colonial rule, the Government is a remote body which passes laws, collects taxes, demands labour corvées, takes away able-

bodied men for military service, and generally enriches itself at the expense of the poor peasant. "Government" is associated in the minds of the villagers with exactions, punishments, unpaid labour, and other unpleasant matters. These people are members of families and members of villages, and their loyalties to both are strong. But these loyalties do not extend beyond the village, nor has any past experience taught the peasants why they should. The idea that the peasants should assume any responsibility for the [extra-village] government themselves would be so alien to their thinking as to·be comic. Educated Vietnamese are well aware of this, as many of their actions show. . . .

Such political parties as existed in Vietnam before the advent of independence were all clandestine, so that any political experience acquired from these by the Vietnamese peasants will have been of secret plotting for the overthrow of the Government. Since independence, they will probably have been subjected to attempted Communist indoctrination by the Viet Cong, but this too will have had an anti-Government slant. Since 1954, the peasants have been fed on a diet of puerile, and frequently offensive slogans by the Ministry of Information. These serve, if indeed they serve any purpose at all, to make the peasant distrust the Government of Ngo Dinh Diem. The peasants, for all their naïveté, are far from foolish and they are not deceived by slogans alleging to be true things which they know, from their own personal experience, to be untrue. Any political experience among the peasantry, then, is more likely to prove a liability than an asset to any Government.

Diem knew that his main political dissent was centered not among his fellow mandarins, in his press, or among his military officers, but in the peasantry. And the prime challenge was, as Diem saw it, communism, precisely because it could and did afford the peasants political experience.

Communism was, from the outset of Diem's rule, his bete noire. In 1955, after the victory over the sects, and just before General John W. O'Daniel ended his tour as Chief, MAAG Vietnam, Diem talked to the General about Vietnam's future:

> He spoke about the decentralization of government that he had been advised to undertake, but felt that the time was not yet right. He felt that, since his country was involved in a war, warlike control was in order. He remarked that the Vietminh propaganda line never mentioned Communism, but only land reform. . . . Diem wants land reform too. . . .

In his message to the American Friends of Vietnam in June, 1956, Diem acknowledged progress, but warned that:

> We have arrived at a critical point. . . . We must now give meaning to our hard sought liberty. . . . To attain that goal we need technicians and machines. Our armed forces which are considerably reduced must however undertake an immense task from the military as well as the cultural and social point of view. It is indispensable that our army have the wherewithal to become increasingly capable of preserving the peace which we seek. There are an infinite number of tasks in all fields to complete before the year's end.

Diem's preoccupation with security paradoxically interfered with his ability to compete with the communists in the countryside. In effect, he decided on a strategy of postponing the politicizing of the peasants until he had expunged his arch-foes. Diem's official biography underscores this point:

> The main concern of President Ngo Dinh Diem is therefore to destroy the sources of demoralization, however powerful, before getting down to the problem of endowing Vietnam with a democratic apparatus in the Western sense of the word.

Madame Nhu, his sister-in-law, was vehement that any political liberalization would have operated to Viet Cong advantage: "If we open the window, not only sunlight, but many bad things will fly in, also." To hold a contrary view does not necessarily argue that democratization was the only way Diem could have met his political opposition in the villages; it does seem, however, that in failing to meet aspirations there by some departure from inefficiently repressive course he adopted, Diem erred. In concluding that he did not have to reckon with peasant attitudes, Diem evidently operated from two related misapprehensions: that somehow the peasants would remain politically neutral while he eliminated the communists, and that the Viet Cong were essentially a destructive force. It was not that Diem could not vocalize a sound estimate of the communist political threat; his own description of communist operations to an Australian journalist was quite accurate:

> In China, during the Indo-China war and now here, the Communists have always sheltered in open base areas of difficult access, in areas where there are no roads. They have made their headquarters in the jungle. Cautiously, sometimes only one man at a time, they move into a village and establish a contact, then a cell until the village is theirs to command. Having got one village, they move to a second village and from a second to third, until eventually they need not live in any of these villages, but merely visit them periodically. When this stage is reached, they are in a position to build training camps and even start crude factories and produce home-made guns, grenades, mines, and booby traps.
>
> This is all part of the first phase. The second phase is to expand control and link up with Communist groups in other bases. To begin with, they start acts of violence through their underground organizations. They kill village chiefs, headmen, and others working for the government and, by so doing, terrorize the population, not necessarily by acts of violence against the people but by demonstrating that there is no security for them in accepting leadership from those acknowledging the leadership of the government. Even with much smaller numbers of troops than the constituted authority, it is not difficult now for the Communists to seize the initiative. A government has responsibility for maintaining supply to the civil population of keeping railways, rivers, and canals open for traffic, of ensuring that rural crops reach the markets and that in turn commodity goods are distributed throughout the country. The Communists have no such responsibility. They have no roads and bridges to guard, and no goods to distribute.

Diem failed to perceive that the "first phase" was crucial, or that the VC were, from the very outset, constructing while they destroyed, building a state within South Vietnam with more effective local government than his own.

Like many another issue in Vietnam, the problem was in part semantics. "Communists" during this period formally recanted for the GVN by the thousands; thousands more "communists" were incarcerated by the GVN for "political reeducation." But Ordinance 47 of 1956 notwithstanding, "communist" is a term which has not been used since the 1940's by Vietnamese serving the Marxist–Leninist Party headed by Ho Chi Minh of the DRV. These referred to themselves as members of the Vietnam Workers Party (Dang Lao Dong), as members of one Front or another, or as resistance fighters, or fighters for national liberation. Nor was "Viet Minh" a useful name, since Viet Minh, a nationalist front, included numerous non-communist, or at least non-party members. In 1956, the Saigon press began to distinguish between the Viet Minh and communists by referring to the latter as "Viet Cong," a fairly precise, and not necessarily disparaging, rendition of "Viet Nam Cong-San," which means "Vietnamese Communist." The National Liberation Front of South Vietnam (NLF) much later condemned the term as "contemptuous," and pointed out that the GVN had applied it indiscriminately to all persons or groups "who are lukewarm toward the pro-U.S. policy even on details." There can be no doubt that Diem and his government applied the term somewhat loosely within South Vietnam, and meant by it North as well as South Vietnamese communists, whom they presumed acted in concert.

2. The Viet Minh Residue

At the close of the Franco–Viet Minh War, some 60,000 men were serving in organized Viet Minh units in South Viet Nam. For the regroupments to North Vietnam, these units were augmented with large numbers of untrained young men—who were later known among the regroupees in North Vietnam as "soldiers of Geneva." A reported 90,000 soldiers were taken to North Vietnam in the evacuated units, while the U.S. and the GVN estimated that 5,000 to 10,000 trained men were left behind as "cadre." If French estimates are correct that in 1954 the Viet Minh controlled over 60 to 90 percent of South Vietnam's villages outside the Cao Dai and Hoa Hao regions, those 5,000 to 10,000 cadre must have represented only a small fraction of the remaining Viet Minh apparatus—cadre, local workers, sympathizers—in the countryside. GVN figures themselves attest to this. In 1955 and 1956 alone, the GVN claimed 100,000 communist "cadre" rallied or surrendered.

Neither Diem's GVN nor the U.S. knew a great deal about the Viet Minh in the period 1954–1960. By 1967, however, new information had begun to accumulate from interrogations of prisoners and defectors, and captured documents. For example, in March, 1967, a study was published of 23 Viet Minh who stayed behind during the regroupment of 1954–1955. All the men of the sample told consistent stories, and although an admittedly narrow basis for generalization, the stories ring true. Upon departure, the Viet Minh leaders assigned some of these stay-behinds active roles; others were simply told to return to their homes as inactives, and wait for further instructions. It is quite clear that even the activists were not instructed to organize units for guerrilla war, but rather to agitate politically for the promised Geneva elections, and the normalization of relations with the North. They drew much reassurance from the presence of the ICC, and up until mid-1956, most held on to the belief that the elections would take place. They were disappointed in two respects: not only were the promised elections not held, but the amnesty which had been assured by the Geneva Settlement was denied them, and they were hounded by the Anti-Communist campaign. After 1956, for the most part, they went "underground." They were uniformly outraged at Diem's practices, particularly the recurrent GVN attempts to grade the populace into lettered categories according to previous associations with the Viet Minh. Most of them spoke of terror, brutality and torture by GVN rural officials in carrying out the Communist Denunciation campaigns, and of the arrest and slaying of thousands of old comrades from the "resistance." Their venom was expended on these local officials, rather than on Diem, or the central government, although they were prepared to hold Diem ultimately responsible. A veteran who had been a Party member since 1936 characterized the years 1955–1959 as the most difficult years of the entire revolution.

What these cadre did in those years is revealing. Only four of the 23 were engaged in military tasks. Most spent their time in preparation for a future uprising, in careful recruitment in the villages—concentrating on the very families with Viet Minh ties who were receiving priority in the GVN's attentions—and in constructing base areas in the mountains or jungles. The Viet Minh activists sought out the inactives, brought them back into the organization, and together they formed the framework of an expanding and increasingly intricate network of intelligence and propaganda. Few spoke of carrying weapons, or using violence before 1959, although many boasted of feats of arms in later years. They felt that they lacked the right conditions to strike militarily before 1959; their mission was preparation. In several instances, the Viet Cong used terror to recruit former Viet Minh for the new movement, threatening them with "treason" and elimination; caught between the GVN and the VC, many old Resistance members joined the "New Resistance." But most spoke of making person-to-person persuasion to bring in new members for the movement, relying mainly on two appeals: nationalism and social justice. They stressed that the Americans had merely substituted a new, more pernicious form of tyranny for that of the French, and that the My-Diem combine was the antithesis of humane and honest government. One respondent spoke of this activity in these terms:

> From 1957 to 1960 the cadres who had remained in the South had almost all been arrested. Only one or two cadres were left in every three to five villages. What was amazing was how these one or two cadres started the movement so well.
>
> The explanation is not that these cadres were exceptionally gifted but the people they talked to were ready for rebellion. The people were like a mound of straw, ready to be ignited. . . .
>
> If at that time the government in the South had been a good one, if it had not been dictatorial, if the agrarian reforms had worked, if it had established control at the village level, then launching the movement would have been difficult.

These interviews underscored three points on which the GVN was apparently in error. First, with respect to the stay-behinds themselves, by no means were all dedicated communists in the doctrinaire sense. Many reported that they resented and feared the communists in the Viet Minh, and apparently might have been willing to serve the GVN faithfully had it not hounded them out of the society. There were several among the group, for example, who had entered Saigon, and there found a degree of freedom which kept them off the Viet Cong roles for years. Second, with regard to the peasants in general, the Viet Minh were widely admired throughout the South as national heroes, and the GVN therefore committed a tactical error of the first magnitude in damning all Viet Minh without qualification as communists. Third, the GVN created by its rural policy a climate of moral indignation which energized the peasants politically, turned them against the government, sustained the Viet Cong, and permitted "communists" to outlast severe GVN repressions and even to recruit during it.

The foregoing precis of the 1967 study presents views which are paralleled in a captured Viet Cong history, written around 1963, which describes the years after 1954 as follows:

EXPERIENCES OF THE SOUTH VIETNAM REVOLUTIONARY MOVEMENT DURING THE PAST SEVERAL YEARS

During the past nine years, under the enlightened leadership of the Party Central Committee, the people and the Party of South Vietnam have experienced many phases along the difficult and complicated path of struggle but they have also gained many victories and experiences while pushing the South Vietnam liberation revolution and creating the conditions for peaceful reunification of the country. . . .

After the armistice, the South Vietnam people reverted to political struggle through peaceful means by demanding personal rights, freedom and negotiations concerning general elections in accordance with the stipulations of the Geneva Agreement so that the country could be peacefully reunified . . . The Party [words illegible] party were changed in order to guarantee the leadership and forces of the Party under the new struggle conditions. . . .

From the end of 1954 until 1956 several important changes occurred in the South Vietnam situation. Imperialist America ousted and replaced imperialist France, turning South Vietnam into a colony (a new type of colony) based on U.S. military power. The Ngo Dinh Diem government was clearly shown to be a government composed of bureaucratic, dictatorial and family-controlled feudalists and capitalists who committed crimes for the American imperialists and massacred the people, massacred revolutionaries and massacred the oppositionists. Both the Americans and Diem made every effort to oppose the implementation of the Geneva Agreement and made every effort to subvert the peaceful reunification of our fatherland. . . .

Immediately after the re-establishment of peace, the responsibility of South Vietnam was to use the political struggle to demand the implementation of the Geneva Agreement. The struggle responsibilities and procedures were appropriate for the situation at that time and corresponded with the desires of the great majority of the masses who wished for peace after nearly 10 years of difficult resistance.

At that time, although the Americans–Diemists used cruel force to oppose the people and the revolution, and the masses struggled decisively against this repression in many places and at many times, the contradictions had not yet developed to a high degree and the hatred had not yet developed to a point where the use of armed struggle could become an essential and popular struggle tactic. In South Vietnam since 1955, thanks to the armed movement of the sects, we were able to avoid the construction of an armed propaganda force, since we only had a few former bases which were needed in the political struggle and for the creation of a reserve force.

From 1957 to 1958, the situation gradually changed. The enemy persistently sabotaged the implementation of the Geneva Agreement, actively consolidated and strengthened the army, security service, and administrative apparatus from the central to the hamlet level, crudely assassinated the people, and truly and efficiently destroyed our Party. By relying on force, the American–Diemist regime was temporarily able to stabilize the situation and increase the prestige of the counterrevolutionaries. At this time, the political struggle movement of the masses, although not defeated, was encountering increasing difficulty and increasing weakness; the Party bases, although not completely destroyed, were significantly weakened, and in some areas, quite seriously; the prestige of the masses and of the revolution suffered. But in reality, the years during which the enemy increased his terrorism were also the years in which the enemy suffered major political losses [words illegible] The masses became more deep seeded and many individuals who formerly supported the enemy now opposed them. The masses, that is to say, the peasants, now realized that it was impossible to live under such conditions and that it was necessary to rise up in drastic struggle. Faced with the fact that the enemy was using guns, assassinations and imprisonment to oppose the people in their political struggle, many voices among the masses appealed to the Party to establish a program of armed resistance against the enemy. Within the Party, on the one hand, the members were saturated with the responsibility to lead the revolution to a successful overthrow of the enemy, but on the other hand, the majority of the party members and cadres felt that it was necessary to immediately launch an armed struggle in order to preserve the movement and protect the forces. In several areas the party members on their own initiative had organized armed struggle against the enemy . . .

Up to 1959, in South Vietnam, the Americans–Diemists had fully constructed a large army, equipped with modern weapons, along with a large and well armed administrative, police and security apparatus. During the years in which the masses were only using political struggle, the Americans–Diemists used the military, security and administrative apparatus to launch various campaigns to terrorize, mop up and oppress the movement, no different from during the period of warfare. Because they were determined to crush the revolution and control the people at every moment, they could not avoid using every type of repression.

In opposing such an enemy, simple political struggle was not possible. It was necessary to use additional armed struggle, but not merely low level armed struggle, such as only armed propaganda, which was used to support the political struggle. The enemy would not allow us any peace, and in the face of the enemy operations and destructive pursuit, the armed propaganda teams, even if they wished to avoid losses, would never be able to engage the enemy in warfare and would never be able to become an actual revolutionary army. This is an essential fact of the movement and the actual movement in South Vietnam illustrates this fact. Therefore, at the end of 1959, when we launched an additional armed struggle in coordination with the political struggle against the enemy, it immediately took the form in South Vietnam of revolutionary warfare, a long range revolutionary warfare. Therefore, according to some opinions at the beginning of 1959, we only used heavy armed propaganda and later developed "regional guerrillas. . . ."

This version of events from 1954 through 1959 is further supported by the report of interrogation of one of the four members of the Civilian Proselyting

Section of the Viet Cong Saigon/Gia Dinh Special Zone Committee, captured in November, 1964; the prisoner stated that:

> The period from the Armistice of 1954 until 1958 was the darkest time for the VC in South Vietnam. The political agitation policy proposed by the Communist Party could not be carried out due to the arrest of a number of party members by RVN authorities. The people's agitation movement was minimized. However, the organizational system of the party from the highest to the lowest echelons survived, and since the party remained close to the people, its activities were not completely suppressed. In 1959 the party combined its political agitation with its military operations, and by the end of 1959 the combined operations were progressing smoothly.

Viet Cong "political agitation" was a cunning blend of the Viet Minh nationalist charisma, exploitation of GVN shortcomings, xenophobia, and terror. Drawing on the years of Viet Minh experience in subversive government and profiting from Viet Minh errors, the Viet Cong appealed to the peasants not as Marxist revolutionaries proposing a drastic social upheaval, but quite to the contrary, as a conservative, nationalist force wholly compatible with the village-centered traditionalism of most farmers, and as their recourse against "My-Diem" modernization. One American authority summed the Viet Minh experience evident in Viet Cong operations as ten political precepts:

> 1. Don't try for too much; don't smash the existing social system, use it; don't destroy opposition organizations, take them over.
> 2. Use the amorphous united front to attack opposition political forces too large or too powerful for you to take over; then fragment their leadership, using terror if necessary, and drown their followers in the front organization.
> 3. At all times appear outwardly reasonable about the matter of sharing power with rival organizations although secretly working by every means to eliminate them. Don't posture in public.
> 4. Divide your organization rigidly into overt and covert sections and minimize traffic between the two. The overt group's chief task is to generate broad public support; the covert group seeks to accumulate and manipulate political power.
> 5. Use communism as dogma, stressing those aspects that are well regarded by the people; don't hesitate to interpret Marxism–Leninism in any way that proves beneficial. Soft-pedal the class-struggle idea except among cadres.
> 6. Don't antagonize anyone if it can be helped: this avoids the formation of rival blocs.
> 7. Bearing in mind that in Vietnam altruism is conspicuous by its absence, blend the proper mixture of the materialistic appeals of communism and the endemic feelings of nationalism. Win small but vital gains through communism, large ones through nationalism. Plan to win in the end not as Communists but as nationalists.
> 8. Use the countryside as the base and carry the struggle to the cities later; in rural areas political opportunities are greater and risks smaller. Avoid the lure of the teahouse.
> 9. But forge a city alliance. Mobilization of the farmer must create a strong farmer-worker bond.

10. Work from the small to the large, from the specific to the general; work from small safe areas to large liberated areas and then expand the liberated areas; begin with small struggle movements and work toward a General Uprising during which state power will be seized.

The same expert termed General Uprising "a social myth in the Sorelian sense, perhaps traceable back to the Communist myth of the general strike," and cited Viet Cong documents which describe how the 2500 villages of Vietnam will be led toward a spontaneous final and determinant act of revolution:

> The Revolution, directed toward the goal of the General Uprising, has these five characteristics: . . . It takes place in a very favorable worldwide setting. . . . It is against the neocolonialism of the U.S.A. . . . The government of Vietnam is unpopular and growing weaker. . . . The people have revolutionary consciousness and are willing to struggle. . . . It is led by the Party, which has great experience.

Ho and Giap thus coated Marx and Mao with French revolutionary romanticism. Diem, the moral reformer, also drew heavily upon the same traditions for "personalism." One of the tragedies of modern Vietnam is that the political awakening of its peasants was to these, the most virulent, and vicious social theories of the era.

But doctrine was not the sole heritage the Viet Cong received from the Viet Minh. Perhaps more important was the "Resistance" organization: the hierarchy extending upward from hamlet and village through provincial to regional authorities capable of coordinating action on a broad scale. The Viet Minh complied with military regroupments under the Geneva Accords but were not obligated to withdraw the "political" apparatus; in fact, the Settlement provided guarantees for it in its provisions against reprisals (Armistice, Article 14c, and Conference Final Declaration, Article 9), and for liberation of political prisoners (Armistice, Article 21). Knowledge of the techniques of clandestine politics, appreciation for the essentiality of tight discipline, and trained personnel constituting a widespread, basic organizational framework were all conferred on the Viet Cong.

3. *Rural Violence and GVN Counters, 1957–1960*

By early 1958, Saigon was beginning to sense that pacification had eluded the GVN even as it had the French. In December, 1957, the ill-fated newspaper, *Thoi Luan,* pointed out that terrorism was on the rise, and that:

> Today the menace is heavier than ever, with the terrorists no longer limiting themselves to the notables in charge of security. Everything suits them, village chiefs, chairmen of liaison committees, simple guards, even former notables. . . . In certain areas, the village chiefs spend their nights in the security posts, while the inhabitants organize watches.
> . . . The most urgent need for the population today is security—a question to which we have repeatedly drawn the attention of the authorities.
> Spectacular assassinations have taken place in the provinces of An Giang and Phong-Dinh [in the Mekong Delta]. In the village of Than-My-Tay, armed men appeared in the dead of night, awakened the inhabitants, read a death sentence, and beheaded four young men whose heads they nailed to the nearest bridge. . . .

The security question in the provinces must be given top priority: the regime will be able to consolidate itself only if it succeeds in finding a solution to this problem.

Besides the incidents cited, there had been a mass murder of 17 in Chau-Doc in July, 1957; in September the District Chief at My Tho with his whole family was gunned down in daylight on a main highway; on 10 October a bomb thrown into a Cholon cafe injured 13 persons, and on 22 October, in three bombings in Saigon, 13 Americans were wounded.

Also in October a clandestine radio in Vietnam purporting to speak for the "National Salvation Movement" was backing armed insurgents against Diem. In Washington, U.S. intelligence indicated that the "Viet Minh underground" had been directed to conduct additional attacks on U.S. personnel "whenever conditions are favorable." U.S. intelligence also noted a total of 30 armed "terrorist incidents initiated by Communist guerillas" in the last quarter of 1957, as well as a "large number" of incidents carried out by "Communist-lead [sic] Hoa Hao and Cao Dai dissident elements," and reported "at least" 75 civilians or civil officials assassinated or kidnapped in the same period.

Robert Shaplen wrote that:

> By 1958, the Vietminh had fully resumed its campaign of terror in the countryside, kidnapping government officials and threatening villagers . . . in an average month the local and regional units were becoming involved in a score of engagements. Usually, these were hit-and-run Communist attacks on Self-Defense Corps or Civil Guard headquarters, the purpose of which was both to seize weapons and to heighten the atmosphere of terror.

Guns should have been plentiful in the countryside of Vietnam. The Japanese, the French and even the GVN armed the sect forces. And both the sects and the Viet Minh had operated small arms factories—for instance, General Lansdale visited a Cao Dai weapons factory at Nui Ba Den in Tay Ninh in 1955. The Viet Minh cached arms as they withdrew from their "liberated areas" in 1954 and 1955. ARVN veterans and deserters from the force reductions of 1954 and 1955 carried weapons into the hinterland. The VC attacked for weapons to make up for losses to the GVN, and to equip units with similar types to simplify logistics.

In January, 1958, a "large band" of "communist" guerrillas attacked a plantation north of Saigon, and in February, an ARVN truck was ambushed on the outskirts of the capital. In March, the Saigon newspaper *Dan-Cung* complained that: "our people are fleeing the villages and returning to the cities for fear of communist guerrillas and feudalistic officials. . . ." Bernard Fall published an article in July, 1958, in which he mapped the pattern of assassinations and other incidents from April 1957 to April 1958, and announced the onset of a new war: Fall's thesis was challenged by a senior U.S. adviser to the GVN, who argued that the increasing casualty figures represented not a structured attempt to overthrow the GVN, but were simply a product of police reporting in the hinterlands. There can be no doubt that the latter view was partially correct: neither the U.S. nor the GVN knew what was "normal" in the rural areas, and police reporting, with U.S. aid, had been improved. But the deadly figures continued to mount. George A. Carver of the CIA, in his 1966 *Foreign Affairs* article, agreed with Fall:

> A pattern of politically motivated terror began to emerge, directed against the representatives of the Saigon government and concentrated on the very bad and the very good. The former were liquidated to win favor with the

peasantry; the latter because their effectiveness was a bar to the achievement of Communist objectives. The terror was directed not only against officials but against all whose operations were essential to the functioning of organized political society, school teachers, health workers, agricultural officials, etc. The scale and scope of this terrorist and insurrectionary activity mounted slowly and steadily. *By the end of 1958* the participants in this incipient insurgency, whom Saigon quite accurately termed the "Viet Cong," constituted a serious threat to South Viet Nam's political stability.

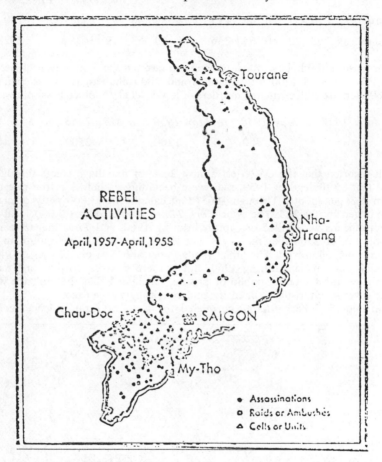

Like most other statistics concerning Vietnam, figures on the extent of the terrorism varied widely. The GVN reported to the ICC that in 1957, 1958, and the first half of 1959, Viet Cong murdered 65 village officials, 51 civilians, 28 Civil Guardsmen, and 10 soldiers. GVN official reports provided the U.S. Embassy in Saigon recorded a significantly greater toll of civilians:

CIVILIAN ASSASSINATIONS AND
KIDNAPPINGS IN SOUTH VIETNAM

By Quarter, From GVN Reports to U.S. Embassy

	1958					*1959*					*1960*
	1	*2*	*3*	*4*	*Total*	*1*	*2*	*3*	*4*	*Total*	*First 5 Months*
Murders	72	51	26	44	193	52	34	46	97	233	780
Abductions	73	32	66	65	236	44	53	67	179	343	282

Journalists and scholars, studying open sources, put the figures even higher. Douglas Pike reported 1700 assassinations and 2000 abductions in the years 1957–1960. Bernard Fall estimated murders of low-level GVN officials as follows:

May 1957 to May 1958	*to May 1959*	*to May 1960*	*to May 1961*
700	1200	2500	4000

Fall reported that the GVN lost almost 20% of its village chiefs through 1958, and that by the end of 1959, they were becoming casualties at the rate of more than 2% per month. Through 1963, Fall calculated, 13,000 petty officials were eliminated by the VC. The *New York Times* estimated that 3,000 local government officials were killed or captured during 1960, and *Time* magazine reported in the fall of 1960 that the GVN was losing 250 to 300 per month to a "new Communist offensive": The U.S. "White Paper" of 1961 cited losses of 1400 local officials and civilians during 1960. But if there was disparity among numerical estimates, most reports, public or private, concluded that the violence was real, anti-government, rising in intensity, and increasingly organized.

In mid-1958 Bernard Fall correlated the locus of rural violence reported in

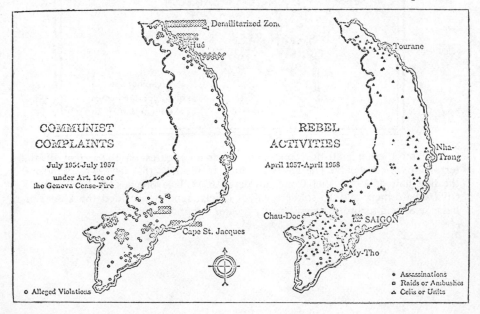

South Vietnam with complaints lodged with the ICC in Hanoi by the DRV on behalf of "Former Resistance members," alleging GVN violations of the "no reprisals" provisions of the Geneva Accords (Armistice, Article 14c). The detail in these complaints indicated an intelligence apparatus in South Vietnam.

"The conclusion is inescapable," he wrote, "that there must be some coordination between the rebels and the North Vietnamese Government." About that same time, U.S. intelligence reported that Viet Cong-bandit operations north of Saigon seemed to be part of a calculated campaign of economic sabotage. According to one description of the village near My Tho which was studied very intensively around mid-1958:

> . . . For the first time [the village] experienced the activities of a relatively new political movement—*Mat Tran Dan Toc Giai Phong Mien Nam Viet Nam* (National Front for the Liberation of Vietnam) referred to by the South Vietnamese government as the Viet Cong or Vietnamese Communists . . . and invariably called the Viet Minh by the villagers. In the vicinity of [the village] the initial efforts of the Viet Cong were largely confined to anti-government propaganda.

One VC pamphlet of late 1958 from the Mekong Delta reads as follows:

> Support the just struggle of the people to overthrow the government of the Americans and Diem [My-Diem], to establish a democratic regime in the South, and to work for general elections which will unify the country by peaceful means.

But, if "struggle" sounds innocuous enough in English, the word fails to carry the intensity of the Vietnamese equivalent, *dau tranh*. A VC rallier put it this way:

> *Dau tranh* is all important to a revolutionist. It marks his thinking, his attitudes, his behavior. His life, his revolutionary work, his whole world is *dau tranh*. The essence of his existence is *dau tranh*.

And, the term "just struggle of the people" sheathed the terror integral to Viet Cong operations. In Pike's estimate:

> Insurgency efforts in the 1958–1960 period involved violence such as assassinations but few actual armed attacks. This was so partly because the cadres had little military capability but chiefly because doctrine counseled against violence. . . .
>
> For the true believers operating throughout the South this was a time of surreptitious meetings, cautious political feelers, the tentative assembling of a leadership group, and the sounding out of potential cadres whose names went into a file for future reference. It meant working mainly with non-Communists and, in many cases, keeping one's Communist identity a secret. . . .

Diem's own party newspaper, the NRM's *Cach Mang Quoc Gia*, published an article in February, 1959 which reported that "the situation in the rural areas is rotten," and described communist cells established in the villages collecting taxes and conducting "espionage," supporting local guerrilla forces responsive to a hierarchy of provincial and regional committees.

From mid-1959 onward, there was a definite upsurge in Viet Cong activity, marked not only by the increase in terrorism noted in the statistics presented above, but also by the fielding of large military units which sought, rather than avoided, engagement with units of Diem's regular army. On 26 September 1959 two companies of the ARVN 23d Division were ambushed by a well-organized force of several hundred identified as the "2d Liberation Battalion"; the ARVN units lost 12 killed, 14 wounded, and most of their weapons.

On 25 January 1960 the same Viet Cong battalion launched an attack coordinated with four guerrilla companies—a total force of 300 to 500 men—which penetrated the compound of the 32d Regiment, 21st ARVN Division at Tay Ninh, killed 23 ARVN soldiers, and netted a large haul of arms and ammunition. On 29 January 1960 an insurgent band seized the town of Dong Xoai, some sixty miles north of Saigon, held the place for several hours, and robbed a French citizen of 200,000 piasters. In the same month, large VC forces opened operations in the Camau peninsula and the Mekong Delta. In Kien Hoa province VC units numbering hundreds effectively isolated the province capital from six of its eight districts. Bernard Fall, in his continuing study of Viet Cong operations, detected a new strategy operating: a shift during 1959 and early 1960 from base development in the Delta to isolation of Saigon. Whether or not the incidents plotted by Fall constituted a strategy as he thought, they were patently more coherent. A U.S. intelligence assessment submitted 7 March 1960 described VC plans, confirmed from a variety of U.S. and GVN sources, to launch large scale guerrilla warfare that year "under the flag of the People's Liberation Movement," which was identified as "red, with a blue star." The VC were reportedly moving into position to exercise one or more of three strategic options by the end of 1960: (1) incite an ARVN revolt; (2) set up a popular front government in the lower Delta; (3) force the GVN into such repressive countermeasures that popular uprisings will follow.

An ARVN coup d'etat did ensue, although it was neither VC incited nor successful; nor was there any general revolt in the ranks. No popular front government was set up. But the GVN was prompted to a succession of repressive countermeasures which may have aided the Viet Cong much as they had expected. Prodded by the rural violence, Diem began his "counterinsurgency" in early 1959 with the reintensification of population classification and relocation programs. On 6 May 1959, the GVN promulgated Law 10/59, which set up three military tribunals which could, without appeal, adjudge death for crimes under Ordinance 47 of 1956—the anti-communist law. In actuality, these tribunals were used sparingly, usually for show-case trials of terrorists. But the existence of Law 10/59 furnished grist for VC propaganda mills for years.

On 7 July, 1959, the GVN launched its "prosperity and density centers"—the "agroville" program—and Ngo Dinh Nhu and his wife plunged into organizing rural youth, women, and farmers' organizations. However, just as the VC Tet offensive of 1968 attenuated "Revolutionary Development," the VC upsurge of late 1959 and early 1960 disrupted the new GVN organizational efforts, and reinforced Diem's conviction that security was the paramount consideration. The U.S. assessment of March 1960 cited widespread abuse of police powers by local officials for extortion and vendetta, and pointed out that arbitrary and corrupt local officials compromised GVN efforts to root out the VC "undercover cadres." Moreover:

> . . . While the GVN has made an effort to meet the economic and social needs of the rural populations through community development, the construction of schools, hospitals, roads, etc., these projects appear to have enjoyed only a measure of success in creating support for the government

and, in fact, in many instances have resulted in resentment. Basically, the problem appears to be that such projects have been imposed on the people without adequate psychological preparation in terms of the benefits to be gained. Since most of these projects call for sacrifice on the part of the population (in the form of allegedly "volunteer" labor in the case of construction, time away from jobs or school labor in the case of rural youth groups, leaving homes and lands in the case of regrouping isolated peasants), they are bound to be opposed unless they represent a partnership effort for mutual benefit on the part of the population and the government. . . .

The situation may be summed up in the fact that the government has tended to treat the population with suspicion or to coerce it and has been rewarded with an attitude of apathy or resentment.

4. The Founding of the National Liberation Front

Despite their expanding military effort, the Viet Cong remained a formless, "faceless" foe until late in 1960, when the National Liberation Front was announced as the superstructure of the insurgent apparatus, and the political voice of the rebellion. Thereafter, the Viet Cong sought publicity, and thereby acquired identity as a South Vietnam-wide organization of three major components: the NLF itself, the Liberation Army of South Vietnam, and the People's Revolutionary Party.

a. Organization and Objectives

The precise dates of the forming of the NLF constitutes one of the puzzles of the war. As mentioned above, in the years 1954 to 1960, peasants, captured documents and prisoners referred frequently to "the Front," meaning the insurgent movement, and "Front" flags had been captured as early as 1959. These were probably references to Viet Minh carry-over organizations, such as they were, rather than a specific leadership group or structure, with a set of defined objectives. Nguyen Huu Tho, the first Chairman of the NLF, stated in a 1964 interview over Radio Hanoi that:

> Although formally established in December 1960, the Front had existed as a means of action without by-laws or program since 1954 when we founded the Saigon–Cholon Peace Committee. . . . Many of the members of the [NLF] Central Committee were also members of the Peace Committee. . . .

Huynh Tan Phat, Tho's Vice Chairman in the NLF, was reported in late 1955 serving on the "Executive Committee of the Fatherland Front" (Mat Tren To Quoc), controlling joint Viet Minh–Hoa Hoa operations against the GVN in the Plain of Reeds. Communists have been joining front organizations linking anti-government minorities. . . . [Examples are] the 'Vietnamese Peoples' Liberation Movement Forces' [and] . . . , the 'Vietnam–Cambodian Buddhist Association.'

A number of authorities, mainly French, have lent credence to an assertion that the NLF was formed by a group of Viet Minh veterans in March, 1960, somewhere in Cochinchina; but the NLF, as such, received no international publicity until after December 20, 1960. On January 29, 1961, Hanoi Radio broadcast in English to Europe and Asia its first announcement concerning the NLF:

> A "National Front for the Liberation of South Vietnam" was recently formed in South Vietnam by various forces opposing the fascist Ngo Dinh

Diem regime. This was revealed by Reuters in Saigon and by different papers published in . . . Phnom Penh, capital of Cambodia. This Front was created after a period of preparation and after a conference of representatives of various forces opposing the fascist regime in South Vietnam. According to these forces, the "National Front for the Liberation of South Vietnam" on December 20, 1960, issued a political program and a manifesto . . . [the manifesto] reads: "For a period of nearly a hundred years, the Vietnamese people repeatedly rose up to fight against foreign aggression for national independence and freedom. . . . When the French colonialists invaded our country for the second time, our compatriots—determined not to return to the former slavery—made tremendous sacrifices to defend national sovereignty and independence. The solidarity and heroic struggle of our compatriots during nine years led the resistance war to victory. The 1954 Geneva Agreements reinstalled peace in our country and recognized the sovereignty, independence, unity and territorial integrity of Vietnam. Under these circumstances, our compatriots in South Vietnam would have been able to live in peace, earn their livelihood in security and build a life of plenty and happiness. However, American imperialists who had in the past helped the French colonialists massacre our people have now replaced the French in subjugating the southern part of our country through a disguised colonial regime. . . . The National Front for the Liberation of South Vietnam calls on the entire people to unite and heroically rise up and struggle with the following program of action:

"NORTH VIETNAM
"Jan. 31, 1961
'1. To overthrow the disguised colonial regime of the imperialists and the dictatorial administration, and to form a national and democratic coalition administration.

'2. To carry out a broad and progressive democracy, promulgate the freedom of expression, of the press, of belief, reunion, association and of movement and other democratic freedoms; to carry out general amnesty of political detainees, dissolve the concentration camps dubbed "prosperity zones" and "resettlement centers," abolish the fascist law 10-59 and other anti-democratic laws.

'3. Abolish the economic monopoly of the United States and its henchmen, protect homemade products, encourage the home industry, expand agriculture, and build an independent and sovereign economy; to provide jobs to unemployed people, increase wages for workers, armymen, and office employees; to abolish arbitrary fines and apply an equitable and rational tax system; to help forced evacuees from North Vietnam who now desire to rejoin their native places; and to provide jobs to those who want to remain.

'4. To carry out land rent reduction, guarantee the peasants' right to till their present plots of land, and redistribute communal land in preparation for land reform.

'5. To eliminate the U.S.-style culture of enslavement and depravation; to build a national and progressive culture and education, eliminate illiteracy, open more schools, and carry out reform in the educational and examination system.

'6. To abolish the system of American military advisers, eliminate foreign military bases in Vietnam, and to build a national army defending the fatherland and the people.

'7. To realize equality between men and women, and among different nationalities, and realize the right to autonomy of the national minorities in the country; to protect the legitimate interests of foreign residents in Vietnam; to protect and take care of the interests of overseas Vietnamese.

'8. To carry out a foreign policy of peace and neutrality; to establish diplomatic relations with all the countries which respect the independence and sovereignty of Vietnam.

'9. To reestablish normal relations between the two zones of Vietnam for the attainment of peaceful reunification of the country.

'10. To oppose aggressive wars, actively defend world peace.

"The manifesto concludes by calling on various strata of the people to close their ranks and to carry out the above program. The appeal was addressed to the workers, peasants, and other working people, to the intellectuals, the industrialists, and trades, national minorities, religious communities, democratic personalities, patriotic armymen, and young men and women in South Vietnam.

"Addressing the Vietnamese living abroad, the manifesto called on them 'to turn their thoughts to the beloved motherland and actively contribute to the sacred struggle for national emancipation.' "

It is clear that the NLF was not intended as an exclusively communist enterprise. Rather it was designed to encompass anti-GVN activists, and to exploit the bi-polar nature of politics within South Vietnam. In the period 1954–1960, prior to the NLF's "creation," the objectives of insurgents in the South, other than overthrow of My-Diem, were vague. Communists in the South no doubt shared the overall objectives of the DRV, and were aiming at unification of all Vietnam under the Hanoi government. Some rebel nationalists were no doubt aware of the communists' ambitions, but would have regarded such an outcome as acceptable, if not desirable. Others, disillusioned by the actions of the Diem regime after 1956, simply looked toward the establishment of a genuine democratic government in the South. Some peasants may have been fighting to rid themselves of government, or to oppose modernization, looking only to village autonomy. The sects, if not struggling for a democratic regime, were fighting for their independence, as were some of the tribal groups who chose to join the NLF. The National Liberation Front formulated and publicly articulated objectives for all these.

George Carver reported that:

> On February 11, 1961, Hanoi devoted a second broadcast to the N.L.F.'s manifesto and program, blandly changing the language of both to tone down the more blatant Communist terminology of the initial version. However, even the milder second version (which became the "official" text) borrowed extensively from Le Duan's September speech [at the Third National Congress of the Lao Dong Party in Hanoi] and left little doubt about the Front's true sponsors or objectives.

The "tone down" of communism was fairly subtle, if Hanoi so intended its revision, since the alterations consisted mainly in additions to the Ten Points of phraseology drawn from the preamble of the Manifesto; references to "agrarian reform," in those terms, were, however, cut. There was a marked increase in condemnatory citations of "My-Diem," so that, in eight of ten points in the action program, expelling the U.S. was clearly identified as the way the desired goal would be reached.

Pike refers to an "organizing congress" of the NLF held in December, 1960, of 60 participants, at which plans were announced for convening the first regular NLF congress within a year. Several postponements obtruded, and the meeting did not take place until February–March 1962. Nonetheless, a Central Committee continued in the interim to further define NLF purposes; the subsequent statements differed from the 1960 Manifesto mainly on points of emphasis. For example, "reunification of the country" (Point 9 of the Manifesto) was downplayed from 1960 through 1962. On the first anniversary of the NLF Manifesto, 20 December 1961, its leaders issued a supplementary series of interim or "immediate action" demands. These called for:

1. Withdrawal of all U.S. military personnel and weapons from South Vietnam and abolition of the Staley Plan.

2. An end to hostilities.

3. Establishment of political freedoms.

4. Release of political prisoners.

5. Dissolution of the National Assembly and election of a new assembly and president.

6. Ending the resettlement program.

7. Solution of Vietnam's economic problems.

8. Establishment of a foreign policy of non-alignment.

Although "immediate action" was probably intended to open the way toward formation of a coalition government and thence to ties with Hanoi, there was no mention of reunification; nonetheless, Hanoi in December, 1961, listed NLF objectives as "peace, independence, democracy, a comfortable life, and the peaceful unification of the Fatherland." One likely reason for the NLF's omission of reunification from "immediate action" was its desire to broaden its base on anti-Diem, anti-U.S. grounds—without alienating anti-Communists who might otherwise support the movement. Again, when the first regular NLF congress met from February 16 to March 3, 1962, the earlier basic objectives of the Front were endorsed, excepting reunification. The Radio Hanoi broadcast on the congress added "advancing to peaceful unification of the Fatherland" to a list from which this objective was conspicuously absent in the NLF releases. On July 20, 1962, the anniversary of the Geneva Accords, the NLF issued a declaration that:

> The Central Committee of the National Liberation Front of South Vietnam believes that in the spirit of Vietnamese dealing with Vietnamese solving their own internal affairs, with the determination to put the Fatherland's interest above all else, the forces that oppose U.S. imperialism in South Vietnam will, through mutual concessions, be able to reach a common agreement for united action to serve the people.

The same statement contained a new "four point manifesto":

> 1. The U.S. government must end its armed aggression against South Vietnam, abolish its military command, withdraw all its troops and personnel, as well as the troops and personnel of U.S. satellites and allies, and withdraw all weapons and other war equipment from South Vietnam.
>
> 2. Concerned parties in South Vietnam must stop the war, re-establish peace, and establish conditions throughout South Vietnam to enable the South Vietnamese to solve their own internal affairs. The South Vietnam authority [that is, government] must end its terror operations.
>
> 3. There must be established a national coalition government, to include

representatives of all political parties, cliques, groups, all political tendencies, social strata, members of all religions. This government must guarantee peace. It must organize free general elections in South Vietnam to choose a democratic National Assembly that will carry out the urgently needed policies. It must promulgate democratic liberties to all political parties, groups, religions; it must release all political prisoners, abolish all internment camps and all other forms of concentration [camps], and stop the forced draft of soldiers and the military training of youth, women, public servants, and enterprise, economic independence. It must abolish monopolies and improve the living conditions of all people.

4. South Vietnam must carry out a foreign policy of peace and neutrality. It must establish friendly relations with all nations, especially with her neighbors. It must not enter any military bloc or agree to let any country establish military bases on her soil. It must accept aid from all countries [if] free of political conditions. A necessary international agreement must be signed in which the big powers of all blocs pledge to respect the sovereignty, independence, territorial integrity, and neutrality of South Vietnam. South Vietnam, together with Cambodia and Laos, will form a neutral area, all three countries retaining full sovereignty.

As the anticipated fall of the Diem government drew near in 1963, NLF statements of goals increasingly stressed the anti-American, probably to shift the focus of NLF attack away from a disappearing objective—the defeat of Diem, and possibly because the NLF could not manipulate or adapt to the Buddhist struggle movement. Demands issued by the NLF five days following Diem's fall in November, 1963, were probably intended to take credit for changes in GVN policy then underway, since, except for halting conscription, the Duong Van Minh government was undertaking every reform the NLF called for. However, the first extensive official statement of the NLF Central Committee following Diem's downfall, issued November 17, 1963, did reassert the reunification objective:

> Concerning the reunification of Vietnam, as was expounded many times by the South Vietnam National Liberation Front, the Vietnam Fatherland Front and the DRV government, it will be realized step by step on a voluntary basis, with consideration given to the characteristics of each zone, with equality, and without annexation of one zone by the other.

Concerning coalition government there was less vacillation in NLF emphasis, although there was some detectable variation in the welcome extended from time to time to anti-communist political movements. Similarly, the objective of "neutralization" was constant. Cambodia was held up as a model, and there was some implication in early NLF statements that it would accept international supervision of "neutralization." Beginning in 1963 NLF statements were couched to convey the notion that "reunification" and "neutralization" were distinct one from the other, apparently out of deference to DRV reaction against proposals to neutralize North Vietnam.

b. *Leadership*

The NLF founders were shadowy figures most of whom had earned modest repute on the murky fringes of Vietnamese politics. They seem to have been chosen with an eye to avoiding known Communists, and to obtaining wide representation from South Vietnam's complicated society. Although the NLF Central Committee reserved places for 52 members, only 31 names were publicized as founding members, indicating either a large covert membership, or, more likely, simple inability to find eligible persons to fill the posts. A U.S. study of 73 NLF leaders in 1965 indicated that almost all were born in South Vietnam, and almost all were highly educated. Most had histories of anti-French political activity, or identification with religious movements, and it appears that if many were not themselves crypto-communists, they had known and worked with communists for years. The prime example of the group is Nguyen Huu Tho, who was the first formally elected chairman of the Presidium of the Central Committee of the NLF. Tho was a Cochinchinese lawyer, once a socialist, who spent some months with the Viet Minh in the Mekong Delta in 1947. He thereafter led anti-French and anti-US demonstrations, defended a number of Vietnamese before Saigon courts for crimes related to the "Resistance," and served some time in French jails. He also edited a clandestine Viet Minh newspaper aimed at Saigon intellectuals. In August, 1954, he became vice chairman of the leftist Saigon Peace Committee, or Movement for the Defense of Peace (MDP). In November, 1954, according to CIA information, Tho and others in the MDP were arrested, and Tho spent the next seven years in Diem's detention centers. Mysteriously released in December, 1961, the CIA reported him elected to NLF office at the congress of March, 1962. Douglas Pike's information has Tho active in Saigon politics through 1958, at which time he was jailed. His NLF biography states that "he was liberated by a daring guerrilla raid on the jail in 1961," but Pike, unable to find any record of such a raid, concludes that Tho was provisional chairman and was selected Central Committee Chairman at the organizing meeting.

c. *Development*

The NLF rapidly took on organizational reality from the Central Committee down through a web of subordinate and associated groups to villages all over Vietnam. Pike estimates that within a few months of its founding in December, 1960, its membership doubled, doubled again by autumn, 1961, and then redoubled by early 1962, at which time 300,000 Vietnamese were on its roles. These were members of the "liberation associations," NLF *per se,* of which there were administrative associations (e.g., provincial headquarters) and functional associations (e.g., Youth Liberation Association); or, they belonged to one of several political parties, including the communist party, affiliated with the NLF; or, they served in the Liberation Army. Normally, each man, woman and child belonged to many organizations simultaneously. A French analysis of Viet Minh organization aptly described the NLF:

> The individual is enchained in several networks of independent hierarchies . . . a territorial hierarchy . . . running from the family and the block to the interprovincial government, and associations that incorporate male and female youth groups, groups of mothers, of farmers, factory, and plantation workers' syndicates . . . they could just as well include clubs of flute players or bicycle racers; the essential thing is that no one escapes from this enrollment and that the territorial hierarchy is crossed by another one, which supervises the first and is in turn supervised by it, both being overseen by police organizations and the [Communist] Party. . . .

The key operational components of the NLF were the Liberation Army and the People's Revolutionary Party, as the communists within the NLF termed themselves. The former had a lien on the services of every NLF member, man, woman or child, although functionally its missions were usually carried out by formally organized and trained paramilitary or full-time units. All "Viet Cong" units were, from 1961 on, regarded as part of the Liberation Army.

There can be little doubt that communists played a major role in organizing the NLF. Although Diem's Communist Denunciation campaign had foreclosed "Front" activity, the communists of South Vietnam possessed the leadership, tight subordination and conspiratorial doctrine necessary for them to survive; moreover, they were, as Milton Sacks characterized them, "the most persevering, most cohesive, best-disciplined, and most experienced political group in Vietnam." The People's Revolutionary Party was not formed until January, 1962; it was explicitly the "Marxist–Leninist Party of South Vietnam," and it purported to be the "vanguard of the NLF, the paramount member." In 1962, it had some 35,000 members. The Lao Dong Party had continued low level overt activity, as well as covert operations, in South Vietnam throughout the years 1955 to 1962. For example, leaflets were distributed over the Lao Dong imprimatur. But the PRP denied official links with the Lao Dong Party of the DRV beyond "fraternal ties of communism." The denial implies the question: What roles did the DRV and the Lao Dong Party play in the years of patient work necessary to bring the NLF to flower in so short a time after 1960? What role did they play in the insurgency overall?

The official U.S. view has been that the PRP is merely the southern arm of the Lao Dong Party, and one instrument by which Hanoi instigated and controlled the revolt against "My-Diem." Douglas Pike's analysis led him to concur, with reservations:

> The Viet Minh elements in South Vietnam during the struggle against the French had of course included many non-Communist elements. . . . After 1954 many Viet Minh entered the ranks of the new Diem government, and even a decade later many of the top military and civilian governmental figures in Saigon were former Viet Minh. Nevertheless the Viet Minh elements, made up chiefly but not entirely of Communists, continued to offer resistance to the Diem government. . . . In terms of overt activity such as armed incidents of the distribution of propaganda leaflets the period was quiet and the Communists within the remnant Viet Minh organization relatively inactive. In addition, much of the activity that did take place apparently was the work of impatient cadres operating in the South independently of Hanoi's orders. . . .
>
> Such action on their part and the religious sects is understandable, and the emergence of a clandestine militant opposition group could be expected. . . . such an effort would be in complete harmony with Vietnamese social tradition and individual psychology. But there is a vast difference between a collection of clandestine opposition political groups and the organizational weapon that emerged, a difference in kind and not just degree. The National Liberation Front was not simply another indigenous covert group, or even a coalition of such groups. It was an organizational steamroller, nationally conceived and nationally organized, endowed with ample cadres and funds, crashing out of the jungle to flatten the GVN. It was not an ordinary secret society of the kind that had dotted the Vietnamese political landscape for

decades. It projected a social construction program of such scope and ambition that of necessity it must have been created in Hanoi and imported. A revolutionary organization must build; it begins with persons suffering genuine grievances, who are slowly organized and whose militancy gradually increases until a critical mass is reached and the revolution explodes. Exactly the reverse was the case with the NLF. It sprang full-blown into existence and then was fleshed out. The grievances were developed or manufactured almost as a necessary afterthought. The creation of the NLF was an accomplishment of such skill, precision, and refinement that when one thinks of who the master planner must have been, only one name comes to mind: Vietnam's organizational genius, Ho Chi Minh.

Volume I   List of Documents

launching of a program of rapid economic aid to Southeast Asia. Secretary of State Dean Acheson letter to R. Allen Griffin, 3 June 1950.

Document 8   (page 372)
North Korea attacks South Korea and President Truman announces U.S. military assistance not only to South Korea but also an "acceleration in the furnishing of military assistance to the forces of France and the Associated States in Indochina and the dispatch of a military mission. . . ." Presidential Statement, 27 June 1950.

Document 9   (page 373)
A summary of existing policy on Indochina reveals the JCS view on NSC 73 that the U.S. give consideration to providing air and naval assistance should the Chinese provide overt support to the Viet Minh. Consultants' Meeting, 25 July 1950.

1952

Document 10   (page 375)
The NSC considers the consequences to the United States of communist domination of Southeast Asia. Loss of Southeast Asia is seen as putting economic and political pressures on Japan, opening sources of strategic materials to the Soviet Bloc, rendering the U.S. position in the Pacific precarious and jeopardizing lines of communication and trade routes to South Asia. If Red China intervenes, the U.S. should take appropriate military action as part of a U.N. action or in conjunction with others but not unilaterally. Annex to NSC 124, 13 February 1952.

Document 11   (page 381)
If the Chinese invade Indochina, "he [Acheson] said it was clear that it was futile and a mistake to defend Indochina in Indochina. He said we could not have another Korea. . . . we could not put ground troops in Indochina. . . . our only hope was of changing the Chinese mind." Secretary of State Note (L. D. Battle), 17 June 1952.

Document 12   (page 382)
Acheson publicly announces optimism over the conduct of the National armies in Indochina and that communist "aggression has been checked" and that the "tide is now moving in our favor." State Department Release 473, 18 June 1952.

Document 13   (page 384)
The President approves NSC 124/2 (NSC 124/1 as amended) on the U.S. objectives and courses of action with respect to Southeast Asia. With respect to Indochina, the U.S. would continue to assure the French of the international interest of the Indochina effort; use U.S. influence to promote political, military, economic, and social policies; provide increased aid in the absence of overt Chinese aggression; oppose French withdrawal; and seek collective action against Red China intervention. NSC 124/2, 25 June 1952.

Document 14   (page 390)
The U.S. and Britain discuss issuing a warning to Red China on intervention in Indochina. French successes could trigger Chinese intervention and the U.S. had "no infantry available for operations within Indochina." The U.S. thinking is

along the lines of a naval blockade of China's coast. London Ministerial Talks, 26 June 1952.

1953

Document 15   (*page 391*)
The Intelligence Advisory Committee concludes that Communist China will not invade Indochina even though hostilities conclude in Korea. The French situation, however, is expected to continue to deteriorate while the Viet Minh prestige increases. National Intelligence Estimate, NIE-91, 4 June 1953.

Document 16   (*page 405*)
The State Department recommends to the NSC an increase in aid to France of $400 million in the current fiscal year. Memorandum for NSC, 5 August 1953.

Document 17   (*page 410*)
The JCS learn that Secretary of Defense plans to forward their 11 August memorandum to Secretary of State so a new memorandum is drafted which makes changes to certain "overly optimistic" statements with respect to "promises of success offered by the Navarre Concept." JCS Memorandum for Secretary of Defense, 28 August 1953.

Document 18   (*page 412*)
President Eisenhower approves the statement of NSC 162/2 as basic national security policy which addresses the Soviet threat to U.S. security. NSC 162/2, 30 October 1953.

Document 19   (*page 429*)
The CIA estimates the Chinese and Soviet reactions to U.S. intervention in Indochina with ground, air, and naval forces. It is anticipated that the Communist Bloc would not overtly intervene even though decisive defeat of the Viet Minh would result but would support and augment the Viet Minh to prolong the resistance. Special CIA Estimate, SE-53, 18 December 1953.

1954

Document 20   (*page 434*)
The President approves the statement of policy in MSC 177, "United States Objectives and Courses of Action with Respect to Southeast Asia," which views the loss of Indochina as having "most serious repercussions on U.S. and free world interests . . ." (NSC 177 was renumbered as NSC 5405) NSC 5405, 16 January 1954.

Document 21   (*page 443*)
The President's Special Committee decides to recommend action on certain urgent French requests for twenty-two B-26 aircraft and two hundred Air Force mechanics for Indochina, and to await General O'Daniel's return before deciding on other requests. It is generally agreed that the importance to the U.S. of winning in Indochina could lead to intervention by U.S. and naval forces—but "not ground forces." ISA Memorandum for the Record, 30 January 1954.

Document 22   (*page 447*)
The JCS express concern over developments in the status of the MAAG Chief to Indochina relative to a considerable increase in personnel and scope of train-

ing responsibilities. The French feel that "it should be clearly understood that neither O'Daniel nor MAAG was to have any powers, advisory or otherwise" in planning operations or training the national armies. The JCS feels a demotion of O'Daniel in deference to Navarre is detrimental to U.S. prestige. JCS Memorandum for Secretary of Defense, 5 March 1954.

Document 23   (page 448)
In the preparation of Defense Department views regarding negotiations on Indochina for the Geneva Conference, the JCS reaffirm their position concerning the strategic importance of Indochina to the security interests of the United States as reflected in NSC 5405. JCS Memorandum for Secretary of Defense, 12 March 1954.

Document 24   (page 451)
General Erskine submits the President's Special Committee recommendations on the military implications of the U.S. position on Indochina at Geneva. The analysis concludes that "no solution to the Indochina problem short of victory is acceptable." The conclusions expressed are felt to merit consideration by the NSC and the President. Erskine Memorandum for the Special Committee, NSC, 17 March 1954.

Document 25   (page 454)
Secretary of Defense, Charles E. Wilson, is fully in accord with the JCS views and General Erskine's recommendations, and recommends to Secretary Dulles that they be carefully considered in preparation for the Geneva Conference. Wilson letter to Dulles, 23 March 1954.

Document 26   (page 455)
General Ely, Chairman of the French Chiefs of Staff, is "unsympathetic" to the JCS view to expand MAAG, Indochina to assist in training Vietnamese. Ely feels it would encroach on French responsibilities, would affect "prestige" and shows lack of confidence in French Leadership. (Annex A, Ely Memorandum for Radford; Annex B, JCS Memorandum for the President) JCS Memorandum for President's Committee, 29 March 1954.

Document 27   (page 460)
The U.S. proposes a coalition of U.S., France, Associated States, U.K., Australia, New Zealand, Thailand, and the Philippines, which would fight in Indochina as an alternative to French Union surrender and as a position of strength going to Geneva. Dulles 3476 to Paris, 3 April 1954.

Document 28   (page 461)
The British consider partition the "least undesirable settlement" for Indochina and had not developed thoughts on a confrontation with a French sell-out. Dulles 5177 to London, 4 April 1954.

Document 29   (page 461)
The French request "immediate armed intervention of U.S. carrier aircraft at Dien Bien Phu" to save the situation. Admiral Radford had previously assured Ely that he would "do his best" to obtain the U.S. support. Paris 3710 to Dulles, 4 April 1954.

Document 30 (*page 462*)
NSC Action No. 1074-A considers the problem of determining the circumstances, conditions, and extent to which the U.S. should commit its resources to save Indochina. The problem involves four issues: (1) the prospect of loss of Indochina; (2) the risks, requirements, and consequences of intervention; (3) desirability and form of U.S. intervention; and (4) the timing and circumstances of intervention. NSC Action 1074-A, 5 April 1954.

Document 31 (*page 471*)
The U.S. Army position on intervention in Indochina cites the military disadvantages of such action. Specifically, the Army views are that air and naval forces alone cannot assure victory; that atomic weapons do not reduce the number of ground troops required; that at least seven U.S. divisions with air and naval support are required to win *if the French withdraw and the Chinese do not intervene;* and that the equivalent of twelve U.S. divisions are required *if* the Chinese intervene. Army Position on NSC Action No. 1074-A (undated).

Document 32 (*page 472*)
The President's Special Committee submits recommendations concerning longer range policy and courses of action for possible future contingencies in Southeast Asia not covered by NSC 5405. It is recommended that the U.S. accept nothing short of military victory, oppose a negotiated settlement at Geneva, pressure the Associated States to continue the war with U.S. support even if negotiations succeed, and seek participation of other nations. Regardless of the outcome of current operations in Indochina, the U.S. in all prudence should develop a regional defense posture incorporating all the Southeast Asian states. Part II, Special Committee Report on Southeast Asia, 5 April 1954.

Document 33 (*page 476*)
"U.S. is doing everything possible . . . . to prepare public, Congressional, and constitutional basis for united action in Indochina." However, such action is considered "impossible" except on a coalition basis with British Commonwealth participation. Dulles 3482 to Paris, 5 April 1954.

Document 34 (*page 476*)
France feels that the time for formulating coalitions has passed as the fate of Indochina will be decided in the next ten days at Dien Bien Phu. Dillon (Paris) 3729 to Dulles, 5 April 1954.

Document 35 (*page 477*)
Eden feels the seriousness of the French military situation is exaggerated— "French cannot lose war between now and the coming of the rainy season however badly they may conduct it." London 4382 to Dulles, 6 April 1954.

Document 36 (*page 477*)
Eden informs Dulles that Britain is strongly opposed to intervention at Dien Bien Phu and intends to lend only diplomatic support to France at Geneva in search of a settlement. DULTE 5 (Geneva) to Washington, 25 April 1954.

Document 37 (*page 478*)
Dulles expresses "dismay that the British are apparently encouraging the French in a direction of surrender which is in conflict not only with our interest but what I [Dulles] conceived theirs to be." DULTE 9, 26 April 1954.

Document 38   (page 480)
Dulles and Eden exchange frank and heated words over the British pressuring
France for a cease-fire. The U.S. indicates that the tripartite position is poor,
i.e., not "very impressive or cohesive" and that "the other side" was worried—
but not about Britain. The U.S. is also concerned over the effects on NATO,
EDC and the entire defense structure in Europe. DULTE 13, 27 April 1954.

Document 39   (page 481)
Dulles makes an estimate of rapidly moving developments: (1) when Dien Bien
Phu falls, the French Government will change, probably to the left, committed
to liquidate China. A withdrawal of forces to defensible enclaves under U.S.
protection with subsequent U.S. training of native armies is considered. Open
intervention at this point would be answered by Chinese intervention, (2) U.K.
attitude is one of increasing weakness, (3) "the decline of France, the great
weakness of Italy, and the considerable weakness of England create a situation
where . . . we must be prepared to take the leadership. . . ." DULTE 21, 29
April 1954.

Document 40   (page 482)
The Intelligence Advisory Committee concludes that the fall of Dien Bien Phu
would have far-reaching and adverse repercussions, but would not signal the
collapse of the French Union political and military situation in Indochina, nor
would it substantially alter relative military capabilities of French and Viet Minh
forces. The French Union could retain control of the cities though there would be
a serious decline in the Vietnamese will to continue the war. NIE 63-54, 30 April
1954.

Document 41   (page 487)
Major General Thomas J. H. Trapnell, former Chief of MAAG, Indochina
comments in his debriefing on the French situation in Indochina. His comments
cover in detail the strategic position of Indochina, the government and its prosecution of the war, the performance of MDAP supported forces, the objectives of
the opposing forces, the organization and tactics of both the French and Viet
Minh forces. In Trapnell's view, few of the aims of the Navarre concept are progressing satisfactorily. "Dien Bien Phu is not only another Na San, but a grave
tactical and strategic error." On the political aspects of the war, Trapnell feels
that "a strictly military solution to the war in Indochina is not possible . . . It is
doubtful if the ordinary people understand the issues at stake between the rebel
and Associated States objectives." The solution in Indochina requires a strong
French assault on the Viet Minh, training of National armies, a defensive alliance
of Asian nations, and a guarantee of the Associated States borders. Trapnell rec-
omends a U.S. training mission for Indochina, and concludes that victory in
Indochina is international rather than local and essentially political as well as military. Major General Trapnell Debriefing, 3 May 1954.

Document 42   (page 499)
The NSC 195th Meeting considers Secretary Dulles pessimistic report on Geneva
to the President: (1) there is no responsible French Government to deal with,
(2) the British reject the "regional grouping," (3) the British want *secret* talks
on Southeast Asia, (4) the expected communist proposal is for foreign troop
withdrawal and elections, (5) and the U.K. wants a settlement based on partition. NSC 195th Meeting, 6 May 1954.

Document 43   (page 500)
Dulles briefs Congressional leaders on the Geneva Conference and reviews the weaknesses of Britain's position. Congress members comments are adverse. Dulles states three conclusions: (1) U.S. should not intervene militarily, (2) U.S. must push rapidly for a Southeast Asia community, (3) and the U.S. should not "write off" the British and French in spite of their weakness in Asia. TEDUL 37, 6 May 1954.

Document 44   (page 501)
President Eisenhower makes it clear that the preconditions for U.S. intervention in Indochina are that the "U.S. would never intervene alone, that the indigenous people must invite intervention, and that there must be regional or collective action The NSC action ot the meeting on 5 April as pertains to paragraph 1.*b.* of the record (organizing a regional grouping) is approved by the President. Memorandum by R. Cutler, Special Assistant, for Secretary of Defense and CJCS and Meeting Minutes, 7 May 1954.

Document 45   (page 504)
May 8–July 21; Geneva Conference on Indochina. The 1st Plenary Session convenes on 8 May and hears proposals by France and the Viet Minh for cessation of hostilities and participation in the conference. (Excerpts) The delegates to the conference are from Great Britain and the USSR (joint chairmen), France, the United States, Communist China, Cambodia, Laos, ano Victnam, and the Viet Minh regime. (Final agreements are signed on July 20 and 21, and the main provisions concerning Vietnam are that (1) Vietnam is to be partitioned along the 17th parallel into North and South Vietnam, (2) regulations are imposed on foreign military bases and personnel and on increased armaments, (3) countrywide elections, leading to the reunification of North and South Vietnam, are to be held by July 20, 1956, and (4) an International Control Commission (ICC) is to be established to supervise the implementation of the agreements. The United States and Vietnam are not signatories to the agreements. The United States issues a unilateral declaration stating that it (1) "will refrain from the threat or the use of force to disturb" the Geneva agreements, (2) "would view any renewal of the aggression in violation of the aforesaid agreements with grave concern and as seriously threatening international peace and security," and (3) "shall continue to seek to achieve unity through free elections, supervised by the UN to insure that they are conducted fairly.") Excerpts from 1st Plenary Session of the Geneva Conference, 8 May 1954.

Document 46   (page 506)
The Defense member of the NSC Planning Board indicates the options available to the U.S. with regard to the Geneva results. General Bonesteel suggests that the increased risks associated with pressuring France to continue the war and possible U.S. intervention to stop the communist advance can "more surely and safely be accepted now than ever again." On the other hand, a compromise at Geneva would lead to communist subversion at a late date and U.S. involvement then might be inhibited by an increased Soviet nuclear capability. "Asia could thus be lost." General Bonesteel Memorandum for Secretary of Defense, 9 May 1954.

Document 47   (page 507)
Secretary Dulles forwards the basic instructions approved by the President for the head of the U.S. Delegation to Geneva. "The United States is not prepared

to give its express or implied approval to any cease-fire, armistice, or other settlement . . . ." which would subvert the local governments, impair territorial integrity, or jeopardize forces of the French Union. Dulles TOSEC 138 to Geneva, 12 May 1954.

Document 48   (page 508)
Secretary Stevens emphasizes the Army's concern over high-level official views that "air and sea forces alone could solve our problems in Indochina" and that the complex nature of these problems would require a major logistical effort— "it explodes the myth that air and sea forces could solve the Indochina problems." Secretary of the Army Memorandum for Secretary of Defense, 19 May 1954.

Document 49   (page 509)
The JCS recommend against a "Korea-type" defense of Southeast Asia as unsound. Accordingly, the U.S. "should adopt the concept of offensive actions against the 'military power of the aggressor,' (in this instance, Communist China) rather than local reaction to the attack. JCS Memorandum for Secretary of Defense, 21 May 1954.

Document 50   (page 511)
The JCS point out their belief that, from the U.S. point of view with reference to the Far East, "Indochina is devoid of decisive military objectives and allocation of more than token U.S. armed forces in Indochina would be a serious diversion of limited U.S. capabilities." JCS Memorandum for Secretary of Defense, 26 May 1954.

Document 51   (page 515)
The White House views the JCS position on intervention in Indochina as not involving any new policy issue relative to NSC 5405. However, a pencilled Secretary of Defense marginal note indicates that the White House "misses the point" —the JCS was considering the "regional grouping" and others in the grouping, i.e., U.K. may object to NSC 5405 policy. Hence the JCS is warning "not to get involved in such a grouping" unless all parties accept direct action. White House Memorandum for Secretary of Defense, 26 May 1954.

Document 52   (page 516)
Ely emphasizes particular points to Trapnell and Dillon: (1) Ely was not in accord with O'Daniel's proposal to reorganize the Vietnamese army on a divisional basis, (2) O'Daniel's operational war plant was unrealistic, (3) the increasing frequency of American criticism of French conduct of the war was not appreciated, (4) Ely was regrouping his forces for defense of the Delta, and (5) One or two U.S. Marine divisions could assure defense of the Delta. Paris 4566 to Dulles, 27 May 1954.

Document 53   (page 518)
General Valluy evaluates the Tonkin Delta military situation: (1) If Tonkin is lost, a military line will not be re-established, (2) in this connection, there are no South Vietnamese who could oppose North Vietnamese, (3) Ho Chi Minh's objective is Tonkin and the political capital Hanoi, to be gained either by negotiation or military force as necessary, (4) if Tonkin is lost, France will not fight in the South, (5) nor would Vietnamese fight against other Vietnamese

and sooner or later the whole of Vietnam will become communist. TEDUL 171, 7 June 1954.

Document 54   (page 519)
Eden cites three major issues emerging on which "we cannot compromise": (1) separate treatment of Laos and Cambodia problem, (2) status and powers of international supervisory authority and (3) composition of the international supervisory authority. Britain feels negotiations have failed and little can be salvaged in Vietnam. DULTE 164, 9 June 1954.

Document 55   (page 521)
"General Ely has twice in my presence stated that his keenest desire is for the United States to enter this war." The purpose of General Valluy's statement (war assessment) is either to bring the U.S. and five other powers into the conflict or to prepare an "excuse before history" for an armistice. Saigon 2714 to Dulles, 10 June 1954.

Document 56   (page 522)
The French impression is that even after all conditions are met, the chances of U.S. participation are "nil." With this attitude it is only a matter of time until the French come to terms with the Viet Minh. The result would be disastrous to French public opinion and the "U.S. would be blamed" for having failed in the crisis. Therefore, it is recommended that the French be informed that "the President is *no longer prepared to request military intervention*" even if France fulfills all conditions. France should strive for an armistice and thus avoid a military disaster. A few months delay in communist takeover in Indochina is not commensurate with "possible collapse of the defense of Western Europe." Paris 4841 to Dulles, 14 June 1954.

Document 57   (page 523)
The French want, and "in effect have, an option on our intervention, but they do not want to exercise it and the date of expiry of our option is fast running out." TEDUL 197, 14 June 1954.

Document 58   (page 524)
Secretary Dulles emphasizes that events have shown that predictions he has made all along on the lack of any real French desire for U.S. intervention but "as a card to play at Geneva." The U.S. does not see that France's bitterness is justified considering "prolonged French and U.K. indecision." Dulles 4579 to Paris, 14 June 1954.

Document 59   (page 525)
The CIA estimates communist reactions to the participation of U.S. air and naval forces at various levels of intensity and on various targets in conjunction with French Union forces in Indochina. Special National Intelligence Estimate, SNIE 10-4-54, 15 June 1954.

Document 60   (page 531)
The "underground military talks" at Geneva are pointing toward a *de facto* partition of Indochina. "There can of course be no repeat no question of U.S. participation in any attempt to 'sell' a partition to noncommunist Vietnamese." TEDUL 212, 17 June 1954.

Document 61   (page 532)
U.S. re-examines possible *de facto* partition of Vietnam in light of five-power staff report suggesting Thakhek-Donghoi line. TEDUL 222, 18 June 1954.

Document 62   (page 532)
The French feel that partition is the best settlement they could have worked for under the conditions laid down by U.S. for intervention which "no French Parliament would approve." Partition should come as no surprise to the Vietnamese since the Viet Minh had made it clear to them—"coalition government or partition." DULTE 195, 18 June 1954.

Document 63   (page 534)
General Smith and Molotov conduct lengthy conversations on "making positions clear." The Soviet tactics were probably to forestall U.S. intervention in the Delta by a compromise formula if intervention appeared imminent. When intervention became improbable, the "ante" in negotiations was raised. DULTE 202, 19 June 1954.

Document 64   (page 537)
In conversations with the French, China recognizes that "two governments" exist in Vietnam and Chou En-lai regards that the final political settlement should be reached by direct negotiations between the two governments. Paris 5035 to Dulles, 24 June 1954.

Document 65   (page 538)
Dulles thinks our present role at Geneva should "soon be restricted to that of observer. . . ." TOSEC 478, 24 June 1954.

Document 66   (page 539)
A French *aide-memoire* indicates the French objective to seek a *de facto* division which leaves a solid territory for the State of Vietnam and further requests that the U.S. do nothing to encourage an anticipated "violent and unreasoning" reaction on the part of Vietnamese patriots who object to an indefinite period of division of the country. Dulles 4852 to Paris, 28 June 1954.

Document 67   (page 540)
French negotiations with Viet Minh are stalled and Mendes-France is perplexed by reference to the "Dong Hoi" line since France was holding out for the 18th parallel. Paris 5117 to Dulles, 30 June 1954.

Document 68   (page 541)
Dulles warns that Ngo Dinh Diem has been "kept in the dark" on French negotiations and fears that if revealed as a *fait accompli* the reaction French wish to avoid will result. Dulles 39 to Paris, 2 July 1954.

Document 68   (page 541)
France apologizes for not keeping the U.S. fully informed of French military withdrawals in the Delta. In addition, while France is holding out for an eighteenmonth period before elections, Diem, to the contrary, has suggested elections within a year. Paris 32 to Dulles, 2 July 1954.

Document 70   (*page 542*)
The U.S. does not want to be associated with a settlement which falls short of the seven-point memorandum on which Britain agreed and now appears to be less than firm. "If either or both the French and Communists are operating on the assumption we will adhere to any settlement they agree to, then we may be headed for serious trouble." Dulles 52 to Paris, 3 July 1954.

Document 71   (*page 543*)
Dillon recommends that if the U.S. attempts to get the best possible settlement, we should (1) maintain a Geneva delegation, (2) have Dulles return to head the delegation, (3) offer French support to sell a settlement to Vietnam if it is satisfactory, and (4) pressure Britain to stick to the seven points of US–UK agreement. Paris 41 to Dulles, 4 July 1954.

Document 72   (*page 545*)
Mendes-France will announce to the National Assembly that if a cease-fire is not agreed to prior to 21 July, it will be necessary for the Assembly to approve the sending of conscripts to Indochina. Paris 66 to Dulles, 6 July 1954.

Document 73   (*page 546*)
Dulles informs Eden that it is "better if neither Bedell nor I went back" to Geneva since the French will probably settle for worse than the 7-point agreement, hence it would be embarrassing to all concerned. Dulles NIACT 101 to London, 7 July 1954.

Document 74   (*page 546*)
The U.S. feels that elections mean eventual unification of Vietnam under Ho Chi Minh and therefore should be held "as long after a cease-fire agreement as possible and in conditions free from intimidation. . . ." Further, the U.S. believes no date should be set now and that no conditions be accepted which would affect international supervision of elections. The U.S. would not oppose a settlement based on the 7 points nor would we seek to upset a settlement by force. Dulles 77 to Paris, 7 July 1954.

Document 75   (*page 547*)
"I have never harbored any thought of wilful concealment . . . there is a certain lack of intimacy . . ." in relations with the present government. The U.S. intends to leave representation at Geneva but not Bedell Smith nor Dulles will return. The U.S. should avoid a "position at Geneva . . ." Dulles 85 to Paris, 8 July 1954.

Document 76   (*page 548*)
The Chinese inform Ambassador Johnson that Chou En-lai had a "very good meeting" with Ho Chi Minh and that "results would be helpful to the French." The French believe that the Sino-Soviet positions have been coordinated with the Chinese views on Asian problems being given major weight. SECTO 578. 9 July 1954.

Document 77   (*page 550*)
President Eisenhower and Secretary Dulles indicate firmly to President Mendes-France the rationale behind not sending Dulles or General Smith back to

Geneva. Essentially, the rationale is based on failure of the U.S., U.K. and France to agree on a joint position at Geneva and lack of agreement on a "united action" proposal if the position is not accepted by the communists. Dulles sees France and U.K. enhancing a communist "whittling-away" process by readily accepting less than the seven points. Dulles 127 to Paris, 10 July 1954.

Document 78   (page 552)

France views the Dulles decision as (1) making the French bargaining position weaker and (2) that Europe would interpret U.S. absence from Geneva as a step in the "return to a policy of isolationism." Paris 134 to Dulles, 11 July 1954.

Document 79   (page 553)

France indicates the "necessity for a clear-cut U.S. guarantee that would protect the Associated States" if the communists did not honor a Geneva settlement. Mendes-France will resign if no cease-fire is reached. Paris 133 to Dulles, 11 July 1954.

Document 80   (page 554)

Secretary Dulles reports on the Paris meeting: (1) an agreed French–United States position paper on Indochina which has the United States respecting terms conforming to a 7-point agreement; (2) the 7 points along the lines which were agreed during the Churchill-Eisenhower conversations; (3) a Mendes-France to Dulles letter which tells Dulles that his absence from Geneva would produce an effect opposite to his intention; (4) a Dulles to Mendes-France letter which informs him of General Smith's return to Geneva; (5) and a letter from Eden to Mendes-France reassuring him of Britain's support. Paris 179 to Dulles, 14 July 1954.

Document 81   (page 558)

Secretary Dulles reports on his trip to Paris at the NSC meeting. Dulles had told Mendes that France's troubles stemmed from lack of a decision on EDC and the Soviets were successful in splitting France and Germany. If the U.S. cannot guarantee the Geneva Conference results or influence France to reject any settlement, the U.S. will be blamed and put a major strain on Franco–United States relations. NSC Minutes, 15 July 1954.

Document 82   (page 559)

At a meeting of Mendes, Eden, and Molotov, the outstanding issues are summarized: (1) demarcation line for Vietnam; (2) elections; (3) control arrangements; (4) regroupment time; (5) prevention of arms importation, and (6) Laotian regroupment areas. France strongly opposes Molotov on holding elections in 1955 and placing the demarcation line at the 16th parallel. SECTO 632, 17 July 1954.

Document 83   (page 560)

The Vietnamese delegation to the Geneva Conference secretly passes the U.S. delegate a note of protest which had been handed to the French. The note complains that the "National Government of Vietnam has been left in complete ignorance" of proposals made by the French to other nations on Vietnam's fate. Vietnam rejects the *de facto* partition proposal, a cease-fire, and requests that

United Nations control be established over all Vietnam territory. SECTO 633, 17 July 1954.

Document 84 (page 561)
The Chinese Communists inform the U.S. of their position via Seymour Topping, Associated Press. The despatch reflects the views of Chou En-lai and demands that the U.S. guarantee a "partition peace plan." Further, China is hopeful of a cease-fire but did not rule out the chance for one even if the U.S. refuses to accept the armistice. SECTO 639, 18 July 1954.

Document 85 (page 563)
The U.S. fears Britain will push France into an agreement short of the 7 points resulting in a situation which had been previously discussed in Paris. TOSEC 565, 18 July 1954.

Document 86 (page 563)
At the 23rd Indochina restricted session, Tran Van Do (Vietnam) states that Vietnam cannot associate iself with the final declaration of the Conference which is to be reviewed. Vietnam does not agree to conditions for cease-fire nor have they as yet advanced proposals for a solution "based on peace, independence, and unity." SECTO 654, 18 July 1954.

Document 87 (page 566)
The Vietnamese delegation requests a plenary session to put forward their position (Document 171, preceding). The U.S. replies that the Vietnamese position is "not practicable" and, in indicating that time is short, suggests that the Vietnamese "speak directly with the French." SECTO 655, 18 July 1954.

Document 88 (page 566)
Seymour Topping again supplies confidential information from a Chinese Communist contact, Huang Hua. "When Huang Hua spoke of the possibility of American bases in Indochina, or anti-Communist pact in Southeast Asia, he became very agitated, his hands shook, and his usually excellent English broke down . . ." Chinese are convinced that France and the U.S. have made a deal. SECTO 661, 19 July 1954.

Document 89 (page 567)
International control commission is to be composed of Poland, India, Canada, or Belgium. The U.S. is satisfied that this is better than Korea and is "within the spirit of Point 7." SECTO 666, 19 July 1954.

Document 90 (page 567)
General Smith makes it clear to France that the U.S. could, under no circumstance, associate itself with the conference declaration and recommends authorization to amend the proposed U.S. declaration of position. SECTO 669, 19 July 1954.

Document 91 (page 568)
Dulles has no objection on Smith's proposal to amend the declaration, but is concerned about including part of paragraph 9 of the Conference declaration, which seems to imply a "multilateral engagement with the Communists" which is inconsistent with the U.S. basic approach. TOSEC 576 NIACT, 19 July 1954.

Document 92   (page 569)
The Vietnamese delegation proposes: (1) a cease-fire on present positions; (2) regroupment into two small zones; (3) disarmament of irregular troops; (4) disarmament and withdrawal of foreign troops; and (5) control by the United Nations. It is noted that there is no provision for demarcation line or partition. SECTO 673, 19 July 1954.

Document 93   (page 570)
The United States, not prepared to sign the Accords, makes a unilateral declaration of its position on the Conference conclusions. The United States declares that it will refrain from the threat or use of force to disturb the agreements and would view any renewal of the aggression with grave concern and as a threat to international peace and security. Unilateral Declaration of the United States, 21 July 1954.

Document 94   (page 571)
Final Declaration of the Geneva Conference, 21 July 1954.

Document 95   (page 573)
Lansdale Team's Report on covert Saigon Mission in 1954 and 1955.

[Document 1]

27 February 1950

REPORT BY THE NATIONAL SECURITY COUNCIL
on
THE POSITION OF THE UNITED STATES
WITH RESPECT TO INDOCHINA

THE PROBLEM

1. To undertake a determination of all practicable United States measures to protect its security in Indochina and to prevent the expansion of communist aggression in that area.

ANALYSIS

2. It is recognized that the threat of communist aggression against Indochina is only one phase of anticipated communist plans to seize all of Southeast Asia. It is understood that Burma is weak internally and could be invaded without strong opposition or even that the Government of Burma could be subverted. However, Indochina is the area most immediately threatened. It is also the only area adjacent to communist China which contains a large European army, which along with native troops is now in armed conflict with the forces of communist aggression. A decision to contain communist expansion at the border of Indochina must be considered as a part of a wider study to prevent communist aggression into other parts of Southeast Asia.

3. A large segment of the Indochinese nationalist movement was seized in 1945 by Ho Chi Minh, a Vietnamese who under various aliases has served as a communist agent for thirty years. He has attracted non-communist as well as communist elements to his support. In 1946, he attempted, but failed to secure French agreement to his recognition as the head of a government of Vietnam. Since then he has directed a guerrilla army in raids against French installations and lines of communication. French forces which have been attempting to restore law and order found themselves pitted against a determined adversary who manufactures effective arms locally, who received supplies of arms from outside sources, who maintained no capital or permanent headquarters and who was, and is able, to disrupt and harass almost any area within Vietnam (Tonkin, Annam and Cochinchina) at will.

4. The United States has, since the Japanese surrender, pointed out to the French Government that the legitimate nationalist aspirations of the people of Indochina must be satisfied, and that a return to the prewar colonial rule is not possible. The Department of State has pointed out to the French Government that it was and is necessary to establish and support governments in Indochina particularly in Vietnam, under leaders who are capable of attracting to their causes the non-communist nationalist followers who had drifted to the Ho Chi Minh communist movement in the absence of any non-communist nationalist movement around which to plan their aspirations.

5. In an effort to establish stability by political means, where military measures had been unsuccessful, i.e., by attracting non-communist nationalists, now followers of Ho Chi Minh, to the support of anti-communist nationalist

leaders, the French Government entered into agreements with the governments of the Kingdoms of Laos and Cambodia to elevate their status from protectorates to that of independent states within the French Union. The State of Vietnam was formed, with similar status, out of the former French protectorates of Tonkin, Annam and the former French Colony of Cochinchina. Each state received an increased degree of autonomy and sovereignty. Further steps towards independence were indicated by the French. The agreements were ratified by the French Government on 2 February 1950.

6. The Governments of Vietnam, Laos and Cambodia were officially recognized by the United States and the United Kingdom on February 7, 1950. Other Western powers have, or are committed to do likewise. The United States has consistently brought to the attention of non-communist Asian countries the danger of communist aggression which threatens them if communist expansion in Indochina is unchecked. As this danger becomes more evident it is expected to overcome the reluctance that they have had to recognize and support the three new states. We are therefore continuing to press those countries to recognize the new states. On January 18, 1950, the Chinese Communist Government announced its recognition of the Ho Chi Minh movement as the legal Government of Vietnam, while on January 30, 1950, the Soviet Government, while maintaining diplomatic relations with France, similarly announced its recognition.

7. The newly formed States of Vietnam, Laos and Cambodia do not as yet have sufficient political stability nor military power to prevent the infiltration into their areas of Ho Chi Minh's forces. The French Armed Forces, while apparently effectively utilized at the present time, can do little more than to maintain the status quo. Their strength of some 140,000 does, however, represent an army in being and the only military bulwark in that area against the further expansion of communist aggression from either internal or external forces.

8. The presence of Chinese Communist troops along the border of Indochina makes it possible for arms, material and troops to move freely from Communist China to the northern Tonkin area now controlled by Ho Chi Minh. There is already evidence of movement of arms.

9. In the present state of affairs, it is doubtful that the combined native Indochinese and French troops can successfully contain Ho's forces should they be strengthened by either Chinese Communist troops crossing the border, or Communist-supplied arms and material in quantity from outside Indochina strengthening Ho's forces.

CONCLUSIONS

10. It is important to United States security interests that all practicable measures be taken to prevent further communist expansion in Southeast Asia. Indochina is a key area of Southeast Asia and is under immediate threat.

11. The neighboring countries of Thailand and Burma could be expected to fall under Communist domination if Indochina were controlled by a Communist-dominated government. The balance of Southeast Asia would then be in grave hazard.

12. Accordingly, the Departments of State and Defense should prepare as a matter of priority a program of all practicable measures designed to protect United States security interests in Indochina.

[Document 2]

March 7, 1950

Dear General Burns:

Embodied below is a brief statement of Department of State policy in Indochina and Southeast Asia. I believe that an examination of this statement will facilitate your consideration of NSC 64.

The Department of State continues to hold that Southeast Asia is in grave danger of Communist domination as a consequence of aggression from Communist China and of internal subversive activities. The Department of State maintains that Indochina, subject as it is to the most immediate danger, is the most strategically important area of Southeast Asia.

The Department of State believes that within the limitations imposed by existing commitments and strategic priorities, the resources of the United States should be deployed to reserve Indochina and Southeast Asia from further Communist encroachment. The Department of State has accordingly already engaged all its political resources to the end that this object be secured. The Department is now engaged in the process of urgently examining what additional economic resources can effectively be engaged in the same operation.

It is now, in the opinion of the Department, a matter of the greatest urgency that the Department of Defense assess the strategic aspects of the situation and consider, from the military point of view, how the United States can best contribute to the prevention of further Communist encroachment in that area.

The military assessment requested above is necessary to a final determination by this Government of the manner in which United States policy in this area shall be executed.

Sincerely yours,

/s/ Dean Rusk
Deputy Under Secretary

Major General James H. Burns,
Office of the Secretary of Defense,
Department of Defense.

[Document 3]

10 April 1950

MEMORANDUM FOR THE SECRETARY OF DEFENSE
SUBJECT: Strategic Assessment of Southeast Asia

The Joint Chiefs of Staff have studied your memorandum, dated 10 March 1950, with its enclosures, in which you requested their views regarding:

a. The strategic importance, from the military point of view, of Southeast Asia;

b. NSC 64, a report by the Department of State on the position of the United States with respect to Indochina, which is now before the National Security Council for consideration;

c. The measures that, from the military point of view, might be taken to prevent Communist expansion into Southeast Asia;

d. The order of magnitude and means of implementation of such measures; and *e.* A French aide-memoire on the subject of aid for Indochina, dated 16 February 1950.

1. In light of U.S. strategic concepts, the integrity of the offshore island chain from Japan to Indochina is of critical strategic importance to the United States.

2. The mainland states of Southeast Asia also are at present of critical strategic importance to the United States because:

   a. They are the major sources of certain strategic materials required for the completion of United States stock pile projects;

   b. The area is a crossroad of communications;

   c. Southeast Asia is a vital segment in the line of containment of communism stretching from Japan southward and around to the Indian Peninsula. The security of the three

[Section missing]

forces are allied with them. In addition, the generally inadequate indigenous forces of the independent states are actively engaged in attempting to maintain internal security in the face of Communist aggression tactics.

5. It appears obvious from intelligence estimates that the situation in Southeast Asia has deteriorated and, without United States assistance, this deterioration will be accelerated. In general, the basic conditions of political and economic stability in this area, as well as the military and internal security conditions, are unsatisfactory. These factors are closely interrelated and it is probable that, from the long-term point of view, political and economic stability is the controlling factor. On the other hand, the military situation in some areas, particularly Indochina, is of pressing urgency.

6. With respect to the measures which, from the United States military point of view, might be taken to prevent Communist expansion in Southeast Asia, the Joint Chiefs of Staff recommend early implementation of military aid programs for Indochina, Indonesia, Thailand, the Philippines, and Burma. Malaya might also be included provided the British by their actions in the areas in Asia where they have primary interest evince a determined effort to resist the expansion of communism and present sufficient military justification for aid. The effectiveness of these military aid programs would be greatly increased by appropriate public statements of United States policy in Southeast Asia.

7. The Joint Chiefs of Staff recommend that the military aid from funds already allocated by the President for the states of Southeast Asia be delivered at the earliest practicable date. They further recommend that the presently unallocated portion of the President's emergency fund under Section 303 of Public Law 329 (81st Congress, 1st Session), be planned and programmed as a matter of urgency.

8. Precise determination of the amounts required for military aid, special covert operations, and concomitant economic and psychological programs in Southeast Asia cannot be made at this time since the financial requirements will, to a large extent, depend on the success of aid and other programs now in the process of implementation. In the light of the world situation, however, it would appear that military aid programs and other measures will be necessary in Southeast Asia at least during the next fiscal year and in at least the same general over-all order of magnitude. The Joint Chiefs of Staff, therefore, strongly recommend that appropriations for over-all use in the general area of Asia be sought for the next fiscal year in terms similar to those under Section 303 of Public Law 329 (81st Congress, 1st Session). It is believed that approximately $100,000,000 will be required for the military portion of this program.

9. In view of the history of military aid in China, the Joint Chiefs of Staff urge that these aid programs be subject, in any event, to the following conditions:

a. That United States military aid not be granted unconditionally; rather, that it be carefully controlled and that the aid program be integrated with political and economic programs; and

b. That requests for military equipment be screened first by an officer designated by the Department of Defense and on duty in the recipient state. These requests should be subject to his determination as to the feasibility and satisfactory coordination of specific military operations. It should be understood that military aid will only be considered in connection with such coordinated operational plans as are approved by the representative of the Department of Defense on duty in the recipient country. Further, in conformity with current procedures, the final approval of all programs for military materiel will be subject to the occurrence of the Joint Chiefs of Staff.

10. The Joint Chiefs of Staff recommend that a Southeast Asia Aid Committee be appointed with State, Defense and ECA representation which will be responsible for the development and implementation of the program for the general area of Southeast Asia. Requests for aid should be screened by the field representatives of the committee in consultation with the local authorities in the countries concerned.

11. Present arrangements for military aid to Indonesia through the military attaches and to the Philippines through the Joint United States Military Aid Group appear to be satisfactory and should be continued.

12. A small military aid group should be established in Thailand to operate in conformity with the requirements in paragraph 9 above. Arrangements for military aid should be made directly with the Thai Government.

13. In view of the very unsettled conditions in Burma, the program for military aid to that country should, for the time being at least, be modest. The arrangements should be made after consultation with the British, and could well be handled by the United States Armed Forces attaches to that country. Arrangements for military aid to Malaya, if and when authorized, should be handled similarly except that request should, in the first instance, originate with British authorities.

14. The Joint Chiefs of Staff recognize the political implications involved in military aid to Indochina. It must be appreciated, however, that French armed forces of approximately 140,000 men are in the field and that if these were to be withdrawn this year because of political considerations, the Bao Dai regime probably could not survive even with United States aid. If the United States were now to insist upon independence for Vietnam and a phased French withdrawal from that country, this might improve the political situation. The French could be expected to interpose objections to, and certainly delays in, such a program. Conditions in Indochina, however, are unstable and the situation is apparently deteriorating rapidly so that the urgent need for at least an initial increment of military and economic aid is psychologically overriding. The Joint Chiefs of Staff, therefore, recommend the provision of military aid to Indochina at the earliest practicable date under a program to implement the President's action approving the allocation of 15 million dollars for Indochina and that corresponding increments of political and economic aid be programmed on an

interim basis without prejudice to the pattern of the policy for additional military, political and economic aid that may be developed later.

15. In view of the considerations set forth in paragraph 14 above, the Joint Chiefs of Staff recommend the immediate establishment of a small United States military aid group in Indochina, to operate in conformity with the requirements in paragraph 9 above. The Joint Chiefs of Staff would expect the senior member of this group to sit in consultation with military representatives of France and Vietnam and possibly of Laos and Cambodia. In addition to screening requests for materiel, he would be expected to insure full coordination of military plans and efforts between the French and Vietnamese forces and to supervise the allocation of material. The Joint Chiefs of Staff believe in the possibility of success of a prompt coordinated United States program of military, political, and economic aid to Southeast Asia and feel that such a success might well lead to the gaining of the initiative in the struggle in that general area.

16. China is the vital strategic area in Asia. The Joint Chiefs of Staff are firmly of the opinion that attainment of United States objectives in Asia can only be achieved by ultimate success in China. Resolution of the situation facing Southeast Asia would therefore, be facilitated if prompt and continuing measures were undertaken to reduce the pressure from Communist China. In this connection, the Joint Chiefs of Staff have noted the evidences of renewed vitality and apparent increased effectiveness of the Chinese Nationalist forces.

17. The Joint Chiefs of Staff suggest the following measures with military implications:

> *a.* An increased number of courtesy or "show the flag" visits to Southeast Asian states;
>
> *b.* Recognition of the "port closure" of Communist China seaports by the Nationalists as a *de facto* blockade so long as it is effective. Such action should remove some of the pressure, direct and indirect, upon Southeast Asia; should be of assistance to the anti-Communist forces engaged in interference with the lines of communication to China; and should aggravate the economic problems and general unrest in Communist China;
>
> *c.* A program of special covert operations designed to interfere with Communist activities in Southeast Asia; and
>
> *d.* Long-term measures to provide for Japan and the other offshore islands a secure source of food and other strategic materials from non-Communist held areas in the Far East.

18. Comments on the French aide-memoire of 16 February 1950, are contained in the substance of this memorandum. The Joint Chiefs of Staff do not concur in the French suggestion for conversations between the "French and American General Staffs" on the subject of Indochina since the desired ends will best be served through conferences in Indochina among the United States military aid group and military representatives of France, Vietnam, Laos, and Cambodia. The Joint Chiefs of Staff are not unmindful of the need for collaboration and consultation with the British and French Governments on Southeast Asia matters and recommend, therefore, that military representatives participate in the forthcoming tripartite discussions on Southeast Asia to be held at the forthcoming meeting of the Foreign Ministers.

FOR THE JOINT CHIEFS OF STAFF:

/s/ OMAR N. BRADLEY
Chairman
Joint Chiefs of Staff

[Document 4]

The Secretary of State   May 4, 1950
Mr. Griffin

Conference on Indo-China—May 2, 1950.

1. *The Indo-China situation cannot be maintained in its present status quo.*

Time is of the essence in the Vietnam situation. Bao Dai and his Government cannot maintain a status quo. Bao Dai must either quickly win additional support and begin showing gains in prestige or there will be a falling away of his present following. There is general cynicism in Vietnam about the French willingness to permit reasonable self-government, and that cynicism spreads to the Bao Dai Government. Bao Dai at present represents a minority group, but he still is potentially capable of achieving substantial majority support if he can prove that he is taking over authority and responsibility and is exercising them. He must be given face. Unless the present trend is materially and almost immediately corrected, Bao Dai's opportunity will be irretrievably lost and his strength will run to water. To salvage the situation a fundamental agreement must be brought about with the French, followed quickly and with certainty with action designed to make Bao Dai a success. If Bao Dai once starts slipping, it will be impossible to restore him.

2. *Problem of a foundation for agreement.*

In order to have a firm basis of agreement with the French regarding U.S. relations with the State of Vietnam and the Kingdoms of Cambodia and Laos, it is almost a necessity to secure from the French a rational evaluation of what they expect of Indo-China, a forecast of the situation they reasonably believe can be brought about that would satisfy the aspirations of the people of Vietnam within the French Union.

The French themselves were forced to the conclusion that a conclusive military solution of their problem was unattainable and they resorted, therefore, to the effort to bring about a political solution. In that effort the United States became involved in the recognition of the Government of Vietnam.

The French also recognize the fact that they cannot afford a continued military cost of hundreds of millions of dollars a year in a campaign that has failed and that has no prospect of bringing about a military solution. As ERP aid is subsequently reduced, it will be impossible for the French to carry this expense. Even today, with the help of ERP, domestic plans of the French Government are deeply affected by this drain, which indirectly but powerfully affects the Government's capacity to deal with labor, social and educational exigencies at home.

The French are also aware, realistically, of the military weakness on the continent due to the maintenance of a military establishment in Indo-China that absorbs half of the regular army and the best cadres for troop training, whose losses are continuous, and whose depletion of French officer strength equals the output of new officers from the French military academies. This, incidentally though importantly, affects the United States position in military assistance to the Continent.

Despite French sentimental aspirations for absorbing colonial areas within the body and spirit of "metropolitan France," there is no doubt that the French are realistic enough, when not emotionally disturbed, to appreciate the fact that the peoples of Vietnam can no longer be "integrated" in that respect.

Therefore it appears that the time has come that an entirely rational French consideration of this problem must take place, that can be the foundation of policy considerations. It is strictly necessary that this consideration be made now, so that U.S. policy may reasonably and justifiably work in cooperation with the French in attempting to make firm and workable a self-governed Vietnam State conditioned to find it desirable and advantageous to be a part of the French Union.

In short, we must find out what the French expect of Vietnam.

3.   *Decisions and actions necessary to create public respect for the Bao Dai government.*

a. A clear definition of the French Union, its meaning, its responsibilities and guarantees including the guarantee of a method for "evolutionary" treatment of countries accepted as partners within the French Union. These conditions have never been defined, and no one knows what the French Union means.

b. Implementation of the provisions of the March 9 agreement. This should not be a mean or petty literal and parsimonious interpretation, but broad and generous. Not only have the French been laggard in carrying out the terms of the agreement but they have been jealous and circumscribed in interpretation of every provision. (In the matter of technical assistance to the Viets, the French Secretariat was adamant in its opposition to any form of American or other foreign aid, stating that such aid was a violation of the agreement.)

c. The attitude of the French towards the Viet Government must be one of acceptance of a fact and a determination to make a success of that Government. This may be contrary to human nature, but it is doubtful if that Government can succeed without the most generous, if not passionate, French assistance. This assistance must be on a subordinate level, thorough and complete. It is indispensable. Until now the French attitude has been to point with scorn at the failures and aberrations of the untrained Viet Government leaders and to take the "I told you so" attitude.

d. Acceptance of the principle of bilateral relations between other governments and the Bao Dai regime. This will be hard for the French to take. They desire to maintain the form or myth of a quadripartite arrangement. While a form of at least tripartite arrangement is necessary among the Vietnam, Cambodian and Laotian Governments—for physical and economic reasons—it is imperative for the prestige of the Bao Dai Government for it to be able to conduct some dealings with other governments. This should apply at least to a substantial part of the proposed economic aid program. When the U.S. and Britain recognized Bao Dai, that recognition was taken as a bilateral action. In itself it established a precedent. This is a vital issue, and one of the most difficult to work out.

e. Turning over to Bao Dai of the No. 1 residence in Saigon, now occupied by the French High Commissioner. This is symbolic as well as practical. This is undoubtedly the reason why it is impossible for Bao Dai to take residence in the capital city, where his presence would be a sign of the reality of his Government. Even Pignon is opposed to this, on the grounds that it would affect French morale. Nevertheless this cannot be overlooked.

f. Statement of the French that their purpose in training and preparing for field operations of a Bao Dai army is part of their plan for the complete protection of the country by Viet forces, which thereafter would enable them to withdraw.

g. There are many other actions, most of them minor in importance in western eyes but highly significant to Orientals, that can be taken to set up the prestige and position of Bao Dai. Some of these proposals have been contained in Gallion's cables.

4. *Current Military Problems.*

A French army of mixed but "regular" troops ot approximately 160,000 men is maintained in Indo-China, chiefly in the Province of Tonkin, to prevent the overrunning of the Province and the Red River Valley by the Viet Minh and to stand guard against Chinese invasion of infiltration.

The presence of this army is indispensable even though many Bao Dai supporters would prefer to have it removed forthwith. These people believe they could settle their differences with Ho Chi Minh by negotiation if the French were withdrawn. The latter point of view is not realistic, and there is good reason to believe that withdrawal of French forces would quickly lend to Communist takeover.

French-trained Viet troops are effective and loyal, and those embodied in the French army are said to be the equal of any colonial troops. The French are vigorously training approximately 80,000 Viet troops for the Bao Dai army. Such units, once tried and found satisfactory, can in time begin to take over French garrisoned areas and make possible the return to the Continent of regular French contingents.

An American arms program can be used to stimulate this training and replacement program.

There is the danger that French public sentiment—and some practical military pressure—might cause the French to threaten to withdraw entirely from Indo China and "cut their losses," if pressure on the French for "evolutionary" treatment of the Viet political problem became too severe. This consideration cannot be overlooked when working for concessions. There is already strong feeling in many French quarters that Indo-China should be written off before more blood and treasure are lost.

As the French are required by the situation and by our insistence to turn over more authority to the Viet Government, it must be recognized that the morale of the French army might be affected. No measure could influence that situation more favorably than if the United States were willing to pledge sea and air support for the Viet-French forces in the event of the threat of invasion of Vietnam from Communist China.

Generals Carpentier and Massandri are officers of the highest calibre. Carpentier's apparent acquiescence to the arming of several Bao Dai battalions with American small arms is an indication that he is willing to yield on some subjects on which he had appeared to be adamant. He speaks frequently of his friendship and great respect for American Generals Gruenther and Mark Clark. In matters affecting important military decisions and American policy in the Indo-China field it might be most useful to send General Gruenther there, after a complete policy briefing, to discuss and review the entire military subject with Carpentier.

[Document 5]

DEPARTMENT OF STATE

FOR THE PRESS   May 11, 1950
                                                     No. 485

At his press conference today, Acting Secretary Webb made the following statement:

AID TO SOUTHEAST ASIA

A special survey mission, headed by R. Allen Griffin, has just returned from Southeast Asia and reported on economic and technical assistance needed in that area. Its over-all recommendations for the area are modest and total in the neighborhood of $60 million. The Department is working on plans to implement that program at once.

Secretary Acheson on Monday in Paris cited the urgency of the situation applying in the associated states of Viet-Nam, Laos and Cambodia. The Department is working jointly with ECA to implement the economic and technical assistance recommendations for Indochina as well as the other states of Southeast Asia and anticipates that this program will get underway in the immediate future.

Military assistance for Southeast Asia is being worked out by the Department of Defense in cooperation with the Department of State, and the details will not be made public for security reasons.

Military assistance needs will be met from the President's emergency fund of $75 million provided under MDAP for the general area of China.

Economic assistance needs will be met from the ECA China Aid funds, part of which both Houses of Congress have indicated will be made available for the general area of China. Final legislative action is still pending on this authorization but is expected to be completed within the next week.

[Document 6]

DEPARTMENT OF STATE

FOR THE PRESS   May 25, 1950
                                                     No. 545

U.S. FORMALLY ANNOUNCES INTENT TO ESTABLISH AN ECONOMIC AID MISSION TO THE THREE ASSOCIATED STATES OF INDOCHINA

On Wednesday, May 24, Charge d'Affaires Edmund Gullion delivered the following letter to the Chiefs of State of Vietnam, Laos, and Cambodia or their representatives at Saigon. Simultaneously, Ambassador Bruce delivered an identical letter to the President of the French Union in Paris.

The text of the letter follows:

"I have the honor to inform you that the Government of the United States has decided to initiate a program of economic aid to the States of Cambodia,

Laos, and Vietnam. My Government has reached this decision in order to assist Cambodia, Laos, and Vietnam to restore stability and pursue their peaceful and democratic development.

"With these purposes in mind, the United States Government is establishing, with headquarters in Saigon and associated with United States Legation, a special economic mission to Cambodia, Laos, and Vietnam. This mission will have the responsibility of working with the Governments of Cambodia, Laos, and Vietnam and with the French High Commissioner in developing and carrying out a coordinated program of economic aid designed to assist the three countries in restoring their normal economic life. The members of the American economic mission will at all times be subject to the authority of the Government of the United States and will not become a part of the administrations of the Associated States.

"The Government of the United States recognizes that this American assistance will be complementary to the effort made by the three Associated States and France, without any intention of substitution. American aid is designed to reinforce the joint effort of France and the governments and peoples of Cambodia, Laos, and Vietnam, on whom rests the primary responsibility for the restoration of security and stability.

"United States economic aid will be granted in accordance with separate bilateral agreements between each of the Associated States and the United States of America. The approval of these agreements will be subject to legal conventions existing between the Associated States and France. Initial economic aid operations, however, may begin prior to the conclusion of these agreements.

"The United States Government is of the opinion that it would be desirable for the three governments and the French High Commissioner to reach agreement among themselves for the coordination of those matters relating to the aid program that are of common interest. The American economic mission will maintain contact with the three Associated States, with the French High Commissioner in Indochina and, if desired, with any body which may be set up by the Associated States and France in connection with the aid program.

"Mr. Robert Blum has been appointed Chief of the United States special economic mission to Cambodia, Laos, and Vietnam.

"Identical letters are being addressed today to the governments of Cambodia, Laos, Vietnam and the President of the French Union."

The letter of intent refers only to economic aid which will be based on the recommendations of the Griffin mission which recently made a survey trip to Southeast Asia and carried on consultations with the leaders and technicians of Indochina.

Secretary of State Dean Acheson announced the policy of United States aid to Indochina at Paris on May 8 when he released this statement following an exchange of views with Foreign Minister Schuman of France:

"The Foreign Minister and I have just had an exchange of views on the situation in Indochina and are in general agreement both as to the urgency of the situation in that area and as to the necessity for remedial action. We have noted the fact that the problem of meeting the threat to the security of Vietnam, Cambodia and Laos which now enjoy independence within the French Union is primarily the responsibility of France and the governments and peoples of Indochina. The United States recognizes that the solution of the Indochina problem depends both upon the restoration of security and upon the development of genuine nationalism and that United States assistance can and should contribute to these major objectives.

"The United States Government convinced that neither national independence nor democratic evolution exist in any area dominated by Soviet imperialism, considers the situation to be such as to warrant its according economic aid and military equipment to the Associated States of Indochina and to France in order to assist them in restoring stability and permitting these states to pursue their peaceful and democratic development."

[Document 7]

DEPARTMENT OF STATE

FOR THE PRESS   June 3, 1950
                                                                        No. 583

The following is the text of a letter of June 2 from Secretary of State Dean Acheson to the Honorable Robert Allen Griffin, upon the conclusion of his assignment as Head of the Special Economic Mission to Southeast Asia:

"Dear Mr. Griffin:

"I congratulate you upon the successful conclusion of the Special Economic Mission to Southeast Asia which you led and extend to you and those on your staff my warmest personal thanks for the careful and thorough job you did. In surveying so large an area under conditions which called for constant diplomatic tact and skillful technical appraisal under the severest time pressure you performed with outstanding ability a most difficult assignment.

"On the basis of your recommendations the United States Government is launching a program which will offer rapid economic aid to those countries for which you drew up plans. The purpose of this assistance, as you well know, is to mobilize the natural and human resources of these countries for the improvement of the general welfare of the people and the strengthening of democratic governments throughout Southeast Asia.

"The fresh approach you took, unhampered by preconceived plans, and the creative ability which you displayed in working out a program with the approval of the Asian governments concerned have contributed much to the auspicious launching of this important program.

                                                        "Sincerely yours,
                                                        "DEAN ACHESON

"The Honorable
"Robert Allen Griffin,
"Pebble Beach, California."

[Document 8]

IMMEDIATE RELEASE   June 27, 1950

STATEMENT BY THE PRESIDENT

In Korea the Government forces, which were armed to prevent border raids and to preserve internal security, were attacked by invading forces from North

Korea. The Security Council of the United Nations called upon the invading troops to cease hostilities and to withdraw to the 38th parallel. This they have not done, but on the contrary have pressed the attack. The Security Council called upon all members of the United Nations to render every assistance to the United Nations in the execution of this resolution. In these circumstances I have ordered United States air and sea forces to give the Korean Government troops cover and support.

The attack upon Korea makes it plain beyond all doubt that Communism has passed beyond the use of subversion to conquer independent nations and will now use armed invasion and war. It has defied the orders of the Security Council of the United Nations issued to preserve international peace and security. In these circumstances the occupation of Formosa by Communist forces would be a direct threat to the security of the Pacific area and to United States forces performing their lawful and necessary functions in that area.

Accordingly, I have ordered the Seventh Fleet to prevent any attack on Formosa. As a corollary of this action I am calling upon the Chinese Government on Formosa to cease all air and sea operations against the mainland. The Seventh Fleet will see that this is done. The determination of the future status of Formosa must await the restoration of security in the Pacific, a peace settlement with Japan, or consideration by the United Nations.

I have also directed that United States Forces in the Philippines be strengthened and that military assistance to the Philippine Government be accelerated.

I have similarly directed acceleration in the furnishing of military assistance to the forces of France and the Associated States in Indo China and the dispatch of a military mission to provide close working relations with those forces.

I know that all members of the United Nations will consider carefully the consequences of this latest aggression in Korea in defiance of the Charter of the United Nations. A return to the rule of force in international affairs would have far reaching effects. The United States will continue to uphold the rule of law.

I have instructed Ambassador Austin, as the representative of the United States to the Security Council, to report these steps to the Council.

[Document 9]

Indo-China

25 July 1950

1. *Existing Policy*

   a. U.S. Policy with respect to Indo-China as approved by the President on 24 April 1950 concludes that:

   (1) Indo-China is a key area of Southeast Asia and is under immediate threat.

   (2) The neighboring countries of Thailand and Burma could be expected to fall under Communist domination if Indo-China were controlled by a Communist-dominated government. The balance of Southeast Asia would then be in grave hazard.

   (3) Accordingly, the Departments of State and Defense should prepare as a matter of priority a program of all practicable measures designed to protect United States security interests in Indo-China.

b. On 10 April 1950 the JCS concurred in the above conclusions and recommended early implementation of military aid programs for Indo-China, Indonesia, Thailand, the Philippines and Burma. Such aid programs to be closely controlled and be integrated with political and economic programs.

c. On 7 July 1950 the JCS (J.C.S. 1924/14) approved the following in their review of NSC 73.

If the Chinese Communists provide overt military assistance to Southeast Asian Communist elements, the United States should prevail upon the British to reverse their proffers of recognition to Communist China and to provide such military assistance as is practicable to assist the Burmese and/or the French in resisting Chinese Communist aggression. In addition:

a. If overt military assistance is provided the Viet Minh forces of Indo-China, the United States should increase its MDAP assistance to the French and urge the French to continue an active defense, with the United States giving consideration to the provision of air and naval assistance.

b. The United States should ask the United Nations to call upon member nations to make forces available to resist the Chinese Communist aggression.

Chinese Communist military moves against Southeast Asia states in the near future are possible and in such an event the U.S. should be prepared to provide military assistance short of actual participation of U.S. Armed Forces at this time.

d. On 14 July the JSPC submitted a report (J.C.S. 1924/20—*Not yet approved*) for consideration by the JCS which included the following with reference to Southeast Asia:

The French military position in Indo-China has continued to improve. . . . No unusual Chinese Communist or Vietminh activities have occurred since the Korean invasion. While the entire East Asia situation is potentially explosive there are no present indications that the situation will be immediately worsened unless the Korean situation further deteriorates. With respect to Burma, Thailand, and Malaya, internal subversive moves will probably remain the chief threats to the established governments. Chinese Communists would probably move against these countries only if first successful in Indo-China. . .

e. Southeast Asia

(1) In the event of Chinese Communist moves against Indo-China or Burma, U.S. military equipment and supplies would be required on an increased scale and U.S. naval and air forces might be called upon to assist the French in Indo-China. It is unlikely that U.S. forces would be employed in Burma. This is considered to be an area of British responsibility.

(2) If Indo-China, Burma and Thailand were to fall under Communist domination, British forces in Malaya should be augmented. Except for possible naval support, it is unlikely that U.S. armed forces would be employed in Malaya since this is an area of British responsibility.

[Document 10]

February 13, 1952

NSC STAFF STUDY

on

*UNITED STATES OBJECTIVES AND COURSES OF ACTION WITH
RESPECT TO COMMUNIST AGGRESSION IN SOUTHEAST ASIA**

THE PROBLEM

1. To determine the policy of the United States toward the countries of Southeast Asia, and in particular, the courses of action which may be taken by the United States to strengthen and coordinate resistance to communism on the part of the governments and peoples of the area, to prevent Chinese Communist aggression, and to meet such aggression should it occur.

ANALYSIS

I. CONSEQUENCES TO THE UNITED STATES OF COMMUNIST
   DOMINATION OF SOUTHEAST ASIA

2. Communist domination of Southeast Asia, whether by means of overt invasion, subversion, or accommodation on the part of the indigenous governments, would be critical to United States security interests. Communist success in this area would spread doubt and fear among other threatened non-communist countries as to the ability of the United States and the United Nations to halt communist aggression elsewhere. It would strengthen the claim that the advance of communism is inexorable and encourage countries vulnerable to Soviet pressure to adopt policies of neutralism or accommodation. Successful overt Chinese Communist aggression in this area, especially if achieved without encountering more than token resistance on the part of the United States or the United Nations, would have critical psychological and political consequences which would probably include the relatively swift alignment of the rest of Asia and thereafter of the Middle East to communism, thereby endangering the stability and security of Europe. Such a communist success might nullify the psychological advantages accruing to the free world by reason of its response to the aggression in Korea.

3. The fall of Southeast Asia would underline the apparent economic advantages to Japan of association with the communist-dominated Asian sphere. Exclusion of Japan from trade with Southeast Asia would seriously affect the Japanese economy, and increase Japan's dependence on United States aid. In the long run the loss of Southeast Asia, especially Malaya and Indonesia, could result in such economic and political pressures in Japan as to make it extremely difficult to prevent Japan's eventual accommodation to the Soviet Bloc.

---

* The term Southeast Asia is used herein to mean Indochina, Burma, Thailand, the Malay Peninsula, and Indonesia.

4. Southeast Asia, especially Malaya and Indonesia, is the principal world source of natural rubber and tin. Access to these materials by the Western Powers and their denial to the Soviet Bloc is important at all times and particularly in the event of global war. Communist control over the rice surpluses of the Southeast Asian mainland would provide the USSR with a powerful economic weapon in its relations with other countries of the Far East. Indonesia is a secondary source of petroleum whose importance would be enhanced by the denial to the Western Powers of petroleum sources in the Middle East. Malaya is the largest net dollar earner for the United Kingdom, and its loss would seriously aggravate the economic problems facing the UK.

5. Communist control of all of Southeast Asia would render the United States position in the Pacific offshore island chain precarious and would seriously jeopardize fundamental United States security interests in the Far East. The extension of communist power via Burma would augment the communist threat to India and Pakistan and strengthen the groups within those countries which favor accommodation. However, such an event would probably result in a stiffer attitude toward communism on the part of the Indian government.

6. Communist domination of mainland Southeast Asia would place unfriendly forces astride the most direct and best-developed sea and air routes between the Western Pacific and India and the Near East. In the event of global war, the development of Soviet submarine and air bases in mainland Southeast Asia might compel the detour of U.S. and allied shipping and air transportation in the Southeast Asia region via considerably longer alternate routes to the south. This extension of friendly lines of communication would hamper U.S. strategic movements in this region and tend to isolate the major non-communist bases in the Far East—the offshore island chain and Australia—from existing bases in East Africa and the Near and Middle East, as well as from potential bases on the Indian sub-continent.

7. Besides disrupting established lines of communication in the area, the denial of actual military facilities in mainland Southeast Asia—in particular, the loss of the major naval operating bases at Singapore—would compel the utilization of less desirable peripheral bases. Soviet exploitation of the naval and air bases in mainland Southeast Asia probably would be limited by the difficulties of logistic support but would, nevertheless, increase the threat to existing lines of communication.

II. REGIONAL STRATEGY

8. The continued integrity of the individual countries of Southeast Asia is to a large extent dependent upon a successful coordination of political and military measures for the entire area. The development of practical measures aimed at preventing the absorption of these countries into the Soviet orbit must therefore recognize this interdependence and must, in general, seek courses of action for the area as a whole.

9. However, it must be recognized that the governments and peoples of Southeast Asia have little in common other than their geographic proximity and their newly awakened nationalism and anti-colonialism. For the most part, their economies are competitive rather than complementary. The countries are divided internally and from each other by language and ethnic differences. The several nationalities and tribal groups are the heirs of centuries of warfare, jealousy, and mutual distrust. In addition, their present governments are sharply divided in their attitudes toward the current East-West struggle. The governments of

the three Associated States of Indochina are not recognized by any other Asian states except Nationalist China and Thailand.

10. In the strategic sense, the defense of Tonkin is important to the defense of mainland Southeast Asia. If Communist forces should succeed in driving the French Union forces from Tonkin, military action in the remainder of Indochina might have to be limited to delaying action and the perimeter defense of certain coastal areas pending reinforcement or evacuation. With the appearance of communist success, native support would probably swing increasingly to the Viet Minh.

11. Thailand has no common border with China and no strong internal communist element. It adjoins areas of Indochina now controlled by the Viet Minh, but the border areas are remote and difficult. Hence, communist seizure of Thailand is improbable except as a result of the prior loss of either Burma or Indochina.

12. Communist control of *either* Indochina or Burma would expose Thailand to infiltration and severe political pressures as well as to the threat of direct attack. Unless substantial outside aid were forthcoming, it is possible that in such a case, political pressure alone would be sufficient to bring about the accommodation of Thailand to international communism within a year. However, substantial aid, together with assurance of support by the United States and the UN might be sufficient to preserve a non-communist government in Thailand in spite of any form of pressure short of overt attack.

13. Thailand would be difficult to defend against an overt attack from the east by way of the traditional invasion route through Cambodia. Thailand is more defensible against attack from Burma owing to the mountainous terrain and poor communications of the Thai-Burmese border. In either case it might be possible to defend an area in southern Thailand centering on Bangkok. Since any attack on Thailand would necessarily be preceded by communist encroachment on Indochina or Burma, the defense of Thailand would probably be part of a broader pattern of hostilities.

14. If the loss of Thailand followed the loss of Burma, the defense of Indochina would be out-flanked; and any substantial communist forces based on Thailand would render the position of the French Union Forces in Indochina untenable in the long run. If the collapse of Thailand followed the loss of Indochina, the psychological and political consequences would accelerate the deterioration of Burma. However, the military consequences in such a case would be less immediate, owing to the difficult terrain of the Thai-Burmese border country.

15. Communist control of Thailand would aggravate the already serious security problem presented by the Thai-Malayan border and greatly increase the difficulties of the British security forces in Malaya. However, assuming control of the sea by the Western Powers, Malaya offers a defensible position against even a full-scale land attack. The Kra Isthmus of the Malayan Peninsula would afford the best secondary line of defense against total communist domination of Southeast Asia and the East Indies. Such a defense would effectively protect Indonesia against external communist pressure. By thus defending Malaya and Indonesia, the anti-communist forces would continue to hold the most important strategic material resources of the area, as well as strategic air and naval bases and lines of communication.

16. The strategic interdependence of the countries in Southeast Asia, and the cumulative effect of a successful communist penetration in any one area, point to the importance of action designed to forestall any aggression by the Chinese

Communists. The most effective possible deterrent would be a joint warning by the United States and certain other governments regarding the grave consequences of Chinese aggression against Southeast Asia, and implying the threat of retaliation against Communist China itself. Such a warning should be issued in conjunction with other nations, including at least the United Kingdom, France, Australia and New Zealand. Participation in such a warning involves all the risks and disadvantages of a precommitment to take action in future and unknown circumstances. However, these disadvantages must be weighed against the alternative of a costly effort to repel Chinese invasion after it has actually occurred. A second, but probably less effective, means of attempting to deter such an invasion would be to focus world attention on the continuing threat of Chinese Communist aggression against Southeast Asia and to make clear to the Soviet and Chinese Communist Governments the fact that the United States views the situation in Southeast Asia with great concern. In fact, statements along these lines have already been made. Such means might also include a Peace Observation Commission, if desired and requested by the countries concerned, public addresses by U.S. officials, and "show the flag" visits by naval and air units.

17. The Chinese Nationalist forces represent considerable reserve upon which to draw in the event of military action against Communist China. The deficiency in equipment and training seriously limits the possible employment of these forces at present, however, continuation of our training and supply efforts should serve to alleviate these deficiencies. The manner of employment of these forces is beset not only with military but also with political difficulties. Hence the decision as to the best use of these forces cannot be made at this time. Nevertheless, we should be prepared to make the best practicable use of this military augmentation in light of the circumstances existing at the time.

III.   INDOCHINA

18. In the long run, the security of Indochina against communism will depend upon the development of native governments able to command the support of the masses of the people and national armed forces capable of relieving the French of the major burden of maintaining internal security. Some progress is being made in the formation and development of national armies. However, the Vietnamese Government has been slow to assume its responsibilities and has continued to suffer from a lack of strong leadership. It has had to contend with: (a) lingering Vietnamese suspicion of any French-supported regime, combined with the apathetic and "fence sitting" attitude of the bulk of the people; (b) the difficulty, common to all new and inexperienced governments, of training the necessary personnel and building an efficient administration; and (c) the failure of factional and sectional groups to unite in a concerted national effort.

19. The U.S. economic aid program for Indochina has as its objectives to increase production and thereby offset the military drain on the economy of the Associated States; to increase popular support for the Government by improving the effectiveness of Government services; to make the Government and the people aware of America's interest in their independence and welfare; and to use economic aid as a means of supporting the military effort. Because of their strained budgetary situation, the Associated States cannot meet the local currency costs of the projects; about 60 percent of the program funds is, therefore, devoted to importing needed commodities which are sold to generate counterpart.

20. The military situation in Indochina continues to be one of stalemate. Increased U.S. aid to the Franco-Vietnamese forces has been an essential factor in enabling them to withstand recent communist attacks. However, Chinese aid to the Viet Minh in the form of logistic support, training, and technical advisors is increasing at least at a comparable rate. The prospect is for a continuation of the present stalemate in the absence of intervention by important forces other than those presently engaged.

21. While it is unlikely under the present circumstances that the French will suffer a military defeat in Indochina, there is a distinct possibility that the French Government will soon conclude that France cannot continue indefinitely to carry the burden of her total military commitments. From the French point of view, the possible means of lessening the present burden include: (1) a settlement with the communists in Indochina; (2) an agreement to internationalize the action in Indochina; (3) reduction of the NATO obligations of France.

22. A settlement based on a military armistice would be more complicated in Indochina than in the case of Korea. Much of Indochina is not firmly under the control of either side, but subject to occasional forays from both. Areas controlled by the opposing sides are interspersed, and lines of contact are fluid. Because of the weakness of the native governments, the dubious attitudes of the population even in areas under French control, and the certainty of continued communist pressure, it is highly probable that any settlement based on a withdrawal of French forces would be tantamount to handing over Indochina to communism. The United States should therefore continue to oppose any negotiated settlement with the Viet Minh.

23. In the event that information and circumstances point to the conclusion that France is no longer prepared to carry the burden in Indochina, or if France presses for a sharing of the responsibility for Indochina, whether in the UN or directly with the U.S. Government, the United States should oppose a French withdrawal and consult with the French and British concerning further measures to be taken to safeguard the area from communist domination. In anticipation of these possibilities, the United States should urgently re-examine the situation with a view to determining:

    a. Whether U.S. participation in an international undertaking would be warranted.

    b. The general nature of the contributions which the United States, with other friendly governments, might be prepared to make.

24. A cessation of hostilities in Korea would greatly increase the logistical capability of the Chinese Communists to support military operations in Indochina. A Korean peace would have an even more decisive effect in increasing Chinese air capabilities in that area. Recent intelligence reports indicate increased Chinese Communist military activity in the Indochinese border area. If the Chinese Communists directly intervene with large forces over and above those introduced as individuals or in small units, the French would probably be driven back to a beachhead around Haiphong. The French should be able to hold this beachhead for only a limited time at best in the absence of timely and substantial outside support.

25. In view of the world-wide reaction to overt aggression in Korea, Communist China may prefer to repeat in Indochina the method of "volunteer" intervention. Inasmuch as the French do not control the border between China and Indochina nor large areas north of Hanoi, it may be difficult to detect the extent of preparation for such intervention. It is important to U.S. security inter-

ests to maintain the closest possible consultation with the French Government on the buildup of Chinese Communist intervention in Indochina. The Government of France has agreed to consult with the United States before it requests UN or other international action to oppose Chinese Communist aggression in Indochina in order that the two countries may jointly evaluate the extent of Chinese Communist intervention.

26. If it is thus determined that Chinese Communist forces (including volunteers) have overtly intervened in the conflict in Indochina, or are covertly participating to such an extent as to jeopardize retention of the Tonkin Delta by the French forces, the United States should support the French to the greatest extent possible, preferably under the auspices of the UN. It is by no means certain that an appropriate UN resolution could be obtained. Favorable action in the UN would depend upon a change in the attitude of those governments which view the present regime in Indochina as a continuation of French colonialism. A new communist aggression might bring about a reassessment of the situation on the part of these governments and an increased recognition of the danger. Accordingly, it is believed that a UN resolution to oppose the aggression could be passed in the General Assembly by a small margin.

27. Even if it is not possible to obtain a UN resolution in such a case, the United States should seek the maximum possible international support for and participation in any international collective action in support of France and the Associated States. The United States should take appropriate military action against Communist China as part of a UN collective action or in conjunction with France and the United Kingdom and other friendly governments. However, in the absence of such support, it is highly unlikely that the United States would act unilaterally. It is probable however, that the United States would find some support and token participation at least from the United Kingdom and other Commonwealth countries.

28. The U.S. forces which would be committed, and the manner of their employment, as well as the military equipment which could be furnished to bolster the French Union forces, would be dependent upon certain factors which cannot now be predicted with accuracy. These include the extent of progress in U.S. rearmament, whether or not hostilities in Korea were continuing, and strategic developments in other parts of the world. It would be desirable to avoid the use of major U.S. ground forces in Indochina. Other effective means of opposing the aggression would include naval, air and logistical support of the French Union forces, naval blockade of Communist China, and attacks by land- and carrier-based aircraft on military targets in Communist China. The latter could be effective against the long, tenuous, and vulnerable supply lines by which Chinese operations in Indochina would have to be supported. In the event of a forced evacuation, U.S. forces might provide cover and assistance. United Kingdom participation in these measures might well result in the seizure of Hong Kong by the Chinese Communists.

29. It is recognized that the commitment of U.S. military forces against Communist China would: (a) increase the risk of general hostilities in the Far East, including Soviet participation under cover of the existing Sino-Soviet agreements; (b) involve U.S. military forces in another Asiatic peripheral action, thus detracting from U.S. capabilities to conduct a global war in the near future; (c) arouse public opposition to "another Korea"; and (d) imply willingness to use U.S. military forces in other critical areas subject to communist aggression. Nevertheless, by failing to take action, the United States would permit the communists to obtain, at little or no cost, a victory of major world consequence.

30. Informed public opinion might support use of U.S. forces in Indochina regardless of sentiment against "another Korea" on the basis that: (a) Indochina is of far greater strategic importance than Korea; (b) the confirmation of UN willingness to oppose aggression with force, demonstrated at such a high cost in Korea, might be nullified by the failure to commit UN forces in Indochina; and (c) a second instance of aggression by the Chinese Communists would justify measures not subject to the limitations imposed upon the UN action in Korea.

31. The military action contemplated herein would constitute, in effect, a war against Communist China which would be limited only as to its objectives, but would not be subject to any geographic limitations. Employment of U.S. forces in a *de facto* war without a formal declaration would raise questions which would make it desirable to consult with key members of both parties in Congress in order to obtain their prior concurrence in the courses of action contemplated.

[Document 11]

DEPARTMENT OF STATE
THE SECRETARY

June 17, 1952

Following his telephone conversation with Sir Oliver Franks today, which is reported separately, the Secretary saw General Bradley and Mr. Perkins. Later Sir Oliver dropped in at the office following a meeting in Mr. Jessup's office. He asked if he could see the Secretary for a few minutes to get the further report on the matter of talks on Southeast Asia. He repeated what he told us earlier that he had had a second message from London following the report which the Embassy had sent of Mr. Perkin's conversation with Mr. Steele.

The Secretary said that he had talked about this matter with General Bradley this afternoon and that Friday was the only day which General Bradley could possibly meet and that was very inconvenient for Mr. Acheson. He said, therefore, he thought that any talks were impossible to arrange. He then said that he would be glad to talk to Sir Oliver right at that moment and see where we stood.

The Secretary reviewed the situation and the talks which took place in Paris. He said that in the earlier meetings which had taken place on Southeast Asia, everyone had started from a different point and there had been little in the way of conclusion reached. He said that he felt what was needed now was political decisions.

The Secretary then analyzed the situation as we saw it. He said that if the Chinese came into Indochina in force, we would have to do something. We could not remain passive. He said that none of the things we could do were very pleasant ones and we felt that a warning was highly desirable. He said that we felt we should not give a warning, however, if there had been no agreement on what we did in the event the Communists moved in anyway. He said this would make us look very silly and would weaken the effect of any other warnings.

He said it was clear that it was futile and a mistake to defend Indochina in Indochina. He said we could not have another Korea. He said it was also true we could not put ground forces in Indochina. We do not have them and we could not afford to immobilize such forces as we had. He said we could take air and naval action, however, and had discussed whether this should be confined to approaches.

He concluded that our only hope was of changing the Chinese mind. He said that we could strike where it hurts China or we could set up a blockade against trade. He said we had concluded that our mission would not be to destroy the Communist regime. He also said that we fully realized the danger of bringing the USSR into the show.

The Secretary concluded that there was no point in getting our military people into any talks. He said we must get political decisions first. He said that if firm decisions could not be reached that we perhaps could reach tentative decisions. He said that it had been clear at Paris that he was somewhat "ahead of the play" while the French and the British had urged us to discuss these matters and had wanted discussions before decisions were made. When the question actually came up, they were not ready to talk.

The Secretary remarked that Mr. Letourneau had said in Paris that the military talks had reached some decision as to how to evacuate the wounded, etc., in the event of difficulties. He said that our Navy had talked to Mr. Letourneau regarding port sizes, capacity of ships, etc., with regard to evacuation.

Sir Oliver said he thought he understood the point, would report back to London and would let us know if there were anything further on it.

Mr. Acheson said that if his analysis were wrong and the British Chiefs of Staff had any different one, he would be glad to hear of it.

S:LDBattle

[Document 12]

DEPARTMENT OF STATE
FOR THE PRESS

JUNE 18, 1952   NO. 473

Secretary Acheson made the following statement at his news conference today:

VISIT OF M. JEAN LETOURNEAU

As you are aware, M. Jean Letourneau, Minister of the Associated States for the French Government, has been spending the last few days in Washington exchanging views with representatives of various agencies of this Government. The Ambassadors of Cambodia and Vietnam have also participated in conversations with M. Letourneau and with our own representatives.

A communique covering the substance of the talks will be issued later today and I will therefore not go into details now. Yet I would like to share with you the feeling of encouragement and confidence which M. Letourneau inspires. His thorough grasp of the situation and his constructive approach to the problems involved—military, political and economic—have impressed us all.

As you know, the Communist aggression in Indochina has been going on for six years. It has been greatly stepped up because of assistance received from Communist China during the past two years. Yet, under French leadership, the threat to this part of the free world has been met with great courage and admirable resourcefulness. The military situation appears to be developing favorably. It has been good to hear from M. Letourneau of the part played in achieving this result by the considerable quantities of American arms and material which the magnificent fighting qualities of the French Union forces, including those of the Associated States, have justified us in devoting to this area of the struggle against Communist aggression. The effort to make of Vietnam, Laos and Cambodia secure and prosperous members of the free world community has made great progress.

I have been particularly impressed by what M. Letourneau has told me of what is being done to enable the people of the three Associated States to play the constantly greater role in their own defense to which they rightly aspire. Much has been accomplished toward the creation, training and equipping of the national armies. Units of these armies have distinguished themselves in battle and are performing vital security functions in many parts of the country. They look forward with confidence and determination to assuming an increasing share of the burden of carrying on the struggle. Their effectiveness fully justifies the program of expansion to which the governments concerned are committed and underlines, I believe the soundness of our own decision, subject of course to the availability of Congressional appropriations, to render increasing assistance in building these armies. M. Letourneau described these programs in the course of his address before the Overseas Writers yesterday.

Favorable developments have not been confined to the fighting fronts and to the national armies. There are increasing evidences of the growing vitality of the Associated States in handling their political, financial and economic affairs. M. Letourneau's account of the manner in which these new member states of the French Union are envisaging and meeting their responsibilities was heartening. I do not think it is generally realized to what extent these new states in fact control their own affairs. Only a limited number of services related to the necessities of the war remain temporarily in French hands.

We in the United States are aware of the vital importance of the struggle in Indochina to the cause of the free world. We have earmarked for Indochina economic and materiel aid to a considerable amount during the past two years. We are doing our best to activate deliveries: as you are aware the 150th ship bearing American arms and munitions to Indochina arrived in Saigon within the last few weeks. We are now bearing a considerable portion of the total burden of the war in Indochina expressed in financial terms, although of course the entire combat burden is being carried by the French Union and the Associated States with the latter assuming a constantly increasing share.

The Communists have made a most determined effort in Indochina. Their aggression has been checked and recent indications warrant the view that the tide is now moving in our favor. Once again the policy of meeting aggression with force is paying off and we can I believe be confident that as we carry out the plans upon which we have agreed we can anticipate continued favorable developments in the maintenance and consolidation of the free world bulwark in Indochina.

[Document 13]

June 25, 1952
NSC 124/2

NOTE BY THE EXECUTIVE SECRETARY

to the

NATIONAL SECURITY COUNCIL

on

UNITED STATES OBJECTIVES AND COURSES
OF ACTION WITH RESPECT TO SOUTHEAST ASIA

References: A. NSC 124/1
               B. NSC 124 and Annex to NSC 124
               C. NSC Action Nos. 597, 614 and 655
               D. Memos for NSC from Executive Secretary, same subject, dated June 24 and June 25, 1952
               E. Memos for NSC from Executive Secretary, subject, "United States Objectives and Courses of Action With Respect to Communist Aggression in Southeast Asia," dated March 4, April 15, April 30 and May 21, 1952
               F. NSC 48/5
               G. NSC 64
               H. SE-22 and SE-27

At the 120th Council meeting with the President presiding, the National Security Council and the Acting Secretary of the Treasury adopted NSC 124/1, subject to changes in paragraphs 2-*a*, 3, 5, 10-*c*-(2), 10-*c*-(3), 11-(1), 11-(3), and 12 thereof, as incorporated in the enclosure (NSC Action No. 655).

In adopting NSC 124/1, as amended, the Council and the Acting Secretary of the Treasury noted the following statement by the Acting Secretary of Defense with respect to the views of the Joint Secretaries regarding NSC 124/1:

> In our opinion, if this policy is to be truly effective, it must be clearly recognized that the U.S. policy "to make it possible for the French to reduce the degree of their participation in the military, economic and political affairs of the Associated States" (par. 8-*d*) must be emphasized and re-emphasized to the French at each and every political, economic or military negotiation which the U.S. Government enters into with the Government of France, especially those negotiations which deal with the providing of U.S. economic or military aid to France or to Indochina.

The report, as amended and adopted, was subsequently submitted to the President for consideration. The President has this date approved NSC 124/1, as amended and enclosed herewith, and directs its implementation by all appropriate executive departments and agencies of the U.S. Government under the coordination of the Secretaries of State and Defense.

Accordingly, NSC 64 and paragraph 14 of NSC 48/5 are superseded by the enclosed report. The enclosure does not supersede, but supplements the statement of the current objective with respect to Southeast Asia contained in paragraph 6-*g* of NSC 48/5.

It is requested that special security precautions be observed in the handling of the enclosure, and that access to it be restricted on a need-to-know basis.

JAMES S. LAY, Jr.
Executive Secretary

cc: The Secretary of the Treasury
The Acting Director of Defense Mobilization

25 June 1952

STATEMENT OF POLICY

by the

NATIONAL SECURITY COUNCIL

on

UNITED STATES OBJECTIVES AND COURSES OF ACTION WITH RESPECT TO SOUTHEAST ASIA*

OBJECTIVE

1. To prevent the countries of Southeast Asia from passing into the communist orbit, and to assist them to develop the will and ability to resist communism from within and without and to contribute to the strengthening of the free world.

GENERAL CONSIDERATIONS

2. Communist domination, by whatever means, of all Southeast Asia would seriously endanger in the short term, and critically endanger in the longer term, United States security interests.

> *a.* The loss of any of the countries of Southeast Asia to communist control as a consequence of overt or covert Chinese Communist aggression would have critical psychological, political and economic consequences. In the absence of effective and timely counteraction, the loss of any single country would probably lead to relatively swift submission to or an alignment with communism by the remaining countries of this group. Furthermore, an alignment with communism of the rest of Southeast Asia and India, and in the longer term, of the Middle East (with the probable exceptions of at least Pakistan and Turkey) would in all probability progressively follow. Such widespread alignment would endanger the stability and security of Europe.
> b. Communist control of all of Southeast Asia would render the U.S. position in the Pacific offshore island chain precarious and would seriously jeopardize fundamental U.S. security interests in the Far East.
> c. Southeast Asia, especially Malaya and Indonesia, is the principal world source of natural rubber and tin, and a producer of petroleum and other strategically important commodities. The rice exports of Burma and Thailand are critically important to Malaya, Ceylon and Hong Kong and

*Southeast Asia is used herein to mean the area embracing Burma, Thailand, Indochina, Malaya and Indonesia.

are of considerable significance to Japan and India, all important areas of free Asia.

  d. The loss of Southeast Asia, especially of Malaya and Indonesia, could result in such economic and political pressures in Japan as to make it extremely difficult to prevent Japan's eventual accommodation to communism.

  3. It is therefore imperative that an overt attack on Southeast Asia by the Chinese Communists be vigorously opposed. In order to pursue the military courses of action envisaged in this paper to a favorable conclusion within a reasonable period, it will be necessary to divert military strength from other areas thus reducing our military capability in those areas, with the recognized increased risks involved therein, or to increase our military forces in being, or both.

  4. The danger of an overt military attack against Southeast Asia is inherent in the existence of a hostile and aggressive Communist China, but such an attack is less probable than continued communist efforts to achieve domination through subversion. The primary threat to Southeast Asia accordingly arises from the possibility that the situation in Indochina may deteriorate as a result of the weakening of the resolve of, or as a result of the inability of the governments of France and of the Associated States to continue to oppose the Viet Minh rebellion, the military strength of which is being steadily increased by virtue of aid furnished by the Chinese Communist regime and its allies.

  5. The successful defense of Tonkin is critical to the retention in non-Communist hands of mainland Southeast Asia. However, should Burma come under communist domination, a communist military advance through Thailand might make Indochina, including Tonkin, militarily indefensible. The execution of the following U.S. courses of action with respect to individual countries of the area may vary depending upon the route of communist advance into Southeast Asia.

  6. Actions designed to achieve our objections in Southeast Asia require sensitive selection and application, on the one hand to assure the optimum efficiency through coordination of measures for the general area, and on the other, to accommodate to the greatest practicable extent to the individual sensibilities of the several governments, social classes and minorities of the area.

COURSES OF ACTION

Southeast Asia

  7. With respect to Southeast Asia, the United States should:

  a. Strengthen propaganda and cultural activities, as appropriate, in relation to the area to foster increased alignment of the people with the free world.

  b. Continue, as appropriate, programs of economic and technical assistance designed to strengthen the indigenous non-communist governments of the area.

  c. Encourage the countries of Southeast Asia to restore and expand their commerce with each other and with the rest of the free world, and stimulate the flow of the raw material resources of the area to the free world.

  d. Seek agreement with other nations, including at least France, the UK, Australia and New Zealand, for a joint warning to Communist China regarding the grave consequences of Chinese aggression against Southeast

Asia, the issuance of such a warning to be contingent upon the prior agreement of France and the UK to participate in the courses of action set forth in paragraphs 10*c*, 12, 14*f* (1) and (2), and 15*c* (1) and (2), and such others as are determined as a result of prior trilateral consultation, in the event such a warning is ignored.

e. Seek UK and French agreement in principle that a naval blockade of Communist China should be included in the minimum courses of action set forth in paragraph 10*c* below.

f. Continue to encourage and support closer cooperation among the countries of Southeast Asia, and between those countries and the United States, Great Britain, France, the Philippines, Australia, New Zealand, South Asia and Japan.

g. Strengthen, as appropriate, covert operations designed to assist in the achievement of U.S. objectives in Southeast Asia.

h. Continue activities and operations designed to encourage the overseas Chinese communities in Southeast Asia to organize and activate anti-communist groups and activities within their own communities, to resist the effects of parallel pro-communist groups and activities and, generally, to increase their orientation toward the free world.

i. Take measures to promote the coordinated defense of the area, and encourage and support the spirit of resistance among the peoples of Southeast Asia to Chinese Communist aggression and to the encroachments of local communists.

j. Make clear to the American people the importance of Southeast Asia to the security of the United States so that they may be prepared for any of the courses of action proposed herein.

Indochina

8. With respect to Indochina the United States should:

a. Continue to promote international support for the three Associated States.

b. Continue to assure the French that the U.S. regards the French effort in Indochina as one of great strategic importance in the general international interest rather than in the purely French interest, and as essential to the security of the free world, not only in the Far East but in the Middle East and Europe as well.

c. Continue to assure the French that we are cognizant of the sacrifices entailed for France in carrying out her effort in Indochina and that, without overlooking the principle that France has the primary responsibility in Indochina, we will recommend to the Congress appropriate military, economic and financial aid to France and the Associated States.

d. Continue to cultivate friendly and increasingly cooperative relations with the Governments of France and the Associated States at all levels with a view to maintaining and, if possible, increasing the degree of influence the U.S. can bring to bear on the policies and actions of the French and Indochinese authorities to the end of directing the course of events toward the objectives we seek. Our influence with the French and Associated States should be designed to further those constructive political, economic and social measures which will tend to increase the stability of the Associated States and thus make it possible for the French to reduce the degree of their participation in the military, economic and political affairs of the Associated States.

e. Specifically we should use our influence with France and the Associated States to promote positive political, military, economic and social policies, among which the following are considered essential elements:

(1) Continued recognition and carrying out by France of its primary responsibility for the defense of Indochina.

(2) Further steps by France and the Associated States toward the evolutionary development of the Associated States.

(3) Such reorganization of French administration and representation in Indochina as will be conducive to an increased feeling of responsibility on the part of the Associated States.

(4) Intensive efforts to develop the armies of the Associated States, including independent logistical and administrative services.

(5) The development of more effective and stable Governments in the Associated States.

(6) Land reform, agrarian and industrial credit, sound rice marketing systems, labor development, foreign trade and capital formation.

(7) An aggressive military, political, and psychological program to defeat or seriously reduce the Viet Minh forces.

(8) US–French cooperation in publicizing progressive developments in the foregoing policies in Indochina.

9. In the absence of large scale Chinese Communist intervention in Indochina, the United States should:

a. Provide increased aid on a high priority basis for the French Union forces without relieving French authorities of their basic military responsibility for the defense of the Associated States in order to:

(1) Assist in developing indigenous armed forces which will eventually be capable of maintaining internal security without assistance from French units.

(2) Assist the French Union forces to maintain progress in the restoration of internal security against the Viet Minh.

(3) Assist the forces of France and the Associated States to defend Indochina against Chinese Communist aggression.

b. In view of the immediate urgency of the situation, involving possible large-scale Chinese Communist intervention, and in order that the United States may be prepared to take whatever action may be appropriate in such circumstances, make the plans necessary to carry out the courses of action indicated in paragraph 10 below.

c. In the event that information and circumstances point to the conclusion that France is no longer prepared to carry the burden in Indochina, or if France presses for an increased sharing of the responsibility for Indochina, whether in the UN or directly with the U.S. Government, oppose a French withdrawal and consult with the French and British concerning further measures to be taken to safeguard the area from communist domination.

10. In the event that it is determined, in consultation with France, that Chinese Communist forces (including volunteers) have overtly intervened in the conflict

in Indochina, or are covertly participating to such an extent as to jeopardize retention of the Tonkin Delta area by French Union forces, the United States should take the following measures to assist these forces in preventing the loss of Indochina, to repel the aggression and to restore peace and security in Indochina.

a. Support a request by France or the Associated States for immediate action by the United Nations which would include a UN resolution declaring that Communist China has committed an aggression, recommending that member states take whatever action may be necessary, without geographic limitation, to assist France and the Associated States in meeting the aggression.

b. Whether or not UN action is immediately forthcoming, seek the maximum possible international support for, and participation in, the minimum courses of military action agreed upon by the parties to the joint warning. These minimum courses of action are set forth in sub-paragraph *c* immediately below.

c. Carry out the following minimum courses of military action, either under the auspices of the UN or in conjunction with France and the United Kingdom and any other friendly governments:

(1) A resolute defense of Indochina itself to which the United States would provide such air and naval assistance as might be practicable.

(2) Interdiction of Chinese Communist communication lines including those in China.

(3) The United States would expect to provide the major forces for task (2) above; but would expect the UK and France to provide at least token forces therefor and to render such other assistance as is normal between allies, and France to carry the burden of providing, in conjunction with the Associated States, the ground forces for the defense of Indochina.

11. In addition to the courses of action set forth in paragraph 10 above, the United States should take the following military actions as appropriate to the situation:

a. If agreement is reached pursuant to paragraph 7-*e*, establishment in conjunction with the UK and France of a naval blockade of Communist China.

b. Intensification of covert operations to aid anti-communist guerrilla forces operating against Communist China and to interfere with and disrupt Chinese Communist lines of communication and military supply areas.

c. Utilization, as desirable and feasible, of anti-communist Chinese forces, including Chinese Nationalist forces in military operations in Southeast Asia, Korea, or China proper.

d. Assistance to the British to cover an evacuation from Hong Kong, if required.

e. Evacuation of French Union civil and military personnel from the Tonkin delta, if required.

12. If, subsequent to aggression against Indochina and execution of the minimum necessary courses of action listed in paragraph 10-*c* above, the United States determines jointly with the UK and France that expanded military action

against Communist China is rendered necessary by the situation, the United States should take air and naval action in conjunction with at least France and the U.K. against all suitable military targets in China, avoiding insofar as practicable those targets in areas near the boundaries of the USSR in order not to increase the risk of direct Soviet involvement.

13. In the event the concurrence of the United Kingdom and France to expanded military action against Communist China is not obtained, the United States should consider taking unilateral action.

[Document 14]

July 14, 1952

MINISTERIAL TALKS IN LONDON, JUNE 1952

Summary Minutes

3.00–4:30 P.M., Thursday, June 26, 1952
British Foreign Office

EXTRACT

MR. EDEN opened the conversation on Indo-China by stating that it might be well, during the bilateral discussions, to go over together what could be said to Mr. Schuman in the trilateral discussions. He anticipated that Mr. Schuman might take the by now familiar line that there was little prospect for victory in Indo-China and that, unless a general settlement were reached, the best we could hope for would be a stalemate. This did not accord to the understanding of the British Government, which has the impression that the situation is improving somewhat; certainly there is a better government, there is wider representation in the government, and active Vietnamese participation. MR. EDEN said that he planned to discuss the situation with Mr. Schuman along such lines in the hope of stimulating his morale and divorcing him from his relatively defeatist attitude. THE SECRETARY replied that he had been discussing Indo-China with the French along the lines he and Mr. Eden had taken in the tripartite discussions in Paris. He expressed the opinion that the only avenue to success in Indo-China is the rapid build-up of native armed forces and the assumption by the people of Vietnam of an increasing share of the financial and military burden. THE SECRETARY announced that the French had been informed that the United States was prepared to increase its military assistance program for Indo-China by $150 million. He added that the United States, feeling that the French military training program was badly strained, had offered to assist them in this respect, but that the French, always skittish over what they might regard as undue American interference, had not taken up this offer. Certainly it is not up to the Americans to press on the French assistance along these lines. THE SECRETARY said that it was obvious that Mr. Letourneau was much encouraged as a result of his visit to Washington. He asked Dr. Jessup to read the text of the Department's telegram 2014, June 18, to Saigon, summarizing the discussions with Mr. Letourneau.

THE SECRETARY said that he had warned the French that success in the military field in Indo-China carried with it certain dangers, including the increased possibility of a large-scale Chinese Communist military intervention.

He said that this in turn points up the question, "How can we prevent this from happening?" He felt it would be desirable to issue a warning statement of some sort, whether public, private, detailed and specific, or otherwise, but it would be essential to have a general understanding as to the action which we might take if the warning were to go unheeded. To issue a warning and take no effective action would be calamitous. Perhaps the United States and the United Kingdom, preferably in conjunction with France, Australia, and New Zealand, can reach a tentative agreement on political policy in this regard which would form a framework for joint military planning. This, in turn, leads to the major question: "What form could retaliation against aggression take?" The American military authorities are of the strong opinion that action only against the approaches to Indo-China would be ineffective. In fact, the first problem which we would likely have to face would be the evacuation of French military and civilians from Tongking. Action confined to the air and naval arms directed against the Chinese Communists in Indo-China would likewise be ineffective and, in the light of world commitments, the United States has no infantry available for operations within Indo-China. The United States thinking is along the lines of a blockade of the coast of China, combined with air action, designed to upset the economy of mainland China and to lessen the will of the Chinese Communists to continue their aggression. Such action would cease when aggression ceased, and this would be made clear to everyone. Every effort should be made to avoid action in the areas of acute sensitivity to the Soviet Union. We are of the opinion that the Soviet Union would probably not enter the conflict if it understood clearly that we had no intention of attempting to overthrow the Chinese Communist regime by force. We must bear in mind that the Chinese Communists have a formidable air force, and we may be forced to attack it wherever it is found. If the Chinese Communists do invade Indo-China in substantial force, it will be a threat to the vital interests of all of us.

MR. EDEN said that he saw no serious objection to the issuance of a warning; he recalled that he had already issued a public warning in his speech at Columbia University. He felt that, whether or not a warning is issued, it would be important to have the Chinese Communists know that retaliation against further Chinese aggression is being urgently considered.

THE SECRETARY reiterated that there was an urgent need for basic political guidance on the basis of which military talks could proceed. MR. EDEN said that he would wish to consult the Cabinet on basic policy, noting that a naval blockade involving Hong Kong was a serious question.

There was general agreement that the Secretary and Mr. Eden would conduct their discussions with Mr. Schuman along the above lines.

[Document 15]

NIE–91, 4 June 1953

PROBABLE DEVELOPMENTS IN INDOCHINA THROUGH MID-1954

THE PROBLEM

To estimate French Union and Communist capabilities and probable courses of action with respect to Indochina and the internal situation throughout Indochina through mid-1954.

ASSUMPTION

There is no major expansion of the Korean war.

CONCLUSIONS

1. Unless there is a marked improvement in the French Union military position in Indochina, political stability in the Associated States and popular support of the French Union effort against the Viet Minh will decline. We believe that such marked improvement in the military situation is not likely, though a moderate improvement is possible. The over-all French Union position in Indochina therefore will probably deteriorate during the period of this estimate.

2. The lack of French Union military successes, continuing Indochinese distrust of ultimate French political intentions, and popular apathy will probably continue to prevent a significant increase in Indochinese will and ability to resist the Viet Minh.

3. We cannot estimate the impact of the new French military leadership. However, we believe that the Viet Minh will retain the military initiative and will continue to attack territory in the Tonkin delta and to make incursions into areas outside the delta. The Viet Minh will attempt to consolidate Communist control in "Free Laos" and will build up supplies in northern Laos to support further penetrations and consolidation in that country. The Viet Minh will almost certainly intensify political warfare, including guerrilla activities, in Cambodia.

4. Viet Minh prestige has been increased by the military successes of the past year, and the organizational and administrative effectiveness of the regime will probably continue to grow.

5. The French Government will remain under strong and increasing domestic pressure to reduce the French military commitment in Indochina, and the possibility cannot be excluded that this pressure will be successful. However, we believe that the French will continue without enthusiasm to maintain their present levels of troop strength through mid-1954 and will support the planned development of the national armies of the Associated States.

6. We believe that the Chinese Communists will continue and possibly increase their present support of the Viet Minh. However, we believe that whether or not hostilities are concluded in Korea, the Chinese Communists will not invade Indochina during this period.[1] The Chinese Communists will almost certainly retain the capability to intervene so forcefully in Indochina as to overrun most of the Tonkin delta area before effective assistance could be brought to bear.

7. We believe that the Communist objective to secure control of all Indochina will not be altered by an armistice in Korea or by Communist "peace" tactics. However, the Communists may decide that "peace" maneuvers in Indochina would contribute to the attainment of Communist global objectives, and to the objective of the Viet Minh.

8. If present trends in the Indochinese situation continue through mid-1954, the French Union political and military position may subsequently deteriorate very rapidly.

---

[1] The Deputy Director for Intelligence, The Joint Staff, believes that the intelligence available is insufficient to permit a conclusion at this time that the Chinese Communists will or will not invade Indochina prior to mid-1954.

DISCUSSION

THE CURRENT SITUATION

9. *Military Situation.*[2] The Viet Minh occupation of the mountainous Thai country of northwestern Tonkin in late 1952 and the follow-up thrust into northern Laos in April 1953 demonstrate that the Viet Minh have retained the military initiative in Indochina. Although the Viet Minh did not defeat any large French Union forces in these operations, they did force the French to withdraw the bulk of their offensive striking power from the Tonkin delta and disperse it in isolated strong points, dependent on air transport for logistic support. At the same time, strong Viet Minh guerrilla elements plus two regular Viet Minh divisions sufficed to contain the 114,000 regular French Union forces remaining in the Tonkin delta. The Viet Minh now appear to have withdrawn the bulk of their regular forces from Laos. They probably have left behind political cadres, some regular forces, and well-supplied guerrilla units in the areas which they overran in order to consolidate Communist political and military control, to prepare bases for future operations, and to pin down French Union garrisons.

10. The invasion of Laos may have been undertaken as part of a long-range Communist design to develop unrest in Thailand and ultimately gain control of all Southeast Asia. Viewed solely in terms of the Viet Minh objective to win all of Indochina, however, the Viet Minh offensive in Laos is an extension of the 1952 winter's offensive in northwestern Tonkin, and represents a shift in Viet Minh military tactics. This shift in tactics is probably largely explained by the inability to defeat the main French Union forces in the Tonkin delta by direct assault. Faced with this position of strength, the Viet Minh began during 1952 to turn the bulk of their regular forces toward the conquest of northwestern Tonkin and northern Laos, areas lightly held by isolated French Union garrisons.

11. In this manner, the Viet Minh probably hope to retain the military and political initiative and, by dispersing French Union forces, to prevent either a clean-up by the French Union in the Tonkin delta or offensive operations by the French Union against Viet Minh troop concentrations and supply installations outside the delta. The Viet Minh may well believe that by gradually extending their base areas in lightly defended regions of Laos, Cambodia, and central Vietnam they can keep French Union forces dispersed and pinned down indefinitely. In time, they probably expect to sap the morale of the Vietnamese and the French and finally so alter the balance of power as to make possible successful Viet Minh attacks against the key areas of Tonkin and south Vietnam.

12. The deployment of four divisions into Laos by the Viet Minh and the fact that the French did not attack their long and exposed lines of communication typify the over-all situation in Indochina. French Union forces still outweigh the Viet Minh in numbers, firepower, and materiel. French ability to air lift troops and equipment, although strained at the present time, provides the French Union with tactical flexibility in planning defensive and offensive operations. The Viet Minh, however, by their skill in guerrilla war, their ability to move rapidly

[2] See Annex A for Estimated French Union Strengths and Dispositions;
See Annex B for Estimated Viet Minh Strengths and Dispositions;
See Annex C for French Far Eastern Air Force Strengths and Dispositions; and
See Annex D for French Far Eastern Naval Strengths and Dispositions.

and to infiltrate and control areas under nominal French occupation, have caused the French to commit large forces throughout Indochina to static defense, thus seriously reducing French ability to take the offensive.

13. Viet Minh regular forces in northern Indochina have continued their gradual evolution from lightly armed guerrilla bands to a regularly organized military force. They have made noticeable advances in the development of field communications, and unit firepower has increased although they still possess only limited amounts of artillery. Viet Minh combat effectiveness is still limited by a lack of medical supplies and an inability to sustain major military operations.

14. Military aid from the US has enabled the French Union to equip adequately their regular ground forces. The French air forces, with US logistical support, and with no air opposition, have maintained a fair degree of effectiveness in paratroop operations, supply by air drops, and daylight attacks on enemy supply dumps. French naval forces have improved in combat effectiveness and have maintained control of the seacoasts and inland waterways. However, the Viet Minh have the continuing capability to threaten control of the inland waterways by a mining campaign. Some Vietnamese National Army units have performed creditably in combat, but desertion and "missing in action" figures remain high. For the most part, Vietnamese National Guard and other local security forces lack the firepower, discipline, and leadership to hold positions alone against regular Viet Minh units which infiltrate the Tonkin delta.

15. Although French Union military capabilities have improved slightly, the French Union military effort has been inhibited by considerations of domestic French politics, French security in Europe, and fear of involvement in a war with Communist China. These considerations have caused French commanders in Indochina to forego aggressive military operations that would entail heavy casualties and have prevented them from obtaining reinforcements on a scale that might make possible the defeat of the Viet Minh.

16. The development of the Vietnamese National Army, promised by the French in 1949, has been retarded by a shortage of officers and non-commissioned officers, by French lack of faith in the Vietnamese and by French fiscal problems. There has also been an unwillingness among many Vietnamese leaders, not including Premier Tam, to undertake a major mobilization effort until the French grant further political concessions and until the Vietnamese character of the new army is fully guaranteed.

17. *Political.* Some political progress has been made in Vietnam during the past year. Premier Tam's administration has enlisted the cooperation of the strongly nationalist Dai Viet leader Nguyen Huu Tri, and nationalist concern over Tam's francophilia has to some extent dissipated. Tam has also added to the political vitality of Vietnam by holding local elections in secure areas of Vietnam. Another Vietnamese program, undertaken with US economic assistance, which involves the relocation of scattered villages in the delta into centralized and defensible sites may be an important step toward the eventual "pacification" of heavily infiltrated areas. The decisions of March 1953 to increase the size of the Vietnamese National Army while expanding the area of Vietnamese strategic and operational responsibility, could also be of major political significance.

18. Despite these advances, Vietnam still lacks the degree of political strength essential for the mobilization of the country's resources. Tam's "action" program remains more shadow than substance. Elected local councils have no real power, promised land reform and other social and economic reforms which might generate popular support have not left the planning stage, and the Vietnamese government is handicapped by incompetent cabinet ministers and the lack of com-

petent administrators. While Bao Dai refuses to assume active direction of the affairs of state, he remains hostile toward new leadership and democratic activities.

19. Of more basic importance in the failure of Vietnamese to rally to the Vietnamese government following the French grant of independence within the French Union in 1949 have been the following:

　　a. Many Vietnamese doubt the ability of French Union forces to defeat the Viet Minh and prefer to remain apart from the struggle.

　　b. The French Government has not dared to promise complete national independence at some future date, as demanded by the Vietnamese, because of the fear that the French national assembly would then refuse to support a war in a "lost" portion of the French Union.

　　c. The Vietnamese, despite many evolutionary steps toward complete independence since 1949, are generally inclined to believe that the French intend to retain effective control over the affairs of Vietnam.

　　d. The nationalist appeal and military prestige of the Viet Minh remains strong among significant numbers of the Vietnamese.

20. In Cambodia, internal political strife has weakened the government, dissident nationalist elements have continued to sap popular loyalty to the throne, and the King is demanding greater independence from the French in order to strengthen his political position at home. Meanwhile, the 9,000 Viet Minh combatants in Cambodia, while under fairly constant attack by French and Cambodian forces, are capable of exploiting disorders which may develop.

21. Laotian stability has been upset by the recent Viet Minh incursion. The Laotians are generally hostile to the Viet Minh but are unable to contribute a great deal to the defense of their homeland. A small group of pro-Communist Laotians returned to Laos with the Viet Minh during the recent incursion. It is led by a disaffected Laotian nobleman, Prince Souphanouvong, and calls itself the "Free Government of Pathet Lao" (Laos).

22. Meanwhile, the Viet Minh leadership, with Chinese Communist material and advisory assistance since 1949, has demonstrated the necessary zeal, ruthlessness, and tenacity to exploit to the maximum the limited resources at their command. The Viet Minh have expanded the area under their complete control and their prestige has probably increased throughout Indochina as a result of military successes in northwest Tonkin and Laos.

23. In the areas of Viet Minh occupation, Viet Minh control is believed to be effective, and minimum food requirements are being met. The Viet Minh have taken on increasingly the conventional characteristics of a "Peoples Republic" and are now engaged in programs to confiscate and redistribute land and to eliminate "traitors" and "reactionaries." Although this departure from national front tactics has increased realization that the Viet Minh are under complete Communist domination, the Viet Minh control many villages within areas of nominal French Union occupation through terror, compulsion, and their continued nationalist appeal.

24. The Viet Minh and the Chinese Communists continue to maintain close relations. It is estimated that there are less than a thousand Chinese Communist advisers and technicians with the Viet Minh in Indochina. The Chinese Communists are providing the Viet Minh with military supplies at an estimated average level of 400 to 500 tons per month, and some Viet Minh troops are sent to Communist China for training. Small Chinese Communist units reportedly have entered the mountainous northwest section of Tonkin on several occasions to assist the Viet Minh against French-supported native guerrillas, but no Chinese

Communist troops have been identified in forward areas. There was some evidence during the past year that Viet Minh policy statements may be "cleared," if not written, in Peiping. Close Viet Minh relations with Communist China are complemented, superficially at least, by equally warm relations with the Soviet Union, but we are unable to determine whether Peiping or Moscow has ultimate responsibility for Viet Minh policy.

PROBABLE TRENDS IN FRENCH UNION
CAPABILITIES AND COURSES OF ACTION

25. French plans for dealing with the war in Indochina now revolve around the development of national armies in the Associated States, particularly in Vietnam. In March 1953, the Franco-Vietnamese High Military Council approved a new program calling for an increase in Vietnamese strength during the current year of 40,000 men, organized in 54 "commando" battalions.[3] A further expansion of 57,000 men has been proposed for 1954 and will probably be undertaken if the initial reinforcement is successful and if equipment is made available by the US. With these additional Vietnamese forces, the French hope to undertake widespread clearing operations and subsequently to organize sufficient mobile groups to begin by early 1955 the destruction of the Viet Minh regular forces in Tonkin.

26. Progress has been made in carrying out the troop reinforcement program thus far, and the Vietnamese may have close to 40,000 reinforcements recruited, trained, and available for combat by early 1954. However, the Viet Minh invasion of Laos and the threat of similar operations will probably keep French mobile reserves deployed outside the Tonkin delta in isolated strong points. The addition of 40,000 untested and lightly armed Vietnamese will not offset the absence of these regular French forces, and effective clearing or offensive operations cannot be undertaken until French Union forces are regrouped. Moreover, the French military leadership has been so dominated by concepts of static defense as to be unable to conduct the planned operations with the vigor necessary for their success. How the new military leadership may alter this we cannot estimate. Finally, unless the French Union forces prove strong enough to provide security for the Vietnamese population, it will not be possible to sweep the guerrillas out of the areas as planned. Not only will the populace fail generally to provide the intelligence required to rout the guerrillas but, as in the past, they will frequently give warning of the presence of the French Union forces, thus permitting the guerrillas to take cover and later to emerge when the danger is past.

27. The French are fearful that they cannot achieve a military decision in Indochina. Unless the French Union military plans achieve great success during the period of this estimate, the conviction will grow in France that the Indochina problem can only be solved through some over-all East-West settlement in the Far East. The difficulties of the French financial position impel the French to seek relief from the mounting costs of the Indochina war, and French apprehensions concerning eventual German rearmament not only make them reluctant to increase the military establishment in Indochina but impel them to seek the early return of French troops to Europe. The French Government will therefore

---

[3] The 40,000 are to be recruited and will represent a net increase in French Union strength. Planned transfers of native units from the French Army to the Vietnamese Army will also strengthen the Vietnamese Army but will not represent any net increase in French Union strength.

remain under strong and increasing domestic pressure to reduce its military commitment in Indochina. On the other hand, the French Government is under strong pressure to maintain its position in Indochina. There is still considerable sentiment against abandoning the heavy investment which France has poured into Indochina. More important, there is great reluctance to accept the adverse effects on the cohesion of the French Union and on French prestige as a world power which would accompany the loss of France's position in Indochina. In these circumstances, we believe that the French will continue without enthusiasm to maintain their present levels of troop strength through mid-1954 and will support the planned development of the National Armies of the Associated States. At the same time, France will probably continue to seek maximum financial and material assistance for the French Union effort while resisting any measures which would impair French pre-eminence among the Associated States, including the making of any commitments concerning the eventual political status of the Associated States.

28. Political strength in Vietnam may grow slightly during 1953 as progress is made toward a stronger national army, as the Vietnamese assume increasing governmental responsibilities, and as Premier Tam's social and political programs serve to decrease distrust of French intentions. There will probably also be a growing understanding, and fear, of the true Communist nature and purpose of the Viet Minh. However, these developments will not bring about a significant increase in Vietnamese will and ability to resist the Viet Minh during the period of this estimate because the Vietnam leadership cannot in this brief period overcome popular apathy and mobilize the energy and resources of the people. Moreover, if events should persuade Vietnam leaders that no progress toward national independence is possible under the French or that French Union forces cannot defeat the Viet Minh, it is probable that the political strength of Vietnam would decline rapidly. Substantial Viet Minh military victories in the Tonkin delta or elsewhere in Indochina would also produce such a decline.

29. In Cambodia, political stability is likely to decline as the result of tension between the monarchy, the politically divided people, and the French colonial administration. Even if French concessions to the King insure his adherence to the French Union, unrest in Cambodia or a Viet Minh penetration into southern Laos might force the deployment of strong French forces to Cambodia.

30. In Laos, political attitudes will be determined almost entirely by military developments. The Laotians will probably remain loyal to the French Union if they are defended aggressively. They will not, however, offer effective resistance to Communist efforts to consolidate political control if French Union forces retreat from the country or if the French Union forces defend only a few strong points.

PROBABLE TRENDS IN VIET MINH AND CHINESE COMMUNIST CAPABILITIES AND COURSES OF ACTION

31. *Viet Minh Capabilities and Probable Courses of Action.* Barring serious Viet Minh military reverses, which could occur if Viet Minh forces should overextend themselves or make frontal attacks on French Union strong points, the Viet Minh regime will probably increase its total strength slightly during the period of this estimate. Viet Minh prestige will be increased by their recent gains in Laos. The organizational and administrative effectiveness of the regime will probably continue to increase with experience and Chinese Communist guidance.

The program of expropriation and distribution of lands to tenants now being carried out probably weakens the Viet Minh appeal among some classes, but will probably strengthen Viet Minh controls at the village level and thus facilitate the collection of rice.

32. Militarily, the Viet Minh are unlikely to expand greatly their armed forces because they are already experiencing manpower difficulties. Their combat efficiency probably will increase, however, as the result of a modest augmentation of their unit firepower and a steady improvement in staff planning and coordination of forces. The Viet Minh probably will continue to receive a steady flow of material assistance from the Chinese Communists, and the amount may increase at any time. The Viet Minh do not have, and probably cannot develop within the period of this estimate, the capability to make such effective use of heavy equipment—artillery, armor, and aircraft—from the Chinese Communists as to permit successful attacks against strong concentrations of regular French forces. Over a longer period, however, a great increase in Viet Minh capabilities, including the development of an air force, is possible.

33. We believe that during the period of this estimate the Communists in Indochina will probably attempt to avoid combat except where they can achieve surprise or great superiority in numbers. They will attempt to consolidate Communist controls in "Free Laos" and will build up supplies in northern Laos to support further penetrations and consolidation in that country. If they reach the Thai border, they probably will attempt to organize guerrilla forces among the Vietnamese in northeastern Thailand, but we do not believe they will have the capability to provide much material assistance to such forces through mid-1954. The Viet Minh forces in Laos may hope to receive assistance from the Vietnamese population in Thailand. The Viet Minh will almost certainly intensify political warfare, including guerrilla activities in Cambodia.

34. We believe that neither the French Union nor the Viet Minh will be able to win a final military decision in Indochina through mid-1954. The Viet Minh, with their principal striking forces operating from the Tonkin base area, will probably retain the initiative during the period of this estimate by maintaining attacks against lightly defended French Union territory. The French Union can hold key positions in Laos and may attempt by attacks against Viet Minh lines of communication, to prevent the Viet Minh from moving southward in force towards southern Laos and Cambodia. We believe, however, that Viet Minh guerrillas in southern Laos will develop sufficient strength to control much of the countryside and that guerrilla activities in Cambodia will be intensified. The French Union probably will reduce, but not eliminate, Viet Minh strength in south Vietnam. Viet Minh infiltration of the Tonkin delta will probably be maintained at a high level and the Viet Minh may undertake major attacks against the delta if they can weaken French defenses by drawing French strength elsewhere.

35. Unless there is a marked improvement in the French Union military position in Indochina, political stability in the Associated States and popular support of the French Union effort against the Viet Minh will decline. We believe that such marked improvement in the military situation is not likely, though a moderate improvement is possible. The over-all French Union position in Indochina therefore will probably deteriorate during the period of this estimate.

36. *Chinese Communist Capabilities and Probable Courses of Action.* The Chinese Communists will have the capability during the period of this estimate

to improve airfields in south China, to train Viet Minh pilots, to continue improvement of transportation facilities, and to increase their present level of logistic support for the Viet Minh. The Chinese Communists will probably retain their present capability to commit and support logistically 150,000 Chinese Communist troops for an invasion of Indochina. The combat efficiency of this potential invasion force could probably be increased considerably by the use of combat-seasoned troops who have been rotated from Korea in the past year. The ability of Chinese Communist forces to sustain offensive operations in Indochina would probably be increased should logistic requirements in Korea remain at low levels for a prolonged period.

37. A Chinese Communist force of 150,000, added to Viet Minh forces, would probably be able to overrun the Tonkin delta area before effective assistance could be brought to bear. The Chinese Communists now have, and will probably continue to have during the period of this estimate, sufficient jet and piston aircraft, independent of operations in Korea, for small-scale but damaging attacks against French Union installations in Tonkin. With surprise, they probably could neutralize the French Air Forces in Tonkin. The Chinese Communist air forces do not appear, however, to possess the capability at present of conducting sustained air operations in Indochina because of a lack of improved airfields in south China and stockpiles of supplies. Such preparations would take several months.

38. We believe that whether or not hostilities are concluded in Korea, the Chinese Communists will not invade Indochina during the period of this estimate.[4] Although they possess the capability, the following considerations militate against intervention by regular Chinese Communist forces or by large numbers of Chinese Communist "volunteers":

   a. The Communists probably consider that their present strategy in Indochina promises success in a prolonged struggle and produces certain immediate advantages. It diverts badly needed French and US resources from Europe at relatively small cost to the Communists. It provides opportunities to advance international Communist interests while preserving the fiction of "autonomous" national liberation movements, and it provides an instrument, the Viet Minh, with which Communist China and the USSR can indirectly exert military and psychological pressures on the peoples and governments of Laos, Cambodia, and Thailand.

   b. Communist leadership is aware that the West, and in particular the US, would probably retaliate against Communist China if Chinese Communist forces should invade Indochina. We believe that fear of such retaliation and of the major war which might result are important deterrents to open Chinese Communist intervention in Indochina.

39. We believe that the Communist objective to secure control of all Indochina will not be altered by an armistice in Korea or by Communist "peace" tactics. However, the Communists may decide that "peace" maneuvers in Indochina would contribute to the attainment of Communist global objectives, and to the objective of the Viet Minh.

[4] The Deputy Director for Intelligence, The Joint Staff, believes that the intelligence available is insufficient to permit a conclusion at this time that the Chinese Communists will or will not invade Indochina prior to mid-1954.

ANNEX A

ESTIMATED GROUND FORCE STRENGTHS
AND DISPOSITIONS AS OF 1 APRIL 1953 [1]

INDOCHINA

A. FRENCH UNION FORCES

Component	Tonkin	Annam & Plateaux	Cochin-china	Cambodia	Laos	Total
Regulars[2]						
French Expeditionary Corps (CEF)	91,000	20,000	45,000	8,000	7,500	171,500 [3]
Associated States Armies	27,000	33,000	20,000	8,500	8,000	96,500
Associated States National Guards	6,000	4,000	10,000	4,000	5,500	29,500
Semi-Military						
CEF Auxiliaries	23,000	6,500	18,000	3,300	2,400	53,200
Vietnam Auxiliaries	8,000	10,000	34,000	....	....	52,000
Other Semi-Military	27,000	7,000	30,000	9,000	6,500	79,500
Totals	182,000	80,500	157,000	32,800	29,900	482,200

[1] These strengths and dispositions were effective before the Viet Minh invasion of Laos. Since that time French Expeditionary Corps (CEF) strength in Laos has been increased to 17,500 and CEF strength in Tonkin reduced to 81,000.

[2] French Union regular forces are organized into a total of 118 CEF battalions and 95 Associated States battalions. The CEF has 83 infantry, 7 parachute, 8 armored, and 19 artillery battalions and 1 AAA battalion. The Associated States have 87 infantry and 4 artillery battalions and 4 parachute battalions.

[3] Does not include 6,000 French personnel detached for duty with the Associated States forces as cadres and advisers. Composition of the 172,000 is as follows: French—51,000; Foreign Legion—19,000; African—17,000; North African—30,000; native Indochinese—55,000.

ANNEX B

ESTIMATED VIET MINH GROUND FORCE STRENGTHS
AND DISPOSITIONS AS OF 1 APRIL 1953 [1]

B. VIET MINH FORCES

Component	Tonkin	Annam & Plateaux	Cochin-china	Cambodia	Laos	Total
Regulars[2]						
Army	81,000	25,000	13,000	1,000	3,000	123,000
Regional Forces (Full-time)	35,000	14,500	7,500	3,000	2,000	62,000
Semi-Military						
People's Militia (Armed)	50,000	34,000	25,000	5,000	1,000	115,000
Totals	166,000	73,500	45,500	9,000 [3]	6,000	300,000

[1] These strengths and dispositions changed during the Viet Minh incursion into Laos in April. An estimated 30,000 Viet Minh regulars moved from Tonkin into Laos and an estimated 10,000 moved from Annam. By mid-May, however, it is believed that all but 15,000 of the Viet Minh regulars had returned to their base areas in Tonkin and Annam.

[2] The Viet Minh are organized into 6 infantry divisions, 1 artillery division, 14 independent regiments, and 15 independent battalions. Regional forces are organized in 44 battalions.

[3] Some 3,000 dissident Khmer Issaraks are also active in Cambodia.

ANNEX C

AIR ORDER OF BATTLE—FRENCH AIR FORCE AND NAVAL AIR ARM, FAR EAST

Unit Designation	Airfield	No. and Type Aircraft Assigned
North Tactical Command		
1st/8 Fighter Squadron	Bach Mai, Hanoi	18 F8F
2nd/8 Fighter Squadron	Cat Bi, Haiphong	20 F8F
Detachment, 1st/21 Fighter Squadron	Cat Bi, Haiphong	7 F8F
1st/25 Lt. Bomber Squadron	Cat Bi, Haiphong	15 B–26
Detachment, 1st/19 Lt. Bomber Squadron	Cat Bi, Haiphong	3 B–26, 1 RB–26
80th Photo Recon. Squadron	Bach Mai, Hanoi	11 F8F
Detachment, 2nd/62 Trans. Squadron	Bach Mai, Hanoi	12 C–47
Detachment, 1st/64 Trans. Squadron	Gia Lam, Hanoi	5 C–47, 3 JU–52
Detachment, 2nd/64 Trans. Squadron	Gia Lam, Hanoi	5 C–47
2nd/62 Trans. Squadron	Do Son, Haiphong	6 C–47
Center Tactical Command		
1st/21 Fighter Squadron	Tourane Afld., Tourane	12 F8F
Detachment 2nd/9 Fighter Squadron	Ban Me Thout Afld., Ban Me Thout	5 F8F
1st/19 Lt. Bomber Squadron	Tourane Afld., Tourane	16 B–26, 3 RB–26
Detachment, 1st/64 Trans. Squadron	Tourane Afld., Tourane	2 JU–52
1st/64 Trans. Squadron	Nhatrang Afld., Nhatrang	5 C–47, 6 JU–52
South Tactical Command		
2nd/9 Fighter Squadron	Tan Son Nhut, Saigon	8 F6F, 10 F8F
2nd/64 Trans. Squadron	Tan Son Nhut, Saigon	16 C–47
Detachment, 1st/64 Trans. Squadron	Tan Son Nhut, Saigon	4 JU–52

Miscellaneous light aircraft and helicopters (used throughout the three tactical commands for liaison, reconnaissance, medical evacuation, and flight training)— 152

TOTAL 345

Naval Air Arm

Carrier based   22 F6F
12 SB2C–5

Miscellaneous other types   28

TOTAL 62

Aircraft (all types) temporarily unoperational because of shortages in personnel and logistics— 179

GRAND TCTAL 586

ANNEX D

FRENCH NAVAL FORCES IN INDOCHINA

Small Aircraft Carrier (CVL)[1]	1
Gunboat (PG)	2
Escort (PCE)	8
Submarine Chaser (PC)	11
Submarine Chaser (SC)	5
Motor Minesweeper (AMS)	6

Amphibious Vessels:

LST	4
LSIL	13
LSSL	6
LCU	19

Miscellaneous small landing craft	211

Auxiliary Vessels:

ARL	1
AG	1
AGS	1
AR	1
AFDL	1
AVP	2
AO	1

Service Craft	54
French Navy Personnel	9,760
Vietnam Navy Personnel	277

Mission Aircraft:

F6F–5[2]	22
SB2C–5[2]	12
PB4Y–2	8
JRF–5	11
S–51	2
Morane 500 "0"	6
C–47A	1

[1] The French have attempted to keep one of their two carriers in Indochina waters, subject to overhaul and repair schedules. The ARROMANCHES (CVL) and the LAFAYETTE (CVL) departed for France in February and May 1953, respectively, for overhaul and repairs.

[2] Carrier-based aircraft.

[Document 16]

NATIONAL SECURITY COUNCIL
WASHINGTON

August 5, 1953

MEMORANDUM FOR THE NATIONAL SECURITY COUNCIL

SUBJECT: Further United States Support for France and the Associated States of Indochina

REFERENCES: A. NSC 124/2
               B. NSC Action Nos. 758, 773 and 780
               C. NIE–63 and NIE–91

The enclosed report by the Department of State on the subject is transmitted herewith for consideration by the National Security Council of the recommendation contained in paragraph 9 thereof at its meeting on Thursday, August 6, 1953.

JAMES S. LAY, Jr.
Executive Secretary

cc: The Secretary of the Treasury
     The Chairman, Joint Chiefs of Staff
     The Director of Central Intelligence

[Opening sections missing]

The winding up of the Indochina war is a necessary condition to enable France to check both these trends and reassume a more confident and positive role on the continent.

4. The lack of success so far in Indochina is traceable largely to French failure:

> *a.* by timely grants of sovereignty and impressive military success, to win a sufficient native support to permit more rapid development of larger and more effective native armies, and to frustrate nationalist appeal of the Viet Minh.
> *b.* to plan and execute aggressive military operations.

5. The present French government is the first in seven years which seems prepared to do what needs to be done to wind up the war in Indochina. Its plans offer the United States at last an opportunity to attack the major Indochinese and Metropolitan French problems as a whole. The French Premier has assured our representatives that his government is anxious to continue the struggle and to press on to win, but he can carry through his program against political opposition only if he offers a "package" solution, not only of Indochina but of the related French weakness in Europe and at home. For this purpose the new government has developed the following program:

> *a. Military Initiative.* A new commander, General Navarre, has taken over in Indochina and is determined to assume the offensive. The initial operations under his command testify to this resolve. He has revised the plan originally presented in outline to us by M. Letourneau in March 1953 for breaking the back of Viet Minh resistance during the campaign season

of 1954–55. His plans include an increase in the native armies by approximately the following figures: 59,600 in 1953; 76,000 in 1954, and 20,000 in 1955 for a total of 331,650 by January 1956. At his request, the French government is prepared, despite popular opposition, to send nine more regular infantry battalions plus ancillary units from France, if the rest of the program is agreed on. The Navarre operational plans drawn up on Indochina were approved by Lt. Gen. O'Daniel, USA, in his report on his recent mission.

b. Political Program. Pursuant to the French declaration of July 3, M. Laniel has assured U.S. representatives of his determination to grant genuine independence to the Associated States without the strings which have marked the previous grants of "independence." He apparently envisages something very much like Dominion status, retaining only such French authority and privileges as may be agreed.

c. Fiscal Rehabilitation. Laniel conceives his project for Indochina as an integral part of a new and supreme effort by France to "put its house in order." He plans to approach a balanced budget during CY 1954. This will involve a cut in French military as well as civil expense for that year. At the same time he contemplates a greater effort in Indochina. To do this he asks the U.S. for additional assistance amounting to about $400 million for FY 1954.

6. *a.* Attached are two tables showing (1) the financing of the Indochina war in CY 1953 and as proposed for CY 1954; and (2) U.S. aid for France and Indochina under 1953 program and 1954 appropriations. They contain tentative figures for 1954.

b. As the first table makes clear, under the proposed program, the United States would assume about 50 per cent of the 1954 budgetary expenditures ($829 million out of $1,676 million) and, if end-item aid is included, would be carrying about 61 per cent of the total financing. This would represent about two and one-third times the amount of U.S. aid for CY 1953.

c. As shown by the second table, this program would entail an increase of $403 million over the assistance now planned for France ($1,286 million). Of the total French military budget for both Indochina and NATO, the presently planned U.S. aid, including end items, would be 26 per cent; if the aid were increased as requested, such U.S. assistance, including end items, would be 34 per cent of the total.

d. Finally, as the first table indicates, under the program, the total expenditures for Indochina for 1954, including end items, would be $2,160 million as compared with $1,700 for CY 1953.

7. The program presents substantial risks. Under it, the French build-up in Europe would be slowed down in some degree, both by the limited troop diversion and the cut in the French military budget. Moreover, in the best of circumstances, the Indo-Chinese war cannot be successfully closed out before the 1954–55 fighting season. Consequently, in addition to any supplemental aid

furnished now, we would have to contemplate a comparable further contribution a year from now to assure a satisfactory conclusion. Furthermore, there is the risk that the French Union forces in Indo-China might suffer reverses before the projected additional effort can be brought to bear.

8. Despite these risks and uncertainties it is believed that the U.S. should agree, in its own security interests, to furnish the additional $400 million of aid to France. Various factors lead to this conclusion:

a. The Laniel government is almost certainly the *last* French government which would undertake to continue the war in Indo-China. If it fails, it will almost certainly be succeeded by a government committed to seek a settlement on terms dangerous to the security of the U.S. and the Free World. The negotiation of a truce in Korea, added to the frustrations and weariness of the seven years' war, has markedly increased the sentiment in France for some kind of negotiated peace in Indo-China. In the recent protracted French governmental crisis, every leading candidate bid for popular support with some kind of promise to reduce the Indo-China commitment in some way. For the first time in seven years, latent defeatist impulses emerged into real efforts by political and parliamentary leaders to "pull out."

b. Under present conditions any negotiated settlement would mean the eventual loss to Communism not only of Indo-China but of the whole of Southeast Asia.

c. The loss of Indo-China would be critical to the security of the U.S. Communist control of Indo-China would endanger vital raw material sources; it would weaken the confidence of other Southeast Asian states in Western leadership; it would make more difficult and more expensive the defense of Japan, Formosa and the Philippines; and complicate the creation of viable Japanese economy. If the French actually decided to withdraw, the U.S. would have to consider most seriously whether to take over in this area.

d. On the other hand, if the proposed program does succeed, and the French are able to achieve victory in Indo-China within two years, the effect will be to strengthen the Free World and our coalition in Europe as well as Southeast Asia. France will be enabled to adopt in Europe the active role which her weakness has undermined in the preceding period.

Recommendation

9. Accordingly it is recommended that the National Security Council agree to an increase in aid to France in the current fiscal year by an amount not exceeding $400 million above that already committed, provided only that (a) the Joint Chiefs of Staff inform the National Security Council that in their view the French plan holds the promise of military success; and (b) the Director of the Foreign Operations Administration ascertain the available sources within currently appointed funds, and the extent to which a special supplementary appropriation will be necessary when Congress reconvenes in January 1954.

TAB A

FINANCING THE WAR IN INDOCHINA

(*millions of dollars*)

	1953	1954
Present estimate of requirements		
French Expeditionary Corps	866	866
Reinforcements under Navarre plan	0	54
French Air Force and Navy	137	137
Total French forces	1003	1057
Associated States forces		
Regular Armies	335	400
Light battalions and support troops	43	196
Air and naval forces	9	23
Total	387	619
Total budgetary requirement	1390	1676
Financing of requirements		
French budget or equivalent		
French fiscal resources	975	690
U.S. financial assistance		
Presently available	258	426
Requirement yet to be financed	0	403
Total	258	829
Total French budget or equivalent including U.S.		
financial assistance	1233	1519
Associated States fiscal resources	157	157
Total budgetary resources	1390	1676
Total U.S. aid for Indochina		
Financial assistance (as above)	258	829
Military end-item program	255	429
Common-use program	30	30
Economic aid to Associated States	25	25
Total	568	1313
Total financing by France, Associated States and the U.S.		
Budgetary	1390	1676
Other	310	484
Total	1700	2160
Total U.S. financing as percent of total program	33%	61%

NOTE: U.S. fiscal year 1954 aid program is related to French calendar year 1954 budget program.

TAB B
U.S. AID TO FRANCE AND INDOCHINA
(*millions of dollars*)

	Program 1953	Proposed 1954	Appropriated 1954
I. Aid related to April memorandum*			
Mutual defense financing			
Attributed French NATO budget	169	100	85
Attributed Indochina budget	48	400	400
Total	217	500	485
Defense support assistance			
Attributed French NATO budget	158	0	0
Attributed Indochina budget	210[a]	0	0
Total	368	0	0
"Kitty" to cover partial costs of expansion Indochina forces	0	100	26[b]
Total aid related to April memorandum	585	600	511
II. Laniel request for aid to finance proposed Indochina program			
Total U.S. aid now available for Indochina in relation to April memorandum			829
			426
Requirement yet to be financed.			403
III. U.S. aid in addition to April memorandum			
Military end-item program: France	0[d]	364	291[c]
Military end-item program: Indochina	255	429	429
Common-use program for Indochina	30	30	30
Economic aid to Associated States	25	25	25
Total	310	848	775
IV. Total U.S. aid for France and Indochina			
Presently available funds	895	1448	1286
Requirement yet to be financed			403
Total			1689
V. Total military program of France and the Associated States, including U.S. assistance in all forms French military budget			
NATO and other areas Indochina	2730		2444
Present French budget plan	1233		1090
Additional U.S. financing requested	0		429
Total	1233		1519
Total French budget with U.S. support	3963		3963
Associated States military budgets	157		157
U.S. aid outside April memorandum	310		775
Total program with U.S. aid	4430		4895

* Memorandum on aid prepared by U.S. delegation to the North Atlantic Council meeting in Paris and handed to the French Government by the U.S. delegation on April 26, 1953.

TAB B (Cont'd.)

	Program 1953	Proposed 1954	Appropriated 1954
VI. *Total U.S. aid as percent total programs financed by U.S., France and Associated States*			
Presently available funds	20%		26%
Including requirement yet to be financed			34%

NOTES:

U.S. fiscal 1954 aid program is related to French calendar 1954 budget program.

   a. Figure arbitrary since attribution has not yet taken place: figure based upon 1952 experience, and also includes counterpart of $60 million provided out of fiscal 1953 appropriation, under April memorandum.

   b. Available from unprogrammed portion of carry-over into fiscal 1954 of unobligated fiscal 1953 appropriations for Far East military aid.

   c. Arbitrarily reduced 20 percent to reflect proportionate reduction in European military aid appropriation below figures proposed to Congress.

   d. This figure shown as zero because of reprogramming which took place in course of the year, because of over-programming for France for the period FY 1950–1953; in effect, no net additional funds were therefore necessary for the French end-item program out of the 1953 appropriations.

[Document 17]

28 August 1953

MEMORANDUM FOR THE SECRETARY OF DEFENSE

Subject: The Navarre Concept for Operations in Indochina.

   1. In a memorandum for you, dated 21 April 1953, subject: "Proposed French Strategic Plan for the Successful Conclusion of the War in Indochina," the Joint Chiefs of Staff pointed out certain weaknesses in the LeTourneau-Allard plan, but felt that it was workable. During the visit of the U.S. Joint Military Mission to Indochina, Lieutenant General Navarre submitted in writing to Lieutenant General O'Daniel, Chief of the Mission, a paper entitled "Principles for the Conduct of the War in Indochina" appended hereto, which appears to correct these weaknesses and which presents a marked improvement in French military thinking concerning operations in Indochina.

   2. In his report Lieutenant General O'Daniel stated that, in his opinion, the new French command in Indochina will accomplish under the Navarre concept the decisive defeat of the Viet Minh by 1955 and that the addition of two or more French divisions from outside of Indochina would expedite this defeat. Additions other than in divisional organization would be in error since it is the divisional team, with its combat proven effectiveness, which is sorely needed in Indochina. Lieutenant General O'Daniel further reported that French military

leaders were most cooperative with the mission, that several agreements were accomplished to improve the effectiveness of the proposed military operations, and that repeated invitations were extended to the U.S. mission to return in a few months to witness the progress the French will have made.

3. Based on past performances by the French, the Joint Chiefs of Staff have reservations in predicting actual results which can be expected pending additional proof by demonstration of continued French support and by further French performance in Indochina. The Joint Chiefs of Staff are of the opinion that a basic requirement for military success in Indochina is one of creating a political climate in that country which will provide the incentive for natives to support the French and supply them with adequate intelligence which is vital to the successful conduct of operations in Indochina. If this is accomplished and if the Navarre concept is vigorously pursued militarily in Indochina and given wholehearted political support in France, it does offer a promise of military success sufficient to warrant appropriate additional U.S. aid required to assist. U.S. support of the Navarre concept should be based on needs of the French Union Forces in Indochina for additional equipment necessary to implement the organization of the "Battle Corps" envisaged by the Navarre concept and necessary support of the planned expansion of indigenous forces, such needs to be screened by the Military Assistance Advisory Group in Indochina. In addition, to improve the chances of success, this support should include continued close liaison and coordination with French military authorities together with friendly but firm encouragement and advice where indicated.

4. In furtherance of the O'Daniel Mission the Joint Chiefs of Staff are receiving Progress Reports from Indochina. Information received from Indochina indicates the French are not pursuing agreements reached between General O'Daniel and General Navarre (including the Navarre concept) as vigorously as expected by General O'Daniel and as contemplated by him in his report. Progress reports state that (a) the French have "no plans for a general fall offensive beyond limited objective operations designed to keep the enemy off balance," (b) reorganization into regiments and division-size units "is still in the planning stages," (c) there is "no sense of urgency in the training of senior Vietnamese commanders and staff officers," (d) the organization of a training command is awaiting the solution of "political problems" and (e) the "organization of the amphibious plan has not gone beyond the planning stages."

5. In light of the apparent slowness of the French in following up the Navarre concept and other agreements reached between General Navarre and General O'Daniel, the Joint Chiefs of Staff believe that additional U.S. support should be conditioned upon continued implementation of French support, demonstration of French intent by actual performance in Indochina, and continued French willingness to receive and act upon U.S. military advice. Further, the French should be urged at all levels to support and vigorously prosecute the Navarre concept to the maximum extent of their capabilities.

> For the Joint Chiefs of Staff:
> ARTHUR RADFORD,
> Chairman,
> Joint Chiefs of Staff.

Enclosure   [material missing]

[Document 18]

October 30, 1953

NOTE BY THE EXECUTIVE SECRETARY

to the

NATIONAL SECURITY COUNCIL

on

BASIC NATIONAL SECURITY POLICY

References: A. NSC 162 and NSC 162/1
          B. NSC Action Nos. 853, 868, 886, 926 and 944
          C. Memo for NSC from Executive Secretary, subject, "Review of Basic National Security Policy," dated October 28, 1953
          D. NSC 153/1
          E. Memo for NSC from Executive Secretary, subject, "Project Solarium," dated July 23, 1953

The National Security Council, the Secretary of the Treasury, the Attorney General, the Director, Bureau of the Budget, the Chairman, Council of Economic Advisers, and the Chairman, Atomic Energy Commission, at the 168th Council meeting on October 29, 1953, adopted the statement of policy contained in NSC 162/1 subject to the changes which are set forth in NSC Action No. 944–*a*.

In connection with this action the Council also noted:

    a. The President's statement that if the Department of Defense hereafter finds that the provisions of subparagraph 9–*a*–(1), when read in the context of the total policy statement, operate to the disadvantage of the national security, the Secretary of Defense should bring this finding before the Council for reconsideration.

    b. That action should be promptly taken to conform existing arrangements regarding atomic weapons to subparagraph 39–*b*.

    c. That the policy in NSC 162/1 does not contemplate any fixed date for D-Day readiness.

    d. That the Planning Board would submit for Council consideration a revision of "U.S. Objectives vis-a-vis the USSR in the Event of War," as presently stated in the Annex, in the light of the provisions of NSC 162/1, as amended.

The President has this date approved the statement of policy contained in NSC 162/1, as amended and adopted by the Council and enclosed herewith, and directs its implementation by all appropriate executive departments and agencies of the U.S. Government. As basic policy, this paper has not been referred to any single department or agency for special coordination.

Accordingly, NSC 153/1 is hereby superseded.

It is requested that special security precautions be observed in the handling of the enclosure and that access to it be very strictly limited on an absolute need-to-know basis.

JAMES S. LAY, Jr.
Executive Secretary

cc: The Secretary of the Treasury
The Attorney General
The Director, Bureau of the Budget
The Chairman, Council of Economic Advisers
The Chairman, Atomic Energy Commission
The Federal Civil Defense Administrator
The Chairman, Joint Chiefs of Staff
The Director of Central Intelligence

REVIEW OF BASIC NATIONAL SECURITY POLICY

Table of Contents

STATEMENT OF POLICY

by the

NATIONAL SECURITY COUNCIL

on

BASIC NATIONAL SECURITY POLICY

GENERAL CONSIDERATIONS

Basic Problems of National Security Policy

1.   *a.* To meet the Soviet threat to U.S. security.
     b. In doing so, to avoid seriously weakening the U.S. economy or undermining our fundamental values and institutions.

The Soviet Threat to the United States

2. The primary threat to the security, free institutions, and fundamental values of the United States is posed by the combination of:

　　a. Basic Soviet hostility to the non-communist world, particularly to the United States.

　　b. Great Soviet military power.

　　c. Soviet control of the international communist apparatus and other means of subversion or division of the free world.

3.　　*a.* The authority of the Soviet regime does not appear to have been impaired by the events since Stalin's death, or to be likely to be appreciably weakened during the next few years. The transfer of power may cause some uncertainty in Soviet and satellite tactics for some time, but will probably not impair the basic economic and military strength of the Soviet bloc. The Soviet rulers can be expected to continue to base their policy on the conviction of irreconcilable hostility between the bloc and the non-communist world. This conviction is the compound product of Marxist belief in their historically determined conflict with, and inevitable triumph over, "world capitalism" led by the United States, of fear for the security of the regime and the USSR, especially in the face of a hostile coalition, of distrust of U.S. aims and intentions, and of long-established reliance on techniques of conspiracy and subversion. Accordingly, the basic Soviet objectives continue to be consolidation and expansion of their own sphere of power and the eventual domination of the non-communist world.

　　b. Soviet strategy has been flexible and will probably continue so, allowing for retreats and delays as well as advances. The various "peace gestures" so far have cost the Soviets very little in actual concessions and could be merely designed to divide the West by raising false hopes and seeking to make the United States appear unyielding. It is possible, however, that the USSR, for internal and other reasons, may desire a settlement of specific issues or a relaxation of tensions and military preparations for a substantial period. Thus far, there are no convincing signs of readiness to make important concessions to this end.

4.　　*a.* The capability of the USSR to attack the United States with atomic weapons has been continuously growing and will be materially enhanced by hydrogen weapons. The USSR has sufficient bombs and aircraft, using one-way missions, to inflict serious damage on the United States, especially by surprise attack. The USSR soon may have the capability of dealing a crippling blow to our industrial base and our continued ability to prosecute a war. Effective defense could reduce the likelihood and intensity of a hostile attack but not eliminate the chance of a crippling blow.

　　b. The USSR now devotes about one-sixth of its gross national product to military outlays and is expected to continue this level. It has and will continue to have large conventional military forces capable of aggression against countries of the free world. Within the next two years, the Soviet bloc is not expected to increase the size of its forces, but will strengthen them with improved equipment and training and the larger atomic stockpile.

　　c. The Soviet bloc now has the capability of strong defense against air attack on critical targets within the USSR under favorable weather conditions, and is likely to continue to strengthen its all-weather air defenses.

5.   *a.* The recent uprisings in East Germany and the unrest in other European satellites evidence the failure of the Soviets fully to subjugate these peoples or to destroy their desire for freedom; the dependence of these satellite governments on Soviet armed forces; and the relative unreliability of satellite armed forces (especially if popular resistance in the satellites should increase). These events necessarily have placed internal and psychological strains upon the Soviet leadership. Nevertheless, the ability of the USSR to exercise effective control over, and to exploit the resources of, the European satellites has not been appreciably reduced and is not likely to be so long as the USSR maintains adequate military forces in the area.

   b. The detachment of any major European satellite from the Soviet bloc does not now appear feasible except by Soviet acquiescence or by war. Such a detachment would not decisively affect the Soviet military capability either in delivery of weapons of mass destruction or in conventional forces, but would be a considerable blow to Soviet prestige and would impair in some degree Soviet conventional military capabilities in Europe.

   c. The Chinese Communist regime is firmly in control and is unlikely to be shaken in the foreseeable future by domestic forces or rival regimes, short of the occurrence of a major war. The alliance between the regimes of Communist China and the USSR is based on common ideology and current community of interests. With the death of Stalin and the Korean truce, Communist China may tend more to emphasize its own interests, though limited by its present economic and military dependence on the USSR, and, in the long run, basic differences may strain or break the alliance. At present, however, it appears to be firmly established and adds strategic territory and vast reserves of military manpower to the Soviet bloc.

6.   *a.* The USSR does not seem likely deliberately to launch a general war against the United States during the period covered by current estimates (through mid-1955). The uncertain prospects for Soviet victory in a general war, the change in leadership, satellite unrest, and the U.S. capability to retaliate massively, make such a course improbable. Similarly, an attack on NATO countries or other areas which would be almost certain to bring on general war in view of U.S. commitments or intentions would be unlikely. The Soviets will not, however, be deterred by fear of general war from taking the measures they consider necessary to counter Western actions which they view as a serious threat to their security.

   b. When both the USSR and the United States reach a stage of atomic plenty and ample means of delivery, each will have the probable capacity to inflict critical damage on the other, but is not likely to be able to prevent major atomic retaliations. This could create a stalemate, with both sides reluctant to initiate general warfare; although if the Soviets believed that initial surprise held the prospect of destroying the capacity for retaliation, they might be tempted into attacking.

   c. Although Soviet fear of atomic reaction should still inhibit local aggression, increasing Soviet atomic capability may tend to diminish the deterrent effect of U.S. atomic power against peripheral Soviet aggression. It may also sharpen the reaction of the USSR to what it considers provocative acts of the United States. If either side should miscalculate the strength of the other's reaction, such local conflicts could grow into general war, even though neither seeks nor desires it. To avoid this, it will in general be desirable for the United States to make clear to the USSR the kind of actions which will be almost certain to lead to this result, recognizing, however, that as general war becomes more devastating for both sides the threat to resort to it becomes less available as a sanction against local aggression.

7. The USSR will continue to rely heavily on tactics of division and subversion to weaken the free world alliances and will to resist the Soviet power. Using both the fear of atomic warfare and the hope of peace, such political warfare will seek to exploit differences among members of the free world, neutralist attitudes, and anti-colonial and nationalist sentiments in underdeveloped areas. For these purposes, communist parties and other cooperating elements will be used to manipulate opinion and control governments wherever possible. This aspect of the Soviet threat is likely to continue indefinitely and to grow in intensity.

8. Over time, changes in the outlook and policies of the leadership of the USSR may result from such factors as the slackening of revolutionary zeal, the growth of vested managerial and bureaucratic interests, and popular pressures for consumption goods. Such changes, combined with the growing strength of the free world and the failure to break its cohesion, and possible aggravation of weaknesses within the Soviet bloc through U.S. or allied action or otherwise, might induce a willingness to negotiate. The Soviet leadership might find it desirable and even essential to reach agreements acceptable to the United States and its allies, without necessarily abandoning its basic hositility to the non-Soviet world.

Defense Against the Soviet Threat

9. In the face of the Soviet threat, the security of the United States requires:

   a. Development and maintenance of:
   (1) A strong military posture, with emphasis on the capability of inflicting massive retaliatory damage by offensive striking power;
   (2) U.S. and allied forces in readiness to move rapidly initially to counter aggression by Soviet bloc forces and to hold vital areas and lines of communication; and
   (3) A mobilization base, and its protection against crippling damage, adequate to insure victory in the event of general war.
   b. Maintenance of a sound, strong and growing economy, capable of providing through the operation of free institutions, the strength described in *a* above over the long pull and of rapidly and effectively changing to full mobilization.
   c. Maintenance of morale and free institutions and the willingness of the U.S. people to support the measures necessary for national security.

10. In support of these basic security requirements, it is necessary that the United States:

   a. Develop and maintain an intelligence system capable of:
   (1) Collecting and analyzing indications of hostile intentions that would give maximum prior warning of possible aggression or subversion in any area of the world.
   (2) Accurately evaluating the capabilities of foreign countries, friendly and neutral as well as enemy, to undertake military, political, economic, and subversive courses of action affecting U.S. security.

(3) Forecasting potential foreign developments having a bearing on U.S. national security.

b. Develop an adequate manpower program designed to:

(1) Expand scientific and technical training.

(2) Provide an equitable military training system.

(3) Strike a feasible balance between the needs of an expanding peacetime economy and defense requirements.

(4) Provide for an appropriate distribution of services and skills in the event of national emergency.

c. Conduct and foster scientific research and development so as to insure superiority in quantity and quality of weapons systems, with attendant continuing review of the level and composition of forces and of the industrial base required for adequate defense and for successful prosecution of general war.

d. Continue, for as long as necessary, a state of limited defense mobilization to develop military readiness by:

(1) Developing and maintaining production plant capacity, dispersed with a view to minimizing destruction by enemy attack and capable of rapid expansion or prompt conversion to essential wartime output.

(2) Creating and maintaining minimum essential reserve stocks of selected end-items, so located as to support promptly and effectively the war effort in areas of probable commitment until war production and shipping capacity reaches the required wartime levels.

(3) Maintaining stockpiling programs, and providing additional production facilities, for those materials the shortage of which would affect critically essential defense programs; meanwhile reducing the rates of other stockpile materials.

e. Provide reasonable internal security against covert attack, sabotage, subversion, and espionage, particularly against the clandestine introduction and detonation of atomic weapons.

11. Within the free world, only the United States can provide and maintain, for a period of years to come, the atomic capability to counterbalance Soviet atomic power. Thus, sufficient atomic weapons and effective means of delivery are indispensable for U.S. security. Moreover, in the face of Soviet atomic power, defense of the continental United States becomes vital to effective security: to protect our striking force, our mobilization base, and our people. Such atomic capability is also a major contribution to the security of our allies, as well as of this country.

12. The United States cannot, however, meet its defense needs, even at exorbitant cost, without the support of allies.

a. The effective use of U.S. strategic air power against the USSR will require overseas bases on foreign territory for some years to come. Such bases well continue indefinitely to be an important additional element of U.S. strategic air capability and to be essential to the conduct of the military operations on the Eurasian continent in case of general war. The availability of such bases and their use by the United States in case of need will depend, in most cases, on the consent and cooperation of the nations where they are located. Such nations will assume the risks entailed only if convinced that their own security will thereby be best served.

b. The United States needs to have aligned on its side in the world struggle, in peace and in war, the armed forces and economic resources and materials of the major highly-industrialized non-communist states. Progressive loss to the Soviet bloc of these states would so isolate the United States and alter the world balance as to endanger the capacity of the United States to win in the event of general war or to maintain an adequate defense without undermining its fundamental institutions.

c. U.S. strategy including the use of atomic weapons, therefore, can be successfully carried out only if our essential allies are convinced that it is conceived and will be implemented for the purpose of mutual security and defense against the Soviet threat. U.S. leadership in this regard, however, does not imply the necessity to meet all desires of our allies.

d. Our allies are, in turn, dependent on the United States for their security: (1) they lack that atomic capability which is the major deterrent to Soviet aggression; (2) most lack political and economic stability sufficient to support their military forces. The United States should be able for the foreseeable future to provide military aid, in more limited amounts than heretofore, to our essential allies. It should be possible in the near future, however, generally to eliminate most grant economic aid, if coupled with appropriate U.S. economic and trade policies.

13. *a.* Under existing treaties or policies, an attack on the NATO countries, Western Germany, Berlin, Japan, the Philippines, Australia, New Zealand, and the American Republics, or on the Republic of Korea, would involve the United States in war with the USSR, or at least with Communist China if the aggression were Chinese alone.

b. Certain other countries, such as Indochina or Formosa, are of such strategic importance to the United States that an attack on them probably would compel the United States to react with military force either locally at the point of attack or generally against the military power of the aggressor. Moreover, the principle of collective security through the United Nations, if it is to continue to survive as a deterrent to continued piecemeal aggression and a promise of an eventual effective world security system, should be upheld even in areas not of vital strategic importance.

c. The assumption by the United States, as the leader of the free world, of a substantial degree of responsibility for the freedom and security of the free nations is a direct and essential contribution to the maintenance of its own freedom and security.

14. *a.* The United States should keep open the possibility of settlements with the U.S.S.R., compatible with basic U.S. security interests, which would resolve specific conflicts or reduce the magnitude of the Soviet threat. Moreover, to maintain the continued support of its allies, the United States must seek to convince them of its desire to reach such settlements. But, in doing so, we must not allow the possibility of such settlements to delay or reduce efforts to develop and maintain adequate free world strength, and thus enable the Soviets to increase their relative strength.

b. It must be recognized, however, that the prospects for acceptable negotiated settlements are not encouraging. There is no evidence that the Soviet leadership is prepared to modify its basic attitudes and accept any permanent settlement with the United States, although it may be prepared for a *modus vivendi* on certain issues. Atomic and other major weapons can be controlled only by adequate and enforceable safeguards which would involve some form of international inspection and supervision.

Acceptance of such serious restrictions by either side would be extremely difficult under existing conditions of suspicion and distrust. The chances for such disarmament would perhaps be improved by agreements on other conflicts either beforehand or at the same time, or by possible realization by the Soviets, in time, that armament limitation will serve their own interests and security.

    c. The United States should promptly determine what it would accept as an adequate system of armament control which would effectively remove or reduce the Soviet atomic and military threat, and on what basis the United States would be prepared to negotiate to obtain it.

*Present State of the Coalition**

15. *a.* The effort of the United States, especially since 1950, to build up the strength, cohesion and common determination of the free world has succeeded in increasing its relative strength and may well have prevented overt military aggression since Korea.

    b. In Western Europe the build-up of military strength and the progress of economic recovery has, at least partially, remedied a situation of glaring weakness in a vital area. NATO and associated forces are now sufficient to make aggressive action in Europe costly for the USSR and to create a greater feeling of confidence and security among the Western European peoples. However, even though significant progress has been made in building up these forces, the military strength in Western Europe is presently not sufficient to prevent a full-scale Soviet attack from overrunning Western Europe. Even with the availability of those German forces presently planned within the framework of EDC, present rates of defense spending by European Nations and present rates of U.S. Military Assistance certainly could not be expected to produce forces adequate to prevent the initial loss of a considerable portion of the territory of Western Europe in the event of a full-scale Soviet attack. Therefore, since U.S. Military Assistance must eventually be reduced, it is essential that the Western European states, including West Germany, build and maintain maximum feasible defensive strength. The major deterrent to aggression against Western Europe is the manifest determination of the United States to use its atomic capability and massive retaliatory striking power if the area is attacked. However, the presence of U.S. forces in Western Europe makes a contribution other than military to the strength and cohesion of the free world coalition.

    c. In the Far East, the military strength of the coalition now rests largely on U.S. military power plus that of France in Indochina, the UK in Malaya and Hong Kong, and the indigenous forces of the Republic of Korea, Vietnam, and Nationalist China. Any material increase will require the revival of the economic and military strength of Japan.

    d. The strength and cohesion of the coalition depends, and will continue to depend, on the continuing strength and will of the United States as its leader, and upon the assumption by each coalition member of a proper share of responsibility.

---

* The term "coalition" refers to those states which are parties to the network of security treaties and regional alliances of which the United States is a member (NATO, OAS, ANZUS, Japan, etc.) or are otherwise actively associated in the defense of the free world.

16. While the coalition is founded on common interest and remains basically sound, certain factors tend to weaken its cohesion and to slow down the necessary build-up of strength.

a. Some of these factors are inherent in the nature of a coalition led by one strong power. The economic and military recovery by our NATO allies from their low point of a few years ago, and the revival of Germany and Japan, has given them a greater sense of independence from U.S. guidance and direction. Specific sources of irritation are trade with the Soviet bloc, the level of the defense effort, use of bases and other facilities, and the prospect of discontinuance of U.S. economic aid without a corresponding change in U.S. trade policies.

b. The coalition also suffers from certain other weaknesses and dilemmas. A major weakness is the instability of the governments of certain NATO partners, such as Italy and France. The colonial issue in Asia and Africa, for example, has not only weakened our European allies but has left those areas in a state of ferment which weakens the whole free world. Efforts by the United States to encourage orderly settlements tend to leave both sides dissatisfied and to create friction within the alliance. Age-old issues such as divide France and Germany, or Italy and Yugoslavia, still impede creation of a solid basis of cooperation against the Soviet threat.

c. Moreover, allied opinion, especially in Europe, has become less willing to follow U.S. leadership. Many Europeans fear that American policies, particularly in the Far East, may involve Europe in general war, or will indefinitely prolong cold-war tensions. Many consider U.S. attitudes toward the Soviets as too rigid and unyielding and, at the same time, as unstable, holding risks ranging from preventive war and "liberation" to withdrawal into isolation. Many consider that these policies fail to reflect the perspective and confidence expected in the leadership of a great nation, and reflect too great a preoccupation with anti-communism. Important sectors of allied opinion are also concerned over developments within the United States which seem to them inconsistent with our assumed role of leader in the cause of freedom. These allied attitudes materially impair cooperation and, if not overcome, could imperil the coalition.

d. Fear of what a general war will mean for them is deeply rooted and widespread among our allies. They tend to see the actual danger of Soviet aggression as less imminent than the United States does, and some have a fatalistic feeling that if it is coming they will not be able to do much about it. In the NATO countries, many have serious doubts whether the defense requirements can be met without intolerable political and economic strains. Certain of our allies fear the rearmament of Germany and Japan on any large scale, and in Germany and Japan themselves strong currents of opinion oppose it as unnecessary or dangerous. Moreover, in certain countries, particularly France and Italy, grave domestic problems have called into question not only the authority of the governments, but also the basic foreign policies and alignments which they have followed. All these factors lead to allied pressure in favor of new major efforts to negotiate with the USSR, as the only hope of ending the present tension, fear and frustration. This pressure has increased with recent "peace gestures" of the new Soviet leadership, which has made every endeavor to exploit it. Whether these hopes are illusory or well-founded, they must be taken into consideration by the United States.

The Uncommitted Areas of the World

17. Despite the Soviet threat, many nations and societies outside the Soviet bloc, mostly in the underdeveloped areas, are so unsure of their national interests, or so preoccupied with other pressing problems, that they are presently unwilling to align themselves actively with the United States and its allies. Although largely undeveloped, their vast manpower, their essential raw materials and their potential for growth are such that their absorption within the Soviet system would greatly, perhaps decisively, alter the world balance of power to our detriment. Conversely, their orderly development into more stable and responsible nations, able and willing to participate in defense of the free world, can increasingly add to its strength.

18. In many of these uncommitted areas, forces of unrest and of resentment against the West are strong. Among these sources are racial feelings, anti-colonialism, rising nationalism, popular demand for rapid social and economic progress, over-population, the breakdown of static social patterns, and, in many cases, the conflict of local religious and social philosophies with those of the West. The general unreliability of the governments of these states and the volatility of their political life complicate the task of building firm ties with them, of counteracting neutralism and, where appropriate and feasible, of responding to requests for assistance in solving their problems. Outside economic assistance alone cannot be counted on either to solve their basic problems or to win their cooperation and support. Constructive political and other measures will be required to create a sense of mutuality of interest with the free world and to counter the communist appeals.

U.S. Ability to Support Security Expenditures

19. The United States must maintain a sound economy based on free private enterprise as a basis both for high defense productivity and for the maintenance of its living standards and free institutions. Not only the world position of the United States, but the security of the whole free world, is dependent on the avoidance of recession and on the long-term expansion of the U.S. economy. Threats to its stability or growth, therefore, constitute a danger to the security of the United States and of the coalition which it leads. Expenditures for national security, in fact all federal, state and local governmental expenditures, must be carefully scrutinized with a view to measuring their impact on the national economy.

20. The economy of the country has a potential for long-term economic growth. Over the years an expanding national income can provide the basis for higher standards of living and for a substantial military program. But economic growth is not automatic and requires fiscal and other policies which will foster and not hamper the potential for long-term growth and which will operate to reduce cyclical fluctuations.

21. Excessive government spending leads to inflationary deficits or to repressive taxation, or to both. Persistent inflation is a barrier to long-term growth because it undermines confidence in the currency, reduces savings, and makes restrictive economic controls necessary. Repressive taxation weakens the incentives for efficiency, effort, and investment on which economic growth depends.

22. In spite of the reimposition of tax rates at approximately the peak levels of World War II, expenditures have risen faster than tax receipts, with a resulting deficit of $9.4 billion in fiscal year 1953. Despite anticipated larger receipts,

without the imposition of new taxes, and assuming substantially unchanged world conditions, a deficit of $3.8 billion is estimated for fiscal year 1954.

23. *a.* Under existing law, tax reductions of $5 billion a year will become effective next January. A proposal to impose substitute taxes therefor would be a reversal of policy.

   b. Additional revenue losses of $3 billion a year are due to occur on April 1, 1954. Congress has not acted on the President's recommendation that these reductions be rescinded. Even if the $3 billion reduction is rescinded, or offset by revenue from new sources, large deficits would occur in FY 1955 and FY 1956 at present levels of expenditures.

   c. The economic problem is made more difficult by the need to reform the tax system in the interests of long-term economic growth. Inevitably, many of the changes necessary to reduce the barriers to growth will lead to a loss of revenue in the years immediately following their adoption.

24. Any additional revenue will have to be secured by new taxation on a broad base.

25. The present high level of the Government debt further complicates the financial and economic problems of the country. Substantial additional borrowing could come only from sources which would be inflationary.

26. There is no precise level or duration of government expenditures which can be determined in advance, at which an economic system will be seriously damaged from inflationary borrowing on the one hand or from repressive taxation on the other. The higher the level of expenditures, the greater is the need for sound policies and the greater are the dangers of miscalculations and mischance. These dangers are now substantial.

27. The requirements for funds to maintain our national security must thus be considered in the light of these dangers to our economic system, including the danger to industrial productivity necessary to support military programs, arising from excessive levels of total Government spending, taxing and borrowing.

28. Modifications of the foregoing fiscal policies to promote long-term growth may be necessitated for a limited period: (1) to deal with short-term cyclical problems or (2) to achieve overriding national objectives that justify departure from sound fiscal policies.

The Situation as to U.S. Manpower

29. *a.* The national security programs of the United States rest upon the manpower to operate them, the economy to produce the material for them, and the financial resources to pay for them.

   b. The qualified manpower annually coming of military age is adequate to carry out our existing military programs. However, the continuing development of more complicated weapons, machines, and devices used by the military greatly increases the need for military manpower possessed of higher skills, and for their better utilization, and emphasizes the need for expanded technical training and retention of technically trained personnel.

   c. Any considerable increase in the need for military manpower would require consideration of:

   (1) Broadening the present criteria governing draft eligibility.

   (2) Broadening the physical requirements for enlistment, particularly to secure technicians.

(3) Extension of the average length of military service, including increased incentives for re-enlistment.

(4) Increased recruitment of long-term volunteers and of women.

(5) Greater use of civilians for technical maintenance work.

(6) Leadership to develop a national response to increased needs, including steps to make military service a matter of patriotic pride and to increase the attractiveness of a military career.

d. Any decisions on these matters should be made in the light of a comprehensive study, to be submitted to the President by the Office of Defense Mobilization by December 1, on manpower availability under varying assumptions as to the degree and nature of mobilization requirements.

Morale

30. Support for the necessary security programs, based upon a sound productive system, is ultimately dependent also upon the soundness of the national morale and the political willingness of the country to support a government which it feels is holding the proper balance between the necessary sacrifices and the necessary defense. Accordingly, the American people must be informed of the nature of the Soviet–Communist threat, in particular the danger inherent in the increasing Soviet atomic capability; of the basic community of interest among the nations of the free world; and of the need for mobilizing the spiritual and material resources necessary to meet the Soviet threat.

POLICY CONCLUSIONS

Basic Problems of National Security Policy

31. *a.* To meet the Soviet threat to U.S. security.

b. In doing so, to avoid seriously weakening the U.S. economy or undermining our fundamental values and institutions.

Nature of the Soviet Threat

32. *a.* With increasing atomic power, the Soviets have a mounting capability of inflicting very serious and possibly crippling damage on the United States. The USSR will also continue to have large military forces capable of aggressive action against countries of the free world. Present estimates are, however, that the USSR will not deliberately initiate general war during the next several years, although general war might result from miscalculation. In the absence of general war, a prolonged period of tension may ensue, during which each side increases its armaments, reaches atomic plenty and seeks to improve its relative power position.

b. In any case, the Soviets will continue to seek to divide and weaken the free world coalition, to absorb or win the allegiance of the presently uncommitted areas of the world, and to isolate the United States, using cold war tactics and the communist apparatus. Their capacity for political warfare against the United States as well as its allies will be enhanced by their increased atomic capability.

33. *a.* A sound, strong, and growing U.S. economy is necessary to support over the long pull a satisfactory posture of defense in the free world and a

U.S. capability rapidly and effectively to change to full mobilization. The United States should not weaken its capacity for high productivity for defense, its free institutions, and the incentives on which its long-term economic growth depends.

b. A recession in the level of U.S. economic activity could seriously prejudice the security of the free world.

Defense Against Soviet Power and Action

34. In the face of these threats, the United States must develop and maintain, at the lowest feasible cost, requisite military and non-military strength to deter and, if necessary, to counter Soviet military aggression against the United States or other areas vital to its security.

a. The risk of Soviet aggression will be minimized by maintaining a strong security posture, with emphasis on adequate offensive retaliatory strength and defensive strength. This must be based on massive atomic capability, including necessary bases; an integrated and effective continental defense system; ready forces of the United States and its allies suitably deployed and adequate to deter or initially to counter aggression, and to discharge required initial tasks in the event of a general war; and an adequate mobilization base; all supported by the determined spirit of the U.S. people.

b. This strong security posture must also be supported by an effective U.S. intelligence system, an adequate manpower program, superior scientific research and development, a program of limited defense mobilization, reasonable internal security, and an informed American people.

c. Such a strong security posture is essential to counter the Soviet divisive tactics and hold together the coalition. If our allies were uncertain about our ability or will to counter Soviet aggression, they would be strongly tempted to adopt a neutralist position, especially in the face of the atomic threat.

35. In the interest of its own security, the United States must have the support of allies.

a. The military striking power necessary to retaliate depends for the foreseeable future on having bases in allied countries. Furthermore, the ground forces required to counter local aggressions must be supplied largely by our allies.

b. The loss of major allies by subversion, divisive tactics, or the growth of neutralist attitudes, would seriously affect the security of the United States.

36. United States policies must, therefore, be designed to retain the cooperation of our allies, to seek to win the friendship and cooperation of the presently uncommitted areas of the world, and thereby to strengthen the cohesion of the free world.

a. Our allies must be genuinely convinced that our strategy is one of collective security. The alliance must be rooted in a strong feeling of a community of interest and firm confidence in the steadiness and wisdom of U.S. leadership.

b. Cooperative efforts, including equitable contributions by our allies, will continue to be necessary to build the military, economic and political strength of the coalition and the stability of the free world.

c. Constructive U.S. policies, not related solely to anti-communism, are needed to persuade uncommitted countries that their best interests lie in greater cooperation and stronger affiliations with the rest of the free world.

d. To enhance the capacity of free world nations for self-support and defense, and to reduce progressively their need for U.S. aid, the United States should assist in stimulating international trade, freer access to markets and raw materials, and the healthy growth of underdeveloped areas. In this connection, it should consider a modification of its tariff and trade policies.

e. In subsequent fiscal years economic grant aid and loans by the United States to other nations of the free world should be based on the best interests of the United States.

37. *a.* In Western Europe, a position of strength must be based mainly on British, French, and German cooperation in the defense of the continent. To achieve a stronger Europe, the United States should support, as long as there is hope of early success, the building of an integrated European Community (including West Germany and if possible a united Germany), linked to the United States through NATO. The United States should press for a strong, united stable Germany, oriented to the free world and militarily capable of overcoming internal subversion and disorder and also of taking a major part in the collective defense of the free world against aggression. The United States must continue to assist in creating and maintaining mutually agreed European forces, but should reduce such assistance as rapidly as United States interests permit.

b. In the Far East, strength must be built on existing bilateral and multilateral security arrangements until more comprehensive regional arrangements become feasible. The United States should stress assistance in developing Japan as a major element of strength. The United States should maintain the security of the off-shore island chain and continue to develop the defensive capacity of Korea and Southeast Asia in accordance with existing commitments.

c. In the Middle East, a strong regional grouping is not now feasible. In order to assure during peace time for the United States and its allies the resources (especially oil) and the strategic positions of the area and their denial to the Soviet bloc, the United States should build on Turkey, Pakistan and, if possible, Iran, and assist in achieving stability in the Middle East by political actions and limited military and economic assistance, and technical assistance, to other countries in the area.

d. In other areas of the free world the United States should furnish limited military aid, and limited technical and economic assistance, to other free nations, according to the calculated advantage of such aid to the U.S. world position.

38. *a.* As presently deployed in support of our commitments, the armed forces of the United States are over-extended, thereby depriving us of mobility and initiative for future military action in defense of the free world.

b. Under present conditions, however, any major withdrawal of U.S. forces from Europe or the Far East would be interpreted as a diminution of U.S. interest in the defense of these areas and would seriously undermine the strength and cohesion of the coalition.

c. Our diplomacy must concentrate upon clarifying to our allies in parts of the world not gripped by war conditions that the best defense of the free world rests upon a deployment of U.S. forces which permits initiative, flexibility and support; upon our political commitment to strike back hard directly against any aggressor who attacks such allies; and upon such allies' own indigenous security efforts.

39.   *a.* In specific situations where a warning appears desirable and feasible as an added deterrent, the United States should make clear to the USSR and Communist China, in general terms or with reference to specific areas as the situation requires, its intention to react with military force against any aggression by Soviet bloc armed forces.

b. (1) In the event of hostilities, the United States will consider nuclear weapons to be as available for use as other munitions. Where the consent of an ally is required for the use of these weapons from U.S. bases on the territory of such ally, the United States should promptly obtain the advance consent of such ally for such use. The United States should also seek, as and when feasible, the understanding and approval of this policy by free nations.

(2) This policy should not be made public without further consideration by the National Security Council.

Defense Against the Threat to the U.S. Economy and Institutions

40.   *a.* A strong, healthy and expanding U.S. economy is essential to the security and stability of the free world. In the interest of both the United States and its allies, it is vital that the support of defense expenditures should not seriously impair the basic soundness of the U.S. economy by undermining incentives or by inflation.

b. The United States must, however, meet the necessary costs of the policies essential for its security. The actual level of such costs cannot be estimated until further study, but should be kept to the minimum consistent with the carrying out of these policies.

c. Barring basic change in the world situation, the Federal Government should continue to make a determined effort to bring its total annual expenditures into balance, or into substantial balance with its total annual revenues and should maintain over-all credit and fiscal policies designed to assist in stabilizing the economy.

d. Every effort should be made to eliminate waste, duplication, and unnecessary overhead in the Federal Government, and to minimize Federal expenditures for programs that are not essential to the national security.

e. The United States should seek to maintain a higher and expanding rate of economic activity at relatively stable price levels.

f. The economic potential of private enterprise should be maximized by minimizing governmental controls and regulations, and by encouraging private enterprise to develop natural and technological resources (e.g. nuclear power).

41. To support the necessarily heavy burdens for national security, the morale of the citizens of the United States must be based both on responsibility and freedom for the individual. The dangers from Soviet subversion and espionage require strong and effective security measures. Eternal vigilance, however, is needed in their exercise to prevent the intimidation of free criticism. It is

essential that necessary measures of protection should not be so used as to destroy the national unity based on freedom, not on fear.

Reduction of the Soviet Threat

42. *a.* The United States must seek to improve the power position of itself and the rest of the free world in relation to the Soviet bloc.

b. The United States must also keep open the possibility of negotiating with the USSR and Communist China acceptable and enforceable agreements, whether limited to individual issues now outstanding or involving a general settlement of major issues, including control of armaments.

c. The willingness of the Soviet leadership to negotiate acceptable settlements, without necessarily abandoning hostility to the non-Soviet world, may tend to increase over time, if the United States and its allies develop and increase their own strength, determination and cohesion, maintain retaliatory power sufficient to insure unacceptable damage to the Soviet system should the USSR resort to general war, and prove that the free world can prosper despite Soviet pressures, or if for any reason Soviet stability and influence are reduced.

d. The policy of the United States is to prevent Soviet aggression and continuing domination of other nations, and to establish an effective control of armaments under proper safeguards; but is not to dictate the internal political and economic organization of the USSR.*

43. As a means of reducing Soviet capabilities for extending control and influence in the free world, the United States should:

a. Take overt and covert measures to discredit Soviet prestige and ideology as effective instruments of Soviet power, and to reduce the strength of communist parties and other pro-Soviet elements.

b. Take all feasible diplomatic, political, economic and covert measures to counter any threat of a party or individuals directly or indirectly responsive to Soviet control to achieve dominant power in a free world country.

c. Undertake selective, positive actions to eliminate Soviet-Communist control over any areas of the free world.

44. *a.* Measures to impose pressures on the Soviet bloc should take into account the desirability of creating conditions which will induce the Soviet leadership to be more receptive to acceptable negotiated settlements.

b. Accordingly, the United States should take feasible political, economic, propaganda and covert measures designed to create and exploit troublesome problems for the USSR, impair Soviet relations with Communist China, complicate control in the satellites, and retard the growth of the military and economic potential of the Soviet bloc.

45. In the face of the developing Soviet threat, the broad aim of U.S. security policies must be to create, prior to the achievement of mutual atomic plenty, conditions under which the United States and the free world coalition are prepared to meet the Soviet–Communist threat with resolution and to negotiate for

* This paragraph does not establish policy guidance for our propaganda or informational activities.

its alleviation under proper safeguards. The United States and its allies must always seek to create and sustain the hope and confidence of the free world in the ability of its basic ideas and institutions not merely to oppose the communist threat, but to provide a way of life superior to Communism.

46. The foregoing conclusions are valid only so long as the United States maintains a retaliatory capability that cannot be neutralized by a surprise Soviet attack. Therefore, there must be continuing examination and periodic report to the National Security Council in regard to the likelihood of such neutralization of U.S. retaliatory capability.

ANNEX

U.S. OBJECTIVES VIS-A-VIS THE USSR IN THE EVENT OF WAR

(The following paragraphs are taken verbatim from NSC 20/4, approved in November, 1948. They also formed an annex to NSC 153/1, approved in June, 1953. This subject is currently under review by the NSC Planning Board.)

1. In the event of war with the USSR we should endeavor by successful military and other operations to create conditions which would permit satisfactory accomplishment of U.S. objectives without a predetermined requirement for unconditional surrender. War aims supplemental to our peace-time aims should include:

   a. Eliminating Soviet Russian domination in areas outside the borders of any Russian state allowed to exist after the war.
   b. Destroying the structure of relationships by which leaders of the All-Union Communist Party have been able to exert moral and disciplinary authority over individual citizens, or groups of citizens, in countries not under communist control.
   c. Assuring that any regime or regimes which may exist on traditional Russian territory in the aftermath of a war:
      (1) Do not have sufficient military power to wage aggressive war.
      (2) Impose nothing resembling the present iron curtain over contacts with the outside world.
   d. In addition, if any bolshevik regime is left in any part of the Soviet Union, insuring that it does not control enough of the military-industrial potential of the Soviet Union to enable it to wage war on comparable terms with any other regime or regimes which may exist on traditional Russian territory.
   e. Seeking to create postwar conditions which will:
      (1) Prevent the development of power relationships dangerous to the security of the United States and international peace.
      (2) Be conducive to the successful development of an effective world organization based upon the purposes and principles of the United Nations.
      (3) Permit the earliest practicable discontinuance within the United States of wartime controls.

2. In pursuing the above war aims, we should avoid making irrevocable or premature decisions or commitments respecting border rearrangements, administration of government within enemy territory, independence for national minori-

ties, or post-war responsibility for the readjustment of the inevitable political, economic, and social dislocations resulting from the war.

[Document 19]

SPECIAL ESTIMATE

PROBABLE COMMUNIST REACTIONS TO CERTAIN
POSSIBLE US COURSES OF ACTION IN
INDOCHINA THROUGH 1954

SE–53

Approved 15 December 1953

Published 18 December 1953

LIMITED DISTRIBUTION

*The Intelligence Advisory Committee concurred in this
estimate on 15 December 1953. The FBI abstained, the
subject being outside of its jurisdiction.*

*The following member organizations of the Intelligence
Advisory Committee participated with the Central Intelligence Agency in the preparation of this estimate: The
intelligence organizations of the Departments of State,
the Army, the Navy, the Air Force, and The Joint Staff.*

CENTRAL INTELLIGENCE AGENCY

THE PROBLEM[1]

To estimate the probable reactions of Communist China and the USSR to:

a. The commitment in Indochina, before the end of 1954, of US ground, air, and naval forces on a scale sufficient to defeat decisively the field forces of the Viet Minh.

b. The commitment in Indochina, before the end of 1954, of US ground, air, and naval forces on a scale sufficient to hold the Viet Minh in check until such time as US-developed Vietnamese forces could decisively defeat the field forces of the Viet Minh.

ASSUMPTIONS[1]

For both a. and b. above:

1. No Chinese Communist intervention in force in Indochina had taken place.
2. Commitment of US forces had been publicly requested by the French and Vietnamese governments.
3. At the time of the US commitment French Union forces still retained essentially their present position in the Tonkin Delta.
4. Communist China and the USSR would have prior knowledge of the US intent to commit its forces in Indochina.

[1] The Problem and the Assumptions have been provided to the intelligence community as a basis for the estimate.

5. Following the US commitment, there would be a phased withdrawal of French forces from Indochina.
6. The US will warn the Chinese Communists that if they openly intervene[2] in the fighting in Indochina, the US will not limit its military action to Indochina.

ESTIMATE

1. We believe that the Communists would assume that the purpose of committing US forces in Indochina was the decisive defeat of the Viet Minh. Consequently, we believe that Communist reactions to such a US commitment would be substantially the same whether it were designed to defeat the Viet·Minh with US forces (Problem a.) or eventually with US-trained Vietnam forces (Problem b.).

In the Event of a Pending US Commitment

2. We do not believe that Communist China, upon learning of a forthcoming commitment by the US, would immediately intervene openly with substantial forces in Indochina. The acceptance by Communist China of an armistice in Korea, its policies to date with respect to Indochina, and its present emphasis on domestic problems seem to indicate a desire at this time to avoid open intervention in the Indochina war or expansion of the conflict to Communist China. US warnings against Chinese Communist intervention in force[3] probably would have a strong deterrent effect. Moreover, the political advantage to be gained by portraying the US as an "aggressor" would probably appear both to Communist China and the USSR to outweigh the military advantage of moving large Chinese Communist forces into Indochina before the arrival of US forces.
3. In addition, Communist leadership would probably estimate that they would have time to take a number of steps which, without a serious risk of expanding the war to China, might deter a US military commitment or seriously impair its effectiveness. Such steps might include:

   a. Increasing logistic and rear area support to the Viet Minh.
   b. Covertly committing Chinese troops to operate as "Viet Minh guerrillas."
   c. Encouraging intensified Viet Minh guerrilla and sabotage operations in Indochina, particularly in and around the Tonkin Delta, designed to inflict such damage on the French Union position as to increase the difficulties of the US operation.
   d. Building up Chinese Communist strength in south China, including Hainan.
   e. Seeking by diplomatic and propaganda means in the UN and elsewhere to forestall US action, to gain the support of non-Communist countries, and to exploit differences between the US and its allies over preparations for this operation.

---

[2] For the purposes of this estimate, open intervention is defined as the commitment of substantial Chinese Communist combat forces, under any guise.
[3] Such warnings would reinforce the warning already given by Secretary of State Dulles, in his American Legion Speech at St. Louis, 2 September 1953:

> Communist China has been and now is training, equipping and supplying the Communist forces in Indochina. There is the risk that, as in Korea, Red China might send its own army into Indochina. The Chinese Communist regime should realize that such a second aggression could not occur without grave consequences which might not be confined in Indochina. I say this soberly in the interest of peace and in the hope of preventing another aggressor miscalculation."

f. Concluding a defense pact with the Viet Minh.

Although, in response to a US military commitment in Indochina, the Communists might threaten to renew hostilities in Korea, we believe that they would not actually take such action as they probably estimate that renewed aggression in Korea would result in expanding the conflict to Communist China itself.

Actual US Commitment

4. In the initial stages of an actual US military commitment, the Communists might not feel compelled to intervene openly in force immediately. They would recognize the difficulties which the US forces would face in operating in the Indochina climate and terrain. They would also realize that the xenophobia of the indigenous population of Indochina might be effectively exploited to the disadvantage of US forces by Communist propaganda; the Chinese Communists would therefore prefer that the US rather than themselves be confronted with this antiforeign attitude. They might estimate that, with increased aid from Communist China, the Viet Minh forces, by employing harassing and infiltrating tactics and avoiding major engagements, could make any US advance at the least slow and difficult. It is probable, therefore, that the Chinese Communists would initially follow a cautious military policy while they assessed the scale, nature, and probable success of the US action, the effect of such action on Vietnamese national morale and military capabilities, the subsequent military and political moves of the French, the temper of US opinion, the reactions of US allies and the neutralist states, and the position of the UN. Even at this early stage, however, the Chinese Communists would probably take strong actions short of open intervention in an effort to prevent the US from destroying the Viet Minh armed forces.[4]

5. In addition to the steps outlined in paragraph 3 above, the Chinese Communists, at this early stage of US commitment, would probably provide an increased number of military advisors, possibly including commanders for major Viet Minh units. Moreover, Peiping might covertly furnish limited air support for Viet Minh ground forces, but would be unlikely to undertake air operations which it estimated would provoke US retaliation against Communist China itself other than retaliation against those airfields from which such air attacks were launched.

6. If the leaders of Communist China and the USSR came to believe that a protracted stalemate in Indochina was likely, they would probably not openly commit Chinese Communist ground, naval, or air forces to an intervention in force in Indochina, nor would they renew hostilities in Korea or commit new acts of armed aggression elsewhere in the Far East. Peiping and Moscow would probably believe that a long and indecisive war in Indochina could be exploited politically and that, in time, US and Vietnamese will to fight might be worn down.

7. If at any time, however, the leaders of Communist China and the USSR came to believe that a decisive defeat of the Viet Minh armed forces was likely, they would be faced with the decision whether Communist China should intervene openly in force in order to avert this development.

[4] The Special Assistant, Intelligence, Department of State, believes that the timing of the Communist reaction to the commitment of US forces in Indochina cannot be estimated with any degree of assurance. He therefore believes that a decision by the Communists to follow a cautious policy in the initial stages of the US action should be presented as a possibility, rather than as a probability.

8. The following considerations might induce the Communists to decide in favor of open intervention in force:

a. Decisive defeat of the Viet Minh armed forces would be a grave blow to Communist prestige throughout the world and would seriously diminish prospects for the expansion of Communism in Asia.

b. A US military commitment in Indochina might form part of a larger plan, possibly involving, in the minds of the Communists, the resurgence of Chinese Nationalist strength, aimed at the destruction of the Chinese Communist regime. In any case, decisive defeat of the Viet Minh armed forces would bring US power to the borders of China.

c. Whatever the initial intention, successful US military action in Indochina might encourage the US to increase pressure on other points of the Communist periphery.

d. Many observers, particularly in the Asian neutralist states, would consider the US in the wrong in Indochina and would condone Chinese Communist intervention as a move to "liberate Indochina from American imperialism." These sentiments could be effectively exploited by Communist propaganda.

e. The US, despite its warnings, might not retaliate strongly against Communist China, because it would fear that such retaliation would alienate its NATO allies, result in wider military deployment of US forces, cause Peiping to invoke the Sino-Soviet treaty, and thereby increase the danger of general war.

f. By intervening openly in force the Chinese Communists might be able to prevent indefinitely both the successful accomplishment of the US mission and the disengagement of substantial US forces from Indochina.

9. On the other hand, the following considerations might deter the Communists from deciding to intervene openly in force:

a. It would be more important to concentrate upon domestic problems including strengthening of Communist China's economy.

b. There would be a grave risk of US reprisals against Communist China and possibly of general war.

c. Indochina is remote from the USSR and the centers of power in Communist China. Accordingly, the establishment of a strong US position in Indochina would not constitute, to the same degree as in Korea, a threat to Chinese Communist and Soviet power in the Far East.

d. Short of actual intervention, the Chinese Communists could acquire a position of strength by reinforcing and rehabilitating the military facilities on Hainan. This position would dominate the Gulf of Tonkin, and pose a distinct threat to sea-air lines of communications of US forces in Indochina and to rear bases.

e. The loss in prestige involved in the defeat of the Viet Minh armed forces could in part be offset by depicting the Viet Minh as an indigenous liberation movement. Moreover, the Viet Minh Government and its armed forces could be preserved on Chinese soil where they could exercise constant military and political pressure on the forces of the US and the Associated States.

f. The military and political nature of the Indochina war is such that even if the US defeated the Viet Minh field forces, guerrilla action could probably be continued indefinitely and preclude the establishment of complete non-Communist control over that area.

g. Under such circumstances, the US might have to maintain a military commitment in Indochina for years to come. Heavy US commitments in Indochina over the long run might cause concern to US allies and might create divergencies between the US and neutralist states.

10. The Director of Central Intelligence and the Deputy Director for Intelligence, The Joint Staff, believe that the Communist reaction to commitment of US forces in Indochina would largely depend upon US posture prior to, and at the same time of, such commitment. If the US posture made manifest to the Communists that US naval and air retaliatory power would be fully applied to Communist China, then Peiping and Moscow would seek to avoid courses of action which would bring about such retaliation. In such circumstances, the chances are better than even that the Chinese Communists would not openly intervene in Indochina, even if they believed that failure to intervene would mean the defeat at that time of the Viet Minh field forces in Indochina. Therefore the Director of Central Intelligence and the Deputy Director for Intelligence, The Joint Staff, believe that in weighing the arguments set forth in paragraphs 8 and 9 Chinese Communist leaders, in such circumstances, would estimate that it was more advantageous to them to support a guerrilla action in Indochina and tie down large US forces in such a war, than to risk US retaliatory action against China itself which open intervention would involve. However, the Communists would almost certainly continue to support the remnants of the Viet Minh, including re-equipping these remnant forces on the Chinese side of the border and possibly augmenting them with Chinese "volunteers" so that Viet Minh resistance could be continued indefinitely. Moreover, they would pursue their objectives in the rest of Southeast Asia by all means short of open military intervention.

11. The Special Assistant, Intelligence, Department of State, the Director of Naval Intelligence, the Assistant Chief of Staff, G-2, Intelligence, Department of the Army, and the Director of Intelligence, USAF, believe that the condition of "decisive defeat of the field forces of the Viet Minh" prescribed for considering this problem would necessarily result in such a serious setback to Communist prestige, security, and expansionism as to lead to the following conclusions. In weighing the arguments presented in paragraphs 8 and 9, the Communist leaders in both Peiping and Moscow would probably give greatest consideration to: (a) the loss of prestige, the threat to Bloc security, and the setback to Communist expansionism in Southeast Asia involved in a decisive defeat of the Viet Minh armed forces and, (b) the risk of direct US action against Communist China. To the Communists, the consequences of the decisive defeat of the Viet Minh armed forces would be both certain and far reaching. In appraising the possible nature and scale of direct US action against the China mainland, the Communists would weigh any US warnings of probable consequences of intervention, the temper of US and free world opinion, and the probable US desire not to expand a local action. It is unlikely that the Communists' appraisal would lead them to the conviction that the US reaction to their intervention in Indochina would take the form of extensive and intense warfare against Communist China. In any case, their overriding suspicion of the ultimate motive of US forces in strength on or near the borders of Communist China would strongly influence their courses of action. Thus, the thought foremost in their minds would most probably be that failure to dislodge US military forces from the Chinese border would lead to increasing challenges to Communist power elsewhere. We therefore believe that the chances are probably better than even that the Communists would accept the risk involved and that the Chinese Communists would intervene openly and in force in an effort to save the Communist position in Indochina.

[Document 20]

NSC 5405   January 16, 1954

NOTE BY THE EXECUTIVE SECRETARY

to the

NATIONAL SECURITY COUNCIL

on

UNITED STATES OBJECTIVES AND COURSES OF ACTION
WITH RESPECT TO SOUTHEAST ASIA

References: A. NSC 177
            B. NSC Action Nos. 897, 1005 and 1011
            C. Memo for NSC from Executive Secretary, same subject,
                dated January 12, 1954
            D. NSC 124/2
            E. NSC 171/1
            F. NIE-63/1 and SE-53

The National Security Council, the Secretary of the Treasury and the Director, Bureau of the Budget, at the 180th Council meeting on January 14, 1954 adopted the statement of policy contained in NSC 177, subject to the deletion of the last sentence of paragraph 1-*a* thereof and to the deletion of paragraph 46 (NSC Action No. 1011-*a*).

In connection with this action the Council also agreed that the Director of Central Intelligence, in collaboration with other appropriate departments and agencies, should develop plans, as suggested by the Secretary of State, for certain contingencies in Indochina.

The Council at its meeting on January 8, 1954, in connection with its preliminary consideration of NSC 177 also (NSC Action No. 1005-*c* and *d*):

   a. Agreed that Lieutenant General John Wilson O'Daniel should be stationed constinuously in Indochina, under appropriate liaison arrangements and with sufficient authority to expedite the flexible provision of U.S. assistance to the French Union forces.
   b. Requested the Department of Defense, in collaboration with the Central Intelligence Agency, urgently to study and report to the Council all feasible further steps, short of the overt use of U.S. forces in combat, which the United States might take to assist in achieving the success of the "Laniel-Navarre" Plan.

The President has this date approved the statement of policy contained in NSC 177, as amended and adopted by the Council and enclosed herewith as NSC 5405; directs its implementation by all appropriate executive departments and agencies of the U.S. Government; and designates the Operations Coodinating Board as the coordinating agency. A financial appendix is enclosed for Council information.

Accordingly those portions of NSC 124/2 not previously superseded by NSC

171/1 are superseded by the enclosed statement of policy. The enclosure does not supersede the current NSC policy on Indoesia contained in NSC 171/1.

JAMES S. LAY, JR.

Executive Secretary

cc: The Secretary of the Treasury
The Director, Bureau of the Budget
The Chairman, Joint Chiefs of Staff
The Director of Central Intelligence

UNITED STATES OBJECTIVES AND COURSES OF ACTION WITH RESPECT TO SOUTHEAST ASIA

Table of Contents

STATEMENT OF POLICY

by the

NATIONAL SECURITY COUNCIL

on

UNITED STATES OBJECTIVES AND COURSES OF ACTION WITH RESPECT TO SOUTHEAST ASIA*

I. GENERAL CONSIDERATIONS

1. Communist domination, by whatever means, of all Southeast Asia would seriously endanger in the short term, and critically endanger in the longer term, United States security interests.

---

* Southeast Asia is used herein to mean the area embracing Burma, Thailand, Indochina and Malaya. Indonesia is the subject of a separate paper (NSC 171/1).

a. In the conflict in Indochina, the Communist and non-Communist worlds clearly confront one another on the field of battle. The lost of the struggle in Indochina, in addition to its impact in Southeast Asia and in South Asia, would therefore have the most serious repercussions on U. S. and free world interests in Europe and elsewhere.

b. Such is the interrelation of the countries of the area that effective counteraction would be immediately necessary to prevent the loss of any single country from leading to submission to or an alignment with communism by the remaining countries of Southeast Asia and Indonesia. Furthermore, in the event all of Southeast Asia falls under communism, an alignment with communism of India, and in the longer term, of the Middle East (with the probable exceptions of at least Pakistan and Turkey) could follow progressively. Such widespread alignment would seriously endanger the stability and security of Europe.

c. Communist control of all of Southeast Asia and Indonesia would threaten the U.S. position in the Pacific offshore island chain and would seriously jeopardize fundamental U.S. security interests in the Far East.

d. The loss of Southeast Asia would have serious economic consequences for many nations of the free world and conversely would add significant resources to the Soviet bloc. Southeast Asia, especially Malaya and Indonesia, is the principal world source of natural rubber and tin, and a producer of petroleum and other strategically important commodities. The rice exports of Burma, Indochina and Thailand are critically important to Malaya, Ceylon and Hong Kong and are of considerable significance to Japan and India, all important areas of free Asia. Furthermore, this area has an important potential as a market for the industrialized countries of the free world.

e. The loss of Southeast Asia, especially of Malaya and Indonesia, could result in such economic and political pressures in Japan as to make it extremely difficult to prevent Japan's eventual accommodation to communism.

2. The danger of an overt military attack against Southeast Asia is inherent in the existence of a hostile and aggressive Communist China. The use of U.S. forces to oppose such an attack would require diversion of military strength from other areas, thus reducing our military capability in those areas, as well as over-all, with the recognized military risks involved therein, or an increase in our military forces in being, or both. Toward deterring such an attack, the U.S. Government has engaged in consultations with France and the United Kingdom on the desirability of issuing to Communist China a joint warning as to the consequences to Communist China of aggression in Southeast Asia. Although these consultations have not achieved a full measure of agreement a warning to Communist China has in fact been issued, particularly as to Indochina, in a number of public statements. (See Annex A for texts.) [Words illegible] Kingdom, Australia, and New Zealand in military talks on measures which might be taken in the event of overt Chinese Communist aggression against Indochina.

3. However, overt Chinese Communist attack on any part of Southeast Asia is less probable than continued communist efforts to achieve domination through armed rebellion or subversion. By far the most urgent threat to Southeast Asia arises from the strong possibility that even without overt Chinese Communist intervention the situation in Indochina may deteriorate anew as a result of weakening of the resolve of France and the Associated States of Indochina to continue to oppose the Viet Minh rebellion, the military strength of which is

increased by virtue of aid furnished by the Chinese Communist and Soviet regimes. Barring overt Chinese Communist intervention or further serious deterioration in Indochina, the outlook in Burma, Thailand, and Malaya offers opportunities for some improvement in internal stability and in the control of indigenous communist forces.

4. The successful defense of Tonkin is the keystone of the defense of mainland Southeast Asia except possibly Malaya. In addition to the profound political and psychological factors involved, the retention of Tonkin in friendly hands cuts off the most feasible routes for any massive southward advance towards central and Southern Indochina and Thailand. The execution of U.S. courses of action with respect to individual countries of the area may vary depending upon the route of communist advance into Southeast Asia.

5. Since 1951 the United States has greatly increased all forms of assistance to the French in Indochina, particularly military aid, and has consulted continuously with France with a view to assuring effective use of this aid. Partly as a result of these efforts, French resumption of the initiative under the "Laniel-Navarre Plan" has checked at least temporarily deterioration of the French will to continue the struggle. Concurrently the French have moved toward perfecting the independence of the Associated States within the French Union. In September 1953 the United States decided to extend an additional $385 million in aid, in return for a number of strong French assurances, including a commitment that the French would vigorously carry forward the "Laniel-Navarre Plan," with the object of eliminating regular enemy forces in Indochina, and on the understanding that if the "Laniel-Navarre Plan" were not executed, the United States would retain the right to terminate this additional assistance. (See NSC Action No. 897, Annex B)

6. The French objective in these efforts is to terminate the war as soon as possible so as to reduce the drain of the Indochina war on France and permit the maintenance of a position for France in the Far East. By a combination of military victories and political concessions to the Associated States, France hopes to strengthen these States to the point where they will be able to maintain themselves against Communist pressures with greatly reduced French aid. In the absence of a change in basic French attitudes, the Laniel-Navarre Plan may be the last French major offensive effort in Indochina. There is not in sight any desirable alternative to the success of a Franco-Vietnamese effort along the lines of the "Laniel-Navarre" Plan.

7. Notwithstanding the commitment and intent of the Laniel Government to seek destruction of Viet Minh regular forces, a successor French Government might well accept an improvement in the military position short of this as a basis for serious negotiation within the next year. Political pressures in France prevent any French Government from rejecting the concept of negotiations. If the Laniel-Navarre Plan fails or appears doomed to failure, the French might seek to negotiate simply for the best possible terms, irrespective of whether these offered any assurance of preserving a non-Communist Indochina. With continued U.S. economic and material assistance, the Franco–Vietnamese forces are not in danger of being militarily defeated by the Viet Minh unless there is large-scale Chinese Communist intervention. In any event, apart from the possibility of bilateral negotiations with the Communists, the French will almost certainly continue to seek international discussion of the Indochina issue.

8. The Chinese Communists will almost certainly continue their present type of support for Viet Minh. They are unlikely to intervene with organized units even if the Viet Minh are threatened with defeat by the Franco–Vietnamese

forces. In the event the United States participates in the fighting, there is a substantial risk that the Chinese Communists would intervene. The Communists may talk of peace negotiations for propaganda purposes and to divide the anti-Communists believing that any political negotiations and any settlement to which they would agree would increase their chances of eventually gaining control of Indochina.

9. Actions designed to achieve our objectives in Southeast Asia require sensitive selection and application, on the one hand to assure the optimum efficiency through coordination of measures for the general area, and on the other, to accommodate to the greatest practicable extent to the individual sensibilities of the several governments, social classes and minorities of the area.

II. OBJECTIVE

10. To prevent the countries of Southeast Asia from passing into the communist orbit; to persuade them that their best interests lie in greater cooperation and stronger affiliations with the rest of the free world; and to assist them to develop toward stable, free governments with the will and ability to resist communism from within and without and to contribute to the strengthening of the free world.

III. COURSES OF ACTION

A. SOUTHEAST ASIA IN GENERAL

11. Demonstrate to the indigenous governments that their best interests lie in greater cooperation and closer affiliation with the nations of the free world.

12. Continue present programs of limited economic and technical assistance designed to strengthen the indigenous non-communist governments of the area and expand such programs according to the calculated advantage of such aid to the U.S. world position.

13. Encourage the countries of Southeast Asia to cooperate with, and restore and expand their commerce with, each other and the rest of the free world, particularly Japan, and stimulate the flow of raw material resources of the area to the free world.

14. Continue to make clear, to the extent possible in agreement with other nations including France, the United Kingdom, Australia, and New Zealand, the grave consequences to Communist China of aggression against Southeast Asia and continue current military consultations to determine the military requirements for countering such Chinese Communist aggression.

15. Strengthen, as appropriate, covert operations designed to assist in the achievement of U.S. objectives in Southeast Asia.

16. Continue activities and operations designed to encourage the overseas Chinese communities in Southeast Asia: (a) to organize and activate anti-communist groups and activities within their own communities; (b) to resist the effects of parallel pro-communist groups and activities; (c) generally, to increase their orientation toward the free world; and, (d) consistent with their obligations and primary allegiance to their local governments, to extend sympathy and support to the Chinese National Government as a symbol of Chinese political resistance and as a link in the defense against communist expansion in Asia.

17. Take measures to promote the coordinated defense of Southeast Asia, recognizing that the initiative in regional defense measures must come from the governments of the area.

18. Encourage and support the spirit of resistance among the peoples of Southeast Asia to Chinese Communist aggression, to indigenous Communist insurrection, subversion, infiltration, political manipulations, and propaganda.

19. Strengthen propaganda and cultural activities, as appropriate, in relation to the area to foster increaased alignment of the people with the free world.

20. Make clear to the American people the importance of Southeast Asia to the security of the United States so that they may be prepared for any of the courses of action proposed herein.

B. INDOCHINA

In the Absence of Chinese Communist Aggression

21. Without relieving France of its basic responsibility for the defense of the Associated States, expedite the provision of, and if necessary increase, aid to the French Union forces, under the terms of existing commitments, to assist them in:

a. An aggressive military, political and psychological program, including covert operations, to eliminate organized Viet Minh forces by mid-1955.

b. Developing indigenous armed forces, including independent logistical and administrative services, which will eventually be capable of maintaining internal security without assistance from French units.

Toward this end, exert all feasible influence to improve the military capabilities of the French Union–Associated States forces, including improved training of local forces, effective command and intelligence arrangements, and the reposing of increased responsibility on local military leaders.

22. Continue to assure France that: (1) the United States is aware that the French effort in Indochina is vital to the preservation of the French Union and of great strategic importance to the security of the free world; (2) the United States is fully aware of the sacrifices France is making; and (3) U.S. support will continue so long as France continues to carry out its primary responsibility in Indochina.

23. Encourage further steps by both France and the Associated States to produce a working relationship based on equal sovereignty within the general framework of the French Union. These steps should take into account France's primary responsibility for the defense of Indochina.

a. Support the development of more effective and stable governments in the Associated States, thus making possible the reduction of French participation in the affairs of the States.

b. Urge the French to organize their administration and representation in Indochina with a view to increasing the feeling of responsibility on the part of the Associated States.

c. Seek to persuade the Associated States that it is not in their best interest to undermine the French position by making untimely demands.

d. Cooperate with the French and the Associated States in publicizing progress toward achieving the foregoing policies.

24. Continue to promote international recognition and support for the Associated States.

25. Employ every feasible means to influence the French government and people against any conclusion of the struggle on terms inconsistent with basic U.S. objectives. In doing so, the United States should make clear:

a. The effect on the position of France itself in North Africa, in Europe, and as a world power.

b. The free world stake in Indochina.

FINANCIAL APPENDIX

POLICY ALTERNATIVE: NO CHINESE COMMUNIST AGGRESSION

Estimated Expenditures in Connection with U. S. Courses of Action in Southeast Asia

(Millions of Dollars)

	1 Total	2 MDAP and Common-use Programs[1]	3 Financial Support through France	4, 5 Technical and Economic Assistance Grant	Loan	6 Information Activities	7 Other[2]
Indochina							
FY 1950–53	969.7	548	375	46	—	.7[3]	—
FY 1954	839.5	304	400–500	25	—	.5	—
FY 1955	1,159.5	333	750–800	25	—	1.5	—
FY 1956	713.5	287	400–500	25	—	1.5	—
Burma							
FY 1950–53	18.6	2	—	16	—	.6[3]	—
FY 1954	4.5	*	—	4	—	.5	[4]
FY 1955	.5	—	—	—	—	.5	[4]
FY 1956	.5	—	—	—	—	.5	—
Thailand							
FY 1950–53	102.7	88	—	13	1	.7[3]	—
FY 1954	49.5	42.5	—	7	—	.5	—
FY 1955	53.0	46.0	—	7[5]	—	1.0	—
FY 1956	52.0	45.0	—	7[5]	—	1.0	—

Malaya

FY 1950–53	.7	—	—	—	.7[3]
FY 1954	.5	—	—	—	.5
FY 1955	.5	—	—	—	.5
FY 1956	.5	—	—	—	.5

Total

FY 1950–53	1,092.7	639	375	75	1	2.7[3]
FY 1954	894.0	346	400–500	36	—	2.0
FY 1955	1,213.5	378	750–800	32	—	3.5
FY 1956	766.5	331	400–500	32	—	3.5

* Less than $500 thousand.

[1] Represents value of end item shipments plus expenditures for packing, handling, crating and transportation, training and common-use items.

[2] Estimated costs of covert operations not available.

[3] FY 1953 only.

[4] Estimated costs to the U. S. of evacuation of Chinese troops from Burma not available.

[5] Additional expenditures of approximately $2.0 million in 1955 and $3.0 million in 1956 might be generated by a proposed road program currently under consideration.

PERTINENT ASSUMPTIONS

Indochina

1. *MDAP and Common-use Programs* (Col. 2) expenditures assume (a) elimination of organized resistance by June 1955; (b) a period of pacification extending for approximately another year; (c) a continuance of U.S. assistance for the duration of the major military operations at approximately the same rate as in FY 1954.

2. *Financial Support through France* (Col. 3) expenditures for FY 1950–53 reflect staff estimates of amounts of aid to France which is attributable to Indochina.

3. *Economic Assistance* (Col. 4) includes no specific estimates for rehabilitation on the assumption that such costs could be offset against reduced military expenditures.

4. *Informational Activities* (Col. 5) are assumed to continue in FY 1956 at a relatively stable rate.

5. *Other* (see footnotes 2 and 3 to table).

c. The impact of the loss of Indochina upon the over-all strategy of France's free world partners.

26. Reiterate to the French:

a. That in the absence of a marked improvement in the military situation there is no basis for negotiation with any prospect for acceptable terms.

b. That a nominally non-Communist coalition regime would eventually turn the country over to Ho Chi Minh with no opportunity for the replacement of the French by the United States or the United Kingdom.

27. Flatly oppose any idea of a cease-fire as a preliminary to negotiations, because such a cease-fire would result in an irretrievable deterioration of the Franco–Vietnamese military position in Indochina.

28. If it appears necessary, insist that the French consult the Vietnamese and obtain their approval of all actions related to any response to Viet Minh offers to negotiate.

29. If the French actually enter into negotiations with the communists, insist that the United States be consulted and seek to influence the course of the negotiations.

30. In view of the possibility of large-scale Chinese Communist intervention, and in order that the United States may be prepared to take whatever action may be appropriate in such circumstances, continue to keep current the plans necessary to carry out the courses of action indicated in paragraphs 31 and 32 below. In addition, seek UK and French advance agreement in principle that a naval blockade of Communist China should be included in the courses of military action set forth in paragraph 31 below.

In the Event of Chinese Communist Intervention

31. If the United States, France and the Associated States determine that Chinese Communist forces (including volunteers) have overtly intervened in Indochina, or are covertly participating so as to jeopardize holding the Tonkin delta area, the United States (following consultation with France, the Associated States, the UK, Australia, and New Zealand) should take the following measures to assist French Union forces to repel the aggression, to hold Indochina and to restore its security and peace:

a. Support a request by France or the Associated States that the United Nations take immediate actions, including a resolution that Communist China had committed an aggression and a recommendation that member states take whatever action may be necessary, without geographic limitation, to assist France and the Associated States to meet such aggression.

b. Whether or not the United Nations so acts, seek the maximum international support for participation in military courses of action required by the situation.

c. Carry out the following minimum courses of military action, either under UN auspices or as part of a joint effort with France, the UK, and any other friendly governments:

(1) Provide, as may be practicable, air and naval assistance for a resolute defense of Indochina itself; calling upon France and the Associated States to provide ground forces.

(2) Provide the major forces to interdict Chinese Communist communication lines, including those in China; calling upon the UK and France

to provide token forces and such other assistance as is normal among allies.

(3) Provide logistical support to other participating nations as may be necessary.

d. Take the following additional actions, if appropriate to the situation:

(1) If agreed pursuant to paragraph 30 above, establish jointly with the UK and France a naval blockade of Communist China.

(2) Intensify covert operations to aid guerrilla forces against Communist China and to interfere with and disrupt Chinese Communist lines of communication.

(3) Utilize, as desirable and feasible, Chinese National forces in military operations in Southeast Asia, Korea, or China proper.

(4) Assist the British in Hong Kong, as desirable and feasible.

(5) Evacuate French Union civil and military personnel from the Tonkin delta, if required.

32. *a.* If, after taking the actions outlined in paragraph 31-*c* above, the United States, the UK and France determine jointly that expanded military action against Communist China is necessary, the United States, in conjunction with at least France and the UK, should take air and naval action against all suitable military targets in China which directly contribute to the war in Indochina, avoiding insofar as practicable targets near the USSR boundaries.

b. If the UK and France do not agree to such expanded military action, the United States should consider taking such action unilaterally.

33. If action is taken under paragraph 32, the United States should recognize that it may become involved in an all-out war with Communist China, and possibly with the USSR and the rest of the Soviet bloc, and should therefore proceed to take large-scale mobilization measures.

[material missing]

[Document 21]

OFFICE OF THE ASSISTANT SECRETARY OF DEFENSE
WASHINGTON 25, D.C.

30 January 1954

INTERNATIONAL SECURITY AFFAIRS

MEMORANDUM FOR THE RECORD

Subject: Meeting of President's Special Committee on Indochina,
29 January 1954

1. The Special Committee met in Mr. Kyes' office at 3:30 p.m. 29 January 1954.

2. The first matter discussed was the disposition of urgent French requests for additional U.S. assistance. The Under Secretary of State, General W. B. Smith, mentioned that there has as yet been no reply to Prime Minister Laniel's letter to President Eisenhower on this subject. It was necessary to answer this substantively as soon as possible.

3. Admiral Radford said he had been in touch with General Ely, French Chief of Staff, through General Valluy. Ten B-26 aircraft are on the way to Indochina this week. These would contribute to filling the French request for aircraft to bring two B-26 squadrons up to a strength of 25 operational aircraft each. However, an additional 12 are needed to fill the full requirement because a total of

22 are needed (12 to fill the annual attrition plus 10 to fill the additional French request). There was some discussion on the seeming differences in requests reaching Washington via Paris and those coming through the MAAG. Subsequently in the meeting it was agreed that the French should be informed that the U.S. would act only on requests which had been approved by General O'Daniel after General O'Daniel was set up in Indochina.

4. Admiral Radford indicated that to fill the entire requirement for 22 B-26's on an urgent basis would mean taking some of them from U.S. operational squadrons in the Far East, but this could be done. The aircraft would not all have "zero" maintenance time on them.

5. As to the additional French request for 25 B-26's to equip a third squadron, it was decided that final decision to furnish them should await the return of General O'Daniel. However, the Air Force has been alerted that they may have to be furnished on short notice.

6. As to the provision of a small "dirigible," it was decided to inform the French that this could not be furnished.

7. Regarding the French request for 400 mechanics trained in the maintenance of B-26 and C-47 aircraft, there was considerable discussion. Admiral Radford said he had informed General Ely, through General Valluy, that the U.S. does not believe the French have exhausted all efforts to get French civilian maintenance crews. He suggested the French try to find them through "Air France." Mr. Kyes mentioned the possibility of obtaining French personnel from their eight aircraft factories or from the big Chateauroux maintenance base where the U.S. employed French mechanics. General Smith inquired about the possibility of lowering French NATO commitments to enable transfer of French military mechanics. Admiral Radford said General Valluy had informed him the French Staff have carefully considered the idea but the French Air Force does not have enough military mechanics trained in B-26 or C-47 maintenance to fill the requirement. Therefore, there would be such a delay while their military mechanics were being trained on these aircraft that the urgent requirement could not be met. He had also said that the employment of French civilian mechanics presented a difficult problem in security clearance.

8. General Smith recommended that the U.S. send 200 U.S. Air Force mechanics to MAAG, Indochina, and tell the French to provide the rest. Admiral Radford said this could be done and that the Air Force is, somewhat reluctantly, making plans to this end. He had let the French know that if American mechanics were sent they must be used only on air bases which were entirely secure from capture. General Smith wondered, in light of additional French requests, if the Committee should not consider sending the full 400 mechanics.

9. Mr. Kyes questioned if sending 200 military mechanics would not so commit the U.S. to support the French that we must be prepared eventually for complete intervention, including use of U.S. combat forces. General Smith said he did not think this would result—we were sending maintenance forces not ground forces. He felt, however, that the importance of winning in Indochina was so great that if worst came to the worst he personally would favor intervention with U.S. air and naval forces—not ground forces. Admiral Radford agreed. Mr. Kyes felt this consideration was so important that it should be put to the highest level. The President himself should decide. General Smith agreed. Mr. Allan Dulles wondered if our preoccupation with helping to win the battle at Dien Bien Phu was so great that we were not going to bargain with the French as we supplied their most urgent needs. Mr. Kyes said this was an aspect of the question he was raising. Admiral Radford read from a cable just received

from General O'Daniel which indicated General Navarre had been most cordial to General O'Daniel at their meeting and had indicated he was pleased with the concept of U.S. liaison officers being assigned to his general headquarters and to the training command. General Navarre and General O'Daniel agreed to try to work out a maximum of collaboration at the military level.

10. Later in the meeting, Mr. Allan Dulles raised the question as to sending the CAP pilots the French had once requested. It was agreed that the French apparently wanted them now, that they should be sent, and CIA should arrange for the necessary negotiations with the French in Indochina to take care of it.

11. Mr. Kyes said that if we meet the French urgent demands they should be tied to two things: first, the achievement of maximum collaboration with the French in training and strategy, and secondly, the strengthening of General O'Daniel's hand in every way possible. General Smith agreed and felt we should reinforce General O'Daniel's position not only with the French in Indochina but also at the highest level in Paris.

12. *Summary of Action Agreed Regarding Urgent French Requests*
It was agreed:

   a. To provide a total of 22 B-26 aircraft as rapidly as practicable.

   b. To provide 200 uniformed U.S. Air Force mechanics who would be assigned as an augmentation to MAAG, Indochina. These mechanics to be provided only on the understanding that they would be used as bases where they would be secure from capture and would not be exposed to combat.

   c. To send the CAP pilots, with CIA arranging necessary negotiations.

   d. Not to provide a "dirigible."

   e. To await General O'Daniel's return to Washington before making a decision on the other French requests. Efforts should continue to get the French to contribute a maximum number of mechanics.

It was further agreed that General Smith would clear these recommended actions with the President.

13. The next item discussed was the status of General O'Daniel. Mr. Kyes said General Trapnell, the present Chief of MAAG, is being replaced at the normal expiration of his tour. General Dabney had been chosen to replace General Trapnell and is about to leave for Indochina. Admiral Radford pointed out that General O'Daniel could be made Chief of MAAG without any further clearance with the French Government. General Smith said this would be all right but should not preclude further action to increase the position of General O'Daniel. General Erskine pointed out that the MAAG in Indochina is not a "military mission" but only an administrative group concerned with the provision of MDAP equipment. He thought the MAAG status should be raised to that of a mission which could help in training. It was agreed that General O'Daniel should probably be first assigned as Chief of MAAG and that, for this reason, General Dabney's departure for Indochina should be temporarily held up. General Dabney should, however, go to Indochina to assist General O'Daniel by heading up the present MAAG functions. Admiral Davis was requested to assure that General Dabney did not depart until further instructions were given.

14. There was some discussion, initiated by Mr. Kyes, about ways by which the French Foreign Legion in Indochina might be augmented. He felt that if the German and French Governments would facilitate it, considerable numbers of Germans might be enlisted to increase the Legion. Mr. Kyes mentioned several other general courses of action he thought should be further considered by

the Special Committee and then suggested that General Erskine read his paper on the subject of Indochina. Mr. Kyes made it plain he considered this paper only a point of departure for further work by the Special Committee. General Erskine then read the paper, copies of which were given to the members of the Special Committee.

15. Admiral Radford said he thought, in general, that the paper covered many important fields but he had one or two reservations. He felt, with regard to the recommendation on regional coordination, that CINCPAC was, and should be, the man to head up regional coordination of the MAAGs. Mr. Kyes reiterated that the paper was only a point of departure and said he felt the basic trouble in trying to help in Indochina was the attitude of the French Government. Mr. Allan Dulles said the French do not want us to become too involved in the conduct of operations in Indochina because they want to keep one foot on the negotiations stool.

16. Admiral Radford said he felt the paper was too restrictive in that it was premised on U.S. action short of the contribution of U.S. combat forces. He said that the U.S. could not afford to let the Viet Minh take the Tonkin Delta. If this were lost, Indochina would be lost and the rest of Southeast Asia would fall. The psychological impact of such a loss would be unacceptable to the U.S. Indochina must have the highest possible priority in U.S. attention. He suggested the paper, when redrafted, should have two parts, one based on no intervention with combat forces and a second part indicating what should be done to prepare against the contingency where U.S. combat forces would be needed. General Smith was generally agreeable to this approach.

17. It was agreed not to use the OCB facilities to support the Special Committee, but instead to set up a working group of representatives of the principals of the Special Committee to revise General Erskine's paper by the middle of the week, 31 January–6 February.

18. The working group would comprise:

> Admiral Davis (OSD)
> Mr. Godel (OSD)
> Captain Anderson (JCS)
> Mr. Bonsal (State)
> Mr. Aurell (CIA)
> General Bonesteel (OSD)

General Smith recommended that a representative of the Air Force be included in the working group.

19. At the close of the meeting, General Smith inquired as to what was being done to speed up the delivery of spare parts for B-26's and C-119's. He was informed that necessary action had been taken.

20. Mr. Allan Dulles inquired if an unconventional warfare officer, specifically Colonel Lansdale, could not be added to the group of five liaison officers to which General Navarre had agreed. Admiral Radford thought this might be done and at any rate Colonel Lansdale could immediately be attached to the MAAG, but he wondered if it would not be best for Colonel Lansdale to await General O'Daniel's return before going to Indochina. In this way, Colonel Lansdale could help the working group in its revision of General Erskine's paper. This was agreeable to Mr. Allan Dulles.

21. Present at the meeting were:

> Department of Defense—Mr. Kyes, Admiral Radford, Admiral Davis, General Erskine, Mr. Godel, B/G Bonesteel, Colonel Alden.

Department of State—General Smith, Mr. Robertson.

CIA—Mr. Allan Dulles, General Cabell, Mr. Aurell, Colonel Lansdale.

C. H. Bonesteel, III
Brigadier General, USA

[Document 22]

THE JOINT CHIEFS OF STAFF
WASHINGTON 25, D.C.

5 March 1954

MEMORANDUM FOF THE SECRETARY OF DEFENSE

Subject: Reappraisal of General O'Daniel's Status with Respect to Indochina

1. Subsequent to decisions made at levels above the Department of Defense concerning enlargement of Military Assistance Advisory Group (MAAG), Indochina, and appointment of a new chief thereof, information has been received which points to the need for a reappraisal of the matters involved.

2. A recent message from the United States Ambassador to Indochina, states that General Navarre informed the Ambassador that Navarre's "very willing acceptance of General O'Daniel [USA] was predicated on the understanding that the latter's functions were limited to military assistance," that "any good ideas the General or any [U.S.] officers might produce would be put into effect wherever practicable [but that] it should be clearly understood that neither O'Daniel nor MAAG was to have any powers, advisory or otherwise, in the conduct and planning of operations, or in the training of national armies and cadres."

3. Information available to the Joint Chiefs of Staff relative to plans of the United States Government indicates that a very considerable increase in MAAG, Indochina, personnel and in the scope of its training responsibilities is contemplated. Recent messages from the U.S. Ambassador to Indochina and the U.S. Embassy, Paris, make it apparent that General Navarre would be strongly opposed to granting increased training responsibility and authority. From this it appears that the Chief, MAAG, Indochina, will not have authority, primarily the authority of command supervision, to accompany the proposed greatly increased responsibility of the MAAG. Without this capability to exercise command supervision, no training program can be assured of success. In the opinion of the Joint Chiefs of Staff, this places a completely different complexion on the entire matter of General O'Daniel's appointment as Chief, MAAG, Indochina.

4. Therefore, the Joint Chiefs of Staff feel that it is more essential than ever, in the interests of the United States, that this basic issue of authority commensurate with responsibility be satisfactorily resolved in advance on a governmental level and in a manner acceptable to the United States.

5. Inasmuch as this basic matter requires reconsideration, we believe that the question of the rank proposed for Lieutenant General O'Daniel, USA, as Chief, MAAG, Indochina, should be reconsidered. The Joint Chiefs of Staff hold it to be distinctly detrimental to the prestige of the United States Military Services in general, and to the United States Army in particular to demote a distinguished

senior United States Army officer already well and widely known in that region. The repercussions of such action in the Orient are well known.

6. In light of the above, the Joint Chiefs of Staff recommend that:

a. The basic issue of increased responsibility of MAAG, Indochina, with respect to training be satisfactorily resolved on a governmental level, and in a manner acceptable to the United States.

b. The despatch of General O'Daniel to Indochina, and his demotion both be held in abeyance until the training issue is satisfactorily settled.

For the Joint Chiefs of Staff:
ARTHUR RADFORD,
Chairman,
Joint Chiefs of Staff.

[Document 23]

THE JOINT CHIEFS OF STAFF
WASHINGTON 25, D.C.

12 March 1954

MEMORANDUM FOR THE SECRETARY OF DEFENSE

Subject: Preparation of Department of Defense Views Regarding Negotiations on Indochina for the Forthcoming Geneva Conference

1. This memorandum is in response to your memorandum dated 5 March 1954, subject as above.

2. In their consideration of this problem, the Joint Chiefs of Staff have reviewed UNITED STATES OBJECTIVES AND COURSES OF ACTION WITH RESPECT TO SOUTHEAST ASIA (NSC 5405), in the light of developments since that policy was approved on 16 January 1954, and they are of the opinion that, from the military point of view, the statement of policy set forth therein remains entirely valid. The Joint Chiefs of Staff reaffirm their views concerning the strategic importance of Indochina to the security interests of the United States and the Free World in general, as reflected in NSC 5405. They are firmly of the belief that the loss of Indochina to the Communists would constitute a political and military setback of the most serious consequences.

3. With respect to the possible course of action enumerated in paragraph 2 of your memorandum, the Joint Chiefs of Staff submit the following views:

a. Maintenance of the status quo. In the absence of a very substantial improvement in the French Union military situation, which could best be accomplished by the aggressive prosecution of military operations, it is highly improbable that Communist agreement could be obtained to a negotiated settlement which would be consistent with basic United States objectives in Southeast Asia. Therefore, continuation of the fighting with the objective of seeking a military victory appears as the only alternative to acceptance of a compromise settlement based upon one or more of the possible other courses of action upon which the views of the Joint Chiefs of Staff have been specifically requested in your memorandum.

b. Imposition of a cease-fire. The acceptance of a cease-fire in advance of a satisfactory settlement would, in all probability, lead to a political stalemate attended by a concurrent and irretrievable deterioration of the Franco-Vietnamese military position. (See paragraph 27 of NSC 5405.)

c. *Establishment of a coalition government.* The acceptance of a settlement based upon the establishment of a coalition government in one or more of the Associated States would open the way for the ultimate seizure of control by the Communists under conditions which might preclude timely and effective external assistance in the prevention of such seizure. (See subparagraph 26b of NSC 5405.)

d. *Partition of the country.* The acceptance of a partitioning of one or more of the Associated States would represent at least a partial victory for the Viet Minh, and would constitute recognition of a Communist territorial expansion achieved through force of arms. Any partition acceptable to the Communists would in all likelihood include the Tonkin Delta area which is acknowledged to be the keystone of the defense of mainland Southeast Asia, since in friendly hands it cuts off the most favorable routes for any massive southward advance towards central and southern Indochina and Thailand. (See paragraph 4 of NSC 5405.) A partitioning involving Vietnam and Laos in the vicinity of the 16th Parallel, as has been suggested (See State cable from London, No. 3802, dated 4 March 1954), would cede to Communist control approximately half of Indochina, its people and its resources, for exploitation in the interests of further Communist aggression; specifically, it would extend the Communist dominated area to the borders of Thailand, thereby enhancing the opportunities for Communist infiltration and eventual subversion of that country. Any cession of Indochinese territory to the Communists would constitute a retrogressive step in the Containment Policy, and would invite similar Communist tactics against other countries of Southeast Asia.

e. *Self-determination through free elections.* Such factors as the prevalence of illiteracy, the lack of suitable educational media, and the absence of adequate communications in the outlying areas would render the holding of a truly representative plebiscite of doubtful feasibility. The Communists, by virtue of their superior capability in the field of propaganda, could readily pervert the issue as being a choice between national independence and French Colonial rule. Furthermore, it would be militarily infeasible to prevent widespread intimidation of voters by Communist partisans. While it is obviously impossible to make a dependable forecast as to the outcome of a free election, current intelligence leads the Joint Chiefs of Staff to the belief that a settlement based upon free elections would be attended by almost cerain loss of the Associated States to Communist control.

4. The Joint Chiefs of Staff are of the opinion that any negotiated settlement which would involve substantial concessions to the Communists on the part of the Governments of France and the Associated States, such as in c and d above, would be generally regarded by Asian peoples as a Communist victory, and would cast widespread doubt on the ability of anti-Communist forces ultimately to stem the tide of Communist control in the Far East. Any such settlement would, in all probability, lead to the loss of Indochina to the Communists and deal a damaging blow to the national will of other countries of the Far East to oppose Communism.

5. Should Indochina be lost to the Communists, and in the absence of immediate and effective counteraction on the part of the Western Powers which

would of necessity be on a much greater scale than that which could be decisive in Indochina, the conquest of the remainder of Southeast Asia would inevitably follow. Thereafter, longer term results involving the gravest threats to fundamental United States security interests in the Far East and even to the stability and security of Europe could be expected to ensue. (See paragraph 1 of NSC 5405.)

6. Orientation of Japan toward the West is the keystone of United States policy in the Far East. In the judgment of the Joint Chiefs of Staff, the loss of Southeast Asia to Communism would, through economic and political pressures, drive Japan into an accommodation with the Communist Bloc. The communization of Japan would be the probable ultimate result.

7. The rice, tin, rubber, and oil of Southeast Asia and the industrial capacity of Japan are the essential elements which Red China needs to build a monolithic military structure far more formidable than that of Japan prior to World War II. If this complex of military power is permitted to develop to its full potential, it would ultimately control the entire Western and Southwestern Pacific region and would threaten South Asia and the Middle East.

8. Both the United States and France have invested heavily of their resources toward the winning of the struggle in Indochina. Since 1950 the United States has contributed in excess of 1.6 billion dollars in providing logistic support. France is reported to have expanded, during the period 1946–1953, the equivalent of some 4.2 billion dollars. This investment, in addition to the heavy casualties sustained by the French and Vietnamese, will have been fruitless for the anti-Communist cause, and indeed may redound in part to the immediate benefit of the enemy, if control of a portion of Indochina should now be ceded to the Communists. While the additional commitment of resources required to achieve decisive results in Indochina might be considerable, nevertheless this additional effort would be far less than that which would be required to stem the tide of Communist advance once it had gained momentum in its progress into Southeast Asia.

9. If, despite all United States efforts to the contrary, the French Government elects to accept a negotiated settlement which, *in* the opinion of the United States, would fail to provide reasonably adequate assurance of the future political and territorial integrity of Indochina, it is considered that the United States should decline to associate itself with such a settlement, thereby preserving freedom of action to pursue directly with the governments of the Associated States and with other allies (notably the United Kingdom) ways and means of continuing the struggle against the Viet Minh in Indochina without participation of the French. The advantages of so doing would, from the military point of view, outweigh the advantage of maintaining political unity of action with the French in regard to Indochina.

10. It is recommended that the foregoing views be conveyed to the Department of State for consideration in connection with the formulation of a United States position on the Indochina problem for the forthcoming Conference and for any conversation with the governments of the United Kingdom, France, and, if deemed advisable, with the governments of the Associated States preliminary to the conference. In this connection, attention is particularly requested to paragraphs 25 and 26 of NSC 5405; it is considered to be of the utmost importance that the French Government be urged not to abandon the aggressive prosecution of military operations until a satisfactory settlement has been achieved.

11. It is further recommended that, in order to be prepared for possible contingencies which might arise incident to the Geneva Conference, the National

Security Council considers now the extent to which the United States would be willing to commit its resources in support of the Associated States in the effort to prevent the loss of Indochina to the Communists either:

  a. In concert with the French; or

  b. In the event the French elect to withdraw, in concert with other allies or, if necessary, unilaterally.

12. In order to assure ample opportunity for the Joint Chiefs of Staff to present their views on these matters, it is requested that the Military Services be represented on the Department of Defense working team which, in coordination with the Department of State, will consider all U.S. position papers pertaining to the Geneva discussions on Indochina.

> For the Joint Chiefs of Staff:
> ARTHUR RADFORD,
> Chairman,
> Joint Chiefs of Staff.

[Document 24]

March 17, 1954

MEMORANDUM FOR THE SPECIAL COMMITTEE, NSC

Subject: Military Implications of the U.S. Position on Indochina in Geneva

1. The attached analysis and recommendations concerning the U.S. position in Geneva have been developed by a Subcommittee consisting of representatives of the Department of Defense, JCS, State, and CIA.

2. This paper reflects the conclusions of the Department of Defense and the JCS and has been collaborated with the State Department representatives who have reserved their position thereon.

3. In brief, this paper concludes that from the point of view of the U.S. strategic position in Asia, and indeed throughout the world, no solution to the Indochina problem short of victory is acceptable. It recommends that this be the basis for the U.S. negotiating position prior to and at the Geneva Conference.

4. It also notes that, aside from the improvement of the present military situation in Indochina, none of the courses of action considered provide a satisfactory solution to the Indochina war.

5. The paper notes that the implications of this position are such as to merit consideration by the NSC and the President.

6. I recommend that the Special Committee note and approve this report and forward it with the official Department of State views to the NSC.

> G. B. Erskine
> General, USMC (Ret)
> Chairman, Sub-committee
> President's Special Committee

Military Implication of U.S. Negotiations on Indochina at Geneva

I. PROBLEM

To develop a U.S. position with reference to the Geneva Conference as it relates to Indochina, encompassing the military implications of certain alternatives which might arise in connection with that conference.

II. MAJOR CONSIDERATIONS

A. The Department of Defense and the JCS have reviewed NSC 5405 in the light of developments since that policy was approved from a military point of view and in the light of certain possible courses of action as they affect the Geneva Conference. These are:

    1. Maintenance of the status quo in Indochina.
    2. Imposition of a cease-fire in Indochina.
    3. Establishment of a coalition government.
    4. Partition of the country.
    5. Self-determination through free elections.

B. The Department of Defense and the JCS have also considered the impact of the possible future status of Indochina on the remainder of Southeast Asia and Japan and have considered the effect which any substantial concessions to the Communists on the part of France and the Associated States would have with respect to Asian peoples as a whole and U.S. objectives in Europe.

C. Indochina is the area in which the Communist and non-Communist worlds confront one another actively on the field of battle. The loss of this battle by whatever means would have the most serious repercussions on U.S. and free world interests, not only in Asia but in Europe and elsewhere.

D. French withdrawal or defeat in Indochina would have most serious consequences on the French position in the world; the free world position in Asia; and in the U.S. on the domestic attitude vis-a-vis the French. It would, furthermore, constitute a de facto failure on the part of France to abide by its commitment in U.N. to repel aggression.

E. Unless the free world maintains its position in Indochina, the Communists will be in a position to exploit what will be widely regarded in Asia as a Communist victory. Should Indochina be lost to the Communists, and in the absence of immediate and effective counteraction by the free world (which would of necessity be on a much greater scale than that required to be decisive in Indochina), the conquest of the remainder of Southeast Asia would inevitably follow. Thereafter, longer term results, probably forcing Japan into an accommodation with the Communist bloc, and threatening the stability and security of Europe, could be expected to ensue.

F. As a measure of U.S. participation in the Indochinese war it is noted that the U.S. has since 1950 programmed in excess of $2.4 billion dollars in support of the French–Associated States operations in Indochina. France is estimated to have expended during the period 1946–1953 the equivalent of some $5.4 billion. This investment, in addition to the heavy casualties sustained by the French and Vietnamese, to say nothing of the great moral and political involvement of the U.S. and French, will have been fruitless for the anti-Communist cause if control of all or a portion of Indochina should now be ceded to the Communists.

III. FACTS BEARING ON THE PROBLEM

A. NSC 5405, approved January 16, 1954, states U.S. policy with respect to Indochina.

B. The French desire for peace in Indochina almost at any cost represents our greatest vulnerability in the Geneva talks.

IV. DISCUSSION

For the views of the JCS see Tab A.

V. CONCLUSIONS

A. Loss of Indochina to the Communists would constitute a political and military setback of the most serious consequences and would almost certainly lead to the ultimate Communist domination of all of Southeast Asia.

B. The U.S. policy and objectives with respect to Southeast Asia as reflected in NSC 5405 remain entirely valid in the light of developments since that policy was approved.

C. With respect to possible alternative courses of action enumerated in paragraph IIA above, the Department of Defense has reached the following conclusions:

1. *Maintenance of status quo in Indochina.* It is highly improbable that a Communist agreement could be obtained to any negotiated settlement which would be consistent with basic U.S. objectives in Southeast Asia in the absence of a very substantial improvement in the French Union military situation. This could best be accomplished by the aggressive prosecution of military operations.

2. *Imposition of a cease-fire.* The acceptance of a cease-fire in advance of a satisfactory settlement would in all probability lead to a political stalemate attended by a concurrent and irretrievable deterioration of the Franco-Vietnamese military position.

3. *Establishment of a coalition government.* The acceptance of a settlement based upon this course of action would open the way for the ultimate seizure of control by the Communists under conditions which would almost certainly preclude timely and effective external assistance designed to prevent such seizure.

4. *Partition of the country.* The acceptance of this course of action would represent at the least a partial victory for the Viet Minh and would constitute a retrogressive step in the attainment of U.S. policy and would compromise the achievement of that policy in Southeast Asia.

5. *Self-determination through free elections.* Many factors render the holding of a truly representative plebiscite infeasible and such a course of action would, in any case, lead to the loss of the Associated States to Communist control.

VI. RECOMMENDATIONS

A. That the U.S. and U.K. and France reach an agreement with respect to Indochina which rejects all of the courses enumerated above (except No. 1 on the assumption that the status quo can be altered to result in a military victory) prior to the initiation of discussions on Indochina at Geneva. Failing this, the U.S. should actively oppose each of these solutions, should not entertain discussion of Indochina at Geneva, or having entertained it, should ensure that no agreements are reached.

B. If, despite all U.S. efforts to the contrary, the French Government elects to accept a negotiated settlement which fails to provide reasonably adequate assurance of the future political and territorial integrity of Indochina, the U.S. should decline to associate itself with such a settlement and should pursue, directly with the governments of the Associated States and with other Allies (notably the U.K.), ways and means of continuing the struggle against the Viet Minh in Indochina without participation of the French.

C. The Special Committee has reviewed the findings and recommendations of the Department of Defense and considers that the implications of this position are such as to warrant their review at the highest levels and by the National Security Council, after which they become the basis of the U.S. position with respect to Indochina at Geneva. The Special Committee recognizes moreover that certain supplementary and alternative courses of action designed to ensure a favorable resolution of the situation in Indochina merit consideration by the NSC. These, and the Special Committee recommendations with respect thereto, are:

1. *The political steps to be taken to ensure an agreed U.S.–U.K.–French position concerning Indochina at Geneva.* That the NSC review the proposed political action designed to achieve this objective with particular attention to possible pressure against the French position in North Africa, and in NATO, and to the fact that discussions concerning implementation of course 2 and 3 hereunder will be contingent upon the success or failure of this course of action.

2. *Overt U.S. involvement in Indochina.* That the NSC determine the extent of U.S. willingness, over and above the contingencies listed in NSC 5405, to commit U.S. air, naval and ultimately ground forces to the direct resolution of the war in Indochina with or without French support and in the event of failure in course 1 above. That in this connection the NSC take cognizance of present domestic and international climate of opinion with respect to U.S. involvement and consider the initiation of such steps as may be necessary to ensure worldwide recognition of the significance of such steps in Indochina as a part of the struggle against communist aggression.

3. *The development of a substitute base of operations.* That the NSC consider whether this course of action is acceptable as a substitute for 1 and 2 above and recognizing that the hope of implementation thereof would be one of major expenditure and long-term potential only.

[Document 25]

THE SECRETARY OF DEFENSE
Washington

March 23, 1954

Dear Mr. Secretary:

Pursuant to a recommendation of the Under Secretary of State, the Department of Defense has considered the military implications of a negotiated settlement to terminate the hostilities in Indochina. The views and recommendations of the Joint Chiefs of Staff on this matter were submitted to me in a memorandum dated March 12, 1954. These views, together with the views of General G. B. Erskine, USMC (Ret), Chairman of the Subcommittee of the President's Special Committee, were submitted to the Special Committee in a memorandum dated March 17, 1954. It is understood that the Department of State is presently considering General Erskine's report.

I am fully in accord with General Erskine's recommendations and the views and recommendations of the Joint Chiefs of Staff in this matter. Accordingly, there is forwarded herewith for your information a copy of the aforementioned documents which represent the views of the Department of Defense. It is recommended that these views be carefully considered in preparation of the United States position on Indochina for the forthcoming conference at Geneva.

Sincerely yours,
C. E. Wilson

[Document 26]

THE JOINT CHIEFS OF STAFF
Washington, D.C.

CM-74-54
29 March 1954

MEMORANDUM FOR THE PRESIDENT'S SPECIAL
COMMITTEE ON INDO-CHINA:

SUBJECT: Discussions with General Paul Ely.

1. During the period 20-24 March I conducted a series of discussions with General Ely, Chairman of the French Chiefs of Staff, on the situation in Indo-China. I am setting forth herein a summary report of these discussions with particular relation to those items which were included in Phase A report submitted by the Special Committee.

2. General Ely requested urgent action for the United States to effect early delivery of various items of material that had previously been requested through the MAAG–Indo-China. These requests were all met to the satisfaction of General Ely with exception of:

  a. 14 C-47 aircraft which are in critical supply and were not in the urgent category.
  b. 20 helicopters and 80 additional U.S. maintenance personnel. An alternative solution is now being worked out through routine channels.

3. In connection with the foregoing is the solution that was evolved to meet the French request for 25 additional B-26 aircraft for a third squadron. There is no doubt that French capabilities for maintenance and aircraft utilization fall far short of acceptable standards and that the supply of additional aircraft alone is not the remedy to inadequate air power in Indo-China. However, in view of the importance of the morale factor at the present time in relation to the struggle for Dien Bien Phu, it was agreed, and the President has approved, to lend the French these aircraft. Certain conditions were imposed which General Ely accepted:

  a. A special inspection team headed by an Air Force General Officer would proceed to Indo-China immediately to examine French maintenance, supply problems, and utilization of U.S. aircraft furnished the French. A report will be made to the Secretary of Defense with a copy being given to General Navarre.
  b. The aircraft will be returned to the U.S. Air Force at the end of the current fighting season about the end of May, or earlier if required for service in Korea. Decision as to permanent acceptance and support of the third B-26 squadron will be made after the report of the special examination (para 3*a* above) has been analyzed.

4. General Ely informed me that steps had been taken by the French Air Force to supply additional aviation mechanics to Indo-China and to replace our 200 U.S. Air Force mechanics along the following lines:

  a. The tour of duty of 200 French mechanics due for early return to France is being extended two months. This will permit the operation of the 25 additional B-26s without need for more U.S. personnel. 15 Air crews now in training in France and North Africa are being sent by air to Indo-China.

  b. Fifty mechanics are being sent from France within the next month and beginning 1 June, one hundred additional per month will be sent to a total of 450.

  c. The 200 U.S. Air Force mechanics can be released "within 8 days of 15 June."

5. General Ely raised the question of obtaining authorization to use the C-119 transports to drop napalm at Dien Bien Phu. Although the U.S. does not expect spectacular results, this was approved on condition:

  a. No U.S. crews were involved.

  b. The French high command requested the diversion of this air lift capability to meet the emergency situation at Dien Bien Phu.

6. I presented to General Ely our views in regard to expanding the MAAG to assist the French in training the Vietnamese, indicating to him the importance which we attach to this action, first, to obtain better results, secondly to release French officers for combat service. General Ely was most unsympathetic to any encroachment on French responsibilities or significant expansion of the MAAG. The reasons given related to French "prestige," possible lack of confidence in French leadership by the Vietnamese, "the political situation in France" etc. The only commitments I was able to get from General Ely were:

  a. He would urge General Navarre to be most sympathetic to the advice given by the officers recently assigned to MAAG (such as Colonel Rosson).

  b. He would request General Navarre to discuss the utilization of U.S. staff officers with General O'Daniel on the spot in a broad, understanding and comprehensive manner." I would make a similar request of General O'Daniel.

  c. He would make some informal soundings in Paris on the subject of increased U.S. participation in training and would communicate further with me—informally—through General Valluy.

I conclude that the French are disposed firmly to resist any delegation of training responsibilities to the U.S. MAAG.

7. Much the same attitude was manifested by General Ely in regard to U.S. operations in the fields of psychological, clandestine and guerrilla warfare. No commitment was obtained except that General Ely would discuss the matter with Mr. Allen Dulles (which he did).

8. General Ely submitted a request in writing, copy attached as Enclosure "A," as to what action the U.S. would take if aircraft based in China intervened in Indo-China. I exchanged the following agreed minute with him on this matter:

> "In respect to General Ely's memorandum of 23 March 1954, it was decided that it was advisable that military authorities push their planning work as far as possible so that there would be no time wasted when and if our governments decided to oppose enemy air intervention over Indo-China if it took place; and to check all planning arrangements already made under previous agreements between CINCPAC and the CINC Indo-China and send instructions to those authorities to this effect."

9. The particular situation at Dien Bien Phu was discussed in detail. General Ely indicated that the chance for success was, in his estimate, "50–50." He dis-

counted any possibility of sending forces overland to relieve the French Garrison. He recognized the great political and psychological importance of the outcome both in Indo-China and in France but considered that Dien Bien Phu, even if lost, would be a *military* victory for the French because of the cost to the Viet Minh and the relatively greater loss to the Viet Minh combat forces. Politically and psychologically the loss of Dien Bien Phu would be a very serious setback to the French Union cause, and might cause unpredictable repercussions both in France and Indo-China.

10. In regard to the general situation in Indo-China General Ely's views were essentially as follows. The loss of Indo-China would open up all of South East Asia to ultimate Communist domination. Victory in Indo-China is as much a political as a military matter. The French hope to get agreement with the Viet Nam in current discussions in Paris which will implement the July 3rd declaration and lead to more enthusiastic cooperation and participation in the war by the Vietnamese. They hope also to get more positive leadership from Bao Dai who, at this time, is the only potential native leader. From the more optimistic point of view, assuming that Dien Bien Phu was held and native support assured, he expected that military successes but not total military victory would be achieved in 1954–1955, following the broad concept of the Navarre Plan and within presently programmed resources. Ultimate victory will require the creation of a strong indigenous army, extending operations to the north and west, manning and defending the Chinese frontier and the commitment of resources greatly in excess of those which France alone can supply. He envisages some sort of a coalition or regional security arrangement by the nations of South East Asia.

11. I raised with General Ely the question of promoting General Navarre in order that General O'Daniel might retain his rank of Lt. General without embarrassment to Navarre. General Ely made no commitment, pointing out that rank in the French Army resulted from a Cabinet action depending upon seniority. He indicated that the Cabinet might possibly consider a promotion for General Navarre if Dien Bien Phu was held.

12. General Ely made quite a point of explaining in "great frankness" actions on the part of the United States which were causes of friction. Those mentioned specifically were:

   a. Americans acted as if the United States sought to control and operate everything of importance; that this was particularly true at lower levels and in connection with FCA operations.

   b. The United States appears to have an invading nature as they undertake everything in such great numbers of people.

   c. French think that McCarthyism is *prevalent* in the U.S. and actually is akin to Hitlerism.

   d. Americans do not appreciate the difficulties under which the French must operate as a result of two devastating wars.

   e. Many Americans appear to favor Germany over France.

   f. U.S. administrative procedures are enormously wasteful, irritating and paper heavy.

   g. In Germany the U.S. forces have the benefit of better weapons and most modern techniques, whereas the French forces do not.

   h. In connection with offshore procurement, the U.S. appeared to lack confidence in the French in the manufacture of most modern weapons and equipment.

I endeavored to set the record straight on each of these particulars and stressed the fact that Americans were growing very impatient with France over its lack of action on the EDC and German rearmament and French tendencies to overemphasize their prestige and sensitivities.

13. General Ely indicated that the leaders of the present French Government were fully aware of the importance of denying Indo-China to the Communists and the prevention of Communist domination of South East Asia. He stated that they would take a strong position at the Geneva Conference but, inasmuch as France could make no concessions to Communist China, they looked to the United States for assistance as the United States could contribute action that the Communist Chinese sought, i.e., recognition and relaxation of trade controls.

14. During the course of the discussions General Ely stressed that, from the military standpoint, one of the major deficiencies in Indo-China was offensive air power. I took this opportunity to pose the proposition of incorporating an air component within the framework of the Foreign Legion or alternatively forming an International Volunteer Air Group for operations in Indo-China. General Ely manifested casual interest but made no commitment to do more than consider the matter further on his return to Paris.

15. As I stated in a brief memorandum to the President, copy attached as Enclosure "B," I am gravely fearful that the measures being undertaken by the French will prove to be inadequate and initiated too late to prevent a progressive deterioration of the situation in Indo-China. If Dien Bien Phu is lost, this deterioration may occur very rapidly due to the loss of morale among the mass of the native population. In such a situation only prompt and forceful intervention by the United States could avert the loss of all of South East Asia to Communist domination. I am convinced that the United States must be prepared to take such action.

ARTHUR RADFORD
Admiral, U.S. Navy
Chairman, Joint Chiefs of Staff

ENCLOSURE "A"

Washington, 23 March 1954

MEMORANDUM FOR: ADMIRAL ARTHUR W. RADFORD
Chairman, Joint Chiefs of Staff

FROM: GENERAL PAUL ELY

The absence of enemy air has been a characteristic of the military situation in Indochina since the beginning of operations. Therefore, an enemy air intervention would carry grave consequences.

On the other hand, the lack of jettable airfields in Vietminh controlled areas leads to the conclusion that any intervention by modern aircrafts would start from Chinese territory.

Without prejudging decisions of a general nature which our governments could take in the event of an air aggression starting from China, it seems to me it will be of some use to study the best way of limiting the effects that such an attack might have on the French Air Force units and on the Corps Expeditionnaire even if it were carried out by aircraft of a doubtful nationality; this last assumption has not been made so far.

Can direct intervention by U.S. aircraft be envisaged and, if such is the case, how would it take place?

Contacts have already been made in the past by CINCPAC and the French CinC Indochina on this problem. I feel they ought to be renewed and pave the way for more precise studies and more detailed staff agreements with a view to limiting the air risk which characterizes the present situation.

/s/ P. ELY
Enclosure "A"

ENCLOSURE "B"

THE JOINT CHIEFS OF STAFF

Washington, D. C.

24 March 1954

MEMORANDUM FOR THE PRESIDENT

SUBJECT: Discussions with General Ely relative to the situation in Indo-China.

1. During the period 20–24 March I conducted a series of discussions with General Ely, Chairman of the French Chiefs of Staff, on the situation in Indo-China. In addition, General Ely conferred with the Secretary of State, Secretary of Defense, the Joint Chiefs of Staff, the Director of CIA and the U.S. Military Representative to NATO.

2. General Ely requested urgent action to make early delivery of various items of material that had previously been requested through the MAAG Indo-China. These were all arranged to the satisfaction of General Ely except for 14 C-47 transport aircraft which are in critical supply and did not come in the urgent category. Noteworthy is the supply of 25 additional B-26s for a third squadron which will be furnished immediately on a temporary loan basis. A recent request for 20 helicopters and 80 additional U.S. maintenance personnel was discussed and he was informed that it was not possible to grant the request at this time.

3. General Ely made no significant concessions in response to suggestions which would improve the situation in Indo-China. He explained French difficulties involving domestic problems and maintenance of prestige as basic reasons for his non-concurrence. He agreed to explore informally the possibility of accepting limited U.S. assistance in training the Vietnamese, but is generally in opposition.

4. General Ely submitted a request in writing as to what action the U.S. would take if aircraft based in China intervened in Indo-China. No commitment was made. The matter is being referred to the Secretary of State.

5. General Ely affirmed the gravity of the situation at Dien Bien Phu stating the outcome as 50–50, and emphasized the great importance of that battle from the political and psychological standpoint. In this I am in full accord but share the doubts of other members of the Joint Chiefs of Staff as to the adequacy of the measures being taken by General Navarre. He was given approval to use C-119 transport aircraft to drop Napalm provided no U.S. crews were involved.

6. General Ely expressed the view that military successes but not total military victory were to be expected in 1954–1955, with the presently programmed resources in pursuance of the Navarre Plan. He considers the problem in Indo-China to be political as well as military. Ultimate victory will require the independence of the Associated States, development of a strong indigenous army, manning and defending the Chinese frontier and commitment of resources greatly in excess of those which France can supply. He envisages some sort of coalition by the nations of S. E. Asia.

7. As a result of the foregoing conferences I am gravely fearful that the measures being taken by the French will prove to be inadequate and initiated too late to prevent a progressive deterioration of the situation. The consequences can well lead to the loss of all of S. E. Asia to Communist domination. If this is to be avoided, I consider that the U.S. must be prepared to act promptly and in force possibly to a frantic and belated request by the French for U.S. intervention.

/s/ ARTHUR RADFORD
Enclosure "B"

[Document 27]

Apr. 3, 1954

SENT TO: AMEMBASSY PARIS 3476
AMEMBASSY LONDON 5175

EYES ONLY DILLON AND ALDRICH

FYI   Following are main points made by Secretary in long conversation with Bonnet this morning.

1) We see no prospect of negotiated settlement at Geneva which does not boil down to one of following alternatives: (a) Face-saving formula to cover surrender of French Union forces, or (b) Face-saving formula to cover surrender of Viet Minh.

2) Division of Indochina impractical. QUOTE Mixed UNQUOTE government would be beginning of disaster. Both would lead to (a).

3) In addition to consequences in Southeast Asia solution (a) would create gravest difficulties for France in Europe and North Africa. Future of France as great power is at stake.

4) If we are strong and resolute enough to make Chinese Communists see clearly that their conquest of Southeast Asia will not be permitted without danger of extending war they may desist and accept (b).

5) This requires strong coalition of nations (U.S., France, Associated States, UK., Australia, New Zealand, Thailand, Philippines) who will recognize threat to their vital interests in area and will be prepared to fight if necessary. This presupposes continuation of French military effort in Indochina.

6) If coalition established U.S. would play its full part.

7) Establishment and announcement of coalition should precede Geneva in order permit us to go there with position of strength.

8) Although UN action not excluded and UN would in any event need to be notified in some formal way, we probably could not count on it. (Soviet veto in SC and long drawn debate in Assembly.)

9) Formal approach to other governments will depend on French desires.

10) Bonnet said he would report immediately to his Government and seek their views.

DULLES

[Document 28]

Apr. 4, 1954

SENT TO: Amembassy LONDON NIACT 5177
RPTD INFO Amembassy PARIS 3478

EYES ONLY ALDRICH AND DILLON

Secretary saw Makins late April 2 and discussed Indochina problem along same general lines his talk April 3 with Bonnet (see Department's 5090 to London rptd Paris 3418 and DEPTEL 3476 to Paris, 5175 to London). Makins indicated our thinking considerably more advanced than British which had apparently not yet gone beyond examination of possible political solutions Indochina under existing conditions.

Partition seemed to London least undesirable settlement according Makins but it was clear UK had not yet developed thoughts for dealing positively and constructively with situation which well may confront us if French determined to sell out.

Secretary emphasized to Makins essentiality of UK and US [Word missing] and at Geneva maintaining solid front to stiffen French attitude. Makins agreed latter point and promised report entire talk fully and urgently. He suggested desirability British military representative here talking promptly to our Chiefs which Secretary said had best wait till later next week.

DULLES

[Document 29]

FROM: Paris

TO: Secretary of State

NO: 3710, April 5, 1 a.m.

LIMIT DISTRIBUTION

URGENT. I was called at 11 o'clock Sunday night and asked to come immediately to Matignon where a restricted Cabinet meeting was in progress.

On arrival Bidault received me in Laniel's office and was joined in a few minutes by Laniel. They said that immediate armed intervention of US carrier aircraft at Dien Bien Phu is now necessary to save the situation.

Navarre reports situation there now in state of precarious equilibrium and that both sides are doing best to reinforce—Viet Minh are bringing up last available reinforcements which will way outnumber any reinforcing French can do by parachute drops. Renewal of assault by reinforced Viet Minh probable by middle or end of week. Without help by then fate of Dien Bien Phu will probably be sealed.

Ely brought back report from Washington that Radford gave him his personal (repeat personal) assurance that if situation at Dien Bien Phu required US naval air support he would do his best to obtain such help from US Government. Because of this information from Radford as reported by Ely, French Government now asking for US carrier aircraft support at Dien Bien Phu. Navarre feels that a relatively minor US effort could turn the tide but naturally hopes for as much help as possible.

French report Chinese intervention in Indochina already fully established as follows:

First.   Fourteen technical advisers at Giap headquarters plus numerous others at division level. All under command of Chinese Communist General Ly Chen-hou who is stationed at Giap headquarters.

Second.   Special telephone lines installed maintained and operated by Chinese personnel.

Third.   Forty 37 mm. anti-aircraft guns radar-controlled at Dien Bien Phu. These guns operated by Chinese and evidently are from Korea. These AA guns are now shooting through clouds to bring down French aircraft.

Fourth.   One thousand supply trucks of which 500 have arrived since 1 March, all driven by Chinese army personnel.

Fifth.   Substantial material help in guns, shells, etc., as is well known.

Bidault said that French Chief of Air Staff wished US be informed that US air intervention at Dien Bien Phu could lead to Chinese Communist air attack on delta airfields. Nevertheless, government was making request for aid.

Bidault closed by saying that for good or evil the fate of Southeast Asia now rested on Dien Bien Phu. He said that Geneva would be won or lost depending on outcome at Dien Bien Phu, this was reason for French request for this very serious action on our part.

He then emphasized necessity for speed in view of renewed attack which is expected before end of week. He thanked US for prompt action on airlift for French paratroops. He then said that he had received Dulles' proposal for Southeast Asian coalition, and that he would answer as soon as possible later in week as restricted Cabinet session not competent to make this decision.

New Subject. I passed on Norstad's concern that news of airlift (DEPTEL 3470, April 3) might leak as planes assembled, Pleven was called into room. He expressed extreme concern as any leak would lead to earlier Viet Minh attack. He said at all costs operation must be camouflaged as training exercise until troops have arrived. He is preparing them as rapidly as possible and they will be ready to leave in a week. Bidault and Laniel pressed him to hurry up departure date of troops and he said he would do his utmost.

DILLON

[Document 30]

SPECIAL SECURITY PRECAUTIONS

April 5, 1954

NSC ACTION NO. 1074-a
(Revision of Report distributed April 3)

Problem

1. To analyze the extent to which, and the circumstances and conditions under which, the United States would be willing to commit its resources in support of the effort to prevent the loss of Indochina to the Communists, in concert with the French or in concert with others or, if necessary, unilaterally.

Issues Involved

2. The answer to this problem involves four issues:

    a. Will Indochina be lost to the Communists unless the United States commits combat resources in some form?

    b. What are the risks, requirements and consequences of alternative forms of U.S. military intervention?

    c. Should the United States adopt one of these forms of intervention rather than allow Indochina to be lost to the Communists and if so which alternative should it choose?

    d When and under what circumstances should this decision be taken and carried into effect?

Prospect of Loss of Indochina

3. The first issue turns on whether the French Union can and will prevent the loss of Indochina and what further actions, if any, the United States can take to bolster or assist the French effort. Some of these questions were covered by the Report of the Special Committee of March 17, 1954. Others are matters of continuous intelligence estimates. At the present time there is clearly a possibility that a trend in the direction of the loss of Indochina to Communist control may become irreversible over the next year in the absence of greater U.S. participation. There is not, however, any certainty that the French have as yet reached the point of being willing to accept a settlement which is unacceptable to U.S. interests or to cease their military efforts. Moreover, regardless of the outcome of the fight at Dienbienphu, there is no indication that a military decision in Indochina is imminent. It is clear that the United States should undertake a maximum diplomatic effort to cause the French and Associated States to continue the fight to a successful conclusion.

Risks, Requirements, and Consequences of U.S. Intervention

4. The attached Annex addresses itself to the second issue: The risks, requirements and consequences of certain alternative forms of U.S. military intervention. In order to permit analysis of military requirements and allied and hostile reactions, this annex assumes that there will be either: (1) a French and Associated States invitation to the United States to participate militarily; or (2) an Associated States invitation to the United States after a French decision to withdraw, and French willingness to cooperate in phasing out French forces as U.S. forces are phased in. If neither of these assumptions proved valid the feasibility of U.S. intervention would be vitiated. If the French, having decided on withdrawal and a negotiated settlement, should oppose U.S. intervention and should carry the Associated States with them in such opposition, U.S. intervention in Indochina would in effect be precluded. If, after a French decision to withdraw, the Associated States should appeal for U.S. military assistance but the French decided not to cooperate in the phasing in of U.S. forces, a successful U.S. intervention would be very difficult.

Desirability and Form of U.S. Intervention

5. The third issue is whether the United States should intervene with combat forces rather than allow Indochina to be lost to the Communists, and which alternative it should select?

a. U.S. commitment of combat forces would involve strain on the basic western coalition, increased risk of war with China and of general war, high costs in U.S. manpower and money, and possible adverse domestic political repercusions. Moreover, the United States would be undertaking a commitment which it would have to carry through to victory. In whatever form it might intervene, the U.S. would have to take steps at the outset to guard against the risks inherent in intervention. On the other hand, under the principles laid down in NSC 5405, it is essential to U.S. security that Indochina should not fall under Communist control.

b. Of the alternative courses of action described in the Annex, Course A or B has these advantages over Course C. Neither Course A or B depends on the initial use of U.S. ground forces. For this reason alone, they obviously would be much more acceptable to the American public. For the same reason, they would initially create a less serious drain on existing U.S. military forces. But either Course A or B may turn out to be ineffective without the eventual commitment of U.S. ground forces.

c. A political obstacle to Course A or Course B lies in the fact that the present French effort is considered by many in Southeast Asia and other parts of the world as essentially colonial or imperialist in character. If the United States joined its combat forces in the Indochina conflict, it would be most important to attempt to counteract or modify the present view of this struggle. This would also be essential in order to mobilize maximum support for the war within Indochina.

d. An advantage of Course B over Course A lies in the association of the Asian States in the enterprise which would help to counteract the tendency to view Indochina as a colonial action. There would be advantages in Course B also in that U.S. opinion would be more favorable if the other free nations and the Asian nations were also taking part and bearing their fair share of the burden.

e. As between UN and regional support it appears that regional grouping would be preferable to UN action, on the ground that UN support would be far more difficult to get and less likely to remain solid until the desired objective was reached.

6. In order to make feasible any regional grouping, it will be essential for the United States to define more clearly its own objectives with respect to any such action. In particular, it would be important to make perfectly clear that this action is not intended as a first step of action to destroy or overthrow Communist China. If the other members of a potential regional grouping thought that we had such a broad objective, they would doubtless be hesitant to join in it. The Western powers would not want to increase the risks of general war which would, in their opinion, flow from any such broad purpose. The Asian countries would be equally reluctant to engage in any such broad activity. Both groups would doubtless want to make very clear that we object essentially to the expansionist tendencies of Communist China and that, if those ceased, we would not go further in attempting to carry on military activities in the Far East. Furthermore, to attract the participation of Asian States in a regional grouping, the United States would undoubtedly have to undertake lasting commitments for their defense.

Timing and Circumstances of Decision to Intervene with U.S. Combat Forces

7. The timing of the disclosure or implementation of any U.S. decision to intervene in Indochina would be of particular importance.

a. In the absence of serious military deterioration in Indochina, it is unlikely that France will agree to the arrangements envisaged in Alternatives A, B, or C in light of the hopes widely held in France and elsewhere that an acceptable settlement can be achieved.

b. On the other hand, inaction until after exhaustive discussions at Geneva, without any indication of U.S. intentions, would tend to increase the chance of the French government and people settling, or accepting the inevitability of settling, on unacceptable terms. Hints of possible U.S. participation would tend to fortify French firmness, but might also tend to induce the Communists to put forward more acceptable terms.

c. On balance, it appears that the United States should now reach a decision whether or not to intervene with combat forces, if that is necessary to save Indochina from Communist control, and, tentatively, the form and conditions of any such intervention. The timing for communication to the French of such decision, or for its implementation, should be decided in the light of future developments.

8. If the United States should now decide to intervene at some stage, the United States should now take these steps:

a. Obtain Congressional approval of intervention.

b. Initiate planning of the military and mobilization measures to enable intervention.

c. Make publicized U.S. military moves designed to make the necessary U.S. air and naval forces readily available for use on short notice.

d. Make maximum diplomatic efforts to make it clear, as rapidly as possible, that no acceptable settlement can be reached in the absence of far greater Communist concessions than are now envisaged.

e. Explore with major U.S. allies—notably the UK, Australia, and New Zealand, and with as many Asian nations as possible, such as Thailand and the Philippines, and possibly Nationalist China, the Republic of Korea, and Burma—the formation of a regional grouping.

i. Exert maximum diplomatic efforts with France and the Associated States designed to (1) bring about full agreement between them, if possible prior to Geneva, on the future status of the Associated States; (2) prepare them to invite U.S. and if possible group participation in Indochina, if necessary.

NSC Action # 1074a
April 5, 1954

ANNEX

I. GENERAL

Scope of This Annex

1. This Annex seeks to assess the risks, requirements, and consequences of alternative forms of U.S. military intervention in Indochina.

Objective of U.S. Intervention in Indochina

2. The immediate objective of U.S. military intervention in any form would be the destruction of organized Vietminh forces by military action limited to the area of Indochina, in the absence of overt Chinese Communist intervention.

However, whether or not the action can be limited to Indochina once U.S. forces and prestige have been committed, disengagement will not be possible short of victory.

Risk of Expanding the War

3. The increased risk of such Chinese Communist intervention is assessed under each alternative form of U.S. military intervention. U.S. action in the event that the Chinese Communists overtly intervene in Indochina is covered by existing policy (NSC 5405).

4. The implications of U.S. intervention go far beyond the commitment and support of the military requirements identified below under the several alternative courses. To meet the increased risk of Chinese Communist intervention and possibly of general war, measures must be taken inside the United States and in areas other than Indochina to improve the defense posture of the United States. Military measures would include the increased readiness of the existing forces and the re-positioning of U.S. forces outside the United States. Domestic measures would include those outlined below under "Mobilization Implications." A reexamination and possibly complete revision of U.S. budgetary and fiscal policies would be required.

Availability of Military Forces

5. The military forecs required to implement the various courses of action described in this paper are presently assigned missions in support of other U.S. objectives. A decision to implement any of these courses would necessitate a diversion of forces from present missions. It would also require the mobilization of additional forces to assume the functions of the diverted forces and to meet the increased risk of general war. The foregoing is particularly true with respect to U.S. ground forces.

Mobilization Implications

6. All the domestic consequences of U.S. intervention cannot be forecast, being dependent on such factors as the degree of opposition encountered, the duration of the conflict and the extent to which other countries may participate, but in varying degree some or all of the following steps may become necessary:

    a. Increase in force levels and draft quotas.
    b. Increase and acceleration of military production.
    c. Acceleration of stockpile programs.
    d. Reimposition of materials and stabilization controls.
    e. Speed-up of readiness measures for all continental defense programs.

Whether or not general mobilization should be initiated, either at the outset or in the course of U.S. intervention, is a major question for determination.

Use of Nuclear Weapons

7. Nuclear weapons will be available for use as required by the tactical situation and as approved by the President. The estimated forces initially to be supplied by the United States under the alternatives in this paper are based on the assumption of availability. If such weapons are not available, the force require-

ments may have to be modified. The political factors involved in the use of nuclear weapons are assessed under the various alternatives.*

Political Conditions

8. U.S. military intervention in concert with the French should be conditioned upon satisfactory political cooperation from the French and French agreement to grant independence to the Associated States in a form that will contribute to their maximum participation in the war. The Associated States undoubtedly would not invite U.S. or allied intervention without lasting guarantees of territorial integrity. U.S. contribution to a full-scale reconstruction and development program in Indochina must also be anticipated.

(No paragraphs 9 and 10)

II. ALTERNATIVE FORMS OF COMMITMENT OF U.S. COMBAT FORCES FOR OPERATION IN INDOCHINA

A. IN CONCERT WITH THE FRENCH

Assumptions

11. The Associated States and France invite the military participation of the United States.

12. It is impracticable to organize a UN or regional military effort.

13. The military situation in Indochina is approximately as at present, i.e., stalemate with elements of deterioration.

14. France and the Associated States will carry forward the scale of military effort envisaged in the Laniel-Navarre Plan.

Military Requirements

15. *Estimated forces to be supplied by U.S. initially.*

    a. Ground forces—(None, provided French Union forces afford adequate security for local defense of U.S. forces in Indochina.)

    b. Naval forces—(Total personnel strength of 35,000).
        (1) 1 carrier task group plus additional units consisting of:
            Amphibious lift for 1 RCT
            Minecraft
            Underway replenishment group
            VPRON's

    c. Air Force forces—(Total personnel strength of 8,600)
        (1) 1 fighter wing (3 sqdns. with integral air defense capability)
        (2) 1 light bomber wing
        (3) 1 troop carrier wing
        (4) 1 tactical control sqdn.
        (5) 1 tactical recon. sqdn.

16. *Command Arrangements: Theater Command*

    a. This should be U.S., since this command must be a combined as well as a joint command and U.S. commanders have had considerably more ex-

---

* State considers the military effect of use or non-use of nuclear weapons should be made clear in the estimates of military requirements to assist in making a decision.

perience in commanding combined and joint commands. Further, should it become necessary to introduce U.S. ground forces, it would be much better to have a U.S. commander already operating as theater commander rather than effect a change at the time U.S. ground forces become involved. All services of the United States, France, and the Associated States will have representatives at the combined headquarters. Similar representation will be necessary at the Joint Operations Center (JOC) to be established.

b. Political considerations and the preponderance of French Union forces may dictate the assignment of theater command to the French, at least during the early phase of U.S. participation.

17. *Logistic Requirements:* This course of action can be logistically supported with the following effects:

a. No delay to NATO deliveries.

b. No drain on Army logistic reserves, negligible drain on Air Force logistic reserves, a partial drain on certain logistic reserves of the Navy, particularly aircraft and ammunition.

c. Some Navy production schedule increases in aircraft and ammunition (depending on extent of operations), some increases in Air Force production schedule with emphasis on ammunition, no effect on Army production schedules.

d. No additional facilities at bases in Indochina required.

18. The training of indigenous forces is crucial to the success of the operation. The United States should therefore insist on an understanding with the French which will insure the effective training of the necessary indigenous forces required including commanders and staff personnel at all levels. The United States must be prepared to make contributions of funds, materials, instructors and training devices as agreed with the French. A United States program for the development of indigenous forces would stress the organization of divisional size units. The battalion organization docs not particularly well fit the approved concept for operations formulated by General Navarre, nor does it represent the best return in striking power for the manpower investment made. A reasonable, attainable goal in Associated States forces which the United States might develop and train is on the order of 330,000 (an increase of 100,000 over the present forces.) This would be accomplished by a re-organization of the presently formed battalions into divisions followed by further training stressing regimental and divisional exercises. New units would be developed as necessary to complete the program.

Political Aspects

19. *French Reaction:* The French would expect U.S. military participation in Indochina:

a. To relieve them from the prospect of defeat or failure in Indochina and to this extent they would welcome U.S. intervention.

b. To highlight the inability of the French to handle the situation alone, with resultant weakening of the general international position of France.

c. To lead to a strengthening of the position of the Associated States as against the French, and a weakening of the French Union concept.

d. To tend to result in channeling U.S. support for the Indochina war directly to the theater of operations, thus reducing the financial benefits to metropolitan France.

e. To increase the risk of Chinese Communist intervention and, through a series of actions and counteractions, to increase the risk of general war with the USSR.

On balance, the French would prefer to find a solution of the Indochina problem which did not involve U.S. military participation, although such solution might in our opinion risk the ultimate loss of Indochina. In the event of U.S. military participation the French could be expected to attempt progressively to shift the military burden of the war to the United States, either by withdrawing their forces or failing to make good attrition.

20. *Associated States Reaction:* The Associated States would not be interested in U.S. intervention unless they were satisfied (1) such intervention would be on a scale which seemed adequate to assure defeat of the Vietminh organized military forces and to deter Chinese Communist aggression, and (2) the United States would assume lasting responsibility for their political independence and territorial integrity. On these terms non-Communist Indochinese leaders would welcome U.S. intervention, and would be unlikely to succumb to Communist peace proposals. The war-weary Indochinese people, however, might be less favorable, particularly if U.S. intervention came at a time when an end to the fighting seemed otherwise in sight. The Associated States would expect to profit from U.S. intervention in terms of increased independence from the French, and would constantly seek to enlist U.S. influence in bolstering their position vis-a-vis France. The Indochinese, however, would be worried over the possibility that U.S. intervention might invite Chinese Communist reaction and make Indochina a battleground of destruction on the Korean scale. Accordingly, they would be expected to oppose the use of nuclear weapons in Indochina.

21. *Free World Reaction:* The U.K., apprehensive of the possibility of war with Communist China, would approve a U.S. intervention in Indochina only if convinced that it was necessary for the prevention of further expansion of Communist power in Asia. Australia and New Zealand would fully support such a U.S. action, and Canada to a lesser extent. Nationalist China and the Republic of Korea would welcome U.S. intervention in Indochina, since both would hope that this would lead to general war between the United States and Communist China. President Rhee, in particular, might be tempted to believe that his chances of involving the United States in a renewal of Korean hostilities were greatly enhanced. Thailand, if assured of U.S. guarantees of adequate permanence would probably permit the use of Thai territory and facilities. The Philippines would support U.S. intervention. Japan would lend unenthusiastic diplomatic support. India and Indonesia strongly, and Ceylon and Burma to a lesser extent, would disapprove U.S. intervention. Other members of the Arab-Asian bloc would be unsympathetic especially because of seeming U.S. support for French colonialism. The NATO countries, other than those mentioned above, would generally support U.S. military action, but their support would be tempered by fear of expansion of the hostilities and the effect on the NATO build-up. The attitude of most of the Latin American countries would tend to be non-committal.

22. *Free World Reaction in the Event of U.S. Tactical Use of Nuclear Weapons:* U.S. allies would almost certainly consider that use by the U.S. of nuclear weapons in Indochina (a) would remove the last hope that these weapons would

not be used again in war, and (b) would substantially increase the risk of general war. Our allies would, therefore, doubt the wisdom of the use of nuclear weapons in Indochina and this doubt would develop into strong disapproval if nuclear weapons were used without their being consulted or against their wishes. On the other hand, France and, if consulted, the UK, Australia, New Zealand, and possibly the Netherlands, might support such action but only if convinced by the U.S. that such action was essential to keep Southeast Asia from falling under Communist control and to preserve the principle of collective security. Other NATO governments, if similarly consulted would probably not publicly disapprove of such U.S. action, if they were persuaded during consultation that such action was essential to prevent collapse of the collective security system. Nationalist China and the Republic of Korea would probably approve such action in the hope that this would result in general war between the U.S. and Communist China. Japan would almost certainly publicly disapprove. Most Asian states and those of the Arab Bloc would probably object strongly to such U.S. action. Certain of these nations led by India, would almost certainly seek to have the UN censure the U.S.

   23. *Soviet Bloc Reaction:*

   a. The Communist Bloc would almost certainly seek to create differences between the United States and the French, and for this purpose would probably put forward "plausible" peace offers to the greatest extent possible in the light of the Geneva Conference. It is unlikely, in the first instance, that the USSR would take any direct military action in response to U.S. participation in the Indochina war. The Soviet Union would, however, continue to furnish to the Chinese Communists military assistance for Vietminh utilization in Indochina.

   b. The Chinese Communists probably would not immediately intervene openly, either with regular or "volunteer" forces, but would substantially increase all other kinds of support. However, if confronted by impending Vietminh defeat, Communist China would tend toward intervention because of the prospect that Communist prestige throughout the world would suffer a severe blow, and that the area of U.S. military influence would be brought to the southern border of China. On the other hand, Communist China's desire to concentrate on domestic problems, plus fear of what must appear to Peiping as the virtual certainty of U.S. counteraction against Communist China itself, would tend to deter overt intervention. The chances are about even that in this situation Communist China would decide upon overt intervention rather than accept the defeat of the Vietminh.*

   c. Soviet Bloc Reaction in the Event of U.S. Tactical Use of Nuclear Weapons. Initial Communist military reactions would probably be substantially the same as in the case of no nuclear weapons. Politically, the Communists would intensify their world-wide campaign to brand the U.S. as an aggressor, with the expectation that considerable political capital could be realized out of the adverse world reactions to U.S. use of nuclear weapons. If U.S. use of nuclear weapons should lead to impending Vietminh defeat, there is a split of opinion within the Intelligence Advisory Committee as to whether the Chinese Communists would accept the risk involved

---

* For fuller discussion of the split of opinion within the IAC on this question, see SE-53, "Probable Communist Reactions to Certain Possible U.S. Courses of Action in Indochina through 1954" (published December 18, 1953).

and intervene overtly to save the Communist position in Indo China: three members believe the chances they would not openly intervene are greater than assessed in par. 23-*b* above; three members believe the chances are better than even they would openly intervene.

24. *Foreign Aid Consideration:* Military assistance to finance the French and Associated States military effort and to supply military hardware would continue at approximately current rates (FY 1954 = $800 million; FY 1955 = $1130 million). Expenditures for economic assistance in Indochina would be substantially increased over the present rate of expenditure ($25 million). These figures do not take into account the cost of U.S. military participation or the possible cost of post-war rehabilitation in Indochina.

[material missing]

C. *IN THE EVENT OF A PROPOSED FRENCH WITHDRAWAL, THE UNITED STATES ACTING IN CONCERT WITH OTHERS OR ALONE*

Assumptions

37. France refuses to continue participation in the war in Indochina.

38. The Associated States invite the military participation of the United States with others or alone.

39. There has been no serious deterioration in the French Union military situation prior to U.S. take-over.

40. The French will so phase their withdrawal as to permit orderly replacement of their forces.

41. The Associated States will cooperate fully with the United States in developing indigenous forces.

42. It may be practicable to organize a UN or regional military effort.

Military Requirements

43. *a. Ground forces.* (Total personnel strength of 605,000)

    (1)   Indigenous forces of 330,000.

    (2)   U.S. or allied forces of six infantry and one airborne division (each the equivalent of a U.S. division in strength and composition) plus necessary support personnel totaling 275,000.

b. Air Force forces. (Total personnel strength of 12,000)

    1 air defense fighter wing

    1 light bomb wing

[Document 31]

ARMY POSITION ON NSC ACTION NO. 1074-A

1. There are important military disadvantages to intervention in Indochina under the assumptions set forth in NSC Action No. 1074-a.

2. A military victory in Indochina cannot be assured by U.S. intervention with air and naval forces alone.

3. The use of atomic weapons in Indochina would not reduce the number of ground forces required to achieve a military victory in Indochina.

4. It is estimated that seven U.S. divisions or their equivalent, with appropriate naval and air support, would be required to win a victory in Indochina if the

French withdraw and the Chinese Communists do not intervene. However, U.S. military intervention must take into consideration the capability of the Chinese Communists to intervene.

5. It is estimated that the equivalent of 12 U.S. divisions would be required to win a victory in Indochina, if the French withdraw and the Chinese Communists intervene.

6. The equivalent of 7 U.S. divisions would be required to win a victory in Indochina if the French remain and the Chinese Communists intervene.

7. Requirements for air and naval support for ground force operations are:

   a. Five hundred fighter-bomber sorties per day exclusive of interdiction and counter-air operations.

   b. An airlift capability of a one division drop.

   c. A division amphibious lift.

8. One U.S. airborne regimental combat team can be placed in Indochina in 5 days, one additional division in 24 days, and the remaining divisions in the following 120 days. This could be accomplished partially by reducing U.S. ground strength in the Far East with the remaining units coming from the general reserve in the United States. Consequently, the U.S. ability to meet its NATO commitment would be seriously affected for a considerable period. The time required to place a total of 12 divisions in Indochina would depend upon the industrial and personnel mobilization measures taken by the government.

[Document 32]

5 April 1954

Special Committee Report On
SOUTHEAST ASIA—PART II

I. THE PROBLEM

To set forth recommendations concerning longer range policy and courses of action for possible future contingencies in Southeast Asia not covered by NSC 5405.

II. MAJOR CONSIDERATIONS

A. The Special Committee has reviewed NSC 5405, "U.S. Objectives and Courses of Action with Respect to Southeast Asia," dated 16 January 1954, and considers that this statement of policy remains valid and should be continued in effect insofar as it concerns the specific contingencies enumerated therein.

B. NSC 5405 covers the contingency of possible Chinese Communist intervention in Indo-China and along with Part I of the Special Committee Report establishes U.S. courses of action designed to secure the military defeat of Communist forces in Indo-China in the absence of Chinese Communist intervention.

C. There are, however, at least two additional factors not covered by NSC 5405 which merit additional policy consideration of the U.S. Government. These are:

   (1) The fact that the Communist threat to Southeas Asia will continue to be a major obstacle to U.S. policy and objectives in Southeast Asia even though a solution to the Indo-Chinese war which is satisfactory to the U.S. may be obtained.

(2) The fact that the threat of Communist domination in Southeast Asia will be infinitely increased in the event that Indo-China should fall under Communist domination despite the present efforts of the U.S. to the contrary.

III.   FACTS BEARING ON THE PROBLEM

A. Southeast Asia comprises some 170 million people in an area just emerging from the colonial era. Standards of living and of literacy are very low. With the exception of Viet Nam, military forces are inconsiderable. The number and quality of leaders, administrators, and technicians is far below minimum requirements. The prospects of political or economic stability during this generation are dim, except in the Philippines and perhaps in Thailand.

B. The peoples of Southeast Asia are accustomed to the rule of the many by the very few at the level of their central government. Their principal national political vitality expresses itself as "anti-colonialism" and the termination of all foreign domination rather than in a desire for political democracy or for the political liberties upon which the Western concept of the world ideological struggle is based.

C. Southeast Asia is a part of and ethnically associated with the Asian continent, principally China. China today is the base of international Communism in the Far East. With the exception of Australia, to which Southeast Asian states are not ideologically oriented, anti-Communist bases are very distant. Certain of them are associated with colonialism in the minds of the people of Southeast Asia. Western influence, both in Southeast Asia and in Korea, has not been effective in preventing the spread of Communism. This results in increased vulnerability of some Southeast Asian countries to Communist influences.

D. Nationalism that expresses itself in Asia as anti-colonialism, if properly guided, is also a potential weapon against Communist imperialism. At the present time, however, some Asians tend to regard "Western colonialism" as more evil and pressing than the possible future threat of Communist imperialism.

E. Economically, the countries of Southeast Asia vary in their products and markets. Many major export products of the area (rubber, tin, copra, etc.) are absorbed by the West. However, rice production is a matter of pan-Asian concern as is oil production.

F. Southeast Asia as a region is less homogeneous than the Atlantic Community or the American Republics in the factors making for real regional consistency and strength. There are major ethnic and religious differences as well as traditional enmities. There is no sense of a common danger as regards Communist imperialism.

G. Current developments, including military operations in the Associated States and the forthcoming Geneva Conference, will have a major influence on future U.S. policy throughout Southeast Asia.

H. U.S. position and policy in the area are most effectively represented in the Philippines and in Thailand, from which countries—outside of Indo-China —any expanded program of Western influence may best be launched.

IV.   CONCLUSIONS

A. The Special Committee considers that these factors reinforce the necessity of assuring that Indo-China remain in the non-Communist bloc, and believes that defeat of the Viet Minh in Indo-China is essential if the spread of Communist influence in Southeas Asia is to be halted.

B. Regardless of the outcome of military operations in Indo-China and without compromising in any way the overwhelming strategic importance of the Associated States to the Western position in the area, the U.S. should take all affirmative and practical steps, with or without its European allies, to provide tangible evidence of Western strength and determination to defeat Communism; to demonstrate that ultimate victory will be won by the free world; and to secure the affirmative association of Southeast Asian states with these purposes.

C. That for these purposes the Western position in Indo-China must be maintained and improved by a military victory.

D. That without compromise to C. above, the U.S. should in all prudence reinforce the remainder of Southeast Asia, including the land areas of Malaya, Burma, Thailand, Indonesia, and the Philippines.

V.　RECOMMENDED COURSES OF ACTION *

A. The Special Committee wishes to reaffirm the following reconmmendations which are made in NSC 5405, the Special Committee Report concerning military operations in Indo-China, and the position paper of the Special Committee, concurred in by the Department of Defense, concerning U.S. courses of action and policies with respect to the Geneva Conference:

(1) It be U.S. policy to accept nothing short of a military victory in Indo-China.

(2) It be the U.S. position to obtain French support of this position; and that failing this, the U.S. actively oppose any negotiated settlement in Indo-China at Geneva.

(3) It be the U.S. position in event of failure of (2) above to initiate immediate steps with the governments of the Associated States aimed toward the continuation of the war in Indo-China, to include active U.S. participation and without French support should that be necessary.

(4) Regardless of whether or not the U.S. is successful in obtaining French support for the active U.S. participation called for in (3) above, every effort should be made to undertake this active participation in concert with other interested nations.

B. The Special Committee also considers that all possible political and economic pressure on France must be exerted as the obvious initial course of action to reinforce the French will to continue operating in Indo-China. The Special Committee recognizes that this course of action will jeopardize the existing French Cabinet, may be unpopular among the French public, and may be considered as endangering present U.S. policy with respect to EDC. The Committee nevertheless considers that the free world strategic position, not only in Southeast Asia but in Europe and the Middle East as well, is such as to require the most extraordinary efforts to prevent Communist domination of Southeast Asia. The Committee considers that firm and resolute action now in this regard may well be the key to a solution of the entire problem posed by France in the free world community of nations.

C. In order to make the maximum contribution to free world strength in Southeast Asia, and regardless of the outcome of military operations currently

---

* The Department of State representative recommends the deletion of paragraphs A and B hereunder as being redundant and included in other documents.

in progress in Indo-China, the U.S. should, in all prudence, take the following courses of action in addition to those set forth in NSC 5405 and in Part I of the Special Committee report:

Political and Military:

(1) Ensure that there be initiated no cease-fire in Indo-China prior to victory whether that be by successful military action or clear concession of defeat by the Communists.

Action: State, CIA

(2) Extraordinary and unilateral, as well as multi-national, efforts should be undertaken to give vitality in Southeast Asia to the concept that Communist imperialism is a transcending threat to each of the Southeast Asian states. These efforts should be so undertaken as to appear through local initiative rather than as a result of U.S. or UK, or French instigation.

Action: USIA, State, CIA

(3) It should be U.S. policy to develop within the UN charter a Far Eastern regional arrangement subscribed and underwritten by the major European powers with interests in the Pacific.

> *a.* Full accomplishment of such an arrangement can only be developed in the long term and should therefore be preceded by the development, through indigenous sources, of regional economic and cultural agreements between the several Southeast Asian countries and later with Japan, Such agreements might take a form similar to that of the OEEC in Europe.

Action: State, CIA, FOA

> *b.* Upon the basis of such agreements, the U.S. should actively but unobtrusively seek their expansion into mutual defense agreements and should for this purpose be prepared to underwrite such agreements with military and economic aid and should [material missing]

D. The courses of action outlined above are considered as mandatory regardless of the outcome of military operations in Indo-China.

(1) If Indo-China is held they are needed to build up strength and resistance to Communism in the entire area.

(2) If Indo-China is lost they are essential as partial steps:

> *a.* To delay as long as possible the extension of Communist domination throughout the Far East, or
> *b.* In conjunction with offensive operations to retake Indo-China from the Communists.

(3) Should Indo-china be lost, it is clear to the Special Committee that the involvement of U.S. resources either in an attempt to stop the further spread of Communism in the Far East (which is bound, except in terms of the most extensive military and political effort, to be futile) or to initiate offensive operations to retake and reorient Indo-China (which would involve a major military campaign), will greatly exceed those needed to hold Indo-China before it falls.

(4) Furthermore, either of these undertakings (in the light of the major set-

back to U.S. national policy involved in the loss of Indo-China) would entail as an urgent prerequisite the restoration of Asian morale and confidence in U.S. policy which will have reached an unprecedently low level in the area.

(5) Each of these courses of action would involve greater risk of war with Communist China, and possibly the Soviet Union, than timely preventive action taken under more favorable circumstances before Indo-China is lost;

[Remainder missing]

[Document 33]

April 5, 1954

SENT TO: Amembassy PARIS 3482

EYES ONLY FOR AMBASSADOR FROM SECRETARY

As I personally explain to Ely in presence of Radford, it is not (rpt not) possible for US to commit belligerent acts in Indochina without full political understanding with France and the other countries. In addition, Congressional action would be required. After conference at highest level, I must confirm this position. US is doing everything possible as indicated my 5175 to prepare public, Congressional and Constitutional basis for united action in Indochina. However, such action is impossible except on coalition basis with active British Commonwealth participation. Meanwhile US prepared, as has been demonstrated, to do everything short of belligerency.

FYI US cannot and will not be put in position of alone salvaging British Commonwealth interests in Malaya, Australia and New Zealand. This matter now under discussion with UK at highest level.

DULLES

[Document 34]

FROM: Paris

TO: Secretary of State

NO: 3729, April 5, 8 p.m.

LIMIT DISTRIBUTION

I delivered message DEPTEL 3482 to Bidault Monday evening. He asked me to tell Secretary that he personally could well understand position US Government and would pass on your answer to Laniel.

He asked me to say once more that unfortunately the time for formulating coalitions has passed as the fate of Indochina will be decided in the next ten days at Dien-Bien-Phu. As I left he said that even though French must fight alone they would continue fighting and he prayed God they would be successful.

DILLON

[Document 35]

FROM: London

TO: Secretary of State

NO: 4382 April 6, 3 p.m.

PRIORITY

EYES ONLY FOR SECRETARY

In compliance with DEPTEL 5090, I saw Eden this morning and made points referred to therein and embodied those in an informal memorandum which I left with him, a copy of which is going forward to you by pouch.

Eden had already seen President's letter to Prime Minister (DEPTEL 5179). Eden stated questions covered would be considered at highest level as soon as possible and that in meantime he wished to say that he felt seriousness of military situation in Indochina had been exaggerated saying, "French cannot lose the war between now and the coming of the rainy season however badly they may conduct it." He will consult with Prime Minister, Cabinet and Joint Chiefs of Staff and will let us know soonest whether it is thought that you or Bedell Smith might profitably come here prior to meeting in Paris.

ALDRICH

[Document 36]

FROM: Geneva

TO: Secretary of State

NO: DULTE 5, April 25, midnight

EYES ONLY ACTING SECRETARY FROM THE SECRETARY

I met with Eden this evening at 10:15 p.m., following his arrival from London. He had consulted Churchill, the Cabinet and British chiefs. He said that the United Kingdom is strongly opposed to any intervention at Dien Bien Phu because it does not think it will have decisive effect and will not be understood by United Kingdom or free world opinion. He indicated that the views of the British chiefs differ with ours and that British chiefs look forward to a discussion and estimate with Radford in London. In summary the British position is as follows: (1) The United Kingdom is prepared now to join with the United States in a secret study of measures which might be taken to defend Thailand and the rest of Southeast Asia if the French capitulate.

Eden saw Bidault at Orly tonight on his way through Paris (where he stopped to pick up Mrs. Eden) and outlined to him the British position as follows: (1) The United Kingdom will give the French all possible diplomatic support in Geneva to reach a satisfactory settlement on Indochina. (2) If such a settlement is reached the United Kingdom will be willing to join with United States and others in guaranteeing that settlement. (3) If Geneva fails the United

Kingdom will be prepared to join the others to examine the situation urgently to see what should be done.

I said to Eden that while I had reservations myself about air intervention at Dien Bien Phu at this moment without an adequate political basis for such action, his reply was most discouraging in that it seemed to leave the French nothing to fall back on. If French are to stand loss of Dien Bien Phu they must be strengthened and a declaration of common intent would do this. In essence the United Kingdom was asking the French to negotiate and at the same time telling them that if the negotiation failed that they would be glad to examine what could be done. Given the present French situation with which Eden is fully familiar, I said to Eden that I doubted that there would be French will to stand up to their adversaries at Geneva.

Eden made quite clear that the United Kingdom is opposed to air intervention at Dien Bien Phu and also opposed to becoming directly involved in any way with the Indochinese war.

Referring to the rest of Southeast Asia, he said the British were confident that they had the situation in Malaya in hand and mentioned that they had 22 battalions there and 100,000 native police. He said that there was no parallel between Indochina and Malaya.

Eden also showed me a map of Indochina prepared by Alexander and the British chiefs. The map indicates that virtually all of Vietnam, Laos, and Cambodia is under or subject to imminent control by the Viet Minh. The British believe that the only way to cope with the situation is to commit a strong force to the Hanoi delta and generally work outward concentrically consolidating their position as they go with loyal natives. This they believe is a "tremendous project involving lots of time and considerable forces."

I said to Eden I felt the position which his Government had taken would have so little in it in way of comfort to the French that the prospect of the latter standing firm here was very slight. It would be a tragedy not to take steps now which would prevent Indochina from being written off.

Eden said that there was obviously a difference in the United States and the United Kingdom estimates and thinking but the United Kingdom proposals which he had outlined above were as far as the British Government could go.

DULLES

[Document 37]

FROM: Geneva

TO: Secretary of State

NO: DULTE 9, April 26, 9 p.m.

SENT DEPARTMENT DULTE 9; REPEATED INFORMATION LONDON 73, PARIS 122.

DEPARTMENT EYES ONLY ACTING SECRETARY FROM SECRETARY

PARIS AND LONDON EYES ONLY AMBASSADOR

I met for about an hour this afternoon with Eden and Bidault at latter's villa. Meeting was called at latter's request with no (repeat no) indication its purpose.

After some discussion procedural problems Indochina conference (reported separately) discussion turned to Bao Dai's declaration in Paris and current attitude. Bidault told us that he understands Bao Dai named as his personal representative and observer a former member Ho Chi Minh's cabinet but that Bidault has not (repeat not) been able to confirm observer's arrival at his station in Evian.

Bidault then launched into rather confused discussion of problem his government faces with regard to establishing position for Indochina negotiation which he said was extremely difficult during progress of Dien Bien Phu battle. He touched lightly on whole range of possibilities including collective defense, cease-fire and partition. He mentioned further deterioration in political situation in Associated States,

Eden picked up the question of cease-fire and encouraged further discussion by Bidault this subject with cryptic remark that a month ago British had felt cease-fire due to general infiltration was dangerous but that now without having any clear view they were not (repeat not) so sure. I pointed out that cease-fire at Dien Bien Phu locally would be in fact surrender and that cease-fire generally would involve serious risk of native peoples' rising with resultant massacre of French. Side conversations later made it clear French believe with support of their military authorities in Indochina that general cease-fire lacking any control or safeguards would make it impossible for French Union forces to resume fighting once cease-fire established. Bidault said that the French Government had queried French High Command in Indochina and had received a reply that there would either have to be a final cease-fire or further reeinforcements would have to be sent to Indochina during the conference.

As indicative of Bidault's continuing courage, he said that when he saw Molotov tomorrow he intended to stand on Laniel's statement of March 5 and attempt to draw Molotov out without ceding ground himself and without getting involved in detailed discussions of substance on an Indochina settlement.

In my judgment, Eden has arrived with instructions actively to encourage French into almost any settlement which will result in cessation hostilities in Indochina. My guess is that behind this lies British fear that if fighting continues, we will in one way or another become involved, thereby enhancing risk Chinese intervention and possibility further expansion of war. This estimate of mine is confirmed by fact that Chauvel told MacArthur the French believe Eden's instructions are to press actively for a cease-fire.

I made clear to Bidault privately that we would have no (repeat no) part in settlement at Geneva of Indochina war which constituted surrender of Indochina to Communists, and that France has better chance by fighting on rather than by attempted withdrawal which would be under most difficult conditions. I intend to see Eden alone tomorrow morning to talk with extreme bluntness to him expressing my dismay that British are apparently encouraging French in direction surrender which is in conflict not (repeat not) only with our interest but what I conceive theirs to be.

DULLES

[Document 38]

FROM: Geneva

TO: Secretary of State

NO: DULTE 13, April 27, midnight

SENT DEPARTMENT DULTE 13 REPEATED INFORMATION LONDON 77 PARIS 127.

EYES ONLY ACTING SECRETARY.

EYES ONLY AMBASSADORS.

I saw Eden and his immediate advisors for a few minutes before his luncheon April 27. I opened by saying that I wanted to speak frankly concerning our own immediate affairs. I said I considered it great mistake to push French in direction cease-fire which I believed would be a disaster. I said I considered it of utmost importance that we both keep French in mood to fight on in Indochina. If that mood is lost surely disaster would follow with little chance of limiting its scope and indeed little chance of French extricating themselves.

Eden replied with some heat that he was not advocating a cease-fire though he admitted that he had told Bidault that he was less sure today than a month ago that a cease-fire was out of the question. He insisted that all he had been thinking of had been a cease-fire with adequate safeguards and controls. His purpose he said had been to concentrate French thinking on latter points.

I interjected that I did not think three of us were presenting a very impressive or cohesive position. I reminded him that I wanted immediate ad hoc plans covering Southeast Asia including Indochina if Geneva failed but that British were against this. French I said had in effect no government and were at a loss as to what to do. They were drifting toward disaster. I was concerned that we were not doing all possible between us to shore up French resolution. I said there was a basic difference between us in that British seemed to think that plans for a joint defense were more apt to spread conflict than absence of any plans.

Eden said that what worried them in London apart from political aspects was that they felt military intervention would be "terrific business," a bigger affair than Korea, which could get us nowhere. They just did not believe that it was a realizable military exercise considering the military means available. Moreover Eden said it would be most unpopular in Asia let alone with British home opinion.

Eden then asked if our tripartite position was really as bad as I had pointed it. He said he felt that other side was properly worried.

I agreed but said in all frankness they were more worried about United States than British.

Eden did not deny this, and said that we must see how things go here in next few days and do what we can to buck French up particularly if Dien Bien Phu falls.

I said I was deeply worried over French situation not alone in its relation with Indochina. NATO was directly affected. The fall of Laniel might result in a left-of-center government coming to power which would exist by Communist sufferance, thereby increasing Communist influence domestically in France and by contagion in Italy which country was also a source of serious concern. I said EDC would be affected, and our entire defense structure in Europe. At this point Bidault arrived and we broke off our conversation.

DULLES

[Document 39]

FROM: Geneva

TO: Secretary of State

NO: DULTE 21, April 29, 10 a.m.

EYES ONLY ACTING SECRETARY FOR PRESIDENT FROM SECRE-TARY.

Developments have been so rapid and almost every hour so filled with high-level talks that evaluation has been difficult. My present estimates follow:

(1) Indochina: Delay in fall of Dien Bien Phu has resulted in some French discounting of this development. Nevertheless, it must be assumed the French will not continue in any long-range operation unless it will definitely relieve the strain on French manpower in Indochina. Present French Government holding on because their Parliament in recess and probably no one eager to take over at this juncture. Bidault given considerable discretion because present Cabinet cannot make up its mind on any course. Therefore, we do not have anyone on French side with whom we can make any dependable agreements. After deputies return and Dien Bien Phu falls, there may well be a change of government, probably to the left, committed to liquidate Indochina. However, this is more easily said than done and it is possible that as this fact develops a French Government might be prepared to sit down with us seriously and consider some joint program which is something that so far they have evaded.

I do not know whether from military standpoint it would be deemed feasible to end the scattering and exposure of military forces for local political reasons and withdraw present forces to defensible enclaves in deltas where they would have U.S. sea and air protection meanwhile retain enough territory and enough prestige to develop really effective indigenous army along lines suggested by O'Daniel. This might, I suppose, take two years and would require in large part taking over training responsibility by U.S. Also full independence and increased economic aid would probably be required to help maintain friendly governments in areas chosen for recruitment.

I do not have any idea as to whether this is militarily feasible and Admiral Davis inclines to view that it is not. However, from political standpoint this type of program appears to offer best hope of France staying in war. If France and U.S. agree on such a plan, there would be fair chance of Australia and New Zealand coming along. However, this estimate can be improved in next day or two after I have conferred further with Foreign Minister Casey and Prime Minister Webb. It is unlikely that the UK would initially participate and would probably use its influence to prevent participation by Australia and New Zealand. The UK situation would be difficult internally and externally, and there would probably be undesirable repercussions upon other NATO partners. Thailand could be expected to cooperate if we act promptly. Foreign Minister Wan gave further assurance today and urges quick military conversations.

The attitude here of Molotov and Chou En-lai's statement yesterday lead me to rate more highly than heretofore the probability that any open U.S. intervention would be answered by open Chinese intervention with consequence of general war in Asia.

(2) UK attitude is one of increasing weakness. British seem to feel that we are disposed to accept present risks of a Chinese war and this, coupled also with their fear that we would start using atomic weapons, has badly frightened them. I have just received a note from Eden referring to my paper read before NATO restricted council where Eden again urges necessity of consultation before any use. He says, "You know our strongly-held views on the need for consultation before any decision is taken."

(3) General: The decline of France, the great weakness of Italy, and the considerable weakness in England create a situation where I think that if we ourselves are clear as to what should be done, we must be prepared to take the leadership in what we think is the right course, having regard to long-range U.S. interest which includes importance of Allies. I believe that our Allies will be inclined to follow, if not immediately, then ultimately, strong and sound leadership. In saying this, I do not underestimate the immense difficulty of our finding the right course in this troubled situation. Nor do I mean to imply that I think that this is the moment for a bold or war-like course. I lack here the U.S. political and NSC judgments needed for overall evaluation.

DULLES

[Document 40]

NIE 63–54
Approved 28 April 1954
Published 30 April 1954

CONSEQUENCES WITHIN INDOCHINA OF THE FALL OF DIEN BIEN PHU

THE PROBLEM

To estimate the probable consequences within Indochina during the next two or three months of the fall of Dien Bien Phu within the near future.

SCOPE

The consequences of the fall of Dien Bien Phu on the political situation in France, and the repercussions of major decisions in France or Geneva on the situation in Indochina, are excluded from the scope of this estimate.

CONCLUSIONS

1. The fall of Dien Bien Phu would have far-reaching and adverse repercussions, but it would not signal the immediate collapse of the French Union

political and military situation in Indochina. As a consequence of the fall of Dien Bien Phu, the morale of French Union forces would receive a severe blow. A crucial factor in the military situation thereafter would be the reliability of native units, particularly the Vietnamese. There would almost certainly be increased desertions, and the possibility cannot be excluded that the native components of French Union forces might disintegrate. However, we believe that such disintegration would be unlikely during the ensuing two or three months, and that for at least this period the major part of the native troops would probably remain loyal.

2. Assuming no such disintegration, the fall of Dien Bien Phu would not in itself substantially alter the relative military capabilities of French Union and Viet Minh forces in Indochina during the next two or three months. The French stand at Dien Bien Phu has produced certain compensatory military results. It has prevented an overrunning of Laos and has resulted in the inflicting of casualties upon the Viet Minh comparable in number to the total French force committed at Dien Bien Phu. The bulk of Viet Minh forces released by the fall of Dien Bien Phu would probably not be able to move, regroup, and re-equip in time to be employed in new major operations during the next two or three months, although some lightly equipped infantry battalions might be made available more rapidly for operations in the Delta region.

3. Although the Viet Minh have a substantial capability to organize demonstrations and carry out sabotage and terrorist activities in the major cities of Indochina, we believe that French Union forces could maintain control in those cities.

4. The political consequences in Indochina of the fall of Dien Bien Phu would be considerably more adverse than the strictly military consequences and would increase the tempo of deterioration in the over-all French Union position in Indochina, particularly in Vietnam. There would probably be a serious decline in the Vietnamese will to continue the war and to support the Vietnamese military programs. However, we believe that general collapse of French and native governmental authority during the next two or three months would be prevented by the continued existence of organized French Union forces and the hope among Indochinese that the U.S. might intervene in Indochina.

5. We believe that although the fall of Dien Bien Phu would not immediately lead to collapse of the French Union position in Indochina, it would accelerate the deterioration already evident in the French Union military and political position there. If this trend were not checked, it could bring about a collapse of the French Union position during the latter half of 1954. It should be emphasized that this estimate does not consider the repercussion of major decisions in France or Geneva and elsewhere, which could have a decisive effect on the situation in Indochina.

DISCUSSION

6. We believe that the fall of Dien Bien Phu, if it occurred as assumed in the problem, would result from: (a) French capitulation; or (b) an overwhelming of the French either by assault or by gradual constriction of the French position.

7. If the French were to capitulate without further heavy fighting, the adverse military and political consequences would be essentially similar in kind, though possibly of greater intensity, to those accompanying the fall of the fortress through heavy fighting. Viet Minh losses in the event of capitulation would be less than those which would be incurred during further heavy fighting.

8. In any event, the Viet Minh would have suffered heavy losses in the prolonged fighting at Dien Bien Phu. Estimated Viet Minh casualties in the fighting there to date are approximately 13,000; roughly 50 percent of this number have been killed or rendered permanently ineffective. Although a few experienced units have been sent as reinforcements, individual replacements for the most part have consisted of partially trained personnel. As a result of the Dien Bien Phu operation, the effectiveness of the Viet Minh offensive striking force will be greatly reduced during the next two or three months.

9. French Union casualties at Dien Bien Phu to date have been approximately 5,500. The defeat of the force now at Dien Bien Phu would add another 11,000, thus bringing the total French Union losses to roughly 17,000. At least two-thirds of these troops are experienced, professional units from Algerian, colonial and foreign legion forces. Moreover, [word missing] of the thirteen parachute battalions in the French Union forces in Indochina are at Dien Bien Phu. The loss of these elite French Union troops would reduce the French Union offensive striking force by approximately one quarter, thus markedly reducing over-all French Union capabilities for offensive operations in Indochina.

10. As a consequence of the fall of Dien Bien Phu, the morale of the French Union forces would receive a severe blow. Their will to win would be diminished, largely because of a widespread belief that military victory was no longer possible. The loss of morale would probably not be sufficient to reduce the effectiveness of the professional soldiers of the French Expeditionary force. However, a crucial factor in the military situation thereafter would be the reliability of native units, particularly the Vietnamese. There would almost certainly be an increase in Vietnam desertions, and the possibility cannot be excluded that the native components of French Union forces might disintegrate. However, we believe that such disintegration would be unlikely during the ensuing two or three months, and that for at least this period the major part of the native troops would probably remain loyal. Therefore, we estimate that the impact upon the morale of the French Union forces would be severe, but not of such severity as to preclude their employment as an effective military force during the next two or three months.

11. The fall of Dien Bien Phu would not in itself substantially alter the relative military capabilities of French Union and Viet Minh forces in Indochina during the next two or three months unless there were large-scale desertions from the French Union forces. The victorious Viet Minh troops at Dien Bien Phu would have suffered heavy casualties and their efficiency would be reduced. In order to bring these forces up to full strength, the Viet Minh would probably move them from Dien Bien Phu to their main supply and training areas adjacent to the Red River delta. Prior to the rainy season, this redeployment would require at least three to four weeks. After the full onset of the rainy season, which is unlikely before mid-May, the movement would take between two and three months to complete. We therefore estimate that the bulk of the Viet Minh troops at Dien Bien Phu would not be available for major operations elsewhere in Indochina during the next two or three months, although some lightly-equipped infantry battalions might be made available more rapidly for operations in the Delta region.

12. Although the over-all capabilities of the Viet Minh would be reduced as a consequence of the losses inflicted upon their main striking force, Viet Minh forces elsewhere in Indochina would have the capability during the rainy season to maintain and in some instances increase military pressure against French Union forces. In the Red River delta, they could intensify efforts to sever land

communications between Hanoi and Haiphong, ambush French detachments, attack villages, air bases, and other installations, and lay siege to isolated French delta strong points. The scale of Viet Minh operations in the Delta, however, would be restricted by the adverse effects of heavy rains on maneuverability. The Viet Minh could use their force concentrated in the Pleiku region in southern Annam to launch fairly large-scale attacks against French forces engaged in the "Atlante" operation. They could also use units from this force for raiding operations in the Mekong River area or to reinforce the Viet Minh battalions now in Cambodia. Combat operations in southern Annam, the Mekong valley, and in Cambodia would be restricted by the tenuous nature of resupply of ammunition and other military equipment for these units. The Viet Minh could at the same time organize demonstrations and carry out sabotage and terrorist activities in the major cities of Indochina. The Viet Minh capability in this regard is probably substantial.

13. French Union forces, assuming no major Vietnamese defections, would have the capability to maintain their present major fortified positions in the Delta, and elsewhere, maintain control in the major cities, prevent the permanent severing of land communications between Hanoi and Haiphong, repulse Viet Minh attacks in southern Annam and the Mekong River area, and retain the area liberated in the "Atlante" operation. If the Viet Minh were to undertake a major military operation against Cambodia, the defense of Cambodia would require troops from other areas. French Union forces would retain the capability to launch limited offensive operations before the full onset of the rainy season, either in the Red River delta region or on the coast of Annam.

14. The political consequences in Indochina of the fall of Dien Bien Phu would be considerably more adverse than the strictly military consequences, although the two are interrelated. The defeat would increase the tempo of deterioration in the over-all French Union position in Indochina, particularly in Vietnam. The principal political consequences would be: (a) a major blow to French prestige among the Indochinese, and an increased conviction on their part that the French were unable to protect them against the Viet Minh; (b) a serious decline in French and Indochinese will to continue the war, and in particular a further decline in popular support in Vietnam for Vietnamese military programs; (c) exacerbation of French–Indochinese relations, partly as a result of increased Indochinese suspicions that the French will "sell out" to the Viet Minh; (d) a sharp increase of "fence sitting" among politically conscious groups previously disposed to support the Vietnam Government; and (e) a sharp increase, particularly among Vietnamese, of covert support of the Viet Minh. However, we believe that a general collapse of French and native governmental authority during the next two or three months would be prevented by the continued existence of organized French Union forces and the hope that the U.S. might intervene in Indochina.

15. The political effect in Laos would probably be similar to that of Vietnam. However, the Laotians would probably display a greater disposition than the Vietnamese to stand by the French and to continue the war effort.

16. The political effect on Cambodia would be extremely uncertain. The internal security of Cambodia and a certain minimum stability might be maintained, but Cambodia's vulnerability to future Viet Minh pressure would increase.

17. The Viet Minh would make every effort to make political capital of their victory at Dien Bien Phu. They would concentrate on increasing the sense of hopelessness in the Associated States, and would seek to convince the Indo-

TROOP STRENGTHS AND DISPOSITIONS

French Union		*Viet Minh*	
Regular and Light Bns 274	402,000	Regular and Regional Bns 155	185,000
Semi-Military	203,500	Semi-Military	106,000
Total	605,500	Total	291,000

MAJOR CONCENTRATIONS *

Delta

65 Regular Bns (35 Fr. Ex. Force)	22 Regular Bns
19 Light Bns	10 Regional Bns
83,000 semi-military	35,000 semi-military

Dien Bien Phu

16 Regular Bns (15 Fr. Ex. Force)	28 Regular Bns
	2 Regional Bns

Northern Tonkin (Less DB Phu Area)

13 Regional Bns

Northern Laos

14 Regular Bns (10 Fr. Ex. Force)	3 Regular Bns
2 Light Bns	2 Regional Bns

Thakhek-Savannakhet

17 Regular Bns (13 Fr. Ex. Force)	8 Regular Bns
3 Light Bns	4 Regional Bns

Central Vietnam

35 Regular Bns (10 Fr. Ex. Force)	14 Regular Bns
16 Light Bns	7 Regional Bns

Cochin China

17 Regular Bns (3 Fr. Ex. Force)	10 Regular Bns
20 Light Bns	2 Regional Bns

Southern Laos and Northeastern Cambodia

8 Regular Bns (3 Fr. Ex. Force)	4 Regular Bns

Western Cambodia

11 Regular Bns (0 Fr. Ex. Force)	Elements
3 Light Bns	

* These dispositions cover only infantry units. The regional breakdown does not include the total number of Viet Minh and French bns.

chinese that the triumph at Dien Bien Phu signalled their imminent "deliverance" from colonial rule by fellow countrymen. They would intensify current efforts to enhance the status of the so-called "People's Governments" of Laos and Cambodia.

18. We believe that although the fall of Dien Bien Phu would not immediately lead to collapse of the French Union position in Indochina, it would accelerate

the deterioration already evident in the French Union military and political position there. If this trend were not checked, it could bring about a collapse of the French Union position during the latter half of 1954. It should be emphasized that this estimate does not consider the repercussion of major decisions in France or Geneva and elsewhere which are likely to have a decisive effect on the situation in Indochina.

[Document 41]

INDOCHINA

The following are comments made by Major General Thomas J. H. Trapnall, Junior, former Chief of the Military Assistance Advisory Group (MAAG) Indochina, at his debriefing, 3 May 1954.

GENERAL

The battle of Indochina is an armed revolution which is now in its eighth year. It is a savage conflict fought in a fantastic country in which the battle may be waged one day in waist-deep muddy rice paddies or later in an impenetrable mountainous jungle. The sun saps the vitality of friend and foe alike, but particularly the European soldier. Torrential monsoon rains turn the delta battleground into a vast swamp which no conventional vehicle can successfully negotiate. It is a war of many paradoxes—

Where there is no popular will to win on the part of the Vietnamese.

Where the leader of the Rebels is more popular than the Vietnamese Chief of State.

Where a sizeable French army is composed of relatively few Frenchmen.

Where the partners of the Associated States regard each other as more dangerous than the enemy.

Where a large segment of the population seeks to expel the French at any price, possibly at the cost of extinction as a new nation.

This is a war which has no easy and immediate solution, a politico-military chess game in which the players sit thousands of miles distant—in Paris, Washington, Peiping, and Moscow.

STRATEGIC POSITION OF INDOCHINA

The autonomous Associated States of Indochina consist of Viet Nam, Laos, and Cambodia. They occupy a blocking position against the expansion of Chinese Communist influence along the principal routes of communication in Southeast Asia. If this area, approximately the size of the state of Texas, defects or is neutralized the frontiers of Burma, Thailand and Malaya would immediately be exposed and eventually the positions of Australia, New Zealand, India, Ceylon, Pakistan, Indonesia and the Philippines would be weakened. A state of Civil War presently exists in Indochina, which pits the Communist Viet Minh against French Union forces essentially devoted to the ideals of freedom. Other issues, such as varieties of Nationalism, are involved as well. Moreover, a state of transition is concurrently underway in which a formerly strong Colonial power is crumbling. France is giving way to a self-determination movement by the indigenous peoples, who, while numbering more than 30 million, lack stability and security. The population of the three states is not completely compatible in matters of economics, culture, religion, ethnic origins, philosophy or [words illegible] compromise position has been reached in which the principal state of Viet Nam, combining the former protectorates of Annam and Tonkin with the ex-colony of Cochin China, has entered into a loose state of alliance with the lesser states of Laos and Cambodia, and with France. This federation is called the French Union. The exact relationship of each autonomous state to France has as yet not been completely determined. This indecision is, moreover, complicated by natural rivalries existing among the states, even extending to political tribal groups within the states.

The topography of Indochina is varied and consists of extensive mountains, jungles, rivers, canals and major deltas. A remarkable compartmentation results. Military operations in a given area may be conducted with almost complete disregard of the situation in the adjacent compartment. While essentially the ground war presently is the dominant military activity, great potentials in amphibious, naval and air warfare by French Union Forces exist which should be exploited increasingly. Poor internal communications and 1,599 miles of coastline are factors dictating the advisability of utilizing more effectively the combat power of the combined arms.

The political situation in France and Indochina requires a complicated system of military administration. Four national armies comprise the French Union Ground Forces. The French Far East Territorial Force, numbering roughly ¼ million troops, equals the combined totals of the three indigenous armies, of which only that of Viet Nam may be considered as significant. Military responsibility is being delegated to the Associated States to the degree that their state of military development and capabilities so warrant. The pentalateral agreement of 23 December 1950 is the authority for existing relationships. The United States is a signatory to this document which extends MDAP into Indochina. Significantly, the conflict in Indochina has not been "internationalized" such as in Korea. Of the French Union partners, only France is a member of the United Nations. France has specifically opposed UN intervention on the presumption that its control of the Union would eventually be weakened by UN participation. On the enemy-side, the rebel army of 300,000 troops could not be supported without the substantial aid presently provided by Red China.

GOVERNMENT OF INDOCHINA

The prosecution of the war against the Viet Minh in Indochina is a joint responsibility of the sovereign governments of Viet Nam, Cambodia, Laos and France, under the leadership and direction of the latter. The local representative of the French Government is the Commissioner General, M. De Jean. He represents M. Marc Jacquet, French Minister of State, in charge of relations with the Associated States. The Ministers of the Associated States, the French Commissioner General and the military Commander in Chief, Lt General Henri Navarre, prescribe the conduct of the war. Existing protocols define the degree of military control enjoyed by the Commander in Chief over the armed forces of the individual Associated States. Essentially, the French exercise operational control over all forces in strategy and tactics. Each of the Associated States maintains a Chief of Staff and a General Staff who are primarily concerned with recruiting, training, personnel actions and limited logistical activities. The long range program envisages a progressive turnover of responsibilities to the Associated States, although a requirement exists that adequate coordinating powers be vested in the hands of the French for many years to come.

Political decisions affecting military operations are reached in sessions of the high committee by representatives of the States, France, and the Commander in Chief. Essentially military problems are resolved in a permanent military committee in which the military chiefs of the Associated States together with the Commanding General of Headquarters, Joint and Ground Forces, Far East, participate.

Although a quadruplication of facilities exist in the form of several national general staffs and territorial organizations, actually a reasonably efficient channel of command is maintained by the French. Diplomatic liaison with the States counterpart organizations is exercised wherever coordination is required. This highly complex arrangement of joint and combined staffs and pooling of national forces may be likened to a miniature NATO at war, except that by necessity, the senior and more professionally qualified partner, France, exercises the dominant role. The governmental structure of each state is more or less oriented toward support of the war against Communism and the principal portion of each State's budget is devoted to defense expenditures. Viet Nam is the most vigorous state in this regard. Laos is cooperative to the French, but without sizeable resources of men or money. Cambodia views the entire struggle as secondary to what it considers more important, the determination of future relationships among the States themselves. In consideration of the fact that hostilities are more or less normal in the life of the Indochinese, the States may be considered as mobilized for war, although with less dislocation to private enterprise and fewer restrictions and austerity measures than would be expected by Western nations in a counterpart situation.

Both Laos and Cambodia are constitutional monarchies, while the Vietnamese respond with less solidarity to the government indirectly controlled by the Chief of State, Bao Dai, nominal descendant of the Emperors of Annam. He is potentially a capable leader but unfortunately out of favor with many extreme Nationalists and non-Communist dissidents.

The overall attitude of the population borders on indifference. The failure of friendly propaganda toward both development of a National attitude and the fostering of patriotism is an important deficiency. The uneducated native is inclined toward himself, his family and his tribe, or stock, in that order. The Japanese-inoculated spirity of Asia for the Asiatics has been adopted by Nationalistic leaders and the intelligentsia. The peasant, whose way of life has not been changed for centuries, is mostly apathetic.

The principal targets for Communism are among the educated classes, whose immediate resentment is the domination of the French through force of arms and political and economic controls. These people, when converted to Communism, muster more effective support from the peasantry and city workers than do the French and the educated Loyalists. Communist influence is strong and its organization very complete, particularly within the large cities. The contending leaders compete with each other for recruits—the Communists holding forth idealistic rewards reinforced by threats, and the Loyalists stressing fear of the enemy as well as other inducements, some of which approach impressment.

The effect of the Ho Chi Minh bid for a negotiated peace and the French inclination to seek a settlement has had strong repercussions among the people, particularly those who pay double taxes, and whose villages are invaded, fought over and destroyed periodically by the opposing forces.

It is natural that the Communists will support the line of negotiation since implementation of any such peace will set the stage for Communist absorption of the entire area, without fail and immediately. The Ho Demarche, and the proven ability of his field forces to threaten seriously the French Union Forces, has had a profound effect on metropolitan France as well, where a considerable portion of the population is in favor of terminating an expensive and seemingly futile war.

PERFORMANCE OF MDAP-SUPPORTED FORCES

French and Associated States Forces have received MDAP equipment in increasing amounts since 1950. French Union Forces conduct modern joint military operations according to professionally accepted tactics and techniques, and in accordance with doctrines approved by the U.S. Armed Services. Applications vary in consonance with difficulties imposed by terrain and the climatic environment. It has been noted that this is a war which pits a modern mechanized army against a large and well-led guerrilla force. However, the character of the Viet Minh forces has been changing during the past year. Therefore, many inefficiencies must be charged against the mechanized army since it lacks complete opportunity to utilize its capabilities fully. Since it is neither practicable nor completely desirable to meet the enemy on the basis of guerrilla versus guerrilla, the ultimate solution will require the isolation of the Viet Minh from his base of supply in Red China and then overwhelming him by materiel superiority. In any instance, a requirement for provision of quantities of MDAP equipment exists and will continue to exist for an indeterminate period. Generally, maintenance standards of MDAP equipment are below those of the U.S. Armed Services, although within well-trained units employing equipment in the intended manner, favorable comparisons may be reached. Since many of the personnel of the French Union Army begin their careers as illiterate peasants, completely unskilled, the training and indoctrination task toward better maintenance is evident. MAAG visiting teams proffer such guidance as is feasible. Specific notification of superior, as well as unsatisfactory units, are made officially to the French military authorities. Under the existing terms of reference, MAAG has no authorized direct contact with armed forces of the Associated States. A significant weakness on the part of the French is their failure to project their system of field operations and staff planning beyond their experience in Indochina. *Imagination is frequently lacking. Also evident is the fact that their limited experience in World War II has stunted their overall development in modern warfare.* This is basically the reason underlying their poor staff work, logistics and operational plans. In addition, the French are sensitive and touchy and loath to accept advice. We frequently encounter outdated techniques dating back to Colonial campaigns and World War I.

Another weakness of the French Union Force is the diversity of troops employed. The French Expeditionary Corps is composed of Foreign Legion, Moroccans, Algerians, Tunisians, Songalese and a small percentage of metropolitan French volunteers. These units are diluted nearly 59 percent by native Indochinese. The Associated States Forces are composed of varieties of native Vietnamese, Laotians and Cambodians. The whole effect is that of a heterogeneous force among whom even basic communication is difficult. Troops require a variety of clothes sizes and diets. They have different religious customs, folkways and mores. They vary in their capacity for different tasks and terrain. Logistically, a great problem exists in the support of such troops.

On the other hand, the Rebels are mostly Vietnamese recruited largely from the hardy stocks of Tonkin and Annam. They are a truly homogeneous army whose capabilities and requirements remain more or less consistent.

The MDAP equipment furnished the French Air Force of Indochina has converted it into a modern air arm capable of performing its combat mission in a highly satisfactory manner. It is an effective offensive or defensive combat weapon, the full potential of which has not been realized.

NATIONAL MILITARY SERVICE

a. French Forces: All French Army personnel in Indochina are serving in the Regular Army. The draftee in France is not required by law to serve in Indochina. However, he may volunteer for such duty. The period of service in Indochina was formerly 24 months, but due to a shortage of replacements, the period currently is extended to 27 months. French personnel receive substantial increases in pay for service in Indochina.

b. Vietnamese Forces: The original law which drafted man for military service required all physically fit males to undergo a period of service for 60 days. Until April 1953, this law was not strictly enforced. In April, it became, with minor changes, the basis for the ordinance drafting 40,000 men for duty with Kinh Quan battalions. Personnel are inducted into the army for the duration. They are selected on the basis of their family situation. Single men are taken first. A man enlisting for the Regular Army is taken on a trial basis for one year. At the end of one year, and if his service has proven satisfactory, he can re-enlist for a period of one, two, three or four years. Recently, the draft laws have been more vigorously enforced to eliminate draft dodging.

INTER-SERVICE BALANCE OF FORCES IN INDOCHINA

While the majority of resources are devoted to ground operations, the following factors must be considered:

a. The enemy has no air forces or naval forces other than junks and sampans.

b. Friendly ground forces maintain a large proportion of river squadrons and light aviation units.

c. Opportunities for employment of large tactical air forces and seagoing naval and amphibious forces are limited.

d. Strategic targets are limited. Terrain and enemy skill in camouflage reduce number of tactical targets.

e. A shortage of trained air personnel exists, with limited prospects for augmentation from metropolitan France resources.

f. Commercial resources satisfy a considerable portion of naval and air logistical requirements.

g. Airfield construction limits composition of air traffic to light and medium transports and propeller-driven fighters and bombers. The balance of forces is considered adequate, although recently the French Air Force, motivated by un-anticipated operational requirements in Laos and Dien Bien Phu, has requested additional B-26 light bombers, an additional C-47 transport squadron, and the loan of U.S. C-119 heavy transports and maintenance personnel. Civilian CAT pilots are presently on contract to the French Air Force for logistical missions. The Army likewise has requested increased air strength in the form of helicopter companies and liaison aircraft.

OBJECTIVES

The missions of the opposing forces may be considered as follows:

VIET MINH—To achieve, by attritive military and political action, a negotiated settlement of the war in Indochina upon such terms as will permit either.

a. Absolute control of a portion of Viet Nam and Laos—generally considered to be north of the 18th Parallel, or

b. Eventual control of the majority portion, or the complete entity, of Indochina as a result of a favorable political position achieved at the peace table.

FRENCH UNION—To achieve, by overwhelming military pressure and political action, a cessation of hostilities upon terms favorable to the French Union which will

a. Restrict the influence of the League of Independent Viet Nam Party–Viet Minh, to that of a controllable minority.

b. Permit the establishment of sound, stable, solvent and harmonious governments within the Associated States.

c. Enable France to maintain its position as the dominant member of the French Union—of the Far East—with extra territorial privileges and commercial benefits.

Naturally, the results of the Geneva Conference may be expected to have a strong influence on future political and military objectives in Indochina for both sides.

ORGANIZATION OF THE FRENCH UNION GROUND FORCES

By the end of 1954, French Union ground forces will consist of four French and one Vietnamese infantry division and one French airborne division. The ground divisions will be formed from 13 French RCTs and 9 Vietnamese ARCTs. The airborne division will be formed from 2 French ARCTs and one Vietnamese ARCT. This force, known as the Battle Corps, will be supported by 5 armored battalions, 5 reconnaissance battalions, 5 amphibious battalions and 3 medium and 1 heavy artillery battalion. This represents the striking force of the French Union Forces, not much larger than a single U.S. type Army Corps. To free this force for independant action against the Rebel strongholds, the French consider that a force of twice that size is necessary for static defense and pacification purposes. By the end of 1955, this surface defense force will reach a total of 86 standard infantry battalions, 132 light infantry battalions, 1100 suppletive companies, the equivalent of 70 artillery batteries and 36 armored car companies. All units of the French Union Army are equipped with a percentage of MDAP material. Amounts vary according to date of activation, depot stocks, mission and replacement factors. A certain percentage of hard items, estimated at 30 percent of gross requirements, is provided by French procurement agencies and may consist of identical items to those of MDAP, having been acquired during World War II, or through other channels by which U.S. surplus stocks were distributed after 1946. Indigenous production is practically negligible, since local industry is not developed and barely sufficient to provide maintenance for civilian requirements. A certain number of paramilitary agencies exist in this theater of operations which are not MDAP supported. These include militia, national police, plantation guards and others. Obviously, MDAP items, mostly small arms and ammunition will find their way by devious channels into unauthorized hands.

Due to the stress of constant warfare, circumstances are such that strict control is impossible. For example, an MDAP rifle, abandoned in battle may be acquired by a Viet Minh soldier, who will forfeit the same weapon upon his death or capture by paramilitary forces.

LOGISTICS OF THE GROUND FORCES

In general terms the organization and operation of the technical services which furnish logistical support to the combat arms is similar to that in the United States Army. The French Forces are handicapped by an insufficient number of units and trained specialists and consequently are unable to furnish the amount and quality of support given by comparable U.S. units. For all technical services MDA Programs have furnished the spare parts and small items necessary to carry out adequate maintenance and repair programs.

French Forces: French Forces are, for the most part, trained prior to shipment to Indochina. Training of individual replacements is done in the units to which they are assigned. French Far East ground forces operate schools for artillery, armor, engineer and transportation for their own forces and additionally provide generous quotas for Associated States personnel. Recently, four tactical training centers have been activated for use as maneuver areas for large tactical formations and battalions rotated out of static positions.

Vietnamese Forces: There are eight training centers for recruits of the Vietnamese Army. Four are for recruits for the Regular Army and four are for personnel to be activated into Kinh Quan (light infantry) battalions and companies. On-the-job training is conducted in technical fields for selected individuals upon assignment to a unit. In addition to this training, a limited number of specialists, technical, non-commissioned and officer schools exist. A considerable number of indigenous officers and men attend French schools both in France and Indochina. Training is not up to American standards.

The Associated States training plan has an annual capacity of about 65,000. It is considered adequate to meet phased build-up requirements. By American criteria, certain training deficiencies are conspicuous, particularly in such areas as standardization of training aids, programs of instruction, troop training programs and training literature. Utilization of plant facilities with greater efficiency is a further requirement. It is apparent that the Associated States forces are developing with more stress on quantity than quality. It is hoped that American guidance will prove acceptable and valuable to the French. The use of MDAP equipment has not generated any critical training problems, however a need exists for management training to encompass stock control; organization of depots and other procedural-type activities.

ORGANIZATION OF THE FRENCH NAVAL FORCES, FAR EAST

French naval strength is approximately 10,000. The only Associated States navy is a 1,000 man Vietnamese force. Naval forces are light units composed of approximately 250 light vessels and 100 small craft. These are supported by an aircraft carrier on loan from NATO and a squadron of privateer aircraft. Command of river operations as well as overall logistic support is the responsibility of the Commander, French Naval Forces ashore. Direct coordination of naval river forces with the respective Army area commands is executed at the Naval area level. Commander, French Naval Forces, afloat, controls coastal operations including surveillance, blockade, and amphibious operations. Naval

Aviation, Indochina, supports the Naval mission as directed. The aircraft carrier force is under Naval administrative command although embarked aircraft operate as directed by the French Air Force area tactical commands.

SUMMARY OF THE NAVAL SITUATION

The French Union naval forces in Indochina are reasonably effective on rivers and inshore areas. They have had much experience in river landings, combating, river ambushes and intercepting junk and small boat traffic on both the ocean and inland waterways. Also, logistic support by water to all services is a constant and heavy undertaking. For guerrilla warfare along the waterways in the Red River and Mekong River deltas, they are uniquely qualified and equipped. In other more orthodox forms of naval warfare such as large amphibious operations, anti-submarine and anti-aircraft warfare, they are neither trained nor equipped. With the establishment of the Joint Amphibious Staff and the formation of an Amphibious Corps, part of this deficiency should be eliminated. Although enemy submarines and aircraft have not been a factor in this war, the possibility does exist. There is little in Indochina to combat the potential menace. Limitations and restrictions for the conduct of the war at present are basically caused by a shortage of personnel rather than a lack of equipment. In addition, concrete and positive steps have been taken in the establishing of a Vietnamese National Navy. This will perform a two-fold purpose—that of easing the serious shortage of personnel and engendering a spirit of pride in the Vietnamese people through increased responsibility and participation in the conduct of the war in their homeland.

ORGANIZATION OF THE FRENCH AIR FORCE

As of 10 April 1954, the French Air Force consisted of 98 Bearcats, organized into 4 squadrons, 16 Bearcat Photo Recon Aircraft organized as a flight, 84 B-26 light bombers, expanding to 3 squadrons, a light tactical reconnaissance flight of modified B-26 bombers, 4 transport squadrons of 114 C-47s—65 MDAP—and liaison aircraft squadrons consisting of 8 C-45s, 12 L-20 Beavers and 8 H-19 helicopters. Additionally, 85 Army liaison aircraft—L-19s—will be delivered by 31 August. 22 C-119 packets with supporting (200) mechanics are on loan during the present emergency.

SUMMARY OF THE AIR FORCE SITUATION

The general MAAG opinion is that the individual flight and ground crews are very well qualified in operating and maintaining their equipment. However, there is not enough of them. Shortages of MDAP supplied equipment of the major categories has not restricted or hampered the operational ability of the FAF combat squadrons and support agencies. Some of the changes in methods and procedures which MAAG believed should be placed in effect are actually beyond the capability of the FAF due primarily to the shortage of personnel and overall restrictions imposed on the FAF by the political and economic situation both in Indochina and in Metropolitan France.

The French are highly operationally minded, however, they do not put proper emphasis on their logistics support requirements to support their operations. In spite of the MDAP equipment and machinery received, the development of this country's self-sufficiency has been abnormally slow.

ORGANIZATION AND TACTICS OF THE REBEL ARMY

The Viet Minh is a well-led, veteran guerrilla army of approximately 300,000 troops organized into 6 infantry divisions, a heavy division of artillery and engineers and numerous regiments, battalions and companies. It has a regional militia component as well as its regular troops. Its equipment and tactics are those of light infantry with a tremendous capability of cross country mobility and endurance. A high command is reputed to contain Red Chinese advisors. Until the pitched battle at Dien Bien Phu, the rebels followed the strategy of hit and run with much of its maneuver dictated by political objectives. The manner in which this force deployed its battle corps into assault infantry, and, with effective artillery support, captured several highly organized and well-defended strong points, indicates a versatility not fully appreciated prior to this campaign season. Additionally, the Viet Minh are skilled in psychological and political indoctrination and have been able to establish bases of operations behind French fortified lines, particularly in the delta. The recent capability of the Viet Minh to seize territory throughout Indochina, albeit temporarily, will have a profound effect upon the conferences at Geneva.

CONDUCT OF THE WAR—MILITARY ASPECTS

In June 1953, General Navarre formulated a set of principles for the conduct of the war in Indochina. This was described in the O'Daniel report as the Navarre concept for *successful conclusion* of the war in Indochina, but it is less a formula for successfully concluding the war than a statement of short term aims, to wit:

a. To retake the initiative immediately through the carrying out, beginning this summer, of local offensives and by pushing to the utmost commando and guerrilla actions.

b. To take the offensive in the north beginning September 15, in order to forestall the enemy attack. To conduct the battle which will take place during the fall and winter of 1953–54 in an offensive manner by attacking the flanks and rear of the enemy.

c. To recover from areas not directly involved in the battle a maximum number of units. To pacify these regions progressively.

d. To build up progressively a battle corps by grouping battalions into regiments and regiments into divisions and by giving to the units thus created the necessary support—artillery, engineers, armor, communications—taking into account the very special character of the war in Indochina, the terrain—the enemy. To bring about a cooperation with the Air Force and the Navy.

e. To maintain a reserve of special type units—armor, commando, light battalion, etc., for attachment to groups and divisions in accordance with terrain and mission.

f. To continue the effort of instructing and organizing the army of the Associated States so as to give them more and more participation as well as more and more autonomy in the conduct of operations.

Note: The above was given to General O'Daniel in writing by General Navarre on 29 June 1953 and was thereafter referred to as the Navarre concept for the successful conclusion of war in Indochina.

Few of these aims are progressing satisfactorily. The training of the National armies is woefully inefficient and the series of tactical offensive operations engaged in during 1953–54 fighting season, instead of retaking the initiative has lost it to the Viet Minh. After a rather encouraging beginning with the Lang Son operation, Navarre's later operations reveal that he is following the same conservative defensive tactics as his predecessor, General Salan. Although Mouette was highly publicized as a successful offensive, it in fact was nothing but a reconnaissance in force with the objective of occupying a strong position and awaiting attack by the enemy in the hope of dealing him a crippling blow. The enemy refused to be taken in. The current campaign season has been dominated by the Viet Minh, and the present position of the French Union Forces is no improvement over that of last year. *Dien Bien Phu is not only another Na San but a grave tactical and strategic error.* The only hope for gain from the battle now raging is that the French can survive. The French have consistently postponed seizure of the initiative through failure to select and pursue vital military objectives such as the obvious enemy troop concentration depot and communications area in the foothills north of the Tonkin delta. Viet Minh leadership, on the other hand, has capitalized on this vacated opportunity by seizing and holding the initiative. The French battle corps, which was built up hopefully by energetic withdrawal of implanted units, has now been dissipated into four sizeable components: (1) Dien Bien Phu—12 battalions—an expensive-supplied airhead, is encircled and under heavy attack. (2) Seno-Savannakhet-Thakhek-Pakse area—15 battalions—partially supported by air with its overland communications threatened. (3) Operation Atlanta—25 battalions—a coastline sweep north from Nha Trang, which has uncovered no appreciable enemy, and (4) the Tonkin delta—18 battalions—where the enemy is increasing his attacks on rear installations and lines of communications. The lack of initiative which the French have is emphasized by the day-to-day reaction of the French to enemy moves and activity as expressed in recent requests for emergency assistance in the way of U.S. equipment and maintenance personnel.

French tactics are based primarily on defense, even though French Union Forces outnumber Viet Minh forces by almost 2 to 1, have overwhelming fire power, and unopposed air force, a balanced naval force and strategic transport capability. The barbed wire concept is exemplified by the fact that the French have established a requirement of 4000 tons of this item per month over and above that furnished by France. The bulk of the C-119 airlift for Dien Bien Phu supply was utilized in dropping barbed wire.

French Union forces do not as a general rule attempt to gain and maintain contact with the enemy, but rather, they wait for the Viet Minh to attack. Patrolling is the exception rather than the rule. Viet Minh regular battle corps troops have been avoided unless the French troops are well dug in behind barbed wire or have astronomical odds in their favor.

Night operations are never employed by French Union forces although the Viet Minh use such operations most successfully. French forces retire to their fortified and secured areas at nightfall, and control only the areas of their fields of fire. Night operations training should be instituted and emphasized in their training programs, and French Union forces should be as adept and successful in such operations as the enemy.

At present there is no evidence that the French staff is working off-detailed plans for the final offensive which General Navarre has indicated to me as Chief MAAG will occur during the next dry season, 1954–55.

Although Navarre demands that his requirement for U.S. equipment should not be challenged by this MAAG, the fact is that the small inadequate French staff handling this function is not capable of accurately presenting requirements for Indochina. Were it not for the screening which these requests undergo by MAAG, material would be wastefully supplied, and many critical and sudden shortages would occur. Many examples of this lack of planning foresight can be found in the files of this MAAG, such as requests for specialized equipment requiring specially trained operators with no companion plan to provide such operators—request for a specific amount of ammunition in January is constitute a year, supply only to double the request in April—not because of an oversight or error but because of poor planning for the operations to occur during the intervening months.

This lack of French staff capability and to a great extent the conservative and defensive attitude of the entire theater of operations, is due in large measure to the fact that many of the officers on duty in this theatre are over age in grade according to U.S. standards, and are lacking in drive and imagination. Lack of command supervision is obvious in all echelons, the best evidence of which is the absence of command inspections and maintenance inspections of equipment of commanders. End-use inspections by members of this MAAG frequently reveal that higher commanders have never made an inspection of equipment in their subordinate units. Shortage of personnel is another contributing factor which cannot be overcome except through more extensive support from metropolitan France.

POLITICAL ASPECTS

A strictly military solution to the war in Indochina is not possible. Military operations are too closely bound to concurrent political problems, and most of the military decisions concerning tactics and strategy have their origin in the politics of the situation here. The governments of the three Associated States are comparatively weak, and are almost as insistent upon complete autonomy from France as they are on liberation from the Communists. It is doubtful if the ordinary people understand the issues at stake between the rebel and Associated States objectives. It probably appears to them that they are being ground between the two political groups, one of which seeks to achieve autonomy by Communist methods. The other by political evolution. They are not aware of the dangers of domination by Communism nor of the difference between democracy and the Communist People's Government as we understand it.

The French have a tremendous investment in Indochina and have made great strides in bringing the advantages of Western civilization to the people. Yet the French are not wanted. Colonialism is still the chief argument against the French and with some substance. The natives are still considered as second-rate people and the French have only made concessions reluctantly and when forced to do so. There is a lack of camaraderie between the native soldier and officer and the French. Separate messes are maintained, due in some measure to the difference in dietary preference, but also due to this lack of friendly association in a common cause.

The Viet Minh, on the other hand, are fighting a clever war of attrition, without chance of a major military victory, but apparently feeling that time is working in their favor and that French and U.S. public opinion will force eventual favorable negotiation.

PSYCHOLOGICAL ASPECTS

In 1949 the French, in a search for Nationalist support against Ho Chi Minh, recognized Bao Dai, playboy scion of the ancient Annamite emperors as Chief of State of Viet Nam which was given its independence within the framework of the French Union. Bao Dai is popularly believed to be very pro-French, and most of the people have a luke-warm feeling toward the Government which they feel is not earnestly working for their complete independence from France. The French promise independence, but only reluctantly give concessions.

The key to this problem is a strong and effective Nationalist army with the support of the Populist behind it. When the people have confidence in their government and in its ability, through the Nationalist army, to give them the protection from Communist terrorism which is necessary for business and commerce, then complete victory will be in sight.

THE U.S. CONTRIBUTION TO THE WAR IN INDOCHINA

The U.S. has greatly contributed to the success of the French in holding Indochina from the beginning. In January 1951, material was rushed from the docks of Haiphong to the battlefield of Vinh Yen, then being fought under the personal direction of Marshall De Lattre himself. Since then, delivery of aid has kept pace with changing French needs, often on a crash basis, down to the present heroic defense of Dien Bien Phu. U.S. aid has consisted of budgetary support, furnishing of end items, military hardware, and of technical training teams. The magnitude and range of this contribution is shown by the following very few examples. All of these figures are as of 31 March this year.

a. 785 million dollars has been allocated for the budgetry support of the French Expeditionary Force and the Vietnamese Army. This will assist in meeting budgetary requirements for pay, food, and allowances for these troops.

b. Under MDA Programs, a total of more than 784 millions of dollars has been programmed for the years 1950–54. Of this, more than 440 million dollars worth of military end items have been received.

c. To date, 31 March 1954, 441 ships have delivered a total of 478 thousands of long tons of MDA equipment to Indochina.

SOLUTION

As in Korea, Iran, Malaya, and Burma, the war in Indochina is not a separate entity. It is another tentacle of the octopus, another brush fire on the periphery of the iron and bamboo curtains. The problem can only be solved completely if the masters of the Kremlin decide that Indochina should be abandoned in favor of more profitable enterprises elsewhere. However, ways and means exist to achieve a degree of success with respect to Indochina, beginning at the political level—specifically at the level of Chiefs of State. What is then necessary is as follows:

a. An agreement must be reached with the French to deliver their strongest possible assault upon the Viet Minh as soon as possible to reduce their efficiency of that force to its lowest potential.

b. Concurrently, the Associated States armies must be put through a training cycle designed to produce leaders and units and to develop confidence through skill and achievement. Such forces must be developed to the level of the ROK or Greek armies under American tutelage and material support for these forces must be in being and capable of replacing the French when they retire.

c. A defensive alliance of democratic nations of the Orient must be developed to provide future stability for the Associated States. The U.S. must establish leadership in this area by relieving the French in a similar manner as was followed in relieving the British for the responsibility of Greece.

d. The sovereignty and territorial borders of the Associated States must be guaranteed—under no circumstances should the country be allowed to divide on an arbitrary parallel such as in Korea.

CONCLUSION

I recommend that the Department of Defense urge that negotiations for agreements to be initiated at the earliest time to achieve the foregoing objectives and that upon reaching an understanding with France and the Associated States, a full-scale U.S. training mission be established with the Associated States forces to achieve an effective training base by Spring of 1956. That the French overwhelm the enemy in the interim is a vital concurrent requirement, and, again, this objective must be achieved by governmental agreement, with the U.S. insisting that the French Government establish military victory as a primary objective and so instruct the field commander, who may then be relieved of his anxieties regarding casualties and indifferent political and moral support from France.

In conclusion, I reaffirm my opinion that victory in Indochina is an international rather than a local matter, and essentially political as well as military.

[Document 42]

NSC 195th Meeting
6 May 1954

ITEM 1 (For Discussion)

REPORT BY MR. DULLES ON GENEVA AND INDO-CHINA

1. Secretary Dulles, who was rather pessimistic, in reporting to the President yesterday morning on the Geneva Conference, made the following points: (a) there is no responsible French Government with which to deal; (b) the British have declined to take a position regarding a Southeast Asia regional grouping until after the Geneva Conference; (c) the British however are willing to proceed with *secret* talks with us regarding the political and military scope of our plans for SEA; (d) the expected Communist proposal re Indo-China will call for evacuation of all foreign troops and elections to be supervised by a joint Vietminh-Vietnam Commission; (e) French have no particular form of settlement in mind; UK is still thinking in terms of partition.

2. It is not clear how the NSC discussion will develop, but it seems desirable that certain questions be clarified at the meeting. They are along this line:

   a. Should the U.S. resign itself to being unable to influence any further the French and U.K. positions at Geneva? (i.e., is it still not possible to stiffen their spines by any conceivable means—Presidential talks, threats, sending Mr. Dulles back with a new mandate, etc.—so as to assure they will not accept a dangerous compromise.)

   b. Is or is not the U.S. prepared to commit its combat forces in the near future, in some form of regional effort if possible, to save the partition or loss of Indo-China? (A decision in principle seems necessary *now*. As the situation is at present we are saying we will consider this if the parliaments of Australia, New Zealand, etc. agree, but it is not clear whether we mean before or after Indo-China is lost.)

c. Is the U.S. prepared to acquiesce in the clearly engineered Communist aggression in and taking over of Indo-China—with Red Chinese support—even though we evaluate this loss as very serious to the free world and even though we have the military means to redeem the situation? (The A-bomb)

3. The Joint Chiefs of Staff sent you a memorandum several days ago (see TAB A) recommending that you "secure governmental acceptance" of the following position:

In the event of a cease fire in Indochina, the shipment of military end items under U.S. MDAP . . . will immediately be suspended, except for such spares and associated maintenance items necessary to the main-tenance of equipment in operations. The entire question of U.S. aid to Indochina will be re-examined in the light of circumstances then existing.

The Office of the Assistant Secretary of Defense (ISA) has suggested you for-ward the memo to the NSC saying you concur, but you have not yet acted on the matter. You may wish to raise it during the discussion.

[Document 43]

May 6, 1954

SENT TO: Amconsul GENEVA
            TEDUL 37

PRIORITY

Secretary held hour and half briefing of 25 leading members Congress yester-day. Generally friendly, constructive atmosphere, no direct criticism, although considerable discussion on future plans and weakness of British and French.

Secretary described set-up of Conference and briefly went over Korean devel-opments. Explained difficulty with Allies on all-Korean elections and trouble finding someone to speak up in defense of U.S. against Communist vilification. Congressmen showed interest in this and asked about positions our various Allies.

Turning to Indochina, Secretary traced developments in our thinking and plans since inception massive aid program last fall. Three prerequisites demanded from French had then seemed to be met: understanding A.S. become independ-ent, effective program for rapid training of natives, aggressive military plan. Prerequisites would lead to our desired objectives. Navarre Plan still sound, but French will for offensive action and even ability govern themselves disintegrated. Following development united action concept and as French military situation deteriorated, we began think of U.S. military intervention. In April 3 meeting with Congressmen agreed objectives of earlier prerequisites must be met to in-creased degree and other interested nations must join in before such intervention could be authorized. Secretary described London–Paris trip and Eden's reneging on communique. Some adverse Congressional comment on latter and Secretary said thought Nehru had pressured British.

Secretary described two informal French requests for U.S. air intervention on April 4 and 22 and his replies thereto. Described French mood of extreme urgency and British Cabinet confirmation of reversal of agreement in communique of April 13. British terrified by H-bomb, pressured by Nehru, contrasted their giving up India with French call for help to keep Indochina, and gave higher rating to risk of Chinese intervention and global war if West intervened. Secretary read from memo of conversation in which he had chastised Eden for British stand. Number adverse Congressional comments on British position, especially Judd.

Secretary said had reached three conclusions. U.S. should not intervene militarily until and unless prerequisites agreed on at April 4 meeting were fulfilled. Conditions must exist for successful conclusion of war and such was not now case. Participation other allies academic since French had not fulfilled prerequisites. Considerable opposition to internationalization of war in France anyway This was Administration position on intervention. No Congressional comments on this.

Secondly, U.S. must push rapidly for development of SEA community, probably without Vietnam but hopefully with Laos and Cambodia. British might come in and they might want Burma and India too. We were agreeable to Burma. This community might offer fair chance quote insulate unquote rest SEA against possible loss of Vietnam.

Third conclusion was we should not write off British and French in spite of their weakness in Asia. Lack of 100 per cent cooperation one of welcome disadvantages of democratic system.

DULTE 51 then received and Secretary read pertinent parts. Considerable discussion ensued on Eden's idea of quote five white powers unquote consultation and conclusions 2 and 3 above. Judd strongly against Eden quote plan unquote, wanted Asians in even without U.K. and France. Knowland agreed on importance of Asians, as did several others. Knowland said we should have commitments from U.K., Australia, New Zealand and others to help us if needed in Korea or Japan, et cetera, if we were to have collective security pact with them for SEA, which he personally favored. Secretary said Burma, Thailand, Philippines plus A.S. would help and that he told Eden he wanted Formosa in if British brought in India. McCormack and Smith supported Secretary on conclusion three and several others did too.

Secretary described effect of Indochina developments on French government and EDC. Russell paid fine tribute to Secretary for briefings and cooperation with Congress and others expressed appreciation.

DULLES

[Document 44]

The White House
Washington
May 7, 1954

MEMORANDUM FOR: SECRETARY OF DEFENSE
CHAIRMAN, JOINT CHIEFS OF STAFF

At a meeting in the President's office with the President, J. F. Dulles and Cutler, the President approved Paragraph 1*b* of the tentative Record of Actions of 5/6/54 Meeting of the National Security Council, but wished that the advice to Smith relative to Eden's proposal should also make clear the following points:

1. Five Power Staff Agency, alone or with other nations, is not to the United States a satisfactory substitute for a broad political coalition which will include the South East Asian countries which are to be defended.

2. Five Power Staff Agency examination is acceptable to see how these nations can give military aid to the Southeast Asian countries in their cooperative defense effort.

3. The United States will not agree to a "white man's party" to determine the problems of the Southeast Asian nations.

> ROBERT CUTLER
> Special Assistant
> to the President

May 7, 1954

At a meeting in the President's office this morning with Dulles, three topics were discussed:

1. Whether the President should approve paragraph 1*b* of the tentative Record of Action of the 5/6/54 NSC Meeting, which covers the proposed answer to the Eden proposal. The Secretary of State thought the text was correct. Wilson and Radford preferred the draft message to Smith for Eden prepared yesterday by MacArthur and Captain Anderson, and cleared by the JCS, which included in the Five Power Staff Agency Thailand and the Philippines. Radford thinks that the Agency (which has hitherto been not disclosed in SEA) has really completed its military planning; that if it is enlarged by top level personnel, its actions will be necessarily open to the world; that therefore some Southeast Asian countries should be included in it, and he fears Eden's proposal as an intended delaying action.

The President approved the text of paragraph 1*b*, but suggested that Smith's reply to Eden's proposal should make clear the following:

1. Five Power Staff Agency, alone or with other nations, is not to the United States a satisfactory substitute for a broad political coalition which will include the Southeast Asian countries which are to be defended.

2. Five Power Staff Agency examination is acceptable to see how these nations can give military aid to the Southeast Asian countries in their cooperative defense effort.

3. The United States will not agree to a "white man's party" to determine the problems of the Southeast Asian nations.

I was instructed to advise Wilson and Radford of the above, and have done so.

2. The President went over the draft of the speech which Dulles is going to make tonight, making quite a few suggestions and changes in text. He thought additionally the speech should include some easy to understand slogans, such as "The U.S. will never start a war," "The U.S. will not go to war without Congressional authority," "The U.S., as always, is trying to organize cooperative efforts to sustain the peace."

3. With reference to the cease-fire proposal transmitted by Bidault to the French Cabinet, I read the following, as views principally of military members of the Planning Board, expressed in their yesterday afternoon meeting:

1. U.S. should not support the Bidault proposal.

2. Reasons for this position:

a. The mere proposal of the cease-fire at the Geneva Conference would destroy the will to fight of French forces and make fence-sitters jump to Vietminh side.

b. The Communists would evade covertly cease-fire controls.

3. The U.S. should (as a last act to save Indo-China) propose to France that if the following 5 conditions are met, the U.S. will go to Congress for authority to intervene with combat forces:

a. grant of genuine freedom for Associated States
b. U.S. take major responsibility for training indigenous forces
c. U.S. share responsibility for military planning
d. French forces to stay in the fight and no requirement of replacement by U.S. forces.
(*e.* Action under UN auspices?)

This offer to be made known simultaneously to the other members of the proposed regional grouping (U.K., Australia, N.Z., Thailand, Associated States, Philippines) in order to enlist their participation.

I then summarized possible objections to making the above proposal to the French:

a. No French Government is now competent to act in a lasting way.
b. There is no indication France wants to "internationalize" the conflict.
c. The U.S. proposal would be made without the prior assurance of a regional grouping of SEA States, a precondition of Congress; although this point might be added as another condition to the proposal.
d. U.S. would be "bailing out colonial France" in the eyes of the world.
e. U.S. cannot undertake *alone* to save every situation of trouble.

I concluded that some PB members felt that it had never been made clear to the French that the U.S. was willing to ask for Congressional authority, if certain fundamental preconditions were met; that these matters had only been hinted at, and that the record of history should be clear as to the U.S. position. Dulles was interested to know the President's views, because he is talking with Ambassador Bonnet this afternoon. He indicated that he would mention these matters to Bonnet, perhaps making a more broad hint than heretofore. He would not circulate any formal paper to Bonnet, or to anyone else.

The President referred to the proposition advanced by Governor Stassen at the April 29 Council Meeting as not having been thoroughly thought out. He said that he had been trying to get France to "internationalize" matters for a long time, and they are not willing to do so. If it were thought advisable at this time to point out to the French the essential preconditions to the U.S. asking for Congressional authority to intervene, then it should also be made clear to the French as an additional precondition that the U.S. would never intervene alone, that there must be an invitation by the indigenous people, and that there must be some kind of regional and collective action.

I understand that Dulles will decide the extent to which he cares to follow this line with Ambassador Bonnet. This discussion may afford Dulles guidance in replying to Smith's request about a U.S. alternative to support the Bidault proposal, but there really was no decision as to the U.S. attitude toward the cease-fire proposal itself.

[Document 45]

Excerpts from the First Plenary Session
The Geneva Conference
Indochina Phase
May 8, 1954

The French Proposals

". . . . The French Government is thus confident that it has done every-thing in its power to put an end to the conflict. Not only has it removed all reason for this conflict to exist by recognizing fully and unreservedly the in-dependence of Viet-Nam, Laos and Cambodia but, furthermore, the French Government has manifested for a long time its readiness and its desire of obtain-ing a reasonable settlement which would allow for the hostilities to be brought to an end. This is the main and primary task assigned to this Conference. . . .

"We propose that the Conference should, first of all, declare that it adopt the principle of a general cessation of hostilities in Indochina based upon the necessary guarantees of security. . . .

". . . . in agreeing upon the withdrawal of the invading forces and the restora-tion of the territorial integrity of those states. . . .

". . . . For France there is a Viet-Nam state of which the unity, territorial integrity and independence must be respected. . . .

". . . . the most just solution of the political problem can be found and finally assured only when the population is in a position to express in complete freedom its sovereign will by means of free elections. For the present moment I repeat the problem is that of bringing about a cessation of hostilities and the guaranteeing of that cessation. These guarantees, in our opinion, must be of two kinds.

". . . . the regular forces of the two parties would be brought together in clearly demarcated regrouping zones . . . . the implementation of the agree-ment should be placed under the supervision of international commissions. . . .

". . . . the agreement . . . . should be guaranteed in appropriate conditions by the states participating in the present Conference. . . .

". . . . The French proposal is as follows:

"I. *Vietnam*

1. All regular units to be assembled in assembly areas to be defined by the Conference on the basis of proposals by the Commanders-in-Chief.
2. All elements not belonging either to the army or to the police forces to be disarmed.
3. All prisoners of war and civil internees to be released immediately.
4. Execution of the above provisions to be supervised by international com-missions.
5. Hostilities to cease as soon as the agreement is signed. The assembly of troops and disarmament of forces as above provided to begin not later than x days (the number to be fixed by the Conference) after the signature of the agreement. . . .

"II. *Cambodia and Laos*

1. All regular and irregular Vietminh forces which have entered the country to be evacuated.
2. All elements which do not belong either to the army or to the police forces to be disarmed.
3. All prisoners of war and civil internees to be released immediately.
4. Execution of the above provisions to be supervised by international commissions.

"III. These agreements shall be guaranteed by the States participating in the Geneva Conference. In the event of any violation thereof there shall be an immediate consultation between the guarantor States for the purpose of taking appropriate measures either individually or collectively.

"This, Mr. President, is the proposal submitted to the Conference on the responsibility of the French Delegation and by that Delegation. Thank you, Sir. . . .

The Viet Minh Proposals

". . . . In the same spirit, expressing the sentiment of the three peoples of Vietnam, Khmer, and Pathet Lao, the delegation of the Democratic Republic of Viet Nam proposes to the conference that it invite the official representatives of the governments of resistance of Khmer and of the government of resistance of Pathet Lao to take part in its work. We submit this proposal having in mind the following:

". . . . the peoples of Khmer and Pathet Lao have liberated vast areas of their national territory. . . .

". . . . These governments represent the great majority of the people of Khmer and Lao, the aspirations of whom they symbolize. . . .

". . . . Alas, the delegation of the Democratic Republic of Viet Nam proposes to the conference that it adopt the following resolution:

> In view of the present situation of the countries of Indochina and in the interests of the thorough and objective examination of the question of the cessation of hostilities and the reestablishment of peace in Indochina, the conference recognizes the necessity to invite the representatives of the governments of resistance of Khmer and Pathet Lao to take part in the work of the conference in regard to the question of the reestablishment of peace in Indochina.

"Having submitted this proposal to the conference, I would ask the President of this meeting to authorize me to continue my statement when the conference has discussed the proposal that I have submitted. . . ."

The United States Proposal

"The United States proposes that any idea of inviting these nonexistent, so-called governments be rejected. . . .

The Red China Position

". . . . The delegation of the People's Republic of China fully supports the views of Mr. Pham van Dong. . . .

The Soviet Union Position

"In view of the aforesaid, the Soviet Delegation supports the proposal of the delegation of the Democratic Republic of Viet Nam to invite the delegates of the Democratic Governments of Pathet Lao and Khmer to take part in our conference. . . ."

[Document 46]

OFFICE OF THE ASSISTANT SECRETARY OF DEFENSE
WASHINGTON 25, D.C.

9 May 1954

INTERNATIONAL SECURITY AFFAIRS

MEMORANDUM FOR THE SECRETARY OF DEFENSE

SUBJECT: Future U.S. Action Regarding Indo-China

1. In light of the French having tabled an armistice proposal at Geneva, the United States must now decide whether:

   a. To intervene actively in the Indo-China war to redeem the situation.
   b. To exercise all feasible pressure to require the French Government to avoid all compromise at Geneva and to take increased effective military and political action against the Viet Minh in Indo-China. This appears realistically possible only if the decision to implement *a* above is also made.
   c. To adopt a passive policy toward the negotiations at Geneva while endeavoring to organize hastily a regional grouping, with U.S. participation, to hold what remains of Southeast Asia.

2. Decisions *a* plus *b* offer the only sure way to stop the Communist advance. They involve substantial risk of war with Red China and increased risk of general war. However, recognizing the steadily increasing Soviet capabilities in nuclear warfare and the consequent steady diminution of the present military advantage of the U.S. over the USSR, these increased risks can more surely and safely be accepted now than ever again.

3. Decision *c* would be a compromise involving clear possibilities for piecemeal advancement of Communist control over the balance of free Asia despite the best efforts of the U.S. to the contrary. The likelihood of further such advancement would be somewhat diminished if the U.S. made publicly clear that the further support by Moscow and Peiping of Communist aggression or subversion, as judged by the U.S., would entail direct military action by the U.S. against the source or sources of this support. However, it might be months or years before further subversion would enable such a U.S. judgment. By then the increased Soviet nuclear capability might well inhibit the U.S. Government from implementing its announced intention. Asia could thus be lost.

4. Therefore, it would appear that the U.S. Government must decide whether to take the steps necessary to contain Communism in Asia within Red China by intervention in Indo-China or accept the probable loss of Asia to Communism.

C. H. BONESTEEL, III
Brigadier General, United States Army
Defense Member, NSC Planning Board

[Document 47]

12 May 1954

SENT TO: AMCON GENEVA TOSEC 138

FOR THE UNDER SECRETARY FROM THE SECRETARY

BEGIN VERBATIM TEXT

The following basic instructions, which have been approved by the President, and which are in confirmation of those already given you orally, will guide you, as head of the United States Delegation, in your participation in the Indochina phase of the Geneva Conference.

1. The presence of a United States representative during the discussion at the Geneva Conference of "the problem of restoring peace in Indochina" rests on the Berlin Agreement of February 18, 1954. Under that agreement the US, UK, France, and USSR agreed that the four of them plus other interested states should be invited to a conference at Geneva on April 26 "for the purpose of reaching a peaceful settlement of the Korean question" and agreed further, that "the problem of restoring peace in Indochina" would also be discussed at Geneva by the four powers represented at Berlin, and Communist China and other interested states.

2. You will not deal with the delegates of the Chinese Communist regime, or any other regime not now diplomatically recognized by the United States, on any terms which imply political recognition or which concede to that regime any status other than that of a regime with which it is necessary to deal on a *de facto* basis in order to end aggression, or the threat of aggression, and to obtain peace.

3. The position of the United States in the Indochina phase of the Geneva Conference is that of an interested nation which, however, is neither a belligerent nor a principal in the negotiation.

4. The United States is participating in the Indochina phase of the Conference in order thereby to assist in arriving at decisions which will help the nations of that area peacefully to enjoy territorial integrity and political independence under stable and free governments with the opportunity to expand their economies, to realize their legitimate national aspirations, and to develop security through individual and collective defense against aggression, from within or without. This implies that these people should not be amalgamated into the Communist bloc of imperialistic dictatorship.

5. The United States is not prepared to give its express or implied approval to any cease-fire, armistice, or other settlement which would have the effect of subverting the existing lawful governments of the three aforementioned states or of permanently impairing their territorial integrity or of placing in jeopardy the forces of the French Union in Indochina, or which otherwise contravened the principles stated in (4) above.

6. You should, insofar as is compatible with these instructions, cooperate with the Delegation of France and with the Delegations of other friendly participants in this phase of the Conference.

7. If in your judgment continued participation in the Indochina phase of the Conference appears likely to involve the United States in a result inconsistent with its policy, as stated above, you should immediately so inform your Govern-

ment, recommending either a withdrawal or the limitation of the US role to that of an observer. If the situation develops such that, in your opinion, either of such actions is essential under the circumstances and time is lacking for consultation with Washington, you may act in your discretion.

8. You are authorized to inform other delegations at Geneva of these instructions.

DULLES

[Document 48]

19 May 1954

MEMORANDUM FOR: THE SECRETARY OF DEFENSE

SUBJECT: Indo-China

1. I am becoming increasingly concerned over the frequency of statements by individuals of influence within and without the government that United States air and sea forces alone could solve our problems in Indo-China, and equally so over the very evident lack of appreciation of the logistics factors affecting operations in that area.

2. Indo-China is almost totally devoid of local resources which would be of use to our Armed Forces. It has a tropical, monsoon climate with pronounced wet and dry seasons and the disease and morale hazards are high for Caucasian troops. The population, when not hostile, is untrustworthy. However, the principal deficiency of Indo-China as a base for the support of large military operations lies in the inadequacy of its facilities for the movement of supplies.

3. The two principal ports are Saigon and Haiphong, with a combined daily capacity of 15,100 short tons. Both are inland river ports requiring considerable dredging before maximum potential can be obtained. There are nine secondary ports whose tonnage capacities vary from 100 to 1,400 tons.

4. Because of the inadequacies of the road, railroad, and waterway systems north from Saigon, this port would be of very little use for the support of operations in the Tonkin Delta. Haiphong could not be used without augmentation of its capacity including full use of secondary ports and all beaches. The tonnage capacity of the road and railroad system from Haiphong to Hanoi is even now less than the port capacity of Haiphong.

5. It would be necessary to make full use of the air for supply and evacuation as well as for tactical support. Much construction, to include lengthening and reinforcing of runways, of extreme difficulty during the rainy season, would be necessary. Only three airfields in Indo-China, Haiphong/Cat Bi, Tourane and Tan Sou Nhut (near Saigon) have runways over 7,500 feet long and have reported pavement strengths which could support B-45 bomber operations. Eight fields can handle transport planes as large as a C-119; an additional seven fields can accommodate C-46's. Sustained operations could not be undertaken on most of these fields in the rainy season. Within the Delta itself, there are ten airfields of all types of which only one, Cat Bi, is currently being used by C-119's or C-54's.

6. Even were it decided to limit the employment of United States forces to naval and air, which in itself would be a basically faulty military decision, it would devolve upon the Army to perform the bulk of the logistical services and it is essential that the magnitude of the effort required be clearly understood.

7. The adverse conditions prevalent in this area combine all those which confronted United States forces in previous campaigns in the South and Southwest Pacific and Eastern Asia, with the additional grave complication of a large native population, in thousands of villages, most of which are about evenly divided between friendly and hostile.

8. The complex nature of these problems would require a major United States logistical effort. It explodes the myth that air and sea forces could solve the Indo-China problems. If United States land-based forces are projected any appreciable distance inland, as would be essential, they would require constant local security at their every location, and for their every activity. The Army would have to provide these forces, their total would be very large, and the time to provide them would be extensive.

ROBERT T. STEVENS
Secretary of the Army

[Document 49]

21 May 1954

MEMORANDUM FOR THE SECRETARY OF DEFENSE

Subject: Defense of Southeast Asia in the Event
of Loss of Indochina to the Communists

1. As a result of recent military and political developments, including certain public statements by high-level officials of the United States, the Joint Chiefs of Staff consider that it is incumbent upon them to determine what military forces and resources would be required to hold Southeast Asia against further Communist aggression in the event Indochina is lost to the Communists.

2. Currently approved United States Government objectives regarding Southeast Asia are based on the considerations that:

a. The passing of the countries of Southeast Asia into the Communist orbit would be inimical to the security interests of the United States, and

b. The loss of Indochina to the Communist orbit could lead to the eventual loss of the other countries of Southeast Asia to the Communist orbit.

3. In the event that Indochina is lost to the Communists, the United States must take as an objective the prevention of the loss of the rest of Southeast Asia (Thailand, Burma, and Malaya) to the Communists.

4. There are two basic military concepts for the defense of Southeast Asia:

a. Static type defense (Korea type).

b. An offensive to attack the source of Communist military power being applied in Southeast Asia.

5. The force requirements and inherent logistic implications for a "static" defense of the remaining countries of Southeast Asia—Burma, Thailand, and Malaya are of the order of magnitude as shown in Appendices "A" and "B" hereto. So long as Burma and Thailand are not under Communist control, the geography of the area and the lack of a Chinese Communist capability for a major overseas attack renders Malaya secure from external attack. Therefore,

the force requirements are limited to those necessary to defend Burma and Thailand and to provide internal security against infiltration and subversion in Malaya. Should Burma and Thailand be lost, to the Communists prior to an Allied decision to hold a line in Southeast Asia, the defensive position would have to be established in Malaya.

6. A study of the above requirements and implications reveals the following extensive and damaging weaknesses inherent in this concept:

> *a.* It is estimated that it would take a minimum of 12 months to build up the necessary base complex and facilities required to support the forces indicated.
>
> *b.* These forces would have to remain for an extended period.
>
> *c.* The commitment in manpower and material incident to maintaining these forces in Southeast Asia for such a period would be unacceptable from the overall viewpoint.
>
> *d.* The presence of large numbers of United States Commonwealth, and French troops in this area would provide a basis for Communist propaganda to develop and intensify anti-Western sentiment.
>
> *e.* The dissipation of allied strength through the commitment of forces of this magnitude to a "static" defense of Southeast Asia would contribute to the realization of the politico-military objectives of the USSR vis-a-vis the free world.
>
> *f.* Execution of static defense plan would result in maldeployment and seriously reduce the flexibility of employment of United States forces. This could seriously jeopardize the United States capability of supporting logistically our present war plans.

7. In view of the foregoing, the Joint Chiefs of Staff consider that from the military viewpoint the concept of a static-type defense is unsound.

8. In stating certain implementing actions to the current military posture of the United States, the Joint Chiefs of Staff stated *inter alia:*

> Certain other countries such as Indochina, to which the United States has no specific commitment, are of such importance to the United States that an attack on them probably would compel the United States to react with military force either locally at the point of attack or generally against the military power of the aggressor.

It is considered that the rest of the Southeast Asian countries are included in the above category.

9. In view of the above, the United States should adopt the concept of offensive actions against the "military power of the aggressor," in this instance Communist China, rather than the concept of "reaction locally at the point of attack," which is the thesis of the action outlined in paragraphs 5 and 6 above.

10. The force requirements and the logistic support for the operations envisaged in paragraph 9 above are being considered but have not been fully developed. However, it is felt that adoption of this concept would provide a more acceptable return for the manpower and resources expended than would be the case in the concept of a static defense.

11. Upon the decision to implement either one or the other of these courses of action, it would be necessary to insure the degree of mobilization required to take care of the increased possibility of a general war.

> For the Joint Chiefs of Staff:
> ARTHUR RADFORD,
> Chairman,
> Joint Chiefs of Staff

[Document 50]

26 May 1954

MEMORANDUM FOR THE SECRETARY OF DEFENSE

Subject: Studies with Respect to Possible U.S.
Action Regarding Indochina

1. Reference is made to the memorandum by the Acting Secretary of Defense, dated 18 May 1954, subject as above, wherein the Joint Chiefs of Staff were requested to prepare certain studies, and agreed outline answers to certain questions relating thereto, for discussion with the Acting Secretary of Defense on or before 24 May, and for subsequent submission to the National Security Council (NSC).

2. *a.* The studies requested by the Acting Secretary of Defense were developed within the parameters prescribed in the memorandum by the Executive Secretary, NSC, dated 18 May 1954, subject as above. This memorandum is interpreted as assuming no concurrent involvement in Korea. This assumption may be quite unrealistic and lead to malemployment of available forces. The Joint Chiefs of Staff desire to point out their belief that, from the point of view of the United States, with reference to the Far East as a whole, *Indochina is devoid of decisive military objectives and the allocation of more than token U.S. armed forces in Indochina would be a serious diversion* of limited U.S. capabilities. The principal sources of Viet Minh military supply lie outside Indochina. The destruction or neutralization of these sources in China proper would materially reduce the French military problems in Indochina.

b. In connection with the above, it may be readily anticipated that, upon Chinese Communist intervention in Indochina, the French would promptly request the immediate deployment of U.S. ground and air forces, additional naval forces, and a considerable increase in MDAF armament and equipment. The Joint Chiefs of Staff have stated their belief that committing to the Indochina conflict naval forces in excess of a Fast Carrier Task Force and supporting forces, as necessary in accordance with the developments in the situation, of basing substantial air forces in Indochina, will involve maldeployment of forces and reduce readiness to meet probable Chinese Communist reaction elsewhere in the Far East. Simultaneously, it is necessary to keep in mind the considerable Allied military potential available in the Korea-Japan-Okinawa area.

c. In light of the above, it is clear that the denial of these forces to Indochina could result in a schism between the United States and France unless they were employed elsewhere. However, it should be noted that the Joint Chiefs of Staff have plans, both approved and under consideration, which provide for the employment of these forces in combat operations outside Indochina. Nevertheless, it is desired to repeat that this particular report is responsive to the question of U.S. intervention in Indochina only.

ASSUMING THE CHINESE COMMUNISTS INTERVENE

3. *Strategic Concept and Plan of Operation*

Seek to create conditions through the destruction of effective Communist forces and their means for support in the Indochina action and by reducing Chinese Communist capability for further aggression, under which Associated States forces could assume responsibility for the defense of Indochina. In the light of this concept the major courses of action would be as follows:

a. Employing atomic weapons, whenever advantageous, as well as other weapons, *conduct offensive air* operations against *selected military targets in Indochina and against* those *military targets in China, Hainan,* and other Communist-held offshore islands which are being used by the Communists in *direct support of their operations,* or which threaten the security of U.S. and allied forces in the area.

b. Simultaneously, French Union Forces, augmented by U.S. naval and air forces, would exploit by coordinated ground, naval, and air action such successes as may be gained as a result of the aforementioned air operations in order to destroy enemy forces in Indochina.

c. Conduct coordinated ground, naval, and air action to destroy enemy forces in Indochina.

d. In the light of circumstances prevailing at the time, and subject to an evaluation of the results of operations conducted under subparagraphs *a* and *b* above, be prepared to take further action against Communist China to reduce its war-making capability, such as:

(1) Destruction of additional selected military targets. In connection with these additional targets, such action requires an enlarged but highly selective atomic offensive in addition to attacks employing other weapons systems.

(2) Blockade of the China coast. This might be instituted progressively from the outset.

(3) Seizure or neutralization of Hainan Island.

(4) Operations against the Chinese mainland by Chinese Nationalist forces.

4. *Forces Required of Each Nation Participating*

The forces which would be employed under current plans during the initial phases of the above operations are those indicated in the Appendix hereto. The duration of the commitment of these forces would depend on the success of French Union forces operations supported by U.S. naval and air operations in defeating communist forces in Indochina.

5. Normal Service logistic arrangement for United States Forces would prevail. CINCPAC would be responsible for providing logistic support. CINCFE would assist by providing material and logistic support as mutually agreed with

CINCPAC, or as directed by the Joint Chiefs of Staff. The facilities of MATS and MSTS would be made available to CINCPAC as directed. Existing U.S. bases in Western Pacific are available. Bases with limited facilities in Indochina and the Philippines (other than U.S.) would be available. Effort would be made to obtain or utilize bases on Formosa, if required. The French would provide their own logistic support within capabilities. United States logistical support of French Union Forces and Associated States would be provided as required. The Military Assistance Advisory Group, Indochina, would coordinate and arrange for utilization of facilities and services and would provide logistic support to the United States Liaison Groups and Training Missions. In the event operations should involve the use of NORC Forces, United States logistic support above the current NORC MDA Program would be provided.

6. *Plan for Command Structure*

In accordance with the Unified Command Plan, CINCPAC would exercise unified command of assigned forces. He would insure the coordination of all operations in Southeast Asia and provide for the necessary ground-air coordination between French Union Forces and U.S. Navy and Air Force forces which operate in support of the land battle. In addition, CINCPAC would select targets and conduct air operations with assigned forces against military targets in Indochina and those in China which directly support Chinese Communist aggression. COMSAC would support CINCPAC in these operations, and in addition would conduct air operations to further reduce the Chinese Communists war-making capability, as directed by the Joint Chiefs of Staff. CINCFE will continue to provide for the security of Japan and the Ryukyus in accordance with his priority mission and in addition would support CINCPAC and COMSAC in their operations as agreed mutually.

7. *Plan for Training Native Troops*

For the United States to initiate training of Associated States Forces, it is estimated that approximately 2,270 U.S. personnel would be required, as an augmentation of the existing Military Assistance Advisory Group, to carry out this program. In addition, U.S. personnel would be required to provide appropriate logistic support. The exact size and composition of the training mission, the logistic support requirements, and the security requirements and arrangements will be determined in light of recommendations which have been requested from CINCPAC and the Chief, MAAG, Indochina. The training of Associated States Forces would be patterned after the training program conducted for RCK forces in Korea.

8. *Plan for World-Wide Military Aid*

The Joint Chiefs of Staff consider that action should be taken to insure appropriate degree of mobilization to provide for the greater risk of a general war and be prudently prepared under this alternate assumption. In view of the increased risk of general war involving the Soviet Bloc, immediate action would have to be taken to strengthen our allies. However, due to the overriding mobilization requirements for U.S. forces, such aid would be limited to those allies who could directly support the U.S. strategic concept for general war. This aid would further be limited to combat essential material, essential replacements, and spare parts which are beyond the capabilities of the individual countries to provide from their own or other allied resources.

ASSUMING THE CHINESE COMMUNISTS DO NOT INTERVENE

9. *Strategic Concept and Plan of Action*

Seek to create conditions by destroying effective Communist forces in Indochina, under which the Associated States Forces could assume responsibility for the defense of Indochina. In the light of this concept, the major courses of action which would be undertaken are as follows:

> *a. Conduct air operations* in support of allied forces in *Indochina.* The employment of atomic weapons is contemplated in the event that such course appears militarily advantageous.
> *b.* Simultaneously, French Union Forces augmented by such armed forces of the Philippines and Thailand as may be committed would, in coordination with U.S. naval and Air Force forces, conduct coordinated ground, naval and air action to destroy enemy forces in Indochina.

10. *Forces Required of Each Nation Participating*

The forces which would be employed under current plans during the initial phases of the above operation would include:

> *a.* French Union Forces currently operating in Indochina.
> *b.* A U.S. Fast Carrier Task Force and supporting forces as necessary in accordance with developments in the situation.
> *c.* U.S. Air Force units operating from present bases outside Indochina as required.
> *d.* Forces as may be contributed by other friendly nations.

The duration of commitment of these forces cannot be determined at this time.

11. *Plan for Logistic Support*

The plan for logistic support would be the same under this assumption as under the assumption that Chinese Communists intervene (see paragraph 5 above)—except for the last sentence of paragraph 5.

12. *Plan for Command Structure*

Although the Allied Commander in Chief in Indochina should be French, there must be a United States Deputy with sufficient staff assistance to provide liaison with the French and coordinate U.S. activities with the over-all operation. CINCPAC would exercise command over all U.S. forces based in Indochina and other forces assigned to him for operations in Indochina. In addition, a U.S. Air Advisor would be provided the French Commander in Chief for the purpose of advising him concerning the air effort. This officer would have no command responsibilities but would be under the direction of the U.S. Deputy.

13. *Plan for Training Native Troops*

The plan for training native troops would be the same under this assumption as under the assumption that Chinese Communists intervene (see paragraph 7 above).

14. *Plan for World-Wide Military Aid*

a. Initially, there would be no requirement for additional material and equipment over and above current IDAP for the French and other allied forces in Indochina. MDA programs, however, would require augmentation within approximately 6 months to provide equipment and support necessary to equip initially and maintain a total of 3 new ROK-equivalent Associated States' divisions. Thereafter, increased MDA programs would be required to support additional Associated States' divisions as developed. The maximum number of such divisions probably would not exceed 20.

b. All other military assistance should proceed as currently programmed.

c. Current programs for equipping and modernizing U.S. forces must not be curtailed as a result of any of the foregoing.

METHOD OF FINANCING COMBAT OPERATIONS

15. Whether or not the U.S. intervenes in Indochina, the Joint Chiefs of Staff consider that it is vital that the war in Indochina be financed by a method separate and distinct from the world-wide MDAP. It is imperative that the commander be provided with the necessary equipment to wage war effectively without the financial and legal restrictions imposed by MDAP procedures. The current practice of diverting MDA funds from approved programs to support emergency requirements such as those resulting from combat operations in Indochina has already had the effect of hindering the attainment of our world-wide strategic objectives. Only by divorcing the fluid requirements which exist in local combat situations from the normal MDA programming methods and procedures can the orderly achievement of our objectives in other world areas be achieved.

For the Joint Chiefs of Staff:
ARTHUR RADFORD,
Chairman
Joint Chiefs of Staff

[Document 51]

May 26, 1954

MEMORANDUM FOR THE SECRETARY OF DEFENSE

1. I wish to acknowledge the receipt of your memorandum, May 25, 1954, subject: "Defense of Southeast Asia in the Event of Loss of Indochina to the Communists," with an attached memorandum to you from the Joint Chiefs of Staff, dated May 21, 1954, same subject.

2. Your memorandum indicates that the paper of the Joint Chiefs of Staff deals with the military defense of the rest of Southeast Asia, if Indochina is lost,

"against an overt Chinese Communist attack" (although these specific words are not used in the paper). Given this clarification, the paper takes the position, in the event of overt Chinese Communist attack, that a static-type defense is militarily unsound and that the proper concept is an offensive against Communist China.

3. It is clear in the current policy of the United States towards Southeast Asia that, in the event of "overt Chinese Communist attack" against Burma, Thailand, or Malaya, the United States will "take appropriate military action against Communist China" (Paragraphs 42, 46, and 48, NSC 5405) rather than employ a static-type defense.

4. In view of this existing policy, the Joint Chiefs' paper does not appear to involve a new policy issue necessarily requiring its circulation to the members of the National Security Council at the present time. On the other hand, if you feel that it would be desirable to circulate the paper on a limited basis, with an appropriate explanatory note as above, I shall be very glad to do so.

ROBERT CUTLER
Special Assistant
to the President

[Document 52]

FROM: Paris

TO: Secretary of State

NO: 4566, May 27, 6 p.m.

SENT DEPARTMENT 4566, REPEATED INFORMATION GENEVA 305, SAIGON 550.

EYES ONLY SECRETARY; GENEVA EYES ONLY UNDER SECRETARY; SAIGON EYES ONLY CHARGE

PASS DEFENSE FOR DEPARTMENT ARMY FOR RIDGWAY

THIS IS JOINT EMBASSY-TRAPNELL MESSAGE

After arriving Paris, Trapnell called first on Ambassador for general background discussion and subsequently on General Gruenther for same purpose. He was originally scheduled to call on Laniel May 28 before seeing Ely but because of Prime Minister's preoccupation with Cabinet meetings and other urgent business meeting was postponed. Trapnell accompanied by Ambassador seeing Laniel at latter's home tomorrow morning. Meanwhile Laniel suggested that Trapnell make direct contact with Ely. This was done this morning when Trapnell, accompanied by Embassy Officer, had hour and half interview with Ely, accompanied by Colonel Brohan.

As conversation opened, it became apparent that Ely was not fully aware of reason behind Trapnell's presence in Paris. After this was explained Ely launched into a general review of the Indochina situation giving particular emphasis to following points:

1. He recounted content of talks he had had in Indochina with O'Daniel. He was agreeable to principle of American instruction Vietnamese forces but not

entirely in accord with O'Daniel's proposal that national army be reorganized on divisional basis. He believed that divisional units were perhaps too weighty and that lighter units of perhaps 6, 7 or 8 battalions per division were more practicable. Yet, he did not wish to press this point as he regarded it as a detail which could be worked out subsequently. He pointed out that if O'Daniel's concept was followed and US instructor-advisers remained with units upon completion of training, they would have to accompany units into battle and, therefore, major question of whether US prepared to participate in combat operations would arise. Only alternate to this would be replacement of US instructor-advisers by French as units were prepared to enter combat. This would be unsatisfactory because training and advising methods of French and Americans were dissimilar.

2. Ely stated that O'Daniel had presented an operational plan for continuing the war but that he found it unrealistic on basis that it gave priority to operations in the south while the principal and immediate threat is in the north.

3. Ely referred to increasing frequency of American criticism of French conduct of war. He explained that it was easy to criticize post facto and when things went wrong. As Trapnell knew, the war in Indochina was of a very special nature and it was unfair for people who perhaps didn't understand this fact as well as he and Trapnell to criticize. It was useless to compare the wars in Korea and Indochina; they were entirely different. He hoped that Trapnell could use his influence to reduce the degree of present US criticism of past and present French performance in Indochina in the interests of good Franco–American working relations in the important joint tasks at hand.

4. At about this stage of the conversation, Ely remarked that it was virtually impossible to discuss specific military questions in Indochina without getting into the major political questions including the possibility of US intervention, the prospects for a Pacific pact and the whole question of where the defense of Southeast Asia was to take place and by whom. Trapnell referred to his terms of reference which prevented him from discussing other than specific military questions, particularly that of the regrouping of existing forces in Indochina for the defense of the Delta.

5. When Trapnell asked Ely what the immediate military prospects were in the Delta, he replied that the five Viet Minh divisions released from Dien Bien Phu were moving rapidly forward and should be at the Delta perimeter between the 10th and 15th of June. Normally at that season they would return to their regrouping areas for rest, "self-criticism" and general revision. Whether they will do so this year or not is still uncertain, although there are indications at the moment that some Viet Minh forces are moving to regrouping areas.

6. When Trapnell asked what Ely was doing to regroup his forces for the defense of the Delta he replied two basic things: First, removing units from pacification and other static missions to the Delta to become part of mobile defense groups; secondly, he was recovering units from inactive posts in Laos, Central Annam and other areas for transfer to the Delta to become part of these same mobile forces.

7. Ely's plan for the defense of the Delta centers around the defense of what he termed the Hanoi–Haiphong axis. No specific detail was given as to the number of units, where they were to be retained, or the exact area to be defended. He was particularly and, no doubt, designedly pessimistic on the aspects for the defense of this axis, stating that if Hanoi had to be surrendered French Union Forces would move to Haiphong, and if Haiphong were lost they would at least be able to move out from there to "possibly another stand in the south." This,

too, depended entirely, according to Ely, on what was decided about US intervention and other pending high-level political decisions.

8. Trapnell pointed out that French superiority in aviation and armor could be extremely effective against a Viet Minh coordinated attack in the Delta because of the terrain. Ely not only admitted this fact but stated that it "is our trump card."

9. When Trapnell pressed Ely for an opinion as to what was required between the period of the immediate threat and the period when, it was hoped, the Vietnamese army would be on an effective footing, Ely replied that the General was obviously thinking of how many US Marines would be required to assure the defense of the Delta. He went on to say that in his opinion, of one or two US Marine divisions intervened "there would be no problem."

Comment: The conversation was largely unsatisfactory from our standpoint because our efforts to obtain specific commitments from Ely, including any statement regarding French intentions concerning despatch of reinforcements from metropolitan France and North Africa to Indochina, were unsuccessful. Nor did Ely appear particularly interested in Trapnell's recommendations concerning the redeployment of forces. We attribute this to the fact that Ely is still busily engaged in consultations with the Prime Minister, Pleven, and the High Council of National Defense, and was probably being very careful not to make any commitments which had not yet been cleared by the government. He was aware that Trapnell is seeing Laniel tomorrow morning with the Ambassador, at which time more specific matters may be discussed. In the meanwhile, Ely requested that Trapnell continue his conversations with Colonel Brohan for the time being and that, of course, Ely would be seeing Trapnell again after the interview with Laniel.

DILLON

[Document 53]

June 7, 1954

SENT TO: Amconsulate Geneva TEDUL 171

EYES ONLY AMBASSADORS

RE SECTO 389.

Defense Dept reports that five-power military conference at its plenary session of June 4, under chairmanship General Valluy, amended and approved Conference Study No. I: "Intelligence Survey of Military Situation in SEA Area."

In connection with review of intelligence survey, Gen Valluy presented his own evaluation military situation Tonkin Delta as follows:

1. If Tonkin is lost, military line will not rpt not be reestablished anywhere.

2. Anyone can find on map a line with tactical characteristics which theoretically should permit reestablishment, such as Laos bottleneck or eighteenth parallel, but Valluy said he could affirm there would be no forces to man this line.

3. Valluy said he was not rpt not speaking of French forces in this connection but meant to indicate that there were no rpt no southern Vietnamese who could oppose northern Vietnamese.

4. Ho Chi Minh's objective is Tonkin, to be attained either by negotiation at Geneva or by assault on Hanoi.

5. Ho Chi Minh wishes to entangle us in negotiations by admitting now, for first time, that there is a Communist northern state and a non-Communist southern state and saying that both might be incorporated in French Union.

6. What Ho Chi Minh seeks is Tonkin and its political capital Hanoi from which he was driven in 1946. He wishes obtain Tonkin either by negotiation (Valluy admitted "among military men" that Ho Chi Minh finds across negotiating table receptive French ears) or by military action. To prepare for such action, he is drawing out negotiations to gain time for his battle corps to be in position and ready, if action is called for.

7. In course of negotiating toward a ceasefire (which is demanded by French public opinion) concept of partition appears, as Ho Chi Minh wants occupy all Tonkin. If conditions are too hard and talks are broken off he will strive to obtain Tonkin by force. In such a military action his chances of success are good.

8. It has been said at this Conference that if Tonkin is lost we will fight in south. However French will not rpt not fight nor will Vietnam. To man line in south, conferees will have to provide own men. Moreover it will be an artificial line for defense of which Laos, Cambodia and Thailand can do nothing.

9. Decisive point in military conference is this: if other conferees do not rpt not underwrite today's battle for Tonkin, tomorrow they will fight without French in Saigon and Bangkok. Valluy said he could affirm that if Tonkin were lost, no Vietnamese would fight against other Vietnamese, and sooner or later (probably sooner) the whole of Vietnam will become Communist.

10. Valluy said he did not rpt not mean to dramatize but only to be realistic among soldiers. Truth cannot be disguised. Each of allies has share of responsibility and if battle for Tonkin is lost, allies will have to fight alone on actual main line of resistance much farther away.

Admiral Carney remarked that Gen Valluy's appraisal was of interest and important to all conferees and suggested it might be put in writing and appended to intelligence survey as representing unilateral views of one representative. End Defense Dept summary.

Foregoing for your own info only. Valluy was speaking in confidence and as an individual. Your comments requested.

DULLES

[Document 54]

FROM: Geneva

TO: Secretary of State

NO: DULTE 164, June 9, 10 p.m.

EYES ONLY SECRETARY

I had a long talk with Eden this morning. He said that we are clearly coming to end here on Indochina. Three major issues have emerged on which we cannot compromise and on which Communists show no intention of receding. These are (1) separate treatment of Laos and Cambodia, which are clearly victims of Viet Minh aggression; (2) status and powers of impartial international supervisory authority; and (3) composition of international supervisory authority.

He is convinced that we can get no further on these issues and should break within next few days. While he feels no useful negotiating purpose would be served, he is inclined to think that for public opinion it would be desirable that he privately see Molotov once more before a break in order to make clear to Molotov firmness our position and obtain Communist position. He is hopeful of forcing Molotov into public rejection Colombo powers for supervisory organization. This will have very beneficial effects in south and southeast Asia I pointed out, and he agreed, that French situation is such that we would probably have to leave the French and Viet Minh military officers here talking about zones in Vietnam.

Immediately following break he feels Cambodia and Laos should put their cases to the UN entirely divorced from Thailand request. (I gathered that he was thinking of something more than just a POC.) He thinks it highly important that they move rapidly after the conference is wound up, but equally important until that time there be no hints or press leaks whatever that such action is contemplated. He feels that if properly handled and appeals are spontaneous on their part, with no implication of US–UK initiative or prodding, they will receive general Asian support. I pointed out, and he agreed, that France might oppose but we should go ahead anyway. In meanwhile he feels very strongly we must not now complicate matter by insisting on broadening Thailand appeal to Laos and Cambodia. He rightly points out that language in Security Council draft resolution is largely academic, as it will in any event be voted. Resolution can be written any way that appears desirable at the time matter comes before General Assembly. He said he would send instructions to Dixon to try to work out with Lodge some language that would meet his point, while not necessarily precluding POC operations outside Thailand. I am sending separate telegram repeated to USUN replying to your TOSEC 378 giving only latter part this paragraph.

Eden said he had not yet put to cabinet his ideas with regard to UN appeal by Cambodia and Laos, and therefore asked that the matter be treated with strictest secrecy.

Eden also said he was considering recommendation reduce strength of Commonwealth division in Korea by about half or one brigade in order to reinforce Malaya. If things eased up in Egypt, he was also hopeful that forces could be spared from there for Malaya. I told him that in view of more critical situation in southeast Asia and our ability within the armistice to train and equip ROK forces as replacements, I thought we would have no objection.

Clear that Eden now considers negotiations here have failed. Believe he is prepared to move ahead quickly in southeast Asia coalition which would guarantee Cambodia and most of Laos under umbrella of some UN action with respect to those two countries. He expects active cooperation from Burma, and hopes for benevolent neutrality from India. He apparently does not feel much can be salvaged in Vietnam.

As you know, Bidault is not here and we will not know where French stand until Assembly debate completed, if then. If French continue negotiations, point will probably arrive shortly when deteriorating military situation will force them accept simple cease-fire in attempt temporarily salvage something. Therefore one question we may shortly face is what we and UK do if France insists on continuing negotiations somewhat longer. It is one thing to withdraw if France negotiates an agreement with which we cannot publicly associate ourselves, and another to withdraw prior to that time.

Eden's tactics recommend themselves very strongly to me.

Chauvel spoke to me after the above was dictated. In Bidault's absence he and others have been considering recommending to Bidault that France and three Associated States together make appeal to UN. He had reports from Valluy, part of which he read to me. He is obviously convinced that things will go badly in Delta. I made no comment except to suggest that Laos and Cambodia commanded a certain sympathy in Asia and Middle East which France plus Vietnam did not. I asked him categorically if France wanted to internationalize on conditions we had tabled some time ago, saying neither you nor I knew where France stood. He replied that he did not know:—that "Bidault still hoped to get something here".

I would appreciate your thoughts and guidance.

With respect Korea, Eden indicated he would probably speak next plenary (which we plan for Friday or Saturday). He would not be adverse to making this last session on Korea. However, not all of sixteen are yet prepared to do this. I do not know whether we will be able get them lined up. If not, one more plenary may be necessary.

SMITH

[Document 55]

FROM: Saigon

TO: Secretary of State

NO: 2714, June 10, 2 p.m.

SENT DEPARTMENT 2714, REPEATED INFORMATION PARIS 967, GENEVA 214.

PARIS FOR AMBASSADOR.

GENEVA FOR UNDER SECRETARY.

General Valluy's appreciation of the situation as set out Department telegram 2527, sent Geneva TEDUL 171, repeated Paris 4448 is exceedingly good—in fact almost too good. Although there are one or two points to which we might take exception from purely military aspect, I desire to confine my comment to political connotations of Valluy's statement. I have impression that under instructions he made this very concise evaluation less with military considerations in mind than with political objectives in view. I think that Valluy was looking as much at the French Parliament as he was at the Tonkin delta when he made his speech. General Ely has twice in my presence stated that his keenest desire is for United States to enter this war. Only yesterday his Chief of Staff, Colonel Brohan, repeated this comment. My belief is that purpose of Valluy statement was either to bring us and, if possible, other five powers into conflict here or, failing that, to prepare excuse before history for an impending armistice which French would then request of Viet Minh.

MC CLINTOCK

[Document 56]

FROM: Paris

TO: Secretary of State

NO: 4841, June 14, 5 p.m.

SENT DEPARTMENT 4841; REPEATED INFORMATION GENEVA 393.

DEPARTMENT EYES ONLY SECRETARY

GENEVA EYES ONLY UNDER SECRETARY

1. In all probability one of first acts of any new French Government will be request precise statement immediate and future US intentions regarding military intervention Indochina.

2. During past week, I have gathered the very definite impression that because of (A) our reluctance to send ground forces to Indochina; (B) deterioration of military and political situation in Indochina during last month; (C) extreme reluctance, if not refusal, of ANZUS partners to consider joining US in any military intervention in Delta area, the chances of US responding favorably to French request for military assistance even after they have met all conditions are approximately nil.

3. Hardening of Communist position in Geneva as indicated by Molotov and Chou En-lai last week would seem to indicate that Communists no longer fear possibility of US military intervention in Indochina provided there is no overt Chinese attack. It would seem, therefore, that Viet Minh and Chinese will not accept any armistice which does not clearly pave the way for Communist takeover in Indochina.

4. Lacking the possibility of US military support, it would seem to be only a question of time, weeks or a few months at very most, before French are forced to accept Viet Minh terms. In the meantime, there is the constant risk of an all-out assault on the Delta which could lead to a serious French reverse, if not total annihilation of expeditionary corps in Tonkin.

I have continually pointed out that such a reverse might have a disastrous effect on French public opinion. Today I am more certain than ever that such would be the case. Rightly or wrongly, US would be blamed by French public opinion for having built up French hopes of intervention and then for having failed in the crisis. The result could well be a neutralist government in France that would reduce French military commitments to NATO and would, at the same time, be completely intransigeant on question of German rearmament. Such a government would also, in all probability, make a strong effort to strengthen relations with the Soviet Union and to recreate the wartime Franco–USSR alliance in order to prevent German rearmament.

From this distance, I cannot judge what the effect of such French actions would be on American public opinion and particularly on our Congress, but I suspect that it might lead to an irresistible demand for the recall of some, if not all, of our troops from Europe, which, in effect, would mean the end of the North Atlantic Alliance followed eventually by the isolation of the Western Hemisphere.

5. In view of these very serious and grave dangers which we will run if we allow the French to be defeated militarily in the Delta, and if my assumption in paragraph 2 above is correct, I recommend that you give serious consideration to promptly informing the French that because of either (A) the deterioration of the military situation in Indochina or (B) the reluctance of the ANZUS powers to take action, or both, the President is no longer prepared to request military intervention from the Congress even if the French should now fully meet our conditions. While such action on our part would hasten what now appears to be the inevitable loss of Vietnam and might cause a certain additional temporary loss of face for the US, it would put the French on notice that they should promptly accept the Viet Minh armistice terms and thus would save the French Expeditionary Corps from possible military disaster. In the event of a withdrawal from Indochina under such circumstances, I would not forsee any serious or long term repercussions on France's position in the North Atlantic Alliance. If we allow the French to continue to fight in the false hope that in the event of a crisis in the Delta, they may get US military assistance, the best we can hope for is to delay the Communist conquest of Vietnam by a few months, while we risk the very existence of the North Atlantic Alliance.

From my viewpoint here in Paris, the possibility of a few months delay in the Communist takeover of Indochina does not seem at all commensurate with the risk of the possible collapse of the defense of Western Europe.

6. While I have several times made it clear, both to Laniel and Maurice Schumann, that, as indicated in paragraph 8 of your TEDUL 185 from San Francisco, our decision would have to be made in the light of "conditions at the time"; this is not at all clear to French public opinion and is not even very clear to Schumann himself, as he has no means of knowing how we will judge "the conditions at the time". Therefore, what I am in effect recommending is that we adopt your suggestion contained in paragraph 8 of TEDUL 185 of putting a time limit on our intervention offer with the additional proviso that I would suggest that the time limit be now.

DILLON

[Document 57]

June 14, 1954

SENT TO: Amconsul GENEVA PRIORITY TEDUL 197

Re DULTE 174

Department is giving this thorough consideration with Defense. My personal opinion is that we should try to carry situation along with avoidance of either formal refusal now train Vietnamese and also without anything like a massive commitment of some two to three thousand MAAG personnel which under present conditions could not but carry strong political overtones and might raise Congressional complications.

With reference to your last paragraph suggestion on QTE expedite conclusion of final agreement with French UNQTE this is quite impossible so long as French have not made up their mind whether or not they want to internationalize war and now are further from internationalizing it than ever before. They want, and in effect have, an option on our intervention but they do not want to exercise it and the date of expiry of our option is fast running out.

DULLES

[Document 58]

June 14, 1954

SENT TO: Amembassy PARIS 4579 PRIORITY

EYES ONLY FOR AMBASSADOR AND UNDER SECRETARY FROM SECRETARY

FYI

It is true that there is less disposition now than two months or one month ago to intervene in Indochina militarily. This is the inevitable result of the steady deterioration in Indochina which makes the problem of intervention and pacification more and more difficult. When united defense was first broached, the strength and morale of French and Vietnam forces were such that it seemed that the situation could be held without any great pouring-in of U.S. ground forces. Now all the evidence is that the morale of the Vietnamese Government, armed forces and civilians has deteriorated gravely; the French are forced to contemplate a fall-back which would leave virtually the entire Tonkin Delta population in hostile hands and the Saigon area is faced with political disintegration.

What has happened has been what was forecast, as for example by my Embassy Paris 4117 TEDUL 78 of May 17. I there pointed out that probably the French did not really want intervention but wanted to have the possibility as a card to play at Geneva. I pointed out that the Geneva game would doubtless be a long game and that it could not be assumed that at the end the present U.S. position regarding intervention would necessarily exist after the Communists had succeeded in dragging out Geneva by winning military successes in Indochina. This telegram of mine will bear rereading. That point of view has been frequently repeated in subsequent cables.

I deeply regret any sense of bitterness on Bidault's part, but I do not see that he is justified in considering unreasonable the adaptation of U.S. views to events and the consequences of prolonged French and U.K. indecision.

I do not yet exclude possibility U.S. intervention on terms outlined PARIS 402 and TEDUL 54. UK it seems is now more disposed to see movement in this direction but apparently the French are less than ever disposed to internationalizing the war.

DULLES

[Document 59]

SNIE 10–4–54
15 JUNE 1954

COMMUNIST REACTIONS TO CERTAIN US COURSES
OF ACTION WITH RESPECT TO INDOCHINA

THE PROBLEM

To estimate Chinese Communist and Soviet reactions to the courses of action and consequent situations indicated below.[1]

THE ESTIMATE

PART I

ASSUMPTIONS

A. The treaties of independence between France and the Associated States will have been signed.

B. A regional security grouping including at least the Associated States, Thailand, the Philippines, Australia, France, and the United States, and possibly including also New Zealand and the United Kingdom, will have been formed.

C. The Associated States will have publicly requested the direct military participation of members of the regional grouping in the war in Indochina.

D. The French will have undertaken to continue at least the present level of their military commitment in Indochina.

REQUIREMENT 1

To estimate the initial Chinese Communist and Soviet reactions to the participation of US air and naval forces with French Union forces and token Thai and Philippine forces in coordinated ground, naval, and air operations designed to destroy the Communist military forces in Indochina. Air operations would be limited to targets in Indochina. Nuclear weapons would be employed if their use were deemed militarily advantageous but nuclear attacks on the Indochinese civil population as a target system would be avoided.

Chinese Communist Reaction

1. The intervention of US and allied forces in Indochina probably would cause the Chinese Communists to believe that sooner or later they would have to decide whether to accept the defeat of the Viet Minh or to intervene in force in order to try to prevent such defeat. Their decision would probably rest mainly, though not exclusively, upon their weighing of the risks and disadvantages arising from the Viet Minh defeat against the likelihood of involvement in

[1] The assumptions and estimative requirements stated herein were furnished to the intelligence community for the purposes of this estimate. We interpret the hypothetical action as occurring within the next twelve to eighteen months.

major war with the US and the probable consequences of such a war for Communist China. Available evidence gives no unmistakeable indication of what the Chinese Communist decision would be. On balance, however, we believe that the chances are somewhat better than even that the Chinese Communist would decide to take whatever military action they thought required to prevent destruction of the Viet Minh, including when and if necessary, open use of Chinese Communist forces in Indochina.[2][3]

2. The nature of the assumed US action is such that ample warning would almost certainly be given in advance of actual operations. The Chinese Communists have the capability now to intervene quickly and in such force as to drive French Union forces out of the Delta. The Chinese Communists might choose to exercise this capability before US intervention could be effected.

3. We believe it somewhat more likely, however, that even if the Chinese Communists had determined not to accept the defeat of the Viet Minh they would not intervene openly immediately following the assumed US intervention. They might estimate that US air and naval forces could not, in the absence of US ground forces, decisively alter the course of the war. They might therefore consider their intervention unnecessary at this point and might postpone final decision as to their course of action until they had observed the initial scale and success of the allied military operations and had estimated the probable nature and extent of US aims in the conflict.

4. In this connection, US use of nuclear weapons in Indochina would tend to hasten the ultimate Chinese Communist decision whether or not to intervene. It would probably convince the Chinese Communists of US determination to obtain a decisive military victory in Indochina at whatever risk and by whatever means, and of the consequent danger of nuclear attack on Communist China. Whether this conviction would precipitate or deter Chinese Communist intervention would depend on the military situation in Indochina at the time, the observed military effect of the use of nuclear weapons, and the observed political and psychological effect of such use, particularly its effect on the coherence of the regional security grouping and the Atlantic alliance.

5. In any case, the Chinese Communists would almost certainly greatly increase their logistic support, delivery of arms and equipment, and technical assistance to the Viet Minh. The Chinese Communists would probably increase their deliveries of AA weapons and might send in Chinese AA gun crews. Moreover, the Chinese Communists would probably deploy ground and air units near the Indochina border in order: (a) to warn the US and its allies, and (b) to have forces ready either to intervene on behalf of the Viet Minh or to defend the southern border of China.

6. While maintaining a posture of military readiness, the Chinese Communists

[2] The Deputy Director for Intelligence, The Joint Staff, recommends deletion of the last sentence of this paragraph and would substitute the following:

"However, their decision would be largely determined by the Chinese estimate of the probable extent and effect of US initial action."

[3] The Director of Intelligence, USAF, believes that the last sentence of this paragraph should read as follows:

"Communist China will probably not choose knowingly any course of action likely to expose its fundamental national strengths in war with a major power. However, we believe that Communist China's strength for conducting various kinds of warfare is such, and the motives and judgment of its leaders are such as to make Communist China's courses of action dangerously unpredictable under outside pressure of any appreciable magnitude."

would intensify political and propaganda activities designed to exploit anti-Western and anticolonial feelings of the indigenous population of Indochina and the war-fears of neutralist Asian nations and of certain US allies. They would also seek to label the US as an aggressor. In the meantime and throughout the period of military operations, the Communists would almost certainly agitate and propagandize for a "cease-fire" and political settlement, which would preserve the Communist position and prospects.

Soviet Reaction

7. In the assumed situation, the USSR probably would estimate that the US action, though limited to air and naval forces, would considerably increase the risks of unlimited war between the US and Communist China. The USSR would probably prefer that such a war not develop out of the Indochina situation. Nevertheless, the USSR would assure Communist China of continuing military assistance. The USSR would also give complete diplomatic and propaganda support to Communist China and the Viet Minh regime.

REQUIREMENT 2

To estimate Chinese Communist and Soviet reactions to the success of the operations envisaged in the assumptions above (i.e., to the impending effective destruction of the Communist forces in Indochina).[4]

Chinese Communist Reaction

8. As stated in Paragraph 1, we believe that the chances are somewhat better than even that the Chinese Communist, in the assumed situation, would intervene militarily to prevent the destruction of the Viet Minh. If they decided to do so, we believe that the exact timing and nature of their action would depend on various factors, but principally on the scope and character of the US/allied operations they were seeking to counter.[5][6]

Soviet Reaction

9. In this assumed situation, the USSR would probably continue to support the Chinese Communists. If the Chinese Communists intervened openly in support

[4] The Assistant Chief of Staff, G–2, Department of the Army, believes that the results in this requirement could not be achieved by the unbalanced and insufficient forces envisaged.

[5] The Director of Intelligence, USAF, believes that this paragraph should read as follows:

"Communist China will probably not choose knowingly any course of action likely to expose its fundamental national strengths in war with a major power. However, we believe that Communist China's strength for conducting various kinds of warfare is such, and the motives and judgment of its leaders are such as to make Communist China's courses of action dangerously unpredictable under outside pressure of any appreciable magnitude."

[6] The Deputy Director for Intelligence, The Joint Staff, believes that paragraph 8 should read as follows:

"Communist China would conclude from the assumed impending destruction of Communist forces in Indochina, by limited forces employing nuclear and conventional weapons, that its open military intervention would invite an extension of similar action to Communist China, and would, therefore, probably not intervene militarily."

of the Viet Minh, the USSR would rapidly increase military assistance to Communist China. The Soviet diplomatic and propaganda campaigns against the US would continue full-scale, and the USSR might ask the UN to condemn the US as an aggressor. Thinly veiled threats of Soviet involvement in the fighting and references to the Sino-Soviet Treaty of 1950 would multiply.

PART II

ASSUMPTIONS

A. The treaties of independence between France and the Associated States will have been signed.

B. A regional security grouping including at least the Associated States, Thailand, the Philippines, Australia, France, and the United States, and possibly including also New Zealand and the United Kingdom, will have been formed.

C. The Associated States will have publicly requested the direct military participation of members of the regional grouping in the war in Indochina.

D. The French will have undertaken to continue at least the present level of their military commitment in Indochina.

E. The Chinese Communists will have openly intervened with military forces in Indochina in order to counter US direct participation as defined in Requirement 1.

REQUIREMENT 3

To estimate Chinese Communist and Soviet reactions to an extension of allied offensive air operations to include military targets in Communist China directly supporting Communist military operations in Indochina or directly threatening the security of Allied forces in the area.[7] Nuclear weapons would be employed in these operations if it were deemed militarily advantageous to do so, but nuclear attacks on the Chinese civil population as a target system would be avoided.

Chinese Communist Reaction

10. We consider it probable that before intervening in Indochina the Chinese Communists would have accepted the likelihood of US air attacks against military targets in China. Consequently, they would not feel compelled to withdraw their forces from Indochina solely as a result of the initiation of the air operations assumed above. At the same time, we believe that the Chinese Communists, in order to prevent further destruction to this area of China and particularly to avoid the spread of unlimited US attacks to the whole of China, would intensify efforts to induce the US to enter negotiations for a settlement which would preserve the Communist position and prospects in Indochina.

11. Meanwhile the Chinese Communists, to the full extent of their capabilities, would prosecute the war on the ground in Indochina and attack allied air bases, aircraft carriers, and other installations directly supporting allied operations in the area. They would, however, probably try to keep the war centered in Indochina and, as a consequence probably would confine their attacks to such directly supporting bases and installations.

[7] In this requirement we interpret targets "directly supporting" Communist military operations to be generally south of the Yangtze River and to consist primarily of transport lines, troop concentrations, and air fields in the area.

12. The use of nuclear weapons under the restrictions given above would greatly increase Chinese Communist concern about US intentions but probably would not by itself cause them to adopt new courses of military action at this time. However, they would threaten nuclear retaliation. They would also exploit to the fullest resultant psychological opportunities and in particular would charge that the US was using weapons of mass destruction on the civilian population.[8]

13. The Chinese Communists would attempt by all means possible to convince other Asian nations that the US had undertaken to destroy the Chinese Communist regime in order to thwart its efforts on behalf of an indigenous independence movement. If the Chinese had not previously done so, they would probably appeal to the UN to brand US action as a threat to the peace.

Soviet Reaction

14. In this assumed situation, the USSR would greatly increase its military assistance to Communist China, especially supplying modern aircraft and small naval vessels, possibly including submarines, with Soviet personnel to train and advise the Chinese and probably to participate in air defense operations. The USSR would probably not openly commit combat units of the Soviet armed forces and probably would not release nuclear weapons for Chinese Communist use.

15. The Kremlin would also continue its diplomatic and propaganda campaigns against the US, undertaking in the UN to brand the US as an aggressor if this had not previously been attempted. The USSR would support Chinese charges concerning the use of nuclear weapons against civilian populations. At the same time, the USSR would probably advise the Chinese Communists to negotiate for a cessation of hostilities on the basis of the status quo at the time and would try to establish a position as peacemaker.

REQUIREMENT 4

To estimate Chinese Communist and Soviet reactions to the following additional allied courses of action, undertaken subsequently to those above:
a. Extension of allied offensive air operations to additional selected military

[8] The Deputy Director for Intelligence, The Joint Staff, believes this paragraph should read:
"Nuclear weapon attacks on Communist China would undoubtedly result in a much greater Chinese Communist reaction than nuclear attacks on the Indochinese battleground. In addition, such attacks would probably indicate to the Chinese Communists a US willingness to exploit its superiority in nuclear weapons and delivery capability to force them out of Indochina. Since the nuclear attack contemplated in this requirement is of a limited nature, the Chinese Communist rulers would retain control of the government and country and, with the initial attacks, they would probably make urgent appeals to the USSR for nuclear weapons and additional military assistance. They might also increase the tempo of their military operations and would undoubtedly endeavor to induce the United States to enter negotiations in the hope of forestalling further attacks. A Chinese Communist decision to withdraw or not would be dependent primarily upon continued or increased US nuclear attacks and other US action as well as upon Soviet reaction. It is believed, however, that the Chinese Communists would be willing to withdraw from Indochina rather than be subjected to further destruction of their homeland."

targets in Communist China, including the use of atomic weapons under the same conditions as above.

    b. Naval blockade of the China coast.

    c. Seizure or neutralization of Hainan.

    d. Chinese Nationalist operations against the Chinese mainland.

Chinese Communist Reaction

16. As a consequence of this allied broadening of the war, the Chinese Communists would probably conclude that the US was prepared to wage unlimited war against them. They would continue to defend themselves to the limit of their capabilities and would probably make vigorous efforts to secure the full participation of the USSR. At the same time, they would intensify their efforts to end the war by negotiations, and might eventually indicate in some way their willingness to withdraw from Indochina in order to obtain a cease-fire.[9] If unable to obtain a cease-fire agreement, the Chinese Communists would accept the fact of unlimited war with the US and would wage such war to the full extent of their remaining capabilities.

Soviet Reaction

17. In this assumed situation, the USSR would continue to provide military assistance to Communist China as indicated above, but would probably refuse Chinese Communist demand for full Soviet participation in the war. The Kremlin would strongly urge the Chinese Communists to negotiate for a cessation of hostilities on the basis of withdrawing from Indochina.[10] If the Chinese Communists could not obtain a cease-fire agreement, the USSR would provide Communist China with military assistance in every way short of openly committing combat units of the Soviet armed forces in operations against US and allied forces outside Communist-held territory. The USSR would provide military resources and equipment for Chinese Communist attacks on US bases or US forces anywhere in the Far East. At this stage of the conflict, the USSR might provide Communist China with nuclear weapons and the technical personnel required for their use.[11] [12]

18. The USSR would continue its diplomatic and propaganda campaigns against the US, insisting that the Soviet aim was purely the defense of China against outright aggression. The USSR would also begin at least partial mobiliza-

---

[9] The Deputy Director for Intelligence, The Joint Staff, and the Director of Intelligence, USAF, suggest that the words "might eventually" in this sentence should be replaced with "would probably."

[10] The Assistant Chief of Staff, G–2, Department of the Army, recommends the deletion of "on the basis of withdrawing from Indochina," believing that at this state of the conflict the Kremlin would not willingly acquiesce in the surrender of any Communist-held territory in Indochina or elsewhere.

[11] The Deputy Director for Intelligence, The Joint Staff, and Director of Intelligence, USAF, believe that this sentence should read:

"We do not believe that the USSR would release nuclear weapons for Chinese Communist use."

[12] The Assistant Chief of Staff, G–2, Department of the Army, substitutes for the last sentence:

"It is also believed that the USSR would give serious consideration to making a substantially greater military contribution including nuclear weapons and the technical personnel required for their use."

tion of its own military forces on a war basis. It would issue thinly veiled threats of general war, suggesting attacks on Western Europe and on the continental US but would probably confine its operations to the defense of China so long as the US did not attack Soviet territory.

REQUIREMENT 5

To estimate Chinese Communist and Soviet reactions to the success of the foregoing operations (i.e., to the impending effective destruction of the Chinese Communist capability to conduct military operations outside the borders of Communist China).[13]

Chinese Communist Reaction

19. Unless the USSR was willing to make an unlimited commitment of Soviet forces to prevent the success of the assumed US and allied operations, we believe that the Communist Chinese, under the assumed circumstances, would accept any US terms for a settlement which preserved the integrity of China under the Chinese Communist regime.

Soviet Reaction

20. In this assumed situation, we believe the USSR would urge the Chinese Communists to accept any US terms for a settlement which preserved the integrity of China under the Chinese Communist regime.[14] So long as the fighting continued, however, the USSR would continue its aid to China.

[Document 60]

June 17, 1954

SENT TO: Amconsul GENEVA TEDUL 212 PRIORITY

From your DULTE 187 it is evident that QUOTE underground military talks UNQUOTE, even more than conference proceedings, are pointing toward de facto partition under conditions such that Communist take-over of all Vietnam looms ahead clearly.

Chauvel's mention of difficulty of QUOTE selling UNQUOTE Vietminh proposal to Vietnamese and his doubt that Hanoi–Haiphong area can be held indicate to us that French may end by accepting any Vietminh proposition which offers hope of extricating Expeditionary Corps. In this connection we note failure of Vietminh thus far to react to French question regarding evacuation French troops and citizens and Vietnamese Catholics.

There can of course be no repeat no question of US participation in any attempt to QUOTE sell UNQUOTE a partition to non-Communist Vietnamese.

DULLES

---

[13] The Assistant Chief of Staff, G–2, Department of the Army, believes that the results assumed in this requirement could not be achieved by the unbalanced and insufficient force envisaged.

[14] The Assistant Chief of Staff, G–2, Department of the Army, would add "and retained a Communist foothold in Indochina."

[Document 61]

\   June 18, 1954

SENT TO: Amconsul GENEVA TEDUL 222 PRIORITY

EYES ONLY UNDER SECRETARY FROM SECRETARY

NO DISTRIBUTION TEDUL 221

Supplementing immediately-preceding-cable, five-power staff report suggesting Thakhek-Donghoi line, coupled with rapid Delta deterioration, is leading us to reexamine possible *de facto* partition Vietnam.

DULLES

[Document 62]

FROM: Geneva

TO: Secretary of State

NO: DULTE 195, June 18, 3 p.m.

SENT DEPARTMENT DULTE 195, REPEATED INFORMATION PARIS 455, SAIGON 177.

PARIS EYES ONLY AMBASSADOR; SAIGON EYES ONLY AMBASSADOR

Johnson saw Chauvel this morning and discussed with him conference situation in light TEDUL 211. Johnson stated seemed to us that such fundamental questions as composition, voting procedures and authority or international control commission should be dealt within conference rather than by committee. If conference reached decision on fundamental principles, working out of details could be done by committee of experts of principally interested parties in same pattern as present Franco–Viet Minh military conversations.

Chauvel said this would be agreeable except that question of authority, which he termed "relationship between international commission and joint committees" could be dealt with by technical committee, thus implying France not (repeat not) prepared to maintain principle of subordination joint committees to international commission. As French have already circulated proposal contained SECTO 460 through secretariat, it was agreed we would make suggestion along foregoing lines at today's restricted meeting. Chauvel said they did not (repeat not) yet have any further indication as to what attitude Chinese would take on French proposal entirely clear from conversation with Chauvel that his main interest is in keeping some conference activity of nine going and that if regardless of level representation we prepared continue some conference meetings would probably meet French point of view. Appears French proposal made on assumption that there would be complete recess of conference with departure of Smith and Eden.

Chauvel made reference to his conversation with Smith yesterday (DULTE 193—last paragraph), making inquiry as to exactly what we had in mind. Johnson in reply read to him paragraphs 5, 6 and 7 basic instructions (TOSEC

138) stating that French willingness surrender even minimum enclave in north of Haiphong would so clearly contravene the principles which the US considered essential as to require our public dissociation with such a solution. In reply to Chauvel's questions, Johnson made it clear we were speaking only of public disassociation from such a settlement. The US had in the past and of course would continue working with and supporting France in every possible way and wherever we could. Chauvel indicated full understanding our position. He said they had come to conclusion that what he termed any "leopard spot" solution was entirely impracticable and unenforceable. From standpoint of future it would be much better to retain a reasonably defensible line in Vietnam behind which there would be no (repeat no) enclaves of Viet Minh and do all possible behind that line to build up effective Vietnamese Government and defense. They had no (repeat no) intention of "any immediate surrender of Haiphong" which in any event must remain under their control for a considerable period for purely military reasons to effect evacuation of French Union Forces from the north. However, if, as appeared likely, choice was giving Viet Minh an enclave in south in exchange for French enclave in Haiphong, they thought it preferable to give up Haiphong. He said no (repeat no) French parliament would approve conditions which the US had laid down for its intervention, and French had no (repeat no) choice but made the best deal they could, obtaining as strong position as possible in south. Chauvel understood fully we would probably not (repeat not) be able to publicly associate ourselves with such a solution, but he hoped that when it came time to put it to the Vietnamese the US would consider it possible very discreetly to let the Vietnamese know that we considered it best that could be obtained under the circumstances and our public disassociation would not (repeat not) operate so as to encourage Vietnamese opposition. Johnson replied he did not (repeat not) see how it would be possible for us to do this, and in any event he would of course have to see what the solution was. Chauvel said that such a solution as partition should come as no (repeat no) surprise to the Vietnamese as Buu Loc had sometime ago indicated to DeJean there had been conversations between Vietnamese and Viet Minh in which Viet Minh had made it clear that only two alternatives were coalition government or partition. Chauvel said Ngo Dinh and Diem are very unrealistic, unreasonable, and would probably prove to be "difficult."

Chauvel said the line French had in mind had been made available to US defense representatives at some five-power talks, but was vague about time and place. He referred to it as "line of the chalk cliffs," which he said was defensible position running from the sea across Vietnam and Laos to the Mekong. Understand this is a line roughly 19 parallel running from vicinity of Dong Hoi to Thakhek. Replying to query, Chauvel said French Union Forces removed from the north would be deployed along that line.

Chauvel said all indications were Mendes-France would succeed in forming government next day or two and would probably himself assume Foreign Minister post. Said he had been in touch with Mendes-France and had sent emissary to Paris this morning to brief him on situation in Geneva. Chauvel said was anxious to show complete continuity of French effort here in Geneva and hoped there could be another restricted meeting tomorrow. Chauvel said, "Under-ground military talks" last night had been completely unproductive, Viet Minh obviously taking strong line in view of French Government situation.

SMITH

[Document 63]

OUTGOING TELEGRAM   1426

June 19, 1954

Sent to: SECSTATE DULTE 202

RPTD INFO: Amembassy Moscow 138 EYES ONLY FOR AMBASSADOR

I saw Molotov at his villa yesterday evening at my request to inform him of my departure, and because I felt time had come to sound a note of warning: Talk lasted more than hour and a half. Molotov asked what I thought would be best thing to do with Conference, to adjourn it temporarily or to keep it going. I replied as far as we concerned should be kept going while there was hope of reaching reasonable settlement, but that there was no use referring to "committees" matters of major policy which must be decided by the Conference as a whole. Before my departure I felt it would be desirable to exchange views, in order that mistakes of the past should not be repeated as the result of misunderstanding of our respective positions. With regard to Korean phase, I had only to say that in reserving our position re final Chinese proposal had not implied to exclude Communist China from future discussions on Korean question. As matter of fact, China was belligerent there against UN and for practical reasons would have to be party to settlement.

Regarding Indochinese phase Molotov said he had impression US avoided reaching solution and cited in this regard Robertson objection in yesterday's restricted session to acceptance Chou's proposal on Laos and Cambodia. I said that while proposal might be satisfactory in some respects it made no mention of Vietminh withdrawal or of adequate supervision. So long as regular Vietminh forces remained in Laos and Cambodia we could not help but view situation in very serious light. Molotov cited Pham Van Dong's remarks regarding withdrawal Vietminh "volunteers" and emphasized importance of beginning direct negotiations regarding Laos and Cambodia of type now taking place regarding Vietnam. I regretted that I was not at all convinced that Pham Van Dong really meant what he said. His statements sounded well enough, but his written proposals did not bear them out.

I said I wanted to make our position on Laos and Cambodia entirely clear. In addition to regular Vietminh forces in these countries, which I enumerated, there were some dissident elements in Laos and a much smaller number in Cambodia. If regular Vietminh forces were withdrawn, elections could be held, with guarantees that individuals would be discriminated against as regards their electoral rights for having supported either side. Dissidents would be able to vote for any candidates they chose, Communists included. However, while Vietminh forces remained in these countries, there could be no peace nor could free elections be held.

In private conversations with Mr. Eden and others, Communist delegates, in particular Chou En-lai, had taken an apparently reasonable view on Laos and Cambodia, but that here again, when we came to the point of trying to get open agreement on specific points we were unable to do so. I specifically mentioned Chou En-lai's statements to Eden in which he said that China would have no objections to recognizing the kingdoms of Laos and Cambodia or to these States having forces and arms sufficient to maintain security, or their remaining in French Union so long as they were not used as military bases by the United States. We could not disagree with any of this, although if we kept out the Chinese would have to keep out, and these small states would have to be allowed to join with their neighbors in whatever regional security arrangements would best protect their integrity without constituting a threat to any one else. Chou En-lai might be anxious about possibility of US bases in Laos and Cambodia. We wanted on our part to be sure that these countries were not handed over to the Chinese. Molotov said that while he did not know about what attitude Chinese might have on other questions in future, he could assure me that Chinese attitude on this particular question was not at all unreasonable, and that there was nothing in it which would give rise to conflicts. He added, however, that if we continued to take a one-sided view and insist on one-sided solutions, he must "in all frankness say that this would not succeed." There were, he said, some differences of view between us on Laos and Cambodia, especially in regard to our refusal to recognize resistance movements; point he wanted to make, however, was that basis for reaching agreement was present and that agreement could be reached so long as neither side "adopted one-sided views or put forward extreme pretensions." This, he said, could only lead to other side's doing same.

Resistance movements existed, in Laos and Cambodia, Molotov asserted. About 50% of the territory of Laos was not under the control of official government. It was true that much smaller resistance movement existed in Cambodia. He said that in fact conditions in all three Indochinese countries were different—large resistance movement controlling three-quarters of territory in Viet Nam, substantial movement in Laos controlling, as he had indicated, about half territory, and much smaller movement in Cambodia. I said, with regard to two latter counts solution was simple. Withdraw invading Vietminh forces and let dissident elements elect communist representatives to general assemblies if they wished. But the elections must be actually "free." Regarding Viet Nam, I said we recognized relative strength of the Vietminh but they were demanding too much. It seems Vietminh demanded all Delta, including both Hanoi and Haiphong. The French were our allies, and we took grave view of this extreme pressure. Molotov said that if French were to have something in South and something in North, and probably in center as well, this would add up to three-quarters of country or better, which was wholly unreasonable. He said there was old Russian proverb that if you try to chase two rabbits at once you are apt to miss both of them, and added that in this case wanting something in North and in South was like chasing two rabbits. If French were to give way to Vietminh in North, they would gain territory probably greater in extent in South in recompense. I said appearance of "partition" was repugnant to US, and that as far as proverb about rabbits went I felt that Vietminh were chasing two rabbits in wanting both Hanoi and Haiphong. Vietminh demands for all the Delta, or efforts take it all by force prior to reaching political solution through elections, was serious matter in view of my Government. Molotov disagreed, stating that present French position in area was due only to Vietminh restraint, and that two cities did not even have normal communications between each other. In regard to US aversion to partition, he said that this problem could easily be solved by holding elections at once, which would decide "one way or the other." He repeated that important thing in reaching agreement on any of these questions relating Indochina was to be realistic about actual facts, and to avoid putting out one-sided views or extreme pretensions. If French were encouraged to disregard actual situation and to ask for too much, he said, one could only expect conflict to continue. (He made it clear that he considered US as party likely to do the encouraging.) I replied that US was not one of principals to Indochinese dispute and did not cast deciding vote, to which Molotov remarked "maybe so, but you have veto, that word I hear you use so often," and went on to say that among other delegations present at Conference there seemed to be real willingness to reach agreement. Agreement had in fact, he added, very nearly been reached, although he hoped I would realize this was not information for publication. (This remark, obviously, referred to private French–Vietminh military conversations which I have mentioned.) I said I must emphasize my Government held serious views on issues involved in Indochina situation, more serious, perhaps, than did some of other governments represented at Conference. I hope he would give consideration to this, and assist in overcoming some of the deep-rooted suspicions of Asiatic participants, which became apparent every time we tried to reconcile formal proposals.

COMMENT:

Throughout conversation Molotov maintained friendly and mild tone evident in all informal conversations. He is completely sure of himself and of his position. What he had to say regarding Delta, Laos and Cambodia confirms Communist intentions to play all the cards they hold. His avoidance of endorsing Chou's remarks to Eden concerning Laos and Cambodia indicated that simple withdrawal of Vietminh forces from these countries was not acceptable and that some form of de facto partition was intended in Laos, at least. His remarks seemed to indicate that Communists have eye on as much as half of country. This conversation, together with the inflexible position which Molotov took during his last conversation with me regarding the composition of a Neutral Nations Supervisory Commission for Indochina, as well as his speech on Tuesday, June 8, and all subsequent speeches on the Communist side, which took firm positions on points the Communists know to be unacceptable to Eden, Bidault and me, are highly significant. The recent emphasis by all three Communist spokesmen that France should carry on direct political as well as direct military negotiations with Vietminh show their interest in having a convenient way of holding out for greater gains in their direct negotiations with the French as well as within the framework of the Conference.

Molotov in effect told France in his June 8 speech that her position and that of the Government she was supporting in Indochina were hopeless and that she had best face up to facts and capitulate in direct negotiations with the Vietminh. His speech, of course, was in large part intended to assist in the destruction of the French Government for the implications that that would have on the European as well as the Asiatic scene. Nevertheless, his harsh and even insulting language seemed to reflect the confident, nearly triumphant mood in which he has been lately. It would be misleading to ascribe the harder line which Molotov brought back with him from Moscow entirely to Soviet tactical considerations in regard to the French Government crisis. While the Soviets may think that the blocking of EDC through the destruction of the French Government would reduce future threats to them in Europe, the fact remains that the Indochina conflict potentially involves a much more immediate threat of general war.

It is probable that initial Soviet tactics were to forestall US intervention in the Delta by some kind of a compromise formula involving Hanoi and Haiphong if it appeared that such intervention were imminent. The recent raising of the ante in the negotiations here by the Communist side probably reflects an estimate on their part that our intervention is improbable and that they are safe to go ahead there, keeping, of course, a sharp eye out for indications of change in our attitude.

While the Communist position on Laos and Cambodia remains more flexible than their position in regard to the Delta, they will get all they can in Laos now. In the whole are the determining factor for the Communists will continue to be their estimate of the likelihood of US or joint intervention and nothing short of a conviction on their part that this intervention will take place will stop them from going ahead with their plans for taking all of it eventually, through military conquest, French capitulation, or infiltration.

Realize much of above is repetitious, but it will serve as final summary.

SMITH

[Document 64]

FROM: Paris

TO: Secretary of State

NO: 5035, June 24, 10 p.m.

SENT DEPARTMENT 5035; REPEATED INFORMATION GENEVA 443.

LIMIT DISTRIBUTION.

Since Mendes was tied up in National Assembly today, he asked me to see Parodi and Chauvel regarding his talk with Chou. Chauvel did all the talking and described the meeting as follows:

He said that Mendes opened the meeting telling Chou that he had been glad to agree to Chou's idea of a meeting and that he was interested to hear anything Chou had to say. Chou then spoke very fully and most of the time at the meeting, which lasted a little over two hours, was taken up by Chou's statements and the necessary translations.

Chou in general followed the same line as he previously had taken with Eden and Bidault, with certain important exceptions, which Chauvel considered to represent a considerable advance over Chou's previous position.

Chou started by talking about Laos and Cambodia. He said that the immediate problem was to obtain the withdrawal of all foreign forces including Viet Minh from the entire territory of both countries. He said that then the governments of the two countries should arrange political settlements within their own countries based on the will of the majority of the people. Chou said that while there should be no persecution of minorities, he had no objection to the two countries retaining their monarchical form of government if they so desired. The one thing upon which he insisted was that there should be no (repeat no) US bases in either Laos and Cambodia. He stated that he saw no objection to Laos and Cambodia remaining within the French Union, provided they so desired.

The talk then turned to Vietnam where Chauvel considered important advances in Chou's position were revealed. Chou said that he recognized that there were now two governments in the territory of Vietnam, the Viet Minh Government and the Vietnamese Government. According to Chauvel, this was the first time that Chou had recognized the valid existence of the Vietnamese Government. Chou then said that the settlement in Vietnam should be reached in two stages.

First, an armistice which should be reached as soon as possible, and second, peace, which would obviously take longer to achieve. Chauvel said that Chou clearly accepted, and for the first time, the French thesis that there should be two phases; first military and second political to the eventual settlement of Vietnam. Regarding military settlement, Chou said that there should be regroupment of troops in large zones in order to stop the fighting. Chou said that he was ready to discuss the division of zones if Mendes so desired. Mendes answered that he was not yet prepared for such a detailed discussion and said he preferred that it be handled by the delegations at Geneva. Therefore, there was no discussion in detail regarding the make-up of the eventual zones.

Regarding the final political settlement, Chou said this should be reached by direct negotiations between the two governments in Vietnam, i.e., the Vietnamese Government and the Viet Minh Government. Chou further said that France might be able to help in these negotiations. He added that he saw no reason why the eventually united state of Vietnam should not remain within the French Union.

Mendes at this point said that since the war had been going on for 8 years and passions were high, it would take a long time before elections could be held as the people must be given a full opportunity to cool off and calm down. Chou made no objection to this statement by Mendes and did not press for early elections.

Mendes then told Chou that negotiations with the Viet Minh for reasons not very clear to the French had been at a practical standstill for the past week or ten days and he suggested that a word from Chou to the leader of the Viet Minh delegation might be helpful in speeding things up which seemed to be Chou's desire as well as Mendes'. Chou agreed to intervene with the Viet Minh and ask them to speed up negotiations.

The conversation never touched on any subject other than Indochina. According to Chauvel, no other item of Far Eastern policy was touched upon, nor was Europe nor the UN or possible recognition of China by France ever mentioned. Chauvel is returning to Geneva tonight and will see the head of the Viet Minh delegation tomorrow in an attempt to get the military talks under way again.

DILLON

[Document 65]

June 24, 1954

SENT TO: Amconsul GENEVA TOSEC 478

Reference SECTO 512.

Our position remains that in TOSEC 461.

The imminence of a settlement between Mendes-France and the Communists, which in some form will probably be brought before a revived conference for its approval, emphasizes the importance of adhering to these instructions. Otherwise we may be involved in committee work leading to the making of decisions which we might be obliged publicly to disavow.

We should avoid being drawn into the French effort to give conference semblance of vitality by means of a series of committee operations.

FYI Our thinking at present is that our role at Geneva should soon be restricted to that of observer, and now that Lord Reading has departed, you should leave in a few days. Bonsal could continue as chief observer in accord with terms of TEDUL 211. Let us have your views.

DULLES

[Document 66]

1954 JUN 28

SENT TO: Amembassy PARIS 4852

TOSEC

Following is translation aide memoire delivered by Bonnet to Secretary and Eden June 26. Text coordinated US–UK reply contained next following message.

"The coming weeks will be of decisive importance insofar as Indochina is concerned. Following his conversation with Mr. Chou En-lai, the head of the French Government has instructed M. Chauvel to approach M. Phan Van Dong with a view to carrying on with him directly negotiations to ascertain whether a basis can be found, in his opinion, for a territorial settlement in Vietnam or not.

"The objective of the French Government is to arrive at a regrouping which will assure the State of Vietnam a territory as solid as possible, and without the *de facto* division which will result being too cut up. That is the reason why the French Government will insist on maintaining Haiphong as long as possible and on obtaining the neutralization of the bishoprics of Bui Chu and Phat Diem.

"It is difficult to predict the result of this negotiation in which the French authorities must face two sorts of difficulties: on the one hand it will be most difficult to obtain concessions from the Viet Minh in the north; and on the other hand the negotiations risk causing, if the agreement is concluded, dangerous reactions by the Vietnamese Government whose citizens are serving at the present time under the orders of the French command, comprising a major proportion thereof.

"The French Prime Minister feels that the allied American and British governments should be as well informed as possible of these possibilities. M. Mendes-France wishes especially to call the attention of these two Governments to the following aspects of the situation:

"(1) If the Viet Minh appears disposed to negotiate, it is for a series of reasons among which figure without doubt the fear of a spreading of the conflict, a spreading which nothing at the present time would lead us to expect, but which the general world situation does not permit us to exclude. Although the fear of such an extension of the conflict may have a determining influence on the decisions of our adversaries, the French Government realizes that precise declarations on this subject are not possible at this time. But it considers it would be very useful if the final communique of the Anglo-American talks in Washington could state in some fashion or other that, if it is not possible to reach a reasonable settlement at the Geneva Conference, a serious aggravation of international relations would result.

"(2) The problem which is posed with regard to Vietnam is different. It is to be feared that any solution providing for an indefinite period a division of the country will cause a violent and unreasoning reaction on the part of the Vietnamese patriots. While this reaction may be in a large measure inevitable, every effort should nevertheless be made to canalize this reaction in a direction in conformity with the interests of Vietnam, France and their allies.

"To this end it appears highly desirable to the Prime Minister of France to obtain the assurance of the United States Government that nothing will be done by the latter which might even implicitly encourage such a reaction. Under present circumstances such action could lead to no result but to ruin any hope of seeing Vietnam consolidate herself in such a fashion as to create in the face of the Viet Minh an authentically national and independent force. It is for this reason that the French Government strongly hopes it can count on the United States at the proper moment to intervene with the Vietnamese to counsel upon them wisdom and self-control and to dissuade them from refusing an agreement which, if it is reached, is dictated not by the spirit of abandoning them, but on the contrary by the desire to save in Indochina all that can possibly be saved, and to give the Vietnamese state, under peaceful conditions, opportunities which have not always been possible heretofore because of the war."

DULLES

[Document 67]

FROM: Paris

TO: Secretary of State

NO: 5117, June 30, 7 p.m.

SENT DEPARTMENT 5117, REPEATED INFORMATION SAIGON 634, GENEVA 449

EYES ONLY MCCLINTOCK SAIGON, JOHNSON GENEVA

Jebb came to see me this morning after his interview with Mendes-France in the course of which he delivered reply to French aide-memoire of June 26 (DEPTEL 4853) in the form of aide-memoire, followed by verbal comments along lines outlined in paragraph 2 reference telegram.

Jebb reported that Mendes was pleased with text reply and stated that Parodi would give us definite French position in day or so. Mendes also confirmed that negotiations with Viet Minh at Geneva were stalled (Geneva SECTO 544, repeated Paris as 519).

Mendes was somewhat perplexed by reference to "line running generally west from Dong Hoi" as possible partition line for while Dong Hoi approximately at 17.5 degrees French had been holding out for 18th parallel in face Viet Minh wanting 13th.

On question of elections, Jebb quoted Mendes as stating that the Viet Minh wanted them to be held in six months but that the French were taking the position that they should be delayed for a year after final settlement and withdrawal of troops had been achieved. This, as presently envisaged, would mean a year and half to two years from now.

As reported EMBTEL 5099, we delivered reply to aide-memoire to Foreign Office this morning.

DILLON

[Document 68]

July 2, 1954

SENT TO: Amembassy PARIS 39

RPTD INFO: Amembassy SAIGON 31
Amconsul GENEVA 9

REDEPTEL 4852, June 28; Saigon 2746; Geneva 489

It seems to me that new Vietnamese Prime Minister Ngo Dinh Diem, who has reputation of uncompromising nationalist, is quite in the dark about developments critically affecting country he is trying to lead. We fear that if results of French negotiations with Communists are revealed to him as a *fait accompli*, the very reaction French wish to avoid will result.

You should therefore indicate our concern to the French and ascertain their own intentions with respect to consulting him or minimizing his resentment and their views with respect to plans and prospects for maintaining order in South Vietnam.

DULLES

[Document 69]

FROM: Paris

TO: Secretary of State

NO: 32, July 2, 8 p.m.

SENT DEPARTMENT 32, REPEATED INFORMATION GENEVA 2, SAIGON 4.

Re DEPTELs 5 and 8.

I took up reference telegrams with Mendes this afternoon. Regarding present withdrawals in the delta Mendes said that these had been planned in May by the Laniel government and he had made no change in the original plan. The withdrawals represent a definite shortening of the French lines to protect Hanoi, Haiphong and the connecting road.

He said he had been much surprised to read in the papers that a State Department spokesman had said that the US had not had prior information regarding these withdrawals. He had assumed, he said, that Ely had fully informed O'Daniel of his plans. He then accordingly asked Ely this morning if that was not the case and Ely had told him that he had not informed O'Daniel. Mendes accordingly offered his apologies and said that he had instructed Ely in the future to keep O'Daniel fully informed on the spot.

Regarding withdrawals themselves he said they were necessary to ensure the safety of the French Expeditionary Corps. He said that the French had offered to take with them those members of the local population who desired protection and that the French forces had provided transportation for such people. He said he had not seen the latest figures but a fairly substantial number of people had availed themselves of this opportunity. On the other hand, there had been many who preferred to stay where they were.

In this connection he said that since Dien Bien Phu the Viet Minh had not conducted reprisals when they occupied new territory but had behaved very well toward the local population. He said that he realized that this might only be a temporary policy to facilitate negotiations at Geneva, but that for whatever it was worth, it was the fact. He then said that the withdrawals were not yet completed and showed me on a rough map where further withdrawals were scheduled. These include the Phu Ly area and a portion of the area to the west of Hanoi.

Regarding the right of population transfer as contained in paragraph 6 of DEPTEL 4853, Mendes said that he was thoroughly in accord that this would be a good thing from the French point of view. He said that it had been mentioned to the Viet Minh in Geneva and that they had made no answer either favorable or unfavorable. When I reiterated the importance that we attach to this subject, Mendes made a note of it and said that he was writing Chauvel tonight and would include in his letter of instruction a reference to this subject. I think it would be useful if Johnson would stress this subject in his next talk with Chauvel.

Mendes then said negotiations in Geneva had been at a standstill and that he had instructed Chauvel to go to Berne for two days to show that the French were in no greater hurry than the Viet Minh. He said that the Soviet representative at Geneva had told Chauvel not to worry about the slow pace of the negotiations as at conferences such as these everything was always settled in last few hours.

Regarding DEPTEL 8, use of word "withdrawal" was intended only to mean deployment agreed regroupment areas. Mendes said that the French on timing of election are holding out for 18 months after completion of regrouping which, he said, would mean 22 or 23 months after cease-fire. Viet Minh are asking for elections six months after cease-fire. Mendes expects the final result will be a compromise somewhere in between.

He then commented that Diem had made an unhelpful speech the other day in Saigon when he was quoted as having said that he was in favor of the elections within a year. Mendes thinks that this is too soon and not in the interests of Vietnam, and it runs counter to what the French were trying to obtain at Geneva.

DILLON

[Document 70]

1954 Jul 3

SENT TO: Amembassy PARIS 52 PRIORITY

EYES ONLY FOR AMBASSADOR FROM SECRETARY

We are considering here what position we should take as regards the French negotiations in Indochina. These negotiations appear to have gone underground and we have little reliable knowledge of what is really in the minds of the French Government or what is likely to emerge. We have ourselves agreed with the British on the 7 points previously communicated to you. However, we have the distinct impression that the British look upon this merely as an optimum solution and that they would not encourage the French to hold out for a solution as good as this. Indeed, during the talks here the British wanted to express these 7 points merely as a "hope" without any indication of firmness on our part. The word "respect" was agreed on as a compromise. The fact is however that the US would not want to be associated in any way with a settlement which fell materially short of the 7 point memorandum.

We fear the French may in fact without prior consultation with us of more than perfunctory character agree to a settlement which though superficially resembling the 7 points will in fact contain such political clauses and restrictions that Laos, Cambodia, and Southern Vietnam will almost surely fall in a few months under Communist control. No doubt such a solution would be accepted with satisfaction by the French people and parliament who would rejoice in the ending of the fighting and close their eyes to the possible future implications of the settlement. At this point the US may be asked as one of the powers which convoked and participated in the Indochina phase of the Geneva Conference to sign or otherwise adhere to the settlement. Also the Communists may insist upon this and take the position that if we did not do so that would be a violation of the understanding upon which the armistice was negotiated and they might even threaten to withdraw their armistice terms if the US did not adhere to them. This Communist tactic would well serve their purpose of creating animosity between France and the US at a time when the defeat of EDC is a major Soviet objective.

We are giving consideration to various possibilities such as the withdrawal of the remnants of our delegation from Geneva or clarification of our position as regards the French position. This latter matter would not (rpt not) serve the desired purpose unless it were public and if it were public it might be looked upon as a threat which would create the French antagonistic reaction which we want to avoid.

Possibly you could find out whether or not there is the danger which we apprehend and whether or not the French are negotiating on the assumption that we may not be a party to the settlement. If the French are operating on this basis and if they know that the Communists also accept this premise, the situation is not dangerous. If either or both French and Communists are operating on assumption we will adhere to any settlement they agree to, then we may be headed for serious trouble. I would like your personal thoughts on this matter.

DULLES

[Document 71]

FROM: Paris

TO: Secretary of State

NO: 41, July 4, 3 p.m.

EYES ONLY SECRETARY

Reference DEPTEL 52.

I can well understand difficulties we face as described in reference telegram. I feel that French position is fairly clear as of now but difficulty may well arise in last days or hours of conference after Ministers have returned to Geneva.

In that connection we face following problem. If we withdraw delegation from Geneva we lose all possibility of influencing French to stand firm, and we also throw away whatever restraining influence we may still have on Communist delegations. French would feel abandoned and, with only Eden to advise, would undoubtedly accept a result more favorable to the Communists than if we stayed at Geneva. The same effect but to a lesser extent would result if neither Under Secretary nor you return to Geneva for closing negotiations.

On the other hand even if we do maintain a full delegation at Geneva headed by you or Under Secretary there is always the possibility and maybe even probability that French will accept a settlement that does not fully accord with 7 points in US–UK agreement. This will be particularly apt to happen if Eden does not stand firm in final negotiations.

I do not feel that public statement of our position would be helpful as it would create the antagonism mentioned in next to last paragraph of reference telegram. Even if we do not consider final settlement satisfactory to us, I feel that unless we agree not to use force to upset it we will be in an untenable position here vis-a-vis Soviet and neutralist propaganda that will picture US as the nation which by its acts clearly shows that it wants war.

Mendes is fully conscious that we may feel that we cannot be a party to the settlement. However, I do not feel that this would necessarily weigh very heavily with him in final settlement, particularly if he can obtain Eden's support. Naturally I have no idea what is in mind of Communists on this score.

We have one strong card which so far we have apparently not cared to use. That is we can trade willingness to give full diplomatic support to French in their effort to sell settlement to Vietnam in return for a settlement that we can support. The indication which French now have that no matter what the settlement may be, we cannot be counted upon for support with Vietnam obviously greatly weakens our influence with French.

In conclusion if we base our actions solely on the attempt to get the best possible settlement I feel that we should (1) maintain our delegation at Geneva, (2) have you or the Under Secretary return to head the delegation when the other Foreign Ministers return, (3) tell the French at once that we will support them in selling settlement to Vietnam provided that settlement is satisfactory to us, (4) maintain close contact with and pressure on Eden so he sticks to 7 points US–UK agreement.

I fully realize that domestic political considerations must also be taken into account, but I am not in a position to evaluate them so I have confined these thoughts to a description of the best method available to US to influence the final settlement at Geneva in the direction we desire.

DILLON

[Document 72]

FROM: Paris

TO: Secretary of State

NO: 66, July 6, 11 p.m.

SENT DEPARTMENT 6, REPEATED INFORMATION GENEVA 8, SAIGON 11.

After finishing discussion of Kerr article, Mendes said that the second major thing which he wished to discuss with me was the question of the resumption of the Geneva talks at the Ministerial level. He said that it was now clear that the Ministers would have to make the decisions as the technical committees had been unsuccessful. Therefore, and in view of his July 20 deadline, he personally hoped that Ministerial discussions could commence as soon as possible.

In this connection he mentioned a report that Molotov might return to Geneva on July 8. He said that Chauvel had tried to confirm this with the Russians at Geneva but they replied that they were without information. Mendes said he very much did not (repeat not) want to be in a position of talking at Geneva with only Molotov and Chou En-lai. Therefore, he would like very much to find out what US intentions and plans were as to when the Secretary or Under Secretary would return to Geneva. He said that Massigli was making similar inquiries of Eden on his arrival today.

I said that I was unfamiliar as to US plans and asked Mendes what his understanding was as to when the conference would resume. He replied that it was his definite understanding that all five Foreign Ministers had agreed to return to Geneva not (repeat not) later than July 12, to recommence their discussions. Referring to US, he indicated that he expected that either the Secretary or the Under Secretary would return at that time. I told him that I was not informed but that I would inquire and let him know as soon as possible.

Mendes then informed me that he will announce tomorrow to the National Assembly that if a cease-fire is not (repeat not) agreed to prior to July 21, it will be necessary for the Assembly to approve the sending of conscripts to Indochina and that the last act of his government before resigning will be to introduce a law to authorize the sending of conscripts to Indochina. This law would be introduced on July 21, and the Assembly would be required to vote on it the same day as they will have had two weeks from the date of his announcement to consider the matter. He said that his government would definitely not (repeat not) resign until such a law had been passed. Mendes also said that the shipping to move the first group of conscripts to Indochina would be ready on July 25, so that his schedule for parliamentary action would cause no (repeat no) delay in the movement of troops.

I then mentioned DEPTEL 39, and Mendes said that he recognized that this posed a real problem. He said that Ely had been instructed to keep Diem as fully informed as possible and that he had stressed the matter again in a telegram to Ely. Mendes said, however, that no (repeat no) matter what occurs or what action is taken, he expects there would be difficulties with Diem, and he said that he wanted again to ask for our assistance at that time. He said he realized that the US would probably be unable to underwrite any settlement which might come out of Geneva. He said he also realized that it would not (repeat not) be easy for us to tell Diem, to accept everything. Mendes said he did not (repeat not) want to ask us to do anything we could not (repeat not) do, but that he hoped we could by unofficial means discourage Diem from being too stubborn and difficult if a solution along general lines of US–UK formula had been reached.

DILLON

[Document 73]

July 7, 1954

SENT TO: Amembassy LONDON NIACT 101

Rptd Info Amembassy PARIS NIACT 68

EYES ONLY ALDRICH AND DILLON FROM SECRETARY

Please deliver following personal message to Eden:
QTE Dear Anthony: We have an inquiry from Mendes-France as to whether or not Bedell or I will return to Geneva and if so when. He apparently contemplates a reunion at the ministerial level July 12. I understand he is making a similar inquiry of you.

It is my present feeling that it would be better if neither Bedell nor I were back. As you know, it would not be feasible for us to be parties to a settlement which fell below the seven point paper which we drew up together in Washington and gave the French through our Ambassadors. Our position in that respect is perhaps a little different from your own. In any event, I fear that the French, whether or not Bedell or I are there, will take a solution considerably worse than this and in that event our high-level presence at Geneva might prove an embarrassment to all concerned. In view, however, of our joint efforts for this area, I wanted to let you know of our present thinking and I would welcome quickly knowing how you yourself visualize this matter working out. Sincerely yours, Foster. UNQTE

DULLES

[Document 74]

July 7, 1954

SENT TO: Amembassy PARIS 77

Re EMBTEL 50

We see no real conflict between paragraphs 4 and 5 US–UK terms. We realize of course that even agreement which appears to meet all seven points cannot constitute guarantee that Indochina will not one day pass into Communist hands. Seven points are intended provide best chance that this shall not happen. This will require observance of criteria not merely in the letter but in the spirit. Thus since undoubtedly true that elections might eventually mean unification Vietnam under Ho Chi Minh this makes it all more important they should be only held as long after cease-fire agreement as possible and in conditions free from intimidation to give democratic elements best chance. We believe important that no date should be set now and especially that no conditions should be accepted by French which would have direct or indirect effect of preventing effective international supervision of agreement ensuring political as well as military guarantees. Also note paragraph 3 of President and Prime Minister joint declaration of June 29 regarding QTE unity through free elections supervised by the UN UNQTE.

Our interpretation of willingness QTE respect UNQTE agreement which might be reached is that we would not (repeat not) oppose a settlement which conformed to seven points contained Deptel 4853. It does not (repeat not) of course mean we would guarantee such settlement or that we would necessarily support it publicly. We consider QTE respect UNQTE as strong a word as we can possibly employ in the circumstances to indicate our position with respect to such arrangements as French may evolve along lines points contained DEPTEL 4853. QTE respect UNQTE would also mean that we would not seek directly or indirectly to upset settlement by force.

You may convey substance above to French.

DULLES

[Document 75]

July 8, 1954

SENT TO: Amembassy PARIS 85 PRIORITY

FOR DILLON, ALDRICH AND JOHNSON

I think it is probably true that if we had put together all of the bits of information given at various times and at various political and military levels at Paris, Geneva, Washington, Saigon and Hanoi, the result would have been a reasonably clear picture of French military intentions as now revealed. I have never harbored any thought of any wilful concealment. Also I have always conceded that the French were clearly within their rights in making their own plans. I have repeatedly said at press conferences that we recognize that the French had the primary position in Indochina and that our role was that of a friendly observer who wanted to help if and when our help was wanted.

I do feel that there is a certain lack of any intimacy which is perhaps due to the fact that we have not in the past worked closely with the personalities of the present Government who have been plunged into an immense and engrossing task. In this respect they have our sympathy and I hope that you will try to remove any impression of carping criticism on our part.

We are quite prepared to agree that France has been overextended in relation to Indochina and we are not quarrelling with present French policy designed to limit its commitments more nearly within the bounds of its strength.

Our present intentions to leave representation at Geneva at the present level of Ambassador Johnson is primarily because we do not want to be the cause of any avoidable embarrassment by what might be a spectacular disassociation of the United States from France. Whatever France may be determined to do, we accept as within its prerogatives. We only regret that we cannot agree to associate ourselves in advance with an end result which we cannot foresee. Equally, we do not want to be in a position of seeming to obstruct an end result which from the French national standpoint seems imperative to its parliament and people.

Since starting to dictate this, I have received through Bonnet a message from Mendes-France strongly urging that either Bedell Smith or I should come back. This apparently based on my today's press conference statement that neither of us had any present plans for returning.

I told Bonnet the substance of the preceding paragraphs to the effect that while we would be only too happy to contribute to a united front, we could do not so without knowing on what position that front was based. If there were a position which France was able to define and state that she would not accept anything else, then we would be able to judge whether or not that afforded the foundation for a united front. At the moment, it seems to me that there is less danger of doing irreparable injury to Franco-American relations if we avoid getting into a position at Geneva which might require a dissassociation under spectacular conditions which would be deeply resented by the French as an effort on our part to block at the last minute a peace which they ardently desire.

We have not yet taken any irrevocable decision and even if no one from here comes over for the 12th, we would be standing by here under circumstances such that if developments at Geneva seem to indicate that our presence there would serve a really constructive purpose one or the other of us could get to Geneva overnight.

Unless you perceive objection, I would like you to explain orally my position to Mendes-France, making clear that we are motivated by our estimate that in the end our presence at Geneva, even though initially it seemed an asset, might subsequently prove a liability to Franco-American relations.

DULLES

Code Room:—Please note

FOR LONDON ONLY

Please show Eden portion of this cable which follows first two paragraphs. Portion begins QTE We are quite prepared, etc. UNQTE

[Document 76]

FROM Geneva

TO: Secretary of State

NO: SECTO 578, July 9, 9 p.m.

LIMIT DISTRIBUTION

PARIS EYES ONLY AMBASSADOR

SAIGON EYES ONLY AMBASSADOR

I called on Chauvel following restricted meeting today. He has just returned from Paris. His impression is that Mendes-France position unchanged and that he does not intend make further concessions to secure agreement with Communists. Mendes-France anticipates active week of discussions followed possibly by last minute agreement on evening July 19. Mendes-France arrives here tomorrow afternoon. He will see Molotov tomorrow evening.

Chauvel dined last night with Communist Chinese. Li Konung and Chang Wen-tien, Vice Minister for Foreign Affairs and Ambassador to USSR who has just returned here, were present. Atmosphere was "very cordial." Chauvel informed Chinese that military discussions with Viet Minh not going well and that latter had made both for Vietnam and for Laos unacceptable proposals wholly out of harmony with what Chauvel had understood Chou En-lai's position to be. Chinese expressed surprise but did not go into details of situation. He told Chauvel that Chou En-lai would probably return here early next week saying it takes three to four days to fly here from Peking depending on weather. Vice Minister stated Chou En-lai had had "very good meeting" with Ho Chi Minh and results "would be helpful to French." Vice Minister has spent last two weeks in Moscow and Chauvel believes Communist Chinese and Soviet positions regarding problem have been coordinated, with Chinese views on Asian problems being given major weight.

There was an "underground" meeting between French Colonel Brebisson and Viet Minh military representative yesterday. At this meeting Viet Minh made two proposals (1) A demarcation line about 40 kilometers north of Tuyhoa line and (2) "neutralization" of delta in order to permit total evacuation of French Expeditionary Corps in three months period. French representative stated both these proposals wholly unacceptable and not even worthy of discussion. He refused to set date for next meeting.

Chauvel saw Molotov this morning. Molotov expressed interest in being informed of progress of conference. Chauvel gave him general review touching particularly on question of demarcation line, attitude of extreme intransigence being adopted by Viet Minh in military talks and problem of international controls. Molotov expressed interest but claimed unfamiliarity with details. Chauvel suggested desirability of contact between French military representatives and members of Soviet delegation in order that Soviet delegation might be fully informed of difficulties being encountered and of attitudes adopted by Viet Minh. Later in day Soviet delegation got in touch with French delegation and these contacts will be set up. Molotov stated that he had seen Chauvel's working paper (SECTO 575) and that while there were points requiring clarification and further study he thought it was a useful contribution.

Chauvel has impression both Russians and Chinese give Viet Minh fairly free hand to see how far they can go but that when they find Viet Minh demands have gone beyond limit which French can be expected to accept, they intervene. Chauvel made point to Molotov that any agreement reached must be acceptable not only to Franco-Vietnamese side and to Viet Minh but also to other conference members. He is hopeful that, as he says occurred previously, Chinese–Russian moderating influence will now be brought to bear on Viet Minh. Chauvel expressed confidence that if he were negotiating only with Russians and Chinese, he could almost certainly achieve a settlement in line with provisions of US–UK aide-memoire.

Chauvel told me that he is having his staff prepare drafts of an armistice agreement and related documents so as to be ready in case ministers reach agreements on major matters. He stated that information we had furnished regarding Korean armistice was most useful to them and was much appreciated.

JOHNSON

[Document 77]

NIACT

SENT TO: AMEMB PARIS 127   7/10/54

FOR AMBASSADOR FROM SECRETARY

LIMIT DISTRIBUTION

Following is personal message from Secretary Dulles to Mendes-France which is to be delivered by Ambassador Dillon to Mendes-France in person as promptly as possible as instructed by separate cable.

BEGIN TEXT: My dear Mr. President:

President Eisenhower (who has been kept closely informed) and I have been greatly moved by your earnest request that I or General Bedell Smith should return next week to Geneva for what may be the conclusion of the Indochina phase of the Conference. I can assure you that our attitude in this respect is dictated by a desire to find the course which will best preserve the traditional friendship and cooperation of our countries and which will promote the goals of justice and human welfare and dignity to which our two nations have been traditionally dedicated. We also attach great value to preserving the united front of France, Great Britain and the United States which has during this postwar period so importantly served all three of us in our dealings with the Communists.

What now concerns us is that we are very doubtful as to whether there is a united front in relation to Indochina, and we do not believe that the mere fact that the high representatives of the three nations physically reappear together at Geneva will serve as a substitute for a clear agreement on a joint position which includes agreement as to what will happen if that position is not accepted by the Communists. We fear that unless there is the reality of such a united front, the events at Geneva will expose differences under conditions which will only serve to accentuate them with consequent strain upon the relations between our two countries greater than if the US does not reappear at Geneva in the person of General Smith or myself.

Beginning early last April the US worked intensively with the French Government and with that of Great Britain in an effort to create a common position of strength. This did not prove possible. The reasons were understandable, and derived from fundamental causes which still subsist and influence the possibility of achieving at the present time a genuine "united front."

During the talks of Prime Minister Churchill and Foreign Secretary Eden with President Eisenhower and me, an effort was made to find a common position which might be acceptable to the two of us and, we hoped, to the French Government. This was expressed in the seven-point memorandum of which you are aware. I believe that this represented a constructive contribution. However, I do not yet feel that there is a united position in the sense that the three of us would be prepared to stand firmly on this as a minimum acceptable solution and to see the negotiations break off and the warfare resume if this position was not accepted by the Communist side. We doubt very much that the Communists will in fact accept this seven-point position unless they realize that the alternative is some common action upon which we have all agreed. So far, there is no such alternative.

Under these circumstances, we greatly fear that the seven points which constitute a minimum as far as the US is concerned will constitute merely an optimum solution so far as your Government and perhaps the UK are concerned, and that an armistice might be concluded on terms substantially less favorable than those we could respect.

We gather that there is already considerable French thinking in terms of the acceptability of departures from certain of the seven points. For example:

Allowing Communist forces to remain in Northern Laos; accepting a Vietnam line of military demarcation considerably south of Donghoi; neutralizing and demilitarizing Laos, Cambodia and Vietnam so as to impair their capacity to maintain stable, non-Communist regimes; accepting elections so early and so ill-prepared and ill-supervised as to risk the loss of the entire area to Communism; accepting international supervision by a body which cannot be effective because it includes a Communist state which has veto power.

These are but illustrations of a whittling-away process, each stroke of which may in itself seem unessential, but which cumulatively could produce a result quite different from that envisaged by the seven points. Also, of course, there is the danger that the same unacceptable result might come about through the Communist habit of using words in a double sense and destroying the significance of good principles with stultifying implementations.

We do not for a moment question the right of the French Government to exercise its own judgment in all of these respects. Indeed, we recognize that the issues for France are so vital that the French Government has a duty to exercise its own judgment. I have from the beginning recognized the preponderant interest of your Government as representing the nation which has borne for so many years the burden of a cruel and costly war. However, my Government equally has the duty not to endorse a solution which would seem to us to impair seriously certain principles which the US believes must, as far as it is concerned, be kept unimpaired, if our own struggle against Communism is to be successfully pursued. At the same time, we do not wish to put ourselves in the position where we would seem to be passing moral judgment upon French action or disassociating ourselves from the settlement at a moment and under circumstances which might be unnecessarily dramatic.

It is also to be considered that if our conduct creates a certain uncertainty in the minds of the Communists, this might strengthen your hand more than our presence at Geneva in a form which would expose probably to the world, and certainly to the Communists themselves, differences which the Communists would exploit to the discomfiture of all three of us.

Under all these circumstances, it seems to us that the interests of both of our countries are best served by continuing for the time being the present type of US representation at Geneva. This consists of able and responsible persons who are in close contact with the President and me.

If circumstances should alter so that it appeared that our common interests would be better served if higher ranking officials became our representatives, than we would be alert to act accordingly.

It is because I am fully aware of the serious and solemn nature of the moment that I have gone into the matter at this considerable length. It is possible that by the first of the week, the Communist position will be sufficiently disclosed so that some of the answers to the foregoing queries can be foreseen. This might clarify in one sense or another the thinking of us all.

In this connection, let me emphasize that it is our ardent hope that circumstances might become such that consistently with the foregoing either General Bedell Smith or I can personally come to Geneva and stand beside you.
END TEXT

DULLES

[Document 78]

FROM: Paris

TO: Secretary of State

NO: 134, July 11, 9 p.m.

SENT DEPARTMENT 134, REPEATED INFORMATION GENEVA 21, LONDON 35

FOR SECRETARY FROM AMBASSADOR

I delivered Secretary's message Department telegram 127 to Mendes in Geneva after lunch Sunday. At same time, I gave him personal message contained in first paragraph Department telegram 128. In view Eden's absence (SECTO 585), I did not (repeat not) see him. Johnson will deliver message to Eden tomorrow, if Aldrich has not (repeat not) already done so.

Mendes was very touched by personal message in Department telegram 128 and twice asked me to be sure and thank Secretary on his behalf for this thought.

Regarding Department telegram 127, Mendes expressed extreme disappointment and gave concern at United States decision not (repeat not) to be represented at Ministerial level. He divided his remarks into two categories, first, the effect of our decision on Conference itself, and second, the overall effect of our decision on world affairs.

Regarding first category, Mendes stated that our absence made French bargaining position far weaker. He stated that if Secretary was present, France would not (repeat not) accept anything at Conference that was unacceptable to United States. As he put it in his own words, presence of Secretary would give United States in effect a veto power on decisions of Conference. He felt it particularly important that we have someone at Geneva who could take strong personal position with Molotov, if and when necessary, and without having to refer to Washington for instructions. Mendes also feels that United States absence at Ministerial level will lead Communists to increase their pressure and be more demanding in order to deepen the obvious rift between the Western powers. He said France had not (repeat not) as yet departed from the Seven Point United States–United Kingdom position and he did not (repeat not) make any commitment to hold to these points during coming week, except for statement regarding United States veto power if Secretary present.

On the overall effect of our decision, Mendes pointed out that this will be first time since the war that United States not (repeat not) represented at equal level with other powers in an important conference. He said he felt certain that Europe would interpret United States absence as first step in return to a policy of isolationism. This, he felt, would have catastrophic effects not (repeat not) only in Far East, but also in Europe and would be great cold war victory for Communism. According to Mendes, we would in effect be saying "do your best, you have our sympathy, but result is no (repeat no) real concern to us."

I tried hard to dissuade Mendes from this viewpoint, but without much success. His statement regarding United States veto power if Secretary present, led me to point out that there must also be an agreed alternative if Conference failed. Mendes promptly replied that only alternative to cease-fire at Geneva would be internationalization of war with United States military forces coming promptly to assistance of French. This aspect of our talk being covered more fully in separate telegram, being repeated to Saigon.

Finally, Mendes asked if there was anything he could do specifically to create a situation that would make it possible for Secretary to come to Geneva. He asked me to pass this question on to Washington. In this connection, he specifically questioned sixth paragraph of Secretary's letter, and said he knew of no (repeat no) French thinking along such lines, except possibly on subject of international supervision. He wondered where United States had got the ideas expressed in this paragraph.

While I was talking with Mendes, Johnson talked with Chauvel and showed him a copy of Secretary's letter. Chauvel showed Johnson a cable from Bonnet which indicated that Bonnet may have given Secretary the impression that French were considering retreating from Seven Point program.

Chauvel and Johnson joined us at the end of our talk, and Johnson and I suggested that if Mendes developed any concrete ideas which would help meet United States fears, it would be helpful if he put them into a reply to Secretary's letter. While Mendes was non-committal as to a formal reply, I rather expect he will make one. In closing, Mendes said he would keep in close touch with Johnson. During talk, Mendes made it clear that while presence of Under Secretary at Geneva would be most helpful, he very much hoped that Secretary himself could come.

DILLON

[Document 79]

FROM: Paris

TO: Secretary of State

NO: 133, July 11, 9 p.m.

PRIORITY

LIMIT DISTRIBUTION

FOR SECRETARY FROM AMBASSADOR DILLON

During conversation with Mendes at Geneva, I informed him of contents of DEPTEL 84 and of our feeling that Vietnam Government should be kept more fully informed by French. I told him that we felt time had now come for Vietnam to be informed of general lines of seven point program. Mendes said he would consider informing Vietnamese after discussing matter with his advisors during afternoon: He said he had originally felt it preferable not to inform them until he could assure them that US was prepared to guarantee them against further aggression or subversion.

He then spoke at length of necessity for a clear-cut US guarantee that would protect Associated States in the event that the Communists did not honor the spirit of any agreement that might be reached at Geneva. Without such a guarantee he said that a settlement would not be worth the paper it was written on. Mendes asked me to inquire as to whether if a settlement within seven point framework was obtained, Secretary would then be willing to come to Geneva to close conference and to work out necessary guarantees to protect Associated States.

He then discussed in some detail the situation which would arise if no settlement was reached at Geneva. He said the sending of conscripts to Indochina would then be debated on July 22 and 23. If the National Assembly approved, the first division would leave on July 25 and the second division about 10 days later. It would take a month to reach Indochina and three more weeks to get troops ready for action. Therefore the first division of conscripts would not be ready in Indochina until about September.

This schedule for reinforcements would be known to Viet Minh and the result would undoubtedly be a massive Viet Minh assault during August prior to arrival of new troops.

Mendes said he doubted if French alone could successfully resist such an assault. He said that French Government would officially inform US of these facts at end of July if no cease-fire reached.

I reminded him of US requirements for action on our part, and he said he could not foretell how French Parliament might react. They might react strongly and request US help to continue the war or they might have what he termed a "nervous breakdown" and push for capitulation at any price to save expeditionary corps.

If no cease-fire, Mendes will resign, but in view of the above, I feel it is possible that if no cease-fire is reached the French Government which will succeed Mendes may appeal for US armed help, and may meet all US terms. Not possible to estimate timing of such an appeal but it could occur during August when US Congress no longer in session.

DILLON

[Document 80]

FROM: Paris

TO: Secretary of State

NO: 179, July 14, 9 p.m.

PRIORITY

Paris Talks—III

In addition to the following agreed texts of Paris meeting, the Secretary's party will bring full memoranda of conversations: (The following documents are classified and not (repeat not) for release.)

A. Agreed French–United States position paper on Indochina.

QUOTE

1. France and the Associated States of Vietnam, Laos and Cambodia are recognized to be those which, on the non-Communist side, are primarily interested in the Indochina phase of the Geneva Conference.

The United States is interested primarily as a friendly nation which desires to assist, where desired, in arriving at a just settlement, but who will not (repeat not) seek, or be expected, to impose its views in any way upon those primarily interested.

2. The attached 7 points constitute a result which France believes to be obtainable by negotiation at Geneva and which would be acceptable to France and, France believes, to the Associated States. The United States, while recognizing the right of those primarily interested to accept different terms, will itself be prepared to respect terms conforming to the attached. The United States will not (repeat not) be asked or expected by France to respect terms which in its opinion differ materially from the attached, and it may publicly disassociate itself from such differing terms.

3. If the settlement is one which the United States is prepared to "respect" its position will be expressed unilaterally or in association only with non-Communist states in terms which apply to the situation the principles of non-use of forces which are embodied in Article 2 (4) and (6) of the Charter of the United Nations.

4. The United States is prepared to seek, with other interested nations, a collective defense association designed to preserve, against direct and indirect aggression, the integrity of the non-Communist areas of Southeast Asia following any settlement.

5. If there is no (repeat no) settlement, the United States and French Government will consult together on the measures to be taken. This will not (repeat not) preclude the United States, if it so desires, bringing the matter before the United Nations as involving a threat to peace as dealt with by Chapter VII of the Charter of the United Nations.

6. France reaffirms the principle of independence for the Associated States in equal and voluntary association as members of the French Union.

UNQUOTE

B. Annex to above document consisting of the 7 points regarding a settlement which could be respected as agreed during Churchill-Eisenhower conversations. (Please note following phrase which has been added with the full consent of Eden and Mendes-France at the beginning of paragraph 2 of the 7 points.) "In connection with the line of military demarcation, preserves—"
"Memorandum of points referred to in paragraph 2 of the France–United States position paper.
An agreement which:
"1. Preserves the integrity and independence of Laos and Cambodia and assures the withdrawal of Viet Minh forces therefrom;
"2. In connection with the line of military demarcation preserves at least the southern half of Vietnam and if possible an enclave in the deltas; in this connection, we would be unwilling to see the line of division of responsibility drawn further south than a line running generally west from Dong Hoi;
"3. Does not (repeat not) impose on Laos, Cambodia or retained Vietnam any restrictions materially impairing their capacity to maintain stable non-Communist regimes; and especially restrictions impairing their right to maintain adequate forces for internal security, to import arms and to employ foreign advisers;
"4. Does not (repeat not) contain political provisions which would risk loss of the retained area to Communist control;
"5. Does not (repeat not) exclude the possibility of the ultimate unification of the Vietnam by peaceful means;
"6. Provides for the peaceful and humane transfer, under international supervision, of those people desiring to be moved from one zone to another of Vietnam; and

"7. Provides effective machinery for international supervision of the agreement."

C. Letter from Mendes-France to Secretary (unofficial translation of French text).

QUOTE

Dear Mr. Secretary:

Following our frank and friendly conversation of last evening, I believe I understand fully the position of the United States with regard to the negotiations at Geneva concerning Indochina.

If I interpret your views correctly, you recognize fully the primary right of France, the Associated States of Vietnam, Laos, and Cambodia, to decide the conditions for the settlement of a war in which they are the only belligerents on the non-Communist side. You wish to aid us through your good offices in obtaining a just and honorable settlement which will take into account the needs of the interested peoples. However, you are not (repeat not) prepared to participate with the Communist countries in any settlement which might appear to retain for them the benefits of aggression or the domination of non-willing peoples. In any case, if a settlement should be arrived at between the parties holding the primary responsibility, you would agree to indicate that you would comply with the principles which are contained in Articles 2 (4) and (6) of the United Nations Charter and you would consider any violation of the settlement by the Communist regimes as being of grave concern.

It being your belief that the continuation of the war would involve a serious risk of an extension of the conflict, both as concerns the combat areas and the belligerent countries, the question of the participation of the United States would be guided by the terms defined in the fourth paragraph of the letter addressed on July 16, 1954, by President Eisenhower to President Coty.

You have indicated to me that you would fear, in the present state of negotiations, that the sending by the United States to Geneva of representatives chosen at a high level and bearing instructions from President Eisenhower to adhere to the principles noted above, could cause a situation capable of giving rise in France, under the most regrettable circumstances, to a feeling that our two countries are divided and that it might risk affecting seriously their good relations which are so important to the whole free world.

I have noted your hesitation to come to Geneva in the fear of having eventually to disassociate yourself from an agreement, or certain of its terms, which you might not (repeat not) be able to respect. This appears to me to be understandable, but in my opinion it does not (repeat not) respond to the situation. In effect, I have every reason to think that your absence would be precisely interpreted as demonstrating, before the fact, that you disapproved of the conference and of everything which might be accomplished. Not (repeat not) only would those who are against us find therein the confirmation of the ill will which they attribute to your government, concerning the re-establishment of peace in Indochina; but many others would read in it a sure sign of a division of the western powers. Finally, the negotiations would thus be deprived of the element of balance indispensable to the seeking of a solution as recommended in the memorandum of June 30.

I consider thus that such an absence would produce an effect diametrically opposed to the intentions which you have expressed and which I have cited above. In a situation as difficult as this only the unity of the western democratic front, supported by the immense potential which we have in common, can bring about the very military and strategic unity which we should seek eventually to establish in that part of the world.

It is in this spirit that the French Government envisages, aside from the assurances which the conference itself could furnish, the establishment of a collective guarantee by virtue of which the signatories would declare themselves prepared to intervene if, in Indochina, one of the three states was a victim of aggression. I am fully conscious of the position of the government of the United States and I have noted with care the consequences which it might imply; but for the reasons which I have just enumerated, I have the profound conviction that the common interests of our two countries and of the three Associated States would be effectively defended only if you, yourself, or the Undersecretary should represent in person your government at Geneva.

If the situation should nevertheless evolve in a manner which would confirm your fears, I engage myself, on behalf of France, to make known publicly the conditions under which you have acceded to my request.

UNQUOTE

D. Letter from Secretary to Mendes-France.

QUOTE

My dear Mr. President:

I have received your letter of July 14 with reference to participation by the United States in the final stages of the Indochina phase of the Geneva conference.

In the light of what you say and after consultation with President Eisenhower, I am glad to be able to inform you that the President and I are asking the Undersecretary of State, General Walter Bedell Smith, to prepare to return at his earliest convenience to Geneva to share in the work of the conference on the basis of the understanding which we have arrived at.

I greatly appreciate the opportunity which we have had to confer together and I believe that it has added a new chapter to the honorable and precious tradition of Franco-American cooperation.

UNQUOTE

E. Letter to Mendes-France from Eden.

QUOTE

My Dear Mr. President:

Thank you for providing me with copies of correspondence exchanged today between yourself and Mr. John Foster Dulles on the present phase of the Indochina conference at Geneva.

I have noted their contents and wish to assure you that, as a friend and ally, I shall do my best to help you to achieve a settlement on the basis set out in this correspondence.

I am sending a copy of this letter to Mr. Dulles.

UNQUOTE

DULLES

[Document 81]

SECRETARY DULLES' REPORT ON HIS RECENT TRIP TO PARIS

At the NSC meeting of 15 July, Secretary Dulles reported on his recent trip to Paris as follows:

1. He had been in practically continuous meetings with Mendes-France and Mr. Eden from the time of his arrival to his departure, sometimes with one or the other individually and sometimes with the two together. He had told Mendes that, in his opinion, most of France's troubles stem from a lack of French decision on EDC. Because of this, the Soviets were being successful in splitting France and Germany. Therefore, he put the greatest urgency on French action on EDC. Mendes said that it might not be possible now to get a constitutional majority of 314 votes in the Assemblé without some face-saving formula. He hoped this could be done through minor amendments which would not require renegotiation, but in any event, Mendes had promised Secretary Dulles action by the Assembly by early August. Mr. Dulles had pointed out that the U.S. public was getting a trifle short-tempered on the EDC topic and that if Mendes was not careful, the U.S. Congress might terminate aid to NATO which would be detrimental to the military effort of all Europe, especially France.

2. a. Regarding the dilemma of U.S. participation in the Geneva Conference, Secretary Dulles had pointed out that if the U.S. participates in the Conference and then finds itself unable to guarantee the results, a violent French public reaction against the U.S. would ensue. Similarly, if the U.S. participates and so stiffens French will that France does not accept the Communist best offer, then again, the U.S. would be blamed and a major strain placed upon U.S.–French relations. Therefore, the U.S. was seeking to play an inconspicuous role.

b. The original VM proposal had been for a partition line along the 14th parallel; their second proposal, along the 16th parallel. Both had been rejected and the French position was to hold out for the 18th parallel, along with the guaranteed independence of Laos and Cambodia.

c. The Secretary had worked up with the French a joint U.S.–French paper along the lines of the seven points of the U.S.–U.K. paper which had resulted from the Churchill–Eden talks. Mr. Dulles had said there would be no U.S. guarantee of the settlement, but rather a unilateral declaration that the U.S. would not attempt to change it by force. Mendes had provided Mr. Dulles with a letter of reply and acceptance of the U.S.–French position paper. Accordingly, Gen. Smith was returning to Geneva with his instructions contained in these two papers.

3. Mr. Dulles said that the Mendes Government put more emphasis on the granting of independence to the Associated States than had the Laniel Government. Mendes even agreed that French functionaries and eventually armed forces would have to leave the area. It was current French planning to hold Haiphong until French forces and their equipment could be evacuated but not to attempt to maintain Haiphong as a permanent enclave.

4. When asked if the VM would agree to the seven points, the Secretary said he was not sure but he could count on support from Laos and Cambodia. Mr. Allen Dulles felt the possibility of VM uprising against the French was a real one.

5. Mendes had assured Secretary Dulles that if the Geneva Conference was a failure, he would send two additional French divisions to Indochina, although they could not arrive before September, 1954.

[Document 82]

FROM: Geneva

TO: Secretary of State

NO: SECTO 632, July 17, 7 p.m.

Following account of Mendes-France–Eden–Molotov meeting last night is based on report of this meeting to Foreign Office made available to Johnson by Caccia. This telegram expands upon and supersedes preliminary account transmitted in first three paragraphs SECTO 630 (repeated information Paris 76, Saigon 48).

At Eden's suggestion, French enumerated documents before conference:

(A) Armistice agreements to be signed by local commanders-in-chief. French have prepared drafts for Vietnam and Laos and Cambodians draft for Cambodia. Viet Minh delegation preparing counter draft for Vietnam.

(B) Control arrangements. French have circulated papers for Vietnam, Laos, and Cambodia.

(C) Political arrangements. After having seen military documents, certain delegations might make unilateral statements. For example, Laos and Cambodia are preparing statements on their willingness to limit their armed forces. Conference as whole would then agree upon common statement taking note of military agreements and unilateral declarations. French have circulated draft of such statement. Soviets have prepared counter draft and French second redraft.

French explained that if conference did not (repeat not) have time to agree on all details of armistice, it might approve only parts providing for cessation of hostilities and first stage of regroupment. Remaining aspects of agreements could be covered by statement of general principles for guidance of experts who would work out details after conference had dispersed.

It was agreed that British, French, and Soviet experts would meet July 17 to consider various drafts.

At Eden's suggestion, Mendes-France summarized main outstanding problems as (A) demarcation line for Vietnam; (B) elections, and (C) control arrangements. Concerning demarcation line, he said French had proposed line near 18th parallel whereas Viet Minh proposed 16th parallel. On elections in Vietnam, he said question was whether to fix firm date now (repeat now) (Soviets had proposed June 1955) or whether, as French proposed, to settle now (repeat now) only manner in which date would be set. Elections in Laos and Cambodia already provided for in constitutions for August and September 1955, respectively. On control, he said main questions were: Whether there should be one commission or three, composition, voting, execution of commissions' recommendations, and freedom of movement for inspection teams.

Molotov added to outstanding issues: (D) time required for regrouping (French have proposed 380 days and Soviets 6 months); and (E) prevention of importation of new arms and military personnel subject to certain exceptions for Laos and Cambodia, prohibition of foreign military bases, and prohibition of military alliances by three states.

Eden added (F) question of regroupment areas for resistance forces in Laos.

Discussion then turned to substantive issues:

(A) *Elections in Vietnam.* Molotov said conference should fix date for elections. He conceded more flexible formula might be found than firm date of June 1955 previously proposed by Soviets and suggested agreement merely that elections be held during 1955 with precise date to be fixed by Vietnamese and Viet Minh authorities.

Mendes-France argued that it would be imprudent to fix date as early as the end of 1955. He suggested two ways of providing necessary flexibility in arrangements: Date for elections might be fixed after completion of regrouping; or exact date might be fixed now (repeat now) and international control commission be given authority to advance date if necessary.

Eden supported Mendes-France on need for flexibility and suggested that two parts of Vietnam fix date after completion of regrouping. Mendes-France agreed to consider this suggestion, but Molotov continued to urge elections during 1955.

(B) *Demarcation line.* Molotov argued that in moving from 13th to 16th parallel, Viet Minh had made substantial concession which called for proper response from French. Mendes-France disagreed, arguing that Viet Minh would be giving up much less in Annam than they would be getting in Tonkin. He said that Pham Van Dong had admitted that line on 16th parallel would require special arrangements for Tourane, Hue, on route No. 9 leading into Laos. Mendes-France stated that necessity for such special arrangements showed how unnatural demarcation line at 16th parallel would be. He said that there was no (repeat no) chance of persuading French Government to accept line which excluded either Hue or route No. 9. Eden supported Mendes-France.

Molotov suggested that discussion move to question of control arrangements. Mendes-France replied might be better to postpone such discussion. He observed that questions of elections and demarcation line had been discussed together and might be linked in sense that conceivably one party might yield on one question and another party on other.

SMITH

[Document 83]

FROM: Geneva

TO: Secretary of State

NO: SECTO 633, July 17, 8 p.m.

Nguyen Huu Chau of Vietnamese delegation handed USDEL copy of note which was given to French delegation today. He said French requested contents be kept secret for moment, and that French not aware copy given to this delegation. Following is unofficial translation:

BEGIN QUOTE

Just as the French High Command in Indochina evacuated, without fighting and in spite of the strongest protests by President Ngo Dinh Diem, zones vital for the defense and the existence of a free Vietnam, the delegation of the Vietnamese National Government learned only by the papers and by the messages which were sent to it yesterday, July 16, that the French delegation appears already to have accepted abandoning to the Viet Minh all of that part situated north of the eighteenth parallel and that the delegation of the Viet Minh might claim an even more advantageous demarcation line.

The National Government of Vietnam has also been left in complete ignorance of the proposals on the fate of Vietnam made by the French Government to the American and British Governments, particularly at the meeting in Paris.

The delegation of the State of Vietnam must express its surprise at this situation. This delegation finds it hard to understand that peace in Vietnam is being negotiated without previously consulting with its qualified representatives.

The de facto partition which seems to have been adopted from the outset by the delegations of France and of the Viet Minh—at discussions bearing only on the materialization of the partition—does not take any account of the unanimous will for national unity of the Vietnamese people.

On the other hand the regroupment of non-national armed forces in the zones resulting from the partition implies their consolidation outside of any danger of combat and thus reinforces the threat that they constitute to the free expression of the will of the people.

Therefore not only does such a cease-fire not lead to a durable peace, since, ignoring the will for national unity, it provokes the people to "unify" the country, but, by the consolidation of the armed forces now facing each other, it violates in advance the liberty of the future elections.

The delegation of the State of Vietnam, which more than any other wishes the return of peace, is pleased with the efforts put forth by the other delegations in favor of this object. However, it greatly fears that the cease-fire, such as it seems to be accepted by certain delegations, far from leading to peace, makes peace improbable and precarious.

Aware of these very grave dangers and certain that it is expressing the profound aspirations of all true Vietnamese, including most of the Viet Minh fighters themselves, and in full accord with the Chief and the Government of the State of Vietnam, the Vietnamese delegation asks not only a cease-fire but the disarmament of all the belligerent forces in Vietnam.

The Vietnamese delegation asks that the entire territory of Vietnam be placed provisionally under the control of the United Nations pending the complete reestablishment of security, of order and of peace in their minds and in their hearts which will permit the Vietnamese people to decide their destiny by free elections.

His Majesty Bao Dai, Chief of State of Vietnam, thus shows once more that he places the independence and the unity of his country above any other consideration, and the National Government of Vietnam would prefer this provisional control by the United Nations over a truly unified and independent Vietnam to its maintenance in power in a country dismembered and condemned to slavery.

The Vietnamese delegation reserves its right to develop its proposal at a later time.

END QUOTE

SMITH

[Document 84]

FROM: Geneva
TO: Secretary of State
NO: SECTO 639, July 18, 1 p.m.
FOR THE SECRETARY FROM THE UNDER SECRETARY
Following despatch given us in advance by Topping of Associated Press apparently represents official Chinese Communist position and was given Topping in order that we would become aware of it. It begins:

QUOTE

The Communist bloc has demanded that the United States guarantee the partition peace plan for Indochina and join in an agreement to neutralize the whole country, a responsible Chinese Communist informant said today.

The informant, who reflects the views of Red China Premier Chou En-lai, said the Communists are hopeful of a cease-fire agreement by next Tuesday's deadline if the Western powers agree to 'bar all foreign military bases from Indochina and keep the three member states out of any military bloc.'

The informant said the Communists are pressing for the stamp of American approval on the armistice agreement—already okayed in principle by Britain and France—which would divide Vietnam between Communist leader Ho Chi Minh's Viet Minh and Bao Dai's pro-Western regime.

'We believe that the US as a member of the conference should and is obligated to subscribe to and guarantee any settlement. Morally, there is no reason for the US to avoid this obligation.'

But the informant did not (repeat not) rule out the chance of an Indochina cease-fire even if the US refuses to okay the armistice agreement.

The Eisenhower administration has told France and Britain that they can go ahead with their plan for an Indochina settlement based on partition of Vietnam. But Washington has made it clear that it is not (repeat not) ready to associate itself formally with the plan which would sanction putting millions of Vietnamese under Red rule.

The Communist informant said the 'crucial issue' now in the Geneva peace negotiations revolves around whether the Western powers will agree effectively to neutralize Indochina.

'Refusal to join in such a guarantee,' the informant said, 'could seriously deter a final settlement. On other important points in the negotiations we are in agreement or close to it. We are hopeful and we believe that there is time to reach a settlement by July 20.'

French Premier Pierre Mendes-France has promised to resign with his Cabinet if he fails to end the bloody eight-year-old war by next Tuesday. Fall of the French Government probably would doom the Geneva negotiations. The informant declared that American efforts to organize a Southeast Asia Treaty organization (SEATO) is 'a threat to any possible Indochina agreement.'

'Success or failure of the Geneva Conference may depend on the attitude of the American delegation in this regard,' he added.

END QUOTE

The above seems to me extremely significant, particularly in view of the fact that in my discussion with Eden last night he expressed pessimism, which he said was now shared for the first time by Krishna Menon. Latter had begun to feel, as I do, that Molotov wishes to force Mendes-France's resignation. Eden remarked that Molotov had now become the most difficult and intransigent member of Communist delegation. You will note obvious intention to place on shoulders of US responsibility for failure of Geneva Conference and fall of French Government if this occurs.

Molotov is insisting on a meeting this afternoon which French and British are trying to make highly restricted as they are apprehensive of what may occur. If such a meeting is held and if demands are made for US association in any agreement, I will simply say that in the event a reasonable settlement is arrived at which US could "respect," US will probably issue a unilateral statement of its own position. If question of participation Laos, Cambodia and Vietnam in security pact is raised, I will reply that this depends on outcome of conference.

Eden has already told Molotov that security pact is inevitable, that he himself favored it some time ago and that he would not (repeat not) withdraw from that position, but he made the mistake of saying that no consideration had been given to inclusion of Laos and Cambodia.

This final gambit is going to be extremely difficult to play and I do not (repeat not) now see the moves clearly. However, my opinion as expressed to you before leaving, i.e., that Molotov will gain more by bringing down Mendès Government than by a settlement, has grown stronger.

SMITH

[Document 85]

July 18, 1954

SENT TO: Amconsul GENEVA TOSEC 565 NIACT

FROM SECRETARY FOR UNDER SECRETARY

Does SECTO 637 fourth paragraph mean that Eden has given away position which Mendes-France took in Paris, namely that he was willing to have Communist state on Control Commission without veto, or unanimity if no Communist state a member, but he would not (rpt not) take both a Communist state and unanimity rule?

Your SECTO 639 received. It may be useful for you to bear in mind that Executive has no Constitutional power to give "guarantee." This can only be done by treaty, ratification of which would surely be rejected. Executive can only reaffirm in relation to Indochina its general undertakings expressed in UN Charter.

Am fearful Eden will try to push Mendes-France into agreement far short of 7 Points which will confront us with dilemma of either agreeing to "respect" it or repudiation which might involve our responsibility for breakup. This precisely result which I apprehended and fully discussed with Mendes-France Paris and I must count on him to strive to protect both our countries against consequences of this Communist maneuver which Eden might unwittingly abet.

DULLES

[Document 86]

FROM: Geneva

TO: Secretary of State

NO: SECTO 654, July 18, 11 p.m.

Twenty-third Indochina restricted session Sunday, July 18, Molotov presiding. This session called at urgent request Soviets; French and British had requested that participants be confined to chiefs of del plus one adviser. This latter relaxed to permit two advisers.

Molotov spoke first, noting that last meeting of Foreign Ministers held on June 19, just one month ago. He believed that today's session presented good opportunity to gauge importance of period which had passed since last meeting and work performed by deputies. He believed that results achieved through private meetings and discussions had been not (repeat not) inconsiderable. Of course, not (repeat not) all of the questions had been resolved nor everything done which had to be done, but one should recognize the value of what had been achieved.

Molotov said first of all he wished to note that as far as the most complicated problem was concerned, that of peace in Indochina, a basis for reestablishment of peace had been achieved as a result private negotiations which had opened possibility of agreement on that question. He believed all participants would attach appropriate significance to this accomplishment. He felt it was also important to recognize the work done with reference to establishment of peace in Laos and Cambodia. In this connection, it is perhaps true that everything had not (repeat not) been done that could be done but it appeared conference was on way to agreement concerning Laos and Cambodia.

Molotov said that all this shows recent private talks have had success and he expressed belief that such success would continue.

Describing situation as it appeared to him, Molotov noted that drafts for agreements on cessation of hostilities in Vietnam and Laos had been presented to conference. Two drafts would be available today. The same was also true for Cambodia. He hoped parties concerned would display goodwill necessary to agree on unresolved points in these drafts.

Molotov noted also were two drafts of Geneva conference declaration dealing with important political matters.

Two drafts have also been presented concerning the question of international control pertaining to implementation of the agreements. Question of control commission has long been discussed and Molotov felt that final agreement on this subject would not (repeat not) require great deal of time.

Molotov concluded by saying that he had made these observations in order to give general picture of the conference at present and that his remarks were naturally not (repeat not) complete. He believed that today's meeting could make progress re the questions under discussion and would contribute to solution of problems facing conference.

After long pause Tran Van Do (Vietnam) spoke next, saying he had learned this morning that today's meeting was to review final declaration of Geneva conference. In order to avoid any misunderstanding, he wished to state firmly that Vietnam del could not (repeat not) associate itself with any discussion of this declaration. Vietnam position based on following points:

1. Vietnam does not agree to conditions advanced for cessation of hostilities.

2. Vietnam delegation has not (repeat not) as yet advanced proposals on behalf of Vietnam Government for solution of problem based on principles of peace, independence and unity.

With regard point number one, Do referred to French draft of July 16 of conference declaration (SECTO 628 repeated Paris 74, Saigon 46). This draft spoke of division of Vietnam into zones. For example, article 6 said settlement must permit Vietnamese people enjoy fundamental liberties guaranteed by democratic institutions formed following free elections supervised by international commission. Elections would take place when in opinion of competent representative authorities in each zone restoration of peace in country has made sufficient progress, et cetera. Article 7 speaks of a settlement which would give Vietnamese people right decide freely as to zone where residence desired.

Vietnamese representative next referred to Soviet draft of July 15 (SECTO 615, repeated Paris 63, Saigon 35). Article 8 of Soviet draft speaks of "consultation between competent representative authorities of northern and southern zones of Vietnam." Article 10 states that representative authorities in northern and southern zones of Vietnam, as well as authorities of Laos and Cambodia, will not permit persecution of persons who have collaborated with other side.

In view Vietnamese delegation, this indicates that Vietnam will be divided into north and south zones. Everyone is talking of the division of Vietnam and mention is even made of parallels at which division will be accomplished. Delegation of Vietnam can only protest the idea of partition. Based on point number one cited earlier in statement of Vietnamese representative, Vietnamese delegation flatly rejects both drafts submitted to conference.

Vietnamese representative then stated that Vietnamese delegation has not had opportunity, on behalf of new Vietnamese Government, to express own views. It reserves its right to submit a draft declaration and to elaborate on it at a plenary meeting in near future. Vietnamese delegation therefore requests a plenary meeting for this. Do noted further that there was no mention of State of Vietnam in either French or Soviet drafts. Vietnamese delegation cannot accept declaration or agreement where Vietnam, which invited to conference as existing state, not even mentioned.

After pause following Molotov's request for other speakers, General made following statement:

"If no one else desires to speak, I think it would be helpful if I made clear position of US in these last critical days of conference. I do this because I have recently seen the advance drafts submitted to the conference and have had a chance to review them.

"One position of the United States with respect to this conference has consistently been that it is willing to assist, where desired, in arriving at a just and honorable settlement which will contribute to the establishment and maintenance of peace in the area. The United States is not a belligerent in this conflict and it has not and will not seek to impose its views in any way upon the belligerents, who are the parties primarily interested.

"If the agreements arrived at here are of a character which my government is able to respect, the United States is prepared to declare unilaterally that, in accordance with its obligations under the United Nations Charter, and particularly Article II(4), it will refrain from the threat or the use of force to disturb them, and would view any renewal of the aggression in violation of the agreements with grave concern.

Since no other representatives requested floor following General Smith's statement, Molotov suggested intermission. After intermission had lasted for 45 minutes, it was informally agreed that meeting should be adjourned without returning to conference room. No communique issued.

Comment: Today's restricted session strangest performance to date. Apparent Molotov had not set stage even with Communist colleagues for any particularly important announcement despite his insistence that meeting be called. Molotov had said to Mendes-France just before meeting that he thought would be well underline progress made and to show how close conference was to reaching agreement.

During recess, Chou En-lai said he had no desire make any statement. He seemed as much in dark as everyone else as to why Soviets had called meeting.

SMITH

[Document 87]

FROM: Geneva

TO: Secretary of State

NO: SECTO 655, July 18, 11 p.m.

At recess after today's meeting Tran Van Do and Tran Van Chuong immediately approached Johnson stating they wished U.S. clearly understand reasons they felt compelled make their statement at today's meeting (SECTO 654) and why they were asking for a plenary session. They said they desired at such a plenary session put forward position contained their note to French (SECTO 633) and asked Johnson's opinion on position. Johnson replied that did not feel it was practicable proposal, to which they responded they fully realized that it was not practicable and would be rejected by other side, but they felt they must make moral position their government clear to world and to Vietnamese people. If other side rejected it, position of their government would have been improved. Upon rejection by other side they would be prepared accept settlement along lines now being discussed.

Johnson pointed out that time was short and it was late for such proposal to which they replied that Mendes could of course ask for and obtain additional time from French Assembly. Johnson expressed strong doubt and urged they speak directly with French. After repeated strong urgings they finally approached Mendes, who listened sympathetically and at length. He suggested and they promised to consider formulation their proposal in writing and circulation to other delegations. He categorically stated he could not even if he so desired ask Assembly for any extension time he has given self.

Johnson told Mendes he was concerned over reaction to Vietnamese statement and reminded Mendes of U.S. position on Vietnamese concurrence with any agreement. Mendes stated he was very conscious of [word illegible] and was asking De Jean immediately go to Cannes to see Bao Dai.

Chauvel said that from De Jean's previous talk with Bao Dai it appeared Bao Dai had no knowledge of Do's conversations with Dong and in general had given delegation here free hand.

SMITH

[Document 88]

FROM: Geneva

TO: Secretary of State

NO: SECTO 661, July 19, 1 p.m.

Re SECTO 639

Topping has supplied in confidence following background information concerning his story on views of Chinese Communist delegation.

He stated his informant was Huang Hua, whom he has known for many years.

Interview was at Huang's initiative, was called on short notice, and was conducted in extremely serious manner without propaganda harangues.

Topping said he had reported Huang's statement fully in his story but had obtained number of "visual impressions" during interview. When Huang spoke of possibility American bases in Indochina or anti-Communist pact in Southeast Asia, he became very agitated, his hands shook, and his usually excellent English broke down, forcing him to work through interpreter. Huang also spoke seriously and with apparent sincerity concerning his belief that I have returned to Geneva to prevent settlement. Topping believes Chinese Communists convinced Americans made deal with French during Paris talks on basis of which Mendes-France has raised price of settlement.

SMITH

[Document 89]

FROM: Geneva

TO: Secretary of State

NO: SECTO 666, July 19, 7 p.m.

NIACT

FOR THE SECRETARY FROM THE UNDERSECRETARY.

The outlines of international control now clearly emerge. Composition will probably be Poland, India, and Canada or Belgium. The French prefer Belgium and so do I. Both Poland and Canada or Belgium will have veto on important questions. Commission will have full freedom of movement in demilitarized zones which will separate forces at each stage of regrouping and in all frontier and seacoast areas.

Taking everything into consideration, I strongly feel this is satisfactory and much better than we were able to obtain in Korea. French feel, and Eden and I agree, that with such composition built-in veto will work to our advantage. This setup is best French or anybody else could get, and I feel it is within spirit of point 7.

SMITH

[Document 90]

FROM: Geneva

TO: Secretary of State

NO: SECTO 669, July 19, 8 p.m.

FOR THE SECRETARY FROM THE UNDER SECRETARY

I had long talk with Mendes-France this afternoon, as I told you. He urgently asked that we expand our proposed unilateral declaration so as take note not (repeat not) only of agreements between military commands, but also take note of paragraphs one to nine proposed conference declaration. (See SECTOs 628 and 647). I made it clear that we could under no circumstances associate ourselves with conference declaration even though it is anticipated it will be only conference document and not signed agreement, nor could we note or otherwise imply any acquiescence in or approval of paragraph 10 which provides for consultation among conference members on questions transmitted to them by international control commissions.

Text of declaration not yet agreed between French and Communists, but I am transmitting immediately by following telegram French estimate probable final text. I am also transmitting texts of unilateral statements to which Laos and Cambodia have agreed which are referred to in paragraph 4 draft declaration and draft French unilateral declaration referred to in paragraph 8.

French position is this conference declaration is integral part of agreements reached at conference and they will be sorely disappointed if we simply disassociate ourselves from declaration without even taking note in same manner as with respect to cease-fire agreements. I recommend that I be authorized amend our proposed declaration (Annex B my instructions) by inserting a brief addition taking note of paragraphs one to nine of conference declaration if its final content does not too greatly differ from that which French have indicated they prepared to accept. I would like some latitude on this, and am sure I know what would be acceptable to you. I will, of course, have to state in conference that the US is unable to join in a multilateral declaration (since the one planned would include the Communists) but it is making a declaration of its own position, et cetera. This may come to a head tomorrow afternoon or evening, and while it would be possible to make our declaration later it is infinitely preferable to do it at the time of settlement. Otherwise we will have to disassociate ourselves with a lengthy and detailed conference declaration without anything of our own to offer except the very brief declaration we already have prepared.

SMITH

[Document 91]

July 19, 1954

SENT TO: Amconsul GENEVA TOSEC 576

FOR UNDER SECRETARY FROM SECRETARY

Your SECTOS 666, 667, 668, 669.

As requested 669 you may expand proposed unilateral declaration so as to take note of paragraphs 1 to 8 of the proposed Conference declaration with understanding that US obligations QTE with regard to aforesaid agreements and paragraphs of Declaration UNQTE are limited to those expressed Subparagraphs 1 and of Annex B of your instructions.

The foregoing is on the assumption that the Declaration in its final form does not materially differ from SECTO 667. As to nonmateriality of differences, would like you to obtain Phleger's legal judgment.

Have no objection to including first portion of paragraph 9 of proposed Conference declaration but am concerned as to effect of including second portion of paragraph 9 as this seems to imply a multilateral engagement with Communists which would be inconsistent with our basic approach and which subsequently might enable Communist China to charge us with alleged violations of agreement to which it might claim both governments became parties.

While we don't want to take responsibility of imposing our views on the French, I feel particularly concerned about provisions of paragraph 6 which gives the Control Commission constituted as per SECTO 666 authority also to control the general elections. The ink is hardly dry on the Declaration of President Eisenhower and Prime Minister Churchill of June 29 to the effect that "In the case of nations now divided against their will, we shall continue to seek to achieve unity through free elections supervised by the UN to insure that they are conducted fairly." It is rather humiliating to see that Declaration now so quickly go down the drain with our apparent acquiescence.

With reference to 668 believe something like this is acceptable if obtainable. Believe that this would not necessitate these states dealing only with or through France as suggested your 650 and 652. We hope that this possibility of direct assistance for genuinely defensive and internal security purposes and not involving any US bases can be preserved as it may very well be that as a result of surrender in Tonkin Delta French will become so highly unpopular that their effort to maintain authority in other areas would in fact lead to these other areas surely falling under Communist domination.

DULLES

[Document 92]

FROM: Geneva

TO: Secretary of State

NO: SECTO 673, July 19, 9 p.m.

Vietnamese DEL handed us late this afternoon their new proposal. It is elaboration of idea in note to French (SECTO 633) and conference was advised of its preparation in yesterday's restricted session. Unofficial translation follows:

QUOTE

French, Soviet, and Viet Minh drafts all admit the principles of a partition of Vietnam in two zones, all of North Vietnam being abandoned to the Viet Minh.
Although this partition is only provisional in theory, it would not (repeat not) fail to produce in Vietnam the same effects as in Germany, Austria, and Korea. It would not (repeat not) bring the peace which is sought for, deeply wounding the national sentiment of the Vietnamese people it would provoke trouble throughout the country, trouble which would not (repeat not) fail to threaten a peace so dearly acquired.
Before discussing the conditions of a de facto partition with disastrous consequences for the people of Vietnam and for the peace of the world, the DEL of the state of Vietnam renews its proposal for a cease-fire without a demarcation line, without partition, even provisionally.
The Vietnamese DEL therefore proposes:

1. A cease-fire on present positions
2. Regroupment of troops in two zones which would be as small possible.

3. Disarmament of irregular troops
4. After a period to be fixed, disarmament of Viet Minh troops and simultaneous withdrawal of foreign troops.
5. Control by the United Nations:

A. Of the cease-fire
B. Of the regroupment
C. Of the disarmament and the withdrawal
D. Of the administration of the entire country
E. Of the general elections, when the United Nations believes that order and security will have been everywhere truly restored.

This proposal made on the formal instructions of His Majesty Bao Dai, and of the President Ngo Dinh Diem, shows that the chief of state of Vietnam once more places the independence and the unity of his country above any other consideration, and that the national government of Vietnam would prefer this provisional UN control over a truly independent and United Vietnam to its maintenance in power in a country dismembered and condemned to slavery.
Vietnamese DEL renews its request that a conference session be devoted to the study of its proposal for a cease-fire without partition.
In adding this proposal to those of other members of the conference, the DEL of the state of Vietnam means to bring a positive contribution to the search for a real and durable peace which conforms to the aspirations of the Vietnamese people.

Geneva, July 19, 1954.

END QUOTE

Comments follow.

SMITH

[Document 93]

(*This unilateral declaration by the United States Government sets forth its position with regard to the Geneva Accords, which it did not sign.*)

STATEMENT BY THE UNDER SECRETARY OF STATE [1]
AT THE CONCLUDING PLENARY SESSION OF THE
GENEVA CONFERENCE, JULY 21, 1954 [2]

As I stated on July 18, my Government is not prepared to join in a declaration by the Conference such as is submitted. However, the United States makes this unilateral declaration of its position in these matters:

Declaration

The Government of the United States being resolved to devote its efforts to the strengthening of peace in accordance with the principles and purposes of the

[1] Walter Bedell Smith.
[2] Department of State *Bulletin*, Aug. 2, 1954, pp. 162–163.

United Nations takes note of the agreements concluded at Geneva on July 20 and 21, 1954 between (a) the Franco-Laotian Command and the Command of the Peoples Army of Viet-Nam; (b) the Royal Khmer Army Command and the Command of the Peoples Army of Viet-Nam; (c) Franco-Vietnamese Command and the Command of the Peoples Army of Viet-Nam and of paragraphs 1 to 12 inclusive of the declaration presented to the Geneva Conference on July 21, 1954 declares with regard to the aforesaid agreements and paragraphs that (i) it will refrain from the threat or the use of force to disturb them, in accordance with Article 2(4) of the Charter of the United Nations dealing with the obligation of members to refrain in their international relations from the threat or use of force; and (ii) it would view any renewal of the aggression in violation of the aforesaid agreements with grave concern and as seriously threatening international peace and security.

In connection with the statement in the declaration concerning free elections in Viet-Nam my Government wishes to make clear its position which it has expressed in a declaration made in Washington on June 29, 1954, as follows:

> In the case of nations now divided against their will, we shall continue to seek to achieve unity through free elections supervised by the United Nations to insure that they are conducted fairly.

With respect to the statement made by the representative of the State of Viet-Nam, the United States reiterates its traditional position that peoples are entitled to determine their own future and that it will not join in an arrangement which would hinder this. Nothing in its declaration just made is intended to or does indicate any departure from this traditional position.

We share the hope that the agreements will permit Cambodia, Laos and Viet-Nam to play their part, in full independence and sovereignty, in the peaceful community of nations, and will enable the peoples of that area to determine their own future.

[Document 94]

21 July 1954

Original: FRENCH

GENEVA CONFERENCE

INDO-CHINA

FINAL DECLARATION, dated the 21st July, 1954, of the Geneva Conference on the problem of restoring peace in Indo-China, in which the representatives of Cambodia, the Democratic Republic of Viet-Nam, France, Laos, the People's Republic of China, the State of Viet-Nam, the Union of Soviet Socialist Republics, the United Kingdom, and the United States of America took part.

1. The Conference takes note of the agreements ending hostilities in Cambodia, Laos and Viet-Nam and organizing international control and the supervision of the execution of the provisions of these agreements.

2. The Conference expresses satisfaction at the ending of hostilities in Cambodia, Laos and Viet-Nam; the Conference expresses its conviction that the execution of the provisions set out in the present declaration and in the agreements on the cessation of hostilities will permit Cambodia, Laos, and Viet-Nam

henceforth to play their part, in full independence and sovereignty, in the peaceful community of nations.

3. The Conference takes note of the declarations made by the Governments of Cambodia and of Laos of their intention to adopt measures permitting all citizens to take their place in the national community, in particular by participating in the next general elections, which, in conformity with the constitution of each of these countries, shall take place in the course of the year 1955, by secret ballot and in conditions of respect for fundamental freedoms.

4. The Conference takes note of the clauses in the agreement on the cessation of hostilities in Viet-Nam prohibiting the introduction into Viet-Nam of foreign troops and military personnel as well as of all kinds of arms and munitions. The Conference also takes note of the declarations made by the Governments of Cambodia and Laos of their resolution not to request foreign aid, whether in war material, in personnel or in instructors except for the purpose of the effective defence of their territory and, in the case of Laos, to the extent defined by the agreements on the cessation of hostilities in Laos.

5. The Conference takes note of the clauses in the agreement on the cessation of hostilities in Viet-Nam to the effect that no military base under the control of a foreign State may be established in the regrouping zones of the two parties, the latter having the obligation to see that the zones allotted to them shall not constitute part of any military alliance and shall not be utilized for the resumption of hostilities or in the service of an aggressive policy. The Conference also takes note of the declarations of the Governments of Cambodia and Laos to the effect that they will not join in any agreement with other States if this agreement includes the obligation to participate in a military alliance not in conformity with the principles of the Charter of the United Nations or, in the case of Laos, with the principles of the agreement on the cessation of hostilities in Laos or, so long as their security is not threatened, the obligation to establish bases on Cambodian or Laotian territory for the military forces of foreign Powers.

6. The Conference recognizes that the essential purpose of the agreement relating to Viet-Nam is to settle military questions with a view to ending hostilities and that the military demarcation line is provisional and should not in any way be interpreted as constituting a political or territorial boundary. The Conference expresses its conviction that the execution of the provisions set out in the present declaration and in the agreement on the cessation of hostilities creates the necessary basis for the achievement in the near future of a political settlement in Viet-Nam.

7. The Conference declares that, so far as Viet-Nam is concerned, the settlement of political problems, affected on the basis of respect for the principles of independence, unity and territorial integrity, shall permit the Viet-Namese people to enjoy the fundamental freedoms, guaranteed by democratic institutions established as a result of free general elections by secret ballot. In order to ensure that sufficient progress in the restoration of peace has been made, and that all the necessary conditions obtain for free expression of the national will, general elections shall be held in July 1956, under the supervision of an international commission composed of representatives of the Member States of the International Supervisory Commission, referred to in the agreement on the cessation of hostilities. Consultations will be held on this subject between the competent representative authorities of the two zones from 20 July 1955 onwards.

8. The provisions of the agreements on the cessation of hostilities intended to ensure the protection of individuals and of property must be most strictly

applied and must, in particular, allow everyone in Viet-Nam to decide freely in which zone he wishes to live.

9. The competent representative authorities of the Northern and Southern zones of Viet-Nam, as well as the authorities of Laos and Cambodia, must not permit any individual or collective reprisals against persons who have collaborated in any way with one of the parties during the war, or against members of such persons' families.

10. The Conference takes note of the declaration of the Government of the French Republic to the effect that it is ready to withdraw its troops from the territory of Cambodia, Laos, and Viet-Nam, at the requests of the Governments concerned and within periods which shall be fixed by agreement between the parties except in the cases where, by agreement between the two parties, a certain number of French troops shall remain at specified points and for a specified time.

11. The Conference takes note of the declaration of the French Government to the effect that for the settlement of all the problems connected with the re-establishment and consolidation of peace in Cambodia, Laos and Viet-Nam, the French Government will proceed from the principle of respect for the independence and sovereignty, unity, and territorial integrity of Cambodia, Laos and Viet-Nam.

12. In their relations with Cambodia, Laos and Viet-Nam, each member of the Geneva Conference undertakes to respect the sovereignty, the independence, the unity and the territorial integrity of the above-mentioned states, and to refrain from any interference in their internal affairs.

13. The members of the Conference agree to consult one another on any question which may be referred to them by the International Supervisory Commission, in order to study such measures as may prove necessary to ensure that the agreements on the cessation of hostilities in Cambodia, Laos and Viet-Nam are respected.

[Document 95]

Reprinted from New York *Times*

LANSDALE TEAM'S REPORT ON COVERT SAIGON MISSION IN 1954 AND 1955

Following are excerpts from the report of the Saigon Military Mission, an American team headed by Edward G. Lansdale, covering its activities in the 1954–55 period. The report accompanies the Pentagon's study of the Vietnam war, which cites it without identifying the author or date. The excerpts appear verbatim, with only unmistakable typographical errors corrected.

I. FOREWORD

. . . This is the condensed account of one year in the operations of a "cold war" combat team, written by the team itself in the field, little by little in moments taken as the members could. The team is known as the Saigon Military Mission. The field is Vietnam. There are other teams in the field, American, French, British, Chinese, Vietnamese, Vietminh, and others. Each has its own story to tell. This is ours.

The Saigon Military Mission entered Vietnam on 1 June 1954 when its Chief arrived. However, this is the story of a team, and it wasn't until August 1954 that sufficient members arrived to constitute a team. So, this is mainly an account of the team's first year, from August 1954 to August 1955.

It was often a frustrating and perplexing year, up close. The Geneva Agreements signed on 21 July 1954 imposed restrictive rules upon all official Americans, including the Saigon Military Mission. An active and intelligent enemy made full use of legal rights to screen his activities in establishing his stay-behind organizations south of the 17th Parallel and in obtaining quick security north of that Parallel. The nation's economy and communications system were crippled by eight years of open war. The government, including its Army and other security forces, was in a painful transition from colonial to self rule, making it a year of hot-tempered incidents. Internal problems arose quickly to points where armed conflict was sought as the only solution. The enemy was frequently forgotten in the heavy atmosphere of suspicion, hatred, and jealousy.

The Saigon Military Mission received some blows from allies and the enemy in this atmosphere, as we worked to help stabilize the government and to beat the Geneva time-table of Communist takeover in the north. However, we did beat the time-table. The government did become stabilized. The Free Vietnamese are now becoming unified and learning how to cope with the Communist enemy. We are thankful that we had a chance to help in this work in a critical area of the world, to be positive and constructive in a year of doubt.

II. MISSION

The Saigon Military Mission (SMM) was born in a Washington policy meeting early in 1954, when Dien Bien Phu was still holding out against the encircling Vietminh. The SMM was to enter into Vietnam quietly and assist the Vietnamese, rather than the French, in unconventional warfare. The French were to be kept as friendly allies in the process, as far as possible.

The broad mission for the team was to undertake paramilitary operations against the enemy and to wage political-psychological warfare. Later, after Geneva, the mission was modified to prepare the means for undertaking paramilitary operations in Communist areas rather than to wage unconventional warfare. . . .

III. HIGHLIGHTS OF THE YEAR

a. *Early Days*

The Saigon Military Mission (SMM) started on 1 June 1954, when its Chief, Colonel Edward G. Lansdale, USAF, arrived in Saigon with a small box of files and clothes and a borrrowed typewriter, courtesy of an SA-16 flight set up for him by the 13th Air Force at Clark AFB. Lt-General John O'Daniel and Embassy Charge Rob McClintock had arranged for his appointment as Assistant Air Attache, since it was improper for U.S. officers at MAAG at that time to have advisory conferences with Vietnamese officers. Ambassador Heath had concurred already. There was no desk space for an office, no vehicle, no safe for files. He roomed with General O'Daniel, later moved to a small house rented by MAAG. Secret communications with Washington were provided through the Saigon station of CIA.

There was deepening gloom in Vietnam. Dien Bien Phu had fallen. The French were capitulating to the Vietminh at Geneva. The first night in Saigon, Vietminh saboteurs blew up large ammunition dumps at the airport, rocking Saigon throughout the night. General O'Daniel and Charge McClintock agreed that it was time to start taking positive action. O'Daniel paved the way for a quick first-hand survey of the situation throughout the country. McClintock paved the way for contacts with Vietnamese political leaders. Our Chief's reputation from the Philippines had preceded him. Hundreds of Vietnamese acquaintanceships were made quickly.

Working in close cooperation with George Hellyer, USIS Chief, a new psychological warfare campaign was devised for the Vietnamese Army and for the government in Hanoi. Shortly after, a refresher course in combat psywar was constructed and Vietnamese Army personnel were rushed through it. A similar course was initiated for the Ministry of Information. Rumor campaigns were added to the tactics and tried out in Hanoi. It was almost too late.

The first rumor campaign was to be a carefully planted story of a Chinese Communist regiment in Tonkin taking reprisals against a Vietminh village whose girls the Chinese had raped, recalling Chinese Nationalist troop behavior in 1945 and confirming Vietnamese fears of Chinese occupation under Vietminh rule; the story was to be planted by soldiers of the Vietnamese Armed Psywar Company in Hanoi dressed in civilian clothes. The troops received their instructions silently, dressed in civilian clothes, went on the mission, and failed to return. They had deserted to the Vietminh. Weeks later, Tonkinese told an excited story of the misbehavior of the Chinese Divisions in Vietminh territory. Investigated, it turned out to be the old rumor campaign, with Vietnamese embellishments.

There was political chaos. Prince Buu Loc no longer headed the government. Government ministries all but closed. The more volatile leaders of political groups were proposing a revolution, which included armed attacks on the French. Col. Jean Carbonel of the French Army proposed establishing a regime with Vietnamese (Nungs and others) known to him close to the Chinese border and asked for our backing. Our reply was that this was a policy decision to be made between the FEC top command and U.S. authorities.

Oscar Arellano, Junior Chamber International vice-president for Southeast Asia, stopped by for a visit with our Chief; an idea in this visit later grew into "Operation Brotherhood."

On 1 July, Major Lucien Conein arrived, as the second member of the team. He is a paramilitary specialist, well-known to the French for his help with French-operated maquis in Tonkin against the Japanese in 1945, the one American guerrilla fighter who had not been a member of the Patti Mission. He was assigned to MAAG for cover purposes. Arranged by Lt-Col William Rosson, a meeting was held with Col Carbonel, Col Nguyen Van Vy, and the two SMM officers; Vy had seen his first combat in 1945 under Conein. Carbonel proposed establishing a maquis, to be kept as a secret between the four officers. SMM refused, learned later that Carbonel had kept the FEC Deuxieme Bureau informed. Shortly afterwards, at a Defense conference with General O'Daniel, our Chief had a chance to suggest Vy for a command in the North, making him a general. Secretary of State for Defense Le Ngoc Chan did so, Vy was grateful and remained so.

Ngo Dinh Diem arrived on 7 July, and within hours was in despair as the French forces withdrew from the Catholic provinces of Phat Diem and Nam Dinh in Tonkin. Catholic militia streamed north to Hanoi and Haiphong, their hearts filled with anger at French abandonment. The two SMM officers stopped a planned grenade attack by militia girls against French troops guarding a warehouse; the girls stated they had not eaten for three days; arrangements were made for Chinese merchants in Haiphong to feed them. Other militia attacks were stopped, including one against a withdrawing French artillery unit; the militia wanted the guns to stand and fight the Vietminh. The Tonkinese had hopes of American friendship and listened to the advice given them. Governor [name illegible] died, reportedly by poison. Tonkin's government changed as despair grew. On 21 July, the Geneva Agreement was signed. Tonkin was given to the Communists. Anti-Communists turned to SMM for help in establishing a resistance movement and several tentative initial arrangements were made.

Diem himself had reached a nadir of frustration, as his country disintegrated after the conference of foreigners. With the approval of Ambassador Heath and General O'Daniel, our Chief drew up a plan of overall governmental action and presented it to Diem, with Hellyer as interpreter. It called for fast constructive action and dynamic leadership. Although the plan was not adopted, it laid the foundation for a friendship which has lasted.

Oscar Arellano visited Saigon again. Major Charles T. R. Bohanan, a former team-mate in Philippine days, was in town. At an SMM conference with these two, "Operation Brotherhood" was born: volunteer medical teams of Free Asians to aid the Free Vietnamese who have few doctors of their own. Washington responded warmly to the idea. President Diem was visited; he issued an appeal to the Free World for help. The Junior Chamber International adopted the idea. SMM would monitor the operation quietly in the background.

President Diem had organized a Committee of Cabinet Ministers to handle the problem of refugees from the Communist North. The Committee system was a failure. No real plans had been made by the French or the Americans. After conferences with USOM (FOA) officials and with General O'Daniel, our Chief suggested to Ambassador Heath that he call a U.S. meeting to plan a single Vietnamese agency, under a Commissioner of Refugees to be appointed by President Diem, to run the Vietnamese refugee program and to provide a channel through which help could be given by the U.S., France, and other free nations. The meeting was called and the plan adopted, with MAAG under General O'Daniel in the coordinating role. Diem adopted the plan. The French pitched in enthusiastically to help. CAT asked SMM for help in obtaining a French contract for the refugee airlift, and got it. In return, CAT provided SMM with the means for secret air travel between the North and Saigon. . . .

b.   *August 1954*

An agreement had been reached that the personnel ceiling of U.S. military personnel with MAAG would be frozen at the number present in Vietnam on the date of the cease-fire, under the terms of the Geneva Agreement. In South Vietnam this deadline was to be 11 August. It meant that SMM might have only two members present, unless action were taken. General O'Daniel agreed to the addition of ten SMM men under MAAG cover, plus any others in the Defense pipeline who arrived before the deadline. A call for help went out. Ten officers in Korea, Japan, and Okinawa were selected and were rushed to Vietnam.

SMM had one small MAAG house. Negotiations were started for other housing, but the new members of the team arrived before housing was ready and were crammed three and four to a hotel room for the first days. Meetings were held to assess the new members' abilities. None had had political-psychological warfare experience. Most were experienced in paramilitary and clandestine intelligence operations. Plans were made quickly, for time was running out in the north; already the Vietminh had started taking over secret control of Hanoi and other areas of Tonkin still held by French forces.

Major Conein was given responsibility for developing a paramilitary organization in the north, to be in position when the Vietminh took over. . . . [His] . . . team was moved north immediately as part of the MAAG staff working on the refugee problem. The team had headquarters in Hanoi, with a branch in Haiphong. Among cover duties, this team supervised the refugee flow for the Hanoi airlift organized by the French. One day, as a CAT C-46 finished loading, they saw a small child standing on the ground below the loading door. They shouted for the pilot to wait, picked the child up and shoved him into the aircraft, which then promptly taxied out for its takeoff in the constant air shuttle. A Vietnamese man and woman ran up to the team, asking what they had done with their small boy, whom they'd brought out to say goodbye to relatives. The chagrined team explained, finally talked the parents into going south to Free Vietnam, put them in the next aircraft to catch up with their son in Saigon. . . .

A second paramilitary team was formed to explore possibilities of organizing resistance against the Vietminh from bases in the south. This team consisted of Army Lt-Col Raymond Wittmayer, Army Major Fred Allen, and Army Lt Edward Williams. The latter was our only experienced counter-espionage officer and undertook double duties, including working with revolutionary political groups. Major Allen eventually was able to mount a Vietnamese paramilitary effort in Tonkin from the south, barely beating the Vietminh shutdown in Haiphong as his teams went in, trained and equipped for their assigned missions.

Navy Lt Edward Bain and Marine Captain Richard Smith were assigned as the support group for SMM. Actually, support for an effort such as SMM is a major operation in itself, running the gamut from the usual administrative and personnel functions to the intricate business of clandestine air, maritime, and land supply of paramilitary materiel. In effect, they became our official smugglers as well as paymasters, housing officers, transportation officers, warehousemen, file clerks, and mess officers. The work load was such that other team members frequently pitched in and helped.

c. September 1954

Highly-placed officials from Washington visited Saigon and, in private conversations, indicated that current estimates led to the conclusion that Vietnam probably would have to be written off as a loss. We admitted that prospects were gloomy, but were positive that there was still a fighting chance.

On 8 September, SMM officers visited Secretary of State for Defense Chan and walked into a tense situation in his office. Chan had just arrested Lt-Col Lan (G-6 of the Vietnamese Army) and Capt Giai (G-5 of the Army). Armed guards filled the room. We were told what had happened and assured that everything was all right by all three principals. Later, we discovered that Chan was alone and that the guards were Lt-Col Lan's commandos. Lan was charged with political terrorism (by his "action" squads) and Giai with anti-Diem propaganda (using G-5 leaflet, rumor, and broadcast facilities).

The arrest of Lan and Giai, who simply refused to consider themselves arrested, and of Lt Minh, officer in charge of the Army radio station which was guarded by Army troops, brought into the open a plot by the Army Chief of Staff, General Hinh, to overthrow the government. Hinh had hinted at such a plot to his American friends, using a silver cigarette box given him by Egypt's

Naguib to carry the hint. SMM became thoroughly involved in the tense controversy which followed, due to our Chief's closeness to both President Diem and General Hinh. He had met the latter in the Philippines in 1952, was a friend of both Hinh's wife and favorite mistress. (The mistress was a pupil in a small English class conducted for mistresses of important personages, at their request. . . .

While various U.S. officials including General O'Daniel and Foreign Service Officer Frank [name illegible] participated in U.S. attempts to heal the split between the President and his Army, Ambassador Heath asked us to make a major effort to end the controversy. This effort strained relations with Diem and never was successful, but did dampen Army enthusiasm for the plot. At one moment, when there was likelihood of an attack by armored vehicles on the Presidential Palace, SMM told Hinh bluntly that U.S. support most probably would stop in such an event. At the same time a group from the Presidential Guards asked for tactical advice on how to stop armored vehicles with the only weapons available to the Guards: carbines, rifles, and hand grenades. The advice, on tank traps and destruction with improvised weapons, must have sounded grim. The following morning, when the attack was to take place, we visited the Palace; not a guard was left on the grounds; President Diem was alone upstairs, calmly getting his work done.

As a result of the Hinh trouble, Diem started looking around for troops upon whom he could count. Some Tonkinese militia, refugees from the north, were assembled in Saigon close to the Palace. But they were insufficient for what he needed. Diem made an agreement with General Trinh Minh The, leader of some 3,000 Cao Dai dissidents in the vicinity of Tayninh, to give General The some needed financial support; The was to give armed support to the government if necessary and to provide a safe haven for the government if it had to flee. The's guerrillas, known as the Lien Minh, were strongly nationalist and were still fighting the Vietminh and the French. At Ambassador Heath's request, the U.S. secretly furnished Diem with funds for The, through the SMM. Shortly afterwards, an invitation came from The to visit him. Ambassador Heath approved the visit. . . .

The northern SMM team under Conein had organized a paramilitary group, (which we will disguise by the Vietnamese name of Binh) through the Northern Dai Viets, a political party with loyalties to Bao Dai. The group was to be trained and supported by the U.S. as patriotic Vietnamese, to come eventually under government control when the government was ready for such activities. Thirteen Binhs were quietly exfiltrated through the port of Haiphong, under the direction of Lt Andrews, and taken on the first stage of the journey to their training area by a U.S. Navy ship. This was the first of a series of helpful actions by Task Force 98, commanded by Admiral Sabin.

Another paramilitary group for Tonkin operations was being developed in Saigon through General Nguyen Van Vy. In September this group started shaping up fast, and the project was given to Major Allen. (We will give this group the Vietnamese name of Hao). . . .

Towards the end of the month, it was learned that the largest printing establishment in the north intended to remain in Hanoi and do business with the Vietminh. An attempt was made by SMM to destroy the modern presses, but Vietminh security agents already had moved into the plant and frustrated the attempt. This operation was under a Vietnamese patriot whom we shall call Trieu; his case officer was Capt Arundel. Earlier in the month they had engineered a black psywar strike in Hanoi: leaflets signed by the Vietminh instructing Tonkinese on how to behave for the Vietminh takeover of the Hanoi region in early October, including items about property, money reform, and a three-day holiday of workers upon takeover. The day following the distribution of these leaflets, refugee registration tripled. Two days later Vietminh currency was worth half the value prior to the leaflets. The Vietminh took to the radio to denounce the leaflets; the leaflets were so authentic in appearance that even most of the rank and file Vietminh were sure that the radio denunciations were a French trick.

The Hanoi psywar strike had other consequences. Binh had enlisted a high police official of Hanoi as part of his team, to effect the release from jail of any team members if arrested. The official at the last moment decided to assist in the leaflet distribution personally. Police officers spotted him, chased his vehicle through the empty Hanoi streets of early morning, finally opened fire on him and caught him. He was the only member of the group caught. He was held in prison as a Vietminh agent.

d. *October 1954*

Hanoi was evacuated on 9 October. The northern SMM team left with the last French troops, disturbed by what they had seen of the grim efficiency of the Vietminh in their takeover, the contrast between the silent march of the victorious Vietminh troops in their tennis shoes and the clanking armor of the well-equipped French whose western tactics and equipment had failed against the Communist military-political-economic campaign.

The northern team had spent the last days of Hanoi in contaminating the oil supply of the bus company for a gradual wreckage of engines in the buses, in taking the first actions for delayed sabotage of the railroad (which required teamwork with a CIA special technical team in Japan who performed their part brilliantly), and in writing detailed notes of potential targets for future paramilitary operations (U.S. adherence to the Geneva Agreement prevented SMM from carrying out the active sabotage it desired to do against the power plant, water facilities, harbor, and bridge). The team had a bad moment when contaminating the oil. They had to work quickly at night, in an enclosed storage room. Fumes from the contaminant came close to knocking them out. Dizzy and weak-kneed, they masked their faces with handkerchiefs and completed the job.

Meanwhile, Polish and Russian ships had arrived in the south to transport southern Vietminh to Tonkin under the Geneva Agreement. This offered the opportunity for another black psywar strike. A leaflet was developed by Binh with the help of Capt Arundel, attributed to the Vietminh Resistance Committee. Among other items, it reassured the Vietminh they would be kept safe below decks from imperialist air and submarine attacks, and requested that warm clothing be brought; the warm clothing item would be coupled with a verbal rumor campaign that Vietminh were being sent into China as railroad laborers.

SMM had been busily developing G-5 of the Vietnamese Army for such psywar efforts. Under Arundel's direction, the First Armed Propaganda Company printed the leaflets and distributed them, by soldiers in civilian clothes who penetrated into southern Vietminh zones on foot. (Distribution in Camau was made while columnist Joseph Alsop was on his visit there which led to his sensational, gloomy articles later; our soldier "Vietminh" failed in an attempt to get the leaflet into Alsop's hands in Camau; Alsop was never told this story). Intelligence reports and other later reports revealed that village and delegation committees complained about "deportation" to the north, after distribution of the leaflet. . . .

Contention between Diem and Hinh had become murderous. . . . Finally, we learned that Hinh was close to action; he had selected 26 October as the morning for an attack on the Presidential Palace. Hinh was counting heavily on Lt-Col Lan's special forces and on Captain Giai who was running Hinh's secret headquarters at Hinh's home. We invited these two officers to visit the Philippines, on the pretext that we were making an official trip, could take them along and open the way for them to see some inner workings of the fight against Filipino Communists which they probably would never see otherwise. Hinh reluctantly turned down his own invitation; he had had a memorable time of it on his last visit to Manila in 1952. Lt-Col Lan was a French agent and the temptation to see behind-the-scenes was too much. He and Giai accompanied SMM officers on the MAAG C-47 which General O'Daniel instantly made available for the operation. 26 October was spent in the Philippines. The attack on the palace didn't come off.

e. *November 1954*

General Lawton Collins arrived as Ambassador on 8 November. . . .

Collins, in his first press conference, made it plain that the U.S. was supporting President Diem. The new Ambassador applied pressure on General Hinh and on 29 November Hinh left for Paris. His other key conspirators followed.

Part of the SMM team became involved in staff work to back up the energetic campaign to save Vietnam which Collins pushed forward. Some SMM members were scattered around the Pacific, accompanying Vietnamese for secret training, obtaining and shipping supplies to be smuggled into north Vietnam and hidden there. In the Philippines, more support was being constructed to help SMM, in expediting the flow of supplies, and in creating Freedom Company, a non-profit Philippines corporation backed by President Magsaysay, which would supply Filipinos experienced in fighting the Communist Huks to help in Vietnam (or elsewhere). . . .

On 23 November, twenty-one selected Vietnamese agents and two cooks of our Hao paramilitary group were put aboard a Navy ship in the Saigon River, in daylight. They appeared as coolies, joined the coolie and refugee throng moving on and off ship, and disappeared one by one. It was brilliantly planned and executed, agents being picked up from unobtrusive assembly points throughout the metropolis. Lt Andrews made the plans and carried out the movement under the supervision of Major Allen. The ship took the Hao agents, in compartmented groups, to an overseas point, the first stage in a movement to a secret training area.

f. *December 1954*

. . . discussions between the U.S., Vietnamese and French had reached a point where it appeared that a military training mission using U.S. officers was in the immediate offing. General O'Daniel had a U.S.-French planning group working on the problem, under Col Rosson. One paper they were developing was a plan for pacification of Vietminh and dissident areas; this paper was passed to SMM for its assistance with the drafting. SMM wrote much of the paper, changing the concept from the old rigid police controls of all areas to some of our concepts of winning over the population and instituting a classification of areas by the amount of trouble in each, the amount of control required, and fixing responsibilities between civil and military authorities. With a few changes, this was issued by President Diem on 31 December as the National Security Action (Pacification) Directive. . . .

There was still much disquiet in Vietnam, particularly among anti-Communist political groups who were not included in the government. SMM officers were contacted by a number of such groups who felt that they "would have to commit suicide in 1956" (the 1956 plebiscite promised in the 1954 Geneva agreement), when the Vietminh would surely take over against so weak a government. One group of farmers and militia in the south was talked out of migrating to Madagascar by SMM and staying on their farms. A number of these groups asked SMM for help in training personnel for eventual guerrilla warfare if the Vietminh won. Persons such as the then Minister of Defense and Trinh Minh The were among those loyal to the government who also requested such help. It was decided that a more basic guerrilla training program might be undertaken for such groups than was available at the secret training site to which we had sent the Binh and Hao groups. Plans were made with Major Bohanan and Mr. John C. Wachtel in the Philippines for a solution of this problem; the United States backed the development, through them, of a small Freedom Company training camp in a hidden valley on the Clark AFB reservation.

Till and Peg Durdin of the N.Y. Times, Hank Lieberman of the N.Y. Times, Homer Bigart of the N.Y. Herald-Tribune, John Mecklin of Life-Time, and John Roderick of Associated Press, have been warm friends of SMM and worked hard to penetrate the fabric of French propaganda and give the U.S. an objective account of events in Vietnam. The group met with us at times to analyze objectives and motives of propaganda known to them, meeting at their own request as U.S. citizens. These mature and responsible news correspondents performed a valuable service for their country. . . .

g. *January 1955*

The Vietminh long ago had adopted the Chinese Communist thought that the people are the water and the army is the fish. Vietminh relations with the mass of the population during the fighting had been exemplary, with a few exceptions; in contrast, the Vietnamese National Army had been like too many Asian armies, adept at cowing a population into feeding them, providing them with girls. SMM had been working on this problem from the beginning. Since the National Army was the only unit of government with a strong organization throughout the country and with good communications, it was the key to stabilizing the situation quickly on a nation-wide basis. If Army and people could be brought together into a team, the first strong weapon against Communism could be forged.

The Vietminh were aware of this. We later learned that months before the signing of the Geneva Agreement they had been planning for action in the post-Geneva period; the National Army was to be the primary target for subversion efforts, it was given top priority by the Central Committee for operations against its enemy, and about 100 superior cadres were retrained for the operations and placed in the [words illegible] organization for the work, which commenced even before the agreement was signed. We didn't know it at the time, but this was SMM's major opponent, in a secret struggle for the National Army. . . .

General O'Daniel was anticipating the culmination of long negotiations to permit U.S. training of the Vietnamese Armed Forces, against some resistance on the part of French groups. In January, negotiations were proceeding so well that General O'Daniel informally organized a combined U.S.–French training mission which eventually became known as the Training Relations & Instruction

Mission (TRIM) under his command, but under the overall command of the top French commander, General Paul Ely.

The French had asked for top command of half the divisions in the TRIM staff. Their first priority was for command of the division supervising National Security Action by the Vietnamese, which could be developed into a continuation of strong French control of key elements of both Army and population. In conferences with Ambassador Collins and General O'Daniel, it was decided to transfer Colonel Lansdale from the Ambassador's staff to TRIM, to head the National Security division. Colonel Lansdale requested authority to coordinate all U.S. civil and military efforts in this National Security work. On 11 January, Ambassador Collins announced the change to the country team, and gave him authority to coordinate this work among all U.S. agencies in Vietnam. . . .

President Diem had continued requesting SMM help with the guard battalion for the Presidential Palace. We made arrangements with President Magsaysay in the Philippines and borrowed his senior aide and military advisor, Col. Napoleon Valeriano, who had a fine combat record against the Communist Huks and also had reorganized the Presidential Guard Battalion for Magsaysay. Valeriano, with three junior officers, arrived in January and went to work on Diem's guard battalion. Later, selected Vietnamese officers were trained with the Presidential Guards in Manila. An efficient unit gradually emerged. Diem was warmly grateful for this help by Filipinos who also continuously taught our concept of loyalty and freedom.

The patriot we've named Trieu Dinh had been working on an almanac for popular sale, particularly in the northern cities and towns we could still reach. Noted Vietnamese astrologers were hired to write predictions about coming disasters to certain Vietminh leaders and undertakings, and to predict unity in the south. The work was carried out under the direction of Lt Phillips, based on our concept of the use of astrology for psywar in Southeast Asia. Copies of the almanac were shipped by air to Haiphong and then smuggled into Vietminh territory.

Dinh also had produced a Thomas Paine type series of essays on Vietnamese patriotism against the Communist Vietminh, under the guidance of Capt. Arundel. These essays were circulated among influential groups in Vietnam, earned front-page editorials in the leading daily newspaper in Saigon. Circulation increased with the publication of these essays. The publisher is known to SMM as The Dragon Lady and is a fine Vietnamese girl who has been the mistress of an anti-American French civilian. Despite anti-American remarks by her boy friend, we had helped her keep her paper from being closed by the government . . . and she found it profitable to heed our advice on the editorial content of her paper.

Arms and equipment for the Binh paramilitary team were being cached in the north in areas still free from the Vietminh. Personnel movements were covered by the flow of refugees. Haiphong was reminiscent of our own pioneer days as it was swamped with people whom it couldn't shelter. Living space and food were at a premium, nervous tension grew. It was a wild time for our northern team.

First supplies for the Hao paramilitary group started to arrive in Saigon. These shipments and the earlier ones for the Binh group were part of an efficient and effective air smuggling effort by the 581st [word illegible] Wing, U.S. Air Force, to support SMM, with help by CIA and Air Force personnel in both Okinawa and the Philippines. SMM officers frequently did coolie labor in manhandling tons of cargo, at times working throughout the night. . . . All . . . officers pitched in to help, as part of our "blood, sweat and tears." . . .

By 31 January, all operational equipment of the Binh paramilitary group had been trans-shipped to Haiphong from Saigon, mostly with the help of CAT, and the northern SMM team had it cached in operational sites. Security measures were tightened at the Haiphong airport and plans for bringing in the Hao equipment were changed from the air route to sea. Task Force 98, now 98.7 under command of Captain Frank, again was asked to give a helping hand and did so. . . .

. . . Major Conein had briefed the members of the Binh paramilitary team and started them infiltrating into the north as individuals. The infiltration was carried out in careful stages over a 30 day period, a successful operation. The Binhs became normal citizens, carrying out every day civil pursuits, on the surface.

We had smuggled into Vietnam about eight and a half tons of supplies for the Hao paramilitary group. They included fourteen agent radios, 300 carbines, 90,-000 rounds of carbine ammunition, 50 pistols, 10,000 rounds of pistol ammunition, and 300 pounds of explosives. Two and a half tons were delivered to the Hao agents in Tonkin, while the remainder was cached along the Red River by SMM, with the help of the Navy. . . .

j. *April 1955*

. . . the Hao paramilitary team had finished its training at the secret training site and been flown by the Air Force to a holding site in the Philippines, where Major Allen and his officers briefed the paramilitary team. In mid-April, they were taken by the Navy to Haiphong, where they were gradually slipped ashore. Meanwhile, arms and other equipment including explosives were being flown into Saigon via our smuggling route, being readied for shipment north by the Navy task force handling refugees. The White team office gradually became an imposing munitions depot. Nightly shootings and bombings in restless Saigon caused us to give them dispersed storage behind thick walls as far as this one big house would permit. SMM personnel guarded the house night and day, for it also contained our major files other than the working file at our Command Post. All files were fixed for instant destruction, automatic weapons and hand grenades distributed to all personnel. It was a strange scene for new personnel just arriving. . . .

Haiphong was taken over by the Vietminh on 16 May. Our Binh and northern Hao teams were in place, completely equipped. It had taken a tremendous amount of hard work to beat the Geneva deadline, to locate, select, exfiltrate, train, infiltrate, equip the men of these two teams and have them in place, ready for actions required against the enemy. It would be a hard task to do openly, but this had to be kept secret from the Vietminh, the International Commission with its suspicious French and Poles and Indians, and even friendly Vietnamese. Movements of personnel and supplies had had to be over thousands of miles. . . .

Justification of the War—Public Statements

Foreword

   This portion of the study consists of an examination of the public statements justifying U.S. involvement in Vietnam. Only official statements contained in either the U.S. Department of State Bulletins or the Public Papers of the Presidents were reviewed. Although conclusions are based primarily on the statements of the President, the Secretary of State and the Secretary of Defense, the statements of other high-ranking government officials were also studied in ascertaining the policy context of the quoted material. This report includes analyses of the Truman and Eisenhower periods. The statements are organized chronologically within each Administration, and are summarized at the head of each section.

A. *TRUMAN ADMINISTRATION*

Contents

B. EISENHOWER ADMINISTRATION

Contents

tion of the civil war; U.S. intervention; French armistice; collective security; possibility of U.S. intervention (7 May 1954).

Public Statement 11   (page 601)
Eisenhower assesses progress at the Geneva Conference; cites plans for collective security arrangement in Southeast Asia (5 May 1954).

Public Statement 12   (page 602)
Eisenhower reaffirms his "domino" concerns in response to press questioning (12 May 1954).

Public Statement 13   (page 603)
Secretary of States Dulles analyzes developments to date in Indochina; he discusses the conditions under which U.S. would intervene directly (11 June 1954).

Public Statement 14   (page 604)
Eisenhower states U.S. position on Geneva Accords (21 July 1954).

Public Statement 15   (page 606)
Text of the declaration (21 July 1954).

Public Statement 16   (page 608)
U.S.–French communique announcing desire to aid directly the newly independent states of Cambodia, Laos, and Vietnam (29 September 1954).

Public Statement 17   (page 609)
Eisenhower informs President of Vietnam's Council that aid will be conditioned on his government's giving the U.S. "assurance as to standard of performance" (23 October 1954).

Public Statement 18   (page 609)
Eisenhower notes but questions the moderation in Soviet policy; refers to Diem's successes in South Vietnam (21 April 1956).

Public Statement 19   (page 610)
Assistant Secretary of State Robertson restates American policy in Vietnam at a time of relative stability (1 June 1956).

Public Statement 20   (page 613)
Eisenhower emphasizes role of aid program in achieving Asian goals; cites susceptibility of underdeveloped nations to communist probings (21 May 1957).

Public Statement 21   (page 614)
Eisenhower justifies foreign aid to American people as necessary for U.S. security; cites its "returns" in Vietnam (21 May 1957).

Public Statement 22   (page 616)
Eisenhower reports to the nation on the Red Chinese shelling of Quemoy; relates U.S. security interests to Formosa; cites lesson of Munich and the militant statements of Chinese Communists as requiring a firm U.S. stand (11 September 1958).

Public Statement 23 (*page 621*)
Eisenhower attempts at news conference to put communist aggression in perspective (1 October 1958).

Public Statement 24 (*page 622*)
Eisenhower in special message to Congress discusses communist threat to developing nations and need for U.S. aid to maintain collective defense (13 March 1959).

Public Statement 25 (*page 624*)
Eisenhower discusses importance of Vietnam to free world; he shows specifically how its economy complements Japan's (4 April 1959).

Public Statement 26 (*page 627*)
Eisenhower stresses threat posed by economic and military power of China and Russia in defense of foreign aid (16 February 1969).

Public Statement 27 (*page 628*)
Eisenhower reminds Diem of the responsibility that the Vietnamese people have in safeguarding their independence (22 October 1960).

TRUMAN ADMINISTRATION

Summary

The statements enclosed are from the period 1950–1952: from the Secretary of State's announcement marking the beginning of the U.S. involvement in Vietnam to the NATO resolution supporting the French fight in Indochina. The justifications advanced for the U.S. commitment in Indochina include the following:
  a. The Soviets are engaged in a "monstrous conspiracy to stamp out freedom all over the world," and Soviet imperialism, with Communist China as its instrument, poses a direct threat to the independence of the Associated States of Indochina.
  b. The defense of Indochina is an integral part of the worldwide resistance by free nations to communist aggression and subversion.
  c. The raw materials and agricultural products of Southeast Asia are "vitally needed" by the free nations of the world.
  d. The United States, in the interest of preventing a third world war, has provided aid to the Associated States and France.

EISENHOWER ADMINISTRATION

Summary

President Eisenhower took office in the context of negotiations for a settlement in Korea and the portending defeat in France in Indochina. His Administration early faced the crisis surrounding the Geneva Conference of 1954, in which direct U.S. intervention in Vietnam was a distinct prospect. Having pressed diplomatically for a constructive outcome at Geneva, the United States threw its support behind Ngo Dinh Diem and the Government of Vietnam. With U.S. support, that government, despite a series of severe tests, succeeded in consolidating itself and making significant progress. U.S. justification for its policy toward Vietnam in this period included the following:

a. The "domino principle": the loss of Vietnam, the most vulnerable state of Southeast Asia, would imperil the other nations of the region, and ultimately lead to a seriously weakened U.S. strategic position. Vietnam was a key to continued free world access to the human and material resources of Southeast Asia.

b. Communist China was pursuing an expansionist foreign policy relying upon subversive aggression, as well as armaments. China thus continued to reflect the unchanging Soviet objective of conquest of the world, and both had manifest designs on Southeast Asia.

c. The United States proposed, through its aid programs, to help the small and weak nations contiguous with communist powers to maintain their freedom and independence lest aggression and expansion be encouraged, and the world moved thereby towards a third world war.

d. In the words of President Eisenhower, "We gave military and economic assistance to the Republic of Vietnam. We entered into a treaty—the Southeast Asia Security Treaty—which plainly warned that an armed attack against this area would endanger our own peace and safety and that we would act accordingly."

e. U.S. aid for Vietnam—economic and military—has made possible not only its survival, but also genuine progress toward a stable society, a modern economy, and internal and external security.

TRUMAN ADMINISTRATION PUBLIC STATEMENTS

1. *Secretary of State Statement on Extension of Military and Economic Aid, May 8, 1950, Department of State Bulletin, May 22, 1950, p. 821:*

* * *

"The United States Government, convinced that neither national independence nor democratic evolution exist in any area dominated by Soviet imperialism, considers the situation to be such as to warrant its according economic aid and military equipment to the Associated States of Indochina and to France in order to assist them in restoring stability and permitting these states to pursue their peaceful and democratic development."

2. *President's Radio Report to the American People on Korea and on U.S. Policy in the Far East, April 11, 1951, Public Papers of the Presidents, p. 223.*

"I want to talk to you plainly tonight about what we are doing in Korea and about our policy in the Far East.

"In the simplest terms, what we are doing in Korea is this: We are trying to prevent a third world war.

* * *

"The Communists in the Kremlin are engaged in a monstrous conspiracy to stamp out freedom all over the world. If they were to succeed, the United States would be numbered among their principal victims. It must be clear to everyone that the United States cannot—and will not—sit idly by and await foreign conquest. The only question is: What is the best time to meet the threat and how is the best way to meet it?

"The best time to meet the threat is in the beginning. It is easier to put out a fire in the beginning when it is small than after it has become a roaring blaze. And the best way to meet the threat of aggression is for the peace-loving nations to act together. If they don't act together, they are likely to be picked off, one by one.

"If they had followed the right policies in the 1930's—if the free countries had acted together to crush the aggression of the dictators, and if they had acted in the beginning when the aggression was small—there probably would have been no World War II.

"If history has taught us anything, it is that aggression anywhere in the world is a threat to the peace everywhere in the world. When that aggression is supported by the cruel and selfish rulers of a powerful nation who are bent on conquest, it becomes a clear and present danger to the security and independence of every free nation.

*   *   *

"I have another secret intelligence report here. This one tells what another Communist officer in the Far East told his men several months before the invasion of Korea. Here is what he said: 'In order to successfully undertake the long-awaited world resolution, we must first unify Asia . . . Java, Indochina, Malaya, India, Tibet, Thailand, Philippines, and Japan are our ultimate targets. . . . The United States is the only obstacle on our road for the liberation of all the countries in southeast Asia. In other words, we must unify the people of Asia and crush the United States.'

*   *   *

"The dangers are great. Make no mistake about it. Behind the North Koreans and Chinese Communists in the front lines stand additional millions of Chinese soldiers. And behind the Chinese stand the tanks, the planes, the submarines, the soldiers, and the scheming rulers of the Soviet Union."

*   *   *

3. *President Truman's Special Message to Congress on Mutual Security Program, May 24, 1951, Public Papers of the Presidents, p. 309:*

*   *   *

"In Asia, in a vast area stretching from Afghanistan to Korea, free countries are struggling to meet communist aggression in all its many forms. Some of these countries are battling the communist armies of Soviet satellites; some are engaged in bitter civil strife against communist-led guerrillas; all of them face the immediate danger of communist subversion.

"Soviet intentions with regard to these countries are unmistakably clear. Using the weapons of subversion, false propaganda and civil war, the Kremlin has already reduced China to the status of a satellite. The Soviet rulers have turned their satellite armies loose on the Republic of Korea. Communist rebellion is raging in Indochina. In Burma, the Philippines, and other places, communist-inspired groups are stirring up internal disorder. In all countries, they are trying to exploit deep-seated economic difficulties—poverty, illiteracy and disease.

"This campaign threatens to absorb the manpower and the vital resources of the East into the Soviet design of world conquest. It threatens to deprive the free nations of some of their most vitally needed raw materials. It threatens to turn more of the peaceful millions of the East into armies to be used as pawns at the disposal of the Kremlin.

"Aside from immediate considerations of security, the continued independence of these nations is vital to the future of the free world. Many of these nations are new to self governments. They have dedicated themselves to the ideals of national independence, of human liberty, and social progress. Their hundreds of millions of citizens are eager for justice and liberty and a stake in the future.

"These countries demonstrate the power and vitality of the ideals of our own American Revolution; they mark the sweeping advance across the world of the concepts of freedom and brotherhood. To lose these countries to the rulers of the Kremlin would be more than a blow to our military security and our economic life. It would be a terrible defeat for the ideals of freedom—with grave spiritual consequences for men everywhere who share our faith in freedom.

"All these considerations make it essential for the United States to help the free countries of Asia in their struggle to make good their independence and bring economic and social progress to their people. Where the governments of these countries are striving to establish free and stable political institutions, to build up their military defenses, and to raise the standard of living above the level of bare subsistence, we can and should give them assistance. We cannot replace their own strong efforts, but we can supplement them.

"This Mutual Security Program is intended to do that. On the military side, it will supply certain of the Asian countries with items of military equipment and the training they need for their defense forces. On the economic side, it will provide a number of the Asian countries with the most urgently needed commodities, machinery, and tools, and with technical advice in such fields as agriculture, industry, health, and governmental administration.

"The assistance I am recommending for Asian countries, 555 million dollars in military aid and 375 million dollars in economic aid, is so planned as to meet the most pressing needs in the various countries, and is intended to provide the crucial margin of resources which will enable them to move forward.

"Military assistance under this program will go to the Chinese armies on Formosa, to help keep that island out of the hands of Communist China. It will go to Indo-China, where over 100,000 French troops are fighting side-by-side with the forces of Viet Nam, Laos, and Cambodia against communist-led forces. It will go to the Philippines and to Thailand, to help build forces strong enough to insure internal security and discourage outside attack. Some of these military assistance funds will also be available for allocation to other countries in the area if a critical need arises.

"The military aid under this program will supplement other military efforts against communism in Asia. The countries we will be aiding, and a number of others, are supporting military forces with their own funds. France is supplying the largest part of the military supplies needed in Indo-China, and Britain is supplying her forces which are fighting guerrillas in the Malay States. The substantial military aid we are giving to the forces of the Republic of Korea is included in the budget for our military services.

"The struggle for security and peace in Asia is far more than a military matter.

In many of the Asian countries, including all the countries which need military aid, economic assistance is also required."

* * *

4. *The Military Aid Program: Statement by the Departments of State and Defense, September 23, 1951, Department of State Bulletin, October 8, 1951, p. 570:*

* * *

"The participants were in complete agreement that the successful defense of Indochina is of great importance to the defense of all Southeast Asia. . . ."

* * *

5. *The Defense of Indochina: Communique Regarding Discussions Between Representatives of the United States, France, Viet-Nam, and Cambodia, June 18, 1952, Department of State Bulletin, June 30, 1952, p. 1010:*

"The principle which governed this frank and detailed exchange of views and information was the common recognition that the struggle in which the forces of the French Union and the Associated States are engaged against the forces of communist aggression in Indochina is an integral part of the world-wide resistance by the Free Nations to Communist attempts at conquest and subversion. . . ."

* * *

6. *Support by NATO of the French Union Defense Efforts in Indochina: Resolution Adopted by the North Atlantic Council, December 17, 1952, Department of State Bulletin, January 5, 1953, p. 4:*

"The North Atlantic Council

"*Recognizes* that resistance to direct or indirect aggression in any part of the world is an essential contribution to the common security of the free world;

"*Having Been Informed* at its meeting in Paris on the 16th December of the latest developments in the military and political situation in Indo-China;

"*Expresses* its wholehearted admiration for the valiant and long continued struggle by the French forces and the armies of the Associated States against Communist aggression; and

"*Acknowledges* that the resistance of the free nations in South East Asia as in Korea is in fullest harmony with the aims and ideals of the Atlantic Community;

"*And therefore agrees* that the campaign waged by the French Union forces in Indo-China deserves continuing support from the NATO governments."

EISENHOWER ADMINISTRATION PUBLIC STATEMENTS

1. *President Eisenhower's Remarks at Governors' Conference, August 4, 1953, Public Papers of the Presidents, 1953, p. 540:*

* * *

"I could go on enumerating every kind of problem that comes before us daily. Let us take, though, for example, one simple problem in the foreign field. You have seen the war in Indochina described variously as an outgrowth of French colonialism and its French refusal to treat indigenous populations decently. You find it again described as a war between the communists and the other elements in southeast Asia. But you have a confused idea of where it is located—Laos, or Cambodia, or Siam, or any of the other countries that are involved. You don't know, really, why we are so concerned with the far-off southeast corner of Asia.

"Why is it? Now, first of all, the last great population remaining in Asia that has not become dominated by the Kremlin, of course, is the sub-continent of India, including the Pakistan government. Here are 350 million people still free. Now let us assume that we lose Indochina. If Indochina goes, several things happen right away. The Malayan peninsula, the last little bit of the end hanging on down there, would be scarcely defensible—and tin and tungsten that we so greatly value from that area would cease coming. But all India would be outflanked. Burma would certainly, in its weakened condition, be no defense. Now, India is surrounded on that side by the Communist empire. Iran on its left is in a weakened condition. I believe I read in the paper this morning that Mossadegh's move toward getting rid of his parliament has been supported and of course he was in that move supported by the Tudeh, which is the Communist Party of Iran. All of that weakening position around there is very ominous for the United States, because finally if we lost all that, how would the free world hold the rich empire of Indonesia? So you see, somewhere along the line, this must be blocked. It must be blocked now. That is what the French are doing.

"So, when the United States votes $400 million to help that war, we are not voting for a giveaway program. We are voting for the cheapest way that we can to prevent the occurrence of something that would be of the most terrible significance for the United States of America—our security, our power and ability to get certain things we need from the riches of the Indonesian territory, and from southeast Asia."

*   *   *

2. *Joint Franco-American Communique, Additional United States Aid for France and Indochina, September 30, 1953, Department of State Bulletin, October 12, 1953, p. 486:*

"The forces of France and the Associated States in Indochina have for 8 years been engaged in a bitter struggle to prevent the engulfment of Southeast Asia by the forces of international communism. The heroic efforts and sacrifices of these French Union allies in assuring the liberty of the new and independent states of Cambodia, Laos and Vietnam has earned the admiration and support of the free world. In recognition of the French Union effort the United States Government has in the past furnished aid of various kinds to the Governments of France and the Associated States to assist in bringing the long struggle to an early and victorious conclusion.

"The French Government is firmly resolved to carry out in full its declaration of July 3, 1953, by which is announced its intention of perfecting the independence of the three Associated States in Indochina, through negotiations with the Associated States.

"The Governments of France and the United States have now agreed that, in support of plans of the French Government for the intensified prosecution of the war against the Viet Minh, the United States will make available to the

French Government prior to December 31, 1954 additional financial resources not to exceed $385 million. This aid is in addition to funds already earmarked by the United States for aid to France and the Associated States.

"The French Government is determined to make every effort to break up and destroy the regular enemy forces in Indochina. Toward this end the government intends to carry through, in close cooperation with the Cambodian, Laotian, and Vietnamese Governments, the plans for increasing the Associated States forces while increasing temporarily French forces to levels considered necessary to assure the success of existing military plans. The additional United States aid is designed to help make it possible to achieve these objectives with maximum speed and effectiveness.

"The increased French effort in Indochina will not entail any basic or permanent alteration of the French Government's plans and programs for its NATO forces."

3. *President Eisenhower's News Conference, February 10, 1954, Public Papers of the Presidents, 1954, p. 253:*

* * *

Q. Daniel Shorr, CBS Radio: "Mr. President, should your remarks on Indochina be construed as meaning that you are determined not to become involved or, perhaps, more deeply involved in the war in Indochina, regardless of how that war may go?"

THE PRESIDENT: "Well, I am not going to try to predict the drift of world events now and the course of world events over the next months. I say that I cannot conceive of a greater tragedy for America than to get heavily involved now in an all-out war in any of those regions, particularly with large units.

"So what we are doing is supporting the Vietnamese and the French in their conduct of that war; because, as we see it, it is a case of independent and free nations operating against the encroachment of communism."

4. *Address by Secretary Dulles before the Overseas Press Club of America at New York City on March 29, 1954, The Threat of a Red Asia. Department of State Bulletin, April 12, 1954, p. 539:*

"This provides a timely occasion for outlining the administration's thinking about two related matters—Indochina and the Chinese Communist regime.

"Indochina is important for many reasons. First, and always first, are the human values. About 30 million people are seeking for themselves the dignity of self-government. Until a few years ago, they formed merely a French dependency. Now, their three political units—Viet-Nam, Laos, and Cambodia—are exercising a considerable measure of independent political authority within the French Union. Each of the three is now recognized by the United States and by more than 30 other nations. They signed the Japanese peace treaty with us. Their independence is not yet complete. But the French Government last July declared its intention to complete that independence, and negotiations to consummate that pledge are actively under way.

"The United States is watching this development with close attention and great sympathy. We do not forget that we were a colony that won its freedom. We have sponsored in the Philippines a conspicuously successful development of political independence. We feel a sense of kinship with those everywhere who yearn for freedom.

"The Communists are attempting to prevent the orderly development of independence and to confuse the issue before the world. The Communists have, in these matters, a regular line which Stalin laid down in 1924.

"The scheme is to whip up the spirit of nationalism so that it becomes violent. That is done by professional agitators. Then the violence is enlarged by Communist military and technical leadership and the provision of military supplies. In these ways, international communism gets a stranglehold on the people and it uses that power to 'amalgamate' the peoples into the Soviet orbit.

" 'Amalgamation' is Lenin's and Stalin's word to describe their process.

" 'Amalgamation' is now being attempted in Indochina under the ostensible leadership of Ho Chi Minh. He was indoctrinated in Moscow. He became an associate of the Russian, Borodin, when the latter was organizing the Chinese Communist Party which was to bring China into the Soviet orbit. Then Ho transferred his activities to Indochina.

"Those fighting under the banner of Ho Chi Minh have largely been trained and equipped in Communist China. They are supplied with artillery and ammunition through the Soviet-Chinese Communist bloc. Captured materiel shows that much of it was fabricated by the Skoda Munition Works in Czechoslovakia and transported across Russia and Siberia and then sent through China into Viet-Nam. Military supplies for the Communist armies have been pouring into Viet-Nam at a steadily increasing rate.

"Military and technical guidance is supplied by an estimated 2,000 Communist Chinese. They function with the forces of Ho Chi Minh in key positions—in staff sections of the High Command, at the division level, and in specialized units such as signal, engineer, artillery, and transportation.

"In the present stage, the Communists in Indochina use nationalistic anti-French slogans to win local support. But if they achieved military or political success, it is certain that they would subject the people to a cruel Communist dictatorship taking its orders from Peiping and Moscow.

"The tragedy would not stop there. If the Communist forces won uncontested control over Indochina or any substantial part thereof, they would surely resume the same pattern of aggression against other free peoples in the area.

"The propagandists of Red China and Russia make it apparent that the purpose is to dominate all of Southeast Asia.

"Southeast Asia is the so-called 'rice bowl' which helps to feed the densely populated region that extends from India to Japan. It is rich in many raw materials, such as tin, oil, rubber, and iron ore. It offers industrial Japan potentially important markets and sources of raw materials.

"The area has great strategic value. Southeast Asia is astride the most direct and best-developed sea and air routes between the Pacific and South Asia. It has major naval and air bases. Communist control of Southeast Asia would carry a grave threat to the Philippines, Australia, and New Zealand, with whom we have treaties of mutual assistance. The entire Western Pacific area, including the so-called 'offshore island chain,' would be strategically endangered.

"President Eisenhower appraised the situation last Wednesday (March 24) when he said that the area is of 'transcendent importance.'

"The United States has shown in many ways its sympathy for the gallant struggle being waged in Indochina by French forces and those of the Associated States. Congress has enabled us to provide material aid to the established governments and their peoples. Also, our diplomacy has sought to deter Communist China from open aggression in that area.

"President Eisenhower, in his address of April 16, 1953, explained that a

Korean armistice would be a fraud if it merely released aggressive armies for attack elsewhere. I said last September that if Red China sent its own army into Indochina, that would result in grave consequences which might not be confined to Indochina.

"Recent statements have been designed to impress upon potential aggressors that aggression might lead to action at places and by means of free-world choosing, so that aggression would cost more than it could gain.

"The Chinese Communists have, in fact, avoided the direct use of their own Red armies in open aggression against Indochina. They have, however, largely stepped up their support of the aggression in that area. Indeed, they promote that aggression by all means short of open invasion.

"Under all the circumstances it seems desirable to clarify further the United States position.

"Under the conditions of today, the imposition on Southeast Asia of the political system of Communist Russia and its Chinese Communist ally, by whatever means, would be a grave threat to the whole free community. The United States feels that that possibility should not be passively accepted but should be met by united action. This might involve serious risks. But these risks are far less than those that will face us a few years from now if we dare not be resolute today.

"The free nations want peace. However, peace is not had merely by wanting it. Peace has to be worked for and planned for. Sometimes it is necessary to take risks to win peace just as it is necessary in war to take risks to win victory. The chances for peace are usually bettered by letting a potential aggressor know in advance where his aggression could lead him.

"I hope that these statements which I make here tonight will serve the cause of peace.

"Let me now discuss our political relations with Red China, taking first the matter of recognition.

"The United States does not recognize the Chinese Communist regime. That is well known. But the reasons seem not so well known. Some think that there are no reasons and that we are actuated purely by emotion. Your Government believes that its position is soberly rational.

"Let me first recall that diplomatic recognition is a voluntary act. One country has no right to demand recognition by another. Generally, it is useful that there should be diplomatic intercourse between those who exercise de facto governmental authority, and it is well established that recognition does not imply moral approval.

"President Monroe, in his famous message to Congress, denounced the expansionist and despotic system of Czarist Russia and its allies. But he said that it would nevertheless be our policy 'to consider the government de facto as the legitimate government for us.' That has indeed been the general United States policy, and I believe that it is a sound general policy. However, where it does not serve our interests, we are free to vary from it.

"In relation to Communist China, we are forced to take account of the fact that the Chinese Communist regime has been consistently and viciously hostile to the United States.

"A typical Chinese Communist pamphlet reads: 'We Must Hate America, because She is the Chinese People's Implacable Enemy.' 'We Must Despise America because it is a Corrupt Imperialist Nation, the World Center of Reaction and Decadency.' 'We Must Look down upon America because She is a Paper Tiger and Entirely Vulnerable to Defeat.'

"By print, by radio, by drama, by pictures, with all the propaganda skills which communism has devised, such themes are propagated by the Red rulers. They vent their hatred by barbarous acts, such as seizures and imprisonments of Americans.

"Those responsible for United States policy must ask and answer 'Will it help our country if, by recognition, we give increased prestige and influence to a regime that actively attacks our vital interests?' I can find only the answer: 'No.' "

*   *   *

5. *Address by Alfred le Sesne Jenkins, Officer in Charge, Chinese Political Affairs, before the American Academy of Political and Social Science, Philadelphia, Pa., Present United States Policy Toward China, April 2, 1954, Department of State Bulletin, April 26, 1954, p. 624:*

"In recent years we have often heard it said that more heat than light has been cast on the China question. I am not surprised at the heat, nor do I object to it, provided there is also sufficient light. The fate of one-fourth of the world's population is not a matter which can be taken lightly, and the addition of China's vast material and manpower resources to the Soviet bloc is a matter involving not only the security interests of the United States but those of the entire free world. I do not see how one can help feeling strongly about these matters. We need not apologize that our thinking about China is charged with feeling. National policies are an expression of national interests concerning which there is naturally much feeling, and our policies are an expression both of what we are and of what we want. We are a nation of free peoples. We want to remain free to pursue in peace our proper national destiny, and we want the same freedom and rights for others.

"We do not believe that the Chinese Communist regime represents the will of the people it controls. First capitalizing on the natural desire of the Chinese people to enjoy full recognition and respect for their importance in the world community, the regime then proceeded by its 'lean-to-one-side' policy to betray the powerful Chinese longings to stand up straight. It has followed slavishly the leadership of the Soviet Union and attempted to emulate it in all its ways. With the aid of thousands of Soviet advisers it has set about methodically to change the entire fabric of traditional Chinese culture, substituting communism's materialistic, atheistic doctrines wherein the state is the be-all and end-all and the individual its pawn.

"The regime at first attracted considerable support, principally through its sponsorship of a land redistribution program, but is now, after establishment of the prerequisite police-state controls, taking the land away from the owners in the same collectivization process which is familiar in other Communist countries and which invariably has brought suffering in its wake. China's much advertised 'New Democracy' is of course in reality 'old communism.'

"From its inception the regime has proclaimed a 'lean-to-one-side' policy in foreign affairs, and has left no doubt about its dedication to the proposition of world Communist revolution under the leadership of the Union of Soviet Socialist Republics. While its 'leaning-to-one-side' has not brought it to the position of complete 'prostration-to-one-side' characteristic of the Eastern European Soviet satellites, there is not the slightest evidence that this indicates any separatist tendencies. The difference in status of Peiping in its relationship with Moscow (as distinguished from that of the Eastern European satellites) is rather due chiefly to its having come to power without benefit, except in Manchuria, of Soviet Army occupation; to the prestige of Mao Tse-tung, arising from his long history of leadership of Chinese communism and his literary contributions to theoretical communism; to China's assumption of the role of leadership. . . ."

* * *

6. *President Eisenhower's News Conference, April 7, 1954, Public Papers of the Presidents, 1954, p. 382:*

* * *

Q. Robert Richards, Copley Press: "Mr. President, would you mind commenting on the strategic importance of Indochina to the free world? I think there has been, across the country, some lack of understanding on just what it means to us."

THE PRESIDENT: "You have, of course, both the specific and the general when you talk about such things.

"First of all, you have the specific value of a locality in its production of materials that the world needs.

"Then you have the possibility that many human beings pass under a dictatorship that is inimical to the free world.

"Finally, you have broader considerations that might follow what you would call the 'falling domino' principle. You have a row of dominoes set up, you knock over the first one, and what will happen to the last one is the certainty that it will go over very quickly. So you could have a beginning of a disintegration that would have the most profound influences.

"Now, with respect to the first one, two of the items from this particular area that the world uses are tin and tungsten. They are very important. There are others, of course, the rubber plantations and so on.

"Then with respect to more people passing under this domination, Asia, after all, has already lost some 450 million of its peoples to the Communist dictatorship, and we simply can't afford greater losses.

"But when we come to the possible sequence of events, the loss of Indochina, of Burma, of Thailand, of the Peninsula, and Indonesia following, now you begin to talk about areas that not only multiply the disadvantages that you would suffer through loss of materials, sources of materials, but now you are talking really about millions and millions and millions of people.

"Finally, the geographical position achieved thereby does many things. It turns the so-called island defensive chain of Japan, Formosa, of the Philippines and to the southward; it moves in to threaten Australia and New Zealand.

"It takes away, in its economic aspects, that region that Japan must have as a trading area or Japan, in turn, will have only one place in the world to go— that is, toward the Communist areas in order to live.

"So, the possible consequences of the loss are just incalculable to the free world."

* * *

Q. Robert G. Spivack, New York Post: "Mr. President, do you agree with Senator Kennedy that independence must be guaranteed the people of Indochina in order to justify an all-out effort there?"

THE PRESIDENT: "Well, I don't know, of course, exactly in what way a Senator was talking about this thing.

"I will say this: for many years, in talking to different countries, different governments, I have tried to insist on this principle: no outside country can come in and be really helpful unless it is doing something that the local people want.

"Now, let me call your attention to this independence theory. Senator Lodge, on my instructions, stood up in the United Nations and offered one country independence if they would just simply pass a resolution saying they wanted it, or at least said, 'I would work for it.' They didn't accept it. So I can't say that the associated states want independence in the sense that the United States is independent. I do not know what they want.

"I do say this: the aspirations of those people must be met, otherwise there is in the long run no final answer to the problem."

Q. Joseph Dear, Capital Times: "Do you favor bringing this Indochina situation before the United Nations?"

THE PRESIDENT: "I really can't say. I wouldn't want to comment at too great a length at this moment, but I do believe this: this is the kind of thing that must not be handled by one nation trying to act alone."

*   *   *

7. *Remarks Made by Under Secretary Smith in Answer to Questions Prepared for Use on "The American Week" over the CBS Television Network, April 11, 1954, on the Importance of Indochina, Department of State Bulletin, April 19, 1954, p. 589:*

Q. "Why is Indochina important to Americans?"

MR. SMITH: "For one vital basic and two special additional reasons. In the first place, the vital basic question is: Shall we or can the free world allow its position anywhere and particularly in Asia to be eroded piece by piece? Can we allow, dare we permit, expansion of Communist Chinese control further into Asia? Propagandists of the Soviet Union and of Communist China have made it clear that their purpose is to dominate all of Southeast Asia. Remember that this region helps to feed an immense population. It stretches all the way from India to Japan. It's a region that is rich in raw materials, full of tin, oil, rubber, iron ore.

"Now, from the strategic point of view, it lies across the most direct sea and air route between the Pacific and South Asia. There are major naval and air bases located in the area. Communist control of Southeast Asia would threaten the Philippines, Australia, and New Zealand directly, would threaten Malaya; it would have a very profound effect upon the economy of other countries in the area, even as far as Japan."

Q. "The President, at his news conference on April 7, described the process of Communist conquest as the 'falling domino' principle. Is that a good description of the threat in Southeast Asia?"

MR. SMITH: "Yes, it is. If Indochina is lost to the Communists, Burma is threatened, Thailand is threatened, the Malay Peninsula is exposed, Indonesia is subject to the gravest danger, and, in addition to these countries and their possible loss, there is the possible loss of food source. I have already mentioned the strategic raw materials, the bases in the area; and, while they are of enormous importance, the most important thing of all is the possible loss of millions and millions of people who would disappear behind the Iron Curtain. There are enough millions behind the Iron Curtain now. So what's at stake in Indochina?

It is the human freedom of the masses of people for all that enormous area of the world."

* * *

8. *Statement by Secretary Dulles Made at Augusta, Georgia, April 19, 1954, on Conversations in London and Paris Concerning Indochina, Department of State Bulletin, May 3, 1954, p. 668:*

"I have reported to President Eisenhower on my recent trip to London and Paris, where I discussed the position in Indochina.

"I found in both Capitals recognition that the armed Communist threat endangered vital free world interest and made it appropriate that the free nations most immediately concerned should explore the possibility of establishing a collective defense. This same recognition had already been expressed by other nations of the Southeast Asian area.

"The Communists in Viet-Nam, spurred on by Red China, have acted on the assumption that a quick, easy victory at Dien-Bien-Phu would open the door to a rapid Communist advance to domination of the entire Southeast Asian area. They concluded they were justified in recklessly squandering the lives of their subjects to conquer this strongpoint so as to confront the Geneva Conference with what could be portrayed as both a military and political victory for communism.

"The gallant defenders of Dien Bien-Phu have done their part to assure a frustration of the Communist strategy. They have taken a toll such that, from a military standpoint, the attackers already lost more than they could win. From a political standpoint, the defenders of Dien-Bien-Phu have dramatized the struggle for freedom so that the free world sees more clearly than ever before the issues that are at stake and once again is drawing closer together in unity of purpose.

"The Communist rulers are learning again that the will of the free is not broken by violence or intimidation.

"The brutal Soviet conquest of Czechoslovakia did not disintegrate the will of the West. It led to the formation of the North Atlantic Treaty alliance.

"The violent conquest of the China mainland followed by the Korean aggression did not paralyze the will of the free nations. It led to a series of Pacific mutual security pacts and to the creation under the North Atlantic Treaty of a powerful defensive force-in-being.

"The violent battles now being waged in Viet-Nam and the aggressions against Laos and Cambodia are not creating any spirit of defeatism. On the contrary, they are rousing the free nations to measures which we hope will be sufficiently timely and vigorous to preserve these vital areas from Communist domination.

"In this course lies the best hope of achieving at Geneva the restoration of peace with freedom and justice."

* * *

9. *Statement by Jameson Parker, Department Press Officer, read to Correspondents April 17, 1954, on U.S. Policy Toward Indochina, Department of State Bulletin, April 26, 1954, p. 623:*

"Certain remarks with regard to United States policy toward Indochina have been attributed to a high Government official [Vice President Nixon]. The contents of the speech referred to and questions and answers which followed were off the record, but a complete report of the speech has been made available to the State Department.

"The speech enunciated no new United States policy with regard to Indochina. It expressed full agreement with and support for the policy with respect to Indochina previously enunciated by the President and the Secretary of State.

"That policy was authoritatively set forth by the Secretary of State in his speech of March 29, 1954, in which he said:

" 'Under the conditions of today, the imposition on Southeast Asia of the political system of Communist Russia and its Chinese Communist ally, by whatever means, would be a grave threat to the whole free community. The United States feels that that possibility should not be passively accepted but should be met by united action. This might involve serious risks. But these risks are far less than those that will face us a few years from now if we dare not be resolute today.'

"In regard to a hypothetical question as to whether United States forces should be sent to Indochina in the event of French withdrawal, the high Government official categorically rejected the premise of possible French withdrawal. Insofar as the use of United States forces in Indochina was concerned, he was stating a course of possible action which he was personally prepared to support under a highly unlikely hypothesis.

"The answer to the question correctly emphasized the fact that the interests of the United States and other free nations are vitally involved with the interests of France and the Associated States in resisting Communist domination of Indochina."

10. *Address by Secretary Dulles Delivered to the Nation over Radio and Television, May 7, 1954, The Issues at Geneva, Department of State Bulletin, May 17, 1954, p. 740 and p. 744:*

*   *   *

"Let me turn now to the problem of Southeast Asia. In that great peninsula and the islands to the south live nearly 200 million people in 7 states—Burma; the three states of Indochina—Laos, Cambodia, and Viet-Nam; Thailand; Malaya; and Indonesia. Communist conquest of this area would seriously imperil the free world position in the Western Pacific. It would, among other things, endanger the Philippines, Australia, and New Zealand, with all of which the United States has mutual-security treaties. It would deprive Japan of important foreign markets and sources of food and raw materials.

"In Viet-Nam, one of the three Indochinese states, war has been going on since 1946. When it began, Indochina was a French colony just liberated from Japanese occupation. The war started primarily as a war for independence. What started as a civil war has now been taken over by international communism for its own purposes. Ho Chi Minh, the Communist leader in Viet-Nam, was trained in Moscow and got his first revolutionary experience in China."

*   *   *

"In Indochina, the situation is far more complex. The present conditions there do not provide a suitable basis for the United States to participate with its armed forces.

"The situation may perhaps be clarified as a result of the Geneva Conference. The French have stated their desire for an armistice on honorable terms and under proper safeguards. If they can conclude a settlement on terms which do not endanger the freedom of the peoples of Viet-Nam, this would be a real contribution to the cause of peace in Southeast Asia. But we would be gravely concerned if an armistic or cease-fire were reached at Geneva which would provide a road to a Communist takeover and further aggression. If this occurs, or if hostilities continue, then the need will be even more urgent to create the conditions for united action in defense of the area.

"In making commitments which might involve the use of armed force, the Congress is a full partner. Only the Congress can declare war. President Eisenhower has repeatedly emphasized that he would not take military action in Indochina without the support of Congress. Furthermore, he has made clear that he would not seek that unless, in his opinion, there would be an adequate collective effort based on genuine mutuality of purpose in defending vital interests.

"A great effort is being made by Communist propaganda to portray it as something evil if Asia joins with the nations of the Americas and Europe to get assistance which will help the peoples of Asia to secure their liberty. These Communist nations have, in this connection, adopted the slogan 'Asia for the Asians.'

"The Japanese war lords adopted a similar slogan when they sought to subject Asia to their despotic rule. The similar theme of 'Europe for the Europeans' was adopted by Mr. Molotov at the Berlin Conference when he proposed that the Europeans should seek security by arrangements which would send the United States back home.

"Great despotic powers have always known that they could impose their will and gain their conquests if the free nations stand apart and none helps the other.

"It should be observed that the Soviet Communist aggression in Europe took place only against countries which had no collective security arrangements. Since the organization of the North Atlantic Treaty, there has been no successful aggression in Europe.

"Of course, it is of the utmost importance that the United States participation in creating collective security in Asia should be on a basis which recognizes fully the aspirations and cultures of the Asian peoples. We have a material and industrial strength which they lack and which is an essential ingredient of security. Also they have cultural and spiritual values of their own which make them our equals by every moral standard.

"The United States, as the first colony of modern history to win independence for itself, instinctively shares the aspirations for liberty of all dependent and colonial peoples. We want to help, not hinder the spread of liberty.

"We do not seek to perpetuate Western colonialism and we find even more intolerable the new imperialist colonialism of communism.

"That is the spirit that animates us. If we remain true to that spirit, we can face the future with confidence that we shall be in harmony with those moral forces which ultimately prevail."

11. *President Eisenhower's News Conference, May 5, 1954, Public Papers of the Presidents, 1954, p. 451:*

*　　*　　*

"United States foreign policy has consistently supported the principles on which was founded the United Nations. The basic expression of this policy was the Vandenberg resolution in 1948. The United States believes in assuring the peace and integrity of nations through collective action and, in pursuance of the United Nations principle, has entered into regional security agreements with other nations. Examples are the Inter-American Agreement, the NATO Agreement, and numerous pacts in the Pacific. These arrangements are invariably to assure the peaceful security of the contracting nations and to prevent likelihood of attack; they are not arrangements designed primarily for waging war.

"The Geneva conference, now 9 days old, has produced no surprises. The expressed fears of some have proved unfounded.

"It has not been a 'Five-Power' conference as the Soviet Union tried to make it.

"It has not involved establishing express or implied diplomatic recognition by the United States of the Chinese Communist aggressors.

"The Korean phase of the conference has been organized. Here the Communists came up with a scheme for Korean unification which was a Chinese copy of the Soviet scheme for the unification of Germany. Under their proposal no election measures could be taken without Communist consent, and there could be no impartial supervision of the election conditions or of the voting.

"This scheme was rejected for Germany. Secretary Dulles tells me that is equally unacceptable to the Republic of Korea and to the United Nations members which took part in the Korean war under the United Nations Command now represented at Geneva.

"The Indochina phase of the conference is in process of being organized and the issues have not yet been clarified. In this matter a large measure of initiative rests with the governments of France, Viet-Nam, Laos, and Cambodia, which are the countries most directly concerned.

"Meanwhile, plans are proceeding for the realization of a Southeast Asia security arrangement. This was publicly suggested by Secretary Dulles in his address of March 29. Of course, our principal allies were advised in advance. This proposal of the Secretary of State was not a new one; it was merely reaffirmation of the principles that have consistently guided our post-war foreign policy and a reminder to interested Asian friends that the United States was prepared to join with others in the application of these principles to the threatened area. Most of the free nations of the area and others directly concerned have shown affirmative interest, and the conversations are actively proceeding.

"Obviously, it was never expected that this collective security arrangement would spring into existence overnight. There are too many important problems to be resolved. But there is a general sense of urgency. The fact that such an organization is in the process of formation could have an important bearing upon what happens at Geneva during the Indochina phase of the conference.

"The countries of the area are now thinking in constructive terms, which include the indispensable concept of collective security. Progress in this matter has been considerable, and I am convinced that further progress will continue to be made."

*   *   *

12. *President Eisenhower's News Conference, May 12, 1954, Public Papers of the Presidents, 1954, p. 473:*

*   *   *

Q. George Herman, CBS Radio: "Mr. President, since we seem to be going into the past, a few weeks ago you told us of your theory of dominoes about Indochina, the neck of the bottle—"

THE PRESIDENT: "Yes."

Q. Mr. Herman: "Since the fall of Dien Bien Phu, there has been a certain amount of talk of doing without Indochina. Would you tell us your administration's position; is it still indispensable to the defense of southeast Asia?"

THE PRESIDENT: "Again I forget whether it was before this body I talked about the cork and the bottle. Well, it is very important, and the great idea of setting up an organism is so as to defeat the domino result. When, each standing alone, one falls, it has the effect on the next, and finally the whole row is down. You are trying, through a unifying influence, to build that row of dominoes so they can stand the fall of one, if necessary.

"Now, so far as I am concerned, I don't think the free world ought to write off Indochina. I think we ought to all look at this thing with some optimism and some determination. I repeat that long faces and defeatism don't win battles."

* * *

13. *Address by the Secretary of State, June 11, 1954 (Excerpt), The Threat of Direct Chinese Communist Intervention in Indochina, Department of State Bulletin, June 28, 1954, p. 971:*

"At the moment, Indochina is the area where international communism most vigorously seeks expansion under the leadership of Ho Chi Minh. Last year President Eisenhower, in his great 'Chance for Peace' address, said that 'aggression in Korea and Southeast Asia are threats to the whole free community to be met by united action.' But the French were then opposed to what they called 'internationalizing' the war. They preferred to treat it as a civil war of rebellion. However, on July 3, 1953, the French Government made a public declaration of independence for the three Associated States, and in September it adopted the so-called Navarre plan, which contemplated a rapid buildup of national native forces. The United States then agreed to underwrite the costs of this plan.

"But last winter the fighting was intensified and the long strain began to tell in terms of the attitude of the French people toward a war then in its eighth year. Last March, after the siege of Dien-Bien-Phu had begun, I renewed President Eisenhower's proposal that we seek conditions which would permit a united defense for the area. I went to Europe on this mission, and it seemed that there was agreement on our proposal. But when we moved to translate that proposal into reality, some of the parties held back because they had concluded that any steps to create a united defense should await the results of the Geneva Conference.

"Meanwhile, the burdens of a collective defense in Indochina have mounted. The Communists have practiced dilatory negotiating at Geneva, while intensifying their fighting in Indochina. The French and national forces feel the strain of mounting enemy power on their front and of political uncertainty at their rear. I told the Senate Foreign Relations Committee last week that the situation is grave but by no means hopeless. The future depends largely on decisions awaited at Paris, London, and Geneva.

"The situation in Indochina is not that of open military aggression by the Chinese Communist regime. Thus, in Indochina, the problem is one of restoring tranquillity in an area where disturbances are fomented from Communist China, but where there is no open invasion by Communist China. This task of pacification, in our opinion, cannot be successfully met merely by unilateral armed intervention. Some other conditions need to be established. Throughout these Indochina developments, the United States has held to a stable and consistent course and has made clear the conditions which, in its opinion, might justify intervention. These conditions were and are (1) an invitation from the present lawful authorities; (2) clear assurance of complete independence to Laos, Cambodia, and Viet-Nam; (3) evidence of concern by the United Nations; (4) a joining in the collective effort of some of the other nations of the area; and (5) assurance that France will not itself withdraw from the battle until it is won.

"Only if these conditions were realized could the President and the Congress be justified in asking the American people to make the sacrifices incident to committing our Nation, with others, to using force to help to restore peace in the area.

"Another problem might, however, arise. If the Chinese Communist regime were to show in Indochina or elsewhere that it is determined to pursue the path of overt military aggression, then the situation would be different and another issue would emerge. That contingency has already been referred to publicly by the President and myself. The President, in his April 16, 1953, address, and I myself, in an address of September 2, 1953, made clear that the United States would take a grave view of any future overt military Chinese Communist aggression in relation to the Pacific or Southeast Asia area. Such an aggression would threaten island and peninsular positions which secure the United States and its allies.

"If such overt military aggression occurred, that would be a deliberate threat to the United States itself. The United States would of course invoke the processes of the United Nations and consult with its allies. But we could not escape ultimate responsibility for decisions closely touching our own security and self-defense.

"There are some, particularly abroad, who seem to assume that the attitude of the United States flows from a desire for a general war with Communist China. That is clearly false. If we had wanted such a war, it could easily have been based on the presence of Chinese aggressors in Korea. But last July, in spite of difficulties which at times seemed insuperable, we concluded a Korean armistice with Communist China. How could it be more surely demonstrated that we have both the will to make peace and the competence to make peace?

"Your Government wants peace, and the American people want peace. But should there ever be openly launched an attack that the American people would clearly recognize as a threat to our own security, then the right of self-preservation would demand that we—regardless of any other country—meet the issue squarely.

"It is the task of statesmanship to seek peace and deter war, while at the same time preserving vital national interests. Under present conditions that dual result is not easy to achieve, and it cannot be achieved at all unless your Government is backed by a people who are willing, if need be, to sacrifice to preserve their vital interests.

"At the Geneva Conference I said: 'Peace is always easy to achieve—by surrender.' Your Government does not propose to buy peace at that price. We do not believe that the American people want peace at that price. So long as that is our national will, and so long as that will be backed by a capacity for effective action, our Nation can face the future with that calm confidence which is the due of those who, in a troubled world, hold fast that which is good."

14. *President Eisenhower's News Conference, July 21, 1954, Public Papers of the Presidents, 1954, p. 642:*

*   *   *

"[Reading] I am glad, for course, that agreement has been reached at Geneva to stop the bloodshed in Indochina. The United States has not been a belligerent in the war in which thousands of brave men, while defending freedom, have died during the past 7 years.

"The primary responsibility for the settlement in Indochina rested with those nations which participated in the fighting.

"Our role at Geneva has been at all times to try to be helpful where desired, and to aid France and Cambodia, Laos and Viet-Nam, to obtain a just and honorable settlement which will take into account the needs of the interested people.

"Accordingly, the United States has not itself been a party to or bound by the decisions taken by the conference, but it is our hope that it will lead to the establishment of peace consistent with the rights and needs of the countries concerned. The agreement contains features which we do not like, but a great deal depends on how they work in practice.

"The United States is issuing at Geneva a statement to the effect that it is not prepared to join in the conference declaration but, as loyal members of the United Nations, we also say that in compliance with the obligations and principles contained in article II of the United Nations Charter, the United States will not use force to disturb the settlement. We also say that any renewal of Communist aggression would be viewed by us as a matter of grave concern.

"As evidence of our resolve to assist Cambodia and Laos to play their parts in full independence and sovereignty, in the peaceful community of free nations, we are requesting the agreement of the governments of Cambodia and Laos to our appointment of an ambassador or minister to be resident at their respective capitals. We already have a Chief of Mission at Saigon, the capital of Viet-Nam, and this embassy will, of course, be maintained.

"The United States is actively pursuing discussions with other free nations with a view to the rapid organization of a collective defense in southeast Asia in order to prevent further direct or indirect Communist aggression in that general area. [Ends reading]"

*   *   *

Q.   Mrs. May Craig, Maine Papers: "Mr. President, President Rhee of Korea will be here soon. Do you regard the partition of Korea as permanent, short of war, and are you including, planning to include, Korea and Free China in any kind of a southeast Asia pact?"

THE PRESIDENT: "Well, of course, Korea is not in southeast Asia.

"Already we have, you know, a treaty of mutual defense with Korea. It has been enacted, it has been approved, by the Senate.

"Now, as I understand it, when the Korean war started, the purpose of the United Nations was to prevent any advance by force into South Korea; they did do that.

"I know of no one that has ever proposed that we go to war to free North Korea.

"As it is, it is an unsatisfactory situation, exactly as exists in Germany, and now apparently is going to exist in part of Indochina.

"These are very unsatisfactory situations and, to my mind, will always give reason for aggravating situations that are difficult, at best. But there is no thought on the part of any of us to start an aggressive move for the freeing of that country."

*   *   *

"I have never felt that, except through these satellite excursions, that the Communist world wants any war at this time; in other words, I don't believe they would deliberately challenge us, challenge the free world, to a war of exhaustion.

"So the problem, no matter whether you happen to be fighting in one of these areas, remains the same. The loss of great areas through propaganda and deceit and subversion and coup d'etat, and every means available to a secret, well-financed conspiracy, they are all there. I personally think that if there is one good that can come out of this whole southeast Asian experience, it is this: to get the free world to looking facts in the face, and to seeing what we must do, what we should do, what sacrifices we are ready to make, in order to preserve the essentials of our system.

"I think that when the freedom of a man in Viet-Nam or in China is taken away from him, I think our freedom has lost a little. I just don't believe that we can continue to exist in the world, geographically isolated as we are, if we just don't find a concerted, positive plan of keeping these free nations so tightly bound together that none of them will give up; and if they are not weakened internally by these other methods, I just don't believe they will give up. I believe we can hold them."

Q. Robert E. Clark, International News Service: "Mr. President, along that line, a number of Congressmen today are branding the Geneva settlement as appeasement. Do you think there are any elements of appeasement in the cease-fire agreement?"

THE PRESIDENT: "Well, I hesitate, Mr. Clark, to use such words, as I have told you so often. I find that so many words mean so many different things to different people. I would say this, as I said in my statement: this agreement, in certain of its features, is not satisfactory to us. It is not what we would have liked to have had.

"But I don't know, when I am put up against it at this moment, to find an alternative, to say what we would or could do. Then if I have no better plan, I am not going to criticize what they have done."

*   *   *

15. *Final Declaration of Geneva Conference, July 21, 1954, IC/43 Rev. 2, July 21, 1954, Original: French:*

"Final declaration, dated July 21, 1954, of the Geneva Conference on the problem of restoring peace in Indo-China, in which the representatives of Cambodia, the Democratic Republic of Viet-Nam, France, Laos, the People's Republic of China, the State of Viet-Nam, the Union of Soviet Socialist Republics, the United Kingdom, and the United States of America took part.

"1. The Conference takes note of the agreements ending hostilities in Cambodia, Laos and Viet-Nam and organizing international control and the supervision of the execution of the provisions of these agreements.

"2. The Conference expresses satisfaction at the ending of hostilities in Cambodia, Laos and Viet-Nam; the Conference expresses its conviction that the execution of the provisions set out in the present declaration and in the agreements on the cessation of hostilities will permit Cambodia, Laos and Viet-Nam henceforth to play their part, in full independence and sovereignty, in the peaceful community of nations.

"3. The Conference takes note of the declarations made by the Governments of Cambodia and of Laos of their intention to adopt measures permitting all citizens to take their place in the national community, in particular by participating in the next general elections, which, in conformity with the constitution of each of these countries, shall take place in the course of the year 1955, by secret ballot and in conditions of respect for fundamental freedoms.

"4. The Conference takes note of the clauses in the agreement on the cessation of hostilities in Viet-Nam prohibiting the introduction into Viet-Nam of foreign troops and military personnel as well as of all kinds of arms and munitions. The Conference also takes note of the declarations made by the Governments of Cambodia and Laos of their resolution not to request foreign aid, whether in war material, in personnel or in instructors except for the purpose of the effective defence of their territory and, in the case of Laos, to the extent defined by the agreements on the cessation of hostilities in Laos.

"5. The Conference takes note of the clauses in the agreement on the cessation of hostilities in Viet-Nam to the effect that no military base under the control of a foreign State may be established in the regrouping zones of the two parties, the latter having the obligation to see that the zones allotted to them shall not constitute part of any military alliance and shall not be utilized for the resumption of hostilities or in the service of an aggressive policy. The Conference also takes note of the declarations of the Governments of Cambodia and Laos to the effect that they will not join in any agreement with other States if this agreement includes the obligation to participate in a military alliance not in conformity with the principles of the Charter of the United Nations or, in the case of Laos, with the principles of the agreement on the cessation of hostilities in Laos or, so long as their security is not threatened, the obligation to establish bases on Cambodian or Laotian territory for the military forces of foreign Powers.

"6. The Conference recognizes that the essential purpose of the agreement relating to Viet-Nam is to settle military questions with a view to ending hostilities and that the military demarcation line is provisional and should not in any way be interpreted as constituting a political or territorial boundary. The Conference expresses its conviction that the execution of the provisions set out in the present declaration and in the agreement on the cessation of hostilities creates the necessary basis for the achievement in the near future of a political settlement in Viet-Nam.

"7. The Conference declares that, so far as Viet-Nam is concerned, the settlement of political problems, effected on the basis of respect for the principles of independence, unity and territorial integrity, shall permit the Viet-Namese people to enjoy the fundamental freedoms, guaranteed by democratic institutions established as a result of free general elections by secret ballot. In order to ensure that sufficient progress in the restoration of peace has been made, and that all the necessary conditions obtain for free expression of the national will, general elections shall be held in July 1956, under the supervision of an international commission composed of representatives of the Member States of the International Supervisory Commission, referred to in the agreement on the cessation of hostilities. Consultations will be held on this subject between the competent representative authorities of the two zones from 20 July 1955 onwards.

"8. The provisions of the agreements on the cessation of hostilities intended to ensure the protection of individuals and of property must be most strictly applied and must, in particular, allow everyone in Viet-Nam to decide freely in which zone he wishes to live.

"9. The competent representative authorities of the Northern and Southern zones of Viet-Nam, as well as the authorities of Laos and Cambodia, must not permit any individual or collective reprisals against persons who have collaborated in any way with one of the parties during the war, or against members of such persons' families.

"10. The Conference takes note of the declaration of the Government of the French Republic to the effect that it is ready to withdraw its troops from the territory of Cambodia, Laos and Viet-Nam, at the request of the governments concerned and within periods which shall be fixed by agreement between the parties except in the cases where, by agreement between the two parties, a certain number of French troops shall remain at specified points and for a specified time.

"11. The Conference takes note of the declaration of the French Government to the effect that for the settlement of all the problems connected with the reestablishment and consolidation of peace in Cambodia, Laos and Viet-Nam, the French Government will proceed from the principle of respect for the independence and sovereignty, unity and territorial integrity of Cambodia, Laos and Viet-Nam.

"12. In their relations with Cambodia, Laos and Viet-Nam, each member of the Geneva Conference undertakes to respect the sovereignty, the independence, the unity and the territorial integrity of the above-mentioned states, and to refrain from any interference in their internal affairs.

"13. The members of the Conference agree to consult one another on any question which may be referred to them by the International Supervisory Commission in order to study such measures as may prove necessary to ensure that the agreements on the cessation of hostilities in Cambodia, Laos and Viet-Nam are respected."

16. *Direct Aid to the Associated States: Communique Regarding Franco-American Conversations, September 29, 1954, Department of State Bulletin, October 11, 1954, p. 534:*

"Representatives of the two Governments have had very frank and useful talks which have shown the community of their views, and are in full agreement on the objectives to be attained.

"The conclusion of the Southeast Asia Collective Defense Treaty in Manila on September 8, 1954, has provided a firmer basis than heretofore to assist the free nations of Asia in developing and maintaining their independence and security. The representatives of France and the United States wish to reaffirm the support of their Governments for the principles of self-government, independence, justice and liberty proclaimed by the Pacific Charter in Manila on September 8, 1954.

"The representatives of France and the United States reaffirm the intention of their governments to support the complete independence of Cambodia, Laos, and Viet-Nam. Both France and the United States will continue to assist Cambodia, Laos, and Viet-Nam in their efforts to safeguard their freedom and independence and to advance the welfare of their peoples. In this spirit France and the United States are assisting the Government of Viet-Nam in the resettlement of the Vietnamese who have of their own free will moved to free Viet-Nam and who already number some 300,000.

"In order to contribute to the security of the area pending the further development of national forces for this purpose, the representatives of France indicated that France is prepared to retain forces of its Expeditionary Corps, in agreement with the government concerned, within the limits permitted under the Geneva agreements and to an extent to be determined. The United States will consider the question of financial assistance for the Expeditionary Corps in these circumstances in addition to support for the forces of each of the three Associated States. These questions vitally affect each of the three Associated States and are being fully discussed with them.

"The channel for French and United States economic aid, budgetary support, and other assistance to each of the Associated States will be direct to that state. The United States representatives will begin discussions soon with the respective governments of the Associated States regarding direct aid. The methods for efficient coordination of French and United States aid programs to each of the three Associated States are under consideration and will be developed in discussions with each of these states.

"After the bilateral talks, the chiefs of diplomatic missions in Washington of Cambodia, Laos and Viet Nam were invited to a final meeting to have an exchange of views and information on these matters. The representatives of all five countries are in complete agreement on the objectives of peace and freedom to be achieved in Indochina."

17. *Aid to the State of Viet-Nam: Message from the President of the United States to the President of the Council of Ministers of Viet-Nam, October 23, 1954, Department of State Bulletin, November 15, 1954, pp. 735–736:*

"Dear Mr. President: I have been following with great interest the course of developments in Viet-Nam, particularly since the conclusion of the conference at Geneva. The implications of the agreement concerning Viet-Nam have caused grave concern regarding the future of a country temporarily divided by an artificial military grouping, weakened by a long and exhausting war and faced with enemies without and by their subversive collaborators within.

"Your recent requests for aid to assist in the formidable project of the movement of several hundred thousand loyal Vietnamese citizens away from areas which are passing under a de facto rule and political ideology which they abhor, are being fulfilled. I am glad that the United States is able to assist in this humanitarian effort.

"We have been exploring ways and means to permit our aid to Viet-Nam to be more effective and to make a greater contribution to the welfare and stability of the Government of Viet-Nam. I am, accordingly, instructing the American Ambassador to Viet-Nam to examine with you in your capacity as Chief of Government, how an intelligent program of American aid given directly to your Government can serve to assist Viet-Nam in its present hour of trial, provided that your Government is prepared to give assurances as to the standards of performance it would be able to maintain in the event such aid were supplied.

"The purpose of this offer is to assist the Government of Viet-Nam in developing and maintaining a strong, viable state, capable of resisting attempted subversion or aggression through military means."

* 　 * 　 *

18. *Address by President Eisenhower before the American Society of Newspaper Editors, April 21, 1956, Public Papers of the Presidents, 1956, p. 417 and p. 423:*

* 　 * 　 *

"The ideas of freedom are at work, even where they are officially rejected. As we know, Lenin and his successors, true to Communist doctrine, based the Soviet State on the denial of these ideas. Yet the new Soviet rulers who took over three years ago have had to reckon with the force of these ideas, both at home and abroad.

"The situation the new regime inherited from the dead Stalin apparently caused it to reappraise many of his mistakes.

"Having lived under his one-man rule, they have espoused the concept of 'collective' dictatorship. But dictatorship it still remains. They have denounced Stalin for some of the more flagrant excesses of his brutal rule. But the individual citizen still lacks the most elementary safeguards of a free society. The desire for a better life is still being sacrificed to the insatiable demands of the state.

"In foreign affairs, the new regime has seemingly moderated the policy of violence and hostility which has caused the free nations to band together to defend their independence and liberties. For the present, at least, it relies more on political and economic means to spread its influence abroad. In the last year, it has embarked upon a campaign of lending and trade agreements directed especially toward the newly-developing countries.

"It is still too early to assess in any final way whether the Soviet regime wishes to provide a real basis for stable and enduring relations."

*   *   *

"For example, why was there such a sudden change in the Soviet policy? Their basic air is to conquer the world, through world revolution if possible, but in any way. Anyone that has read any of their books knows that their doctrine is lies, deceit, subversion, war if necessary, but in any way: conquer the world. And that has not changed.

"But they changed their policies very markedly. They were depending on force and the threat of force only. And suddenly they have gone into an entirely different attitude. They are going into the economic and political fields and are really wearing smiles around the world instead of some of the bitter faces to which we have become accustomed.

"Now any time a policy is winning and the people are completely satisfied with it, you don't change. You change policies that markedly, you destroy old idols as they have been busy doing, only when you think a great change is necessary. So I think we can take some comfort; at least we can give careful consideration to the very fact they had to change their policies.

"And I think the whole free world is trying to test and determine the sincerity of that plan, in order that the free nations themselves, in pursuing their own policies, will make certain that they are not surprised in any place.

"We look at some of the advances we think they have made, but let us remember: they did not conquer Korea, which they announced they were going to do. They were stopped finally in the northern part of Vietnam; and Diem, the leader of the Southern Vietnamese, is doing splendidly and a much better figure in that field than anyone even dared to hope.

"The Iranian situation which only a few short years ago looked so desperate that each morning we thought we would wake up and read in our newspapers that Mossadegh had let them under the Iron Curtain, has not become satisfactory, but that crisis has passed and it is much better."

*   *   *

19. *United States Policy with Respect to Viet-Nam: Address by the Assistant Secretary of State for Far Eastern Affairs (this address by Assistant Sec-*

retary of State Robertson restated American policy and was delivered at a time of relative stability in South Viet-Nam), Washington, June 1, 1956, Department of State Bulletin, June 11, 1956, pp. 972–974:

"This past March, I had the pleasure of accompanying the Secretary of State on his visit to Saigon where we conversed with President Diem on the present and future problems of Viet-Nam. I was struck, as so many other recent observers have been, at the progress Free Viet-Nam has made in a few short months toward stability, security, and strength. President Diem seemed to reflect this progress in his own person. On the occasion of our earlier visit some 15 months ago, he seemed tense and gravely concerned about the problems facing Viet-Nam. This time he was reposed, poised, and appeared confident of the future of his country.

"Among the factors that explain the remarkable rise of Free Viet-Nam from the shambles created by 8 years of murderous civil and international war, the division of the country at Geneva and the continuing menace of predatory communism, there is in the first place the dedication, courage, and resourcefulness of President Diem himself. In him, his country has found a truly worthy leader whose integrity and devotion to his country's welfare have become generally recognized among his people. Asia has given us in President Diem another great figure; and the entire free world has become the richer for his example of determination and moral fortitude. There is no more dramatic example of this fortitude than President Diem's decisions during the tense and vital days of the battle against the parasitic politico-religious sects in the city of Saigon in the spring of 1955. These decisions were to resist the multiple pressures to compromise that were building up around him, and to struggle to the victorious end for the sake of a just cause. The free world owes him a debt of gratitude for his determined stand at that fateful hour.

"Consider Viet-Nam at three stages in its recent history:

"First, in mid-1954, partitioned by fiat of the great powers against the will of the Vietnamese people, devoid of governmental machinery or military strength, drifting without leadership and without hope in the backwash of the defeat administered by the combined weight of Communist-impressed infantry and of Chinese and Russian arms.

"Secondly, in early 1955, faced with the military and subversive threat of the Communists north of the 17th parallel, confronted with internal strife, its government challenged by the armed, self-seeking politico-religious sects, its army barely reformed and of uncertain loyalty, assailed from within by the most difficult problems, including that of having to absorb the sudden influx of three-quarters of a million refugees who would rather leave their ancestral lands and homes than suffer life under Communist tyranny:

"And finally Viet-Nam today, in mid-1956, progressing rapidly to the establishment of democratic institutions by elective processes, its people resuming peaceful pursuits, its army growing in effectiveness, sense of mission, and morale, the puppet Vietnamese politicians discredited, the refugees well on the way to permanent resettlement, the countryside generally orderly and calm, the predatory sects eliminated and their venal leaders exiled or destroyed.

"Perhaps no more eloquent testimony to the new state of affairs in Viet-Nam could be cited than the voice of the people themselves as expressed in their free election of last March. At that time the last possible question as to the feeling of the people was erased by an overwhelming majority for President Diem's leadership. The fact that the Viet Minh was unable to carry out its open threats to sabotage these elections is impressive evidence of the stability and prestige of the government.

"The United States is proud to be on the side of the effort of the Vietnamese people under President Diem to establish freedom, peace, and the good life. The United States wishes to continue to assist and to be a loyal and trusted friend of Viet-Nam.

"Our policies in Viet-Nam may be simply stated as follows:

"To support a friendly non-Communist government in Viet-Nam and to help it diminish and eventually eradicate Communist subversion and influence.

"To help the Government of Viet-Nam establish the forces necessary for internal security.

"To encourage support for Free Viet-Nam by the non-Communist world.

"To aid in the rehabilitation and reconstruction of a country and people ravaged by 8 ruinous years of civil and international war.

"Our efforts are directed first of all toward helping to sustain the internal security forces consisting of a regular army of about 150,000 men, a mobile civil guard of some 45,000, and local defense units which are being formed to give protection against subversion on the village level. We are providing budgetary support and equipment for these forces and have a mission assisting the training of the army. We are also helping to organize, train, and equip the Vietnamese police force. The refugees who have fled to South Viet-Nam to escape the Viet Minh are being resettled on productive lands with the assistance of funds made available by our aid program. In various ways our aid program also provides assistance to the Vietnamese Government designed to strengthen the economy and provide a better future for the common people of the country. The Vietnamese are increasingly giving attention to the basic development of the Vietnamese economy and to projects that may contribute directly to that goal. We give our aid and counsel to this program only as freely invited.

"I do not wish to minimize the magnitude of the task that still remains and of the problems that still confront this staunch and valiant member of the free world fighting for its independence on the threshold of the Communist heartland of Asia.

"The Communist conspiracy continues to threaten Free Viet-Nam. With monstrous effrontery, the Communist conspirators at Hanoi accuse Free Viet-Nam and its friends of violating the armistice provisions which the Vietnamese and their friends, including ourselves, have scrupulously respected despite the fact that neither the Vietnamese nor ourselves signed the Geneva Accords while they, the Communists who have solemnly undertaken to be bound by these provisions, have violated them in the most blatant fashion.

"The facts are that while on the one hand the military potential of Free Viet-Nam has been drastically reduced by the withdrawal of nearly 200,000 members of the French Expeditionary Corps and by the reduction of the Vietnamese Army by more than 50,000 from the time of the armistice to the present as well as by the outshipment from Viet-Nam since the cessation of hostilities of over $200 million worth of war equipment, we have on the other hand reports of steady constant growth of the warmaking potential of the Communists north of the 17th parallel.

"Our reports reveal that in complete disregard of its obligations, the Viet Minh have imported voluminous quantities of arms across the Sino-Viet Minh border and have imported a constant stream of Chinese Communist military personnel to work on railroads, to rebuild roads, to establish airports, and to work on other projects contributing to the growth of the military potential of the zone under Communist occupation.

"As so eloquently stated by the British Government in a diplomatic note released to the press and sent to Moscow in April of this year, and I quote:

" 'The Viet Minh army has been so greatly strengthened by the embodiment and re-equipment of irregular forces that instead of the 7 Viet Minh divisions in existence in July 1954 there are now no less than 20. This striking contrast between massive military expansion in the North and the withdrawal and reduction of military forces in the South speaks for itself.'

"By lies, propaganda, force, and deceit, the Communists in Hanoi would undermine Free Viet-Nam, whose fall they have been unable to secure by their maneuverings on the diplomatic front. These people, whose crimes against suffering humanity are so vividly described in the book by Lt. Dooley who addressed you this morning, have sold their country to Peiping. They have shamelessly followed all the devious zigzags of the Communist-bloc line so that their alliance with Communist China and the Soviet Union is firmly consolidated. These are the people who are now inviting President Diem to join them in a coalition government to be set up through so-called 'free elections.'

"President Diem and the Government of Free Viet-Nam reaffirmed on April 6 of this year and on other occasions their desire to seek the reunification of Viet-Nam by peaceful means. In this goal, we support them fully. We hope and pray that the partition of Viet-Nam, imposed against the will of the Vietnamese people, will speedily come to an end. For our part we believe in free elections, and we support President Diem fully in his position that if elections are to be held, there first must be conditions which preclude intimidation or coercion of the electorate. Unless such conditions exist there can be no free choice.

"May those leaders of the north in whom the spirit of true patriotism still survives realize the futility of the Communist efforts to subvert Free Viet-Nam by force or guile. May they force the abandonment of these efforts and bring about the peaceful demobilization of the large standing armies of the Viet Minh. May they, above all, return to the just cause of all those who want to reunify their country in peace and independence and for the good of all the people of Viet-Nam."

20. *Special Message to the Congress on the Mutual Security Programs, May 21, 1957, Public Papers of the Presidents—Eisenhower, 1957, p. 373.*

*   *   *

"First is defense assistance—our and other free nation's common effort to counter the Soviet-Chinese military power and the drive to dominate the world. That power continues to grow—in armaments, in nuclear capability, in its economic base. The Communist goal of conquering the world has never changed.

"For our nation alone to undertake to withstand and turn back Communist imperialism would impose colossal defense spending on our people. It would ultimately cost us our freedom.

"For other free nations to attempt individually to counter this menace would be impossible.

"We in our own interest, and other free nations in their own interest, have therefore joined in the building and maintenance of a system of collective security in which the effort of each nation strengthens all. Today that system has become the keystone of our own and their security in a tense and uncertain world."

*   *   *

"The second major element of our mutual security programs is economic development assistance and technical cooperation.

"This part of the programs helps less developed countries make the social and political progress needed to preserve their independence. Unless these peoples can hope for reasonable economic advance, the danger will be acute that their governments will be subverted by Communism.

"To millions of people close to the Soviet and Chinese Communist borders political freedom is still new. To many it must still prove its worth. To survive it must show the way to another and equally essential freedom—freedom from the poverty and hopelessness in which these peoples have lived for centuries. With their new freedom their desire and their determination to develop their economies are intense. They are fixed upon raising their standards of living. Yet they lack sufficient resources. Their need for help is desperate—both for technical know-how and capital.

"Lacking outside help these new nations cannot advance economically as they must to maintain their independence. Their moderate leaders must be able to obtain sufficient help from the free world to offer convincing hope of progress. Otherwise their peoples will surely turn elsewhere. Extremist elements would then seize power, whip up national hatreds and incite civil dissension and strife. The danger would be grave that these free governments would disappear. Instability and threats to peace would result. In our closely-knit world, such events would deeply concern and potentially endanger our own people.

"The help toward economic development that we provide these countries is a means to forestall such crises. Our assistance is thus insurance against rising tensions and increased dangers of war, and against defense costs that would skyrocket here at home should tragedy befall these struggling peoples.

"These revolutionary developments in distant parts of the world are borne on the crest of the wave sent out a century and a half ago by the example of our own successful struggle for freedom. The determination of the people of these nations to better their lot and to preserve their newly gained liberty awakens memories of our own noblest traditions. Our helping hand in their struggle is dictated by more than our own self-interest. It is also a mirror of the character and highest ideals of the people who have built and preserved this nation."

*   *   *

"In the many unstable regions of the world, Communist power is today probing constantly. Every weakness of free nations is being exploited in every possible way. It is inevitable that we shall have to deal with such critical situations in the future. In America's own interest, we must stand ready to furnish special assistance when threatened disaster abroad foretells danger to our own vital concerns."

*   *   *

21.   *Radio and Television address to the American People on the Need for Mutual Security in Waging the Peace, May 21, 1957, Public Papers of the President—Eisenhower, 1957, p. 386.*

*   *   *

"The common label of 'foreign aid' is gravely misleading—for it inspires a picture of bounty for foreign countries at the expense of our own. No misconception could be further from reality. These programs serve our own basic national and personal interests.

"They do this both immediately and lastingly.

"In the long term, the ending or the weakening of these programs would vastly increase the risk of future war.

"And—in the immediate sense—it would impose upon us additional defense expenditures many times greater than the cost of mutual security today.

"This evening it is my purpose to give you incontestable proof of these assertions.

"We have, during this century, twice spent our blood and our treasure fighting in Europe—and twice in Asia. We fought because we saw—too late to prevent war—that our own peace and security were imperilled, by the urgent danger—or the ruthless conquest—of other lands.

"We have gained wisdom from that suffering. We know, and the world knows, that the American people will fight hostile and aggressive despotisms when their force is thrown against the barriers of freedom, when they seek to gain the high ground of power from which to destroy us. But we also know that to fight is the most costly way to keep America secure and free. Even an America victorious in atomic war could scarcely escape disastrous destruction of her cities and a fearful loss of life. Victory itself could be agony.

"Plainly, we must seek less tragic, less costly ways to defend ourselves. We must recognize that whenever any country falls under the domination of Communism, the strength of the Free World—and of America—is by that amount weakened and Communism strengthened. If this process, through our neglect or indifference, should proceed unchecked, our continent would be gradually encircled. Our safety depends upon recognition of the fact that the Communist design for such encirclement must be stopped before it gains momentum—before it is again too late to save the peace.

"This recognition dictates two tasks. We must maintain a common worldwide defense against the menace of International Communism. And we must demonstrate and spread the blessings of liberty—to be cherished by those who enjoy these blessings, to be sought by those now denied them.

"This is not a new policy nor a partisan policy.

"This is a policy for America that began ten years ago when a Democratic President and a Republican Congress united in an historic declaration. They then declared that the independence and survival of two countries menaced by Communist aggression—Greece and Turkey—were so important to the security of America that we would give them military and economic aid.

"That policy saved those nations. And it did so without the cost of American lives.

"That policy has since been extended to all critical areas of the world. It recognizes that America cannot exist as an island of freedom in a surrounding sea of Communism. It is expressed concretely by mutual security treaties embracing 42 other nations. And these treaties reflect a solemn finding by the President and by the Senate that our own peace would be endangered if any of these countries were conquered by International Communism.

"The lesson of the defense of Greece and Turkey ten years ago has since been repeated in the saving of other lands and peoples. A recent example is the Southeast Asian country of Viet-Nam, whose President has just visited us as our honored guest.

"Two years ago it appeared that all Southeast Asia might be overrun by the forces of International Communism. The freedom and security of nations for which we had fought throughout World War II and the Korean War again stood in danger. The people of Viet-Nam responded bravely—under steadfast leadership.

"But bravery alone could not have prevailed.

"We gave military and economic assistance to the Republic of Viet-Nam. We entered into a treaty—the Southeast Asia Security Treaty—which plainly warned that an armed attack against this area would endanger our own peace and safety, and that we would act accordingly. Thus Viet-Nam has been saved for freedom.

"This is one of the nations where we have been spending the largest amounts of so-called 'foreign aid.' What could be plainer than the fact that this aid has served not only the safety of another nation—but also the security of our own.

"The issue, then, is solemn and serious and clear.

"When our young men were dying in the Argonne in 1918 and on the beaches of Normandy and in the Western Pacific in 1944 and at Pusan in 1950—and when the battlefields of Europe and Africa and Asia were strewn with billions of dollars worth of American military equipment, representing the toil and the skills of millions of workers—no one for an instant doubted the need and the rightness of this sacrifice of blood and labor and treasure.

"Precisely the same needs and purposes are served by our Mutual Security programs today—whether these operate on a military or an economic front. For on both fronts they are truly defense programs."

*   *   *

22. *Radio and Television Report to the American People Regarding the Situation in the Formosa Straits, September 11, 1958, Public Papers of the Presidents—Eisenhower, 1958, p. 694.*

"My Friends:

"Tonight I want to talk to you about the situation, dangerous to peace, which has developed in the Formosa Straits, in the Far East. My purpose is to give you its basic facts and then my conclusions as to our nation's proper course of action.

"To begin, let us remember that traditionally this country and its government have always been passionately devoted to peace with honor, as they are now. We shall never resort to force in settlement of differences except when compelled to do so to defense against aggression and to protect our vital interests.

"This means that, in our view, negotiations and conciliation should never be abandoned in favor of force and strife. While we shall never timidly retreat before the threat of armed aggression, we would welcome in the present circumstances negotiations that could have a fruitful result in preserving the peace of the Formosa area and reaching a solution that could be acceptable to all parties concerned including, of course, our ally, the Republic of China.

"On the morning of August 23rd the Chinese Communists opened a severe bombardment of Quemoy, an island in the Formosa Straits off the China Coast. Another island in the same area, Matsu, was also attacked. These two islands have always been a part of Free China—never under Communist control.

"This bombardment of Quemoy has been going on almost continuously ever since. Also Chinese Communists have been using their naval craft to try to break up the supplying of Quemoy, with its 125,000 people. Their normal source of supply is by sea from Formosa, where the government of Free China is now located.

"Chinese Communists say that they will capture Quemoy. So far they have not actually attempted a landing, but their bombardment has caused great damage. Over 1,000 people have been killed or wounded. In large part these are civilians.

"This is a tragic affair. It is shocking that in this day and age naked force should be used for such aggressive purposes.

"But this is not the first time that the Chinese Communists have acted in this way.

"In 1950 they attacked and tried to conquer the Republic of Korea. At that time President Truman announced the intention of protecting Formosa, the principal area still held by Free China, because of the belief that Formosa's safety was vital to the security of the United States and the free world. Our government has adhered firmly ever since 1950 to that policy.

"In 1953 and 1954 the Chinese Communists took an active part in the war in Indo-China against Viet Nam.

"In the fall of 1954 they attacked Quemoy and Matsu, the same two islands they are attacking now. They broke off that attack when, in January 1955, the Congress and I agreed that we should firmly support Free China.

"Since then, for about four years, Chinese Communists have not used force for aggressive purposes. We have achieved an armistice in Korea which stopped the fighting there in 1953. There is a 1954 armistice in Viet Nam; and since 1955 there has been quiet in the Formosa Straits area. We had hoped that the Chinese Communists were becoming peaceful—but it seems not.

"So the world is again faced with the problem of armed aggression. Powerful dictatorships are attacking an exposed, but free, area.

"What should we do?

"Shall we take the position that, submitting to threat, it is better to surrender pieces of free territory in the hope that this will satisfy the appetite of the aggressor and we shall have peace?

"Do we not still remember that the name of 'Munich' symbolizes a vain hope of appeasing dictators?

"At that time, the policy of appeasement was tried and it failed. Prior to the second World War, Mussolini seized Ethiopia. In the Far East, Japanese warlords were grabbing Manchuria by force. Hitler sent his armed forces into the Rhineland in violation of the Versailles Treaty. Then he annexed little Austria. When he got away with that, he next turned to Czechoslovakia and began taking it, bit by bit.

"In the face of all these attacks on freedom by the dictators, the powerful democracies stood aside. It seemed that Ethiopia and Manchuria were too far away and too unimportant to fight about. In Europe, appeasement was looked upon as the way to peace. The democracies felt that if they tried to stop what was going on, that would mean war. But because of these repeated retreats, war came just the same.

"If the democracies had stood firm at the beginning, almost surely there would have been no World War. Instead they gave such an appearance of weakness and timidity that aggressive rulers were encouraged to overrun one country after another. In the end the democracies saw that their very survival was at stake. They had no alternative but to turn and fight in what proved to be the most terrible war that the world has ever known.

"I know something about that war, and I never want to see that history repeated. But, my fellow Americans, it certainly can be repeated if the peace-loving democratic nations again fearfully practice a policy of standing idly by while big aggressors use armed force to conquer the small and weak.

"Let us suppose that the Chinese Communists conquer Quemoy. Would that be the end of the story? We know that it would not be the end of the story. History teaches that when powerful despots can gain something through aggression, they try, by the same methods, to gain more and more and more.

"Also, we have more to guide us than the teachings of history. We have the statements, the boastings, of the Chinese Communists themselves. They frankly say that their present military effort is part of a program to conquer Formosa.

"It is as certain as can be that the shooting which the Chinese Communists started on August 23rd had as its purpose not just the taking of the island of Quemoy. It is part of what is indeed an ambitious plan of armed conquest.

"This plan would liquidate all of the free world positions in the Western Pacific area and bring them under captive governments which would be hostile to the United States and the free world. Thus the Chinese and Russian Communists would come to dominate at least the Western half of the now friendly Pacific Ocean.

"So, aggression by ruthless despots again imposes a clear danger to the United States and to the free world.

"In this effort the Chinese Communists and the Soviet Union appear to be working hand in hand. Last Monday I received a long letter on this subject from Prime Minister Khrushchev. He warned the United States against helping its allies in the Western Pacific. He said that we should not support the Republic of China and the Republic of Korea. He contended that we should desert them, return all of our naval forces to our home bases, and leave our friends in the Far East to face, alone, the combined military power of the Soviet Union and Communist China.

"Does Mr. Khrushchev think that we have so soon forgotten Korea?

"I must say to you very frankly and soberly, my friends, the United States cannot accept the result that the Communists seek. Neither can we show, now, a weakness of purpose—a timidity—which would surely lead them to move more aggressively against us and our friends in the Western Pacific area.

"If the Chinese Communists have decided to risk a war, it is not because Quemoy itself is so valuable to them. They have been getting along without Quemoy ever since they seized the China mainland nine years ago.

"If they have now decided to risk a war, it can only be because they, and their Soviet allies, have decided to find out whether threatening war is a policy from which they can make big gains.

"If that is their decision, then a Western Pacific Munich would not buy us peace or security. It would encourage the aggressors. It would dismay our friends and allies there. If history teaches anything, appeasement would make it more likely that we would have to fight a major war.

"Congress has made clear its recognition that the security of the Western Pacific is vital to the security of the United States and that we should be firm. The Senate has ratified, by overwhelming vote, security treaties with the Republic of China covering Formosa and the Pescadores, and also the Republic of Korea. We have a mutual security treaty with the Republic of the Philippines, which could be next in line for conquest if Formosa fell into hostile hands. These treaties commit the United States to the defense of the treaty areas. In addition, there is a Joint Resolution which the Congress passed in January 1955 dealing specifically with Formosa and the offshore islands of Free China in the Formosa Straits.

"At that time the situation was similar to what it is today.

"Congress then voted the President authority to employ the armed forces of the United States for the defense not only of Formosa but of related positions such as Quemoy and Matsu, if I believed their defense to be appropriate in assuring the defense of Formosa.

"I might add that the mandate from the Congress was given by an almost unanimous bipartisan vote.

"Today, the Chinese Communists announce, repeatedly and officially, that their military operations against Quemoy are preliminary to attack on Formosa. So it is clear that the Formosa Straits Resolution of 1955 applies to the present situation.

"If the present bombardment and harassment of Quemoy should be converted into a major assault, with which the local defenders could not cope, then we would be compelled to face precisely the situation that Congress visualized in 1955.

"I have repeatedly sought to make clear our position in this matter so that there would not be danger of Communist miscalculation. The Secretary of State on September fourth made a statement to the same end. This statement could not, of course, cover every contingency. Indeed, I interpret the Joint Resolution as requiring me not to make absolute advance commitments, but to use my judgment according to the circumstances of the time. But the statement did carry a clear meaning to the Chinese Communists and to the Soviet Union. There will be no retreat in the face of armed aggression, which is part and parcel of a continuing program of using armed force to conquer new regions.

"I do not believe that the United States can be either lured or frightened into appeasement. I believe that in taking the position of opposing aggression by force, I am taking the only position which is consistent with the vital interests of the United States, and, indeed with the peace of the world.

"Some misguided persons have said that Quemoy is nothing to become excited about. They said the same about South Korea—about Viet Nam, about Lebanon.

"Now I assure you that no American boy will be asked by me to fight *just* for Quemoy. But those who make up our armed forces—and I believe the American people as a whole—do stand ready to defend the principle that armed force shall not be used for aggressive purposes.

"Upon observance of that principle depends a lasting and just peace. It is that same principle that protects the Western Pacific free world positions as well as the security of our homeland. If we are not ready to defend this principle, then indeed tragedy after tragedy would befall us.

"But there is a far better way than resort to force to settle these differences, and there is some hope that such a better way may be followed.

"That is the way of negotiation.

"That way is open and prepared because in 1955 arrangements were made between the United States and the Chinese Communists that an Ambassador on each side would be authorized to discuss at Geneva certain problems of common concern. These included the matter of release of American civilians imprisoned in Communist China, and such questions as the renunciation of force in the Formosa area. There have been 73 meetings since August 1955.

"When our Ambassador, who was conducting these negotiations, was recently transferred to another post, we named as successor Mr. Beam, our Ambassador to Poland. The Chinese Communists were notified accordingly the latter part of July, but there was no response.

"The Secretary of State, in his September fourth statement, referred to these Geneva negotiations. Two days later, Mr. Chou En-lai, the Premier of the Peoples' Republic of China, proposed that these talks should be resumed 'in the interests of peace.' This was followed up on September eighth by Mr. Mao Tse-tung, the Chairman of the Peoples' Republic of China. We promptly welcolmed this prospect and instructed our Ambassador at Warsaw to be ready immediately to resume these talks. We expect that the talks will begin upon the return to Warsaw of the Chinese Communist Ambassador who has been in Peiping.

"Perhaps our suggestion may be bearing fruit. We devoutly hope so.

"Naturally, the United States will adhere to the position it first took in 1955, that we will not in these talks be a party to any arrangements which would prejudice rights of our ally, the Republic of China.

"We know by hard experiences that the Chinese Communist leaders are indeed militant and aggressive. But we cannot believe that they would now persist in a course of military aggression which would threaten world peace, with all that would be involved. We believe that diplomacy can and should find a way out. There are measures that can be taken to assure that these offshore islands will not be a thorn in the side of peace. We believe that arrangements are urgently required to stop gun fire and to pave the way to a peaceful solution.

"If the bilateral talks between Ambassadors do not fully succeed, there is still the hope that the United Nations could exert a peaceful influence on the situation.

"In 1955 the hostilities of the Chinese Communists in the Formosa area were brought before the United Nations Security Council. But the Chinese Communists rejected its jurisdiction. They said that they were entitled to Formosa and the offshore islands and that if they used armed forces to get them, that was purely a 'civil war,' and that the United Nations had no right to concern itself.

"They claimed also that the attack by the Communist North Koreans on South Korea was 'civil war,' and that the United Nations, and the United States were 'aggressors" because they helped South Korea. They said the same about their attack on Viet Nam.

"I feel sure that these pretexts will never deceive or control world opinion. The fact is that Communist Chinese hostilities in the Formosa Straits area do endanger world peace. I do not believe that any rulers, however aggressive they may be, will flout efforts to find a peaceful and honorable solution, whether it be by direct negotiations or through the United Nations.

"My friends, we are confronted with a serious situation. But it is typical of the security problems of the world today. Powerful and aggressive forces are constantly probing, now here, now there, to see whether the free world is weakening. In the face of this, there are no easy choices available. It is misleading for anyone to imply that there are.

"However, the present situation, though serious, is by no means desperate or hopeless.

"There is not going to be any appeasement.

"I believe that there is not going to be any war.

"But there must be sober realization by the American people that our legitimate purposes are again being tested by those who threaten peace and freedom everywhere.

"This has not been the first test for us and for the free world. Probably it will not be the last. But as we meet each test with courage and unity, we contribute to the safety and the honor of our beloved land—and to the cause of a just and lasting peace."

23. *The President's News Conference of October 1, 1958, Public Papers of the Presidents—Eisenhower, 1958, p. 715.*

* * *

THE PRESIDENT: "Well, sir, all I can tell you about that is that I conceive of no possible solution that we haven't studied, pondered, discussed with others in the very great hope that a peaceful solution can come about.

"As you well know, the basic issue, as we see it, is to avoid retreat in the face of force, not to resort to force to resolve these questions in the international world. And we believe if we are not faithful to that principle in the long run we are going to suffer.

"Now, Mr Dulles, who had a very long conference yesterday morning and almost solely on this subject, did one thing that I would commend to all of you: he quoted paragraphs, two paragraphs I think, from Mr. Spaak's speech recently in the United Nations, where Mr. Spaak said: 'The whole free world must realize that it is not Quemoy and the Matsus that we are talking about, we are talking about the Communists' constant, unrelenting pressure against the free world, against all of it.'

"As a matter of fact, a magazine just, I guess, out last evening, U.S. News and World Report, gives quite a detailed and documented story of Communist aggression and activities in 72 countries.

"I commend that to your reading, because we are very apt, by focusing our eyes on some geographical point, to neglect the great principles for which a country such as ours has stood, for all these years, and for which Western civilization has largely stood.

"So, I should say, we want to get these things in perspective.

"Now, you mentioned the question of it would be foolish for them keeping large forces there for a long time.

"I believe, as a soldier, that was not a good thing to do, to have all these troops there. But, remember, we have differences with our allies all over the world. They are family differences, and sometimes they are acute; but, by and large, the reason we call it 'free world' is because each nation in it wants to remain independent under its own government and not under some dictatorial form of government. So, to the basic ideals, all of us must subscribe."

Q. *Peter Lisagor, Chicago Daily News:* "In the light of Mr. Spaak's statement, can you tell us what your view is of why so many of our allies fail to see this point you have just made?"

THE PRESIDENT: "Well, it's a very difficult thing, and of course an answer is speculative. But when we go back to the Manchurian incident of 1931, when we go back to Hitler's marching into the Rhineland, when we take his taking over the Sudetenland and the Anschluss with Austria by force, when finally he took over all of Czechoslovakia, where was the point to stop this thing before it got into a great major war?

"Why did not public opinion see this thing happening?

"Now, in hindsight, most of us have condemned these failures very bitterly, going right back to 1931 in Manchuria. I don't know why the human is so constructed that he believes that possibly there is an easier solution—that you can by feeding aggression a little bit, a teaspoonful of something, that he won't see that they are going to demand the whole quart.

"I don't know any real answer to that thing; it is puzzling. And, of course, for those who have to carry responsibility, it is a very heavy weight on their spirits and minds; there is no question about that. But there it is."

*   *   *

24. *Special Message to the Congress on the Mutual Security Program, March 13, 1959, Public Papers of the Presidents—Eisenhower, 1959, p. 256.*

*   *   *

"I believe that these events of the past year and the stern, indeed harsh, realities of the world of today and the years ahead demonstrate the importance of the Mutual Security Program to the security of the United States. I think four such realities stand out.

"First, the United States and the entire free world are confronted by the military might of the Soviet Union, Communist China, and their satellites. These nations of the Communist Bloc now maintain well-equipped standing armies totaling more than 6,500,000 men formed in some 400 divisions. They are deployed along the borders of our allies and friends from the northern shores of Europe to the Mediterranean Sea, around through the Middle East and Far East to Korea. These forces are backed by an air fleet of 25,000 planes in operational units, and many more not in such units. They, in turn, are supported by nuclear weapons and missiles. On the seas around this land mass is a large navy with several hundred submarines.

"Second, the world is in a great epoch of seething change. Within little more than a decade a world-wide political revolution has swept whole nations—21 of them—with three-quarters of a billion people, a fourth of the world's population, from colonial status to independence—and others are pressing just behind. The industrial revolution, with its sharp rise in living standards, was accompanied by much turmoil in the Western world. A similar movement is now beginning to sweep Africa, Asia, and South America. A newer and even more striking revolution in medicine, nutrition, and sanitation is increasing the energies and lengthening the lives of people in the most remote areas. As a result of lowered infant mortality, longer lives, and the accelerating conquest of famine, there is underway a population explosion so incredibly great that in little more than another generation the population of the world is expected to double. Asia alone is expected to have one billion more people than the entire world has today. Throughout vast areas there is a surging social upheaval in which, overnight, the responsibilities of self-government are being undertaken by hundreds of millions, women are assuming new places in public life, old family patterns are being destroyed and new ones uneasily established. In the early years of independence, the people of the new nations are fired with a zealous nationalism which, unless channelled toward productive purposes, could lead to harmful developments. Transcending all this there is the accompanying universal determination to achieve a better life.

"Third, there is loose in the world a fanatic conspiracy, International Communism, whose leaders have in two score years seized control of all or parts of 17 countries, with nearly one billion people, over a third of the total population of the earth. The center of this conspiracy, Soviet Russia, has by the grimmest determination and harshest of means raised itself to be the second military and economic power in the world today. Its leaders never lose the opportunity to declare their determination to become the first with all possible speed.

"The other great Communist power, Red China, is now in the early stages of its social and economic revolution. Its leaders are showing the same ruthless drive for power and to this end are striving for ever increasing economic output. They seem not to care that the results—which thus far have been considerable in materialistic terms—are built upon the crushed spirits and the broken bodies of their people.

"The fact that the Soviet Union has just come through a great revolutionary process to a position of enormous power and that the world's most populous nation, China, is in the course of tremendous change at the very time when so large a part of the free world is in the flux of revolutionary movements, provides Communism with what it sees as its golden opportunity. By the same token freedom is faced with difficulties of unprecedented scope and severity—and opportunity as well.

"Communism exploits the opportunity to intensify world unrest by every possible means. At the same time Communism masquerades as the pattern of progress, as the path to economic equality, as the way to freedom from what it calls 'Western imperialism,' as the wave of the future.

"For the free world there is the challenge to convince a billion people in the less developed areas that there is a way of life by which they can have bread *and* the ballot, a better livelihood *and* the right to choose the means of their livelihood, social change *and* social justice—in short, progress *and* liberty. The dignity of man is at stake.

"Communism is determined to win this contest—freedom must be just as dedicated or the struggle could finally go against us. Though no shot would have been fired, freedom and democracy would have lost.

"This battle is now joined. The next decade will forecast its outcome.

"The fourth reality is that the military position and economic prosperity of the United States are interdependent with those of the rest of the free world.

"As I shall outline more fully below, our military strategy is part of a common defense effort involving many nations. The defense of the free world is strengthened and progress toward a more stable peace is advanced by the fact that powerful free world forces are established on territory adjoining the areas of Communist power. The deterrent power of our air and naval forces and our intermediate range missile is materially increased by the availability of bases in friendly countries abroad.

"Moreover the military strength of our country and the needs of our industry cannot be supplied from our own resources. Such basic necessities as iron ore, bauxite for aluminum, manganese, natural rubber, tin, and many other materials acutely important to our military and industrial strength are either not produced in our own country or are not produced in sufficient quantities to meet our needs. This is an additional reason why we must help to remain free the nations which supply these resources."

*   *   *

"Two fundamental purposes of our collective defense effort are to prevent general war and to deter Communist local aggression.

"We know the enormous and growing Communist potential to launch a war of nuclear destruction and their willingness to use this power as a threat to the free world. We know also that even local aggressions, unless checked, could absorb nation after nation into the Communist orbit—or could flame into world war.

"The protection of the free world against the threat or the reality of Soviet nuclear aggression or local attack rests on the common defense effort established under our collective security agreements. The protective power of our Strategic Air Command and our naval air units is assured even greater strength not only by the availability of bases abroad but also by the early warning facilities, the defensive installations, and the logistic support installations maintained on the soil of these and other allies and friends for our common protection.

"The strategy of general defense is made stronger and of local defense is made possible by the powerful defensive forces which our allies in Europe, in the Middle East, and the Far East have raised and maintain on the soil of their homelands, on the borders of the Communist world."

*   *   *

25. *Address at the Gettysburg College Convocation: The Importance of Understanding, April 4, 1959, Public Papers of the Presidents—Eisenhower, 1959, p. 310.*

*   *   *

"I shall not attempt to talk to you about education, but I shall speak of one vital purpose of education—the development of understanding—understanding, so that we may use with some measure of wisdom the knowledge we may have acquired, whether in school or out.

"For no matter how much intellectual luggage we carry around in our heads, it becomes valuable only if we know how to use the information—only if we are able to relate one fact of a problem to the others do we truly understand them.

"This is my subject today—the need for greater individual and collective understanding of some of the international facts of today's life. We need to understand our country's purpose and role in strengthening the world's free nations which, with us, see our concepts of freedom and human dignity threatened by atheistic dictatorship.

"If through education—no matter how acquired—people develop understanding of basic issues, and so can distinguish between the common, long-term good of all, on the one hand, and convenient but shortsighted expediency on the other, they will support policies under which the nation will prosper. And if people should ever lack the discernment to understand, or the character to rise above their own selfish short-term interests, free government would become well nigh impossible to sustain. Such a government would be reduced to nothing more than a device which seeks merely to accommodate itself and the country's good to the bitter tugs-of-war of conflicting pressure groups. Disaster could eventually result.

"Though the subject I have assigned myself is neither abstruse nor particularly difficult to comprehend, its importance to our national and individual lives is such that failure to marshal, to organize, and to analyze the facts pertaining to it could have for all of us consequences of the most serious character. We must study, think, and decide on the governmental program that we term 'Mutual Security.'

"The true need and value of this program will be recognized by our people only if they can answer this question: 'Why should America, at heavy and immediate sacrifice to herself, assist many other nations, particularly the less developed ones, in achieving greater moral, economic, and military strength?'

"What are the facts?

"The first and most important fact is the implacable and frequently expressed purpose of imperialistic communism to promote world revolution, destroy freedom, and communize the world.

"Its methods are all-inclusive, ranging through the use of propaganda, political subversion, economic penetration, and the use or the threat of force.

"The second fact is that our country is today spending an aggregate of about 47 billion dollars annually for the single purpose of preserving the nation's position and security in the world. This includes the costs of the Defense Department, the production of nuclear weapons, and mutual security. All three are mutually supporting and are blended into one program for our safety. The size of this cost conveys something of the entire program's importance—to the world and, indeed, to each of us.

"And when I think of this importance to us, think of it in this one material figure, this cost annually for every single man, woman, and child of the entire nation is about 275 dollars a year.

"The next fact we note is that since the Communist target is the world, every nation is comprehended in their campaign for domination. The weak and the most exposed stand in the most immediate danger.

"Another fact, that we ignore to our peril, is that if aggression or subversion against the weaker of the free nations should achieve successive victories, communism would step-by-step overcome once free areas. The danger, even to the strongest, would become increasingly menacing.

"Clearly, the self-interest of each free nation impels it to resist the loss to imperialistic communism of the freedom and independence of any other nation.

"Freedom is truly indivisible.

"To apply some of these truths to a particular case, let us consider, briefly, the country of Viet-Nam, and the importance to us of the security and progress of that country.

"It is located, as you know, in the southeastern corner of Asia, exactly halfway round the world from Gettysburg College.

"Viet-Nam is a country divided into two parts—like Korea and Germany. The southern half, with its twelve million people, is free, but poor. It is an under-developed country—its economy is weak—average individual income being less than $200 a year. The northern half has been turned over to communism. A line of demarcation running along the 17th parallel separates the two. To the north of this line stand several Communist divisions. These facts pose to South Viet-Nam two great tasks: self-defense and economic growth.

"Understandably, the people of Viet-Nam want to make their country a thriving, self-sufficient member of the family of nations. This means economic expansion.

"For Viet-Nam's economic growth, the acquisition of capital is vitally necessary. Now, the nation could create the capital needed for growth by stealing from the already meager rice bowls of its people and regimenting them into work battalions. This enslavement is the commune system—adopted by the new overlords of Red China. It would mean, of course, the loss of freedom within the country without any hostile outside action whatsoever.

"Another way for Viet-Nam to get the necessary capital is through private investments from the outside, and through governmental loans and, where necessary, grants from other and more fortunately situated nations.

"In either of these ways the economic problem of Viet-Nam could be solved. But only the second way can preserve freedom.

"And there is still the other of Viet-Nam's great problems—how to support the military forces it needs without crushing its economy.

"Because of the proximity of large Communist military formations in the North, Free Viet-Nam must maintain substantial numbers of men under arms. Moreover, while the government has shown real progress in cleaning out Communist guerrillas, those remaining continue to be a disruptive influence in the nation's life.

"Unassisted, Viet-Nam cannot at this time produce and support the military formations essential to it, or, equally important, the morale—the hope, the confidence, the pride—necessary to meet the dual threat of aggression from without and subversion within its borders.

"Still another fact! Strategically, South Viet-Nam's capture by the Communists would bring their power several hundred miles into a hitherto free region. The remaining countries in Southeast Asia would be menaced by a great flanking movement. The freedom of twelve million people would be lost immediately, and that of 150 million others in adjacent lands would be seriously endangered. The loss of South Viet-Nam would set in motion a crumbling process that could, as it progressed, have grave consequences for us and for freedom.

"Viet-Nam must have a reasonable degree of safety now—both for her people and for her property. Because of these facts, military as well as economic help is currently needed in Viet-Nam.

"We reach the inescapable conclusion that our own national interests demand some help from us in sustaining in Viet-Nam the morale, the economic progress, and the military strength necessary to its continued existence in freedom.

"Viet-Nam is just one example. One-third of the world's people face a similar challenge. All through Africa and Southern Asia people struggle to preserve liberty and improve their standards of living, to maintain their dignity as humans. It is imperative that they succeed.

"But some uninformed Americans believe that we should turn our backs on these people, our friends. Our costs and taxes are very real, while the difficulties of other peoples often seem remote from us.

"But the costs of continuous neglect of these problems would be far more than we must now bear—indeed more than we could afford. The added costs would be paid not only in vastly increased outlays of money, but in larger drafts of our youth into the Military Establishment, and in terms of increased danger to our own security and prosperity.

"No matter what areas of Federal spending must be curtailed—and some should—our safety comes first. Since that safety is necessarily based upon a sound and thriving economy, its protection must equally engage our earnest attention.

"As a different kind of example of free nation interdependence, there is Japan, where very different problems exist—but problems equally vital to the security of the free world. Japan is an essential counterweight to Communist strength in Asia. Her industrial power is the heart of any collective effort to defend the Far East against aggression.

"Her more than 90 million people occupy a country where the arable land is no more than that of California. More than perhaps any other industrial nation, Japan must export to live. Last year she had a trade deficit. At one time she had a thriving trade with Asia, particularly with her nearest neighbors. Much of it is gone. Her problems grow more grave.

"For Japan there must be more free world outlets for her products. She does not want to be compelled to become dependent as a last resort upon the Communist empire. Should she ever be forced to that extremity, the blow to free world security would be incalculable; at the least it would mean for all other free nations greater sacrifice, greater danger, and lessened economic strength.

"What happens depends largely on what the free world nations can, and will, do.

"Upon us—upon you here—in this audience—rests a heavy responsibility. We must weigh the facts, fit them into place, and decide on our course of action.

"For a country as large, as industrious, and as progressive as Japan to exist with the help of grant aid by others, presents no satisfactory solution. Furthermore, for us, the cost would be, over the long term, increasingly heavy. Trade is the key to a durable Japanese economy.

"One of Japan's greatest opportunities for increased trade lies in a free and developing Southeast Asia. So we see that the two problems I have been discussing are two parts of a single one—the great need in Japan is for raw materials; in Southern Asia it is for manufactured goods. The two regions complement each other markedly. So, by strengthening Viet-Nam and helping insure the safety of the South Pacific and Southeast Asia, we gradually develop the great trade potential between this region, rich in natural resources, and highly industrialized Japan to the benefit of both. In this way freedom in the Western Pacific will be greatly strengthened and the interests of the whole free world advanced. But such a basic improvement can come about only gradually. Japan must have additional trade outlets now. These can be provided if each of the industrialized nations in the West does its part in liberalizing trade relations with Japan."

*　　*　　*

26. *Special Message to the Congress on the Mutual Security Program, February 16, 1960, Public Papers of the Presidents—Eisenhower, 1960, p. 178.*

*　　*　　*

"*The Mutual Security Program is a program essential to peace.* The accomplishments of the Mutual Security Program in helping to meet the many challenges in the mid-20th Century place it among the foremost of the great programs of American history. Without them the map of the world would be vastly different today. The Mutual Security Program and its predecessors have been an indispensable contributor to the present fact that Greece, Turkey, Iran, Laos, Vietnam, Korea and Taiwan, and many nations of Western Europe, to mention only part, remain the home of free men.

"While over the past year the Soviet Union has expressed an interest in measures to reduce the common peril of war, and while its recent deportment and pronouncement suggest the possible opening of a somewhat less strained period in our relationships, the menace of Communist imperialism nevertheless still remains. The military power of the Soviet Union continues to grow. Increasingly important to free world interests is the rate of growth of both military and economic power in Communist China. Evidence that this enormous power bloc remains dedicated to the extension of Communist control over all peoples everywhere is found in Tibet, the Taiwan Straits, in Laos and along the Indian border.

"In the face of this ever-present Communist threat, we must, in our own interest as well as that of the other members of the free world community, continue our program of military assistance through the various mutual security arrangements we have established. Under these arrangements each nation has responsibilities, commensurate with its capabilities, to participate in the development and maintenance of defensive strength. There is also increasing ability of other free world nations to share the burden of this common defense.

"Obviously, no one nation alone could bear the cost of defending all the free world. Likewise, it would be impossible for many free nations long to survive if forced to act separately and alone. The crumbling of the weaker ones would obviously and increasingly multiply the threats to those remaining free, even the very strongest.

"Collective security is not only sensible—it is essential."

*　　*　　*

27. *U.S. Sends Greetings to Viet-Nam on Anniversary of Independence, White House Press Release dated October 25, 1960, Department of State Bulletin.*

"The White House on October 25 made public the following message from President Eisenhower to Ngo Dinh Diem, President of the Republic of Viet-Nam.

"OCTOBER 22, 1960
"DEAR MR. PRESIDENT: My countrymen and I are proud to convey our good wishes to you and to the citizens of Viet-Nam on the fifth anniversary of the birth of the Republic of Viet-Nam.

"We have watched the courage and daring with which you and the Vietnamese people attained independence in a situation so perilous that many thought it hopeless. We have admired the rapidity with which chaos yielded to order and progress replaced despair.

"During the years of your independence it has been refreshing for us to observe how clearly the Government and the citizens of Viet-Nam have faced the fact that the greatest danger to their independence was Communism. You and your countrymen have used your strength well in accepting the double challenge of building your country and resisting Communist imperialism. In five short years since the founding of the Republic, the Vietnamese people have developed their country in almost every sector. I was particularly impressed by one example. I am informed that last year over 1,200,000 Vietnamese children were able to go to elementary school; three times as many as were enrolled five years earlier. This is certainly a heartening development for Viet-Nam's future. At the same time Viet-Nam's ability to defend itself from the Communists has grown immeasurably since its successful struggle to become an independent Republic.

"Viet-Nam's very success as well as its potential wealth and its strategic location have led the Communists of Hanoi, goaded by the bitterness of their failure to enslave all Viet-Nam, to use increasing violence in their attempts to destroy your country's freedom.

"This grave threat, added to the strains and fatigues of the long struggle to achieve and strengthen independence, must be a burden that would cause moments of tension and concern in almost any human heart. Yet from long observation I sense how deeply the Vietnamese value their country's independence and strength and I know how well you used your boldness when you led your countrymen in winning it. I also know that your determination has been a vital factor in guarding that independence while steadily advancing the economic development of your country. I am confident that these same qualities of determination and boldness will meet the renewed threat as well as the needs and desires of your countrymen for further progress on all fronts.

"Although the main responsibility for guarding that independence will always, as it has in the past, belong to the Vietnamese people and their government, I want to assure you that for so long as our strength can be useful, the United States will continue to assist Viet-Nam in the difficult yet hopeful struggle ahead.

"Sincerely,
"DWIGHT D. EISENHOWER."

Glossary

AAA   Antiaircraft Artillery
ACR   Armored Cavalry Regiment
ABM   Antiballistic Missile
ABN   Airborne
ADP   Automatic Data Processing
AFB   Air Force Base
AID   Agency for International Development
AIROPS   Air Operations
AM   Airmobile
AMB   Ambassador
ANG   Air National Guard
APB   Self-propelled barracks ship
ARL   Landing craft repair ship
ARVN   Army of the Republic of [South] Vietnam
ASA   U.S. Army Security Agency
ASAP   As soon as possible
ASD   Assistant Secretary of Defense
BAR   Browning automatic rifle
BDE   Brigade
BLT   Battalion Landing Team
BN   Battalion
BOB   Bureau of the Budget
B-52   U.S. heavy bomber
B-57   U.S. medium bomber
CAP   Combined Action Platoon
CAS   Saigon Office of the U.S. Central Intelligence Agency
CDC   Combat Development Command
CG   Civil Guard
CHICOM   Chinese Communist
CHMAAG   Chief, Military Assistance Advisory Group
CI   Counterinsurgency
CIA   Central Intelligence Agency
CIDG   Civilian Irregular Detachment Group
CINCPAC   Commander in Chief, Pacific
CIP   Counterinsurgency Plan
CNO VNN   Chief of Naval Operations, Vietnamese Navy
CJCS   Chairman, Joint Chiefs of Staff
CMD   Capital Military District
COMUS   U.S. Commander
COMUSMACV   Commander, U.S. Military Assistance Command, Vietnam

CONARC   Continental Army Command
CONUS   Continental United States
CORDS   Civil Operations and Revolutionary Development Support [pacification]
COS   Chief of Station, CIA
CPR   Chinese Peoples Republic
CPSVN   Comprehensive Plan for South Vietnam
CTZ   Corps tactical zone
CY   Calendar year
DCM   Deputy Chief of Mission
DCPG   Defense Command Planning Group
DEPTEL   [State] Department telegram
DESOTO   Destroyer patrols off North Vietnam
DIA   Defense Intelligence Agency
DMZ   Demilitarized Zone separating North and South Vietnam
DOD   Department of Defense
DPM   Draft Presidential Memorandum [from the Secretary of Defense]
DRV   Democratic Republic of [North] Vietnam
DULTE   Cable identifier, from Secretary of State Dulles to addressee
ECM   Electronic Countermeasures
EXDIS   Exclusive (high level) distribution
FAL and FAR   Royal Armed Forces of Laos
FARMGATE   Clandestine U.S. Air Force unit in Vietnam, 1964
FE and FEA   Bureau of Far Eastern Affairs in the State Department
FEC   French Expeditionary Corps
FLAMING DART   Code name of bombing operations, in reprisal for attacks on U.S. forces
FOA   Foreign Operations Administration
FWMA   Free World Military Assistance
FWMAF   Free World Military Assistance Force

FY   Fiscal Year
FYI   For your information
GRC   Government of the Republic of China (Nationalist China)
GVN   Government of [South] Vietnam
G-3   U.S. Army General Staff, Branch for Plans and Operations
HES   Hamlet Evaluation System
HNC   High National Council
HOP TAC   Program to clear and hold land around Saigon, 1964
IBP   International Balance of Payments
ICA   International Cooperation Administration
ICC   International Control Commission
IDA   Institute for Defense Analyses
IMCSH   Inter-ministerial Committee for Strategic Hamlets
INR   Bureau of Intelligence and Research in the Department of State
ISA   Office of International Security Affairs in the Department of Defense
I Corps   Northern military region of South Vietnam
II Corps   Central military region in South Vietnam
III Corps   Military region in South Vietnam surrounding Saigon
IV Corps   Southern military region in South Vietnam
JCS   Joint Chiefs of Staff
JCSM   Joint Chiefs of Staff Memorandum
JGS   Vietnamese Joint General Staff
JOC   Joint Operations Center
Joint Staff   Staff organization for the Joint Chiefs of Staff
JUSPAO   Joint United States Public Affairs Office, Saigon
J-2   Intelligence Branch, U.S. Army
KANZUS   Korean, Australian, New Zealand, and U.S.
KIA   Killed in action
LANTFLT   Atlantic Fleet
LOC   Lines of communications (roads, bridges, rail)
LST   Tank Landing Ship
LTC   Lt. Col.
MAAG   Military Assistance Advisory Group
MAB   Marine Amphibious Brigade
MAC   Military Assistance Command
MACCORDS   Military Assistance Command, Civil Operations and Revolutionary Development Support
MAF   Marine Amphibious Force
MAP   Military Assistance Program

MAROPS   Maritime Operations
MEB   Marine Expeditionary Brigade
MEF   Marine Expeditionary Force
MIA   Missing in action
MDAP   Mutual Defense Assistance Program
MOD   Minister of Defense
MORD   Ministry of Revolutionary Development
MRC   Military Revolutionary Committee
MR5   Highland Area
NATO   North Atlantic Treaty Organization
NCO   Non-commissioned officer
NFLSV   National Front for the Liberation of South Vietnam
NIE   National Intelligence Estimate
NLF   National Liberation Front
NODIS   No distribution (beyond addressee)
NSA   National Security Agency (specializes in electronic intelligence, i.e. monitoring radio communications)
NSAM   National Security Action Memorandum (pronounced nas-sam; described presidential decisions under Kennedy and Johnson)
NSC   National Security Council
NVA   North Vietnamese Army
NVN   North Vietnam
OB   Order of battle
OCO   Office of Civil Operations [pacification]
O&M   Operations and Management
Opcon   Operations Control
OPLAN   Operations Plan
Ops   Operations
OSA   Office of the Secretary of the Army
OSD   Office of the Secretary of Defense
PACFLT   Pacific Fleet
PACOM   Pacific Command
PAT   Political Action Team
PAVN   People's Army of [North] Vietnam
PBR   River Patrol Boat
PDJ   Plaine Des Jarres, Laos
PF   Popular Forces
PFF   Police Field Force
PL   Pathet Lao
PNG   Provisional National Government
POL   Petroleum, oil, lubricants
POLAD   Political adviser (usually, State Department representative assigned to a military commander)
PRV   People's Republic of Vietnam

PSYOP   Psychological Operations
qte   Quote
RAS   River Assault Squadron
RCT   Regimental Combat Team
RD   Rural (or Revolutionary) Development
RECCE   Reconnaissance
Reclama   Protest against a cut in budget or program
RF   Regional Forces
RLAF   Royal Laotian Air Force
RLG   Royal Laotian Government
RLT   Regimental Landing Team
ROK   Republic of [South] Korea
Rolling Thunder   Code name for sustained bombing of North Vietnam
rpt   Repeat
RSSZ   Rung Sat Special Zone (east of Saigon)
RT   Rolling Thunder Program
RTA   Royal Thai Army
RVN   Republic of [South] Vietnam
RVNAF   Republic of Vietnam Air Force or Armed Forces
RVNF   Republic of Vietnam Forces
SA   Systems Analysis Office in the Department of Defense
SAC   Strategic Air Command
SACSA   Special Assistant [to the JCS] for Counterinsurgency and Special [covert] Activities
SAM   Surface-to-air missile
SAR   Search and Rescue
SDC   Self Defense Corps
SEA   Southeast Asia
SEACOOR   Southeast Asia Coordinating Committee
SEATO   Southeast Asia Treaty Organization
SecDef   Secretary of Defense
SECTO   Cable identifier, from Secretary of State to addressee
Sitrep   Situation Report
SMM   Saigon Military Mission
SNIE   Special National Intelligence Estimate
SQD   Squadron
STRAF   Strategic Army Force

SVN   South Vietnam
TAOR   Tactical Area of Responsibility
TCS   Tactical Control System
TEDUL   Cable identifier, overseas post to Secretary of State Dulles
TERM   Temporary Equipment Recovery Mission
TF   Task force
TFS   Tactical Fighter Squadron
TO&E   Table of organization and equipment (for a military unit)
TOSEC   Cable identifier, from overseas post to Secretary of State
TRIM   Training Relations and Instruction Mission
TRS   Tactical Reconnaissance Squadron
34A   1964 operations plan covering covert actions against North Vietnam
T-28   U.S. fighter-bomber
UE   Unit equipment allowance
UH-1   Helicopter
UK   United Kingdom
USAF   U.S. Air Force
USARAL   U.S. Army, Alaska
USAREUR   U.S. Army, Europe
USASGV   U.S. Army Support Group, Vietnam
USG   United States Government
USIA   U.S. Information Agency
USIB   U.S. Intelligence Board
USIS   U.S. Information Service
USOM   U.S. Operations Mission (for economic assistance)
VC   Viet Cong
VM   Viet Minh
VN   Vietnam
VNA   Vietnamese National Army
VNAF   [South] Vietnamese Air Force or Armed Forces
VNQDD   Vietnam Quocdandang (pre-independence, nationalistic political party)
VNSF   [South] Vietnamese Special Forces
VOA   Voice of America
WESTPAC   Western Pacific Command
WIA   Wounded in action